A Cultural History of the Atlantic World, 1250–1820

A Cultural History of the Atlantic World, 1250–1820, explores the idea that strong linkages exist in the histories of Africa, Europe, North America, and South America. John K. Thornton provides a comprehensive overview of the history of the Atlantic Basin before 1830 by describing political, social, and cultural interactions between the continents' inhabitants. He traces the backgrounds of the populations on these three continental landmasses brought into contact by European navigation. Thornton then examines the political and social implications of the encounters, tracing the origins of a variety of Atlantic societies and showing how new ways of eating, drinking, speaking, and worshipping developed in the newly created Atlantic World. This book uses close readings of original sources to produce new interpretations of its subject.

John K. Thornton is Professor of History and African American Studies at Boston University. He is the author of *Warfare in Atlantic Africa, 1500–1800* (1999), and *Africa and Africans in the Making of the Atlantic World, 1400–1800* (Cambridge University Press, 1992, 1998), and the coauthor, with Linda M. Heywood, of *Central Africans, Atlantic Creoles and the Foundation of the Americas, 1585–1660* (Cambridge University Press, 2007).

A Cultural History of the Atlantic World, 1250–1820

JOHN K. THORNTON

Boston University

CAMBRIDGE
UNIVERSITY PRESS

CAMBRIDGE UNIVERSITY PRESS
Cambridge, New York, Melbourne, Madrid, Cape Town,
Singapore, São Paulo, Delhi, Mexico City

Cambridge University Press
32 Avenue of the Americas, New York, NY 10013-2473, USA

www.cambridge.org
Information on this title: www.cambridge.org/9780521727341

First published 2012

Printed in the United States of America

A catalog record for this publication is available from the British Library.

Library of Congress Cataloging in Publication data
Thornton, John K. (John Kelly), 1949–
  A cultural history of the Atlantic world, 1250–1820 / John K. Thornton.
    p.   cm.
  Includes bibliographical references and index.
  ISBN 978-0-521-89875-1 (hardback) – ISBN 978-0-521-72734-1 (paperback)
  1. Atlantic Ocean Region – History.   2. Atlantic Ocean Region – Civilization.
  3. Civilization, Modern.   I. Title.
  D210.T54   2012
  909'.09821–dc23   2012006482

ISBN 978-0-521-89875-1 Hardback
ISBN 978-0-521-72734-1 Paperback

To

Jack Fischel, colleague and friend

Contents

Figures

Maps

Preface

In 1995, Jack Fischel, the chair of the Department of History at Millersville University, asked me if I could develop a new class that would be interdisciplinary and multiregional in scope. Since I had already published a book that more or less met that requirement in *Africa and Africans in the Making of the Atlantic World* in 1992, I thought that perhaps I could expand the ideas and methods of that book to include not just Africans but all the people of the Atlantic Basin – Africans, Europeans, and the indigenous people of the Americas. Like all such broad-based courses, it floundered at first, and it took me a good three years of teaching it to determine how I should structure the class, what organization it should have, and how such a vast field could be rendered intelligible to undergraduate students at a regional university.

From the very beginning of the course, I was determined that Atlantic history as I was conceiving it would not simply be anchored on the story of European expansion and conquest. Much as I admired the French "big histories" that were my initial guides to doing large-scale history, such as the work of Fernand Braudel, Pierre Chaunu, or Frédéric Mauro, I wanted to include all the actors in the game, and on their own terms. I also decided that I would focus on cultural themes as well as political economy, which I felt had dominated the questions of contact and exchange to the detriment of other elements of human interaction.

More than that, however, I also wanted the class to be regionally comprehensive, to cover the Caribbean and Latin America as well as North America, and not to neglect Africa, my own special interest. I wanted to look at what might be considered fringe areas as well as what are largely conceived as the areas of main activity such as North America, Mexico, and Peru. I hoped to discover patterns of interaction away from the mainstream of historical research that would help us see larger patterns of human interaction, so I wanted to look at Central America as well as the Southern Cone of South America with Chile and Argentina. I wanted to understand the small-scale societies of the North American Midwest or the Mexican Northwest as much as the great empires of the Aztecs and Incas, or the African powerhouses like Mali.

With these grand intentions I waded into teaching the class. Well over my head for much of the time, I struggled to find material to fulfill my plans. As I gradually got some control of the subject matter, I decided that I would write up my lecture notes, because there was no truly comprehensive textbook that covered many of the themes I was dealing with, and the students were frequently lost or bewildered. So during the Spring term of 1998, I wrote up my notes to form a sort of textbook. As an ephemeral publication (it was printed at the college bookstore and sold "at cost" to the students), I was free to revise and update it at will, and indeed I did so every term I taught the course. Thus, over the course of the next few years, I developed a sort of synergy between student feedback, responses to the course, and my own research interests that drove content in the course and was promptly reflected in revisions to the textbook.

By 2001, I started to add footnotes to the work, at first as much for my own reference as for the students to benefit from. However, the task of footnoting turned out to change the work. I had to be more certain of things I had lectured on; looking up things necessarily forced me to present more detail and to anchor the facts more in their historical context. I was embarrassed that I had initially included information I had culled from encyclopedia articles, or less than reputable sources, and so I had to chase down legitimate scholarly offerings. Bit by bit, the text became less a written form of lecture notes and more and more a formally written text. It also increasingly became a scholarly work on its own as well as a summary of existing scholarship.

In 2003, I moved from Millersville to Boston University, and in the environment of a research university I decided to place greater emphasis on the scholarly aspects of the book, and to build my lectures from the text rather than to build the text from my lectures. The book and its apparatus increasingly became more like the model I had used in *Africa and Africans* and its origins as a text became less obvious.

During the early 2000s, however, other developments helped shape the way the book grew. Gallica, the Bibliothèque Nationale de France's Web site, began offering vast numbers of books for download, and I discovered that books I had once only been able to consult in large libraries were available on my computer in a matter of minutes. That marvel was soon joined by other incredible research resources, including JSTOR, an unbelievable (at the time) database of journal articles (and its companions like Project Muse or Persée). These wonders were capped by Google Books, which opened up an even larger store of older publications.

All of a sudden, I could consult huge numbers of primary sources directly – sources I had only been able to read in summer jaunts to the Library of Congress, overseas in Paris or Lisbon, or perhaps at Harvard University after I moved to Boston. But with downloaded and soon annotated copies on my desktop, I did not need to spend time and resources to go to these repositories. If that were not enough, I was also presented with raw archival material; the Spanish National Archives put hundreds of thousands of pages of original unpublished material at my fingertips through PARES, as did the National Archives in Portugal. The Projeto Resgate made countless records of Brazil available to me.

This flood of new material altered my approach to the text. I began to turn increasingly to primary sources to write, and I tried to tackle problems anew. Where once an area that had a historiography that did not fit the aims of my course was simply overlooked, I now found that I could integrate themes directly from the primary sources into my teaching schemes. With the aid of the Internet, I could usually locate primary sources that allowed me to build almost from scratch and that, in turn, allowed me to pursue larger themes in more areas and with greater depth than before.

Throughout the 2000s, my textbook–scholarly research project grew and changed, taking in more regions, engaging more themes, dealing with many topics in greater depth than I could before. At the same time, the relentless demands to make the work accessible to my students forced me to revise constantly, explaining, simplifying, and as always cutting, cutting, cutting, new details wrested from the ever increasing and ever more available store of primary sources I could use.

Finally, I took a sabbatical leave in the spring of 2010 to pull what had become a somewhat unwieldy text together, to ensure that my issues of coverage were met and to fill in areas I knew were still weak. Thanks to the good graces of Henry Louis Gates and Vera Grant, in particular, I was allowed to use a desk in a common use area of the W. E. B. Dubois Institute as my research space. In that environment, enriched by conversations of passing Fellows and workers at the institute, I wrote my final draft. Curiously, thanks to the new electronic environment in which I was working, I often sat at the desk with not one book or piece of paper before me; everything I used or needed was lodged in my computer.

In spite of this long history, this book is in many ways still an incomplete project – in fact, really a first step. I am not embarrassed by this; it is far too large a project to be completed in any meaningful way in one human lifespan, and I only hope that it can point the way for others to work. It was also assembled in a somewhat haphazard way, and readers should note this. I conducted considerable archival research for this project in London, the Netherlands, Brazil, Portugal, Italy, and other locations, including a good deal that was originally performed for other projects. Thus some themes, periods, and areas have been much more thoroughly researched than others. Brazil is one such case, because repeated trips to Brazilian and Portuguese archives gave me a solid base there. Others, such as Mexico and Peru, are not so deeply studied, but thanks to my online research, many older editions of chronicles, collections of documents, and other resources were still available. Such a pattern necessarily creates an unevenness in the treatment of these regions.

I also have relatively less treatment of Europe and most Euro-Americans than to other groups in the Atlantic. This is in some measure a recognition that, on the whole, Europe and Euro-Americans have already been deeply studied by many other scholars. The majority of the source material, and usually the best-quality material, pertains far more to them than to others. I therefore have less to contribute, although I have tried to be attentive to not leaving them out. They are a vitally important part of the whole project, and my including them as much as I do is in recognition of that, but also to ensure that the theoretical ideas I develop apply to them also. In many cases, especially as relates to general cultural issues, the matters can be more deeply and thoroughly explored with that group.

Another point I must make is that after about 2001 or so, I did much more research in primary sources than in secondary ones. A large-scale project overwhelms the capacity of a single researcher to cover all the available literature, and in the interests of timeliness I opted to decide at a certain point to say that I had written enough to make a plausible case for the arguments I present, at which point I would stop writing because otherwise, the project may never be completed. But if one imposes a time limit of this sort, it then requires a certain amount of triage, decisions about how much one can read and about what to read first and what to put off. For better or for worse, I opted to read primary sources before or in lieu of the existing secondary sources. In many cases I was moved this way because the more recent literature, especially in book form or written outside the English-language world, was not readily available online, whereas many of the primary sources were.

I was also moved in this case by a sense of security that one gets from reading primary sources. If one is able to read the most important primary sources and to sample, at least, a range of lesser ones, there is an inevitable feeling that one cannot stray too far from what is known or knowable about a region or period. Knowing that one is reading the words of an eyewitness, a contemporary, or the person closest to the events in question is reassuring. This does not mean that reading primary sources without paying heed to the sometimes substantial critical analysis of these sources that secondary literature provides is always a good idea, only that in the process of triage, I felt more comfortable with the primary literature and more willing to sacrifice the secondary.

In this instance I wish to apologize to the many scholars whose work I appear to have ignored. I know the sense of irritation that arises when one reads a bibliography or notes in a scholarly work and finds that one's own work on that very topic is not there. It may also appear as a sort of arrogance that I should be reinventing the wheel in many places. I can only beg forgiveness for this, and plead in my defense my decisions about triage.

Attentive readers of footnotes may also note that I frequently cite older editions of works that are available in more modern form, and this is, in fact, a product of my research strategy – where a nineteenth-century edition of a chronicle was available through Google Books or Gallica, I might prefer that to a more modern edition. In some cases, albeit not in too many, the more recent edition has a better text – employs additional manuscript material, perhaps reads the paleography better. But often the modern editions were simply a means of making a text available to modern readers because the original edition had become a bibliographic rarity. Today's Internet-driven world has curiously reversed this situation – old editions are now more readily available than the more recent ones.

Finally, I have a penchant for reading sources in the original languages if I can read them myself, and of course if they are available to me. I have found time and time again that sources, especially the types of sources that underlie a book like this one, can yield the most information when read very carefully and closely, and particularly when the semantic field of each word is considered very carefully. In many languages, there is not a perfect fit between the semantic field of a word in one language and the semantic field in another, and thus even the best translators must choose one out of two or perhaps even more words that fit into that field. Yet sometimes, it is a tiny gain in knowledge to be able to sort out the exact field, and so I prefer to read originals. Unfortunately, it also means that I tend to cite original language texts even when there are fine English translations available. I sometimes use the translation and only revert to the original when it seems necessary, but for citation I prefer the original. I have tried when possible to alert readers to English translations, and in citing this work to seek, whenever possible, to use a method that allows the reference to be retrieved across editions and languages. Thus, for older literature, I have preferred book chapter citations to page number citation, as the strategy of older writers was to have relatively short chapters, and my modern readers would be able to find my reference reasonably quickly.

I must take this opportunity to thank a great number of people who made this work possible. The first thanks go to the approximately 600 students who took my course over the period when I developed this book. Their questions, querulous expressions, student reviews, term paper choices, and answers (both good and bad) on examination questions helped me refine, shape, and conceptualize the course. Several graduate students also helped me by more intense discussion, most notably Sarah Westwood, Eric Cooper, and Andrea Mosterman. A special thanks to Mosterman, whose knowledge of German and Dutch (and Dutch paleography) was often of great help.

I want to give Linda Heywood special thanks for the intellectual role she has played in the development of this book and indeed my whole professional life since we met, corresponded, and married in Lisbon in 1978–79. We discussed Atlantic history first in Cleveland in 1982 as a way to take ourselves beyond being Africanists and reaching a larger audience by including the diaspora within our field. My first book-length venture into Atlantic history, *Africa and Africans* was born in her office at Cleveland State, as she wrestled with new ways of integrating Africa into African-American history. Apart from coauthoring one book and a half-dozen articles with me, Heywood has been a constant source of debate, discussion, argument, and consensus building over the past thirty-some years. Thanks to Jonathan Zatlin for organizing a seminar at Boston University to discuss the book, and especially to Barbara Diefendorf and Brendan McConville for their comments.

I benefited from the services of some research assistants while at Boston University, notably Lehong Weng and Andrea Mosterman, as well as Marta Roiz of the University of Coimbra, Portugal.

Much of the research that went into this book took place within the confines of Heywood's and my joint book project, started in 2000 and completed in 2007 with the publication of *Central Africans, Atlantic Creoles and the Foundation of the Americas*. That work was funded by Howard University, Millersville University, Boston University through travel and research grants, the U.S. Park Service, and especially a three-year grant from the W. E. B. DuBois Institute of Harvard University. The DBI also granted me work space in their building during my final writing stages in 2010.

Abbreviations

ACL	Academia das Cienças (Lisbon)
AGI	Archivo General de Indias (Seville)
AHN	Archivo Historico Nacional (Madrid)
AHNA	Arquivo Histórico Nacional de Angola (Luanda)
AHU	Arquivo Histórico Ultramarino (Lisbon)
AIHGB	Arquivo do Instituto Historico e Geografico Brasileiro (Rio de Janeiro)
ANF	Archives Nationales de France (Paris)
ANTT	Arquivo Nacional de Torre do Tombo (Lisbon)
Inq Lx	Inquisição de Lisboa
APEB	Arquivo Público de Estado da Bahia (Salvador)
APF	Archivio "De Propaganda Fide" (Rome/Vatican)
APM	Arquivo Público Mineiro (Belo Horizonte)
AUC	Arquivo da Universidade de Coimbra (Coimbra)
BIFAN	*Bulletin, Institut Foundamental de l'Afrique Noire*
BL	British Library (London)
Add	Additional Manuscripts
BN	Colombia Biblioteca Nacional de Colombia
BNA	Barbados National Archives (Bridgetown)
BNRJ	Biblioteca Nacional de Rio de Janeiro
BSGL	Biblioteca da Sociedade de Geografia de Lisboa (Lisbon)
CDI	*Coleccion de Documentos de Indias*
CDHC	*Coleccion de Documentos para la historia de Chile*
DAESP	*Documentos do Arquivo de Estado de São Paulo*

DTA	Digital Text Archive
GB	Google Books
JR	Reuben Gold Thwaites, *The Jesuit Relations and allied Documents* (73 vols., Cleveland, OH, 1899–1903)
LC	Library of Congress (Washington, DC)
LRO	Liverpool Record Office (Liverpool)
LW	Jaroslav Pelikan and Helmut T. Lehmann, eds., *Luther's Works* (55 vols., St. Louis, MO, and Philadelphia, 1955–1986)
MAB	Moravian Archives, Bethlehem (Bethlehem, PA)
MMA	António Brásio, ed. *Monumenta Missionaria Africana* (1st series, 15 vols., Lisbon, 1952–1988)
MMA²	2nd series, 7 vols., Lisbon, 1958–1985).
NAN	Nationaal Archief Nederland (The Hague)
OWIC	Oude West Indische Compagnie
NAUK	National Archives of the United Kingdom (Kew)
PARES	Portal de Archivos Españoles
SD	Santo Domingo
TUO	Tuohy Papers

Introduction

This book grew out of my desire to see Americans, living on both continents, develop a new understanding of their past and their heritage, one that was multicentered, complex, and interactional. While my thinking was initially directed in particular toward North America, I also realized that other countries in the Americas, especially as I witnessed in my experience in the English-speaking Caribbean and Brazil, shared in their own ways variants of the collective memory I hoped to change. As Maurice Halbwachs originally envisioned it, our collective memory is our sense of ourselves as having a memory that extends beyond our personal recollections and includes the memory of the whole of society.[1] Others, notably Pierre Nora, who have expanded the concept, have noted the role that national symbols, cherished historical events, monuments, and, for my purposes above all, the curriculum of schools have in shaping the collective memory.[2]

I felt that our contemporary collective memory is often unidirectional, anchored in Europe and focused on a relatively few incidents and locations in the Americas. The locations and narratives vary from country to country; in Mexico more than many others, the indigenous heritage joins that of Europe, for example. My way to address, and hopefully to change, our collective memory is through Atlantic history.[3] I see an Atlantic basin focus not as replacing the Western civilization approach to our heritage, but as augmenting and extending it. While Atlantic history as a subdiscipline has a fairly long and respectable lineage, its earliest manifestation was in fact simply to recognize

---

[1] Maurice Halbwachs, *The Collective Memory* (New York, 1980 [French original 1950]), and Paul Ricoeur, *Memory, History, Forgetting* (tr. Katherine Blamey and David Pellauer, Chicago, 2004) have influenced me in this pursuit, although this list could easily be expanded.

[2] Pierre Nora, interpretative remarks as editor in *Realms of Memory: Rethinking the French Past* (3 vols., New York, 1996).

[3] A very good overview and survey of the historiography and literature of the recent history of the Americas is Eric Hinderaker and Rebecca Horn, "Territorial Crossings: Histories and Historiographies of the Early Americas," *William and Mary Quarterly*, 3rd series, 57 (2010): 395–432.

that Europe and the Americas shared a common history.[4] However, in the early 1990s, new conceptions of Atlantic history were emerging. The new Atlantic history deliberately decentered Europe and gave much more attention to non-European regions.[5] Furthermore, Atlantic history's new formulation has been struggling to move from using modern countries as a unit of analysis to look at regional or continental trends.[6]

My approach to Atlantic history in this book, however, has been guided not only by a desire to reshape the collective memory, but also to anchor it in a different approach that in some ways departs from the collective memory model altogether. I started with ideas that Linda Heywood presented in an address to the American Historical Association in which she described three roles that historians fulfill.[7] The first role has been as keeper and restorer of a nation's, group's, or community's heritage, reminding members of how they began, how they progressed, and how time changed or reaffirmed their principles. It is what many people think of as history's primary task, and it is the task most often cited in the theoretical and philosophical literature on collective memory.

The second role, though not much practiced today, especially by professional historians, but still very much a part of popular conceptions of the historian's role, is that of an assessor, making judgments, both moral and practical, on the role of actors in history. History can be seen as a guide to the present, a source of inspiration or a warning of the consequences of incompetence, vanity, or foolishness in human affairs. The role is important, if for no other reason than that political leaders might actually refrain from wickedness, fearing the judgment of history. It is also a role that I have largely eschewed in this book.

The final role has been greatly on the ascendance since the end of the Second World War, and that is the historian as social scientist. History can be seen as the ultimate in social comparison, not only examining societies in the present, but also in the past. If the goal of social science is to study the human experience exhaustively, then the past must be considered as well as the present. Historians have learned to use statistics, to construct counterfactual models, and to use the language of sociology, political science, and psychology to understand their subject.

My approach in this book is to work with history primarily as a social science, but along the way to create the sort of inclusive, multicentric, and multiregional approach that I hope might revise our collective memory and thus

---

[4] For an assessment of its earlier history as essentially recognizing Europe as important for understanding America, or as a branch of Imperial history, see Philip Morgan and Jack Greene, "Introduction: The Present State of Atlantic History," in Jack P. Greene and Philip Morgan, eds. *Atlantic History: A Critical Appraisal* (Oxford, 2009).

[5] The New Atlantic history is well represented in several new textbook treatments – for example, Thomas Benjamin, *The Atlantic World: Europeans, Africans and Indians and their Shared History, 1400–1900* (Cambridge, 2009).

[6] See Hinderaker and Horn, "Territorial Crossings," pp. 405–410.

[7] Heywood's paper, presented the late 1980s, is unpublished, but our discussions of it have been fundamental to my vision of the historian's craft.

address the issue of heritage. Initially, the work opens with an exploration of the development of the Atlantic World, from early European explorations and contacts (in the first chapter) to a survey of the cultures of the Atlantic Basin: a chapter each on Europe, Africa, and the Americas. In this section the approach is comparative but also comprehensive. The advantage of the comparative approach is that it does not require the writer to use the criteria of heritage to choose the most important regions to study or highlight. That is, if one is North American, one does not have to justify, consciously or unconsciously, a description of events in Brazil through their relevance to the heritage of North America. Rather, as Chapter 4 demonstrates, understanding the comparative political systems of the Iroquois and Tupi makes sense as a social science exercise. It provides a solid, comprehensible reason for comparing widely disparate societies; indeed, in many ways, it demands disparity. But the discussion by itself also exposes the reader to material that can contribute to an understanding of the heritage of those societies.

The next section assesses the nature of the encounters between expanding Europe and other societies in the Atlantic World. The approach is thematic, defining three types of encounters – conquest, colonization, and contact – and within each one there are comparative models: the Spanish conquest of Mexico and Peru is different from the Portuguese conquest in Brazil, and that again is different from Spanish conquest in the Rio de la Plata basin, just as Portuguese conquests in Angola differ from those of Brazil. By including contact among the categories, I am able to retain a theoretical and systematic unity, but also include regions that are often left out: Atlantic Africa, the American West, or the Western Caribbean where Europeans came as guests or were roughly expelled.[8] It allows a North American–centered history to continue to include Native Americas in the story, and thus to include it in the collective memory, if not as a part of the heritage of the United States, at least as a society to be discussed and considered and thus within the collective memory of the United States.

Although this book is dedicated to culture, in most respects the first portions of it, more than half, in fact, are political and social rather than cultural. However, the next section does take on cultural issues, again comparatively. We learn of the fate of languages, for example, by seeing the difference between the survival of French in English Canada and that of any African language in the Caribbean, and once again the comparative approach allows us to include regions and times that are usually outside the heritage track of any given area. In exploring aesthetic culture, we use the concept of virtuosity to explode regional cultures and study culture change in a way that departs from most heritage models, which all too often attempt to place value on specific aesthetic forms. In the chapter on religion, the concept of revelation and co-revelation

---

[8] Again, the problems of "borderlands" and inter-European competition versus an indigenous center definition is a problem being confronted today; see Hinderaker and Horn, "Territorial Crossings," pp. 410–412.

likewise invite a comparative approach that cross-cuts regional and sectarian/religious divisions, but manages to intersect with the encounter models.

The last section of the book, dedicated to the revolutions that set most of the Americas free from European control, is much more conventional. Aside from being comparative and problem-oriented (the central problem being how revolutionary leaders dealt with forming alliances with subordinate groups they hoped to dominate), it is primarily narrative-driven and ultimately is a fundamental part of the collective memory of all the counties in question. Its basically chronological organization also reinforces its refocus on cherished stories of resistance and independence on a regional level. Only by working comparatively and being deliberately comprehensive does the work expand any individual heritage.

By abandoning much of the narrative approach so characteristic of heritage history, this book takes a deliberate chance in becoming confusing. There is little doubt that chronology is a powerful tool that helps bind diverse elements in any story, and narrative is more accessible than social-science-oriented comparative history. It is a chance I am taking, not just because I think it is the best strategy for achieving my goals, but also because it is much more in keeping with my own training and predilections as a historian. I hope that the work that follows allows inhabitants of all parts of the Atlantic basin to reconsider their collective memory.

PART I

THE ATLANTIC BACKGROUND

The formation of the Atlantic world was the result of Columbus's voyages to America and subsequent discoveries in navigation that allowed European sailors, for the first time in history, to reach every other part of the world. It is not any surprise, then, that 1492, the date of Columbus's crossing of the Atlantic, is a signal year in the history of the world, for the creation of the Atlantic world involved one of history's great intercontinental migrations and the most massive cultural encounter and engagement that the world had seen up to that time. It is easy to give too much credit for this to European achievement, for a great deal of what happened was as much accident and happy circumstance as it was part of a deliberate plan. And although Europeans initiated the Atlantic navigations, others also benefited from or exploited the opportunities that the navigations created.

Europeans did not possess decisive advantages over any of the people they met, even though their sailing craft were indeed capable of nautical achievements that no other culture up to that time was able to perform. But although we focus on the Atlantic as a maritime highway that connected cultures, the real stuff of human interaction took place on land. There, often enough, sailing advantages were not much help.

The book that follows examines the cultural consequences of European navigation and settlement outside of Europe in three parts. The first part traces the backgrounds of the three continental landmasses whose populations were brought into contact by those navigations. The second section examines the primarily political and social implications of the contact and traces the origins of a variety of Atlantic societies. Only in the third part are specifically cultural issues addressed, in an attempt to see how new ways of eating, drinking, speaking, and worshipping developed in the newly created Atlantic world.

I

The Formation of the Atlantic World, 1250–1600

It is easy to forget in the age of motorized travel that before the middle of the nineteenth century, the easiest, fastest, and cheapest way to move cargo of any significant size and people in any numbers was by water. Only extraordinary effort with horses and draught animals could move goods faster, and then only at considerably more expense. This simple fact goes a long way to explaining why river and sea travel was so important, and why humans worked hard to master maritime and nautical technology.

Given this fact, it may seem extraordinary that the Atlantic Basin was the last large body of water to be mastered for navigation. The vast Pacific was being crossed by Polynesians in increasingly more elaborate watercraft from the time of Christ, following remarkable breakthroughs in oceanic navigation and watercraft construction. The Indian Ocean was crisscrossed with trading boats long before the Common Era began, as the *Periplus of the Erythrean Sea*, a guide to navigation of the first century, shows. Ancient navigators voyaged into the Mediterranean even before historical records marked their journeys, and Europe's northern seas saw ports and trade long before the Romans conquered Gaul.

It was not as though the Atlantic Basin was without those who might sail on it. Roman ships had ventured out into the Atlantic in the early centuries AD, exploring the north coast of Africa and visiting the Canary Islands, the "Fortunate Isles" of ancient geographers. Archaeologists confirm that even before Christ, people of the Orinoco Basin were building seaworthy craft and were beginning to move from the river into the Caribbean.[1] By the time European sailors visited its waters, there was substantial shipping there. Columbus saw a boat whose length he estimated at 96 palms, which carried, by his estimate,

---

[1] Desmond V. Nicholson, "Pre-Columbian Seafaring Capabilities in the Lesser Antillies," *Proceedings of the Sixth International Congress of Pre-Columbian Cultures of the Lesser Antillies* (Pointe-à-Pitre, 1976), 98–105.

150 people off Hispaniola; on another occasion, he saw a watercraft large enough to have a superstructure, a "house" on its decks. A quarter-century later, the first visitors to North America, such as Giovanni de Verrazano, noted quite a sophisticated maritime culture; one of the local boats that visited him was some twenty feet long, sailing outside the Chesapeake Bay in 1524. Native North Americans regularly traveled by water between modern-day New Jersey and the Chesapeake on boats powered by sails.[2]

European travelers to the Atlantic coast of Africa were regularly met by local watercraft. Early descriptions speak of craft that could hold up to a ton of cargo and dozens of sailors all along the coast. Alvise da Mosto, visiting the coast in 1455, thought the local watercraft were good "barche," and he met a fleet of seventeen of them at one point.[3] His contemporary, Diogo Gomes, saw 2 such craft carrying 38 men each;[4] slightly later sources mention as many as 100 fighting men in such craft, which were as long as the European ships, along the coast from Senegal to modern-day Sierra Leone; others might carry several head of cattle.[5] The early traveler Duarte Pacheco Pereira marveled at the Ijo canoes he met off the coast of modern day Nigeria, equal in size and capacity to those he and others met off the coast of Senegal or Sierra Leone.[6]

For all the elaboration of watercraft found throughout the coastal Atlantic, even those cultures that made regular voyages on open seas, like the Europeans or people of the Caribbean basin, it was not until the fifteenth century that the Atlantic became a regular channel of navigation. There were crossings before, and even perhaps on some scale, but they had not made the Atlantic the sort of highway that other large bodies of water had become centuries earlier.

The best known of these early crossings were the north Atlantic explorations of the Scandinavians. In the eleventh and twelfth centuries, they had succeeded in pioneering trade and settlement with Iceland, Greenland, and even North America. But as promising as this start had been, expanding ice and increasing difficulties in navigation made it only a temporary breakthrough. By 1400, the northerners had long since ceased to travel across the Atlantic, and their brave, tenuous settlements were abandoned.[7]

---

[2] Examples cited in Jack Forbes, *Africans and Native Americans: The Language of Race and the Evolution of Red-Black Peoples* (2nd ed., Urbana and Chicago, 1993), pp. 6–14.

[3] Alvise da Mosto, "Mondo Novo," in Tullia Gasparrini Leporace (ed.) *Le Navigazioni atlantiche del Veneziano Alvise da Mosto* (Milan, 1966), p. 82.

[4] "De prima inuentione Guine," in António Baião (ed.) *O Manuscrito 'Valentim Fernandes'* (Lisbon, 1940), fol. 28ov (original foliation marked in this edition).

[5] Valentim Fernandes, "Descripçã da Cepta e sua Costa" (MS of c. 1508), fols. 102v, 117v in Baião, *Manuscrito* (I have followed António Brásio's reading of the text, which he presents, recording original foliation in *Monumenta Missionaria Africana*, 2nd series, 6 volumes, Lisbon, 1958–1991) 1: 672–739.

[6] Duarte Pacheco Pereira, *Esmeraldo De Situ Orbis* (MS of ca. 1506), Book 2, chapter 9, modern ed. from two eighteenth-century MSS, Augusto Epifânio da Silva Dias (Lisbon, 1905, reprinted 1975).

[7] For a good overview of the archaeology and documentation of these settlements, see Helge and Anne Stine Ingstad, *The Viking Discovery of America: The Excavation of a Norse Settlement in L'Anse aux Meadows* (New York, 2001).

It would be surprising if Native American watercraft had not crossed the Atlantic in the opposite direction. The Caribbean in particular had an impressive tradition of building and using watercraft, and even inter-island voyages might go astray, thus resulting in accidental trans-Atlantic voyages. As early as the first century BCE, the Roman writer Pliny noted the shipwreck of some people whom he described, with strange unintended irony, as "Indians" who were wrecked in Germany, from, in his assessment, an ill-fated "trading voyage." A medieval Spanish account notes the stranding of a man, "red and strange," who arrived there from the east in a craft described as a hollowed out log. Unfortunately, he died before anyone could learn enough of his language to discover who he was or where he came from. When he was considering his own trans-Atlantic crossing, Christopher Columbus collected information about human travelers coming to Europe. He had learned of strange people arriving in Ireland from the west, while settlers in the Azores Islands of the central Atlantic told of boats with dead men in them washing up on their shores. One of these was an elaborate craft with a house on it. While none of this evidence is strong enough to confirm even accidental voyages from the Americas to Europe, it provides a circumstantial case.[8]

Africans may also have sought a highway across the Atlantic and not just used its shores. The celebrated case of Mansa Qu, ruler of the powerful medieval empire of Mali, is quite explicit. Mansa Musa, his successor to the throne, revealed the story of his mysterious predecessor's Atlantic adventures to his host Abu'l Hasan Ali b. Amir Hajib, when staying in Cairo while the pious Muslim emperor took a pilgrimage to Mecca in 1324. As they were chatting about succession to power in Mali, Musa revealed to his startled host that his predecessor "did not believe that it was impossible to discover the furthest limit of the Western [Atlantic] Ocean and wished vehemently to do so." He equipped a voyage with 200 ships of men and provisions, and when it failed, he followed it with a second voyage. "Then that sultan got ready 2,000 ships," Musa told the official, "one thousand for himself and the men whom he took with him and 1,000 for water and provisions. He left me to deputize for him and embarked on the Western Ocean with his men. That was the last we saw of him and all those who were with him."[9] More than one scholar has wondered what might have become of such a voyage, and it certainly seems unlikely that at least some of these craft would not have made the trip safely, if the voyage did indeed take place as Mansa Musa related.[10]

---

[8] Forbes, *Africans and Native Americans*, pp. 7–14.

[9] Al-'Umari, *Masalik al absar fi mamalik al-amsar*, text of 1337/38 (BN Paris, MS 5868, fols. 32b–33a [other MSS exist]) as translated in Nehemiah Levtzion and J. F. P. Hopkins, *Corpus of Arabic Texts of West African History* (Cambridge, 1982), pp. 268–269.

[10] It is possible that the voyage was a means of covering up a coup d'etat by Musa, who was not in direct line to succeed, as was clearly related by shaykh 'Uthman, a fakih of Ghana, who told ibn Khaldun during 'Uthman's pilgrimage in 1394 that a line of successors followed the founder of the dynasty up to Qu, "then after him his son Muhammad b. Qu. After him their kingship passed from the line of Mari Jata to that of his brother Abu Bakr in the person of Mansa Musa b Abi

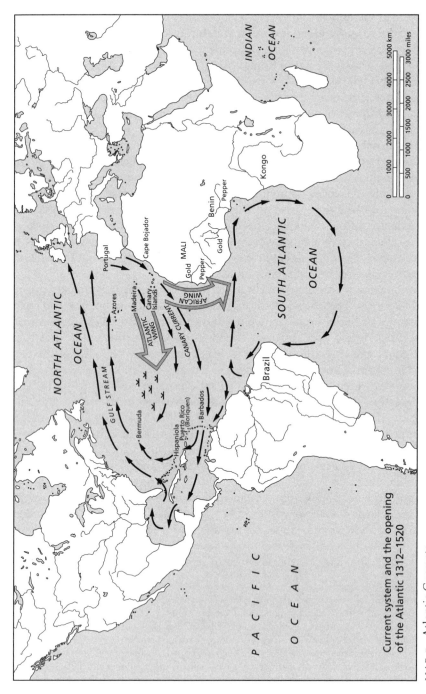

MAP I. Atlantic Currents.

Current system and the opening of the Atlantic 1312–1520

NORTH ATLANTIC OCEAN

SOUTH ATLANTIC OCEAN

INDIAN OCEAN

PACIFIC OCEAN

GULF STREAM

CANARY CURRENT

ATLANTIC WING

AFRICAN WING

Portugal

Cape Bojador

Azores

Madeira

Canary Islands

Bermuda

Hispaniola

Puerto Rico (Boriquen)

Barbados

Brazil

MALI

Gold

Pepper

Gold

Pepper

Benin

Kongo

5000 km

4000

3000

2000

1000

0

3000 miles

2500

2000

1500

1000

500

0

To understand why such voyages often failed and why it took so long to master the Atlantic, one must understand the nature of navigating the Atlantic in the age of sail. A simple glance at most maps does not reveal the difficulties of sailing wind-powered ships on such a body of water. The Atlantic Ocean has strong, consistent currents that run through it, and no sailor can ignore these. Sailing ships are not at liberty to go anywhere they can plot on a map, the way steam and diesel power has made modern ships able to plot straight courses. A contrary wind might make it impossible for a ship to land on a visible coast, and indeed drive it far out to sea. Even when the intricacies of Atlantic navigation were known in the seventeenth century, winds could ruin voyages. The case of the *Black Bess*, an English ship cruising the Caribbean in 1625, is one of many examples, as it was unable to complete its plans to land in Cuba even though the shore was in sight, because offshore winds made it simply impossible to make landfall. The ship had to travel north, carrying with it two unfortunate Cuban pilots, and made landfall only in the Chesapeake, having failed to land them in Florida as well.[11] These were not explorers only partially aware of the geography of the region they visited; these were seasoned sailors accustomed to the region and its ways.

The tyranny of wind and current is the easiest explanation for the length of time it took to make the Atlantic a highway, and also for accounting for its regional development.[12] In the Old World, the Atlantic is dominated by the Canary current, which runs south along the coast of Portugal, down the Atlantic coast of Africa, and past the Canary Islands that gave it its name. From a point about Senegal, it veers off into the Atlantic north of the Equator and enters the Caribbean in the region of the Lesser Antilles. The Canary current drives the Atlantic storm track that brings hurricanes from the Atlantic coast of Africa across to the Caribbean. The current, unlike the monsoons in the Indian Ocean, is a one-way, constant flow that does not reverse.

The Canary current is matched on the other side of the ocean by the Gulf Stream, which flows northward out of the Caribbean, crosses the Atlantic, and then moves to the European coast, bringing warm winds to keep England from being as cold as Canada and producing a distinctly warmer western side than the eastern side of the island. Like the Canary current, the Gulf Stream is a one-directional flow for the whole year.

Bakr"; ibn Khaldun, *Kitab al-'ibar wa-diwan al mubtada wa-'l khabar* (mod. ed. 1924, vol. 6, p. 200), as translated in Levtzion and Hopkins, *Corpus*, p. 334. His disappearance on a voyage, after leaving Musa as a "deputy," might allow the usurper to gain and hold power in the long period of uncertainty while the emperor was on the Atlantic voyage. Thus Qu may have been forced to take a voyage that was doomed to fail to get him out of the way. It would not be surprising that the topic would come up in a discussion of succession, especially when Musa himself said, "We belong to a house which hands on the kingship by inheritance" (*Corpus*, p. 268).

[11] Virginia, Court of 11 July 1625, Henry Read McIlwaine (ed.) *Minutes of the Council and General Court* (Richmond, 1924), pp. 66–67.

[12] The classic study is Raymond Mauny, *Les navigations médiévales sur les côtes sahariennes antérieures à la découverte portugaise (1434)* (Lisbon, 1960).

Countercurrents flowing in the opposite directions drive both the extreme north and extreme south ends of the Atlantic. The possibilities of north Atlantic navigation were exploited by the Norsemen in the eleventh century, and also more recently by fishermen from northern Europe (and even Portugal), but the storminess and ice made them much less attractive after about 1350.

The south-flowing Canary current might easily seem to be an ideal entry to the coast of Africa for Mediterranean people. Indeed, since the sixth century, Mediterranean people have been in contact with sub-Saharan Africa by means of the arduous trans-Saharan trade, made possible by the camel. Gold from West African mines flowed to Byzantine Europe and then to the Arab Caliphates on the backs of these ships of the desert. From at least the eleventh century, maritime people from the Mediterranean have dreamed of finding a sea route to the West African source of the gold trade.

The Sicilian Muslim geographer al-Idrisi related the story of seven cousins from Lisbon (then a Muslim country) who, sometime before 1154, decided to freight a direct voyage to West Africa. The trip down the coast went smoothly enough, but upon reaching their destination, the cousins discovered the constant Canary current did not permit their return. Eventually, they made their way back by means of the overland route.[13] Christians also sought to use the current: in 1291, the Vivaldi brothers from Venice hoped to sail around Africa, beginning their voyage with the deceptive help of the current. Whether they succeeded in reaching West Africa, or whether they tried to return – we cannot say, for they were not heard from again, although Portuguese travelers 150 years later claimed to have found them.[14] The famous Catalan atlas, made by a Jewish cartographer for the king of France in 1375, reveals the equally ill-fated voyage of Jaime Ferrer, shown sailing in 1346 for the "River of Gold," as the Senegal was known to European cartographers, also never to return. Some Christians thought that the Muslims had fared better; an anonymous Franciscan, writing in 1350, described regular voyages conducted by North African Muslims to the gold fields of West Africa, but it was fantasy.[15]

If the Canary current forbade Mediterranean voyagers from reaching Africa, it was even more problematic for Africans who might have wanted to sail northward. Al-Idrisi noted that shipping from the Senegal turned north a few kilometers to the Saharan salt mines of Idjil, but no Africans went by sea any farther north than that.[16] If the strong countercurrent was not enough to deter

---

[13] Abu 'Abd-Allah Muhammad b. Muhammad al-Sharif al-Idrisi, "Muzhat al-mushtaq fi iktiraq al-afaq," (1154) in Levtzion and Hopkins, *Corpus*, pp. 130–131.

[14] See Jaime Cortesão, *Os Descobrimentos portugueses* (2 vols., Lisbon, 1960) 1: 304–305.

[15] Anon., "Libro del consçimiento de todas las tierras y señorios que son por el mundo y de las señales y armas que han cada tierra y señorio," in Youssouf Kamal, *Monumenta Cartographica Africae et egypti* (Leiden, 1926–53) 4: fols. 1259–1259v. Recently, a Portuguese historian has proposed the Muslim voyagers traveled as far as the islands of the Gulf of Guinea: São Tomé, Príncipe, and Bioko (Fernando Po); Sara Santiago and Fernanda Durão Ferreira, "O redescobrimento das ilhas do Golfo da Guiné," *História* 71 (2004): 48–51.

[16] Al-Idrisi, in Levtzion and Hopkins, *Corpus*, pp. 106–107.

further adventures, the waterless, barren coast that stretched northward for hundreds of miles with no point worth visiting would serve as well. The lack of possibilities alone on the Saharan coast was probably enough to discourage would-be African travelers to Europe from departing.

Africans faced the same problems going across the Atlantic that Europeans faced voyaging south to Africa. The Canary current certainly provided a veritable highway across the Atlantic, one that African fishermen may well have taken by accident for centuries. We know from archaeology that Africans exploited the fish of the Canary current, venturing some distance out to sea to do so from very ancient times. Their mounds of fish bones, some dating to millennia before Christ, are piled all along the African coast.[17] Surely the unfortunate fisherman who got caught too far into the current, or was driven there by a chance storm, was bound, whether he wanted to or not, for the Americas. Even today, fishermen are caught this way, and some made the accidental voyage to Brazil in the last century, starved, thirsty, but alive. No doubt a small trickle of the predecessors did as well. The problem for any such trans-Atlantic voyager was that there was no way back, unless one knew how to master the circular patterns of winds that tied America to Europe and then to Africa.[18]

In Mansa Musa's account of his predecessor's exploration of the "Western Ocean," he related a telling point about the Atlantic. When Qu sent out his first expedition of 200 craft, only one returned. When they questioned the captain about his decision to return, he said, "Yes, O Sultan, we traveled for a long time until there appeared in the open sea a river with a powerful current. Mine was the last of those ships. The ships went on ahead but when they reached that place they did not return and no more was seen of them and we do not know what became of them. As for me, I went about at once and did not enter that river."[19] The Canary current must have appeared that way to such a mariner, a small detail that lends credence to Musa's tale.[20]

The problems of the Canary current were mirrored by the Gulf Stream, and perhaps that handful of possible American voyages to Europe were victims of the same peculiarity of the sea – the current made an outgoing voyage easy, even unavoidable, but the return impossible. Practical considerations of this sort made even successful adventures of exploration unattractive, if they did not preclude them entirely.

[17] David Calvocoressi and Nicholas David, "A New Survey of Radiocarbon and Thermoluminiscent Dates for West Africa," *Journal of African History* 20 (1976): 8–9.

[18] The problem of return voyages using African technology is the stumbling block, I think, to Ivan van Sertima's (and a number of other) attempts to see pre-Columbian African voyages and even commerce in the Atlantic; see *They Came Before Columbus: The African Presence in Ancient America* (New York, 1976).

[19] Al-'Umari, *Masalik* in Levtzion and Hopkins, *Corpus*, p. 268.

[20] The existence of the current must also have been common knowledge to the coastal people of the region, and perhaps also the Mansa Musa. Perhaps knowing of this current of no return would have reassured him that Qu would not return to claim his heritage.

The key to crossing and recrossing the Atlantic in sailing craft lies in a special feature of the two opposing currents. In the central Atlantic, not far from the Azores Islands, the outlying eddies of the currents come close to each other. If one is aware that there is an "outbound" current at the Canaries that will take one out into the Atlantic, and that relatively close by to the north there is an "inbound" current in the form of the Gulf Stream, by tacking from one to the other, one can be reassured of a safe return voyage. This simple trick was the key that unlocked the whole of the ocean, and was used, with variants, for the whole Age of Sail. Columbus discovered it; as chance would have it, he was married to a Portuguese woman who made her home in the Azores, and he had traversed most of the seas to the north.[21] There, from the Azores, he made the simple discovery that would allow him to dare to sail straight out into the Atlantic, assured that if he found nothing he could at least return home alive. Had he not known this (and perhaps had it not also been quite common knowledge to sailors of the day and place), he would never have even attempted his voyage. And his sailors in the celebrated story of his first crossing would have seen no point in begging him to turn back, for no sailing ship can ever turn back into a prevailing wind.

In fact, the events that put Columbus on that tiny island in the Azores were the culmination of a long string of accidents and profitable opportunities. A combination of circumstances and fixed features of the Atlantic made it the lot of Mediterranean people to be the first to make successful and practical sustained Atlantic commerce. Exploration of the Atlantic was not a part of some early modern scientific research, akin to a space shot, or the romantic quest that historians of the earlier part of the twentieth century gave it. The tales of Prince Henry the Navigator, the "Sage of Sagres," looking dreamily out into the Atlantic might have fired the imagination of Portuguese nationalists in the nineteenth century, but it did not carry much weight in the thirteenth century, when a series of accidents led to the discovery of the key to a successful crossing.[22]

The exploration of the Atlantic begins, prosaically, not with dreamers, but with the development of the grain trade in the late thirteenth century. Mediterranean cities, growing and expanding with the renewed trade of the early Renaissance, soon outstripped the grain supplies of their immediate hinterlands. They began to reach for other sources of cheaper grain in coastal regions farther and farther afield, because moving grain by ship was cheap enough to be worthwhile, even over long distances, in the increasingly wealthy world of the Mediterranean. By 1277, Mediterranean shipping had outgrown the sea itself, and the first trading voyages, under Genoese captains, passed through the Pillars of Hercules and into the Atlantic to find cheaper grain in

[21] Thornton, *Africa and Africans*, pp. 19–24.
[22] A classic statement in English is C. R. Beazely, *Prince Henry the Navigator* (London, 1901, reprinted 1968).

Atlantic France, England, the Low Countries, and the Rhine Valley. Eventually, ships from Italian and Spanish cities would find their way to the Vistula in Poland to load up with grain.[23]

The grain trade drew more shipping into the waters off the coast of Portugal and Morocco, and with the increase in shipping came an increased chance of accidental discovery. In 1312, in fact, a Genoese merchant Lanzarotto Malocello, bound for northern Europe, was blown off course and found himself in the Canary Islands. Malocello, who had interests in cloth as well as grain, noticed that the rocks of the island had deposits of orchil, a lichen used for making a fast blue dye. He decided to return and exploit these sources, as well as do whatever business there might be with the inhabitants of the islands. A map of 1339 shows the Canary group of islands on it, festooned with the arms of Genoa and a tiny picture of Malocello's castle, rediscovered for Christians (Muslims in North Africa knew the islands and made occasional forays there) more than a millennium after the first Romans had visited the Fortunate Isles.[24] The first small but decisive steps into the Atlantic had been taken, and soon it would bear fruit.

THE TWO WINGS OF EUROPEAN ATLANTIC EXPANSION

The possibility of trade in orchil, and subsequently in wool and in capturead people, brought more European visitors to the islands. Throughout the rest of the fourteenth century, the Canaries became a regular point to visit. Europeans made their first unsuccessful attempts to conquer the islands, and made numerous raids on them for cattle, sheep, and slaves. By century's end, missionaries were visiting them to convert these strange people, who lived on islands but made no boats, who had social stratification and small states but did not use metals, to Christianity.

Europeans dubbed the waters that connected Europe, the Canaries, and northern Africa the "Little Sea" (*Mar Pequeña*) after it became a part of regular navigation. In time, these accidental discoveries led to two great wings of discovery. One wing led southward into Africa, as knowledge of the winds and currents around the Canaries finally allowed Europeans to discover the key to the round-trip voyages to Africa. The other wing led straight into the Atlantic, first to the small islands of Madeira and the Azores, and then ultimately to the Caribbean and the Americas.

These European pioneers were not scientists or explorers. Although many higher nobles in Portugal saw vast strategic goals that might be realized by sailing in the Atlantic, they were hamstrung by the cost of such adventures

---

[23] Pierre Chaunu, *L'expansion européen du XIIIe à XVe siècles* (Paris, 1969), pp. 92–93.

[24] Charles de la Roncière, *La découverte de l'Afrique au moyen age: Cartographes et exploateurs* (3 vols., Cairo, 1925–26) 2: 3–4. A medieval Muslim description is found in al-Idrisi's twelfth-century account, in Levtzion and Hopkins, *Corpus*, p. 106.

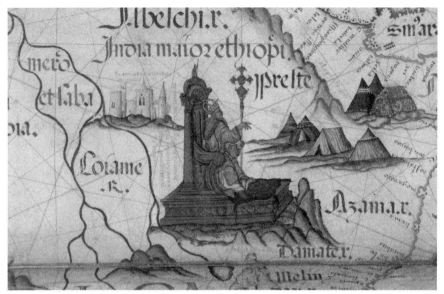

FIGURE 1. "John Prestor as Emperor of Ethiopia," from *Queen Mary's Atlas*. © The British Library Board.

and ill-equipped to pay for them. Thus, when Gomes Eannes de Zurara, the official chronicler of Prince Henrique (known in English as Prince Henry the Navigator), wrote about his motives for sailing into the Atlantic and down the African coast, he included strategic ideas like encircling the Muslims in North Africa, making contact with Prester John, a Christian prince in the faraway east, or converting the people of Africa to Christianity.[25]

Prince Henry was particularly interested in establishing contact with Prester John. Prester John was supposed to be a beleaguered Christian monarch who allegedly sent messengers to the Papal Curia through Crusaders in the Middle East at the end of the twelfth century. The original letter and account of this king was elaborated and circulated in ever-more fantastic versions, making his a land of unbelievable majesty and power.[26] Whether the original letter was from him or not, by 1250 or so, Prester John's land was believed to be in Ethiopia. Wolfram von Eschenbach, author of the most important of the German versions of the stories of King Arthur's knights, associated the Holy Grail with dark-skinned people, and one of his continuators held that the Grail

[25] Gomes Eanes de Zurara, *Crónica do descobrmento e conquista de Guiné*, ed. Torquato de Sousa Soares (2 vols., Lisbon, 1978), cap. 7. I have cited the chapters to facilitate comparisons of the many editions and translations.

[26] The letter may well have been imaginary, and there are literally hundreds of extant versions in many languages. Scholars have sought since the nineteenth century to reconstruct the original text. For a valuable study, and reconstruction of a composite early version, see Manuel João Ramos (editor) and Leonor Buescu (trans.), *A Carta do Preste João das Índias: Versões medievais Latinas* (Lisbon, 1998).

was in Prester John's lands.[27] In 1306, these stories were consolidated when an Ethiopian mission arrived in the Spanish court, seeking an alliance against Egypt and other Muslim powers. Ethiopian monks visited Europe regularly; they attended the Church Council of Florence in 1415, and established a community in Rome. In 1428, there were active negotiations to create a double marriage between the King of Aragon and the King of Ethiopia.[28] Portugal was caught up in the same stories, and when he sought to explain Prince Henrique's sponsorship of some Atlantic voyages, the chronicler Gomes Eanes de Zurara held that making contact with "other Christian princes," of whom Prester John would clearly be one, was one of his most important priorities.[29]

In the end, however, the crown – and Prince Henry in particular – was poor, and these strategic dreams would be expensive to undertake. A young son unlikely to succeed his father as king, Prince Henry had been compensated by being named Grand Master of the Order of Christ, a crusading order established from the Portuguese elements of the Knights Templar. The order was not wealthy, and whatever they wished to accomplish across the seas had to be paid for, so that the capture of slaves or the locating of valuable commodities accompanied their military aims. Not surprisingly, Zurara did not forget to mention commercial objectives and the discovery of gold, known to be mined in West Africa and exported to Europe for centuries, in his list of Prince Henry's motivations.

The earliest explorers were often minor nobles, anxious to win their spurs in combat and prove their names, especially in the spin-off of military activity that accompanied the Portuguese invasion of Morocco in 1415. But they were joined by merchants from Lisbon and other Portuguese ports, who saw potential for profit in trading, or even in raiding, in the Atlantic. The merchants provided the financial backing, the knights provided the military protection that made raiding possible and defended the effort, and Prince Henry provided sponsorship. This sponsorship was largely legal and protective rather than financial, although in the longer run, the sponsors as well hoped to reap financial rewards through taxation. For example, when a large group of people from Lagos in southern Portugal proposed an expedition to Guinea in 1445, their numbers included local officials, merchants, and members of the lesser nobility who pooled their resources and appealed, in the high language of feudal loyalty, to Prince Henrique for his patronage. He gave his consent, claiming, however, one-fifth of their profits.[30]

---

[27] Wolfram von Eschenbach, *Parzival*, which has a number of black-skinned persons connected with the Holy Grail. A continuation, by Albert van Schaffenberg, *Der Jüngere Titurel* (ed. Karl August Hahn, Quedlindburg and Leipzig, 1842 [GB] mod. ed. Werner Wolf, 2 vols., 1968), actually places the Grail in the lands of Prester John in "India" (lines 5915, 6086–6088).

[28] For an overview of this, from the Ethiopian perspective as well as European, see Mordechai Abir, *Ethiopia and the Red Sea: The Rise and Decline of the Solomonic Dynasty and Muslim-European Rivalry in the Region* (London, 1980), pp. 19–40.

[29] Zurara, *Chronica*, cap. 7.

[30] Zurara, *Crónica*, caps. 49 (the appeal), 51 (the wide range of participants). In the end, the voyage resulted in one of the earliest extensive raids in the Senegal area and netted a number of captives.

In the end, the voyaging into the Atlantic was not part of a grand scheme, but a haphazard collection of adventures organized by lower knights and merchants willing to take some risks for profits. As it was the merchants who paid the bill, it was they who really determined where, when, and how fast expansion would take place. And they were guided much more by practical considerations of travel and commerce than the far-reaching goals or even the knightly derring-do that motivated the people they sponsored.

Thus, it was probably an accident that revealed the position of Madeira and the Azores, first visited by a fleet of mixed nationalities under the guidance of a Portuguese in 1341 that sought to raid the Canaries and was recorded by the Italian literary humanist Boccacio.[31] It took some time to demonstrate the value of the Atlantic islands. They were covered with volcanic soil that had tall hardwoods that could be useful in shipbuilding. Small, mostly unrecorded expeditions exploited the trees on a seasonal basis in the late fourteenth century, and in 1420, the Portuguese government supported the first colonization of them, begun in earnest in 1425. The original settlers were sawyers, cutting down the trees and selling them to visiting ships, while also gathering wax, honey, and wild dyestuffs.[32] As they cleared Madeira's land, they found that they could raise cattle, which they were already doing by 1446, and the rich soil could produce wheat for the markets in Lisbon and the Mediterranean at a competitive price.[33] The success of wheat farming led to more settlement, often by noble entrepreneurs who brought settlers from their estates in Portugal. By the 1450s, however, the settlers in Madeira discovered that sugarcane could grow and bring even higher profits than wheat could. Soon Madeira became a major producer of sugar, and often the larger estates were repopulated by slaves brought from raids on the Canary Islands. When the Italian visitor Alvise da Mosto described the islands in 1455, there were already a considerable number of Canarians there, enough to establish a recognizable subgroup.[34]

As the Madeiran planters began clearing the hillsides, they made another important discovery – that the slopes could produce grapevines in great abundance. Madeira wines became world-famous, and wine competed with and eventually passed sugar as its primary export.[35] Thus in the space of less than a century, this small Atlantic islands showed that even uninhabited islands in the tropics could produce substantial profits. No doubt Maderia's success led

---

[31] "De Canaria et insulla reliquis, ultra Ispanium, in occeano nouiter repertis," in *Monumenta Henriciana* (14 vols., Lisbon, 1960–74) 1: 202–206, a voyage that was equipped both to raid and to trade in hides and dyestuffs. These visitors were not the first, for the island appears on the map of Dulcert in 1339; see Kamal, *Monumenta* 4: fol. 1222.

[32] Zurara, *Crónica*, cap. 5.

[33] Zurara, *Crónica*, cap. 83 on both cattle farming and high yields of wheat; Alvise da Mosto [often referred to as Cadamosto], "Mondo Novo," p. 16.

[34] Recounted in detail in John Thornton, *Africa and Africans in the Making of the Atlantic World, 1400–1800* (2nd ed., Cambridge, 1998), pp. 33–34.

[35] Thornton, *Africa and Africans*, p. 34.

to Portuguese colonization of the Azores. These less promising islands laying farther out in the Atlantic were discovered, possibly accidentally, in 1427.[36] The islands, colonized later in the fifteenth century, still managed to produce some sugar and wheat for Portuguese and European markets. The prospect of finding more islands like Madeira would lead to the Atlantic wing of European expansion, aimed primarily at locating islands. A Portuguese request for royal permission in 1486 to sail farther into the Atlantic (which led nineteenth-century Portuguese historians to argue that they had already visited America) spoke of various islands, as did Columbus's charter in 1492.[37] Maps of the late fifteenth century placed several islands just beyond the Azores in the mid-Atlantic bearing names like "Brazil" and "Antilla," probably imaginary places that would subsequently be bestowed on American locations.

THE AFRICAN WING OF EXPANSION

While one group of Portuguese was demonstrating the value of uninhabited lands in the Atlantic, another group was using these discoveries to learn the secret of sailing to Africa. In 1434, Gil Eanes, who was experienced in navigation to the Canaries and Azores, realized that it might be possible to overcome the problems of going against the Canary current that had thwarted earlier attempts at round trips beyond Cape Nao, the cape of no return, in southern Morocco that was traditionally known as a place from which one could journey south but never north. Eanes's men showed that by sailing straight out to sea from beyond this point, one could reach one of the Atlantic islands, and from there it was possible to catch the southernmost ends of the Gulf Stream to sail back to Europe.

This sailing trick, known by the sailors of the period as the Little Wheel, was the precursor to a similar maneuver on a much larger scale, called the Great Wheel, that allowed Columbus and all who followed him to traverse the Atlantic both ways. Once this discovery was made, it would be possible to sail out into the Atlantic knowing that a return current would allow a trip back home.

The sailors exploited the Little Wheel first because the end target of the Little Wheel – round-trip voyages to sub-Saharan Africa – connected merchants to a known objective of proven commercial value. European maps of the day regularly revealed the course of the major rivers (although they joined the Senegal and Niger Rivers into a single stream often called the Nile of the Blacks) and correctly named the towns. A handful of Europeans had even traveled across the desert to Africa, and of course many Muslims from North Africa had as well. In the early fifteenth century, for example, a French knight, Anselm d'Ysalguier,

---

[36] Oliveira Marques, "Expansão no Atlântico," pp. 52–56.
[37] Donation to Fernão Dulmo, 3 March 1486, in José Ramo Coelho, ed. *Alguns documentos do Archivo Nacional da Torre de Tombo àcerca das navigações e conquistas portugueses* (Lisbon, 1892), pp. 58–59.

had crossed to Gao, a rich town on the Niger River, where he met and married a noblewoman named Salacasis. After eight years of residence, he returned to Europe with his wife and a train of African servants and settled in Marseilles. Their son, Eustache de Faudoas, was surnamed *le Maure* (the Moor).[38]

Even with the knowledge of the possibility of round trips to West Africa, no one followed up Eanes' demonstration for another ten years, when Antão Gonçalves made the first round trip to Senegal. This breakthrough was widely hailed, but commercial problems held up full exploitation of the region for another fifteen years.

When the Portuguese first began to arrive in West Africa, they learned from reports of João Fernandes, who spent seven months in the desert, that they could lure trans-Saharan caravans to the otherwise desolate harbor at Arguim and purchase Sudanese gold at near source-level prices there.[39] At the same time that some sailors were examining the prospects of using Arguim, others were arriving in the waters off Senegal with more military intentions in mind. Rather than moving quickly to establish trading relations with Africans there, the Portuguese instead focused on raiding the coastal population and capturing people to take back as slaves. The leader of the first party to land in Senegal, Estevão Afonso, managed to ambush and capture a young man and stole some goods that amounted to little more than souvenirs.[40]

In their initial contact with Africa, the Portuguese were drawing on a long-standing tradition of the western Mediterranean. There the coasts, divided into a Christian north and a Muslim south, were the scene of regularized piracy involving attacking posts on shore as well as taking ships at sea. Trading vessels from the north visiting North Africa were well armed and manned, a precaution against hostile Muslim vessels they might meet at sea. But if they arrived in a Muslim port and found its garrison too small, poorly armed, or inattentive, they might simply put aside commercial strategies and raid the place, carrying off as many goods as they could and capturing as many people as possible to enslave. Muslim shipping often did the same in Europe, and one result was the constant movement of captives from one shore to another. Indeed, at least one Christian charity was established with the entire purpose of redeeming Christians captured by Muslim pirates. In the sixteenth century, as many as 15,000 people from one or the other shore were thus enslaved.

It might have been no different in Africa, except that there, the local people were taken completely by surprise and there was no garrison or coastal protection at all. These were easy pickings for the Portuguese, who dropped the commercial intentions of their sponsors for the pirates' calling. Such armed

---

[38] On the story and its documentation, see Kemal, *Monumenta* 4: fols. 1371–71v. Most of the narrative sources are of seventeenth-century date, but there are records from the late fifteenth century that reveal something of the family, including the son's name.

[39] Zurara, *Crónica*, cap. 77. For a summary of early Portuguese knowledge, see da Mosto's report of 1455 on the desert, "Mondo Novo," ed. Gasparrini Leporace, pp. 26–29, 37–48.

[40] Zurara, *Cronica*, cap. 60.

encounters were followed by many others in the next few years, as Portuguese ships raided fishing villages along the coast above and below the Cape Verde peninsula. The young men in these Portuguese vessels, squires in search of deeds of derring-do that might earn them a knighthood, thought of attacks on fishermen and poorly armed villages as feats of knightly courage, and indeed several were knighted for their participation.[41]

In the end, however, these attacks were both fruitless and counterproductive. Although the Africans were surprised and shocked at first to meet navigators from an unexpected quarter, they had the means to resist the attacks. Early reports from the sailors indicated that the Africans carried much lighter armor than the Portuguese, and their bows were weaker than crossbows. But Africans poisoned their arrows, making even a small scratch anywhere on the body potentially fatal. Against this weapon the Portuguese had no response – in 1447, Nuno Tristão, leading a landing party near Beziguich in the Cape Verde region, lost nineteen of twenty-two men of the party to poisoned arrows and had to limp back to Portugal with a skeleton crew.[42] Other Portuguese mariners met stiff resistance, often even before they landed, by Africans who piled into large naval craft that outnumbered the invaders, while constantly attacking with the dreaded poisoned arrows.

By 1456, the Portuguese crown decided that they had had enough of the raids. They had netted few captives and had cost a substantial toll in Portuguese lives. Deciding that they needed to repair damaged relations with the Africans, they dispatched Diogo Gomes, a nobleman and a member of the royal household, to negotiate with political authorities for a new start in West Africa. Gomes took two voyages to Guinea, in 1456 and in 1462, meeting with political elites and winning agreements for peaceful trade.[43]

In the following years, as Portuguese caravels reached farther and farther along the coast, they showed that they have learned from the lessons in the Senegambian region by the early knightly adventurers. Not even attempting to raid the coasts, they went immediately to establish diplomatic contacts with the political authorities they met, inviting them to send ambassadors to Lisbon and encouraging them to have their younger relatives educated in Portugal with the hope that this might spread Christianity and create alliances. In these negotiations, the Portuguese treated the African rulers with most of the same courtesies they extended to European monarchs, even those, such as on the Gold Coast, who ruled quite small domains.[44] They even went farther, sending embassies far inland to contact the emperor of Mali in the 1490s, and were in

---

[41] Zurara, *Cronica*, caps. 75, 87–88, 94; for an insightful commentary, see Marian Malowist.

[42] Zurara, *Cronica*, cap. 86. For dates, see Gomes, "Prima Inuentione," fol. 274v; and MS "Valentim Fernandes," fol. 89. Also João de Barros, *Decadas de India* (Lisbon, 1552, mod. facsimile ed. 1938), Decade I, Book 1, cap. 14.

[43] Gomes, "Prima Inuentione," fols. 276–277, 280v, 281v–282.

[44] An interesting study of this diplomacy can be found in Ivana Elbl, "Cross-Cultural Trade and Diplomacy: Portuguese Relations with West Africa, 1441–1521," *Journal of World History* 3 (1992): 165–204.

the process of seeking to contact even the ruler of Songhai in Timbuktu when the Moroccan invasion captured the city in 1491.[45] In all this, their most spectacular success was in Kongo, where conversion was won and alliances made.

Once won, the peace was commercially effective. Portuguese traders found that West Africans, with a long tradition of slavery and a well-established slave trade to North Africa clients across the desert, were prepared to sell slaves in much larger numbers than the Portuguese could ever capture at a high human cost. The effect of the transfer of markets was telling – the customs records in Seville recorded a shift in origins of slaves from trans-Atlantic sources away from those arriving through North African merchants after having endured the Saharan crossing to those of the same ulitatme origin but having been brought on Portuguese ships. Portuguese successes in this field have been described as the victory of the "caravel over the camel."[46]

The Portuguese military-naval failure was probably rooted in the possibilities of land-sea warfare in the time. While Portuguese vessels large enough to withstand Atlantic navigation brought them to Atlantic Africa, these vessels were too large and deep-drafted to navigate effectively in the shallow coastal waters and estuaries of the Atlantic coast. Forced to land smaller bodies of men in longboats, which could barely hold a dozen men with their equipment, they were faced with much larger craft (holding dozens and even up to forty men each) that were specially designed to have shallow drafts and operate in the coastal environment. Outnumbered, and all defensive advantages neutralized by poisoned arrows, the Portuguese had to accept a new relationship.[47]

The Portuguese would not attempt naval raiding again on the African coast for many years. The rest of the push around African was a study in diplomatic negotiations with African powers for rights to trade and the keeping of the peace. But these new lessons, fully absorbed by 1460, did not do much to speed up Portuguese advance around Africa. Although the basic navigational breakthroughs necessary to sail around Africa were made in the 1440s, no Portuguese ship actually did so until the very end of the century. Portuguese advance along the coast was not a steady gradual advance, but a series of long leaps, followed by long pauses. This pattern was dictated by the commercial nature of the expansion, because the Portuguese actually doing the sailing were not explorers with curiosity as their motive, but merchants looking for sure profits, especially after the end of the early periods when exploration was linked with military exploits and slave raids. Once the possibilities of reaching an area by sea were demonstrated, the political barriers overcome, and market

---

[45] Avelino Teixeira da Mota, "A malogrado viagem de Diogo Carreiro a Tombuctu em 1565," *Boletim Cultural da Guiné Portuguesa* 25 (no. 97) (1970): 5–25 (and as a separate from the Agrumamento de estudos da Cartografia Antiga, no. 57).

[46] Avelino Teixeira da Mota, "Alguns aspectos da colonização e do comércio maritime dos Portugueses na África occidental nos séculos XV e XVI," *Anais do clube militar naval* 106 (1976): 679–681.

[47] John Thornton, *Warfare in Atlantic Africa, 1500–1800* (London, 1999), p. 29; *Africa and Africans*, pp. 36–39.

possibilities demonstrated, there was little incentive for merchants to push on to the risks and dangers of further navigation.

The profitability of the Guinea coast trade, however, did offer up possibilities for further expansion, with a little push from the crown. Once the Portuguese crown discovered that there were developed and profitable markets in the area, they moved quickly to tax and control them. Claiming the title "Lords of the Navigation of Guinea," the Portuguese crown claimed that it had the right to determine who could sail to the region. As soon as they were able, they insisted visitors, like the Venetian da Mosto who sailed to Senegambia in 1455, obtain a license and pay a tax in Lisbon before they could trade. Even under those circumstances, however, merchants would prefer certain markets to exploration. Thus, the crown granted a monopoly and the right to collect duties to a wealthy Lisbon businessman, Fernão Gomes, in 1469. Gomes paid handsomely for his rights – 200,000 reis initially and 300,000 reis a year for the next four years – which might guarantee profits for years to come, but he also had to accept the burden of agreeing to explore the coast further on, at the rate of 100 leagues a year.[48] When other merchants protested the grant in the Portuguese Cortes (a representative assembly) in 1472, the king responded that the grant was for "the good of the kingdom."[49]

Thus, it was the profits of the first successes that led to real exploration, not under royal auspices, but through the work of a private trader, who could be effectively rewarded for the efforts he made on behalf of the king and his strategic goals. As it turned out, the exploration consistently yielded additional profitable goods. The pioneers that Gomes supported reached beyond Sierra Leone and discovered they could buy a new African pepper, called malagueta pepper, on the modern-day Ivory Coast; then, just a few years later, the found a new outlet for the gold trade on the Gold Coast (modern-day Ghana). Gomes grew rich on the trade he controlled and had gained and was eventually knighted and declared noble. On his new coat of arms, Gomes fixed an image of the heads of three Africans, each adorned with gold ear and lip rings and a wearing a gold collar in recognition of the role the gold and slave trade played in his ennoblement.[50] Meanwhile, voyages sponsored by Gomes continued to explore the African coast, reaching probably as far as modern-day Gabon by 1474, when his lucrative contract ended and his monopoly was assumed by the crown.

Just as the wealth discovered in Senegambian trade had permitted the financing of the voyages of Gomes, so the wealth of the Gold Coast would underwrite further exploration. In the interim, however, war with Castille led to

---

[48] De Barros, *Decadas de India*; Peres, *História*, pp. 144–145.

[49] "Reclamação" in Cortes, 1472, Brásio, *Monumenta* 2nd series, 1: 451–454.

[50] De Barros, *Ásia*, Dec. 1, Book 2, cap. 2, fol. 22. Although de Barros' description of the coat of arms says the figures were "negros" and hence male, a sixteenth-century illustration of coats of arms, the *Livro de Nobreza* of António Godinho, has them as women, illustrated in Brásio, *Monumenta*, 2nd series, vol. 1, facing p. 440.

widespread attacks on Portuguese positions by Spanish ships, and armed fleets began to visit the Gold Coast to get their share of the profits. In the end, given the significance of the trade, the Portuguese crown decided to build a fortress base in the coast to keep foreign shipping out and enforce the royal monopoly. In 1482, shortly after the end of the Portuguese-Castillian war, Diogo de Azambuja was dispatched with a fleet to construct a fortress on the coast, which was dedicated to Saint George, or São Jorge da Mina (Saint George of the Mine in Portuguese).[51]

During this period, the Portuguese also made contact with the Kingdom of Benin, the other powerful coastal African kingdom, and one that promised an important trade in pepper.[52] When Benin established diplomatic relations with Portugal, its first ambassador told the king of Portugal that a powerful king named Ogané, whose lands lay east of Benin, was held as the "Supreme Pontiff" among all the countries of the region. Among Ogané's symbols were crosses, "like the cross worn by the Knights of Saint John," which the ambassador himself wore. The court officials in Portugal compared these accounts with those of Ethiopian diplomats who had been in Spain and even with Ptolomey's ancient geography and concluded that Benin must be very near Prester John's lands.[53] For the first time in the history of Portuguese exploration of Africa, the crown, rather than private merchants, financed voyages.

In 1482, Diogo Cão was dispatched to search for Prester John. Unfortunately for him, the conventional wisdom of the time understood that the coast continued more or less in a west-to-east line from Benin to Prester John's kingdom of Ethiopia. Of course, this was mistaken, and Cão soon discovered the coast veered sharply southward shortly after passing Benin. Cão's ships reached as far as the Cape of Good Hope, a voyage that might have been fruitless had they not contacted the powerful Kingdom of Kongo, which showed both an inclination to become Christian and to be a profitable trading partner. A promise of good relations resulted in an exchange of ambassadors, and by 1491, Nzinga a Nkuwu, king of Kongo, had been baptized as João I of Kongo, and a promising new relationship had been formed. Kongo showed that it was a worthwhile market, and soon Portuguese traders were buying copper, ivory, exotic creatures (like grey parrots and civet cats), and above all slaves from the central African kingdom.[54]

---

[51] For details, see Oliveira Marques, "Expansão no Atlântico," pp. 92–98.

[52] According to the contemporary chronicler, Rui de Pina, however, the promise of a rich trade in pepper was not fulfilled and the commercial factory planned for the country was abandoned; Rui de Pina, *Cronica delRei D. Joham Segundo*, cap 24.

[53] De Barros, *Ásia* Dec. 1, Book 3, cap. 4. Some Benin bronze sculptures bear such a cross, for an argument that Ogané was in fact the Igala kingdom of the Niger-Benue confluence; John Thornton, "Tradition, Documents and the Ife-Benin Relationship," *History in Africa* 15 (1988): 351–362.

[54] Cão's initial encounter with Kongo is found in a near contemporary account of Rui de Pina (known only in an Italian translation), which formed the basis for his account in "Cronica del-Rey D Joham..." both published in Carmen Raudolet, *O cronista Rui de Pina e o 'relação de reino de Congo'* (Lisbon, 1992). For a detailed study, see Ilido do Amaral, *O Reino de Congo,*

The quest for Prester John was not halted by Cão's unfortunate voyage, because the prospect of lucrative trade with Kongo made a longer voyage still possible. The information which they had gleaned from Benin's ambassador about Ogané, and Cão's discovery of the length of Africa, encouraged Portugal's planners in their belief that they had been "shown the way to the Indies" and encouraged by the thought that the voyages of Diogo Cão had indeed shown the way to "the Indies" (a vague term that included Ethiopia as well as the more eastern lands of the Indian Ocean), João II fitted out the explorations of Bartolomeu Dias (in 1488) to seek Ethiopia by the African sea route and the same year dispatched Pero de Corvilhão to Egypt to make contact with Prester John by an overland route.[55] Dias did not manage to reach the Indies, but eventually Vasco da Gama did, in 1498. It was not until 1520 that a Portuguese expedition made it to Ethiopia, and when they did, they found Pero de Corvilhão living there, with great estate and honor, but not allowed to leave the country.[56]

THE ATLANTIC WING OF EXPANSION

The whole of the development of relations with Africa passed before Columbus sought his fortune in the central Atlantic. While commercial possibilities were followed by strategic goals in Africa, the tiny Atlantic islands went through their growth as agricultural colonies. Even with the success in Africa, Columbus met with little favor in the Portuguese court. His plan to sail to "Cipangu," which he knew from Marco Polo's geography, fell on deaf ears in Portugal, even though the contemporary revisions to the Ptolemy's version of the world persuaded them to sponsor a trip around Africa. He had somewhat more luck in Spain.

The Spanish crown had not participated in African exploration much at all, but instead focused great attention on conquering the Canary Islands, which had been ceded to Luis de Cerda, a Spanish nobleman, by Papal Bull in 1344.[57] As with the Portuguese, the Spanish crown allowed much of the work and expense of this conquest to be born by the would-be conquerors. Thus, in 1404–05, they sponsored the first successful conquest of two of the Canaries by Jean de Bettancourt and Gadifer de la Salle, French nobles who raised their

---

os Mbundus (ou Ambundos), o Reino de Angola (ou Ngola) e a presença portuguesa de finais do século XV a meados do século XVI (Lisbon, 1996).

[55] Oliveira Marques, "Expansão no Altântico," pp. 106–111. The account in Thornton, *Africa and Africans*, p. 32, attributes Diogo Cão's voyage to this inspiration, but Barros notes that follow-up voyages commenced in 1486, meaning those of Bartolomeu Dias.

[56] Corvilhão's story is told in Francisco Álvares, *Ho Prestre Joam das Indias* (Lisbon, 1540), cap. 104 (see the translation of a fuller edition compiled from several sources by Charles Beckingham and G. W. B Huntingford, *The Prester John of the Indies* (2 vols., London, 1961)).

[57] *Tu devocionis sinceritas*, November 15, 1344, *Monumenta Henriciana* 1: 209. The Portuguese crown protested the grant, claiming that they had sponsored earlier and more successful expeditions to the islands; see Protest of King Afonso IV, 1345, *Monumenta Henricina* 1: 231–234.

own funds. However, when the war with Portugal broke out, a number of Castillian ships advanced into Africa and dealt in gold with the Gold Coast, whose rulers had no interest in supporting either the Portuguese king's or Fernão Gomes's claims to monopoly. Spain again abandoned the African wing, however, when peace was established by the treaty of Alcaçova in 1479.[58]

The Canaries may have seemed an easy mark. Their inhabitants were divided into several hostile polities, they made no watercraft, and they had no useful metals. Canarians fought to defend themselves with hardened staffs and by throwing stones. Both Portugal and Spain at various times tried to subdue the Canarians, and raided them in between to stock slave plantations in Madeira or on the conquered islands (which also turned to sugar production).

But the Canarians proved to be tough fighters. They could throw stones with enough force to knock an armored knight off his horse, and could hurl the spent arrows and crossbow bolts fired at them back with enough force to pierce light armor. They defeated a very large Portuguese army, of 2,500 foot-soldiers and 120 mounted knights sent to subdue the larger islands in 1424, and again in 1425. In 1460, they ejected another group of Portuguese claimants from Grand Canary Island. Only by allying themselves with some Canarians against the others were the Spanish finally able to win the submission of all the islands in the archipelago, and that only in 1497, five years after Columbus's first voyage.[59]

In the midst of the fight for the last of the Canaries, Columbus approached the Spanish court with a plan to sail to Asia across the Atlantic, using the combination of the Canary Current and the Gulf Stream. The court granted his request, but their charter showed that the most they really expected of him was to meet more islands like the ones already discovered.

Indeed, the first trans-Atlantic voyages met just that. The islands of the Greater Antilles, and Hispaniola, the first Spanish colony in the New World, were essentially an extension of the Canaries. The local people were divided into polities with social classes and dependent populations, and the Spanish soon learned that they could conquer them the same way they had conquered the Canarians, by using alliance with one power against another. This strategy not only worked in the islands of the Greater Antilles, Hispaniola, Jamaica, Cuba, and Puerto Rico, but it would work even against the great empires that were to be found on the mainland. The Aztecs and the Incas, for all their large populations, were vulnerable to political manipulation.

In comparing the behavior of the Spanish and the Portuguese in the late fifteenth century, it might be possible to describe two distinct national styles: a Portuguese one anchored on their African experience and focused on developing

---

[58] J. B. Blake, *European Beginnings in West Africa, 1454–1578: A Survey of the First Century of White Enterprise in West Africa* (London, 1937), still a worthwhile survey. For more specific details, see P. E. H. Hair, *The Founding of the Castelo de São Jorge da Mina: An Analysis of the Sources* (Madison: University of Wisconsin, 1994).

[59] For fuller details on this conquest and its problems, see Chapter Five in this book.

commercial contact with local powers, and a Spanish one, inspired by their long effort in the Canaries, that paid more attention to conquest. While the analogy is not exact, for the Portuguese only gave up on conquest when defeated in Africa, and the Spanish did launch a number of purely commercial ventures, the Brazilian example seems to bear it out.

Portuguese historians sometimes maintain that the Portuguese had visited Brazil as early as 1498, although there is no question that the first voyage to Brazil, led by Pedro Álvares Cabral, took place in 1500. Cabral was actually intending to go to India to follow up Vasco da Gama's contacts, and was driven by storms too far into the Atlantic to make the usual "Great Wheel" route. In any case, he considered the landfall to be sufficiently important that he dispatched one of his ships back to Portugal to give the news to the king.

In the following years, however, the Portuguese showed a great reluctance to colonize or even fight with the local inhabitants. Rather they traded, especially giving iron goods in exchange for tropical hardwoods (Brazil wood). It was only when French sailors, tipped off by news of Cabral's voyage, entered in the trade in competition that the Portuguese became involved at all in the life on shore.[60] In the face of this competition, the Portuguese crown determined that they would have to establish a landed presence, and to that end between 1534 and 1536 began a system of large grants to wealthy or powerful private individuals, each of which would finance the protection of the coast, including some settlements, in exchange for tax exemptions (for a time) and the right to considerable local jurisdiction and power.[61] The system worked in areas where the colonizing expeditions were able to achieve a good local military alliance (usually with cooperating indigenous groups) and where they were able to develop exports which allowed them to finance their expenses and make profits.

The crown used a similar system to grant Paulo Dias de Novais the right to build a colony in Angola in 1575. The colony's primary purpose was not so much to prevent foreign interference in trade, but to manage to control trade from a section of the central African coast, focused on the area around the mouth of the River Kwanza, one of the few African rivers that can be navigated for some distance inland. Dias de Novais provided the capital and manpower from his own resources, and largely paid for it with the export of slaves that he obtained from wars, first on behalf of African powers and later on his own.[62]

---

[60] Jorge Couto, *A construção do Brasil: Amerindios, portugueses e africanos do início do povamento a finais do quinhentos* (Lisbon, 1995).

[61] The history of these captaincies were traced in several classic treatises by João Fernando de Almeida Prado, *Pernambuco e as capitanias do norte do Brasil* (São Paulo, 1939); *A Bahia e as capitanias do centro do Brasil* (São Paulo, 1945), and *São Vicente e as capitanias do sul do Brasil* (São Paulo, 1961).

[62] A good exposition of Dias de Novais's financial arrangements and a comparison with Brazilian legal techniques is in Ilídio do Amaral, *O consulado de Paulo Dias de Novais: Angola no ultimo quartel do século XVI e primeiro do século XVII* (Lisbon, 2000).

The rhythm of Spanish exploration in the Americas was very much like that of the Portuguese in Africa. It took fully a quarter-century to get from the islands of the Greater Antilles to the Aztec Empire, even though most of the geography of the Caribbean basin was known by 1504, just after the end of the first decade of Spanish presence.[63] It was only when the possibilities of economic and commercial exploitation of the great islands were exhausted that the more adventurous sought to find their fortunes on the mainland. Conquest was not always a goal in areas, such as the north coast of South America or the Panama region, where it was possible to deal with local powers through commercial transactions. As with the Portuguese in Africa, it would take royal intervention and favoritism to make the disfavored turn to further expansion.

Geographical location, fortunate accidents, and lucky discoveries played a major role in the European discovery of Atlantic navigation. But simply discovering how to sail from Europe to these distant destinations did not by itself lead to the creation of the Atlantic world that would develop. In the end, Europe's states, not private merchants, came to dominate the region; conquest and settlement rather than trade characterized large segments of it, and inter-regional migrations, voluntary and forced, would ultimately join the early pioneering efforts. To understand how those factors came together, we must turn to understanding the political and social system into which the early European voyagers fit, and ultimately the systems they met and their characteristics to see how the Atlantic world that did develop came to be.

---

[63] For a summary of these voyages, see Sauer, *Early Spanish Main*, pp. 104–141, and more recently, Hugh Thomas, *Rivers of Gold: The Rise of the Spanish Empire from Columbus to Magellan* (New York, 2003).

PART II

THREE ATLANTIC WORLDS

The accidental voyages of European knights and merchants brought three worlds into contact with each other. In many cases the encounter was startling, even a shock. Columbus was as surprised as the Tainos were when his ships arrived in the Caribbean in 1492. If West Africans and Europeans had some knowledge of each other before the first Portuguese ships inched down Africa's Atlantic coast, thanks to the Saharan trade, the surprise for Portuguese and Kongolese was probably mutual when they met at the mouth of the Congo River in 1483. Yet none of the participants took very long to realize that the people they met shared their common humanity, and did not resemble any of the monsters that European fantasy writers – precursors to the modern creators of science fiction – imagined might be in the remote corners of the world. If European exploration revealed nothing else, it was that there were no one-legged men with a single eye in the middle of their foreheads as described in the celebrated fantasy-adventures of John of Mandeville.

Europeans, Americans, and Africans discovered a common humanity in their physical forms and in their lives, for in many ways the world of the Age of Exploration and its aftermath had more commonalities than today's world does. Their preindustrial world was united by common rhythms of life and death, bound by the limits of a constricted food supply, beset by diseases that could not be cured. In this world of the sixteenth or eighteenth century, for example, no society had a life expectancy more than about forty years, and many had less. One out of three or four babies did not survive their first year of life, and on the whole, only half of those who were born managed to live long enough to reproduce themselves. This immense human wastage, sometimes made even worse in the harshest labor and social regimes, such as slavery, rack-renting, or heavy taxation, meant that even birthrates far in excess of those today produced relatively little population growth.

Fernand Braudel, the great French historian with a global view, published a map of the world in 1500 in his monumental work on capitalism and material life, which purported to reveal a world of substantial regional inequalities. Three levels marked this inequality, defined by basic economic factors, much as industrialization defines the developed and underdeveloped world today. At the lowest levels were the people who made their living by hunting and gathering – the foragers of Canada or some parts of Brazil, for example, whereas in the middle were farming populations that used the hoe as their principal instrument. Finally, Braudel proposed that the richest civilizations were those that farmed using the plow.[1] This three-part scheme is reminiscent of similar representations of the world today, with its rich industrialized (or even post-industrial) Northern countries, a group of mid-level industrializing nations in Latin America or Asia, and perhaps the "basket cases" with seriously underdeveloped economies, mostly in Africa. Indeed, the stark differences of the modern levels can be documented in basic conditions of human life. Life expectancy, infant mortality, quality of housing, morbidity – all these indices show clearly the startling differences in basic quality of life worldwide and reveal substantial inequalities in today's world and necessarily shape our own understanding of the past worlds, as it did for Braudel.

But this model of developed and underdeveloped only applies to the modern world, and projecting it back to the sixteenth century is a mistake. The evidence, limited though it is, does not show us that the life expectancy of foragers in Canada or Brazil was substantially lower than they were in France or England, as they might be today. Today, in developed countries of Western Europe, North America, or Japan, average life expectancy hovers around eighty years, whereas in much of Africa it barely passes sixty years in a few countries, generally wavers around fifty years and goes even into the low forties in a few troubled lands. South and Southeast Asia, for their part, have life expectancies around sixty years, South American countries in the high sixties and low seventies. Infant mortality, another frequently used guide to general health, shows a similar result. In the developed world, infant mortality is generally below 10‰, but in Africa it is frequently as high as 100‰ and even reaches 150‰ in a few disfavored regions. South and Southeast Asian infant mortality runs between 50‰ and 60‰, and South American rates are generally lower than 30‰.[2] Thus, in today's world, both life expectancy and infant mortality reveal quite a startling gap between the richest and the poorest countries, as well as a noticeable gap between the highly developed European, North American, and Japanese countries and the middling countries of South America and South Asia.

---

[1] In the one-volume presentation of 1966, Braudel used technology to define the levels, but when he revised the work in 1979, the levels remained, but the hoe/plow distinction was no longer as explicitly determinant; *Capitalism and Material Life* (3 vols., trans. Siân Reynolds, New York, 1983 [original French 1979]) 1: 58–59. On this map, however, the plow continues to be the determinant factor.

[2] I have obtained this information from the United Nations' *World Population Prospects: The 2006 Revision, Highlights* (New York, 2007) (http://www.un.org/esa/population/publications/wpp2006/WPP2006_Highlights_rev.pdf) tables A 17 (life expectancy), A 18, and A 19 (infant mortality). The report notes that HIV/AIDS has caused some of the very low levels of life expectancy found especially in Southern Africa.

But there was no startling gap in 1600. Thanks to baptismal records kept by priests in the Christian Kingdom of Kongo, it can be shown to have had a life expectancy of only about thirty-five years in the seventeenth century, and its infant mortality rate of some 250‰ is dismal by today's standards.[3] In fact, in Angola, where the old kingdom was located, the life expectancy of forty-one years and infant mortality of less than 132‰ are meaningfully better than in the kingdom, but put Angola close to the bottom of today's vital rates.[4]

Yet, Western Europe in the seventeenth century had vital rates that were, if anything, slightly worse than Kongo at the same time. According to decades of careful research in parish registers, historians put Western European life expectancies in the same mid-thirties range that Kongo had, and the infant mortality rate, which was closer to 300‰, was even worse.[5] As with Africa, so too it seems that the indigenous people of the Americas also had life expectancies in the same range as those of Europe; for example, the life expectancy of the people of Pecos Pueblo before 1700, as measured fairly imprecisely by methods of estimating the age at death of people buried in the cemetery, also hovers around thirty years.[6] Urban areas in indigenous Ameica, such as Teotihuacan, the city that flourished in central Mexico at the beginning of the Common Era, were also comparable in life expectancy to those found in the Old World at the same time, such as ancient Rome.[7] The impact of the Industrial Revolution, the development of modern medicine, and especially public health explain the dramatic changes made in Western Europe that totally transformed the region vis-á-vis its own past and the rest of the world. Angola's slightly better modern

---

[3] John Thornton, "Demography and History in the Kingdom of Kongo, 1550–1750," *Journal of African History* 18 (1977): 507–30, and "An Eighteenth Century Baptismal Register and the Demographic History of Manguenzo" in C. Fyfe and D. McMaster (eds.) *African Historical Demography* (Edinburgh: Centre of African Studies, 1977): 405–16, for the reconstruction of basic demography in Kongo; and John Thornton, "Early Kongo-Portuguese Relations, 1483–1575: A New Interpretation," *History in Africa* 8 (1981): 183–204 for comparisons with Europe.

[4] United Nations, *World Population*, table A 17 (life expectancy) A 18 (infant mortality).

[5] For early modern Europe (and some limited extra-European examples), see the classic study by E. A. Wrigley, *Population and History* (New York, 1969), resting largely on the techniques of family reconstruction based on parish registers pioneered by Louis Henry, which wrought a revolution in social history, see the reflective essay, Paul-André Rosental, "The Novelty of an Old Genre: Louis Henry and the Founding of Historical Demography," *Population* 58 (2003): 97–130.

[6] Charles M Mobley, "Demographic Structure of Pecos Indians: A Model Based on Life Tables," *American Antiquity* 45 (1980): 518–30; "A Comment on Mobley's 'Demographic Stucture of Pecos Indians'," *American Antiquity* 48 (1983): 142–47. There is a long dispute about the results of paleodemography research, which generally tends to produce low life expectancies; see the discussion in Andrew Chamberlain, *Demography in Archaeology*, pp. 81–100.

[7] Rebecca Story, "An Estimate of Mortality in a Pre-Columbian Urban Population," *American Anthropologist* 87 (1985): 519–35; urban life expectancies in both Old and New Worlds was lower than in the rural areas; she also compares more rural areas where paleodemography had been done and shows the higher levels there.

rates are probably owing to the use of modern public health techniques as well.[8] So the gap that Braudel read back, using varying subsistence strategies as his guide and with plow agriculture as a stakeholder for the Industrial Revolution, simply did not exist before the nineteenth century.

Consequently, there was really no economic Third World at the time of European expansion in the fifteenth and sixteenth century, if one uses proxy measures of average quality of life as a guide. The crucial quality-of-life determinant was, in fact, social and economic stratification. The greater the social and economic distance between the richest and poorest, the lower the average standard of living. Pierre Goubert, in his classic study of Bouveignes (France) in the seventeenth century, points this discrepancy out clearly.[9] He noted that in the richest parts of the region – that is, the ones that had deep and productive soil, produced large surpluses of crops and contained the wealthiest of the rural population – the vital rates such as infant mortality and life expectancy were lower than they were in the rocky hills usually deemed to be poor. The cause of this unexpected difference appears to have been the merciless exploitation that the average poor farmer of the district experienced at the hands of the upper class – state, church, and wealthier landowner.[10]

This insight can work at the world level as well. In some areas, such as Canada, where the Montaignais of the seventeenth century lived by foraging in a punishingly harsh environment, the average quality of life probably equaled or exceeded that of the average (poor) Frenchman. The Montaignais produced enough food and had adequate clothing and adequate shelter to support themselves, whereas many Frenchmen did not, thanks to their taxes, rents, and tithes. The anthropologist Marshal Sahlins, reading the accounts of French Jesuits who worked in this region in the early to mid-seventeenth century, was so impressed with the way in which these foragers lived that he dubbed their lifestyle (along with other similar groups) the "original affluent society."[11] This was not because they were literally as affluent as the wealthy French landowner might have been, but because they met their needs adequately with relatively little effort. This was achieved in large measure because they kept all that they produced, sharing none with an economic and social elite.

Inequality in the emerging Atlantic world is also sometimes measured by military matters, making military power and success a proxy measure for the strength and efficiency of a larger economy and general prosperity of the people. It is a reasonable position for the modern world, where the economically

[8] Robert William Fogel, Richard Smith, and Jan De Vries, *The Escape from Hunger and Premature Death, 1700–2100* (Cambridge, 2004).

[9] Pierre Goubert, *Beauvais et le Beauvaisis de 1600 à 1730: contribution à l'histoire sociale de la France du XVIIe siècle* (2 vols, Paris, 1960).

[10] For a stark reading of this situation, see Peter Laslett, *The World We Have Lost: England Before the Industrial Age* (London, 1965) and his later book, *The World We Have Lost – Further Explored* (London, 2000, a revision of the 3rd edition).

[11] Marshall Sahlins, *Stone Age Economics* (Edison, NJ, 1972), pp. 1–40, quoting a number of modern as well as historical sources involving populations of foragers or hunters and gatherers.

well-developed countries are militarily superior to the rest, but of course this might be tempered by the notable failures of Great Powers, such as the United States or the Soviet Union, to beat down persistent insurgencies in Vietnam, Iraq, or Afghanistan. And it does not work particularly well in the earlier periods, where technical advantages that come with industrialization were not available.

Jared Diamond makes the case for the defeat of the Incas by Pizarro (but only the capture of Atahuallapa in 1532, as we shall see; their final defeat was far more problematic) as a symptom of the uneven development that gave Europeans huge advantages over even apparently civilized Americans.[12] If we follow this logic, the success of thirteenth-century Mongols or seventeenth-century Manchus against China would indicate that these nomadic equestrian cultures were at a higher level of development than China. The military argument is also problematic for the Atlantic world, in spite of Diamond's enthusiasm for Pizarro's victories. The loosely organized indigenous societies of North America, the Caribbean, and Brazil, which could deal defeat to British, French, and Portuguese armed forces, must therefore have been more developed. When stone-throwing Canary Islanders defeated Spanish knights in the late fifteenth century, they must also have been considered, for that time at least, as somehow ahead. Kongo, upon defeating the Portuguese at the Battle of Mbanda Kasi in 1622 or Kitombo in 1670, must have taken the lead on that European country as well.

The three chapters that follow will look in greater depth at these three worlds that would meet as European explorers visited their coasts or worked their way into the interiors, often not reaching the far interior of both North America and South America until well into the eighteenth century. Throughout each chapter, the goal is to locate those elements of the cultures and societies that would be relevant to the encounter, rather than to attempt a comprehensive social and economic reconstruction.

---

[12] Jared Diamond, *Guns, Germs and Steel: The Fates of Human Societies* (New York and London, 1998), pp. 67–82.

2

The European Background

The involvement of European governments in overseas expansion was rendered urgent by a long-standing struggle over power and authority at home, one that the specific character of European expansion helped meet. This European political structure would determine how the Atlantic world developed politically as it was created by European exploration and commerce. The power struggle in question was particularly between the kings of emerging states and the nobility in those same areas, complicated by the role of a powerful and wealthy ecclesiastical establishment with local power and significant international connections.

The crucial element of European political structure that shaped its politics was the struggle between the kings, or other officials who wished to hold supreme sovereign executive authority (titled princes, dukes, or other noble titles, or alternatively emperors), and the nobility. Monarchs wished to centralize power, income, and decision making in their own hands or in the hands of officials who they controlled exclusively; nobles contested this and sought a more decentralized decision-making process, involving one or another sort of deliberative body that could check or instruct the monarch. Control of military power was essential to this balance, and the period of European expansion corresponded to major shifts in the nature of war and, more importantly, of armies.

KINGS AND SOLDIERS

Military developments dating back to before 1000 had shaped the power of the nobility, especially the initiation of cavalry warfare employing heavily armored knights that became the essential art of war in the medieval period. Their impact can be seen quite clearly in the literature of the times: detailed descriptions of knights' armor and deeds were an important part of the verbal art that was sung by troubadours and subsequently recorded in literature and chronicles. Arthurian romances spent considerable time describing combats, and even historical chronicles dwelled at great length on wars and even on single combats within wars.[1]

The origins of the armored knight went back to the Frankish heartland in the Germanic- and French-speaking lands lying along the Lower Rhine valley and northern France, and a long period of development that allowed a relatively small but highly restricted class of warriors to dominate politics. Developments in armoring and horse training and breeding placed the armored knight, who reached crucial development by the late eleventh century, in a position to dominate European battlefields.

To become a knight required long training, commencing almost in childhood, and considerable capital, because ownership of horse, armor, and the service necessary to keep a knight in the field was expensive. While in many parts of the world, rulers managed to keep highly trained cavalry forces under state control, in Western Europe, the older nobility became knights, creating a remarkable military nobility that would be one of its hallmarks. But no political authority could be without them, and in effect they charged a high price. The price was not simply payable in money, for the continuation of knight's services required that they have lifetime – and heritable – income, grounded in land. Thus, knights had been paid by giving them long-term, effectively perpetual grants of land, in exchange for promises to serve whoever, king or other noble, supplied the land. Nobles who were also knights and often had other knights in their service also demanded and received more: they also wanted the right to effective sovereignty over the lands they owned, and often over those of the neighboring peasants. In the earlier feudal period, knights gradually forced the tax-paying peasantry (whose income thus went to the king) to surrender their lands to them, and in countries like France and Germany especially, they created small, state-like jurisdictions around their lands.

Another set of developments also placed the church in league with the nobles and against any attempt to centralize royal power. The rule of celibacy in the medieval church ensured that priests could not be a self-perpetuating class, and their ranks were filled by younger sons or weaker members of the knightly class. The heads of these noble families then claimed the right to patronage – that is, to place members of their families in the clergy and by extension also into the ecclesiastical hierarchy in decision-making positions, such as heads of monasteries (abbots), religious orders, parish vicars, and bishops. Thus the great noble families not only owned their own lands and often also controlled local governments, but their collateral branches controlled the church, at least at the local level.

Because senior clerics were related to the nobility, they often joined with nobles to oppose any growth of royal power. Their position was complicated by the fact that the papacy had sought, since the eleventh century, to control

---

[1] For what follows, I am inspired by Robert Bartlett, *The Making of Europe. Conquest, Colonization and Cultural Change, 950–1350* (Princeton, 1993), pp. 60–83.

the church and its incomes and thus often had grounds to interfere in the local politics where those interests were involved. The great struggle over control of the church between the rulers of Italy and Germany and the Popes had ended inconclusively; although the Popes claimed the right to appoint bishops, they often had to yield for practical reasons to powerful noble families that aided the Popes in their struggle, and in the process extended their power and protection against kings. In other parts of Europe, however, kings usually managed to win control over the senior and decision-making parts of their church establishment, albeit not without stubborn and sometimes effective rearguard action on the part of the local authorities and their noble allies.

A final element in the larger struggle was the various chartered and exempted corporations that were eventually called the Third Estate in France but were present everywhere. Many towns and cities, and even some rural areas, had been granted charters, sometimes by the king, sometimes by lesser authorities. These charters often included fixed taxes, or exemptions from various services and other duties (such as military service). Although most of the privileged corporations of the Third Estate were not completely tax exempt, the crown had to seek their permission to raise taxes beyond certain limits. There were many classes of people within the Third Estate, such as manufacturing workers organized in guilds, but as most merchants lived under the jurisdiction of towns, and many towns included both privileges and exemptions relevant to trade and commerce, the Third Estate was especially dominated by the merchant class. In Spain and Portugal in particular, the chartered towns and municipalities were also expected to raise soldiers, both infantry and mounted knights. These corporate bodies were originally created to bolster royal power and give kings access to more military power outside the reach of the noble knights, but soon they were demanding rights of their own, often in exchange for support for this or that contender for the throne, or as a reward for the ongoing struggle against Muslim powers that were only driven from Iberia at the end of the fifteenth century.

In Portugal, kings always maintained a certain set of overarching rights, however much they were compromised in practice. In France, and even more so in the former Kingdom of Germany, this power was all but lost in the Early Middle Ages. To ensure their dominance, and to protect themselves in the endemic local and private warfare that marked the feudal period, knights – at least the most successful and wealthy ones – built castles on their lands. The castles, which were invulnerable to cavalry assault and very difficult to take with infantry, provided a base from which one noble, usually one holding extensive lands as well as a political title, could support and host a group of other knights who would then be attached to him for service. Castles could rarely be taken by direct assault, and were most often captured by surprise, betrayal, or through lengthy sieges in which the defenders were worn down by starvation. Knights or nobles who held castles could keep kings or their officials at bay, and became close to effectively self-governing territories, with the military element being the last of a series of economic and political elements. Because of the significance of castles, many of the medieval military campaigns were in fact a series of sieges. This was abundantly clear in the Hundred Years' War, which lasted intermittently from 1337 until 1453, where siege warfare was the dominant factor everywhere.

Rulers of states were themselves descendants of this military equestrian class, and often intermarried with them. Indeed, a survey of chronicles of the period quickly reveals how important the marriages of these nobles and the kings were considered, for most of them dedicated considerable space to these developments. Nobles were anxious about the marriages of kings and the consequences these might bring. The chronicler Hernando de Pulgar noted that when Joana, the wife of Enrique IV, the allegedly impotent king of Castille, gave birth in 1462, it was grounds for a significant division among the nobles and indeed a civil war after he declared this daughter, also named Joana, his heir.[2] Likewise, when his sister Isabella decided to marry Fernando of Aragon, her decision upset the king, who for geostrategic considerations wanted the marriage to be with a Portuguese or French noble.[3] Indeed, had Henrique had his way in his sister's marriage, Castille and Portugal might have united, leaving Aragon in the position of the "other" Iberian kingdom. Royal marriages had resulted in rival claims of England and France that led to the Hundred Years' War; similar arrangements led to the near development of a Rhine Valley kingdom in Burgundy; and of course the House of Hapsburg eventually won claims to the lower Rhine Valley, Austria, and Spain (among other places) through similar conjunctions of marriage and inheritance in the early sixteenth century.

Thus, just as royal offices might be inherited and substantial empires suddenly appear through the vagaries of inheritance, the ultimate capacity of these unions to become effective and permanent relied on more local arrangements with families and other powerful forces in each area. When Castile and Aragon were joined by the marriage of Fernando and Isabella, the two kingdoms had very different governments when the two began ruling them as a single unit in 1479. Castile had a strong monarch, and the nobles, while locally powerful, had relatively little role in decision making; Aragon, on the other hand, found both nobles and the towns exercising substantial power, and even within Aragon there were separate and fiercely independent representative councils in Catalonia and Valencia.[4]

One of the impacts of the development of noble property and jurisdiction is the creation of a wild, patchwork geography for most of Western Europe by 1500. A look at maps of fourteenth- to seventeenth-century Europe is revealing, as such maps tend to show large blocks of territory as "kingdoms." The Catalan Atlas, drawn in 1375 by Abraham Cresques, a Mallorcan cartographer, has no borders, just kingdom names written in the middle of their territory.[5]

[2] Hernando del Pulgar, *Crónica de los señores reyes católicos Don Fernando y Doña Isabel de Castilla y de Aragon* (mod ed. Valencia, 1780) (BVCervantes), Prologue, Cap 1–2.
[3] Pulgar, *Crónica*, Prologue cap 8, Part 1, cap.1–2.
[4] John Lynch, *Spain Under the Hapsburgs* (2nd ed., 2 vols., New York, 1984), pp. 8–11.
[5] Published on the Web at http://expositions.bnf.fr/ciel/catalan/index.htm.

Erhard Etzlaup's late-fifteenth-century map intended to show the routes to Rome, has large colored blocks indicating kingdoms – Germany, for example is a single color, France another, a convention that is maintained in Abraham Ortelius' celebrated *Theatrum Orbis Terrarum* of 1612 (although he places broad provincial names without borders in France).[6] It was only in the eighteenth century that lines consistently began to represent borders and that subdistricts were delineated.[7] In the nineteenth century, historical cartographers sought to recreate a political geography of earlier periods; as a result, their maps were incredibly complex, far more than the contemporary ones.

Such maps, of course, tend to make us think of modern states, which the polities represented on these unicolored map figures emphatically were not. In a modern state, there is a single government with more or less uniform authority over all its lands. Local and regional governments may create local statutes and taxes, but the whole is still harmonized under a uniform structure. Higher levels, in any case, can override or modify whatever happens at the lower levels. This did not happen in any of the European polities shown on the maps of the day.

Instead, these territories were a patchwork of fractured partial sovereignties and jurisdictions. Royal officials could not even enter lands belonging to some noble families and towns. Many districts had their own inviolable laws that could not be contradicted by legislation at higher levels. The area of royal authority might include parts of the whole country designated as France or Spain, but it was constantly interrupted by other discordant and powerful counterjurisdictions. Royal officers might be able to travel, in France for example, to many places and exercise authority over the people there, but their journeys would also take them past various noble territories, exempt ecclesiastical lands, chartered towns, and other districts where the royal writ was limited or nonexistent, where no taxes could be collected, and even where no royal officer was permitted to step. No king could simply raise an army by issuing commands; rather, a wide range of nobles, commanding various groups of men at arms (armored horsemen of lower rank, even non-noble), who they supported with grants of land, and peasants or archers from their estates might answer the call. Furthermore, they did not come without making some demands, so that power and jurisdiction that might be increased in a war were whittled away almost immediately afterward.

The noble knight and his descendants won the right to maintain substantial governmental activity as private property. They could offer or withhold money, allow or disallow royal officials to visit them, agree or refuse to perform

---

[6] "Der Romweg" (1497) at http://nbn-resolving.de/urn:nbn:de:bvb:12-bsb00033752–7; Ortelius, *Theatrvm Orbis Terrarus* at http://www.deventerboekenstad.nl/?sid=sab:lib_rep&pid=ppn:0662 06014&zoom=65&x=0.08&y=-0.05&page=29&zoomin=true

[7] For example, Robert de Vaugondie, whose maps of the mid-eighteenth century are found at http://www.davidrumsey.com/luna/servlet/view/search?sort=Pub_List_No_InitialSort%2CPub_Date&q=+Pub_List_No%3D%273353.000%27%22+LIMIT%3ARUMSEY~8~1&pgs=50& res=1

military service. If kings wanted their service, they had to ask and be granted permission. Growing out of this relationship was the right that the nobility claimed to advise the king, especially on matters pertaining to war. This right gave nobles, church officials, and the heads of chartered towns increasingly strong participation in basic decision making. Nobles claimed exemption from taxation and immunity from royal law, instead demanding that only bodies of their peers could condemn them. The representative assemblies, courts, parliaments, and the like that were created in the Middle Ages were designed to protect their rights from royal harassment and ensure that their incomes and interests were secure from their would-be patrons. Such assemblies existed in multiple layers – kingdoms had them, but so to did smaller polities that were formally subunits of kingdoms, provinces in France, duchies, and other such units in the German lands.

European monarchs began adding representation by chartered towns and associations to their royal councils, among the earliest being those in Iberia. Leon's in 1188 was perhaps the earliest, although by the mid-thirteenth century, most Iberian countries had established this tradition: Castille in 1250, Portugal in 1254. In France, such meetings began at the provincial level at the same time, and in the fourteenth century, during the crisis of the Hundred Years' War, the kings often summoned the "Estates General" to which all the various exempt groups responded, both to raise funds and decide issues of sovereignty; the first such assembly took place in 1301.

In England, the growth of these representative assemblies can be said to have started in 1215 when rebellious noble knights, or barons, forced John (1166–1216) to sign the Magna Carta, guaranteeing wide-ranging liberties to the nobility.[8] It was reissued several times in the following period, often with revisions as king and nobles asserted and reasserted themselves. A noble rebel, Simon de Montfort summoned a gathering of nobles, church leaders, and urban elites to a Parliament to present an organized front to the king in 1265, and set forth a stronger document placing power in the hands of a parliament representing baronial and ecclesiastical interests.[9] Although this did not produce long-ranging results, King Edward I, in fact, summoned what is largely regarded as the first Parliament in England in 1295 for the purposes of obtaining funds for his wars by arranging for them to raise special taxes for his efforts.[10] However, as elsewhere, the nobles and urban elites demanded the right to present grievances to the king and thus the exchange of taxation for redress was established.[11] In England, Parliament consolidated much of its

---

[8] Carl Stevenson and Frederick Geogre Marchum, eds., *Sources of English Constitutional History* (New York, 1937), pp. 115–126.

[9] The rebellion is described in Mathew of Westminister, *The Flowers of History* (trans. C. D. Yonge II, London, 1853[GB]), pp. 414–417 and 436–438. The documents of this period are in Stephenson and Marchum, eds, *Sources*, pp. 142–153.

[10] Documents in Stephenson and Marchum, eds., *Sources*, pp. 159–161.

[11] See the Parliamentary Bill of 1301 (in Stephenson and Marchum, eds, *Sources*, pp. 165–166) for the nature of grievances.

control of revenue and certain other matters pertaining to the royal house by 1399, and consolidated the idea of the three estates meeting together.[12]

ROYAL ASSERTION

The ultimate power of the nobility rested firmly in their ability to dominate battlefields with armored cavalry and territory with castles. Knightly armies were relatively small, a few thousand at most, and were not particularly well disciplined even in battle. Indeed, the problems of European heavy cavalry were sharply revealed when they proved completely incapable of handling the Mongol cavalry, organized along different principals in eastern Europe during the brief Mongol incursion in 1241. The same social programs that had given them political power reduced their overall effectiveness, but in the end it only meant that no one knightly power could dominate the others. It would be changes in the art of war that would ultimately change the balance of power between monarchs and nobles.

The military developments that would shift the balance started in the fourteenth century, but began reaching their fulfillment in the fifteenth – just as European ships were reaching into the Atlantic – and the Atlantic possibilities would contribute to the victory of the kings. Military historians often point to the Hundred Years' War period of the fourteenth and fifteenth centuries as a turning point, when small, compact formations of infantry, equipped with long pikes and effective armor-piercing missile weapons (powerful English-style longbows or crossbows at first and then gunpowder weapons later on), were able to defeat cavalry forces, and would eventually lead to a time when armor was abandoned altogether. In addition, the development of effective artillery using gunpowder, which could batter down castle walls and cramp the military independence of the nobility, took place at about the same time. These developments favored those who could afford gunpowder weapons, and, combined, helped place more power in the hands of commoners and to expand the size of some states.[13]

These infantry forces were recruited at first from peasants, often from marginal areas like Switzerland, Scotland and Wales, or the Pyrenees, sometimes from densely populated regions like Flanders. Sometimes they were raised by levy, but often they were recruited by military entrepreneurs who formed them into military companies. Such mercenary units were not necessarily cheaper to raise and maintain than cavalry were in the short run, but they were unable to make long-term financial or political demands. As mercenaries they could be employed for the duration of a war and then dismissed, without land grants, concessions of jurisdiction, or rights over peasants.

---

[12] See the Parliament of 1399 in Stephenson and Marchum, eds. *Sources*, pp. 250–257.
[13] Clifford J. Rogers, "The Military Revolutions of the Hundred Years' War," *Journal of Military History* 57 (1993): 241–278.

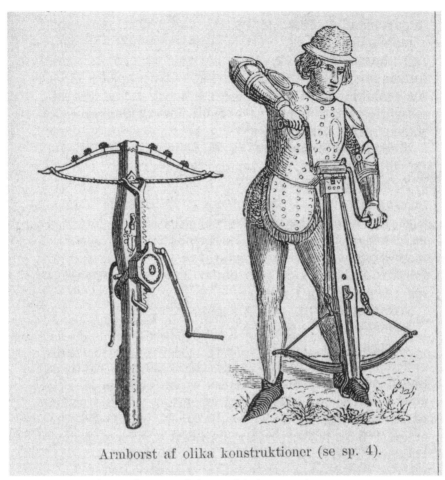

Armborst af olika konstruktioner (se sp. 4).

FIGURE 2. "Armborst" from *Nordisk Famijlebok*, 1904 edition.

The political benefits of employing mercenary companies of infantry had another cost, however, and that was that they needed to be paid in cash – that is, in monetary substance like silver or gold. It was precisely the use of the cash payment system that made it possible for the political impact of military forces to be reduced and placed once again in the hands of centralizing authorities. Without cash payments, military units would refuse to fight, or might decided to change sides, or even to riot and rebel, looting the countryside. Indeed, many thinkers of the period recognized that the cheapness of mercenaries had a serious disadvantage in that their loyalty could not be counted on. No less an authority than Niccolò Machiavelli, in his book, *The Art of War*, argued that princes were ill advised to rely on mercenaries because of their changeable and negotiable loyalty.

The expense of raising soldiers and the fragmented authority of kings created very complex problems in organizing armies. The contemporary writer Luis de Ávila y Zúñiga described the way in which Charles V raised troops to fight in the German war of 1546–1547. First he sent four colonels to raise German infantry companies of 4,000 men each, which were then grouped "following custom" in two regiments, which were then subdivided in 25 smaller units, each with its own flag. Then Álvaro de Sande of Hungary arrived with a tercio (an infantry company) of 2,800 Spaniards, and Arce came with 3,000 infantry from Lombardy. The marquis Albrecht of Brandenburg "immediately sent the horsemen he was obliged to provide, who were 2,500" when called. Juan, the brother of the Marquis of Brandenburg, reported with 600 horse, the master of Prussia with 1,000, Duke Heinrich of Braunschwig with 400, and the prince of Hungary, Archduke of Austria, a further 1,500 cavalry. This complex force including commoners in infantry units and noble horsemen was scattered all over Charles's vast holdings in Spain and central Europe and could not actually assemble in time to fight in all the engagements.[14]

French kings emerging from the Hundred Years' War, which ended in 1453, found that the unemployed bands of mercenaries could prove to be very troublesome, and came to adopt a military policy that every other major power would eventually adopt – they bought out the private companies and guaranteed employment for some 100 companies of soldiers. They then used this permanent army to round up and crush the other companies and to ensure the powers of the king. Such a policy, however, required large outlays of cash.

Early European monarchs were not rich in cash. They received a good deal of the revenue from their own lands in kind – products of the field or herd, and these might not always be convertible to cash. Then too, they often had limited power to tax; thanks to noble concessions, the exemption of church income, and the tax-limiting privileges of the Third Estate, they could only obtain the right to tap these incomes with the consent of the taxpayers, typically by calling them to an assembly and asking for money. While the assemblies would grant taxes and even pay them in money, they demanded a price. That price was to continue or deepen their power. They demanded more from the kings for their taxes, the right to permanent representation in parliamentary bodies, the right to choose kings, even limited rights to depose them, along with a plethora of lesser demands (often including further exemptions from taxation in the future).

In response, kings turned to indirect taxes; rather than asking the assemblies to pay them taxes and accept their counterdemands, they sought to raise cash by taxing trade and production. Salt taxes, tolls, transaction taxes – all became the tools of revenue raising in the emerging monarchies of the fifteenth century. These taxes fell heavily on the merchants, especially because the nature of their occupations caused them to have supplies of cash, and they were not able to

---

[14] Luis de Ávila y Zúñiga, "Commentario de la Guerra de Alemania hecha por Carlos V, máximo emperador romano, rey de España, en el año de 1546 y 1547" (Venice, 1548) (digital version www.cervantesvirtual.com/historia/CarlosV/7_2_avila.shtml).

protect it. Although merchants were often citizens of chartered towns or had won various privileges, they were the least capable of all the estates to resist taxation, and they became the source of royal revenues in cash, which in turn went to fund the new infantry armies and their equipment.

Cash revenues were not only useful for paying the new armies; they also could purchase the services of officials. By paying officials, drawn from the impecunious ranks of the lower nobility or the merchants, in cash, the crown ensured that they would be dependent on these payments, and thus unable to negotiate their services for permanent wealth. With these dependent officials, the kings could be assured of loyal and consistent service that they could control, much better than the services in government that nobles rendered earlier for free, but with their own agenda in mind. If these officials could not be paid in cash, kings would have to rely on self-sufficient nobles, or wealthier but less dependent people, to carry out these tasks, and to accept a lesser degree of ultimate control over them.

The degree to which an early modern monarch could centralize authority was thus highly dependent on his or her ability to raise cash, or to obtain the critical services by barter that did not involve cash services. The more successful one, such as the Castilian monarchs in the late fifteenth century or the Portuguese crown after 1500, managed to persuade the nobility to serve as salaried officials (although they actually paid little salary) so that they would not be excluded from military or political service altogether. But in serving in this way, with or without pay, these nobles gave up their political privileges in decision making and served as dependent officers of the king, subject to dismissal at will. In creating the means to centralize authority and participate in the new, infantry-based armies, European rulers developed what modern historians have termed the fiscal-military state – that is, a state whose primary goals are to raise revenue by whatever means possible in order to wage war.[15]

The concern for finance and its connection to war is well illustrated by the reports sent back home by Venetian ambassadors, dispatched since the early sixteenth century to all the countries with which the Italian city-state had relations. Such reports regularly feature detailed breakdowns of the revenues available to rulers and the problems they might have in collecting these funds, as well as assessments of their military strength. Indeed, for many of their reports, this is the single most important topic dealt with. Even though the numbers were clearly only estimates, and modern historians can correct them sometimes by recourse to archival data, the emphasis they received in these reports underlines the importance of these matters in the health of the states in question.[16]

Vincenzo Quirini wrote his report in 1506 from Burgundy (root of modern Belgium and Holland), the core of Charles V's empire that included Spain as

---

[15] There is a substantial literature on the concept of "fiscal-military" states; for a recent overview and contribution, see Jan Glete, *War and Society in Early Modern Europe: Spain, the Dutch Republic and Sweden as Fiscal-Military States, 1500–1660* (London and New York, 2002).

[16] For a detailed study and bibliography, as well as many datasets, see Richard Bonney, director and editor, "European State Finance Database," http://www.le.ac.uk/hi/bon/ESFDB/frameset.html

FIGURE 3. "The Battle of Breitenfeld on 17 September 1631" from 'Theatrum Europaeum' volume II, engraved by Matthaus Merian the Elder (1631). Image courtesy of the Deutsch Historisches Museum.

well as holdings in the Rhine valley. After carefully noting the cash salaries of the Duke's principal court officers, drawn from his closest family, and including the courts of his queen and children, his armed retainers and secretarial staff and their food and that of their horses – some 360,000 ducats – he also noted that Charles paid a "pension to all the lords of the lands subjected to him" amounting to a further 50,000 ducats. He also had to spend between 15,000 and 20,000 ducats for all the paid officials he had posted throughout the country, by "districts [*terre*], castles and fortresses."[17] This survey of royal income and expense was followed by a notice of noble revenues ranging from the Count of Nassau's 15,000 ducats per year, to the lesser nobles who gained only 2,000 or 3,000: "[A]ll subjected to the duke, but not obliged to give him anything from their income," even though the duke gave them each a pension from his income. They were obliged, however, to give him fighting men at their expense.[18] After estimating the income from the markets of the largest towns, "around a million in gold," Quirini went on to note that even though they had to make account of their public expenses to the Duke, they did not have to pay him anything from it. They did however, give various sums to the Duke to aid in wars, and these had become sources of income, amounting to some 350,000 ducats, although he had to visit each place at least once in four years to receive it. In emergency, too, as in the war between Burgundy and Gelderland, additional extraordinary sums could still be raised.[19]

The tyranny of cash revenues shaped policy. Crowns wished to protect and extend the range and effectiveness of their merchants because their prosperity would ensure that they could pay heavier cash payments, as indeed Quirini's estimates of market incomes in Burgundy reveals. They tried to ensure that trading relationships would maximize cash return payments whenever possible, and they tried their best to accumulate supplies of cash, both for their payments and for emergencies, especially wars, which demanded large and immediate outlays of the precious specie. Many of the royal policies that came to be defined as mercantilism – the interest in the concentration of bullion, the zero-sum trade policies, the privileged monopoly companies – all originated in the need for the monarchs to maximize cash flows. The foolishness of some of these policies in terms of the overall economic health of the nation, as the early economists of the seventeenth and eighteenth centuries would demonstrate, were irrelevant. Kings were not interested in the overall economic health of the nation as much as they were in maintaining the supplies of cash that were the lifeblood of centralized authority.

Atlantic expansion played a critical role in creating the cash flow necessary to centralizing authority, as is well demonstrated in the case of Portugal,

---

[17] "Relazione di Borgogna con aggunti di alcuni particulari da Vincenzo Quirini l'anno 1506," in Eugenio Albèri, ed., *Relazioni degli ambasciatori veneti al Senato* (15 vols., Florence, 1839–63 [GB]) ser 1, vol. 1: 7–10.

[18] Quirini, "Relazione," 1: 12.

[19] Quirini, "Relazione," 1: 16–18.

the country that benefited quickly from the Atlantic and developed policies to maximize the crown's gains from it. Portugal's early gains are revealed by the report, submitted in 1505 by Venice's ambassador to Lisbon, Lunardo da Ca' Masser, which surveyed the incomes of the nobility and the crown. According to his report, the total income of the Portuguese nobility represented some 350,000 Venetian ducats, an income the kings could tap only by summoning the Cortes, the noble-controlled parliamentary body that represented their interests (and the church's) to the king. In contrast, the king also controlled some 350,000 ducats in revenue from Portugal, including income from lands that the crown owned, or was able to tax, "which is a little thing, especially as he has made many grants." Thus, although he was much richer than any single noble – the Dukes of Braganza and Coimbra, the richest among their peers, only accounted for 16,000 and 17,000 ducats of income, respectively – without the extra that they could pay him, the king could not do much more than meet normal administrative costs.[20]

Because of this financial situation, the history of fifteenth-century Portugal clearly reveals that the crown was never able to fight a war – and they fought many in the fifteenth century – without summoning the Cortes. Between 1385, when the ruling House of Aviz had come to power with the support of the Third Estate, until 1495, when King Manuel I took the throne, the Cortes had met roughly every other year, although some kings, like Afonso V (1475–81) met with the Cortes every year. Even so, the principal reason for the Cortes meeting less than annually had as much to do with the mechanics of organizing the assembly as any royal control over its meeting. In addition to votes for money to pay for dowries and for wars, the kings heard complaints against his officials and accepted the control that the Cortes insisted it had over royal marriages that might affect the sovereignty of the state.[21]

But the situation was changing thanks to Portuguese expansion. Ca' Masser also noted that the crown had a very large new source of income from overseas revenues. In 1505, these amounted to another 500,000 ducats, drawn from revenues of the trade of Madeira and the Azores, the gold trade of the Gold Coast, and the incipient slave trade.[22] This considerable revenue would soon be joined by the income from the Indian Ocean trade, just then being reached, and Brazil, first visited just five years earlier. These revenues would have their effect: the Cortes met in 1502, and then not again until 1525, 1535, 1544, and finally in 1562. Furthermore, these Cortes were unable to make as thorough-going demands for power as the fifteenth-century Cortes had done.[23] Overseas

[20] G. Scopoli, ed., "Relazioni di Leonardo da Ca' Masser alla serenissima Repubblica di Venezia…" *Archivio Storico Italiana* 2, appendix 10 (1845 [GB]): 37–43.

[21] A good overview of the Cortes in Portugal is found in Serrão, *História* 2: 211–216, 221–223; 225–233. There is no continuous record of their proceedings, and what is known has been assembled piecemeal from many sources.

[22] Ca' Masser, "Relazione," pp. 44–45.

[23] Serrão, *História* 3: 16, 42–44; 60–62. King Sebastião, who called the last of these Cortes, only called one; subsequently, the Portuguese crown passed to Spain (in 1580), and Portugal's history was disrupted until the reestablishment of independence in 1640.

revenues ensured that the Portuguese nobility would be cowed, and Portugal, though small, would be the most centralized state in Western Europe in the early sixteenth century.

Spain also benefited from overseas cash flows. This was already apparent when Bernardo Navagero submitted his report on Spain to Venice in July 1546. After carefully noting the complex revenues of the Spanish crown in Iberia, Naples, and "Lower Germany," the ambassador turned to the "Indies," about which "people say great things," and noted that it was yielding "at a minimum 500,000 ducats per year," or almost as much as the Iberian kingdoms of Aragon, Catalonia, and Valencia combined (at 600,000 ducats). He noted that there was a wildly different set of opinions, and that there were those who held the American revenues were already "the fourth part of all the income of the emperor."[24] In 1595, after the production of revenue from the silver mines of Mexico and Peru were in full swing, the Venetian ambassador, Francesco Venarmino, noted that while in Charles V's time, the Indies yielded about 500,000 scudi (a Venetian coin) on average, at century's end, it was "of the greatest utility [*grossima utilità*] to the king," and in three years had rendered "ten million in gold," while the revenues from Iberia and Italy amounted to about 10 million annually.[25] In these circumstances, it is not surprising that the Spanish Cortes was curtailed. The revenue not only spurred centralization within Iberia; it encouraged Phillip II to pursue a centralizing policy in lands that were not fully integrated into Spain, such as the Low Countries, Italy, and Sicily, using the military means that the revenue flow assured him he could use. To complicate Spain's financial problems even more, throughout the sixteenth century, Spain waged a costly sea (and sometimes land) war against the Ottoman Empire.

Indeed the flow of overseas revenue would embolden monarchs to expand their powers, as the Portuguese kings did by hiring many officials on salaries of one kind or another, or the Spanish kings did by seeking to impose a more uniform order on the far-flung territories that had come under nominal Spanish control when Charles V united all the lands owned by the Hapsburg family. These included not just southern Italy, but also the whole of modern Belgium and the Netherlands and huge German possessions in Austria and the Holy Roman Empire. Both monarchies used overseas revenue flows to assist in their plans for more power, but both also overstepped their capacities, borrowing heavily from various merchant groups (using tax revenues and overseas income as collateral) and then, when income still fell short of the higher expenses, restructuring loans and even declaring bankruptcy, as the Spanish crown did several times in the late sixteenth century. Thus overseas revenue did not guarantee stable finances, but it did encourage and promote vigorous moves to break the feudal impasse and create a very expensive state and army.

[24] Bernardo Navigero, "Relazione di Bernardo Navigero ritornato ambasciatore da Carlo V..." (July 1546) in Albèri, ed., *Relazioni* series 1, 1: 297; Paolo Tiepolo, writing in 1563, and perhaps with more certain figures, given the detail he provides for other elements of Spanish revenue, put the income of the Indies (in silver alone) between 1553 and 1561 at 3.2 million ducats, or 500,000 ducats per annum; "Relazione di Paolo Tiepolo, 1563," in Albèri, *Relazioni* series 1, 5: 37.
[25] "Relazione de Francesco Vendramino, 1595" in Albèri, ed., *Relazioni* series 1, 5: 450–454.

FINANCE AND EXPANSION

To ensure that the revenue flow would come, these European monarchs were careful to manage the politics of expansion in the most cost-effective way. From the very beginning, the rulers tried to avoid granting privileges and exemptions from taxes to those representing them overseas, or to limit these as much as possible. At the same time, the risks were great enough that the state regularly sought to entice private citizens with money who were willing to take risks if the potential rewards were great enough. Thus, Spain and Portugal both encouraged private citizens to undertake public projects in exchange for privileges. Merchants, for example, might use their own ships to be a sort of navy if they were given the right to a share of spoils captured from prizes taken in the war. They might be willing to take risks if the crown could promise them monopolies or agree to protect their business. In this way, a monarch could persuade them to take risks, and then, only when merchants had demonstrated the risk could pay off, the crown would step in and charge revenue.

Charters that were given to early explorers in both Spain and Portugal serve as a good example. Portuguese charters usually required the grantee to supply some or all of the start-up capital; for example, he would supply the ships, or perhaps pay the personnel, recruit settlers, provide for their transportation, or supply munitions from his own capital. In exchange, the crown agreed to allow the grantee to operate tax-free for a period of years, and then to pay taxes, often at a reduced rate, for more years. Such charters might include the rights to exercise law over areas that might be conquered, to govern the affairs of settlers, and to rule territories almost as if they were sovereign lords. Sometimes the charters allowed the powers to be hereditary and transmitted on to heirs. In general, however, the powers granted in charters were limited, and in the long run, European states were successful in avoiding making permanent concessions of income or jurisdiction to those to whom they granted charters.

If the charter holders were successful, then most often, the crown sought to resume its rights to the newly lucrative trading area or conquest as soon as possible and by any means, just as the success of Prince Henrique's navigations in Guinea led the crown to take direct control of the trade in 1460. Similarly, Fernão Gomes's exploration and trade contract was allowed to lapse when the wealth of the Gold Coast was revealed. Crown lawyers often found defects in the charters, or at times the charter holders were unable to fulfill all the terms of the charter. In such a case, the crown could step in and supply its own officials as governors, and the chartered territory became a colony. Charters were often generous, as it was only by promising big benefits that the crown could persuade private citizens to take up the risks. The same generosity, however, ultimately would defeat the purpose of the crown to obtain better and higher revenues. Therefore, the crown pursued its interest in the more successful colonies vigorously, while often not bothering much about it in the less successful areas.

The Portuguese crown's grant of captaincies to various worthy people along the coast of Brazil between 1534 and 1536 called on them to develop resources and defend the regions and gave their captains wide powers, but the most successful of them were resumed by the crown in 1549; likewise, the charter made to Paulo Dias de Novais for the conquest of Angola in 1571 was revoked, for technical reasons, upon his death in 1589, as the conquest had begun yielding substantial profits.[26]

Columbus's generous charter, given to him prior to his voyage to America in 1492, became the basis for his attempts to develop its commerce, and from the time when the settlement in Hispaniola began to pay off, the crown moved in to revoke the charter. His son Diego fought the crown tooth and nail over the charter's privileges, finally losing in 1525. On a smaller scale, the *encomienda* grants that the crown gave to Spanish subjects who took over areas in America, which were never seen as permanent grants of land, people, or income, were soon under attack, often for allegations that the tax-paying Native American subjects were being abused. Attempts to revoke *encomiendas* and renegotiate their privileges began as early as 1502, and were pressed hardest with the establishment of the New Laws in 1542, ostensibly a move to create justice for Native Americans, but just as much a reassertion of crown authority over ever-more lucrative land held in private contract. On the whole, the Spanish crown was successful in returning these charters to its authority, at least in areas that produced significant amounts of revenue.

The idea of having private citizens do public service in exchange for privileges was not limited to explorers. It might also apply to fundamental parts of defense, and it was through the farming out of military and especially naval activities that the northern European countries like France, the Netherlands, and England – and later Sweden, Denmark, Courland (now Latvia), and Prussia – also joined in colonization or developed commerce. All these powers initially granted rights to deal in the Atlantic for purposes of defense much more than for exploration. There were English, Dutch, and French traders in the early Atlantic, to be sure, but most of them were private traders working markets explored by Spanish and Portuguese merchants and explorers, often paying the crowns of those countries for access to their markets. As merchants, they had little or no interest in exploration or even in high-seas navigation. More often then not, these northern Europeans simply bought the newly arriving African and American products in Seville or Lisbon, thus avoiding the risks of sailing the Atlantic Ocean or engaging in long-distance commerce.

A series of wars would change that, however, the origins of which ultimately lay in Spanish ambitions, especially as they were fueled by income from their conquests. With the output of American mines beginning in 1540 and becoming larger and more regular every year after that, Spanish silver not only allowed

---

[26] For a worthwhile comparative study of the charter in Brazil and Angola, see Ilidio do Amaral, *O Consulado de Paulo Dias de Novais. Angola no último quartel do século XVI e primeiro do século XVII* (Lisbon, 2000), pp. 49–72.

the Spanish crown to dispense meeting with the Cortes to decide policy or declare taxes. It also allowed Hapsburgs, the Austrian royal family that took over the Spanish throne, to follow up on its potential claims to control in other parts of Europe, using the military power that access to large quantities of silver could allow. A series of military and dynastic adventures, often connected with Spanish claims to champion the Catholic Church against Protestants, were fueled by Spanish silver.

As its ships made their first tentative discoveries in America, Spain was at odds with France over power in Italy, kicked off by a French invasion of the north in 1494 and Spanish attacks on the French in Naples in 1502. In 1519, Charles V, of the Austrian house of Hapsburg, became king of Spain and Holy Roman Emperor at the same time, thus challenging France both in northern Europe – his possessions in Burgundy bordered France on the northeast – and in Italy. Wars between the two in the Low Countries (modern Belgium and the Netherlands) and in Italy continued until they were resolved in Spain's favor by the treaty of Cateau Cambrisis in 1559. Thereafter, following the death of King Henri II, France was thrown into chaos for the rest of the century. Henri left a minor heir, François II, and when François died the next year, ten-year-old Charles IX succeeded him, leading to various factions contending to control his regency. At the same time that factional rivalry was disturbing the country, religious rivalry that matched Calvinists against Catholics overlay the existing blocs. Spain supported some Catholic factions and did some limited intervention in the later phases of the civil war, but mostly it used the opportunity presented by French disunity to operate in the Low Countries more freely than it might have had there been a strong France.

Spanish policy in the Low Countries was designed as much to hem in France as to expand its own power, but the combination of French weakness and Spanish perceptions of strength as they garnered ever more Atlantic resources allowed the Spanish crown to tighten its power in the territory at the mouth of the Rhine River that had fallen to its dynasty through the Duchy of Burgundy. Spain sought to limit and even eliminate privileges of taxation and self-government exercised by the towns of the region, and coupled that with a rigorous campaign against Lutherans and Calvinists. A revolt of commoners, led by preachers who called on a destruction of images in churches in the name of Calvinist reform, began in 1566 and was followed by a civil rebellion. Draconian suppression of the rebellion by the Spanish Duke of Alba led to further unrest, and refugees eventually established a rebel province in the northern part of the region – the future Netherlands – in 1572. War between this entity and Spanish forces, with various interventions on both sides from France and England and further revolts in the south, was only ended by an uneasy truce in 1609.

The Spanish were able to maintain substantial forces – upward of 60,000 men – in the Low Countries for such a length of time because of the arrival of Spanish silver from mines in Mexico and Peru. Phillip's revenue in silver from America rose from 12.5 million ducats in the period between 1560 and 1580 to 52 million ducats in the period between 1580 and 1605.[27] By this time, nearly 40 percent of the incoming revenue was spent on the war in the Low Countries.[28] In 1580, Philip inherited the crown of Portugal and with the union of the two was able to combine two mighty streams of overseas revenue, even though Portuguese tried hard to keep their resources out of Spanish adventures. Spanish dynastic aims in England and the threat of a firmly Spanish Netherlands soon brought England into the war. In 1588, the Spanish sought to invade England, launching a mighty fleet, the Spanish Armada (much of it Portuguese), to ferry an equally powerful army to England, but fortunately for the English, their seamanship and bad weather thwarted the Spanish attack and sank most of the fleet.

Considering the significance of revenue to the war, increasing, protecting, or stopping income flows became of vital strategic importance, much as with the oil supplies were in World War II. The Spanish silver fleet, bringing the wealth of the New World back to aid its wars, could not help but be a target. French privateers and their leaders were already considering how to take the fleet in the 1560s when Spain and France were at war.[29]

The war in the Netherlands became a lynchpin for Europe, matching Spain against the Dutch and English. The French watched helplessly as they waged their own civil war, but once Henry IV reestablished order in France before his death in 1610, France became a powerful check on the combatants in the Low Countries. Although the war was cooled by a partition of the country into the Spanish-held Spanish Netherlands (eventually Belgium) and the Dutch Republic by the truce of 1609, Spanish plans for a renewed attack played a part in the politics of Germany. In Germany, the Hapsburg family claimed the power of the Holy Roman Emperor and hoped to use it to increase imperial authority at the expense of the German towns and states, while pushing Catholic interests. A struggle over the succession of Bohemia, which brought Rhine Valley politics to central Europe, kicked off the Thirty Years War (1618–1648). During this war, ambitious northern European powers like Sweden and Denmark intervened to support both the Protestant and anti-Spanish causes and their own ambitions to take over the southern shores of the Baltic Sea.

Throughout this key period in European history, the wars had an Atlantic dimension as well as a European one. While the fighting in the Atlantic was relatively limited compared to the devastating wars in Europe, these naval wars led directly to the colonization of the Americas by France and the northern European countries, as well as their increased participation in the trade of Africa. From the very start of the Hapsburg-Valois wars, the Calvinist parties

---

[27] Basic data on the flow of "Spanish silver" was accumulated in the 1920s by Earl J. Hamilton, and is still the basis for understanding the dynamics of its flow and impact on revenue; *American Treasure and the Price Revolution in Spain, 1501–1650* (Cambridge, MA, 1934).

[28] See graph in Fernand Braudel, *The Mediterranean and the Mediterranean World in the Age of Philip II* (trans. Sîan Reynolds, 2 vols, New York, 1972 [1966]), 1: 476–482 and chart p. 477.

[29] K. R. Andrews, *The Spanish Caribbean: Trade and Plunder, 1530–1630* (New Haven, 1978), pp. 84–87; 128–130; 134–150.

in France, which were situated in commercial areas and port cities, waged a relentless, albeit limited, naval war against Spain, which also involved Portugal. An important part of the overall Protestant strategy in the war was to seek to boost their own incomes and to hurt Spanish efforts by attacking Spanish shipping on the high seas.

The French partisans lacked funds to finance a navy for this naval war, and so the crown issued special licenses to merchantmen, called "letters of marque," allegedly permitting them to seek violent compensation for losses by opposing fleets, which allowed them to seize Spanish shipping and take its cargoes, in exchange for the right to keep the cargoes after paying certain taxes.[30] The considerable costs of fitting out ships intended for war and the risks of taking on the Spanish shipping were borne by the private merchant, thus sparing the state the expense, while at the same time the state benefited from rights to tax the merchants who might otherwise simply be hung as pirates for what they did. To separate these activities from those of pirates in the old-fashioned criminal sense, the French established special courts that had to hear testimony to ensure that the rules established by the system of letter of marque were kept, and to determine the values and distributions of profits from prize ships (ships taken by the raiders). French privateers, as such citizen-raiders were called, became famous and were soon doing significant damage to Spanish shipping. They fanned out well into the Atlantic, attacking Portuguese shipping in the Atlantic as far as Brazil and continuing such attacks until 1536.[31] Renewed attacks on Portuguese shipping began in 1544; some 220 Portuguese vessels were seized in 1549–1550 alone.[32]

As the French civil wars began, the Protestant Admiral Coligny, who was appointed Admiral of France, sponsored voyages, not only to raid Spanish ships and harbors, but also to establish colonies to serve as bases for these attacks. Coligny was particularly interested in areas that had no strong Spanish presence, such as the coast of North America north of Florida, or the regions along the southern coast of Brazil. In 1555, the French established a colony at what is today Rio de Janeiro under Coligny's direction, which they called "Antarctic France," encroaching on space that the Portuguese regarded as their own.[33] A Portuguese attack on the colony in 1560 ended its brief existence, but the French were back and settled another colony in what is today South Carolina in 1562. This outpost was also quickly destroyed by Spanish counterattacks. French privateering continued to be active throughout, even without other

[30] Letters of marque went back to the Hundred Years War epoch at least; see Charles de la Roncière, *Histoire de la Marine Français* (5 vols, Paris, 1899–1920) 2: 159–162.

[31] Documents on these early privateering attacks in Brazil are found in Mário Brandão, *O Processo na Inquisição de Mestre João da Costa* (Coimbra, 1944), pp. 301–3028.

[32] Serrão, *História* 3: 47–49.

[33] For a firsthand account of the colony, see Jean de Léry, *History of a Voyage to the Land of Brazil* (ed. and trans. Janet Whatley, Berkeley and Los Angeles, 1990, the original French was published Lyons, 1578); see also André Thevet, *Les Singularités de la France Antarctique* (1557) mod. ed. Frank Lestringant (Paris, 1997).

colonial enterprises, until Henri IV agreed to limited toleration of Protestant political power in the edict of Nantes in 1598. But many of the old privateers never really gave up their activities, and for a time even turned to outright piracy. Dunkirk, on the border of what is today France and Belgium, was the most famous pirate hideout in Europe, terrorizing shipping of all nationalities well into the seventeenth century.

The French pioneers at this endeavor were joined in the 1580s by Dutch and then English privateers as the territory held by the Spanish crown at the mouth of the Rhine River revolted. Like France before it, the government of the Dutch Republic looked to its commercial classes to build a privately funded navy to carry on war against Spain. At first, these were the "Sea Beggars," a group of raiders who tried to harass Spanish shipping in the mouth of the Rhine, but increasingly they began taking the war to the Atlantic. Already in the 1570s they were raiding as far away as the Caribbean,[34] and in the 1590s were working off the coast of Africa.

As England was drawn into the Dutch war, it too turned to private navies and issued letters of marque to wage a sea war. Soon English privateers were prowling the lands of the Spanish, taking prizes and even seizing coastal towns for brief periods. The great English "Sea Dogs" like Francis Drake, Walter Raleigh, or Thomas Cavendish were able to mount fleets and attack Spanish shipping. They forced the Spanish to divert naval forces to protect their American possessions and thus to weaken their war effort in the Low Countries or against England.[35]

English raiders in the Caribbean found rich pickings, but the distance made it difficult to sustain their operations without land bases on the American side. Even more than the French bases in Brazil and South Carolina, the English looked for bases in the Americas. Walter Raleigh, one of the early pioneers, sought to build a base at Roanoke, now in North Carolina, in 1585, with the express purpose of helping supply fleets from England bound to the West Indies. The colony only sporadically fulfilled its mission, but did serve this important function when Raleigh left the Caribbean in 1590, taking the remaining colonists with him.

Raleigh tried again after 1590, this time in the southern Caribbean. He built a base in Trinidad for a few years after 1595 and explored, with the aim of colonizing, the coast north of Brazil around the mouth of the Amazon and Orinoco Rivers. These colonies also failed to be permanent settlements, and the Spanish proved to be capable of enlisting allies among the Native Americans living in the areas to defend their interests.

---

[34] Museu Naval, Coleccion de MSS Navarete, MS 480, vol 25, fol. 114, "Aviso de la poderosa armada compuesta de 70 o 80 navios que preparan en la Rochella y otros," 1571.

[35] For this and what follows, see the various publication of Kenneth R. Andrews, *Elizabethan Privateering:English Privateering during the Spanish War, 1588–1603* (Cambridge, 1964); Kenneth R. Andrews, *Trade, Plunder and Settlement: Maritime Enterprise and the Genesis of the British Empire, 1480–1630* (Cambridge, 1984).

As the English were seeking colonies to support their operations, so were the Dutch, who made significant attempts to colonize the coast along the Atlantic coast of South America in the early seventeenth century, more or less in the same regions where the English tried building their own colonies.[36]

The military aspects of these early colonies were muted in the early seventeenth century, when England and the Netherlands signed truce agreements with Spain, and privateering stopped legally after 1609. But while the privateers had pillaged Spanish and Portuguese shipping, private merchants had also come to the Americas to trade.

We have noted before that English, French, and Dutch merchants had visited the Americas in the early sixteenth century, often with official permission from Spain or Portugal, but during the war period, such official visiting stopped. Indeed, the Spanish crown began the policy of "arresting" shipping in Spanish ports in the 1580s as a war measure and as retaliation for privateering attacks. Thus, merchants who wanted to deal in New World commodities were forced to develop their own commercial links in Africa and America, which they did, sometime in the wake of the privateers, sometimes on their own.

In the process, English, French, and Dutch consumers became used to American commodities like tobacco and sugar, or found, as the Dutch did, abundant supplies of vital commodities like salt, which previously had been purchased from Portuguese suppliers but was now being supplied from salt pans on the islands off the coast of South America. These commercial enterprises continued after the truce, but with considerable resistance. The Spanish crown never fully accepted the foreign merchants and refused to allow them to trade. When the merchants came to trade anyway, Spanish officials seized their ships and accused them of piracy. Many merchants were hung by Spanish officials for nothing more than trading in salt from Aruba or tobacco and hides off Cuba.

Often, in the climate of the early seventeenth century, merchants formed companies with the aim of protecting their interests, convoying ships to defend against piracy or against the Spanish who still regarded trading in their domains (and this included even West Africa in their eyes) as piracy. The Dutch and English both formed East India Companies at the turn of the century to protect their trade in Indian Ocean markets. Dutch traders on the Gold Coast formed companies to protect themselves against Portuguese attack.

During the truce, these merchants also decided to follow up on colonization. No longer looking for naval bases, the merchants still thought they could build commercial centers in areas that were out of range of Spanish fleets, which might supply the American commodities direct from American producers, either Native Americans or farming colonists who would grow tobacco or other products.[37]

[36] Cornelis Goslinga, *The Dutch in the Caribbean and on the Wild Coast, 1589–1680* (Goricum, 1971).

[37] Linda Heywood and John Thornton, *Central Africans, Atlantic Creoles and the Foundation of the Americas, 1585–1660* (Cambridge, 2007), pp. 5–48.

English commercial colonies were tried in the area of modern-day Maine in 1602 and successfully in Jamestown in 1607. The English were less successful in Grenada in 1609, while French merchants worked on the first colonies in what would become Canada in 1609. Dutch merchants penetrated the Hudson River and founded Fort Orange (now Albany) in 1614. Similar Dutch and English colonies began to sprout in the mouth of the Amazon and along the coast north of that river and the Orinoco River in the future Guianas.

When war broke out again in Europe, first in the Bohemian phase of the Thirty Years War in 1618 and then as the truce ended in 1619, privateers swarmed out once again into the Caribbean and the Americas. The commercial bases could be converted into naval bases easily, and these bases, with an economy grounded on commercial enterprises, could be self-sustaining and not require the sort of financial investments that earlier naval-oriented colonial bases had. The most successful of these colonies were founded on growing tobacco in some areas, in trading with Native American producers of tobacco in other areas (especially in the Amazon and the Guianas), or in tapping the vast potential of the Native Americans in North America to deliver furs to the European market.

English privateers were soon using Bermuda, founded as an offshoot of the early Virginia colony in 1609, as a base, and ships under the enterprising Earl of Warwick, England's most active privateering family, were raiding the Caribbean. Robert Rich, the earl in these years, and his associates founded a private company to promote simultaneously privateering and colonization in 1631, and then used it to build two bases at Providence Island (off the coast of Nicaragua) and Ascenion Island (now Tortuga) in 1633. The Spanish managed to overwhelm both bases in 1641–1645, but their existence demonstrated the way in which privateering base and tobacco producing economy could work.

The Riches and their privateering interests were instrumental in establishing colonies in the southern Caribbean. They had interests in the Amazon, and one of their allies established an English colony in St. Christopher (modern day St. Kitts) in 1624, and then two years later another colony in Barbados. These colonies had less to do with privateering than with growing crops, focusing on tobacco in their earliest years. The Spanish knew their dangers, and on one occasion, in 1629, they managed to capture and depopulate St. Christopher (although the colonists soon reoccupied it).

If the English used this combination of privateering and producing in tandem in small companies like the Rich's Providence Island Company, the Dutch went much bigger. In 1621, a group of powerful Dutch merchants and privateers formed the Dutch West India Company with the express purpose of carrying the war into the Spanish Caribbean. The West India Company sent out large and powerful fleets to harass the Spanish, soon capturing hundreds of prizes and thousands of tons of goods. In 1628, one of their most notable admirals, Piet Heyn, managed to capture the entire Spanish silver fleet off the coast of Cuba. It was the highlight of the Dutch campaign, and produced a dividend greater than the entire revenue of the Dutch Republic.

The West India Company was not as much interested in building colonies from scratch as the English were. Instead, they hoped to use their military strength to take over whole, fully developed colonies. In 1624, a Dutch fleet temporarily occupied Bahia, a rich, sugar-exporting part of Portuguese Brazil. Although they were driven out, they continued their campaign, and in 1630 managed to conquer key parts of another rich province, Pernambuco, which lay north of Bahia. Soon the wealth of Brazilian sugar harvests was being shipped in Dutch holds as they had taken over working colonies. To secure the supply of slaves to Brazil, they crossed over the Atlantic, taking Angola in 1641, and then took a second Portuguese sugar colony at São Tomé the same year. It was only after the Portuguese drove the Dutch from Pernambuco in 1654 that they built their own colonies producing sugar in the Guianas.[38]

The Dutch West India Company became a model for other countries. Some of the people associated with the company found that its monopoly policies discouraged them and cost them income. Thus Willem Usselinx, one of the founders of the company, feeling that he did not get his just rewards from it, offered his services to Sweden in 1623. Initially the company was directed more to trading, as a charter granted by the Swedish king Gustavus Adolphus for a General Trading company in 1626 was, but it included a proviso for the taking of prizes and the disposal of such profits, though limited to action only when attacked.[39] However, as Sweden became more deeply involved in the Thirty Years War in which Spain was the principal enemy, the idea of a trading/naval warfare company that might pay for its operations (without state input) through privateering or commerce was applied to the Swedish navy in 1629, which was built and purchased through the promises of trading ventures and privateering aimed at Spanish shipping.[40] Another former Dutch West India Company officer, Samuel Bloomaert, proposed a more focused company in 1635, whose principal goal would be to trade German copper and Swedish iron to West Africa, where some believed that copper was sold for its weight in gold.[41]

The various West India Companies that Bloomaert formed gradually expanded the operations to include trade with the Spanish colonies in the Caribbean, also seen as consumers of copper, and then the development of

---

[38] C. R. Boxer, *The Dutch in Brazil, 1624–1654* (Oxford, 1957); Evaldo Cabral de Mello, *Olinda Restaurada: Guerra e açúcar no Nordeste, 1630–1654* (Rio de Janeiro, 1975).

[39] An English translation of the charter is published in *Documents on the Colonial History of New York* 14: 1–7.

[40] A convenient summary is Amandus Johnson, *The Swedish Settlements on the Delaware, 1638–64* (2 vols, Philadelphia, 1911, reprinted Baltimore: Genealogical Society, 1969 [GB]), pp. 69–73.

[41] His suggestions are laid out in a series of letters to Axel Oxenstierna, the Swedish minister from 1635 to 1641; the basic plan and its background is in Samuel Bloomaert to Axel Oxenstierna, June 3, 1635, in G. W. Kernkamp, "Zweedsche Archivalia," *Bijdragen en Mededeelingen van het Historish Genootschap te Utrecht* 29 (1908), pp. 67–75. The copper-for-gold concept is found in Konrad van Falkenburg to Axel Oxenstierna, October 28, 1628, in *Rikskanslern Axel Oxenstiernas skrifter och brevväxling* (Stockholm, 1905) 2/11, p. 560.

colonies in American regions that might be beyond Spain's naval reach, which in this case meant North America. Bloomaert's company went on to found New Sweden on the banks of the Delaware River, in what is now Delaware and Pennsylvania, in 1638.[42] But if New Sweden was to be a settlement, the prospect of it as a naval base was never lost, for throughout his letters, Bloomaert focused often on the successes the Dutch company had in privateering. When questions of profitability of the American settlement came up, Bloomaert proposed that these could be met by privateering against the Spanish.[43] The ship bearing the first colonists to New Sweden followed their disembarking by continuing on a successful privateering run against Spanish shipping in the Caribbean, making the profits that the settlers could not yet muster.[44] Another plan of 1644 pointed out that New Sweden was an ideal location for raiding the Caribbean – better, the planners argued, than the Dutch West India Company's holdings in New Netherlands (New York) to which they had learned that, on two occasions, Dutch ships had brought four Spanish prizes.[45] The colony managed to develop a mildly profitable enterprise growing tobacco and exporting Native American products and furs, but the Dutch Company attacked and took it over in 1655. Meanwhile, the plans for a more purely commercial company aimed at the gold trade off the Gold Coast were more successful. The first trading ventures were organized by the Dutch merchant (and now Sweden-based industrialist) Louis de Geer in 1645–1648, which was subsequently incorporated into the Swedish West Africa Company, which established some posts on the Gold Coast and managed to trade from there until the Dutch forced it out of business by raiding its shipping in 1663.[46]

Like the Swedish kings, Duke Jakob of Kurland (modern-day Latvia) saw in the Dutch model a possible way of enhancing naval power through self-supporting companies, although his company was much more oriented to trade than privateering. The Dutch merchant Firck became the founder of the duke's navy in 1640, and focused his attention initially on trade with the East Indies. In 1650, however, the company turned to trade on the African coast, especially the Gambia region, where there was perceived to be a valuable gold trade. Its first trading voyage in 1645 had failed, but the renewed efforts were more successful, and the company founded a colony there to engage in trading for gold and other African products. The Kurland African Company quickly turned to American possessions, like the Swedish Company. Unlike the Swedes, however, the Kurlanders went to the Caribbean. In 1654, the Kurlanders founded a colony on the island of Tobago, the site of a Dutch colony from about 1629 to

[42] Johnson, *Swedish Settlements*, 1: 92–139.

[43] Bloomaert to Oxenstierna, August 22, 1637 in Kernkamp, "Zweedsche Archivalia," p. 129.

[44] Blommaert to Oxenstierna, September 4, 1638, January 28, 1640, Kernkamp, "Zweedsche Archivalia," pp. 157–158, 174–176.

[45] Rigsarchivet, Stockholm, Eric Oxenstierna Sammlungen, Instructions to Printz, June 11, 1644.

[46] For details of the company's trade and its organization, see György Nováky, *Handelskompanier och kompanihandel. Svenska Afrikakompaniet 1649–63. En studie i feodal handel* (Uppsala, 1990).

1635. The Kurland colony remained for a few years before it met the same fate as the Dutch had: wiped out by the Caribs.[47]

With the ending of the Thirty Years War in 1648, the compelling military reasons for Dutch West India Company style naval war/trading companies diminished. But the earlier efforts of Dutch and English privateers and merchants had created a new commercial situation, and more commercially oriented companies were founded to exploit it. For example, Danish, Dutch, and German merchants working from the port of Glückstadt formed a commercial company to work the Gold Coast trade in 1658. The purposes of the company were to protect the valuable cargo and to built forts and trading points on the coast.[48] Heinrich Carloff, who had formerly served on the Dutch West India Company, had subsequently transferred his loyalty to the Swedish company and founded a number of trading posts. He subsequently turned them over to the new Danish company and managed them for the Danes. Eventually the Danish crown participated in forming a royal company in 1674 from the Glückstadt posts.[49] The new Danish company then moved from the gold trade in Africa to see what could be done in the Caribbean, and quickly acquired a small chain of islands – the modern-day Virgin Islands – and developed them as sugar plantations.

Brandenburg (subsequently Prussia) also chartered a commercial company to engage in the gold trade. Like the earlier companies, the Brandenburg company emerged out of naval necessity, not for war against the Spanish, but in the Baltic wars. The Elector of Brandenburg, Friedrich Wilhelm (1640–1688) appointed a Dutch merchant named Benjamin Raule to form a navy for the principality in 1672. To finance this enterprise, Raule immediately proposed forming a trading company, although it was not until 1680 that the idea of a commercial relationship with the African coast was entertained. After a first experimental voyage, the company was formed in 1682. They founded a number of posts on the Gold Coast, as well as on the island of Arguin off the coast of Senegal, where they hoped to deal in desert products like gum Arabic, which was used as a dyestuff. But it was difficult to trade on the Gold Coast, especially to maintain forts. The company's ships were frequently seized by other European powers, and the Brandenburgers became involved in African wars, which sapped their resources. Although the Brandenburg crown maintained little interest in the unprofitable company, it was not finally wound up (by being sold to the Dutch company) until 1721.[50]

---

[47] For a study of the company and its relationships, as well as the texts of many crucial documents, see Otto Heinz Mattiesen, *Die Kolonial- und Überseepolitik Herzog Jakobs von Kurland, 1640–1660* (Stuttgart, 1939).

[48] Heinrich Sieveking, "Die Glückstädter Guineafahrt im 17. Jahrhundert. Ein Stück deutscher Kolonialgeschichte," *Vierteljahrschrift für Sozial- und Wirtschaftsgeschichte* 30 (1937): 19–71.

[49] Georg Norregaard, *Danish Settlements in West Africa* (Boston, 1966).

[50] Richard Schück, *Brandenburg-Preussens Kolonial-Politik unter dem Grossen Kurfüsten und seinen Nachfolgern (1647–1721)* (2 vols., Leipzig, 1889). Many of the documents of the company have been published with English translation in Adam Jones, ed. and trans. *Brandenburg Sources for West African History* (Wiesbaden, 1985).

There is no compelling reason why Europeans had to colonize in the Americas in the sixteenth and seventeenth century. They might have had very profitable enterprises simply with merchants' contacts, as they did in most of Africa. The specific way in which conquest took place, however, was dictated by European concerns of state and of warfare. European governments looked to commercial ventures to increase state revenue, and saw that this could be increased for their purposes by sponsoring colonization. Then again, private commercial ventures could be enlisted in the struggle to increase the reach of the state by making special profit-sharing and cost-distributing arrangements. These arrangements led to the specific nature of colonization.

Initially the Spanish and Portuguese benefited from the overseas revenues, and the interventions of northern Europeans were driven by defensive war and the hope that they could disrupt the revenue flow. The need to involve merchants in this enterprise eventually led to the founding of commercial colonies. Before 1650, these colonies, while sometimes prosperous, did not contribute much to revenue, and were primarily seen not as sources of revenue, but rather as strategic outposts.

However, beginning in the 1650s, as the English and French began cultivating sugarcane in Barbados and the Lesser Antillies, the profitability of these Caribbean colonies increased. By the early eighteenth century, they had become significant sources of cash revenues to all the northern countries, but especially to England and France. By the mid-eighteenth century, revenue from the Caribbean was a vital element of royal incomes and significant in programs of national defense, much as they had been earlier in Spain and Portugal.

Europe's military transformation and its effect on social and political structures was therefore crucial in determining what the nature of overseas expansion would be. While merchants may well have been willing to deal with distant markets in the Atlantic, the potential for revenue, and the various European's government's interest in enhancing revenue to expand its military resources, led to a different sort of expansion. Private capital led the way and took the risks, but the rulers of the state took over once the profitability had been guaranteed. Although Spain and Portugal were the first to realize the importance of overseas income for state centralization, their very success ultimately dragged their rivals and enemies from northern Europe into the Atlantic as well. At first the northerners entered aggressively, to cut vital routes of silver to embattled Europe in the war over the Rhine Valley, and later, as a means to fund these outposts, as merchants. Ultimately their commercial success would underwrite a new expansion in military power in Europe.

The eighteenth century would show the development of newer and ever more expensive means of fighting war for Europeans, and to that end, their rulers turned again to the Atlantic colonies for fiscal relief. As we shall see in the final chapters of this book, this new grasping for overseas resources would backfire and lead many of their colonies to obtain independence.

3

The African Background

As the Portuguese pioneers circled Africa in the late fifteenth century, the many societies that bordered the Atlantic entered into the larger economy that developed with the first voyages to the Americas. While not all of Africa was drawn into this network of interactions even in 1800, a sizable zone extending inland from the coast did. This zone included not only those societies in direct or indirect contact with the Atlantic coast, but also a substantial section of the East African coast and the island of Madagascar, which were bordering on or found in the Indian Ocean. While the Indian Ocean network that the Portuguese created in their Estado da India (State of India) in the sixteenth century had frequent maritime contact with Europe, the African states along the East African coast and Ethiopia had little to do with the Atlantic world as it developed with the creation of an American network.

Africa's participation in the Atlantic world was largely through trade. Unlike the Americas, where dramatic conquest, settlement, and transformation under European direction took place, Africa was not conquered or settled during this time. Portugal managed to build a small colony in Angola in the seventeenth century and colonized the offshore island groups of São Tomé and Príncipe, the Cape Verde Islands, and the islands of Madeira and the Azores; elsewhere along the Atlantic coast, Europeans barely clung to small, vulnerable trading posts, acquiring their slaves from African sellers while often paying taxes and rents to African rulers for the right to do so.

Although Africans dealt in many commodities, by the middle of the sixteenth century, slaves had become an important component of its trade with merchants from the Atlantic. It would soon grow to enormous proportions, rising rapidly after 1700 to reach as many as 50,000 people per year. Between 1500 and 1830, by most estimates, somewhere between 11 million and 15 million Africans crossed the Atlantic to be settled in the Americas.[1]

---

[1] The total number has been the subject of considerable debate and discussion. Numbers have varied even more widely that this one, so that one school of thought suggests 100 million (but such estimates usually include deaths and indirect losses in Africa as well as exports). The pioneering

The slave trade determined that Africans rather than Europeans were the majority of the non-Americans who settled in the Western Hemisphere. North Americans often miss the point as the African slave trade barely touched the continent (less than 6 percent of all the slaves who crossed the Atlantic went to North America), and the flood of European immigrants to many South American countries such as Colombia, Argentina, and Brazil in the nineteenth century have masked these countries' African pasts. Nevertheless, roughly three Africans crossed the ocean for every European between 1500 and 1800, and the demography of the New World quickly showed it. In his mid-sixteenth-century account of the history of the Indies, Gonzalo Fernández Oviedo described Hispaniola as a "new Guinea [Africa]" from the large percentage of Africans found there.[2] Similar language was used to describe Brazil half a century later,[3] and it is still clearly seen in the Caribbean where, on many islands such as Barbados, virtually the entire population today is of African descent, and most of the others (for example, Cuba or Puerto Rico) were "new Africas" in 1800.

The slave trade was no ordinary trade. Apart from the fact that it involved human suffering on a scale that was significant even to European observers used to the brutality of the premodern world, it also involved the export of important human resources. This dual cost, in suffering and in the loss of resources has made the trade of Africa problematic for historians, for it appears as so inherently bad for Africa that its continuation, and especially the African role in furthering it, requires explanation. For that reason, the principal aim of this chapter is to explore the complex role of the slave trade to African decision making, state building, and resource allocation.

SLAVERY'S SPACE: THE GEOGRAPHY OF THE SLAVE TRADE

The trade routes that extended inland from the trading points along the coast reached varying distances inland, depending on political situations, African trading systems, and transportation corridors. In Senegal, for example, the Senegal River provided a highway that reached deep into West Africa, while along the southern regions of West Africa that the Europeans dubbed Lower Guinea, commerce did not extend nearly as deeply.

modern effort, still valuable and valid for some aspects of the trade, was Philip Curtin, *The Atlantic Slave Trade: A Census* (Madison, 1969). For the best recent efforts, see Paul Lovejoy, *Transformations in Slavery: A History of Slavery in Africa* (2nd edition, Cambridge, 2000), Herbert Klein, *The Atlantic Slave Trade* (Cambridge, 1999), and David Eltis, *The Rise of African Slavery in the Americas* (Cambridge, 2000). The W. E. B. DuBois Institute, Harvard University, has also been compiling statistics, and a first effort at identifying slaving voyages is in David Eltis, Stephen D. Behrendt, David Richardso, and Herbert S. Klein, eds., *The Trans-Atlantic Slaver Trade: A Database on CD-ROM* (Cambridge, 1999), since revised and on the Internet at http://www.slavevoyages.org/tast/index.faces

[2] Gonzalo Fernández Oviedo y Valdez, *Historia general y natural de las Indias* (ed. Juan Pérez de Tudela Bueso, 5 vols., Madrid, 1959 [1851 ed GB]) Book 4, chapter 8.

[3] Ambrósio Fernandes Brandão, *Diálogos das Grandezas do Brasil* (2nd edition, José Antonio Gonçalves de Mello, Recife, 1968 [written 1612]), dialogue 2, p. 44

We can gauge the depth of this contact by using as a guide the origins of slaves landed in the Americas. In many European colonies, slaves were known by "nations" or "countries," most of which can be identified with a particular African location, and in a few cases, European missionaries took some pains to locate these places using their and their informants' geographical knowledge. In the early 1620s, Alonso de Sandoval, a Jesuit priest working among incoming slaves in the city of Cartagena (in present-day Colombia), made such a survey, and plotting on a map the origins of the slaves he knew gives us the extent of the contact between Africa and the Atlantic world in his day.[4] In 1767, Georg Christian Andreas Oldendorp, a Moravian missionary working on the Danish Virgin Islands, compiled a similar geography of the lands from which slaves came there. [5] Finally, in the mid-1840s, another missionary, Sigismund Koelle, established a linguistic map of Africa created by interrogating slaves that had arrived in the English colony of Sierra Leone, representing the Atlantic face of Africa in the early nineteenth century.[6] These maps can be expanded by additional information and reveal to us a picture of the growth of the extent of African participation.

In Upper Guinea, the region between modern Senegal and Liberia, the zone established by 1550 or so did not grow at all; slaves from as far inland as the Niger Valley could be found in the Americas in all the surveys. In Lower Guinea, which extended from the Ivory Coast around to Cameroon, intercontinental trade did grow, for inland regions in the northern parts of Ghana, Togo, and Nigeria were added to the zone dealing with the Atlantic during the eighteenth century. Likewise, in West Central Africa, the zone established by trade with Kongo in 1500, grew substantially in the seventeenth century, with Portuguese military activity from their colony of Angola established in 1575. It grew again in the eighteenth century, crossing the Kwango River – its furthest extent in the seventeenth century – and reaching as far inland as modern day eastern Zambia.

South and east of West Central Africa, Africa's participation in the Atlantic world was more sporadic. The Portuguese barely touched the coast of South Africa, stopping occasionally and doing little or no business. The east of South Africa was visited most reluctantly, only by shipwrecked sailors on the India-to-Europe route, until the end of the eighteenth century. On the other hand, the island of Madagascar, reached by Europeans in the early sixteenth century, had

[4] Alonso de Sandoval, *Natrualeza, Policia Sagrada i Profana, Costumbres i Ritos i Catechismo Evangelico de Todos Ethopes* (Madrid, 1627 and second augmented edition, 1647 [Gallica]), fols. 6v–9v; 38v–46; 50v–65.

[5] Christian Georg Andreas Oldendorp, *Historie der caribischen Inseln Sanct Thomas, Sanct Crux und Sanct Jan, inbesondere der dasigen Neger und der Mission der evangelischen Brüder under denselben* (mod. ed. Gudrun Meier, Stephan Palmié, Peter Stein and Horst Ulbricht. 2 parts in 4 volumes, Berlin, 2000–2002) 1: 368–465.

[6] Sigismund Koelle, *Polyglotta Africana* (London, 1854, new annotated edition, P. E. H. Hair and David Dalby, Sierra Leone, 1963).

a brief but quite intense involvement in the Atlantic commerce through the slave trade, which flourished there from about 1670 until the second decade of the eighteenth century, when its international connections were restricted to Indian Ocean neighbors.[7] Further north, in Southeast Africa, the Portuguese established trading posts in the early sixteenth century at Sofala and Mozambique Island, and later in the century began the "conquest" of the Zambezi Valley. While deeply involved in the Indian Ocean trade, these outposts of the State of India did not become involved in the Atlantic world, like Madagascar, as a supplier of slaves until the early nineteenth century, sending human cargos almost exclusively to Brazil. In Koelle's geography of the mid-1800s, slaves hailing from northern Mozambique and exiting Africa through the Zambezi came from areas not so far from those leaving eastern Zambia and departing through the West Central African ports of Luanda, Benguela, Cabinda, and Malemba, where they might have met each other in Brazil. In such a case, the zone of Atlantic contact spread right across the continent.

AFRICA AND THE SLAVE TRADE: A PARADOX

The Atlantic slave trade rests on a giant paradox. It is not difficult to see that at a continental and even at a regional level, the slave trade was bad for Africa. The demographic impact of the removal of so many people alone affected labor regimes and gender relations and helped shape the nature and direction of warfare. Yet at the same time, it is equally easy to see that this same trade, bad as it was at a regional level, was controlled by the political and economic elite of Africa, and not by their European trading partners. Thus the paradox is to explain why the African elite allowed this to take place.

African rulers generally controlled access to their coasts, and were able to prevent direct enslavement of their subjects and citizens by Europeans, except in Angola, where the Portuguese colony, founded in 1575, was often a center for Portuguese-led attacks that netted thousands of slaves. Even there, although direct attacks accounted for a substantial quantity of enslaved people, there was always also a thriving business in buying slaves from African rulers and merchants from neighboring, independent kingdoms. Elsewhere along the African coast, the delivery of enslaved people to European shippers was an African business, managed by African commercial and political elites.

European commercial records reveal this clearly. The records of the Dutch West India Company, which was first formed in 1621 and ran with greater or lesser degrees of commercial success until the nineteenth century, provide clear support. If one takes the company's business on the Gold Coast in the eighteenth century, the period of fullest records and greatest export of people – a record which probably exceeds 100,000 pages in length – there is scarcely any

---

[7] Arne Bialuschewski, "Pirates, Slavers, and the Indigenous Population in Madagascar, c 1690–1715," *International Journal of African Historical Studies* 38 (2005): 401–425.

mention of direct enslavement of Africans.[8] The records of French, English, and Danish companies, less complete and voluminous, but responsible for carrying many more slaves than the Dutch, tell us very much the same story. European merchants or companies acquired their slaves by purchase from African buyers, usually with the active participation of African states, both as taxing agencies and in their own right as commercial sellers.

It is equally obvious that African states had the upper hand if the game of force was to be played. Although Europeans often fortified their "factories," as trading posts were usually called, these fortifications could not resist an attack by determined African authorities. For example, the French director at Whydah, on the coast of modern-day Benin, wrote in the early eighteenth century that he believed the Africans allowed Europeans to build forts on the African coast so that the European traders could be more easily plundered.[9] Francisco Pereira Mendes, the Portuguese factor at the same post, took great lengths to explain to his home government why it was impossible for him to resist the demands of the King of Dahomey when the latter's armies appeared on the coast in 1727.[10]

Yet, although Africans controlled the trade, and could have stopped it within their own lands at virtually any time, they let it continue for centuries. Some areas were never a part of the slave trade, although they lay on the coast and occasionally traded with Europeans in other commodities. The stretch of coast from southern Liberia to eastern Ivory Coast, for example, never exported more than a handful of slaves. Similarly, the coast from southern Cameroon to Gabon was a marginal producer of slaves at best. Some entered and subsequently left the trade: the Kingdom of Benin is a fine example of this. Benin participated in the slave trade in the early sixteenth century, but then around 1550 abruptly broke it off, while continuing to deal with European merchants in other commodities like pepper and ivory. Then, from about 1715 until 1735, it participated again, astonishing the Dutch merchants who were not prepared to purchase slaves at that source. But after 1735, Benin again stopped selling slaves while continuing its commerce in other commodities.[11]

---

[8] The records in question are housed in the Algemeen Rijksarchief (now Nationaal Archief) in the Hague. They are found especially in the documents of the First (Old) and Second West India Companies. This estimate is based on the size of files in the most important collections, the Nederlands Bezittingunen ter Kust Guinea (local records once held on the coast), and the various minutes and plans of the West India Companies in their European offices.

[9] Jean-Baptiste Labat, *Voyage du Chevalier des Marachais en Guinée, isles voisines, et à Cayenne, fait en 1725, 1726, & 1727* (4 volumes, Amsterdam, 1731) 2: 192.

[10] Arquivo do Estado de Bahia, 23, fol. 90, Francisco Pereyra Mendes, 30 June 1728, quoted in Pierre Vergier, *Fluxo e refluxo do Trárico de Escravos entre o Golfo de Benin e a Bahia de Todos os Santos dos seculos XVII a XIX* (trans. Tasso Gadazis, 2nd ed, São Paulo, 1987), p. 144 (I have examined the original and note that this edition of Verger's work quotes the text directly from the original and is not a retranslation from Verger's French translation in the first edition of the work).

[11] The history of Benin's involvement with Europe and the slave trade is presented in A. F. C. Ryder, *Benin and the Europeans, 1485–1897* (New York, 1969).

As for the second half of the paradox, African political and economic elites sold slaves even though it is quite clear that the trade had a devastating effect on the African population. As we have seen, only a portion of Africa participated in the trade, and thus for much of its history, the slave trade drew most heavily on populations within about 200 kilometers of the coast.[12] In this zone, the damage of removing so many people could not help but have a devastating effect on the population.

The damage was done through two processes. The first one was the sheer numbers. At its height in the eighteenth century, the slave trade was removing more than 50,000 people each year.[13] It is unlikely that the population in the region affected by this trade ever had more than about 20 million people, and so this was a tremendous impact on its own.[14] The second process was one of demographic transformation. Slave buyers did not want to purchase people who could not work productively on the other side of the Atlantic. Between instructions to slave buyers, runs of statistics, and other sources, it seems likely that the overwhelming majority of the slaves were taken from people in the most productive age groups, between the ages of eighteen and thirty-five. Thus the population was deprived of its best and most productive workers, not just reduced by total numbers. In addition, the slave buyers wished to have a largely male labor force, and the same statistical sources show us that roughly two men were taken from African for every woman (though with notable variations). In the long run, these two processes produced substantial changes in the age structure and the sex ratios of the remaining African population.[15]

A census taken in Angola in 1777 and 1778 reveals something of the impact of the slave trade on the population as a whole. The Angola census was taken only in areas where the Portuguese government had sufficient authority to count the population, and undoubtedly it was as much an estimate in some areas as a count. But it is likely to be the best gauge that we have today to estimate the impact of the trade in Africa. There is good reason to believe that the

---

[12] The best and most extensive of these surveys was published in Koelle, *Polyglotta Africana* based on interviews in the 1830s including life histories of recaptives in Sierra Leone. Because Koelle was assembling a linguistic inventory, he obtained information from as many different groups as possible. This created some quantitative distortions; see the analysis of this source in Philip D. Curtin and Jan Vansina, "Sources of the Nineteenth Century Atlantic Slave Trade," *Journal of African History* 5 (1964): 185–208 and P. E. H. Hair, "The Enslavement of Koelle's Informants," *Journal of African History* 6 (1965): 193–203. A similar source from the mid-eighteenth century (also a linguistic survey and inventory) by Oldendorp reveals a pattern of enslavement of people living in a more restricted area closer to the coast, Oldendorp, *Historie* 1: 365–456.

[13] Best illustrated in the appendix of Klein, *Slave Trade*.

[14] For estimates of African population affected, see Patrick Manning, *Slavery and African Life: Occidental, Oriental and the African Slave Trade* (Cambridge, 1990); John Thornton, "The Demographic Effect of the Slave Trade on Western Africa, 1500–1850" in C. Fyfe and D. McMaster, *African Historical Demography*, vol. 2 (Edinburgh: Centre of African Studies, 1981): 691–720.

[15] Klein, *Atlantic Slave Trade*, pp. 17–47; 130–160.

regions enumerated by the census takers included areas that had been ravaged by the slave trade and those that had suffered less, but the impact, ironically, was pretty much the same.

The officials broke the population down by age (into categories that were, more or less, infant, child, working adult, and elder) and by sex. They immediately show an alarmingly high dependency ratio – that is the ratio of working adults to the dependent population (mostly children who required care and could not work productively). This is to be expected given the tendency of the slave trade to affect the adult population only and not the dependent groups, especially children (or the dependent elderly).

A second visible impact in the Angolan data is in the sex ratios. Among adults, according to my analysis of the census, there were only 43 men to every 100 women. This is a startling statistic, for it means that adult women outnumbered men by more than two to one. It seems likely that this fact alone might explain the high rates of polygamy (men having multiple wives) in the Angolan (and African) population, so that families could continue even in the shortage of men. In fact, the fertility rate for the women was close to what might be considered normal, strongly suggesting that women were staying connected to men in families that had to be polygamous.[16] But beyond its impact on marriage, Angolans, like people everywhere else, had a sexual division of labor, a conventional idea of what constituted men's work and what constituted women's work. Furthermore, the idea of a set sexual division of labor undoubtedly shaped the sort of work that people were trained to do. In Angola, for example, women did the work of cultivation, but men had the job of field clearance. Women prepared food, whereas men prepared drinks and oils as well as did much of the manufacturing.[17] How did Angolans deal with the imbalances? We do not know, but it is likely that productivity fell as people were forced to do work they were unaccustomed to doing.

Women suffered the most from this demographic imbalance. Their agricultural labor was very probably less fully supported by men, and moreover, the high dependency ratio would have put a considerable strain on them, for they also had child-care responsibilities. Because there were fewer women than normal, and the birth rate remained stable, fewer women had to take care of more children while still managing to do their agricultural labor with insufficient male support. Even in West Africa, where the imbalances were probably less pronounced than in Angola, women took over some of the work that elsewhere was done by men. In the Bijagos Islands, where the imbalances were caused both by losses of males (and perhaps by the importation of females), women seemed to do all the work, according to seventeenth- and eighteenth-century witnesses.[18]

[16] John Thornton, "The Slave Trade in Eighteenth Century Angola: Effects on Demographic Structures" *Canadian Journal of African Studies* 14 (1980): 417–428.

[17] For this division in Kongo, Thornton, *Kingdom of Kongo*, pp. 28–32.

[18] John Thornton, "Sexual Demography: The Impact of the Slave Trade on Family Structure," in Claire Robertson and Martin Klein (eds.) *Women and Slavery in Africa* (Madison, 1983): 39–48.

Angola was, by all accounts, particularly hard hit. There were probably more people enslaved per capita in Angola than in any other place in Africa. But simulations and other exercises done by modern scholars suggest that these types of problems may well have taken place in many other areas, especially the changes in age and sex structure. Women had to work harder, and families had to do without. There is good reason to believe that those who were not enslaved suffered a great deal for the loss of those who were exported during the slave trade.[19]

These impacts were certainly noticeable, even to those who did not have statistics on the changes. Those who made decisions about engaging in the slave trade had to be aware of the long-term population consequences as well. Because of this, some scholars have suggested that European merchants were able to force African leaders to participate in the trade through indirect pressure.

One source of pressure might be the arms trade, because many African armies, especially after 1680, used imported European weapons to fight their wars, and these wars in turn fed the slave trade. In the late eighteenth century, European opponents of the slave trade argued that there was a "gun-slave cycle" in which Europeans would sell guns with the understanding that their African owners would then use them to acquire slaves, which would pay for the weapons. Should Africans resist the ploy, Europeans would sell the weapons to their neighbors who would then use them to enslave the recalcitrant group. Sometimes these weapons were bought on credit, and repaid in slaves, suggesting the same sort of pressure.

A second explanation contends that Africans were more generally dependent economically on Europeans for the supply of vital nonmilitary goods. In this argument, African economies were relatively underdeveloped, producing fewer goods with lower efficiencies than Europe did. Economic historians have thus argued that the value of goods and services produced by African workers in Africa was less than the amount that they produced in America as slaves, and this imbalance made it economically rational to export workers and import (indirectly) their products. In another variant of this theme, the underdeveloped state of the African economy relative to that of Europe gave European merchants a commercial upper hand that allowed them not only to profit handsomely from the sale of their goods, but also to demand payment in slaves, even if Africans did not wish to sell them.[20]

---

[19] Manning, *Slavery and African Life*; a second model using different approaches but obtaining similar results, Thornton, "Demographic Effect."

[20] Manning, *Slavery and African Life*, pp. 32–37, Manning makes his arguments concerning African productivity, which he contends was lower than that of Europe, thus lowering the price of labor. He attacks an article of Stefano Fenoaltea, "Europe in the African Mirror: The Slave Trade and the Rise of Feudalism," *Revista Italiana da storia economica* (1999). See also the debate on productivity and its connections to the slave trade in the *African Economic History Review* 9 (1992), led by John Thornton, "Pre-Colonial African Industry and the Atlantic Trade, 1500–1800," and comments by Patrick Manning and others.

Neither explanation can work fully, however. To address the productivity issue first, although modern Africa is one of the poorest continents in the world today, this general poverty was not to be found in the preindustrial period. Africans produced what they consumed, and international trade made up only a small portion of that consumption. Furthermore, if one uses the limited information that we have about such things as life expectancy and infant mortality as a measure of the ability of the economy to meet basic needs, Africans were on par with Europeans. Statistics from Kongo, where baptismal records allow some estimates of vital rates, show that the average life expectancy in that country in the mid-seventeenth and eighteenth centuries was about thirty years – dismal by today's standards to be sure, but every bit as good as those of France or England in the same period. Likewise, infant mortality rates of around 250 per 1,000 also compared favorably with European ones that were generally somewhat higher.[21] In short, the modern image of Africa as a poverty-stricken, disease-ridden, technology-poor region is a creation of more recent times, and not a picture of the earlier period.

African economic strength was particularly notable in what might be termed "essential commodities" among manufactured goods like steel or textiles. African production strategies often relied on skill or on the utilization of the free time of agricultural populations (rather than developing full-time specialists in production) and did not use much technology. But statistics, when they are available, show that African textile production reached very high levels, and the trade in locally made cloth was substantial, far more than any imported cloth. Local statistical information from the early seventeenth century shows that the quantity of local cloth in the Angolan market was equal to production of similar-sized productive zones in Europe. West Africans exported cotton goods to America, often in significant quantities, until the Industrial Revolution fundamentally altered patterns of textile production and trade. Similarly, archaeology shows that Africans could produce high grades of steel in significant quantities, and archaeological investigation of production in places like Bassar, in modern-day Togo, shows that production rose throughout the period.[22]

European trade with Africa was thus marginal to overall trade, and, while valuable to those who sought imports, not so vital to the economy as to represent a source of pressure. Similarly, African leaders' decision to participate in the slave trade is not simply a question of Europeans making demands for slaves in exchange for weapons, as the "gun-slave cycle" supposes. On one hand, a fairly remarkable number of African armies, even those that exported numbers of slaves, made relatively little use of European weapons. Certainly in some areas, most notably in the arc of African states that occupied the region Europeans called Lower Guinea (roughly from modern-day Ivory Coast to

[21] John Thornton, "Demography and History in the Kingdom of Kongo, 1550–1750," *Journal of African History* 18 (1977): 507–530. For European rates, see E. A. Wrigley, *Population and History* (New York, 1969)

[22] For a fuller documentation, see Thornton, *Africa and Africans*, pp. 43–53.

Cameroon), firearms were the main battle weapon by the opening decades of the eighteenth century. In other areas, however, firearms were less important. In Angola, even the Portuguese army that fought against African opponents and sold the captives as slaves (when it was victorious) equipped only about half of its soldiers with firearms, the remaining troops carrying bows and arrows even in the late eighteenth century. Neighboring African states, such as Kongo to the north or Matamba to the east, had a similar mix of firearms and bows among their soldiers. The armies of the Lunda Empire, for example, which invaded the eastern parts of Angola in the mid-eighteenth century, resulting in a flood of captives for the American markets, not only did not employ firearms, but actively eschewed them as "coward's weapons." In the plains of West Africa – from modern-day Senegal to Liberia and inland to Mali – cavalry held the day and often did not use firearms. Some cavalries carried pistols or carbines by the end of the eighteenth century, but others still relied on lance and bow. When differently equipped armies met in battle as they occasionally did, the outcome was not necessarily decided by who had firearms or who had the most firearms.[23]

European commercial records also do not suggest that the dependence of African states that did employ firearms on imported materiel were subject to pressure to capture slaves by European policies. In the Gold Coast area, corresponding to modern-day Ghana and bordering regions in Ivory Coast and Togo, for example, African leaders were early in adopting firearms (they were already in common use in the early seventeenth century, well in advance of many areas in Africa and even in Europe), and had switched over to firearms as their principal projectile weapon by the end of the century. As both weapons and gunpowder were usually imported, this region is an excellent test case for the role of munitions trade in creating policy.[24]

If one European merchant house or country managed to control the arms trade, they might well use this control to force African leaders to accept terms of trade to their liking. In fact, the idea of developing a monopoly was central to European merchants on the Gold Coast region since the sixteenth century when the Portuguese sought to prevent other Europeans, such as the French and English, from trading there, with only moderate success. At this time, however, the Gold Coast was exporting primarily gold, and moreover was actually importing slaves brought from other parts of African (Kongo and the region around the mouth of the Niger River in modern-day Nigeria) from European merchants.[25] By the early seventeenth century, Dutch and English merchants had broken the Portuguese commercial policy completely and were busy

---

[23] For more information and full documentation, see John Thornton, *Warfare in Atlantic Africa, 1500–1800* (London, 1999).

[24] Thornton, *Warfare*, pp. 61–64.

[25] For the early period, see Avelino Teixeira da Mota and P. E. H. Hair, *East of Mina: Afro-European Relations on the Gold Coast in the 1550s and 1560s* (Madison, 1988); John Vogt, *Portuguese Rule on the Gold Coast, 1469–1682* (Athens, GA, 1979); for more detail, see J. Bato'ra Ballong-wen-Mewuda, *São Jorge da Mina, 1482–1637* (Paris, 1993).

competing with each other. When the Dutch captured the Portuguese fortified trading posts and their Gold Coast capital at Elmina in 1637, they could claim no monopoly – even though this was decidedly their aim – because English merchants held their own.[26] As long as there was this competition, African rulers would be able (and indeed did) play the two off against each other, not only for firearms but for other imports as well. In any case, the region was still not a slave-trading center at the time.

English and Dutch efforts to create monopolies were aided by the formation of large-scale companies; both the Dutch and English set up chartered companies to control trade and exclude their rivals, while negotiating treaties with African rulers as if these trading companies were sovereign powers. But the chartered companies failed to prevent others from entering, and by the second half of the century there were also Brandenburger (Prussian), Swedish, and Danish commercial companies, organized on lines similar to the Dutch and English companies, operating in the Gold Coast. A French company worked on the western part of the zone by the end of the century, and the Portuguese returned in the early eighteenth century.

The trading companies were bitterly resented in Europe, and private merchants sought to have the right to trade in the Gold Coast without supervision from the companies. Indeed, dissatisfied Dutch merchants were significant players in creating the Danish and Swedish African Companies. By the end of the seventeenth century, the companies had to relinquish their monopolies and allow some private trading, and what was a leak soon became a flood. In the early eighteenth century, when Gold Coast African states began to sell slaves in large numbers for the first time, and even to import gold from Portuguese Brazil – a remarkable reversal of trading patterns – there were three important national companies (Dutch, English, and Danish) operating posts on the coast.[27] In addition, however, there was a swarm of private traders, whose activities are intermittently recorded in the account books of the companies and sometimes in notarial archives or private papers in Europe. These various merchants engaged in ferocious competition, often undercutting each other, and certainly not restricting the flow of firearms to serve some larger purpose. Indeed, the companies, always interested in monopolizing trade, were engaged in commercial wars with each other, often enlisting Africans to help them, or alternatively involving themselves in African wars in hopes of gaining an advantage over their commercial rivals from Europe. Here they certainly found grounds to complain that this or that rival sold weapons to Africans, typically those they hoped to fight. But this hardly amounts to the sort of manipulation of weapons that would force unwilling African leaders to sell slaves against their will or interest.

[26] For inter-European commercial rivalries and African participation, see Kwame Daaku, *Trade and Politics on the Gold Coast 1600–1720* (London, 1970).

[27] Noted, with substantial material on the deeper causes, in Ray Kea, *Settlements, Trade, and Polities on the Seventeenth Century Gold Coast* (Baltimore, 1982).

If we have removed the possibility of large scale and systematic force in setting the stage for African participation in the slave trade, we still need to answer the basic paradox: Why would African rulers, in command of their coasts, their economies, and their politics, be willing to engage in a trade that had such disadvantages in the long term? The answer lies in Africa and in the politics of the slave trade rather than its economics.

THE DYNAMICS OF ENSLAVEMENT

The first issue to resolve is the basic issue of enslavement. How were Africans enslaved? Records from Africa are not very helpful – most African societies did not keep written records of their activities, whereas Europeans, who did, were often vague on the precise mechanics of the trade, even in Portuguese Angola, where one would think that a records-keeping, commercially oriented colony that typically enslaved thousands of captives from its wars with African neighbors might describe the process in detail, at least for themselves. Remarkably, however, such documents scarcely exist in the surviving historical record.[28]

One of the best sources remains the testimony of Africans who were enslaved and reached America. While few of them wrote anything, they did on occasion describe their experience to literate people. Alonso de Sandoval, whose description of Africa helped frame the scope of African's involvement in European trade, was one of the first to write a description of the experiences of Africans who he sought to Christianize over an eighteen-year career. De Sandoval believed that most of his informants were enslaved in war, many were also enslaved by bandits or pirates (on rivers or coasts), and sometimes people were punished for crimes by enslavement and transportation – often, in the Jesuit's opinion, by judicial findings that were only questionably just and often involved enslaving innocent family members along with the guilty.[29]

Oldendorp's description of the enslavement of his informants was one of the most systematic of such descriptions from the high period of slave trading.[30]

---

[28] This observation is based on reading materials in the Arquivo Histórico Ultramarino (Lisbon) the principal metropolitan repository, which includes governor's correspondence and attached notes and documents (often quite lengthy) as well as the Arquivo Histórico Nacional de Angola (Luanda), which includes additional governor's reports (Oficios para o Reino) as well as with the interior. Occasional runs of governor's received correspondence (from officials in the interior) are also relevant, the Fernão de Sousa collection from 1624–1630 at the Palacio da Ajuda (published by Beatrix Heintze) and the documents of Innocencio de Souza Coutinho from 1765–1674 in the Biblioteca Nacional de Lisboa, Códices 8742–8744, and ANTT, Conde de Linhares, maços 42–58 and 99. Although numbers of captives are occasionally mentioned, there was clearly no statistical mechanism to report on battlefield captives, only on export statistics. A few surviving military after-action reports, which might also provide this data, do not report either enemy casualties or captives.

[29] De Sandoval, *Naturaleza*, Book 1, chapter 17, fols. 65v–70v.

[30] Oldendorp wrote a very long manuscript of his research upon his return from America, which has only recently been published in its entirety; Christian Georg Andreas Oldendorp, *Historie*

One of Oldendorp's tasks in the West Indies was to determine the linguistic policy of the Moravians, a small Protestant religious group that was very active in evangelization, and to survey the languages Africans who were delivered to the West Indies spoke. Oldendorp interviewed many slaves in the West Indies, sometimes providing biographies, but often not. Among the questions he put to his informants, beside obvious linguistic ones, were the ones that concerned their enslavement.

The Danish West Indies were supplied with slaves not only by the Danish company and its base on the Gold Coast, but slavers from French and English companies and private traders as well. Thus Oldendorp's informants came from all areas and had the experience of all the major traders behind them. He provided information on forty-four different individuals, who he described but unfortunately did not name, who were drawn from some nineteen "nations" or ethnolinguistic groups – the whole range of his informants. It is a small sample – one might wish for several hundred such stories before making more definitive statements – but Oldendorp's is still valuable.

There were a wide range of accounts, but some regularities appear. Nearly two-thirds of the informants were taken violently, either in war or by bandits and robbery. Of these violent enslavements, kidnapping on the road and other forms of robbery accounted for about a quarter of the cases reported by Oldendorp. For example, one Akan man went with his friends to Fante to buy maize and was waylaid on the road while traveling and taken to the "white man's fort"; in another case, a Congo man was captured by "man stealers" while traveling on business.[31] An interesting case was that of a man sent by the "regents" of his country to inquire about runaway slaves, but was himself captured and sold into slavery by them.

A bit more than a third of the informants were captured in open warfare – for example, an Amina man who was taken in a civil war by "his own country people" and sold to the fort on the coast as a slave, even though he was the king's brother. In another case from the Gold Coast, a Tembu woman noted that following a victory, the Amina captured her and other women, stuffing a cloth in her mouth and putting children in a sack. Many of the prisoners were not sold, moreover, but killed by the rampaging troops. In the Niger Delta area at about the same time as Oldendorp's informants were enslaved, another Moravian slave who did not figure in Oldendorp's account, named Joshua, who was from the "Ybo Kingdom in the province of Schomma in the village

der caribischen Inseln Sanct Thomas, Sanct Crux und Sanct Jan, inbesondere der dasigen Neger und der Mission der evangelischen Brüder under denselben (mod. ed. Gudrun Meier, Stephan Palmié, Peter Stein and Horst Ulbricht, 2 parts in 4 volumes, Berlin, 2000–2002). Nearly 3,000 pages long, this manuscript was deemed unpublishable, and a much shorter, reorganized, and poorly edited version was published in 1777 by Johann Jakob Bossart as *Geschichte der Mission der evangelischen Brüder auf den Caraibischen Inseln S. Thoas, S. Croix und S. Jan* (Barby, 1777, reprinted, Hildesheim, 1995); an English translation of this edited work is by Arnold Highfield and Vladimir Barac, *A Caribbean Mission* (New York, 1987).

[31] Oldendorp, *Historie* 1: 481.

of Umoque" and was the son of a "peasant," (*Bauer*) was "taken in war."[32] Olaudah Equiano, another Igbo, was taken as a ten-year-old by bandits who came over the wall of his compound – a fate similar perhaps to another Igbo child named Ofodobendo Wooma, who later told Oldendorp his story, and who also was kidnapped sometimes before 1741 at a young age.[33]

Not all Africans were enslaved as a result of open violence. About one in six were sold by creditors to defray a debt, such as the unfortunate Igbo who went to travel to another country to engage in commerce where he met a creditor who sold him to pay his debt. Another sixth were sold by family members for one reason or another, like the Mokko man who was sold by his own father, apparently because he was too "arrogant and audacious." Five percent of the informants were sold as a result of judicial proceedings, and finally a small number were taken through one or another form of treachery, like the Congo man whose associates tricked him into going to a place where bandits took him.[34]

Other explicit life history testimony confirms this general survey. One of the most thoroughgoing bodies of evidence on enslavement came from the survivors of the Spanish ship *Amistad*, which was seized off Cuba by a revolt among its enslaved cargo and ended up being interned in New Haven, Connecticut, in 1839. All the slaves on the *Amistad* came from the same area in Africa (Mende region in modern-day Sierra Leone) and they each gave a detailed biography to an interested Yale University professor who worked for their defense against re-enslavement and deportation to Cuba.[35] While about two-thirds were enslaved violently, conforming to Oldendorp's model, another third fell victim to judicial enslavement, typically for debt or adultery, in an environment where most major crimes and some minor ones were punishable by enslavement.

Finally, another survey, like Oldendorp's and de Sandoval's, linked to linguistic work by a missionary, was conducted by Sigismund Koelle in the 1840s among Africans who had been taken off slave ships by the British Anti-Slavery Squadron, charged at this time, in the waning years of the slave trade, with suppressing the trade.[36] Koelle's 179 named informants were chosen for their linguistic diversity rather than as a random sample. Paul Hair, calculating from Koelle's list notes, finds that among them, 34 percent were captured in

---

[32] MAB, Lebenslauf of Josua, taken 1761 (images, transcriptions, and translations of these documents are found at http://bdhp.moravian.edu/personal_papers/memoirs/Joshua/Joshua.html). The archive's translation renders this German word as "farmer," although, given eighteenth-century German usage, "peasant" seems more appropriate.

[33] MAB, Lebenslauf of Andrew the Moor, March 13, 1779, which gives his original name and enough details to make it clear he is the same "Negro from Pennsylvania" from whom Oldendorp drew details on Igbo country, *Historie*, 1: 431–434.

[34] Oldendorp, *Historie* 1: 480–490.

[35] Detailed, along with a profile illustration of each person in John Barber, *A History of the Amistad Captives...* (New Haven, CT, 1840) pp. 9–15 (including a biography of James Covey, who was not among the *Amistad* captives but was from the same country and served as an interpreter).

[36] Sigismund Koelle, *Polyglotta Africana...* (London, 1854, new annotated edition, P. E. H. Hair and David Dalby, Sierra Leone, 1963).

war and another 30 percent were kidnapped. Eleven percent were enslaved as a result of judicial proceedings, and 7 percent each for debt or sold by relatives, whereas the remaining 9 percent were enslaved for a wide range of reasons, which again shows broad agreement with the data from Oldendorp a century earlier.[37]

None of these data are statistically representative; often those who wrote these accounts had particular points to make, or chose dramatic and interesting stories. But it is probably safe to say that war was one of the most significant sources of enslavement. Bandits operating outside the law represented another major source of enslaved individuals. A minority was enslaved through a myriad of other possible routes reported by these witnesses, most notably through judicial proceedings for alleged crimes.

This evidence points to the role of the African state in enslavement. On one hand, states were the parties that declared wars and thus led to the military enslavement that took a significant number of Africans from their homes. On the other hand, the failure of African states to maintain order (often, as we shall see, as a result of civil war) allowed bandits to carry off many additional people. Finally it was African states that ultimately controlled the judicial apparatus that enslaved the bulk of those not enslaved violently. When we add to this that African states also controlled the trade in their waters and regulated how Europeans conducted it, it is obvious that the answer to the paradox lies in African politics.

STATE AND NATION: AFRICAN POLITICS

Africa in the sixteenth century provides interesting parallels and contrasts to the homeland of the Europeans who were then visiting their shores and establishing their first relations. As in Europe, most Africans lived in societies with social classes and in which decision making was limited to a fairly small number of people. In Africa, too, the powers of government and decision making were in some cases very dispersed and contested, in other cases quite centralized and defined. In fact, in many ways, African rulers had less problems with limits on their power to act than European equivalents did.

African society after 1500 could be divided in two ways. The first was by "nations" (one of the terms widely used in the seventeenth and eighteenth centuries) or "tribes" (as nineteenth-century and modern popular usage has it) – that is, along ethnolinguistic lines (people with common languages and customs grouped together). The second way was the division along political lines – that is, by states. The two ways did not match – that is, linguistic groups were not units of identity in precolonial Africa, some ethnic groups were divided between more than one state, and some states included multiple ethnicities. Thus, however much modern images of Africa see it as a land of "tribal" loyalties or

---

[37] P. E. H. Hair, "The Enslavement of Koelle's Informants," *Journal of African History* 6 (1965): 193–203.

identities, the evidence does not suggest that these ethnolinguistic divisions were the primary ones before 1900, for ethnolinguistic units did not make decisions or divide resources. When the time came to render loyalty or service, people did so to the state and not to the nation. Considering that African states rendered justice, demanded service, and defined borders, it should not be surprising that people also saw them as their primary membership.

When Oldendorp surveyed Africans held as slaves in the Danish West Indies in the mid-eighteenth century, he was interested in learning about their "nations." For his purposes, which were determining what languages were best to use for teaching Christian religious knowledge, he had no difficulty in locating linguistic groups, but his informants gave a wide range of answers when asked about their nation, which many interpreted in ways other than people speaking the same language. Whereas his informants from the Niger Delta region seemed happy to define their identity by language, and to define their neighbors along those lines as well, not all thought of language as their primary means of identification.[38] For Ofodobendo Wooma, one of his Niger Delta informants who spoke a language Oldendorp called Ibo, the fundamental division among the people he knew was the presence of absence of circumcision, but he, like the others, suggested that their political divisions were much smaller entities.[39]

For example, Oldendorp identified one language, which he called Amina but which would be called either Akan or Twi today, spoken in the Gold Coast region (modern-day Ghana), and interviewed five different men about their identity. While they spoke the same language and agreed about most customs, they described eight "nations," including Fante, Adansi, and Akkim (all of which would properly be called states), that warred among themselves, and thus these men understood their identity as being defined by political and not ethnolinguistic units.[40] They recognized the commonality of the language and customs, but did not use that as a vector of identity. In addition to their language, some of the Aminas had tattoo-like scars on the face and upper body, which made up an important indication of identity, but here also along the political rather than cultural lines – for there was only one "Amina" nation, but one of Oldendorp's informants, who identified himself as Akkim, had distinctive markings that set him apart from the other Aminas, although he spoke that language as his primary one.[41]

African political units can be called states even though many were very small in territory and population (mini-states). They seem to have been the units that

---

[38] Oldendorp, *Historie* 1: 426.
[39] Oldendorp, *Historie* 1: 487. The identity of his informant, described in the book as only being a Moravian in Pennsylvania, is that he was "Andrew the Moor" whose life history resembles that presented in Oldendorp, and can be found in the Moravian Archives, Bethlehem, PA, and online (photo, transcription, and translation) at http://bdhp.moravian.edu/community_records/register/deaths/andrew/andrew.html
[40] Oldendorp, *Historie* 1: 383.
[41] Oldendorp, *Historie* 1: 392.

Oldendorp's informants from what he called the Wawu nation (modern-day Ewe-Fon) used. For example, when defining her neighbors, one woman mentioned five nations, including the kingdom of Dahomey; another man listed six nations, all different from the woman's list, and in both cases the nations corresponded to local political units.[42] The mini-state, an entity that was completely sovereign but was often no larger than a county in the United States, was very common; in the early seventeenth century, about 70 percent of the African population lived in such units.[43] But these entities, small as they were, had all the characteristics of a state. They had boundaries, made decisions, demanded resources (including taxes, labor, and products) from their subjects, and provided a final say in adjudicating disputes.[44] In Europe, large, very loosely structured states existed, including kingdoms like France or Spain, in which sovereign authority was divided between the kingdom, provinces, and the territories of church and nobles. In Africa, there were fewer such cases; instead, there were large areas of remarkably splintered sovereignty in which the local powers were completely independent. In some ways such regions resembled Germany or Italy, with tiny all-but-sovereign territories, but in many parts of Africa there was not even the overarching claims of Emperor or Pope.

In 30 percent of Africa, larger states or empires dominated the political geography, as they did in the region drained by the Senegal River and its inland neighbor the Niger River. When Europeans arrived, the Empire of Mali controlled much of the Senegal valley and the Niger, as well as the hinterland down to the coast in modern Guinea, although they were contesting the middle reaches of the Niger with another large empire called Songhai. In the later sixteenth century, this configuration changed. The Senegal valley was taken over by the Empire of Great Fula, and its reach extended as far as the middle Niger and south to the mountains in the interior of Sierra Leone. Although Great Fula lost its unity in the seventeenth century, the Niger valley and its surrounding areas became the core of two sizable kingdoms named Segu and Kaarta.

If the interior of Senegambia was dominated by large kingdoms and empires, the coastal fringe of this region was mostly divided into smaller political units, as was the whole coast right around to what would be modern-day Bénin. This was the land of the small and sovereign mini-state, of which the polities of the Gold Coast left the most documentation and whose history is best known. In the eighteenth century, however, the inland regions behind this coast did begin to coalesce into larger political units, such as the kingdoms of Asante, Denkyira, and Akwamu, and as the century drew to a close, Asante had become

[42] Oldendorp, *Historie* 1: 423–424.
[43] Thornton, *Africa and Africans* pp. 103–105.
[44] The idea that African polities might be called states is controversial; at least some anthropologists would be inclined to call some of them "chiefdoms," by which they mean a somewhat less well integrated polity. I am not convinced that the definition proposed is sufficiently important to deny African polities status as states, and for me, at least, the crucial elements are the right to demand resources and provide final adjudication of disputes.

predominant, although not in complete control. Likewise, the eighteenth century saw the rise of the larger kingdom of Dahomey centered in modern-day Bénin. Its partial conquest of the region to its south in 1724–1726 marked the start of an era of its highly contested domination of the coast.

The interior behind Dahomey was dominated by the largest political entity in that part of West Africa, the Oyo Empire, whose emergence as a great power in the late seventeenth century continued until well into the nineteenth century, when it was torn apart by internal dissention and foreign invasion from even farther in the interior. The Kingdom of Benin, which dominated the western end of the Niger Delta and a good stretch of coast down to the modern city of Lagos, was the only large coastal kingdom that the Europeans met in all of Lower Guinea in the sixteenth century.

The coast beyond Benin was again divided into small, even tiny ministates in the Niger delta and then along the forested coast of Cameroon and Gabon until one reaches the region north of the mouth of the Congo River. In the sixteenth century, there was no dominant power in that area; toward the end of the century, the kingdom of Loango emerged as a large entity, but the real power on the coast from before the arrival of Portuguese sailors in 1483 was the Kingdom of Kongo. Kongo controlled the coast from the mouth of the Congo River (and claimed areas north of the river as well) down to the region south of the mouth of the Kwanza River just south of modern-day Luanda. There were fairly sizable kingdoms in the interior behind this coast as well; Ndongo was a rising power in the sixteenth century, reaching its peak at the time the Portuguese began their colonization, first around Luanda and then by century's end along the Kwanza. Wars between the Portuguese and Ndongo resulted in the partition of the latter country between the Portuguese and Matamba, another larger interior polity. In the late seventeenth century, the Empire of Lunda, which would grow in the nineteenth century to the largest polity in central Africa and equivalent to the biggest of the great West African empires, began its westward expansion that would bring it to the edge of the Kwango River by the middle of the eighteenth century.

Large kingdoms also dominated the interior mountainous region that lay to the south of the Portuguese colony, although so little is known of their earlier history that it is difficult to know their extent. By the seventeenth century, much of central Angola was dominated by the Grand Feque, a mysterious power that Portuguese knew of only by reputation. As Portuguese trade spread inland from the coast port of Benguela and south from the Kwango in the early eighteenth century, they learned of several large kingdoms – Mbailundu, Viye, and Wambu – as well as a few lesser ones in the area once dominated by the Grand Feque.

South Africa, known to us in detail only from the establishment of the Dutch colony there near Cape Town in 1652, had very small polities of semi-nomadic pastoral people, the Khoikhoi, and only the eastern third of modern-day South Africa had polities of moderate size, but in a region that had little or no contact with the Atlantic.[45] Portuguese expansion in the Zambezi, on the other hand, was wedged between a fairly sizable kingdom of Mwenemutapa, south of the river, and the smaller but still sizable Maravi kingdom to the north. These regions were not involved in the Atlantic trade, even when the Portuguese were pinned in the valley by the expansion of the Rozwi kingdom in the late seventeenth century. When the region joined the Atlantic world as a supplier of slaves, the political situation was of a divided zone of smaller polities.

Finally, the island of Madagascar, whose participation in the Atlantic trade was confined to the last decades of the seventeenth and first decades of the eighteenth century, was divided into small polities, much like those of the Guinea Coast, in that period. Political consolidation would take place, but not until the late eighteenth and early nineteenth centuries.

Thanks to the lack of detailed local documentation, we know something of the political structure and history of only a relatively small handful of these various states, and even some of the larger ones are quite mysterious. In a few regions, like the Gold Coast and its neighboring region in modern-day Togo and Bénin, where the factors of locally established European trading posts took a necessary interest in the politics of their neighboring African mini-states, we know quite a bit about the government and changes in the area. West Central Africa is also well known, not only through the records of the Portuguese colony of Angola, which was deeply involved in the political life of its neighbors, but also through the Kingdom of Kongo, thanks to its own literate elite and the visitations of missionaries who ministered to the faithful in a Catholic kingdom, converted by Portuguese missionaries in 1491. The Dutch colony at the Cape of Good Hope also left an abundant documentary record of the region they colonized and its near neighbors, and the Senegal region is described thanks to French traders who established themselves on the coast and along the Senegal River. But other areas – for example, the Niger delta and those regions that did not export slaves, like the modern-day Ivory and Gabon coasts – are so poorly documented that we know scarcely anything about them. It is ironic that in spite of hundreds of visits by English ships to the Niger delta, resulting in the exportation of tens of thousands of slaves, our only accounts of life in the interior come from the slaves themselves, such as the notable Abolitionist writer Olaudah Equiano, or the informants of the Moravian missionaries like Oldendorp.

In 1600 or so, we can identify some 200 known independent states along the African coast or in the inland areas where people who came into the slave trade lived, and perhaps half as many whose existence can be surmised but

---

[45] The area is very poorly known. In 1592, a Portuguese description named three kingdoms – Virongune, Vambe, and Mokolopapa – and no other source describes the area until the early nineteenth century, when states of roughly the same size existed there as well; see Monica Wilson, "The Nguni People," in Leonard Thompson and Monica Wilson, eds., *The Oxford History of South Africa* (2 vols., New York and Oxford, 1969), pp. 79.

whose names or histories are as yet unknown.[46] Thus decisions about war and peace, trading or not, were made by the political elite of all these polities. If one considers further that these 250–300 polities were ruled by roughly 10 generations of political authorities in this time, one can begin to grasp the problems of making any generalizations about African political processes. Yet there were some similarities among them, and if we seize on what is known about these processes in those that are well documented, we might be able to make reasonable guesses about the processes among others.

Throughout the entire zone, with the possible exception of South Africa, decision making was done by states – or, more exactly, by those people within states who exercised decision-making authority over matters of war and peace, internal security, and justice. The state in Africa was separate from and not associated with family or other kinship organizations, although state offices might be filled by familial factions, as they were, for example, in the central African Kingdom of Kongo, where the distinction is clearest, thanks to an abundant local documentation.[47]

Although there was a wide range of political constitutions and sizes among African states, virtually all those about which we have information had rich people and poor people. Goods and services were not equally divided among them, and these divisions were systematic and generally hereditary. Some regions provided quite a bit of latitude for social mobility, so that someone born poor could, through effort, skill, and luck, rise in status and become rich – and pass on the fruits of that success to the following generation. Even in these regions, however, the majority of the poor segment of the population remained poor, and most of the wealthy remained wealthy over generations.

In some cases the decision-making elite represented a fairly large proportion of the population; for example, in the many polities that dotted the lower courses of the Niger River – perhaps forty to fifty independent polities, according to the seventeenth-century writer Alonso de Sandoval – government was by a collective body.[48] Olaudah Equiano, born about 1745 in a territory named Essaka, according to his memoirs published in 1789, was taken as a slave to America when he was about ten, where he was educated and eventually freed. When discussing government in his memoirs, Equiano recalled that some members of his society had special facial marks that set them apart from others, and they were called Embrenché [Mbreechi, or probably today's ozo title society, who are characterized by facial marks]. Equiano described this group "as I remember, importing the highest distinction, and signifying in our language a mark of grandeur." While the position was not necessarily hereditary, if modern practice is a guide, a member was well positioned to get children to qualify.

---

[46] John Thornton, *Africa and Africans in the Making of the Atlantic World, 1400–1800* (2nd ed, Cambridge, 1998), pp. xii–xiv, xviii–xxxviii contain a map, survey, and documentation of states in the early seventeenth century.

[47] For the Kongo case, see John Thornton, *The Kingdom of Kongo: Civil War and Transition, 1641–1718* (Madison, 1983), pp. 38–55.

[48] De Sandoval, *Naturaleza*, Book 1, chapter 1, fol. 7v; chapter 16, fol. 59.

Equiano told readers that "my father was one of those elders or chiefs," and that most of what he called "elders and senators" (using a classical analogy that his readers would recognize) "were thus marked; my father had long borne it: I had seen it conferred on one of my brothers, and I also was destined to receive it by my parents." Equiano held that "every transaction of government was conducted by the chiefs or elders," and that the "Embrenché, or chief men, decided disputes, and punished crimes; for which purpose they always assembled together."[49]

These "elders or chiefs" made decisions to fight wars, in which people were enslaved, and also sanctioned merchants who sometimes bought the slaves and on occasion, the ardent Abolitionist Equiano maintained, persuaded the elders to fight in order to do so. The members of the ruling societies like the Mbreechi owned slaves themselves, and although there were not large gaps in material wealth between such a group and the rest of society, the gaps did exist, as Equiano noted.[50]

Other polities might be much more autocratic, with a single person or a very small group having much more power than anyone else over the decisions of their states, including deciding on wars that might yield slaves. The Kingdom of Dahomey, for example, which came together in the late seventeenth century through the consolidation of several smaller polities and then rose to dominance in the region of modern-day Bénin, was much larger than tiny Essaka, Equiano's home state. Dahomey had more than 200 towns or village clusters like Essaka under its control and ruled somewhat more than 300,000 people by the 1720s.[51] In 1726, King Agaja of Dahomey, fresh from a victory over the coastal town of Allada, dictated a letter for the King of England George I to the English merchant Bullfinch Lambe. He wished to introduce himself to the English, whose trading posts his army had destroyed, and at the same time reassure his European counterpart:

I have no disturbances or controversies whatever, either amongst my wifes or other subjects, every one knowing thare duty, place, and station, for if any transgress against my laws or customs, or att least them of my fore-fathers, thay must suffer death and sometimes not in my power to save them, without violating the laws of my gods, kingdom,

[49] Olaudah Equiano, *The Interesting Narrative of Olaudah Equiano, or Gustavus Vasa, the African* (2 vols. London, 1789), ed. and annotated by G. I. Jones, "The Early Travels of Olaudah Equiano," in Philip Curtin, ed. *Africa Remembered* (Madison, 1968), pp. 70–71. Vincent Carretta has recently proposed, based on new documentary evidence, that Equiano may not have been African-born, and others suggest that he could not know all that he claims based on personal experience as, in his account, he was only ten years old when enslaved. But if he were indeed not an eyewitness, he must surely have drawn his information from Igbo informants, and thus been at least as good a source as Oldendorp.
[50] Equiano, *Interesting Narrative* (ed. Jones), p. 77.
[51] John Thornton, "The Historian and the Precolonial African Economy: John Thornton Responds," *African Economic History* 19 (1990–1991): 51–52. Using Agaja's statistics in this argument, I made a case for Dahomey having some 8,000 square kilometers occupied at an average density of 39 persons per square kilometer, for a total of 312,000 people.

and predecessors, and bring thare curse on me and country; however I never give sentence without sufficient proof.[52]

While Agaja was still subjected, in his reckoning, to Dahomey's laws and customs, he clearly had ample leeway to make decisions. He and a portion of Dahomean society enjoyed a much superior standard of living to the rest of his subjects, reflected in housing, clothing, food. and especially the power to make decisions.

There was a plethora of other sorts of arrangements of power and decision making, ranging from absolute to republican, within Africa and its several hundred polities, following potentially as many different constitutions and laws. However, most systems of African law that we have knowledge of today supported slavery and the sale of people into slavery. This institution was both widespread and legally accepted, albeit with important reservations and safeguards. African elites held slaves; in many cases, even nonelites owned them. This right of slavery was anchored, I have argued elsewhere, on Africa's legal system in which land is not an object of property. Because Africans did not own land, the ownership of people was the primary means of private wealth (states obtained wealth by taxation, again of people and not of land). Hence slavery was widespread, albeit very varied in its conditions. Because so many people were slaves, and because they were employed in so many different ways, African slavery was often like medieval serfdom in Europe. In some areas, in fact, there were laws against selling such people freely to anyone, although clearly in many other places, owners were free to transfer their slaves to whomever they chose.[53]

An excellent example of the legal status of slavery in Africa comes from the correspondence of King Afonso I of Kongo, especially in his early letters to the king of Portugal dating from 1514 to 1526.[54] Afonso's letters, mostly

[52] This letter is signed "Trudo Audato Povesaw Daujerenjon Suveveto Ene-Mottee Addee Pow, a Pollo Cow Hullow Neccressy, Emperor of Dahomey" and is dated January 1726, *The Parliamentary History of England, from the Earliest Period to the Year 1803* (vol 23 [1789–91] London, 1816), p. 86. Spelling irregularities are a product of Lambe's peculiarities, not Agaja's. A facsimile and critical edition was published by Robin Law, "Further Light on Bulfinch Lambe and the 'Emperor of Pawpaw': King Agaja of Dahomey's Letter to King George I of England, 1726" *History in Africa* 17 (1990): 211–226. Many scholars regard this text as a forgery, first because the king of Dahomey was not literate, and second because it was not published or known until 1789 when it was entered into the English parliamentary gazette at a time when there were ferocious debates between pro- and antislavery advocates in parliament. My belief that the basic tone is authentic is based on reasoning presented by Law, as well as the fact that a message of a very similar tenor was presented to the French factor and recorded at about the same time (1726), ANF C6. Dahomean monarchs were not averse to using foreigners to present themselves in writing.

[53] Thornton, *Africa and Africans*, pp. 74–91; Joseph E. Inikori, "Slavery in Africa and the Transatlantic Slave Trade," in Alusine Jalloh and Stephen E. Maizlish, eds. *The African Diaspora* (College Station, 1999), pp. 40–72.

[54] All known letters of Afonso were published by António Brásio in *Monumenta Missionaria Africana* (1st series, 15 vols., Lisbon 1952–1988), vols. 1, 2, 4, 15. A well-annotated French

complaints to the king of Portugal about the behavior of Portuguese subjects, make it clear that he regarded the holding of slaves as legal. His own army captured people who were designated as slaves, so clearly forcible seizure in war was one route that he recognized to the status.[55] There were also markets in Kongo where one could purchase slaves for money, as his correspondence mentions the purchase of slaves with money.[56] From a legal standpoint, therefore, in Kongo, like most other states in Atlantic Africa, the concept that a person could be a slave – that is, the entire private property of another person – was accepted, as was the corollary idea that this right could be transferred via sale to anyone, even a foreigner.

Afonso wrote another set of letters that show both the problems and limitations of the slave trade as it developed in the early sixteenth century. In 1526, Afonso wrote to complain that some Portuguese resident in his kingdom had purchased slaves who had been wrongfully taken, by "thieves and people of low condition," which, scandalously enough, included some royal kinsmen. This suggests that he was having problems controlling the activities of bandits or outlaws, or at least that it was a problem he needed to address. He also argued that some of his subjects had been seduced by the foreign goods brought to Kongo by these merchants so that they had come to disobey him, and some, he argued, were becoming wealthier than the king himself. At first Afonso proposed banning the slave trade altogether, but eventually decided on a policy of inspecting all slaves through a committee of appointed officials to ensure that all were legally enslaved.[57]

Afonso, and Kongo law, clearly regarded enslavement as a state business, controlled by the laws of the country. When the rights of property in slaves collided with the interests of state, however, Afonso did not hesitate to regulate and even forbid the trade. Later Kongo kings would go so far as to retrieve slaves who had been wrongly taken and indeed, as Linda Heywood has shown, were serious and effective in defending their own people from enslavement from outside throughout the sixteenth century.[58]

---

translation of these and related documents is found in Louis Jadin and Mireille Dicorato, *Correspondance de Dom Afonso, Roi du Congo, 1506–1543* (Brussels, 1974).

[55] Afonso to Manuel, October 5, 1514, Brásio, *Monumenta* 1: 312–315. For Afonso's attitudes to slavery and slavery in Kongo, see John Thornton, "African Political Ethics and the Slave Trade" in Derek Peterson, ed. *Abolition, Imperialism and the Slave Trade in Britian, Africa and the Atlantic* (Athens, Ohio, 2010), pp. 38–47.

[56] Afonso to Manuel, October 5, 1514, Brásio, *Monumenta* 1: 300–301, noting that priests that he gave money in 1508 used them to buy slaves; on 304–305, 306, 317, he says the same about masons and other Portuguese in his employ who used their salaries for the same purposes.

[57] Afonso to King João III, July 6, 1526, same to same, October 18, 1526, Brásio, *Monumenta* 1: 470–471; 489–490. On the question of the degree to which Afonso's letters present a kingdom falling apart as a result of slave trading, a common one in its earlier historiography see in John Thornton, "Early Kongo-Portuguese Relations: A New Interpretation," *History in Africa* (1981).

[58] Linda Heywood, "Slavery and Its Transformation in the Kingdom of Kongo, 1491–1800," *Journal of African History* 50 (2009): 1–7.

THE FATE OF STATES AND ENSLAVEMENT

Whatever the legal status of slavery in Africa, the existence of an enslaved group within the continent was not the primary source of slaves. The evidence of American slaves reported by Sandoval, Oldendorp, or Koelle strongly supports the idea that most Africans who crossed the Atlantic in slave ships were recently enslaved in Africa. African law and custom only provided a legal framework for the transfer, not a source of the slaves. If we continue with the evidence, we also note that war was the principal form of enslavement, and thus in some respects we must understand war and banditry in Africa to understand the solution to the paradox of African leaders who might sell thousands of people to Europeans even though it was harmful to the continent and even to regions within Africa.

It is not surprising in this regard that war would be such an important means of enslavement, because rulers are, by definition, not selling their own subjects when they make war on their neighbors – instead, they are selling their opponents' subjects, and whatever damage is done is not done in their own country. Indeed, their lands and power may well be enlarged and deepened by warfare.

Philip Curtin proposed that African warfare might be divided into two types as it related to the slave trade. On one hand, he argued, there was what he called economic warfare, in which the acquisition of slaves to trade and acquire various sorts of wealth was the primary motive. The other type fit into a political model, in which war was waged primarily for political aims, and the acquisition of slaves was secondary to it. Economic wars were wasteful and exploitative; political wars needed to be analyzed in terms of their objectives and not simply because people were captured.[59]

These distinctions are easier to conceive than they are to demonstrate. War is always very expensive, and the possibilities of defraying the costs of military operations by selling captives had to be an important consideration in any planning for war. Similarly, war involves inherent risks to both aggressor and attacked. Who is to say that aggressors with economic motives will be successful in war? And even if they are successful, will they be able to do so without suffering casualties, potentially of important people?

Curtin went on to apply these models to Senegambia – the West African region that was watered by the Senegal and Gambia Rivers – yet it is not always easy to distinguish exactly which model applied at any given time, although on the whole he tended to lean toward the political model, suggesting that slaves were a by-product of the political economy and diplomacy of the region rather than the driving engine behind political decisions. In this, his approach has been hotly contested, notably by Boubacar Barry, who makes a good case for seeing an economic model.[60]

---

[59] Philip Curtin, *Economic Change in Pre-Colonial Africa: Senegambia in the Era of the Slave Trade* (2 vols., Madison, 1975) 1: 156–157.

[60] Boubacar Barry, *Senegambia and the Atlantic Slave Trade* (Cambridge, 2002), pp. 31–32; 60–63, *et passim*.

In fact, it might be easier to comprehend the slave trade and its connection to the state if one thinks of African states as having the same fiscal-military structure as was dominating the history of Europe at the time. Warfare, weapons, and mobilization of resources all counted in the fiscal-military system, and thus the slave trade fitted into the politics of the contest over power, centralization, and revenue. For African elites who wished to centralize authority, the sale of enemy captives to Europeans represented the sort of outside resources that colonization provided for European rulers, although with a number of twists that made African strategies different, in that incomes from exportation of captives allowed both the bolstering of militaries (and the conduct of war) possible while sparing subjects potentially divisive attempts to raise revenue.

In Senegambia, which Curtin used as a model, this dynamic is visible in the construction of fiscal-military states in the eighteenth century. At the start of the trans-Atlantic slave trade in the late fifteenth century – and Senegambia was the first African region to participate in that trade – the Jolof Kingdom dominated the Senegal basin and the Empire of Mali dominated the hinterland. In the later sixteenth century, however, both large units crumbled, and short-lived successors ruled, like the Empire of Great Fula, in the early seventeenth century. Then for much of the later period after about 1680, Jolof broke permanently into smaller units, and the Empire of Mali also dissolved.[61] The heritage of the older and larger political units was not lost, and so there was a certain thrust in the region to create larger units, or to consolidate centralized control in otherwise fairly decentralized polities. Two small successors of the old Jolof Kingdom, Kajoor and Bawol, often sought to unite into a larger unit, while Kaarta and Segu sought to unite the Niger Valley into a new Mali in a series of eighteenth-century wars. Thus, a certain number of wars in Senegambia were attempts to consolidate power and unite politically independent units.

At the same time, there were also civil wars and contentions within the polities, especially over the question of succession, so that brothers fought brothers, or uncles fought nephews, over the crown. Furthermore, rulers had tried to centralize power by developing special military and administrative functions in the hands of slaves. These slaves, who often commanded armies of other slaves, or headed secretariats, had their own interests, and at times these might allow them to overshadow the legitimate hereditary rulers. The slaves' interests were particularly tricky in time of civil war.

Finally, Senegambia was subject to raiding from the nomads who lived in the southern part of the Sahara Desert that bordered on their region and, after the mid-eighteenth century, by parties from larger states that were based on the Niger River valley, deeper in the interior. These raiders might join the parties in the civil wars, and sometimes were invited to participate in these wars by one side or the other more or less as mercenaries who might be paid by the spoils of war. In other cases, where warfare or civil strife had weakened the authority

---

[61] For an overview of the slave trade and politics in the region see Barry, *Senegambia*.

of the state, they might intervene on their own, in raids whose most important objective was the capture of slaves.

Senegambian wars usually involved enslavement of the losing participants, and often involved raiding. Sometimes, a party would agree to pay for the intervention of outsiders, especially the nomads, by allowing them to pillage and strip their opponents' lands of people who would then be enslaved. The enslavement of opponents' subjects would strip them of income and soldiers, while payments for exported slaves might help acquire munitions and also pay for other expenses. Thus, while sponsored interventions certainly appear to be the economic model in its purest form, it would not have taken place without the political objectives of the parties involved being forwarded by the outcome. So in that sense it also looks like a political model. Likewise, weak parties to civil wars, lacking resources to pursue their goals, might often turn to Europeans to help them, agreeing to pay in slaves. In some cases these wars were made to satisfy earlier debts that themselves had been incurred in the context of wars. Therefore, it is not easy to reduce African politics to simple raiding in order to acquire slaves, although abolitionist writers often used Senegambian pillaging expeditions as examples of military operations that were nothing more than raids to acquire slaves.[62]

It is also possible to see the expansion of the Lunda Empire from its base deep in central Africa (Shaba Province in the Democratic Republic of Congo) nearly 1,000 kilometers from the coast as a response to the development of the slave trade farther east. Portuguese settlers in Angola heard of the "Mozuas," as they called Lunda sometime before 1680 as a country lying in the far interior that traded intermittently with Kasanje, their furthest inland contact. But the dynamic monarchs of Lunda in the early eighteenth century launched a series of expansive attacks, both eastward, where they founded a new kingdom at Kazembe in modern-day northern Zambia, and westward as far as the Kwango River in modern-day Angola.[63] The Portuguese-Angolan diplomat Manoel Correia Leitão visited Kasanje and Holo, two kingdoms whose territories lay along the river in 1756, with the expressed purpose of creating a link with the empire.[64] In Holo, Correia Leitão learned that the Matianbo's (Mwata Yamvo, the royal title) capital lay seven months' travel to the east, "who all

---

[62] Thornton, *Warfare*, pp. 41–53, 129–130.

[63] John Thornton, "Lunda Expansion to the West: Causes and Consequences, 1680–1852," *Zambia Journal of History* 1 (1981): 1–16.

[64] There are several documents and reports from his mission, the final report, "Viag.ᵐ que eû o Sarg.ᵗᵒ Mor dos Moradores...fiz as remotes partes de Cassange e Óllos, no anno de 1755 the o seg.ᵗᵉ de 1756..." in c. 1757 after his return was published first in 1937 by Gastão Sousa Dias, and subsequently re-edited and published with an English translation by Éva Sebastyén and Jan Vansina, "Angola's Eastern Hinterland in the 1750s: A Text Edition and Translation of Manoel Correia Leitão's 'Voyage' 1755–56," *History in Africa* 26 (1999): 299–364 (original foliation marked in text and translation). His original correspondence, written while still in the field, is found among the papers of the governor who sent him, António Álvares da Cunha, in Arquivo da Universidade de Coimbra, AUC VI-3ª-1-2-13 and VI-3ª-1-2-14. These original documents tend to reduce the criticism of the trustworthiness of his observations given by Sebastyén and Vansina in their introduction.

these people (*gentio*) hold as their king" and to whom all "pay vassalage." The Lunda ruler, he learned, was in contact with Portuguese from Mozambique, and he "very much wanted to do business with the whites, whom they call Mueneputo."[65] "This Mulua is very powerful and from his lordships and dominions he dispatches captains with troops of many people to the West, the North and the South and other parts to make conquests of slaves [*conquistas de escravos*] which they sell to the place closest to where they are captured." He even argued that "surely, were it not for them we would not have so many slaves" and they have become "terrestrial Eagles, raiding countries so remote from their Fatherland to make themselves lords of other peoples."[66]

Lunda's expansion was, then, perhaps the epitome of an economic model, except that Correia Leitão thought their ambition to rule was a primary motive as much as simply acquiring trade goods, although he noted their desire to trade with Europeans as well. Lunda traditions, collected and written over a century later, describe the expansion to the west primarily as the pursuit, by the tightly woven elite, of dissident nobles who both spread the empire's authority and were eventually incorporated into it.[67] Interestingly, Correia Leitão noted that the Holos who occupied lands across the Kwango from Lunda had fled there from Canbunda, also a subject of Lunda.[68] Conquest was a crucial motive as well, for he observed that "they give quarter to all sorts of people that they make tributaries in so far as they can arrange it." Moreover, while the Lunda case might appear as a fine test of the guns-for-slaves model, in fact the Lunda armies eschewed firearms to the point of turning captured guns into swords, for "they say they are worthless [*ruins*] weapons as they are a handicap to valor." Indeed, increasing tax and tribute payments may also have served as a significant incentive for conquests: Correia Leitão noted that "they pay a tithe [*dizimo*] to their sovereign of everything they obtain during their conquests."[69]

Undoubtedly the state that fits the model of economic enslavement best is the Portuguese colony of Angola, and in some sense, given Portugal's own dependence on overseas revenue to finance its fiscal military state, it was also the best example of the model. Although it was founded ostensibly as a means to control trade and even as a settlement, according to the royal charter that its founder, Paulo Dias de Novais received in 1571, and even though governors regularly received instructions ordering them not to make wars except when

---

[65] AUC VI-3ᵃ -1-2-14, doc. 301, "Declaração dos apotentados que estão alem do Rio Coango..." 1756. This document is the notes Correia Leitão mentions jotting down on fol. 16 of "Viagem," but did not include there.

[66] Correia Leitão, "Viagem", fols. 13–13v. I have modified Sebastyén and Vansina's quite literal translation.

[67] For a discussion of tradition, collected by Henrique Dias de Carvalho in 1885, see Thornton, "Lunda Expansion," critiquing earlier literal readings of what was probably a composite account. Although the pursuit of Kinguri is counted as mythical, exoduses and pursuits in the chronicle portion of it clearly relates to real movements.

[68] AUC VI-3ᵃ-1-2-14, doc. 301, "Declaração dos apotentados." Canbunda was located along the Luangui River.

[69] Correia Leitão, "Viagem," fol. 13v–14. Translation modified.

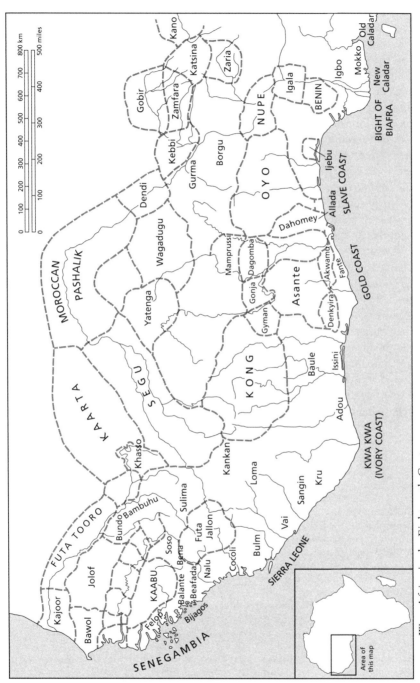

MAP 2. West Africa in the Eighteenth Century.

87

directly attacked, Angola lived on the slave trade and waged frequent wars.[70] In an unusually frank statement, the City Council of Luanda wrote to the Portuguese crown in 1652 explaining that royal prohibitions on offensive wars limited its income, as "slaves are the only source of capital in this kingdom," and on this basis asked permission to make war on the neighboring kingdom of Kongo.[71] Indeed, before departing to be governor of Angola in 1653, Luis Mendes de Sousa Chicorro announced that he would make wars against all of Angola's neighbors for precisely this purpose.[72]

But even in Angola, things were not always so clear. In his initial wars, Dias de Novais served as a mercenary for the Kingdom of Ndongo, and even after Ndongo tried to drive him out in 1579, one might put the fighting of the first governor down to defensive actions. By 1590, however, Portuguese Angola had won a secure place and even settled into a fairly peaceful existence. But most of the early-seventeenth-century governors, like Luis Mendes de Vasconcelos (1617–1621) were committed to making war, often on the thinnest of pretexts, and clearly for the purpose of capturing slaves.[73]

Whatever the governors' sentiments might have been, at times the settlers who came to Angola were not as enthusiastic about wars as their governors. In 1623, for example, settlers expelled Governor João Correa de Sousa because he made an illegal war on Kongo that ruined their business, and in fact the King of Portugal ordered some of the captive slaves restored to Kongo.[74] On another occasion, settlers who had been forced to engage in an endless series of wars by Governor João Fernandes Vieira (1658–1661) revolted and refused to fight, subsequently arguing that the governor waged war only for his own profit and to fill plantations he owned in Brazil.[75] Similarly, Elias Alexandre da Silva Corrêa, a Brazilian military officer who served in the Angolan wars in the eighteenth century, produced a litany of financial burdens imposed on the local

---

[70] On the earliest charters, see the detailed examination of Ilídio do Amaral, *O Consulado de Paulo Dias de Novais. Angola no último quartel do século XVI e primeiro do século XVII* (Lisbon, 2000), pp. 49–72; the charter itself is printed in pp. 49–72. The whole charter's text is found in Brásio, *Monumenta* 3: 36–51; for instructions against fighting offensive wars, see the instructions to Manuel Pereria Forjaz, 26 March 1607, Brásio, *Monumenta* 5: 270; Regimento of September 22, 1611, supposed to be for Francisco Correia da Silva, who actually never went to Angola, Brásio, *Monumenta* 6: 21–39; and also for João Correia da Silva, September 3, 1616, who also did not go at the time, Brásio *Monumenta* 6: 257–259.

[71] Consulta of Conselho Ultramarino, December 14, 1652, Brásio, *Monumenta* 11: 245.

[72] AHU Angola, Cx 6, doc. 92 (11 January 1657) enclosing statement of Luis Mendes de Sousa Chicorro, September 16, 1653.

[73] Linda Heywood and John Thornton, *Central Africans, Atlantic Creoles and the Foundation of the Americas, 1585–1660* (Cambridge, 2007), pp. 109–168.

[74] Graziano Saccardo, *Congo e Angola con la storia dell'antica missione dei Cappuccini* (3 vols., Venice, 1982–1983) 1: 174–182.

[75] AHU, Angola, Cx 8, doc 8, Report of Bartholemeu Paes Bulhão, May 16, 1664; for context see António de Oliveira de Cadornega, *História geral das guerras angolanas, 1680* (3 vols., ed. José Matias Delgado and Manuel Alves da Cunha, Lisbon, 1940–1942, reprinted 1972) 1: 150–157.

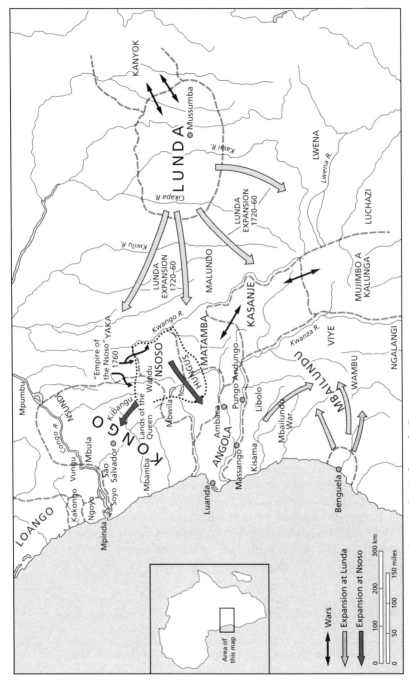

MAP 3. West Central Africa in the Eighteenth Century.

settlers by wars that governors waged to enrich themselves.[76] Wars might often be bad for business and agriculture, and the tensions between the settlers and governors often revolved around this. Angola was unusual in that it was ruled by people who did not live there for very long – governors typically served only a three-year term – and who therefore did not have to consider the other consequences of war for diplomatic relations or nonmilitary commerce.

Another instance of fairly direct European participation in capturing slaves was the several-decade-long involvement of European pirates in Madagascar, which resulted in a noticeable slave trade, largely directed to English and Dutch North America and the Caribbean.[77] In the seventeenth and early eighteenth centuries, when slaves from Madagascar were carried to North America, much of the trade was handled by English pirates, such as Nathaniel North, John Halsey, and Robert Drury. North Americans later joined Englishmen in the pirate trade, but pirates always cooperated with local rulers.

In the late seventeenth century, Madagascar was divided, according to the Sieur de Flacourt, a French resident and historian, into "several provinces and regions governed by diverse nations of the same language." Indeed, he counted twenty-two "provinces" in the region known to the French, assessing each as about the size of the French province of Brie. These provinces were ruled by "tyrants" and were perpetually at war, primarily to raid cattle.[78] These provinces, however, had their own subdivisions, and petty nobles even within one province often quarreled. The province of Vohitsbanh, Fracourt maintained, had a quarrelsome group of nobles who carried on "old quarrels which they never forget." Sometimes – for example, during famine – the people might threaten the nobles to get relief, as happened to Rabertau, the ruler of Amboule, a region known, according to Flacourt, for its libertinage and lawlessness.[79]

The pirates, who came to the Indian Ocean to prey especially on the pilgrimage trade between India and Mecca, often took prizes that included high-ranking Moghul royalty, as Captain Avery captured in his day. The pirates saw Madagascar as a safe haven, where they could withdraw following their activities to divide loot, rest, refit, and live. Charles Johnson, whose 1724 history of the pirates speaks at length of them, noted that they were able rise in power as their well-armed crews, who he believed had unique possession of firearms, could overawe the indigenous people who were organized in relatively small polities. As a result, the pirates took many wives and established themselves in scattered towns like a great flock of powerful nobles, of which a number are

[76] Elias Alexandre da Silva Corrêa, *História de Angola* (mod. ed., 2 vols., Lisbon, 1937) 2: 49–51, 54–55, 60–62.
[77] A recent article, citing earlier literature is Arne Bialuschweski, "Pirates, Slavers and Indigenous Population in Madagascar, 1690–1715," *International Journal of African Historical Studies* 38 (2005): 401–425.
[78] Étienne Sieur de Flacourt, *Histoire de la grande isle Madagascar* (2nd ed, Paris, 1661), pp. 3–4.
[79] De Flacourt, *Madagascar*, pp. 9–10.

known.[80] They allied themselves with local rulers, entered into their disputes, and sheltered many as allies. By Johnson's day, these pirates had become well ensconced, some having three generations in place.

They took slaves in these armed encounters, following a local custom in which losers were enslaved, and thus sold them to more commercially minded traders and visitors such as Frederick Phillipse of New York, whose ships carried a good number to the Hudson valley.[81] These pirates and merchants thus did not restrict themselves to the coast, but also went into the interior along with their local Malagasy allies to raid for slaves and cattle. The Malagasy themselves also held slaves, who were employed in agricultural labor, and raised cattle, and so raiding for slaves and cattle was a well-established local custom, but the presence of well-armed pirates who supplied additional weapons increased the power of some groups to raid successfully against others. Whether in response to the emergence of pirate domains, a result of the importation of muskets and military techniques by pirates, or other causes, the late seventeenth and early eighteenth century witnessed the consolidation of power in several regions on the island. These emerging kingdoms purchased weapons in considerable quantities and sold slaves in exchange – the trade that continued into the eighteenth century, when the connections to the Atlantic Ocean trade diminished.[82]

The period of piracy ended in the early eighteenth century, when colonial governors in America no longer tolerated pirates or gave them letters of marque, and aggressive anti-piracy efforts, such as that of Captain Kidd, managed to force them from the region. Along with the end of piracy, the slave trade from the Indian Ocean to North America ended, although the slave trade from Madagascar continued, directed to South Africa and the smaller colonial islands of France in the Indian Ocean, Réunion, Ile Bourbon, and the Mascarenes.

Elsewhere in Africa there was less involvement of Europeans in war, although in the Gold Coast Europeans occasionally became involved in African wars as mercenary soldiers, or sought to gain commercial advantages over other European rivals for the trade, and at times even to seek to move politics in their direction. In all these operations, however, the opportunities for European participation were conditioned by the political objective of the African rulers who participated with them or invited them in. The most significant and complicated of these arrangements resulted in the Komenda War, a lengthy and complex affair waged in the last years of the seventeenth century, which involved largely English and Dutch merchants and their allied or slave soldiers and private but powerful African merchants, like John Konny, who had a private army as well as business dealings with all the participants.

---

[80] Bialuschweski, "Pirates," pp. 413, 418–420; see also Robert Drury, *Madagascar: or Robert Drury's Journal during Fifteen Years' captivity on that Island* (London, 1729), pp. 432–435.
[81] Charles Johnson, *A General History of the Pyrates...* (London, 1724), pp. 58–62.
[82] Bialuschweski, "Pirates," pp. 414–419.

In short, Europeans were rarely as engaged in warfare in Africa as in Angola or Madagascar, and even there the colonies were more like trading posts and controlled little land. Portuguese governors and pirates might be relatively uninterested in the politics of the region where they stayed, seeing themselves as sojourners in search of quick profits, but elsewhere such an attitude could not prevail (and even in those places ultimately the aggressors became involved in local politics). African rulers could not afford to be cavalier about diplomacy, and the true pariah state committed to slave raiding was more or less impossible.

The kingdom of Dahomey, for example, is often regarded as a classic example of a militarized state committed to the slave trade, and indeed it is also a fine example of a fiscal-military state. In 1724, when Dahomey began a series of conquests that took over coastal states that bordered the inland country on the south, its vigorous king Agaja (1716–1740), in his letter to George I of England, boasted that during his reign he conquered no less that 209 "countries." Reading this declaration, one certainly gets the impression of a militaristic aggressor, bent on conquest and expansion. Some scholars argue, however, that Agaja was actually conquering the coast to restore order that had been frayed by earlier episodes of the slave trade and would have liked to suppress it; others argue that he was in fact seeking a coastal outlet for his own captives.[83] Although he does not mention the slave trade in his letter, he does mention that "I am gret admirer of fire armes, and have allmost intirle left of the use of bows and arrows," suggesting that his army was dependent on these weapons.[84] Certainly his agents sold slaves, in 1716, when Agaja managed to break free from control of Allada, his men captured some 2,800 people who were exported "in two months by two French ships, two Portuguese and a Dutchman."[85] His army took 8,000 more in its victory over Allada in 1724, and between 10,000 and 11,000 in his defeat of Whydah in 1727.[86] The proceeds of these sales surely helped support his purchase of firearms and defrayed the other costs of the war.

Militaristic as it might have been, however, Dahomey was scarcely making costless raids against hapless neighbors and carrying them off into slavery. Dahomey's neighbors were as well armed as Agaja and his successor were, and in fact, his conquest of the coastal regions was incomplete. The ruling

[83] Both ideas were presented by European writers of the time. Among modern historians, the former position is especially associated with I. A. Akinjogbin, *Dahomey and its Neighbours, 1708–1818* (Cambridge, 1967); for a larger assessment of the historiography and its sources as well as a position leaning towards the second possibility, see Robin Law, "Dahomey and the Slave Trade: Reflections on the Historiography of the Rise of Dahomey," *Journal of African History* 27 (1986): 237–267, and also Law, *The Slave Coast of West Africa* (Oxford, 1992).

[84] Agaja to George I, *Parliamentary History*, p. 85. The creative spelling belongs to Bullfinche Lamb, its writer, rather than Agaja, the author.

[85] ANF B.1/9 19, Bouchel, Whydah January 30 and June 22, 1716.

[86] Bullfinch Lambe, Abomey, November 27, 1724 in Smith, *New Voyage*, 186–187 (Allada); APEB, 21, doc. 58, Francisco Pereyra Mendes, April 4, 1727 (Whydah).

dynasties of Allada, conquered in 1724, and of Whydah, taken in 1727, both managed to flee to safe havens in the islands and lagoons of the coast. From there they waged frequent wars against Dahomey, and the Dahomean rulers, lacking an adequate navy to take the islands, were constantly frustrated. Agaja and his equally vigorous successors were frequently at war, sometimes offensively, sometimes defensively, with these tenacious coastal rulers.[87]

Dahomey were engaged in two other types of war, neither of which was easy. On the one hand, their attack on Allada led Oyo, a powerful interior empire, to send a large cavalry army into Dahomey to punish it in 1726. Although the Dahomean rulers were able to defend their key towns and keep their army intact, they were unable to defeat the cavalry of Oyo, and Dahomey lacked horses because they were unable to breed them in their environment, most likely because of the presence of the tse-tse fly.[88] These wars were uniformly disastrous for Dahomey, but finally King Tegbesu agreed to pay Oyo tribute in 1747 and thus stopped the periodic devastations.

Dahomey's second war front grew out of an attempt to impose a dynasty related to the royal family of Dahomey on the land of the Mahi, a loosely governed confederation that bordered on Dahomey's interior.[89] Dahomey also hoped to centralize the authority of this king, but without much effect. Dahomey invaded Mahi frequently, sometimes with success, sometime without, and usually at considerable cost in effort and manpower. Even so, Mahi was able to launch embarrassing counterattacks, including one in 1755 that nearly cut Dahomey in half.[90]

Given its difficult military situation, Dahomey's wars cannot be regarded simply as extended slave raids, nor were they always successful. Werner Peukert, making a careful study of the wars waged by King Kpengla (1774–1789) concluded that about one-third were victories and resulted in the taking of slaves, another third were successful militarily but did not bring slaves, and a further third were defeats in which Dahomeans themselves were enslaved.[91] In this environment, it is not surprising to hear the report of the English factor Lionel Abson, who lived at Whydah and married into the Dahomean royal family. Accustomed to reporting news from Europe to the king, in around 1789, Abson told King Agongolo about the abolitionist movement, which was then presenting its case in the English Parliament. The ruler was exasperated. "We

---

[87] John Thornton, *Warfare in Atlantic Africa, 1500–1800* (London, 1999), pp. 75–97.

[88] Robin Law, "Horses, Firearms, and Political Power in Pre-Colonial West Africa," *Past and Present* 72 (1976), p. 120.

[89] On the origins of these claims, see Robert Norris, *Memoirs of the Reign of Bossa Ahádee, King of Dahomey an Inland Country of Guiney* (London, 1789, reprint London, 1968), pp. 17–26. See also ANF, C6/25 Conseil de direction to Compagnie des Indes, February 18, 1753 on the motives.

[90] Norris, *Memoirs*, p. 23.

[91] Werner Peukert, *Der Atlantische Sklavenhandel von Dahomey, 1740–1797: Wirtschaftsanthropolgie und Socialgeschichte* (Wiesbaden, 1978), see especially pp. 73–76 and appendix III, pp. 300–304.

Dahomans are surrounded by enemies who make incursions," he said, "we must defend ourselves. Your countrymen, therefore, who allege that we go to war for the purpose of supplying your ships with slaves, are grossly mistaken." Finally he declared, "In the name of my ancestors and myself I aver, that no Dahoman man ever embarked in war merely for the sake of procuring wherewithal to purchase your commodities."[92] Be that as it may, Agonglo wrote a letter in 1795 noting that he would pay for imports of silk, gold, or silver by "excess captives there [at the coastal port of Whydah], and more of them that can be sold against tobacco and aguardente [a strong alcoholic beverage]."[93] King Agongolo's successor Adandozan wrote to Portugal in 1797 promising that if ships from that country brought in many rolls of tobacco, he would pay "in good captives."[94]

Likewise, there can be little doubt that, Dahomean protestations notwithstanding, the financing of these wars, especially the procurement of munitions, was funded in some measure by the sale of thousands of captives. Adandozan wrote in 1800 to request powder and muskets (being very specific about the design, caliber, and quality of the guns) and promising to pay "in excellent captives."[95] In describing a war he waged in 1804 against king Vucanim, ruler of neighboring Porto Novo, for a treason he had done, the king remarked that "it is customary among our nations to capture and seize all that we find" in making war.[96] The strategic and political motivations of the wars do not change the fact that a successful war might well pay for itself in the sale of captives, and an unsuccessful one would have had to be waged anyway. Certainly this is how Adandozan described two wars he waged sometime before 1810, one against Porto Novo and the other against Oyo and its allies. Here he was taking the offensive, he argued, to defend his small country against the might of Oyo, and when he won a major victory, he sacrificed a number "to terrorize the others not to come against me"; then he "ordered the great and small sold." This important documentation does suggest that, as the Dahomean elite saw it, war and weapons were necessary for strategic purposes, and that the trade in slaves

---

[92] Archibald Dalzel, *History of Dahomy An Inland Kingdom of Africa* (London, 1793, 2nd ed, London: Cass, 1967), p. 217. The speech, reported in a work by a man who was a slave trader and thus obviously pro–slave trade has been held to be a forgery to make the case against the abolitionists. Yet it is quite in character of the spirit of Dahomean discourse and the actual situation of the kingdom.

[93] BNRJ 552, Agongolo note, March 20, 1795 (printed in Verger, *Fluxo*, p. 287). Agongolo's letters were written for him by the local Portuguese resident Francisco Xavier Alvares do Amaral, although it is clear that he represented the king's intentions.

[94] APEB Secção Colonial, Correspondência Recebida de Autoridades Diversas, Maço 197, Cx. 76, doc. 2, Adanruzâ X to Fernando José, n. d. [dated to 1791 in the archive, but signed by Adandozan, suggesting that the correct date must be after 1797, when Adandozan began his rule].

[95] APEB 89, fol. 345, Adandozan to Prince João de Bragança, nd (c. 1800), printed in Verger, *Fluxo*, p. 261.

[96] BNRJ 846, Adandozan to João Carlos de Bragança, November 20, 1804, in Verger, *Fluxo*, p. 310 (the reason for the war is given on p. 311).

was essential to that – indeed, Adandozan asked in the same letter to obtain "artifices of war" as well as "firey bombs that go off in the air at high altitude" and to insist that he will only buy "quality arms." [97] It seems likely that the sale of slaves figured in the overall strategic planning of Dahomean expansion, as much as the expectation of silver inflows figured in the ambitions of Spain in seventeenth-century Europe.

The demographic effects of warfare and the slave trade, were, as we have pointed out earlier, bad for Atlantic Africa as a whole. African decisions makers might be aware of the consequences of removing population, and this in turn could be a weapon in warfare. It certainly seems to have been so on the eighteenth-century Gold Coast (modern-day Ghana). Here the sovereignty was split into many small, independent states, many not much larger than an American county, and with perhaps a few tens of thousands of inhabitants each. In the sixteenth and much of the seventeenth century, these petty domains made frequent war on each other, but rarely sought to create larger entities. Such wars were to resolve trading disputes or marital matters. Indeed, the region exported gold rather than slaves until the end of the seventeenth century, and Europeans who flocked to the coast to buy this gold often served as mediators in these wars because they disrupted the flow of gold.

In the late seventeenth century, however, warfare changed, as did the nature of many of the states. Muskets replaced all other projectile weapons in the armies, and armies were composed of drafted conscripts rather than professionals. The older professional armies were small and employed a good deal of hand-to-hand fighting, whereas the larger armies of the late period tended to avoid close fighting and instead blazed away at each other with muskets. The size of the army was important, and various kingdoms sought to increase their demographic base so as to increase the number of potential recruits. At the same time, however, there was a powerful incentive to export slaves, because the new armies relied heavily on musketry, and the best way to get muskets was by selling – or by paying for them with – slaves.

In 1730, two of these new emerging larger states, Akwamu and Akyem, went to war with each other. European factors on the coast anxiously awaited the outcome, expecting that the winner would export thousands of captives. They referred to a well-established military custom of the time, called "eating the country," in which the winners used their victories to strip the losers' country of people, simultaneously exhausting its population (and hence it ability to resist or make trouble in the future) and also paying for the costs of the war through exports. Much to everyone's surprise, Akyem won a decisive victory, but then, to the consternation of the European observers, decided not to "eat" Akwamu. The reason for this, they were told, was that Akyem hoped to capitalize on the unpopularity of Akwamu's former king and win the loyalty of the

---

[97] IHGB, Lata 137, pasta 62, fol. 2v, 5, Adandozan to João Carlos de Bragança, October 9, 1810. This letter mentions at least five distinct wars, including fairly detailed descriptions of his operations.

FIGURE 4. Kongolese soldiers have their weapons blessed before going to war. *Missione in praticca, Padri cappuccini ne Regni di Congo, Angola, et adiacenti.* Biblioteca civica centrale, Torino, MS 457.

population over to itself. In this way they would have a larger and potentially loyal army to face Akyem's other rival in the region, the kingdom of Asante. While this aspect of the population dynamics of the slave trade is explicitly discussed in the case of the Gold Coast, it is likely to have figured in the military planning of many other African polities.[98]

Just as the state made war, the failure of a state could create the conditions of instability and lawlessness that contributed to the slave trade as well. This is well demonstrated in the case of Kongo. Although the country was centralized and powerful when the Portuguese first encountered it in the sixteenth century, starting in the late seventeenth century, it entered into an increasingly difficult period of civil war. By 1680, the rivals had sacked and depopulated the large royal capital of São Salvador, and established themselves in fortified mountains on the edges of the country. Using these forts as bases, they waged endless wars against the other pretenders, while all the time hoping to defeat them, reoccupy the abandoned capital, and restore the kingdom. A patched-up solution that recognized the territorial claims of these would-be kings while reestablishing the kingdom arranged by King Pedro IV (1694–1718) worked for a while, but was regularly interrupted by outbreaks of violence.[99] Linda Heywood shows

[98] Thornton, *Warfare*, pp. 55–74.
[99] A fuller version of this history is in John Thornton, *The Kingdom of Kongo: Civil War and Transition, 1641–1718* (Madison, 1983), pp. 68–113.

how in the civil-war period, the Kongo state gradually moved from being a protector of its people and an indifferent participant in the Atlantic slave trade to becoming one in which war fed the export of slaves. Rival kings in the civil wars bent laws and allowed rebels to be enslaved, at first gradually so that the process began under Garcia, and then much more profoundly as civil war engulfed the country.[100]

In the steady disorder of the eighteenth century, the police power of the state was broken, especially in the often lawless lands that lay between the centers of the great pretenders. It now became licit to enslave all rebels, and soon each rival was waging war on his neighbor, and in the anarchy of the era parents even sold their own children. Bandits flourished in these areas and pillaged all and sundry (especially travelers on the roads) to sell as slaves.[101] An attempt to reestablish general control by King José I (1778–1785) failed, and when his brother Afonso V died – rumored to be poisoned – shortly after becoming king, an even greater disorder prevailed.[102]

In these chaotic times, bandit gangs established camps and raided the countryside around them. It is probably not surprising that both of the Kongolese who described their enslavement in the 1760s to Oldendorp were captured by bandits or enslaved through trickery.[103] When Afonso's successor Álvaro XII tried to assert his authority, he found that there were many such camps, and he sent a priest named Rafael Castello de Vide around to offer them pardon in exchange for agreeing to stop raiding and selling slaves.[104] One of these bandits, known as Mbwa Lau ("Mad Dog"), a nobleman who perhaps had started his career in the army of one or another of the pretenders, had set up shop for himself in an armed camp.[105] His men actually shot at the priest, setting off a scandal within the country that eventually led to some reforms.[106] Thus war and banditry might be closely linked. In Kongo and elsewhere, warfare, especially civil war, led to a breakdown of order, and the armed men once recruited for war now became bandits. Their activities were unrestrained because the civil war had broken down the order of the state.

---

[100] Heywood, "Slavery and Its Transformation," pp. 10–15.

[101] Heywood, "Slavery and Its Transformation," pp. 16–22

[102] The general situation in Kongo at the time is laid out in detail from the travels of Rafael Castello de Vide, whose letters written between 1781 and 1788 were gathered together in ACL, MS Vermelho 396, "Viagem do Congo do missionario Fr. Raphael de Castello de Vide…" 1800, mod. ed. Arlindo Correia in "Viagem e Missão no Congo do Fr. Rafael de Castelo de Vide (1780–88)," online edition with original pagination marked at http://arlindo-correia.com/161007.html

[103] Oldendorp, *Historie* 1: 522 (two witnesses).

[104] de Vide, "Viagem," pp. 287–292. De Vide did not give the name of the king, but it is know from a letter addressed to him found in AHNA, Codice A-17-5, fol. 67v, Governor of Angola to King of Congo Dom Antonio, August 11, 1787.

[105] His name is a common appellation even today in Kongo for anyone who is seriously antisocial and regarded as generally out of control; testimony of Luzolo Kiala, Mbanza Kongo, September 27, 2002.

[106] de Vide, "Viagem," pp. 292–296.

In Kongo, a powerful state broke down, giving rising to banditry. In the Lower Niger River, just north of its delta, the problem was more the lack of a single authority that could ever guarantee order. Seventeenth-century accounts of the region describe a vast zone of micro-polities, at least fifty within the bounds of the fairly small district. Indeed, sovereign authority was held over political units that amounted to little more than a series of hamlets. There were organizations that bound these units together and helped resolve disputes, but their authority was limited. Oldendorp, for example, relying on testimony of five slaves from what he called Kalabari, in the 1750s noted that they had a "king," whom they called Drelemongo, who appointed "captains" in every district, but when disputes arose, the king allowed these captains to fight, and those who were captured were sold as slaves.[107] Equiano also noted that sometimes local leaders – incited, he said, by merchants – might fall upon their neighbors in war.[108] Religious authorities such as priests and oracles might also resolve disputes, but they were themselves slave-holding and -trading organizations, like the Aro association, curiously called "Egypt" (but also Alo) by Wooma, where one could buy many things, and also have cases judged by supernatural means; both he and Equiano held that these people were "red" or "brown."[109]

Beyond fragmented authority, many branches, creeks, and effluents of the Niger River penetrated much of the region, making it possible for brigands to move quickly from one place to another by boat. Equiano noted that in addition to the small wars waged between the fragmented polities, they were victimized by bandits. He himself was captured by bandits who came into the compound where he lived and stole him away.[110] Such widespread theft was common in the region, and was beyond the capacities of any of the small states to control. Both Equiano and his countryman Ofodobende Wooma, who was enslaved in the late 1740s, as well as many other people thus enslaved might pass through dozens of masters in a local slave trade before having the misfortune of facing trans-Atlantic transportation.[111]

The paradox of the slave trade thus lies deeply in African politics, from which it is not easily disentangled. Decision makers in Africa probably always considered political considerations – how to consolidate and centralize power, how to increase security for their realms – first, but in making wars certainly had to consider ways of defraying costs. The role of munitions, though not in the simplistic form of the gun-slave cycle, was a crucial factor in this decision, for slaves could defray military costs in the most direct way. But many people were also enslaved by non-state actors, particularly bandits and outlaws,

---

[107] Oldendorp, *Historie* 1: 427.

[108] Equiano, *Interesting Narrative* (ed. Jones), p. 83.

[109] Oldendorp, *Historie* 1: 428 (among Kalabari), 432, 434 (among Ibo), MAB, testimony of Ofodobenda Wooma, 1779.

[110] Equiano, *Interesting Narrative* (ed. Jones), pp. 84–86.

[111] Oldendorp, *Historie* 1: 427–428, 434 (Ofodobende Wooma); Equiano, *Interesting Narrative* (ed. Jones), pp. 84–85.

and there the considerations must have been entirely economic, but only when state authority as weak or corrupt enough for bandits to operate. Finally, in the highly fragmented areas, the incapacity of any authority to control the area also contributed to banditry.

The example of Benin, however, shows us that African states could and did opt not to participate in the slave trade, as did numerous poorly documented groups in those parts of Atlantic Africa that did not participate either. Our knowledge of leaders' motivations, while partial and problematic, nevertheless reveals a complicated set of considerations and constraints.

4

The American World, 1450–1700

The indigenous societies of the Americas had a wide – indeed, bewildering – variety of social organizations. This great variety included everything from societies organized on a very small scale, with very little social differentiation and highly democratic decision making, to vast empires ruling millions of people under the tight supervision of a controlled bureaucracy. Precisely how the Europeans interacted with Americans, their ability to shape relationships and to settle, was directly dependent on the type and structure of these Native American societies. Indeed, the fundamental structure of the resulting American societies was determined in large measure by the social structure of the indigenous people at the time of European arrival.

One great divide separates American societies according to their political organization. This divide separates a type of polity I am calling an egalitarian democracy or a free association, where there is not a formal state organization and no permanent social classes, and a type of polity that has both hierarchical state structures and social classes. Among the latter, I have made a second division separating those with small-scale and often fairly weak levels of authority and socioeconomic differentiation, which I am calling mini-states (often called chiefdoms in anthropological literature), and those I call imperial states, which were larger, more complex, highly integrated, and often very inegalitarian in both political organization and division of wealth. This scheme is heuristic, and the division between categories is often quite blurred in reality. In fact, if one takes size and level of authority alone, there are many subgradations among them.

It is important to emphasize that this scheme of political organization is not necessarily one that reflects their mode of subsistence or standard of living. For example, some American societies did not farm crops at all but subsisted by foraging, whereas others farmed crops with varying degrees of intensity. Although all the foragers were also free associations, there is not a straightforward connection between political organization and intensity of agriculture. Nor is there much connection between political organization, settlement pattern, and subsistence strategy. Some free associations both farmed and lived in

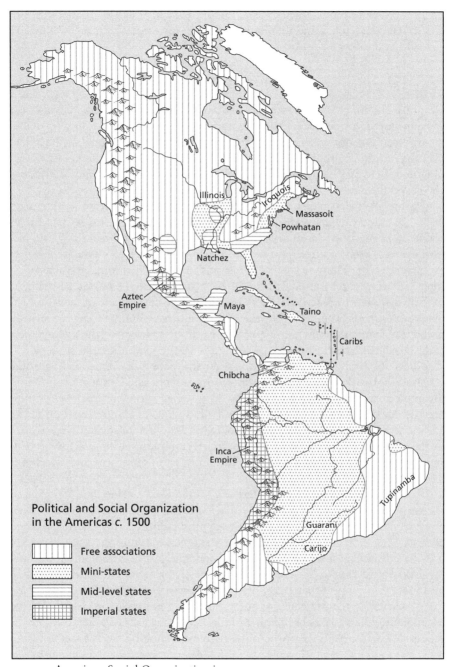

MAP 4. American Social Organization in 1500.

fairly large and compact settlements, as the Tupi in Brazil or the Iroquois of North America did; some mini-states' populations practiced fairly extensive agriculture and lived in scattered hamlets or villages.

EGALITARIAN DEMOCRACIES

Egalitarian democracies were usually small in scale; their basic and often only social grouping rarely exceeded a few thousand and was often concentrated in a single settlement or group of closely related settlements. Such societies had very little authority that was permanent and binding on its members, although obviously in such small groups the disapproval of neighbors could be effective checks on deviant or overly individualistic behavior.

But for all their small scale and lack of hierarchy, egalitarian democracies were not poor or backward remnants of ancient people who had failed to progress. Strongly evolutionary trends in social science, anthropology, and history over the past century have tended to see free association type of societies as "primitive" or alternatively as "pre-state" or "pre-chiefdom," implying that their lack of hierarchy and class was a transitory state to be passed through, or that their failure to reach what was perceived as higher levels of development was the result of failings within their own cultures.[1] But, as we have already noted, the standard of living in free associations, at least for the average person, may have exceeded that of Europeans if one uses a simple proxy measure like life expectancy as a guide to general prosperity. Paleodemographic research that seeks to reconstruct important indices like infant mortality and life expectancy from the remains of the dead found in cemeteries does not support the idea that foragers were poor and inhabitants of empires were rich. The all-important division of society into social classes often pushed down the level of the average inhabitant in larger and more complex societies below that of free associations that had a more egalitarian division of income and a communal solidarity that let no one go hungry.

If one takes what people around the world today value as important in society, namely large-scale political participation and equality of incomes, then egalitarian democracies were the most advanced cultures of their day. Indeed, citizens of egalitarian democracies clearly shared these notions and were quite unwilling to accept a situation in which their egalitarian system might become more disciplined along lines that were manifestly present in Europe and Africa, and indeed in many other parts of the Americas. European social and political theorists of the sixteenth century, such as Thomas More or Michel de Montaigne, often used the democratic system of egalitarian democracies as models to cast their own theories of political participation, and in fact to frame

---

[1] For a fervent critique of the idea of the state as an evolutionary goal of society, see Pierre Clastres, *Society Against the State: Essays in Political Anthropology* (tr. Robert Hurley, ed. Abe Stein, Cambridge, 1987 [original French, 1974]), which often uses American examples of this period.

debates that would come to be important in the democracy movement of the late eighteenth century.

For example, in 1562, a group of Tupinambá people from the Rio de Janeiro area of what is today Brazil was brought to France in order to impress them with the wealth and power of that country. They, however, were significantly unimpressed with the concentrated wealth of France, quite to the surprise and dismay of their hosts. According to Montaigne, who interviewed some of them, "they had noticed that there were among us men full and gorged with all sorts of good things, and that their other halves were beggars at their doors, emaciated with hunger and poverty; and they thought it strange that these other halves could endure such an injustice, and did not take the others by the throat and set fire to their houses."[2] The French, not deterred by this sort of attitude, later tried a similar visit with Savignon, an Iroquois brought to France by Samuel de Champlain in 1609. Upon his return to Canada, he eschewed going back to France, for he told his friends that although France had wonders, he was upset by the "great number of needy and beggars," and that people were sometimes "whipped and hanged without distinction of innocence or guilt."[3]

It was this idea, sometimes militantly held, that made egalitarian democracies what they were, or at least imagined themselves to be: associations, made voluntarily by free people with others for their joint interests. Because they were voluntary, such associations could be severed at any time as the society had no mechanism for enforcing them, save the general opinion of the community and the sanctions that it could impose by isolating or expelling miscreants.

The absence of a state structure made face-to-face democracy the basic means for arriving at group decisions, although it also prevented definitive resolution of disputes, especially intergroup disputes where community sanctions could not be applied effectively. In such situations, groups might split, with dissidents moving away together, or aggrieved parties might seek to get vengeance against those they felt had wronged them. For this reason, egalitarian democracies all across the Americas were torn by vendettas, which often created very long-lasting feuds, particularly between neighboring groups. Such enmities prevented effective group action by large numbers, even when threatened by powerful external forces, such as the Europeans.

At the same time, however, the absence of a state structure also made it impossible for egalitarian democracies to surrender to outsiders, including Europeans. Egalitarian democracies made themselves famous for being unable to enforce treaties that their leadership negotiated with foreigners against their own numbers. Leaders could only speak for themselves and had to persuade their community to accept their decisions. It was impossible, therefore,

---

[2] Michel de Montaigne, *Essais* (1580, modern critical edition, Dezeimeris and H. Barckhausen, 2 vols, Bordeaux, 1870 [Gallica]) 1: 181.

[3] Quoted in James Axtell, "Through Another Glass Darkly: Indian Views of Europeans," in *After Columbus: Essays in the Ethnohistory of Colonial North America* (Oxford, 1988), p. 141.

for a leader to betray his community for personal gain beyond his individual resources.

While in theory, free associations or egalitarian democracies had complete equality, in fact, they varied from that norm quite a bit. Some allowed considerable slavery, which introduced an element of coercion and inequity; others had temporary leaders who could exercise considerable, if limited, power.

CARIBS

Among the Island Caribs of the eastern Caribbean, the free-association organization was tempered by the existence of a class of slaves, often largely female, not fully integrated into the body politic, and by power exercised by "captains" who enjoyed greater wealth than others in their society. The Caribs' oral traditions recorded in the mid-seventeenth century recalled their "father" Kulinago moving from the Orinoco Valley of today's Venezuela northward into the islands of the Eastern Caribbean, in search of new lands, settling first in Dominica and then advancing from there.[4] By the time of Columbus, Caribs had spread northward into the small islands of the Caribbean and were raiding the larger islands of Puerto Rico and Hispaniola. When Columbus undertook his second voyage to the Americas, he had been warned previously by Tainos on Hispaniola that the Caribs were hostile and militant, and for that reason, early accounts of their life are sketchy.[5]

Although the Caribs moved frequently and lived as much off marine resources as agriculture, their villages were not small. Columbus's men stopped at Guadeloupe and noted the pattern of villages of 20–30 houses around a central square, suggesting a population of perhaps 150 to 200 people.[6] The Caribs also had elaborate trading networks that went along with their raiding patterns, which connected the islands to the mainland and rivers of South America, where they traded tobacco, hammocks, and other goods.[7] These trading links were so important, for example, the French learned in 1649 that the Caribs of St. Lucia were planning to attack their nascent settlement in Grenada because the island "was their great passage to the mainland (*terre ferme*),"and the settlement would cut off their place of resting and refreshment.[8]

---

[4] Raymond Breton, "Relation de l'isle de Guadeloupe" (1647), mod. ed. in *Relations de 'ile de la Guadeloupe* (Basse Terre, 1978), pp. 52–53; Jean-Baptiste du Tertre, *Histoire générale des Antilles habitées par les Français* (4 vols, Paris, 1667–1671) 2: 350.

[5] Dr. Diego Alvarez Chanca, Letter of c. 1494, translation in Peter Hulme and Neil Whitehead, eds. *Wild Majesty: Encounters with Caribs from Columbus to the Present Day. An Anthology* (Oxford, 1992), pp. 32–33; Goncalo Fernandez de Oviedo, *Historia* Book II, Cap 8.

[6] Pietro Martire, *De Orbo Novo*, dec 1, book 2.

[7] Marc de Civrieux, "Los Caribes y la Conquesta de la Guayana Española," *Montalban* 5 (1976): 875–1021.

[8] [Bénigne Bresson], "L'Histoire de L'isle de Grenade en Amerique," f. 47v, ed. Jacques Petitjean Roget in *Histoire de l'isle de Grenade en Amérique, 1649–59* (Montréal, 1975), which marks the original foliation.

The earliest travelers describe the Caribs as an archetypical free association, in which every man regarded himself as effectively sovereign and bound to no other person in a political way. Amerigo Vespucci, who reported on Caribs on the coast of modern Venezuela as he saw them in 1501, wrote that they "have no private goods, but all is common, they gather together without a king, without an emperor and each one is his own lord."[9] Of course, family bonds might tie people together, but these were no guarantee of automatic alliance or acceptance.

Father Raymond Breton, a French missionary, provided particularly detailed accounts of the Caribs in 1647. According to Breton, Caribs made group decisions and plans that affected groups larger than the simple family were made in informal, unstructured meetings called *wikus*.[10] Many *wikus* were simply social gatherings, as was the carefree party that the French of Grenada surprised on June 1, 1650, at which the revelers were not "thinking at all about what was to become them," and upon being attacked leaped to their death off the hill that is known even today as "Sauteurs" or "Leapers' Hill."[11] More important, they were also places where marriages were arranged, disputes aired, or joint activities anticipated, and particularly, as Breton noted, captains were chosen for war.[12]

To retaliate against the French for chasing their vessels in 1654, Caribs of St. Vincent organized a *wiku*, "where they took the resolution, that since they could not obtain vengeance against those who had so rudely attacked and pursued them," they would attack the nearest French outpost in Grenada, and recruited 500 followers to carry it out.[13] When French settlers on Martinique violated the peace they made with the Caribs of that island, they vowed vengeance, but finding themselves too weak to do it there, "they concluded at a vin [*wiku*] to turn their arms against us [French settlers in Grenada]."[14] But whatever might be brought together at a *wiku* was just as quickly abandoned once the specific goal had been achieved.

The institution of slavery checked the apparent untrammeled local democracy of Carib free associations to some extent, however. Caribs, militant raiders that they were, also captured people and returned to their homes with them. Some of these people were subsequently integrated into Carib society, often not as equals in the free association. Caribbean folklore had it that the Caribs, reputed to be inveterate cannibals, ate all their male captives and retained only women and children, although in fact this was not true. Nevertheless, Caribs

---

[9] Fracanzo de Montalboddo, *Paesi novamente retrovati et Novo Mondo da Alberico Vesuputio Florentino* (Vicentia, 1507 [Gallica)], cart. ccvii.

[10] This is a phonetic rendering of *ouikou* in French spelling, actually the name of an alcoholic beverage, and hence sometimes called *vins* or "wines' (through translating into French); another name was *carbets*.

[11] [Bresson], "Histoire," fol 52v.

[12] Breton, "Relation," pp. 73, 76.

[13] [Bresson], "Histoire," fol. 64.

[14] [Bresson], "Histoire," fol. 90v.

did seem to capture many more women than men, and integrated them through the mechanism of marriage.

Dr. Chanca, one of Columbus's passengers on his second voyage, gave a woman's-view account of Carib society in 1494 based on what he had been told by a Taino woman from Hispaniola they took from her Carib captors, who described her life as a captive wife among them as a hard one, with few rights and considerable abuse.[15] Luisa de Navarette, an African slave captured from Puerto Rico by Caribs in 1576 and returned four years later, seconded her opinions. Women, especially those taken as captives, grew tobacco and wove cotton cloth, especially manufactured into hammocks, which were widely traded; they were also responsible for cooking and food preparation tasks.[16]

On the other hand, the French clerical witnesses believed that native-born Carib women enjoyed considerable equality within the free association, so the issue was not so much one of an abusive institution of marriage as a disguised institution of slavery. Carib women and their children were something of an elite class, along with the men, and the captives formed a laboring class that supported them. Certainly the Caribs of Grenada regarded Africans they had captured as slaves, and when some ran away to the French, complaining that as baptized Christians, they could not live among people "who lived like beasts," the Carib Captain Buisson demanded that he could not remain at peace with the French "if they held their slaves without subject and without reason, against the public faith that he had given them that he would not do anything against their persons or their goods or anything that belonged to them."[17]

The slave society analogy may not be pressed too far, however, for there is little in Carib society that suggests that slavery was permanent or inheritable, or that any significant concentrations of wealth passed on intergenerationally. Africans were fully integrated into Carib society in the long run, and some groups, such as the "Black Caribs" (or Garífuna) of Saint Vincent, eventually became highly mixed.

The most visible concentrations of power were held in the hands of people known in European sources as "captains," who were war leaders, but such people were elected on the basis of their military skill and valor, and they had no command in peacetime. Baco, a captain of the Galibis (a Carib group) on the South American mainland, was such a war leader, known far and wide as "their God Mars for war and their God Apollo for its conduct," and to whom defeated Caribs from Grenada addressed themselves in 1650, complaining that the French were "driving them out, to the point where they spared no one's life," and if the French were not opposed, the Caribs would be "without land and without country."[18]

---

[15] Chanca in Hulme and Whitehead, *Wild Majesty*, p. 34.

[16] Breton, "Relation," p. 72; on their commerce, see p. 75; on the hammock trade for Tobago, see Willelm Mollens to Duke Jacob of Kurland, August 11, 1654, published in Otto Heinz Mattiesen, *Die Kolonial- und Überseepolitke Herzog Jakobs von Kurland, 1640–1660* (Stuttgart, 1939), p. 451.

[17] [Bresson], "Histoire," fol 81.

[18] [Bresson], "Histoire," fol. 55v.

Only experienced people were elected captains, and thus often the young sons of captains were passed over. Although a captain might convoke a *wiku* in order to start a war, no one was constrained to go with them, as befitted a free association.[19] To be a successful captain one had only to have a reputation. Captain Warner, son of the English governor of Saint Christopher (St. Kitts) and a Carib wife, was a redoubtable leader in Dominica in the mid-seventeenth century.[20] He was able to bring 600 men under his command, in 17 canoes, to aid the English in an attack on St. Lucia in 1663.[21]

The mark of a captain was ownership of a canoe. In his description of Tobago in 1654, the Dutch captain Willem Mollens related that there were "five captains of the Savages [*willden*] each Captain has 25 men and each captain has his own canoe." The captains were important, but Mollens added "no one who is lord over all."[22] Nevertheless, there were certainly some captains who, by reputation at least, led larger groups of Caribs because they routinely did raise forces larger than the compass of a single captain. The Caribs' canoes, *piraguas*, were large watercraft, capable of carrying thirty-five to more than forty men as well as a sizable cargo. The first French settlers in St. Christophe met a fleet of 13 canoes in 1639, in good order, "like a navy," carrying 600–700 men.[23] When the Caribs of St. Vincent decided to invade Grenada in 1649, they fit 500 fighters in 11 canoes, and in their attack on the French fort in 1655, some 1,100 men were carried by 23 such craft, while just 5 canoes carried some 200 in a 1657 war.[24]

Canoes were made by craftsmen, took a good deal of time to produce, and were thus expensive.[25] Those who owned them were effective commanders over any who rode in them, and it was captains who commissioned, owned, and commanded them. Because ownership conferred extra shares of trading surplus and captives, captains could easily parlay military or commercial success into more stable wealth by obtaining additional wives, and eventually descendents to support them, because Caribs were polygamous and at least some of them had many wives.[26] On the other hand, a firmly held belief in partible inheritance, and the absence of any state to hold estates together, generally meant that a permanent class of captains did not exist, although a powerful captain could certainly set his favored children on the way to obtaining their own wealth and *piraguas* before he died.

[19] Breton, "Relation," p. 76.
[20] [Bresson], "Histoire," fol. 90v–91 reveals him leading 100 men (probably two canoes or more) in 1659.
[21] Du Tertre, *Histoire* 3: 82–86.
[22] Mollens to Duke of Kurland, in Mattiesen, *Kolonial*, p. 451.
[23] Du Tertre, *Histoire* 1: 149. Other early French observations from 1639 in Guadeloupe include 200–300 men in 13 pirouges (p. 89) and 15 pirouges carrying 700–800 men (p. 90) in 1636.
[24] [Bresson], "Histoire," fol. 48. The same numbers are also given for another force in 1654; fol. 64v, 67v, and 76v. Not all canoes were this large; elsewhere, Bresson mentions a force of only 212 in some 24 canoes; fol. 67.
[25] Breton, "Relation," p. 69; Mollens to Duke of Kurland, in Mattiesen, *Kolonial*, p. 451.
[26] Breton, "Relation," p. 65.

THE MISKITO KINGDOM

Sketchy Spanish accounts tell us that the Caribbean coast of Central America was divided among free associations and more complex societies. According to Francisco Vazquez, a late-seventeenth-century chronicler, the lands of the province of Taguzgalpa were loosely attached to more powerful ministates of the interior. He wrote that Taguzgalpa was politically diverse; some areas were "republics" governed by "lords" while others were governed by "factions" (*parcialidads*) and families" and lived in a nomadic style.[27] Archaeological research confirms the existence of quite ancient polities, especially in the river valleys behind modern-day Trujillo and into the interior mountains, although the coastal regions are less visible to archaeology.[28] However, the Miskito Kingdom that English privateers operating out of Providence Island, a colony off the coast of Central America in 1636, contacted appears to be more of a free association than a complex society. While the relations are murky, the English took the "king" of the nation to England to solidify the alliance that they made sometime before 1641.[29] Although the kingdom's social structure is not revealed in the early sources, an account of the pirate Alexandre Exquemelin, who visited in 1671, described their rule as a republic, in which land was held in common, leadership was vested in a temporary war captain who had no authority outside of war, and collective decision making was practiced.[30] The kingdom was clearly some sort of federation, the geography of which was outlined by another pirate, only known as M.W., in 1699, and showed a network of "captains" with villages of their followers who owed obedience to a king who lived south of Cape Gracias a Dios.[31]

The Miskito made an alliance with Great Britain in order to fend off attacks by the Spanish, and provided material support for many privateering and then piratical activities throughout the end of the seventeenth century and early eighteenth century. They engaged in slave raiding and sold many of their captives into the Caribbean slave trade, especially to Jamaica; in fact, they even helped Jamaican slave owners to hunt down runaway slaves. In 1740, they

---

[27] Francisco Vázquez, *Crónica del Provincia de Santísimo Nombre de Jesús de Guatemala* (4 vols., Guatemala, 1937–44) Book 5, tratado 1, cap. 1.

[28] An archaeological survey and review of evidence suggests that greater levels of complexity could be found more generally in the area before 1200, and like the Mississippian societies of U.S. Southeast, there was a move to decentralization of wealth and authority, Thomas Cuddy, *Political Identity and Archaeology in Northeast Honduras* (Boulder, 2007), pp. 6–16, 33–36, 42–44.

[29] Michael Olien, "The Miskito Kings and the Line of Succession," *Journal of Anthropological Research* 39 (1983): 200–202.

[30] A[lexandre] O. Exquemelin, *Die Americaensche Zee-Rovers* (Amsterdam, 1678), p. 150. The English translation of this text made in 1684 and the source for most modern editions is unreliable; the new translation of 2000 is superior.

[31] M. W., "The Mosqueto Indian and his Golden River," in Awnsham Churchill, ed. *A Collection of Voyages and Travels, some now printed from original manuscripts for the first time...* (6 vols., London, 1732), p. 6.

made a formal treaty with Britain and permitted a British official to live in their territory, as well as fairly extensive settlement by Englishmen and their slaves.[32] While there is little to suggest substantial changes in social organization, the African ex-slave Olaudah Equiano, who lived on the coast in 1776, noted that the governor – an official appointed by the king – traveled his domains dispensing justice, perhaps in this way maintaining a barrier against vendettas that threatened stability in most free associations.[33]

The kingdom was remarkably durable, surviving as a reasonably cohesive entity until its final absorption into Nicaragua in 1894. The Miskitos enslaved people who they took in war, like the Caribs, and thus elements of social stratification may have entered the picture, although the fate of a group of African slaves who took over their ship and wrecked it on the coast of Honduras around 1640 is instructive. The slaves were initially held in some servile capacity, but by the time Exquemelin arrived, most had attained some freedom, and in the early eighteenth century their mixed-race descendents came to rule the kingdom.[34] Unlike most free associations, the monarchy of the Miskito appears to have been hereditary, certainly after the Mosquitos Zambos, as the mixed-race component of the population was called, took over the office.[35]

FREE ASSOCIATIONS IN BRAZIL

Brazil, home of the Tupinambá that Montaigne met, had many egalitarian democracies, and they appear to have had less inequality than the Caribs. They stretched from north to south all along the Brazilian coast, and indeed much of the interior. They spoke a variety of languages, those on the coast closely related languages of the Tupi family, while behind a low coastal range that separates the coast from the interior, along the valley of the Rio São Francisco, Gê speakers predominated. The latter were first called Aimoré, but by the seventeenth century they were usually called Tapuya by the coastal people and the Portuguese, meaning "those who do not speak Tupi." In spite of linguistic and cultural similarity, as the early chronicler Pero de Magalhães (1576) said, "even

[32] Germán Rivero Vargas, *Las sociedades del Atlántico de Nicaragua en los siglos XVII y XVIII* (Managua, 1995), pp. 67–97; Mary Helms, "Miskito Slaving and Culture Contact: Ethnicity and Opportunity in an Expanding Population," *Journal of Anthropological Research* 39/2 (1983): 179–197.

[33] Olaudah Equiano, *The Interesting Narrative of the Life of Olaudah Equiano, or Gustavus Vassa* (2 vols., London, 1789) 2: 184–186.

[34] Exquemelin, *Zee-Rovers*, p. 150; the French translation of this text is so substantially different from the original that it must have used another, more or less contemporary source, and adds important details; Alexandre Olivier Oexmelin, *Histoire des avanturiers que se sont signalez dans les Indes* (2 vols., Paris, 1688, the 1686 edition is identical), p. 201; for a variant on their fate, Sieur Lussan de Raveneau, *Journal d'un voyage fait `a la mer du Sud avec les filibustiers d'Amerique...* (Paris, 1690), p. 265 (there is an English translation, 1930, that is unreliable).

[35] Karl Offen, "The Sambu and Tawira Miskitu: The Colonial Origins of Intra-Miskitu Differentiation in Eastern Nicaragua and Honduras," *Ethnohistory* 49/2 (2002): 337–340; Olien, "Miskito Kings."

though they are divided and have various names and nations among them, because of the similarity of condition, customs and heathen rites all are one." These nations included the Tamoios in the Rio de Janeiro area, Tupinambás around Bahia, Amaupiras in the inland areas behind Bahia, and Potiguaras from there north to the Amazon.[36]

Just as they had various nations, they also had various settlement patterns. The coastal Tupi lived in large villages. Hans Staden, a German gunner who served the Portuguese and is one of the earliest witnesses on record of Tupi society, was captured and lived among Tupinambá on the coast of Brazil south of Rio de Janeiro in the early 1550s. During his stay among them, he noted that their villages typically had seven communal houses, each of which might be 150 feet long.[37] Jean Léry, Staden's contemporary who resided near modern day Rio de Janeiro in 1555–1556, reported that the villages around the area held 500–600 people,[38] while the later writer Vicente do Salvador, who resided farther north in Bahia, knew of houses holding 70–80 families, making villages as large as 600 families – perhaps 3,000 people.

On the other hand, the Gê-speaking people of the interior, such as the Aimorés, lived in small, scattered houses, according to historian do Salvador (1627).[39] Martin de Nantes, who arrived in Brazil in 1671 and became one of the first observers of those living in the midst of the valley of the São Francisco, made the same observations of those he called Cariri.[40] Their social groups were also tiny and in constant flux, for earlier writers left lists of "nations" in the interior that seem to be always different and never quite fit the idea of fixed, single tribes, even though the modern manifestation of identity in Native Brazil is now established in such tribes.[41]

Europeans were struck with the apparent lack of political authority even in the fairly sizable settlements of the coast. Staden noted that "they have no

---

[36] Vicente do Salvador, *Historia do Brazil* (Bahia, December 20, 1627, mod. ed. João Capistrano de Abreu, Rio de Janeiro, 1889[BNL]) Book 1, cap. 12, pp. 24–25; Pero de Magalhães de Gandovo, *Historia da provincial de Santa Cruz* (Lisbon, 1576[BNL]), p. 33. For a summary of modern views on the linguistic situation, see the excellent overview by John Monteiro, in *Cambridge History of the Native Peoples of the Americas* (6 parts in 3 volumes, Cambridge), vol. 2, pt. 1, pp. 972–981.

[37] Hans Staden, *Warhaftige beschreibung einer Landschaffe der wilden, nacketen, grimmigen menschenfresser leutyen in der newen welt America gelegen* (Marpurg, 1557[BNRJ]; mod. ed. Karl Klüpfel as *N. Federmann und H. Stades Reisen in SüdAmerica, 1529 bis 1555*, Stuttgart, 1859 [GB]), Part II, chapter 4 (this book has no pagination, chapter citation allows various editions and translations to be consulted, but note that Staden's original chapters were sometimes misnumbered, Klüpfel's edition supplies pagination).

[38] Jean de Léry, *Histoire d'vn voyage fait en la terre dv Bresil...* (Geneva, 1611[Gallica]), p. 359.

[39] Do Salvador, *Historia*, Book 1, chapter 13, p. 25.

[40] Martin de Nantes, *Relation succinte et sincere. De la Mission du Pere Martin de Nantes, Prédicateur Capucin, Missionaire Apostolique dans le Brezil parmy les Indiens appellés Cariris* (Quimper: Perier, nd [1707], approval in back from 1706]). A modern facsimile edition published by Frederico G. Edelweiss (Bahia: Tipografia Benedita, 1952).

[41] Julie Cavagnac, "A etnicidade encoberta: 'Indios', e 'Negros' a Rio Grande do Norte," http://www.antropologia.com.br/arti/colab/abanne2003/a10-jcavignac.pdf

special rule or laws," and "one can do whatever one wants." Léry described the customs he observed of different groups of Tupi, noting that they had no respect for law and were "only guided by their nature, each one does what he wishes."[42] Do Salvador regarded this apparent anarchy in both secular and religious life as so striking that he repeated the well-known adage of his day, namely that because the Tupi language lacked sounds corresponding to the Portuguese letters L, F, or R, it was as if they had no words for Law, Faith, or King (*lei*, *fe*, and *rei* in Portuguese).[43]

Staden believed that authority was limited to such an extent that there was really no central justice either. "When someone kills or injures one of them, their friends and family get together to kill that one," although at the village level, he admitted, "this never happens."[44] Léry elaborated on this, noting that should a fight break out (even though he only saw two such incidents in nearly a year's residence), the people simply allowed the two parties to fight, and that if injuries occurred, the families and friends of the injured sought to injure the perpetrator in exactly the same way. On the whole, however, Léry believed, Tupis lived within their village with an astonishing degree of love, mutual aid, and solidarity.[45]

Léry noted, however, that while there may have been a notable lack of animosity and conflict among the inhabitants of a village, the Tupis felt an implacable hatred for those they perceived as their enemies, who lived farther away from them.[46] In the absence of any authority to pronounce final resolution on disputes, especially ones involving the spilling of blood, and with the lack of community pressure that worked only at the village level, intervillage disputes could only be resolved by war, just as violence within the village was alleged to be resolved by an "eye for an eye" sort of justice rendered by the families of those wronged, even if it rarely was. Magalhães de Gandovo related just this history, perhaps rendered by Tupi leaders, when he observed that "they did not fight for any material interest, but because in ancient times, if someone killed another … his relatives gathered together against the killer and his family, and pursued him with such mortal hate one against the others, that from then they came to be divided into various bands and remain enemies as they now are."[47] Staden, asking rhetorically why it was that Tupis ate their captives, wrote "it is not for hunger," but for hatred and revenge. "It is to avenge the death of my friends," went one Tupi battlefield cry, "that I am here."[48]

The urge for this revenge, whose implacability put Léry off, given the Tupis great mutual love in local settings, was what led to the virtually incessant wars.

---

[42] Léry, *Histoire*, p. 358.

[43] For example, do Salvador, *Historia*, Book 1, Cap 12, p. 25; see also Magalhães de Gandovo, *Santa Cruz*, fol. 33v.

[44] Staden, *Wafhaftige beschreibung*, Part II, cap. 12.

[45] Léry, *Voyage*, p. 358.

[46] Léry, *Voyage*, p. 358.

[47] Magalhães de Gandovo, *Santa Cruz*, fol. 34.

[48] Staden, *Warhaftige beschreibung*, Part II, cap 26 (misnumbered in original for 25).

The revenge had cycled upward, with ever more grisly revenges exacted and demanded, so that it had finally settled on what, in Tupi eyes, was the most horrible possible: to be killed and eaten. As soon as prisoners were taken, they were taunted with their eventual demise and fate to be eaten, even though they might be held for a long time before the sentence was carried out. The execution was typically an elaborate ceremony, much described by witnesses, in which the whole village participated. The Tupi eating ceremony was designed to make the consumption of the victim as humiliating as possible and to drive home the vengeance element of its origin. This feature had created an etiquette of death for the victims, to limit the humiliation and turn it against their antagonists, while gleefully anticipating the revenge that his own relatives would exact in the future.[49]

In this way Tupi society was effectively defined by war. "That is their honor," Staden wrote, "to take many enemies prisoners and to kill them."[50] Constant war created geography. When Staden spoke of the geography of the Tupinambá group around the Portuguese captaincy of São Vicente, all their neighbors were enemies, with whom there was nothing but war: "[T]o the north are the Weitakka, their enemies, to the south their enemies the Tuppi Iken, and inland were the Karayan also their enemies."[51] Elsewhere he gave a similar description of the enemies of the Tuppi Iken, the Tupinambá on the north and the Carijo to the south, who they called simply "Tawijar, which means enemies."[52]

In a society driven by war, what authority there was devolved on those who might lead in war, for effective war is best waged with discipline and obedience, even if civil society was characterized by neither. Staden noted the small local authority, for "each house has a captain [*obersten*], who is their king [*Künig*]"; this person, however, was simply the head of a family, as within each village they were all of the same lineage [*Stam*].[53] In one village where he was kept prisoner, Staden observed that two of the house "kings" were brothers of the ruler.[54] Village leaders directing these household leaders were typically referred to in Portuguese as "captains" to refer to their military status, and that military ability was as important as family ties in their selection, according to do Salvador, as his primary duties were "more for war than peace" because "as regards the punishment of their errors, he could do nothing against their will."[55] In his duties for making war, leaders were assisted in decision making by "the principal men of the houses, and other discrete Indians." Although the decision to go to war

---

[49] Léry devoted a whole chapter (*Voyage*, chapter XV) to this description; Staden not only described the ceremony in general (*Warhaftige beschreibung*, Part II, cap. 25), but noted the specifics of the eating of a number of captives; more details are in Magalhães Gândavo, *Santa Cruz*, fols. 40v–45.

[50] Staden, *Warhaftige beschreibung*, part II, cap. 22 (misnumbered).

[51] Staden *Waſhaftige beschreibung*, Part II, cap 4.

[52] Staden, *Warhaftige beschreibung*, Part I, cap. 14.

[53] Staden, *Warhaftige beschreibung*, part II cap. 12.

[54] Staden, *Warhaftige beschreibung*, part I, cap. 34.

[55] Magalhães Gândavo, *Santa Cruz, fol.* 34; do Salvador, *Historia*, Book 1, cap. 13, pp. 25–26.

was made by a council composed of house captains and not by every adult, it was binding on the rest, for once made, a spokesperson went to every house to declare "the obligation that they had to make this war."[56] Without at least this discipline, war would have been impossible and defeat likely.

This scant military authority was not accompanied by much in the way of inequality of wealth: "[T]here is no division of goods among them, they know nothing to say of money," wrote Staden, "for each man and wife has their own [manioc] roots which feeds them."[57] In spite of this limited governmental authority, there was a certain amount of economic status connected with it, for the "principals" in Tupi society were polygamous and possessed somewhat more material goods.[58] Staden gave some indication of the nature of polygamy and status: "Most have only one wife," he wrote, "but the principals have 13 or 14."[59] Rich men in this society had the ability to marry more wives, and enjoyed wearing status symbols in the form of jewelry, which did not pass along as an estate and were thus the earned badges of honor.

Given the great peace within villages, these captains represented them to the outside world, where disputes were not so easily settled, and where the deadly rule of revenge reigned. But so far as the sources reveal it, Tupi society was not simply village against village, for military necessity virtually always required larger groupings still. These groupings were the "nations" of the political geography of Brazil. These nations might have what Staden called a king (*Künig*). When he was carried to Arribab, the village of Konyan Bebe, "the foremost king" of the Tupinambá, Staden congratulated him on his reputation, noting that the Portuguese feared him for his many wars. He wore elaborate jewelry marking him as the highest nobility, and his house was decorated with fifteen skulls of dead enemies. His ambition, he told Staden, was to capture the fortified Portuguese post of Bertioga (near São Vicente) where Staden had served.[60] Staden accompanied Konyan Bebe on a raid in 1554, which captured a few people around the fort, that involved 38 canoes of 18 people each (684 fighters) – perhaps the number that he could mobilize from a group of his villages, but probably not the whole nation.[61] A similar raid a few years earlier had brought 70 canoes – perhaps 1260 fighters – at similar levels of equipment.[62] A fully mobilized nation in a time of crisis, or where heads of all the villages could agree, might be able to assemble several thousand fighters, if Staden was not simply exaggerating when he said that some 8,000 Tupi besieged Pernambuco in 1548.[63] As a military leader, however, neither Konyan Bebe nor others of his

---

[56] Do Salvador, *Historia*, Book 1, Cap. 16, pp. 24–25; Magalhães de Gandovo, *Santa Cruz*, fol. 34.
[57] Staden, *Warhaftige beschreibung*, Part II, cap. 20.
[58] Do Salvador, *Historia*, Book 1, Cap. 14, pp. 27–28.
[59] Staden, *Warhaftige beschreibung*, Part II, cap. 18.
[60] Staden, *Warfaftige beschreibung*, Part I, cap. 28.
[61] Staden, *Warhaftige beschreibung*, Part I, cap. 41.
[62] Staden, *Warhaftige beschreibung*, Part I, cap. 15.
[63] Staden, *Warfatige beschreibung*, Part I, cap. 3. It seems likely that he, and others, estimated combatants by making use of a boat count, as Tupis typically traveled this way, in which case this number might actually be correct.

status had arbitrary power; his voice was simply listened to more than that of others, and even then, when they made war, Staden said that they "confederate as they ought to."[64]

The same social system applied in the more poorly described Gê-speakers of the interior. The missionary de Nantes observed that the "captains or governors" who ruled their villages had no authority except in time of war.[65] The position was held by election; in one village where de Nantes worked, the community was divided over the selection of the next one, one party wishing to choose a worthy son, the other claiming that the position could never be held by a near relative.[66] The most significant feature of the interior was that its ecology did not generally support the large settled villages of the coast, so that the people lived in smaller groups and had more mobility, but socially they were just as much free associations.[67]

IROQUOIANS

The Iroquois and Huron of North America mirror the Tupi case closely, for there, too, violence and warfare shaped much of social life in a group with little or no civil authority. Archaeologists can trace the origins of the militant Iroquoians to radical changes that took place in a large zone from the Great Lakes to modern New England following the adaptation of maize agriculture around 1000. Along the coast, the formerly scattered, small villages of horticulturalists and hunters of what is called the Late Woodland Period, that had characterized much of the northeast part of North America, gradually evolved into petty states, culminating in such polities as the Powhatan Empire, to be discussed in more detail later in the chapter. In the interior, however, south of the Great Lakes, the new economy witnessed the reorganization into large, highly fortified, and increasingly concentrated populations as large-scale violence, attested to in burials and fortifications, emptied the countryside and created no-man's lands between clusters of fortress-towns.[68] Archaeologists can attest to the spread of this sort of culture towards the east and south, and the earliest European documents noted the arrival of these free-associated military bands both in New England and the Chesapeake.

Early visitors, like Samuel de Champlain (1609), attested to widespread violence at the time of his arrival, and his French crew assisted one group of people in their attack on another. A series of visitors in the next decades provide a glimpse into the lives of the free associations that included most Iroquoian-speaking peoples, such as the Hurons, and even many of their neighbors who

---

[64] Staden, *Warhaftige beschreibung*, Part II, caps. 12, 26.

[65] De Nantes, *Relation*, p. 8.

[66] De Nantes, *Relation*, p. 79.

[67] For a careful assessment of the situation, see Cristina Pompa, *Religião como tradução: Missionários, Tupi e Tapuia no Brasil colonial* (Bauru, 2003), pp. 240–269.

[68] For an excellent overview, see Linda Cordell and Bruce D. Smith, "Indigenous Farmers," in *The Cambridge History of the Native People of the Americas* (3 vols., Cambridge, 1996), vol 1, part 1, *North America*, Bruce Trigger and Wilcomb Washburn, eds, pp. 234–257.

spoke other languages. Iroquoian social structure was very egalitarian at base, even though cohabiting social groups were much larger than they were for the Caribs to the south, but equal perhaps to those of the Tupi. Iroquoian people lived in multiple-family longhouses, in a mixture of small, scattered villages and large fortified settlements. Early Dutch visitors called the fortified settlements "castles" to reflect their fortifications and the concentration of population – at one of these near Fort Orange (modern-day Albany, New York) in 1634, Harmen Meydertsz van den Bogaert counted 36 houses, each between 80 and 100 feet long, aligned along streets; at Tenotoque, he saw 55 houses of 100 feet in length each, surrounded by a powerful triple palisade; the castle at the Seneca's main settlement had 66 houses and a double palisade that measured nearly 800 yards around.[69] Such houses, according to Adrien van der Donck, a resident since 1641 and regarded by the Dutch as their greatest expert on the native people, held some 16–18 families, or perhaps 60–80 people each, making the larger settlements hold as many as 3,500 people in conditions of great crowding. Although they did have some settlements in open land, even there they constructed small forts as quick refuges in case of attack.[70] Among the Hurons of Canada, also Iroquoian-speaking people, the same sort of housing arrangements was found; Jean de Brébeuf in 1635–1636 spoke of 50–100 cabins in each town holding 300–400 households.[71]

There were leaders to be sure, but witnesses attested that they held little independent power and their authority was not binding over anyone. Johannes Megapolensis, writing about his experiences between 1642 and 1644, described this leadership: "[G]overnment consists of the oldest, the most intelligent, most eloquent and warlike men." They made decisions that younger men carried out, but they received no income; indeed, Megapolensis believed they were the poorest as they gave out to the "mob," as indeed he felt that their government was like mob rule, so little authority did the leaders manage.[72] Van der Donck noted that they possessed a system of ranks, including chiefs (*oversten*) of higher levels "to whom others submit," and a system whereby there were chiefs of "tribes, villages, and localities [*Geschlachten, vlecken, en plaetsen*]" down to each longhouse "so that every house has its chief."[73] They were not

---

[69] Harmon Meyndertsz van den Boogaert, translation in Dean Snow, Charles Gehring and William Starna, eds. *In Mohawk Country. Early Narratives about a Native People* (Syracuse, 1996), pp. 2–13 *passim*.

[70] Adriaen Cornelissen van der Donck, *Beschrijvinge van Nieuww Nederlant* (Amsterdam, 1655), pp. 58–60. An English translation is in Snow, Gehring, and Starna, *Mohawk Country*, pp. 104–130.

[71] Jean de Brébeuf, "Relation de ce qui s'est passé dans le Pays des Hurons en l'année 1636," in Reuben Gold Thwaites, ed. and trans., *The Jesuit Relations* (73 vols., Cleveland, 1896–1901+) 10: 210–211 (the page range indicated both the original language and its facing-page English translation, which I have modified from place to place).

[72] Johannes Megapolensis, "A Short Account of the Mohawk Indians, 1644" in Snow, Gehring, and Starna, *Mohawk Country*, p. 46.

[73] Van der Donck, *Beschrijvinge*, p. 67.

obsessed with rank of this sort, and thought little of the European concern about it, although they did see a general division of the population into noble and common. On the other hand, real authority in wartime might go to anyone "on merit without regard to family or standing," and rank was not hereditary; "rank dies with the person," as Van der Donck said.[74]

Brébeuf, speaking of Huron "captains," noted the same sort of division with regional and village leaders, and at the family level as well. But these offices were not filled by hereditary succession, for "those who have first rank," he wrote, "have acquired it by their spirit, eloquence, generosity [*magnificence*], courage and wise conduct," and it was to these people that decisions were addressed. Elections were held each year, and the assent of the community was essential for any captain to hold office, or at least to achieve anything.[75] Van der Donck described the lengthy process of discussion that went into community decisions, with many people represented, and when the decision was announced, the general public still had to be persuaded to follow it, because the "community [*Gemeente*] has to carry out what has been decided, and without its consent things will not work out well." For this reason the decision makers worked hard to persuade their own families to follow decisions.[76] Huron captains also, in Brébeuf's words, "do not govern their subjects in an imperious way and absolute power; they have no force whatsoever at hand to compel them to their duty."[77]

Iroquoian violence arose out of the absence of authorities to resolve disputes, especially violent ones, much as it had for the Tupi. At the local level, community pressure and the wisdom of the leadership seems to have been remarkably effective without having much authority. Hence Megapolensis wrote that "there is no punishment here for murder or other villainies, but every one is his own avenger." Punishment for such crimes was carried out by the families of the aggrieved, if they could, until peace was made with families of those committing the injuries. As was often the case, he was surprised at how few crimes there were, and that they were remarkably at peace among themselves.[78] Van der Donck believed that there was no legal authority to punish crimes at all, although like his predecessor he observed the remarkable order of their societies with very low levels of crime and violence among themselves. The chiefs deployed no more than scolding words to redress crimes against public order, and nevertheless, "it is incredible how much they fear this." Most crimes, even serious ones, were settled by compensation and negotiation conducted by neighbors and friends.[79] Brébeuf thought that the same system in Huron villages did constitute a system of laws, albeit not a formal one, and noted the

74 Van der Donck, *Beschrijvinge*, pp. 71–72.
75 Brébeuf, "Relation," pp. 230–231; 234–235.
76 Van der Donck, *Beschrijvinge*, pp. 75–76.
77 Brébeuf, "Relation," pp. 232–233.
78 Megapolensis, "Short Account," in Snow, Gehring and Starna, *Mohawk Country*, p. 46.
79 Van der Donck, *Beschrijvinge*, p. 73.

role of the village as well as the family in bringing wrongdoers to justice. In describing the ceremony of compensation, he made it clear that the interests of the aggrieved families and the whole community were addressed.[80]

Iroquoian wars, like those of the Tupi, were wars of revenge, to inflict losses on others who had injured them in the past as a form of compensation, for beyond the castle-village and its nearby allies there was no community pressure and even less authority. Brébeuf noted that the most common cause of wars in Huron territory was "when some Nation refuses to give satisfaction for the death of someone." Even though the affair might be a private one, the villages and allies stand behind the injured party.[81] To render compensation for murder more effective, the people who were captured in revenge were tortured, often excruciatingly, before being put to death. When, Brébeuf noted, a band of "resolute young men" captures people of an enemy nation, "they treat them with all the cruelty they can devise," burning them to death over a slow fire and torturing them horribly in other ways. As an ultimate humiliation, the remains of the tortured person were eaten.[82] The families and friends of the victim, learning of the torture, then tortured those captives they took from their enemies in return, and a long cycle of increasingly violent revenge gradually led to the virtually uniform application of torture to prisoners taken in war.

However, the cycle of torture and revenge was intersected by another cycle, that of replacement for losses. In an environment where maintaining a large social group was important for defense, Iroquoian towns could not afford to lose too many people, be it from natural mortality, disease, or warfare. Thus, all Iroquoians had the concept of a "mourning war" as a way to increase their population, even as they were torturing and killing their captives.

In theory, the relatives of a victim of murder or violence demanded a mourning war. The victim's wives, family, or children went to a prescribed mourning ritual in which they demanded replacement of the lost family member. Others in the family and town agreed, and they decided to capture people to serve as replacement. Thus wars were simultaneously to capture victims to torture and to recruit forcibly new people to replace those who had been lost. The decision as to how to handle captives was made when the returning war party arrived at the town. There, prisoners were subjected to humiliation and the first stages of torture as the mourning relatives looked on. Should they spot a person they knew to be responsible for their suffering in the past, that person or his friends or allies were likely to be tortured unmercifully to death. But other captives might remind the mourners of their lost one, or perhaps simply seem a good replacement. While these might also be tortured, in the end the mourners would take them in as replacement.

The replacement process was something like brainwashing. Pierre Espirit Radisson, captured by the Mohawks in 1651, was an excellent witness to the

[80] Brébeuf, "Relation," pp. 214–217.
[81] Brébeuf, "Relation," pp. 224–225.
[82] Brébeuf, "Relation," pp. 226–229.

process, for he underwent it and describes it frankly. He was apparently chosen to be integrated from the beginning, for he was well treated during his journey from captivity to the village.[83] While many of those who were captured with him were tortured upon arrival, the would-be new family gradually placed themselves as intermediaries with the adoptee, causing their torture to be lessened, and then eliminated, and indeed Radisson was almost immediately led away from the others when he arrived in the village, even as the other captives were beaten. After six weeks residing there, the woman who had taken Radisson in (and who he consistently called his "mother" in his account) gave him the name "Orihina, her son who before was killed," and who he was clearly intended to replace.[84] Even after he murdered some of his captors and escaped, he was still accepted back and "I was as beloved of my parents as before."[85] Eventually, his adoptive father told him that he "was Iroquoite as himself," although, in spite of this encouragement, Radisson eventually did run away to Albany.[86] The process of integration of captives has led a number of investigators to question whether or not mourning wars were to produce slaves as much as replacements.[87] Radisson's testimony suggests that full integration was possible, even a likely outcome, given that he was forgiven even when he first sought to escape.

In any case, the success of the Iroquois was in large measure a result of the formation among them of the Five Nations, or the League of the Iroquois, or the League of Haudenosaunee. This league was formed probably in the fifteenth century, quite possibly as a means to limit violent reprisals between five nearby groups of towns. By forming a council that could resolve disputes, the Iroquois League managed to keep their level of violence down. The Hurons also formed a league, and their council proceedings were described in detail by Brébeuf. In organizing these leagues, both Iroquois and Hurons also created an organization that could, and did, mobilize larger armed forces than their neighbors, and made the Iroquois predatory. The league's success was particularly notable after about 1648, when Iroquois leaders decided to launch systematic raids on their neighbors, especially the Hurons to the north. Scholarly opinion differs on the overall motivation, some stressing the replacement aspects and labeling them as "mourning wars," others seeing it a response to commercial pressure and labeling them "Beaver Wars."[88]

---

[83] Pierre Espirit Radisson, "The Relation of my Voyage…" in Snow and Gehring, *Mohawk Country*, pp. 62–92.

[84] Radisson, "Relation," ed. Snow and Gehring, p. 70.

[85] Radisson, "Relation," ed. Snow and Gehring, p. 80.

[86] Radisson, "Relation," ed. Snow and Gehring, p. 81.

[87] Most notably William Starna and Ralph Watkins, "Northern Iroquoian Slavery," *Ethnohistory* 38 (1991): 34–57. Note, however, the Starna and Watkins' concept of slavery, derived from the work of Orlando Patterson, is a distinctly noneconomic conception, involving the loss of personhood as much as anything that might be described as exploitation.

[88] For a convincing case against a commercial motivation, see José António Brandão, "*Your Frye Shall Burn No More*": *Iroquois Policy toward New France and its Allies* (Lincoln, 2000).

MAPUCHE

A large group of linguistically related free associations lived in the southern part of modern-day Chile in the sixteenth century, but like other such associations, elements of authority moderated their democracy. The authority elements allowed the Mapuche to mobilize effectively for self-defense, as they did when they defeated the Inca Tupac Yupanqui (c. 1471–1793), in the Battle of Maule.[89] They were just as successful against other Inca incursions that followed; indeed, when the great Inca civil war broke out just before the arrival of the Spanish, there was an Inca army operating against the Mapuche region. The Spanish assisted in yet another invasion in the earliest years of their presence in Peru, and sought after 1544 to conquer the region. This conquest met the same determined resistance, and eventually, by 1598, the Spanish were driven out of the area south of the Biobio River. A second attempt to take back the area in the seventeenth century also failed, making the river an effective boundary until the last part of the nineteenth century.

Mapuche mobilization capabilities were found in otherwise democratic institutions. The Jesuit priest Alonso de Ovalle, writing in the mid-seventeenth century during the wars against the Spanish, believed that not only did they not accept subordination to outsiders like the Incas or the Spanish, but would not allow kings or governors of their "own nation" as the "voice of liberty prevailed among them." Each one, or each "family or kinship group," followed its "own road" and choose one of the eldest and most worthy among them to be their leader, who they recognized as the "head of the lineage, without paying pecho or giving them more obedience than the respect of relatives."[90]

Mapuche loyalty to military elites underlay their discipline and capacity to mobilize. In his epic poem dedicated to the Mapuche in 1569, Alonso de Ercilla y Zuñiga, a Spanish soldier who had seen them personally during military service in the area between 1554 and 1561, noted their higher organization. Seventeen "caciques" (a Spanish word of Caribbean origin often used to describe a ruler with real political power) ruled in Aruacania, as the Spanish called the region, but no one was preferred for these offices unless they distinguished themselves militarily. Such offices were not given for "quality or inheritance, nor for wealth or being better born," but only for the "virtues of their arms and excellence." The lords could count on no personal service from their "vassals" except on the vassals' own volition.[91]

In giving a list of leaders, Ercilla y Zuñiga noted that each generally commanded several thousand (generally 3,000) followers, who "obey him like a

---

[89] Garcilaso de la Vega, *Commentarios Reales de los Incas* (Madrid, 1609–1616), Part II, Book 7, caps. 18–20.

[90] Alonso de Ovalle, *Historica relacion del Reyno de Chile...* (Rome, 1646 [GB]), p. 85. Ovalle was born in Chile in 1602.

[91] Alonso Ercilla y Zuñiga, *La Araucana* (ed. Cayetano Rosell, Madrid, 1851 [GB] and other editions), Canto I.

king."[92] On the other hand, he did seem to make a distinction between "those who dedicate themselves to war" and had no other duty or service to perform and "those of low condition [who] were obliged" to support them. Ercilla y Zuñiga said that the higher lords might meet as a "senate" to determine how to fight against more determined enemies, and indeed they were capable of raising armies from among their fighters, organized in companies and under a chain of command.[93] Another seventeenth-century Jesuit, Diego de Rosales, described this mobilization process by noting that even though each cacique was completely independent in his own jurisdiction, when the Toque general, called the Lepan, sent a bloody arrow, it was an indication to mobilize for war.[94] Their law was not codified but justice was rendered by "men reputed wise."[95]

In spite of their resistance to Spain and their potential to mobilize substantial forces to meet the Spanish challenge, like free associations elsewhere, the Mapuches were troubled by near-constant internal civil war, as, according to Rosales, "they do not have among themselves judges to hold them back, nor have any other way for one to have justice against another or punish or avenge their grievances, except with arms."[96] As elsewhere, these wars were accompanied by gruesome scenes of torture and sacrifice.[97] If the limited authority granted their leaders defended them, it could not give them peace.

MINI-STATES

While egalitarian democracies were characterized by their lack of authority and democratic decision-making process, many Americans lived in some form of state. States were characterized by having permanent decision-making authorities whose determinations were binding on their subjects. These decisions could be enforced by restraint and violence if necessary. States were also divided by social strata and classes in that wealth was passed down through generations and protected by public authorities. A minority of the inhabitants of each state participated in decision making and this minority usually also possessed the greatest amount of personal wealth. The rulers or the state itself enforced labor, service, or tribute requirements on the subjects, which were

---

[92] Ercilla y Zuñiga, *Araucana*, Canto II.

[93] Ercilla y Zuñiga, *Araucana*, Canto I, described in greater detail by Rosales for the period a century later, *Historia general*, Book 1, cap 18, 1: 114–115, at a time when the Mapuches were mounted and war waged quite differently from the days of the first Spanish attacks.

[94] Diego de Rosales, *Historia general del Reyno de Chile. Flandes Indiano* (1674, mod ed. Benjamín Vicuña Mackenna, 3 vols., Valparaíso, 1877–1878 [GB]), Book 1, cap 18, 1: 113–114. Rosales came to Chile in 1629 and resided there for forty-three years. In this section he often quotes Ovalle directly (see p. 87), although he frequently augments the earlier Jesuit's comments as here.

[95] Ercilla y Zuñiga, *Arauacia*, Canto I.

[96] Rosales, *Historia general*, Book 1, cap. 22, 1: 133.

[97] Rosales, *Historia general*, Book 1, cap. 20.

used for the benefit of the elite, although also potentially for the benefit of the whole community.

States varied widely, however, with regards to their size, scope, centralization of decision making, or concentration of wealth. Some states, such as those of the Algonquian-speaking people of New England, were scarcely more authoritarian than egalitarian democracies, and very small in scale. Larger states existed in the Chesapeake region, but were still greatly restrained by elements of democracy and local autonomy. The various states that resulted from the Arawakian diaspora in the Amazon, Orinoco, and Caribbean were larger and more fully integrated, as were the states of the southern part of the present-day United States, and the chains of states in the basins of the Rio de la Plata, Paraguay, and Paraná. Still larger polities existed in modern-day Colombia and in the Mayan regions of Central America. I have labeled these small polities mini-states to contrast them with the imperial states, such as those built by the Aztecs in the Valley of Mexico and its surroundings, or by the Incas in Peru. These later polities, because of their size and special complexity, are considered later.

EMERGING MINI-STATES: THE ALGONQUIAN WORLD: LOW AUTHORITY

In eastern North America, social differentiation came quite late on the scale of time, much later than it did in the Southeast and the Mississippi valley. In the Chesapeake Bay region, the first archaeologically identifiable societies that can be said to have social classes and differentiation of wealth and status only appear in the Potomac valley and surrounding regions around 1200 or perhaps a bit later, and in New England they appear so late that some scholars believe their origin lay in the trade with the first European visitors in the early seventeenth century, who encouraged competition that led to economic and social stratification.[98]

Of these New England groups, Roger Williams, writing about the Narragansett region in modern-day Massachusetts and Rhode Island, described their government as monarchial, and absolute under their sachems, the local term for leader. But this monarchy was very limited in scope and scale, hardly much different from the egalitarian Iroquoian societies to the north and west; Williams wrote, "the Sachims, although they have absolute Monarchie over the people, yet they will not conclude of ought that concernes all, either Lawes, or Subsidies or warres, unto which the people are averse, and by gentle perswasion cannot be brought."[99] The sachem class was hereditary, because sachems

---

[98] For the emergence of complexity in the Chesapeake, see Stephen R Potter, *Commoners, Tribute, and Chiefs: The Development of Algonquian Culture in the Potomac Valley* (Charlottesville, 1993), pp. 138–170; for New England, see William Starna, "The Pequots in the Early Seventeenth Century," in Laurence Hauptman and James Wherry, *The Pequots in Southern New England* (Norman, 1990), pp. 33–47.

[99] Roger Williams, *A Key into the Language of America* ... (London, 1643; facsimile reprint, New Bedford, 1936), p. 142.

only married within that class, and the government was, according to Edward Winslow, another early English observer, "successive, not by choice."[100] Other Englishmen, like William Wood, who also wrote in the early seventeenth century, noted, however, that sachems who did not perform well would be soon "unsepter[ed]."[101]

But these small states did make claims on their subjects' production and labor. Sachems took regular tribute of any game killed in their territory, and, according to Winslow, once a year, under the urging of religious leaders, the people brought them heaping quantities of corn.[102] In his speech to the English around 1620, the sachem Massasoit, who controlled lands around the early English settlement at Plymouth, Massachusetts, cried, "And should they not bring their skins unto us?"[103] Dues of this sort created a higher standard of living for the sachem class; at least their houses were, according to Williams, "farre different from the other house, both in capacity or receipt; and also the fineness and quality of their mats."[104] Moreover, this elite had clothing and adornments made from sewan or wampum, which in other instances was used as money.[105] There were special terms and words of respect in the languages of New England, reserved for this class, while there were those among them who were "obscure" and "had not names."[106] The territories of sachems were well bounded, and within his bounds, a sachem had jurisdiction, taking care of strangers and the helpless (such as widows and orphans).[107] There were many such territories; Williams thought one might meet 12 such towns in a voyage of 20 miles.[108]

Early English settlers at Plymouth saw a loose hierarchy of sachems, some obeying others, or at least restrained in their own sovereignty by superior ones. This was why Emmanuel Altham in 1623 thought Massasoit, the local authority, an "Emperor."[109] Massasoit certainly expressed such ideas, for when visited by the English in 1621, he gave a public speech in which he asked, "Was he not Massasoit, commander of the country about them? Was not such a town his and the people of it?" to which the people agreed. English visitors thought the

---

[100] Edward Winslow, *Good Newes from New England: A True Relations of Things very Remarkable at the Plantation of Plimoth in New England* (London, 1624, annotated edition, New Bedford, nd), pp. 61–62.

[101] William Wood, *New England's Prospect* (London, 1634, mod. Ed. Alden T. Vaughn, Amherst, 1977) p. 97. The class from which sachems were drawn were called "Ataúskawawáuog" in Williams' orthography, which he rendered as "lords"; *Key*, p. 141.

[102] Winslow, *Good Newes*, p. 62.

[103] G. Mourt [George Morton], *A Relation or Journal of the Beginning and Proceedings of the English Plantation settled at Plimouth …* (London, 1622, mod. ed. Dwight Heath, New Bedford, 1963), p. 66.

[104] Williams, *Key*, p. 141.

[105] Williams, *Key*, p. 157; on its commercial uses, see pp. 159–165.

[106] Williams, *Key*, pp. 2, 5.

[107] Winslow, *Good Newes*, p. 62.

[108] Williams, *Key*, p. 3.

[109] Emmanuel Atham to Edward Altham, September 1623, in Samuel Eliot Morrison, ed., *Three Visitors to Early Plymouth* (Plymouth, 1963), p. 29.

other sachems in his jurisdiction were but "petty governors," and in his speech Massasoit named some thirty towns that were subject to him.[110] John Pory provided a quick geography for 1622: to Massasoit's north lay the lands of Cohasset and Massachusetts, and to the south lay Pamet, Nauset, Capawack, and others.[111] Williams spoke of the local sachems as the people's "particular protectors," who, like the greater sachems, received tribute.[112] The more powerful sachems had their rivalries; when the English arrived, they learned that the Narraganset were at odds with Massasoit, and the lesser sachems – notably Corbitant, supposedly one of Massasoit's – were switching sides and arguing over who to support, Massasoit or Corbitant, suggesting that these "empires" were not held together by more than convenience.[113] Indeed, the English settlers built themselves a little empire by getting various sachems to swear to be "King James' men," and soon became involved in the plots and quarrels of the sachems.[114]

Further south, power was less pronounced. News received by Nicholas van Wassenaer from the earliest Dutch settlers in New Amsterdam in 1624–1628 noted that there was "little authority among them" and that while they obeyed their leaders (*sakema* in that dialect) when the "villages assembled for war," "the fight once ended his authority ended." Leaders had no great material advantages, moving along with their followers, and only gaining small tokens of support when they visited, although usually obtaining great respect.[115] Another early Dutch visitor to Manhattan, Isaac de Rasieres, thought the people in 1628 were under the control of sachems, but that the government was "democratic," as the sachem was chosen "by election," usually of the richest person. As the sachem in New England, Manhattan sachems were responsible for entertaining visitors, and also was a judge in marital disputes.[116] They may therefore have had a less aristocratic form than that found farther north or south, since de Rasieres thought the Algonquin-speaking natives of the English colony in New England better disciplined.[117] *Novus Orbis*, a 1633 publication, noted "they have no form of political government" except for their sachems, who "are not much more than the heads of families, for they rarely exceed the limits of one family connection."[118] The Reformed Pastor Jonas Michaëlius

---

[110] Mourt, *Relation*, p. 66.
[111] John Pory to the Earl of Southampton, January 12, 1622/3, in James, *Three Visitors*, p. 11–12.
[112] Williams, *Key*, p. 141.
[113] Mourt, *Relation*, pp. 71, 73.
[114] Mourt, *Relation*, pp. 77–79; 82–83. Morton printed, in 1669, a document authenticated by nine sachems dated September 13, 1621 (n. 5, p. 83); on one complex quarrel, see Altham to Altham, in James, *Three Visitors*, pp. 30–31 and Winslow, *Good Newes*, pp. 8–16.
[115] Van Wassenaer, *Historische verhael* February 1624, April 1625 (trans. In Jameson, *Narratives of New Netherland*, pp. 69–70; 78, 80).
[116] Nationaal Archief (Netherlands) Verspreide West Indische Stukken, 1–20, doc. 2, Isaack de Rasieres to Samuel Bloomaert, c. 1628 (unpublished in Dutch, an English translation is in James, *Three Visitors*, p. 73), Sachems were called Sackema in Dutch orthography.
[117] De Rasieres to Bloomaert in James, *Three Visitors*, p. 78.
[118] Novum Orbis... in J. Franklin Jameson, *Narratives of New Netherland* (New York, 1909), pp. 57–58.

thought in 1628 that the "sakema" had a few hundred followers at most.[119] Peter Lindeström, who lived in the Swedish colony of New Sweden (Delaware), had a somewhat ambiguous idea of government there in the 1650s, but suggested that it was more like the New England model than that of the area around New Amsterdam (New York). On the one hand, he thought that the sachems of the region were strictly obeyed, followed each other in heredity succession, and had power of life and death over their subjects. Yet at the same time he noted that "they show no reverence or honor for their ruler," and that sachems might "sit down last as well as first" and others showed them no preference. Not only that, but he also noted the law of revenge, not only against other neighboring groups, but also among themselves: "they follow no other law or justice" as, if "anyone suffers from the other, they immediately revenge on one another, like for like."[120]

In the Chesapeake Bay region, on the other hand, empires like those of Masassoit were both firmer and more centrally controlled than any other along the Algonquian-speaking east coast. Perhaps it was because of the somewhat longer history of this sort of social organization in the Chesapeake region. Oral traditions, proudly recited by the Emperor Vttapoingassinem to the governor of Maryland in 1660, told of an "Empire of Pascattoway," which ruled a considerable territory on both shores of the Chesapeake Bay and up the Potomac River for some distance, founded some thirteen generations before the unnamed ruler who died in 1636. The scope of this empire is consistent with the archaeological remains of the earliest stratified societies in the whole region, and with a date as early as the late fifteenth century.[121]

When Europeans first penetrated this region, they saw the sort of social organization that such an empire was based on. The English intending to settle at Roanoke in 1584 described a geography of small towns, under leaders known as a *werowances*, that dotted the countryside and lined the rivers and creeks. Thomas Hariot, describing the area around Roanoke (North Carolina) in 1585, thought their towns small, ten to twelve houses at the small end and no more than thirty at the larger end. Politically, some werowances controlled only one town, but others, according to Hariot, controlled two or three, others six or eight, or even more, and the most powerful had eighteen under his authority, but still could not "make above six or eight hundred fighting men at the most."[122] In March 1586, Richard Greenevill captured and briefly interviewed Menatonon, the ruler of Chawanook, located some 130 miles northwest of Roanoke: "[T]he greatest Province and Seigniorie lying upon that River, and

[119] Jonas Michaëlius to Jan Smotius, August 11, 1628 (trans. Jameson, *Narratives of New Netherland*, p. 127).

[120] Peter Lindeström, *Geographica Americanae with an Account of the Delaware Indians...* (trans. Amandus Johnson, Philadelphia, 1925), pp. 205–206.

[121] Memorandum of 20th of December 1660, *Archives of Maryland* (Baltimore, 1883) 3: 402–403. See Potter, *Commoners*, pp. 149–150 and *passim*.

[122] Thomas Hariot, *A briefe and true report of the new found land of Virginia...* ([1588] ed. Theodorus de Bry, Frankfurt, 1590), pp. 36–37, 40, 322.

the very Towne it selfe is able to put 700 fighting men into the field besides the force of the Province it selfe." At that time, he told the Englishman of even more powerful countries lying inland.[123]

As in New England, there were rivalries and even wars between the various towns, and many were palisaded. Wingina, the werowance with whom the English stayed, was wounded in a war with a neighboring country, and most of the neighboring places formed "leagues" or two, three, or more towns. The ruler in Wingina was able to summon people to come to trade with visiting Englishmen and to control the terms they had in trading. The common people showed these rulers great deference and respect, and the leaders, in turn, wore distinctive clothing and jewelry.[124]

Farther north, settlers at Jamestown after 1607 met a much larger political configuration in the domain of Powhatan, the "emperor" of those parts. This polity was probably the largest and the most integrated of any of the Algonquian-speaking coastal people. The empire was ruled in those days by Wahunsonacock, who had expanded his domain from some six towns to about thirty in the mid- to late sixteenth century. John Smith, whose 1612 account of the region was based on considerable firsthand experience, thought that "they have amongst them such government, as that their Magistrats for good commanding, and their people for due subjection and obeying, excel many places that would be counted very civill." He described this "civill" rule as "monarchiacall government" in which "One as Emperor ruleth over many kings or governours."

This rule appeared absolute to Smith: "[W]hen he listeth, his will is a law and must bee obeyed." Powhatan had inherited his position and his authority, and would pass it on through inheritance as well, to which he had added many that he had conquered. He had constructed storehouses for his own use in "all his ancient inheritances," including storehouses of "Treasure, as skinnes, copper, perale, and beades," and, moreover, weapons. In Smith's account, the "inferior kings, whom they call werowances," were "tyed to rule by customes" but had power of life and death over their subjects, and had to pay tribute to Powhatan, by virtue of "hold[ing] all" (as if in feudal tenure) of him.[125] William Strachey, whose account supplements that of Smith, noted that the werewances owe "8 parts of 10 tribute" – a burden that was so heavy that Strachey thought it "robbes the poore in effect of al they have even to the deares Skyn, wherewith they cover them from Could."[126]

[123] Richard Greenevill, "An Account of the Particularities of the Imployments of the English men Left in Virginia," in Richard Hakluyt ed. *The Principal Navigations Voyages and Discoveries of the English Nation…* (London, 1591, mod. ed., James MacLehose, New York, 1904), p. 322.

[124] "The First Voyage Made to the Coast of America … in 1584," in Hakluyt, *Principal Navigations*, pp. 302, 306–308.

[125] John Smith, "A Map of Virginia, with a description of the countrey…" (Oxford, 1612), no pagination, this section is drawn from his account of government.

[126] William Strachey, *The Historie of Travel into Virginia Brittania* (London, 1612, mod. ed, edited Louis Wright and Virginia Freund, London, 1952), p. 87. In many places Strachey's account is

THE RIVER VALLEY CIVILIZATIONS: AMAZON,
ORINOCO, AND RIO DE LA PLATA

Mini-states with relatively low authority were prominent in the sixteenth-century valleys of the three great South American river systems, the Orinoco, Amazon, and Rio de la Plata. In all of them, the inequality rested on the labor of captured people, and the search for slaves may have been a prime cause for war. Slavery would allow a fairly democratic society to incorporate subordinate laborers without risking the rights of those who were free, and thus introduce the permanent inequalities that were latent but not realized in some of the free associations, such as the Caribs and Iroquois.

According to Michael Heckenberger, the northern system of social complexity probably first emerged in the middle reaches of the Orinoco valley around 500 BCE and was possibly associated with people who today speak languages of the Arawakian family, and with a pottery style called Saladoid/Barrancoid. Between the beginning of the Common Era and about 500 CE, these complex societies underwent a sort of diaspora, starting from the original homeland in the middle Orinoco and then expanding down the Orinoco and into the Caribbean. They followed the island chain northward and were established in the Greater Antilles islands of Hispaniola, Cuba, Jamaica, and Puerto Rico by the beginning of the Common Era. At about the same time they also occupied the many rivers that flowed out of the Andes into the Orinoco, in an area called the Llanos or flatlands, where water control was an important strategy. The next step was to move from the Orinoco to the Amazon, probably down the corridor of the Negro River, whose headwaters are very close to the headwaters of the Orinoco. The Arwakan expansion continued along these rivers, reaching their headwaters around 500 CE, where archaeological research has shown their arrival at the southern Xingu River in modern-day Brazil.[127]

The Orinoco-Amazon system was characterized by fairly weakly centralized and small mini-states. Nicholas Federmann, a German agent of the Fugger family who explored the interior of Venezuela on behalf of the Spanish crown and his employers, was among the first to encounter the Arwakan complex when he visited the Llanos of the Orinoco in 1530. He called the whole region the Caquetos, and his informants from the coast and the mountains thought

    word-for-word the same as Smith's, so differences are probably additional information deriving from Strachey's own observations. Modern scholars, finding this an unbelievably heavy burden, have suggested that the charges were against the total tribute collected by werewances and not against the people, although the text itself is quite unambiguous and even pointed on this issue; see Stephen Potter, *Commoners, Tribute and Chiefs: The Development of Algonquian Culture in the Potomac Valley* (Charlottesville, 1993), pp. 17–18, quoting Haynes's 1984 MA thesis at the University of Virginia.

[127] Michael Heckenberger, *The Ecology of Power: Culture, Place and Personhood in the Southern Amazon, AD 1000–2000* (London, 2005), pp. 37–66 for an overview, and the remainder of the book for specific exploration of the Xingu River cultures; see also Heckenberger, J. Christian Russel, Carlos Fausto, et al., "Pre-Columbian Urbanism: Anthropogenic Landscapes, and the Future of the Amazon," *Science* 321 (August 29, 2008): 1214–1217.

them very brave and warlike. They had, he was told, driven all the other people of the region into the mountains "so that they alone could have the most level and fruitful land." They only maintained good relations with the Coro, who lived near the sea, so that the latter would bring the Caquetos salt.[128]

The Caquetos was not politically unified – in fact, it was divided into mutually hostile mini-states with varying political systems. Varquecemeto, where Federmann made his base for a time, counted twenty-three villages, all well fortified, aligned along the river, and was more or less at war with all its neighbors.[129] Similarly Federmann thought nearby Hacarygua could put 16,000 men capable of bearing arms in the field, and although they regarded themselves as two separate "nations," they lived peacefully under a single authority. Vararida, another small polity in a different valley, was really a conjunction of loose federations, generally of three or four large villages; they could cooperate to attack external enemies, but they were generally hostile to each other.[130] Federmann noted, after being rebuffed in an attempt to buy a slave, that in fact the Caquetos were accustomed to buy, sell, and hold people as slaves.[131] Stratification in the region was thereby enhanced by the constant wars that enslaved many people; indeed, it is fair to argue that the constant mutual exchange of captured people was at the root of the social structure.

The Arawakan population of the large islands of the Caribbean was perhaps more centralized and stratified than the Orinoco. The early Spanish accounts of the island of Hispaniola suggest a multilevel aristocracy, in a society in which at the bottom were slaves and common people, and then the nobles ruling small sub-districts, while above them other noble classes controlled larger and larger districts until one reached the "kingdoms," of which there were five on the island at the time of Columbus.[132] The Taino word for ruler, *cacique*, was eventually used by the Spanish to refer to any indigenous ruler anywhere in the Spanish Indies.[133]

Tainos lived in large, circular multifamily houses that might hold ten or more householders and their families, and some twenty to fifty such houses made up a village. Caciques often had their own larger houses that included ceremonial and judicial spaces surrounded by smaller houses of their retainers. These villages with their caciques, numbering perhaps 3,000 people each, were the lowest unit of Taino society. For Peter Martyr and other early Spanish observers, however, there was little authority at the lower level; Peter described

[128] Nicholas Federmann, *Indianische Historia. Ein schöne kurtzweilige Historia* (Hagenau, 1557, mod. ed, Karl Klüpfel as *N. Federmann und H. Stades Reisen in SüdAmerica, 1529 bis 1555*, Stuttgart, 1859, which marks Federmann's original pagination that I cite [GB]), pp. 47–48.

[129] Federmann, *Historia*, pp. 50–52.

[130] Federmann, *Historia*, pp. 99–101.

[131] Federmann, *Historia*, p. 60. Federmann calls the slaves "navoria" – actually a word lent to Spanish from the languages of the central Caribbean.

[132] An excellent reconstruction of the precolonial geography, using the original sources and maps is found in Sauer, *Early Spanish Main*, pp. 39–48.

[133] Peter Martyr describes the meaning of this term as "good men, not cannibals"; *De Orbo Novo*, dec 1, book 2.

a country without laws or judges, which later testimony does not bear out, but he was probably correct in saying that the land was held in common, without private property in land.[134]

Walter Raleigh, visiting Guiana in the 1580s, reported a similar situation of stratified but fairly decentralized polities in the Guiana region around the mouth of the Orinoco. Much of the region was divided into "civill townes" ruled by "kings," of whom one, named Morequito, was the greatest, ruling over some of the other towns.[135] Robert Harcourt, another early English traveler, provided similar details of "lords" and "seigneurs" over towns, some of whom had risen to regional rulers.[136] Another report of 1665 – while somewhat late for the purposes of this specific discussion – presents some population data suggesting that larger provinces might hold as many as 6,000 or even 10,000 families, although smaller provinces could hold less than 1,000, all suggesting that provincial populations would number as high as 50,000 people.[137]

But these rulers were not particularly powerful and could not be said to exercise centralized authority, even at the local level. Harcourt noted that although they recognized both regional and town rulers, they had "no settled government" and each person "obey as they choose." The rulers had little power, but could punish murder and adultery and perhaps had greater say in resolving conflicts in a definitive way, and thus avoiding some of the endless violence that characterized free associations. Much surplus seems to have been generated by the labor of wives, so that polygamy was an important source of resources, although Harcourt also mentioned slaves, who presumably also served to generate revenue for the "captains" and "seigneurs."[138]

Arwakans of the northern Amazon system were first visited in passing several Spanish expeditions in the mid-sixteenth century, who described a series of "provinces" – Omagua (or Aparia), Machifaro, and Solimões – that lay along the banks of the western end of the Amazon, although without much depth into the interior.[139] They had large towns, continuous settlement or cultivation along the river and its islands, and the appearance of governmental authority;

134   Martyr, *Orbo Novo*, dec 1, book 3.
135   Walter Raleigh, *The Discovery of the Large, Rich and Beautiful Empire of Guiana* (London, 1595, mod. Ed. Robert H. Schombrugk, London, 1848, reprinted, New York, n. d.), p. 36, civill towne.
136   Robert Harcourt, *Relation of a Voyage to Guiana* [1613] (London, 1620, mod. ed. C. Alexander Harris, London, 1928), pp. 79–85.
137   "The Description of Guiana" in Vincent Harlow, ed. *Colonizing Expeditions to the West Indies and Guiana, 1623–67* (London, 1925), p. 136.
138   Harcourt, *Voyage*, p. 86; p. 93 where "servants" and "slaves" were killed at their master's death.
139   The Orellana expedition was described in the work of Gaspar de Carvajal, *Descubimiento de Rio de las Amazonas* (ed. José Toribio Medina, Seville, 1894[GB]) [critical ed from version in Oviedo and an incomplete copy in the Real Academia de la Historia]; informants in Omagua told the Orsúa expedition that the interior was uninhabited and they only dealt with the people of the river; Diego de Zúñiga, "Relacion muy verdadera de todo lo que sucedido en el Rio del Marañon…," *CDI*, 4: 226.

in 1540, the chronicler Gaspar de Carvajal noted some twenty-six caciques subject to the authority of Omagua.[140]

There was considerable enmity between the various polities on the river; even though Machiparo was separated from Omagua by a great depopulated space, the two were often at war. During Pedro de Orsúa's stay in 1560, 17 canoes from Omagua with some 200 fighters came to "to attack them and rob them and capture them [Machiparo's people]."[141] Carvajal believed that at the time of his visit in 1540, Machiparo could muster 50,000 men between the ages of 30 and 70, as younger ones did not go to war.[142] Christoval de Acuña's description, from the late 1630s, notes the same levels of authority and extent, as well as frequent wars, so much so that both sources note the presence of fortified frontier villages at the edges of their domains.[143] While the wars may have had many causes, one of the outcomes was the enslavement of captives, who were employed as dependent workers, to the point that slaveholders in Omagua refused to sell any to Europeans.[144] Mauricio de Heriarte, writing about the same people as he observed them in 1638, reported that there were many villages under "principals" who ruled over extended families, but who looked to a king of the whole district. Villages were fortified and raiding parties took many slaves, "some of which were sacrificed, but most serve in their fields."[145] When Father Laureano de la Cruz came to Omagua in 1647, he met some fifty fighters in ten canoes on their way to the Icagnates to "kill and rob, which we supposed they customarily did"; presumably these wars were small-scale raids that netted people among the other things that they robbed.[146]

As in the Orinoco, there was less centralization toward the mouth of the Amazon than at its source. Heriate's survey of the Amazon revealed this clearly, for he knew the whole length of the river. Near the coast and along the lower course of the Amazon, he noted that government was decentralized, being exercised by "principals" who were the heads of families. These principals governed their "relatives."[147] Higher up the river, at the mouth of the Tapajos, was "the largest village and population," where a ruler could bring, de Heriarte believed,

---

[140] Carvajal, *Descubrimiento*, p. 23.

[141] Francisco Vasquez, *Relacion de todo lo que sucedió in la Jornada de Omagua y Dorado hecha por el Governador Pedro de Orsúa* (mod. ed., Feliciano Ramirez de Arellano, Madrid, 1881 [GB]), p. 25. This expedition took place in 1560–1561.

[142] Carvajal, *Descubrimiento*, pp. 30–31.

[143] Christoval de Acuña, *Nuevo Descubrimiento del Gran Rio de las Amazonas* (Madrid, 1641[GB]), cap. 36, 51, 55 (fortified village);

[144] Acuña, *Nuevo Descubrimiento*, caps. 36, 51 (refusal to sell captives).

[145] Mauricio de Heriarte, "Descriçam do Estado do Maranham-Para-Corvpa Rio das Amazonas" (facsimile ed., Karl Antono Nowotny, Graz, 1964), pp. 72–74 (pagination of original manuscript). The manuscript was written in 1648, but as de Heriarte was chronicler to the expedition of Pedro Teixeira in the Amazon in 1638, his information about these distant regions probably derived from the earlier period, especially as he cites testimony he heard in this section.

[146] Laureano de la Cruz, *Nuevo descrbrimiento del Rio de Manañon llamado de las amazones...*(1653, mod. ed. Madrid, 1900) [GB], p. 79.

[147] De Heriarte, "Descriçam," p. 15.

"sixty thousand bowmen" to fight. In this country, "principals" governed villages of twenty to thirty large houses, and "had many slaves among them," and above all them was a "great principal" who was "very well obeyed."[148] There was another such polity at the mouth of the Negro River, governed by a principal named Tabapari whom de Heriarte decided to call a "king," who was "much obeyed" and had "diverse nations" under his authority.[149]

Slavery was an important component of the social inequality of even the smaller scale mini-states. Yves d'Evreux, a Capuchin priest who accompanied the French expedition to the island of Maranhao at the mouth of the Amazon in 1612–1615, noted the extensive local rules concerning slave behavior and marriages they were allowed or not allowed to make. The slaves were readily integrated into the society of the region, albeit as dependents, and undoubtedly with labor obligations that allowed the "principles," or elite, to live in relative luxury.[150] Such conditions were found all along the Amazon, as de Heriarte's survey reveals. But the families in question were undoubtedly swelled by slaves, as were those around Maranhão Island: de Heriarte noted that in their wars they customarily captured slaves, "who serve them or are sold to other nations [*naçõems*]."[151]

Conquest played a role in the political economy of the Amazon as well as slavery, for an interior province of Tapinambana was conquered, around 1600 according to de Heriarte, by Tupinambás from the coast, who had come into the interior in "search of the Terrestrial Paradise" and overcome the local people, while intermarrying with them so that "the two people became one."[152] Such conquests and unions of population may well have characterized the longer history of the valley as well, and, as we shall see, would continue when the Portuguese and Spanish came to conquer the region.

The southern end of the great complex was not unknown to the early European visitors and settlers; all along the eastern side of the Andes, in lands watered by the Amazon system, mini-states were flourishing in the sixteenth century. Archaeological work in the lowlands of the area reveals substantial earthmoving and water management strategies. These have ranged from creating special soils to increase the productivity of a difficult natural environment to constructing networks of raised terraces, settlements, and causeways, sometimes stretching for miles. The system, which stretches from the northern Gran Chaco in the borderland between modern-day Bolivia to Brazil and Paraguay dates back at least 2,000 years.[153]

---

[148] de Heriarte, "Descriçam," p. 41.

[149] De Heriarte, "Descriçam," p. 55.

[150] Yves d'Évreux, *Voyage dans le Nord du Brésil fait Durant les années 1613 et 1614* (Paris, 1615, mod. ed. M Ferdinand Denis, Paris, 1864 [GB]), fols. 48–51 (foliation of original marked in this edition).

[151] De Heriarte, "Descriçam," p. 17 in this case de Heriarte is probably relating information from the 1660s; on the revenge concept around Maranhao, see Claude d'Abbeville, *Voyage*, fol. 287v.

[152] De Heriarte, "Descriçam," pp. 48–49.

[153] Mann, Charles C., "Ancient Earthmovers of the Amazon," *Science* 321 (2008): 1150.

But while archaeologists occasionally speak of cities, the earliest visitors to describe the regions, while not placing them in the range of free associations, suggested a scattered population without a great deal of authority. Diego de Eguiluz, the Jesuit who recorded the establishment of Jesuit missions in the Mojos region – the core of the vast earthwork system that archaeologists have revealed – described a very scattered population: 4,000 people in more than 50 settlements (*pueblos*). Moreover this scattered population had very little authority: "all are independent of each other" and even though each one "recognizes a cacique, it was with such little subordination, that no one thinks they need to obey him." In fact, even wives did not obey their husbands or children their parents.[154]

The Arwakan-speaking inhabitants of the Amazon-Orinoco system thus generally lived in mini-states, perhaps because their expansion was related to the development of that form, but to the south of these great rivers, the Rio de la Plata system including the Salado, Paraguay, Paraná, and Uruguay Rivers was dominated by people speaking Tupi languages. The region serves as a reminder that common language and even some common customs do not necessarily create a common political culture. Although the people of the Rio de la Plata basin belong to the same Tupi linguistic (Guaraní in Spanish and Carijó in Portuguese) stock as the free associations of the coast north of São Paulo, they have been organized as mini-states for a long time, although these have also coexisted with free associations. Recent archaeological work has confirmed that social complexity, as manifested in archaeology by settlement hierarchies with patterns of larger and smaller settlements, groupings around large public plazas, and social differences among gravesites, which can be found at various places in the region as early as 1000 BCE, and reaching greater complexity in the early centuries CE in the region just north of the mouth of the Rio de la Plata.[155]

The early French voyage of Gonneville, around 1503, may well have visited this area. The people he met lived in towns of between thirty and eighty houses, each like a hall with multiple families in each. The land was divided into multivillage "cantons," each with its own king (*Roi*), none of which, however, enjoyed any particular material advantage over the others, as Gonneville saw it. Kings were well obeyed, he was told, and they had power of life and death over their subjects. Gonneville befriended one such king, named Arosca, and as a result he allowed the Frenchman to take his son back to France. In France, the young man was received as a nobleman, and eventually settled in Normandy, taking a French wife and founding a noble line.[156] This region was

---

154 Diego de Eguiluz, *Historia de la Mision de Mojos* (1696), mod. ed. Enrique Torres Salmando (Lima, 1884), p. 6; also AGI Charcas 25 ramo 5 no. 22, fols. 1–1v, Eguiluz, "Relacion summaria de la Apostolica Mision de los Mojos..." 1696.

155 José Iriate, "Landscape Transformation, Mounded Villages, and Adopted Cultigens: The Rise of Early Formative Communities in Southeastern Uruguay," *World Archaeology* 38 (2006): 644–663.

156 "Déclaration du voyage du Captaine Gonneville & ses compagnions ès Indes..." in Leyla Perrone-Moisés, *Le voyage de gonneville (1503–1505) & la découverte de la Normandie par*

probably also traversed by Alvar Núñez Cabeza de Vaca on his way to Asunción in 1542, where he described a multitude of fairly small mini-states.[157]

Substantial mini-states lined the upper courses of the Paraguay River, even as the lower course was dominated by egalitarian democracies. When Ulrich Schmidel traveled up the river during his nearly twenty years of travel and adventure with Pedro de Mendoza's expedition some time after 1536, he passed through a number of areas where people lived only on "fish and meat" before reaching the first mini-states, where the people grew corn and other agricultural products – perhaps a quick shorthand that reflected social organization.[158] The first of these mini-states he called Carijos (following Portuguese terminology). There the Spanish came to Lamberé, a large fortified town that Schmidel called a "city" (*stat*), near where the first Spanish municipality of Asunción was to be built.[159] From there northward up the river were additional mini-states, such as Xarayos, which had a king [*könig*] who was obeyed, holding court "in his own manner, like the greatest lord [*herr*] in the country."[160] Xarayo's king, named Camire, according to Pero Hernández in 1542, had a capital with 1,000 residents, and dominated at least four other nearby settlements.[161] Continuing along the river, Spanish met the Syberiss, like the Xarayos in "language and other matters."[162]

Further west, and along the Pilcomaya River, Schmidel met the Maieless nation, whose rulers had "their subjects [*unterthann*] who must hunt and fish for them and do as they are ordered, just as peasants [*pauern*] are subject to a nobleman [*Edelman*]."[163] Their country was extensive, having all the Chandés and "Thobonna" also subordinate to them "as vassals [*baisailles*] or subjects ... as peasants are subject to their lords," in all probability a group of mini-states collectively called Chiguanos in which a Guarani-speaking elite dominated a Arawakan-speaking peasantry.[164]

les Indiens du Brésil (Paris, 1995) pp. 21–23 (for a description of the country) and pp. 83–105 for the son's descendants in France.

[157] Pero Hernandez, *Comentarios de Alvar Nunez Cabeza de Baca* (Zamora, 1542), mod. ed. Serrano y Sanz) in *Relación de Naufragios y commentarios de Alvar Núñez Cabeza de Vaca* (2 vols. Madrid, 1906 [GB]) 1, caps. 6–7 (but this account gives few details on social structure).

[158] Ulrich Schmidel, *Warhaffigte Beschreibung aller schönen Historien von erfindung viler unbekanten Königreichen, Landschafften, Insulen unnd Stedten...* (Frankfurt, 1567, mod ed. Valentin Langmantel, Tübingen, 1889 [including emendation from MSS versions, marking 1567 pagination][GB]), "fish and meat" eaters: pp. 6 (Zechuruass/Charus) and Carendis (Querandis), 11 (Tiembus/Timbos),13 (Gulgeissen/Calchaquis), 14 (Zechennaus Saluaischco/Chanas), 15 (Kueremagbus/Macobis and Aigeiss/Agazes), and others as well. Agricultural people: p. 16 (Carijos). The English translation of the 1567 edition by Luis Dominguez in *The Conquest of the River Plate (1535–1555)* (London, 1891) is often unreliable.

[159] Schmidel, *Warhafftigte Beschreibung*, pp. 16–17.

[160] Schmidel, *Wafhafftigte Beschreibung*, pp. 34–36.

[161] Hernandez, *Comentarios*, cap. 59.

[162] Schmidel, *Warhafftigte Beschreibung*, p. 36.

[163] Schmidel, *Wafhafftigte Beschreibung*, p. 49 (Dominguez's English translation is quite misleading here).

[164] Schmidel, *Warhafftigte Beschreibung*, p. 51; for an interpretation of this system and its antecedents, see, for example, Tierry Saignes and Isabelle Combès, *Alter Ego: Naissance de l'identité chiriguano* (Paris, 1991).

In referring to the Guaraní along the Paraná River, the Jesuit Antonio Ruiz de Montoya noted, at the start of the seventeenth century when Jesuit missionaries were seeking to convert them, that they lived "in very small settlements … but not without government," a description which fills out the quick notes that Cabeza de Vaca made in crossing the region in 1542. Each one had "caciques" that all recognized as noble, "inherited from their ancestors, founded in having vassals and governing people." They were served by their people who farmed for them, made their houses, and gave their daughters to them when they needed them. Caciques had many wives, up to thirty, but they did not marry common people.[165]

There are no descriptions of the upper reaches of the Rio de la Plata system or the adjoining regions of the upper Amazon system until Portuguese arrived in the gold fields of Cuiaba in 1718. Here, and probably throughout the Rio de la Plata system, raiding and slavery played a critical role in social stratification. Antonio Pires de Campos, the first literate witness to describe the region around 1728, found a number of mini-states, such as the Cayapó who lived in "villages, each village with its cacique." The Cayapó lived by "raiding," with capturing people as an important goal; they ate the adults, Pires de Campos thought, but kept the youth as their "captives" and presumably to work their lands as slaves.[166] The Sarayez also lived in large villages, or perhaps small towns, as one consisted of more than 900 houses. These followed similar villages of which Pires de Campos named a dozen along with "many other nations."[167] The "Kingdom of Pirecis," he continued, contained a dense population, "so numerous that one cannot count their settlements or villages, many times in one day one passes ten or twelve villages," although he thought them not aggressive, fighting only defensive wars.[168] They were ruled by "caciques, or principals" who wore special insignia of carved jasper, but did not have "one head whom all obey like a king or cacique" but instead were divided into many independent polities. The "nation" of Mahibarez had the same language and customs as Pirecis, forming a similar stratified regional polity.[169]

Just as the Rio de la Plata region shows us that not all Tupi speakers were in free associations, so the kingdom of Janduim in Ceará shows us that the Gê speaking people also had mini-states as well as free associations. As with other Gê-speakers, the inhabitants of Janduim lived in small, mobile settlements,

[165] Antonio Riuz de Montoya, *Conquista Espiritual hecha por los Religiosos de la Compañia de Jesus en las provincias del Paraguay, Paraná, Uruguay y Tape* (Madrid, 1639, mod ed. Bilbao, 1892 [GB]), chapter 10, p. 49.

[166] Antonio Pires de Campos, "Breve noticia que dá Antonio Pires de Campos do gentio barbaro…" 1728, in *Revista do Instituto Histórico e Geographico Brasileiro* 25 (1862): 437 (the date in the heading is given as 1723, but internal evidence suggests a date of 1728).

[167] Pires de Campos, "Breve noticia," p. 443.

[168] Pires de Campos, "Breve noticia," p. 444; see also João Antonio Cabral Camello, "Noticias praticas das minas do Cuyabá e Goyazes…" (1734), in *Revista do Instituto Historico Geografico Brasileiro* 4 (1863): 496, who thought them incapable of fighting.

[169] Pires de Campos, "Breve noticia," 444–445.

having no "set dwellings, and moved them from time to time," because the arid climate and inhospitable environment required them to move according to "the time of year and the ease in finding food," according to a Dutch account of 1631.[170] The Dutch interpreter Rouloux Barro reported in 1647 that this mobility even included the king's capital.[171]

Still, Janduim had the characteristics of a mini-state. Johannes Rabi, who lived among Jandovi's people for four years, thought the king told his subjects "when they should rise and sleep, where they should go, when they should move their camp."[172] Janduim had a multitiered hierarchy of offices; a Portuguese land document of 1630 noted that the king's domains included five subdivisions, one ruled by his brother while another leader named Vvariju had twenty-four lesser leaders under his command.[173] In 1692, when Janduim surrendered to Portugal, the domains of its king Canindé consisted of 22 villages with some 13,000–14,000 souls, from whom 5,000 archers could be mobilized.[174]

Janduim included a hereditary nobility, "transmitted by blood," in which "magnates ate magnates" during a religious ceremony in which dead bodies were eaten. Military leadership was from the royal family, and the king's command passed on by heredity.[175] Beyond the nobility were servants, for when playing a game involving two teams carrying a heavy log, the group was accompanied by "women, servants [*famuli*], and children."[176] Royal taxation was usually expressed in the form of gifts in exchange for counter-gifts: Baro described one village leader who had been given his land by Janduim, "for him and his followers," and paid part of what he sowed to Janduim in exchange for seeds.[177]

WESTERN CARIBBEAN MINI-STATES

The coasts and immediate interior of modern-day Venezuela, Colombia, Panama and Nicaragua also hosted a wide range of small mini-states in a region where most people spoke languages of the Chibchan family. In some cases, the level of authority was high even when the territorial extent of the polity was not. Most of what is modern-day Panama in the early sixteenth century was divided

---

[170] De Laet, *Iaerlijck verhael* p. 402 (first quote) Barlaeus, *Rerum in octennium*, p. 419 (second quote).

[171] Rouloux Baro "Relation dv voyage de Rovlox Baro, interprete et ambassadeur ordinaire de la Compagnie des Indes d'Occident, de la part ... des Prouinces Vnies au pays des Tapuies dans la terre ferme du Brésil ... 1647," published as an annex to Pierre Moreau, *Histoire des derniers trovbles dv Bresil; entre des Hollandois et les Portugais* (bound in Augustin Courbé, *Relations veritables et cvrieuses de l'isle de Madagascar et dv Brésil...* [Paris, 1651]), p. 207–241.

[172] Barlaeus, *Rerum per octennium*, pp. 419–420; 432 (Johannes Rabii as source).

[173] Baro, "Voyage," p. 225.

[174] Ennes, *Guerra dos Palmares*, p. 422; see also Camara Coutinho to King, July 4, 1692, *DH* 34: 64.

[175] Barlaeus, *Rerum per octennium*, p. 424. The marginal note says "Nobilibus"; p. 428, "Magnatum cadavera à magnitibus devorantur." On royal succession, see De Laet, *Iaerlijck verhael*, pp. 403–405.

[176] Barlaeus, *Rerum per octennium*, p. 420.

[177] Baro, "Voyage," p. 214.

into quite small mini-states according to Pascual de Andagoya, who wrote an account of them as he saw them in 1514. They did not have, according to his description, "great pueblos, except that each principal person has three or four houses in his land," and furthermore, "the lords are small, as they have many lords, and they have great conflicts over fighting and hunting in which many are killed," which also included boundary disputes.[178] However, there were larger settlements as well: Gonçalo Fernández de Oviedo, who also lived in the area in the early sixteenth century, noted that the town of Nata, near the Pacific coast, had forty-five to fifty houses.[179]

There was a social hierarchy, for Oviedo noted that a lord was called quevi or tiba, a "lord of vassals," and subordinates were called saco. In any case, there was a ruling class "like knights or nobles [*hijos-dalgos*], separated from the common people." This division also included a slave class, as although many enemies were killed in wars, they also sought to "take and brand them to serve as slaves, and every lord has own brand," and high status people were carried on litters by these slaves.[180]

The surest sign of authority in mini-states was the power to decide disputes. "The lords settled disputes in person, and for this no judge had anyone other than alguaciles [an official] who go to seize people." Procedure was simple: each side stated their case, no witnesses were deemed necessary, the lord decided the case immediately, "and there was no further dispute."[181] Their jurisdiction was sufficient that they could put thieves and murderers to death.[182] As in mini-states elsewhere, the lords of Panamá had the power to demand an income from their subjects; even though Andagoya said he received no tribute or rent, he added, "except for personal service, which when ever the lord needs to build a house or sow fields or fish or make war, all have to come and do it." The hunting element probably involved large-scale communal hunts, assisted by fires to drive the animals into a killing zone. This labor was not repaid, but the lord typically had a festival with food and drink for the participants. Thanks to this system, the lords of the region "lacked nothing." However, nearby in the same "province," he noted that there were people who had no lords at all – "the heads of families were the lords among the people, and all lived in friendship with each other."[183]

---

[178] Pascual de Andagoya, "Relación de los sucesos de Pedrarias Dávila en las Provincias de Tierra Firme o Castilla del Oro," in Navarrete, *Colección de viages* 3: 393–395. There is an English translation by Clements Markham, *Narrative of the Proceedings of Pedrarias Davila*…(London, 1865 [GB]) p. 12; see also independent testimony of Oviedo, *Historia*, Book 29, cap. 26. Oviedo was both an eyewitness to the region and read copiously from writing left by others, including Vasco Nuñez de Balboa who left his papers to the historian on his death.

[179] Oviedo, *Historia*, Book 29, cap. 27.

[180] Oviedo, *Historia*, Book 29, cap. 26.

[181] De Andagoya, "Relación," (Eng. tr. p. 12) -13 (justice and revenue), 17 (hunting). Oviedo noted that the judge's assistants were responsible for executions; *Historia* Book. 29, cap. 26.

[182] Oviedo, *Historia* Book 29, cap 27 in which he maintains that theft was the most important crime.

[183] De Andagoya, "Relación" (English, p. 13.)

The pattern of mini-states in Panamá continued into Costa Rica. Although early Spanish visitors did not know the area, and it repelled their numerous invasions, a temporary occupation of Santiago de Talamanca in 1605 allowed a report of 1610 to record that they country was divided into many small polities, each anchored on a fortified *palenque* or village, and torn with constant wars. They were, according to the report, "very obedient to that which their caciques ordered," even in cases where they risked their lives in carrying the orders out, possibly an indication of some hierarchy but perhaps only suggesting that the caciques played primarily a military role.[184]

Farther north, in Nicaragua, the Pacific coast was home to a host of mini-states, some from Chibchan origins and others, called Pipil, that were related linguistically to the Nahua-speaking people of central Mexico who built the Aztec Empire. Oviedo, whose account of the region as he saw it in 1528–1529 is by far the most detailed, noted that there were two forms of rule: the Chibchan-speaking ones in the form of what he called "republics" dominated by councils of elders who rotated in office, but who were both wealthy and slave holders; and the Pipil-speakers who were characterized by dynastic rule of a single family. Both sets exercised state power, appointed officials, and delineated territory in two and three levels of authority, even though domains were usually only a few thousand people.[185]

If the coast of today's Colombia was dominated by fairly small mini-states, the interior behind it was in the process of creating much larger and more complex mini-states. The largest of the consolidated mini-states lay in the Muisca region around Bogotá in modern-day Colombia, for here the size and density of population suggest that the emerging political units of the sixteenth century were approaching imperial proportions. The region, which the Spanish initially called the "New Kingdom," did not have a common name for itself, nor a common language.[186] It had, however been the site of expanding political authority for perhaps a century before the arrival of the Spanish.[187] Two kingdoms had

[184] "Memorial para el Rey nuestro señor a la descripción y calidades de la provincial de Costa Rica," 1610 in Léon Fernández, ed. *Colección de documentos para la historia de Costa Rica* (10 vols, Paris, 1881–1907) 1: 157–158.

[185] Oviedo *Historia* Book 42, cap 1. See the thoroughly annotated French translation of Book 42 ed. Louise Bénat-Tachot, *Singularités de la Nicaragua de Gonzalo Fernández de Oviedo (1529)* (Paris, 2002) for interpretive information.

[186] Pedro Simón, *Noticias historiales de la conquista de tierra firme en las Indias Occidentales* 2nd Part, (1628, mod ed., Bogotá, 1891 [GB]), Noticia 2, cap 1, p. 114.

[187] This region is described in several different levels, first the initial accounts, some of which have survived, with few details but great immediacy, such as the account of Juan de San Martin and Antonio Lebrija, "Relación sbore la Conquista del Nuevo Reino de Granada," c. 1539 and Gonzalo Jiménez de Quesada, "Epitome de la Conquista del Nuevo Reino de Granada," c. 1539 in Juan Friede, ed. *Descubrimiento del Nuevo Reino de Granada y Fundación de Bogotá (1536–39)* (Bogotá, 1960), pp. 184–186; 253–273; then early chronicle accounts that take post-conquest reflection into consideration, such as that of Oviedo y Valdéz, *Historia general*, Books 25–26, written in the 1550s, and the first visitas, such as that of 1560, which delineated tribute payments and political arrangements for the Spanish but inquired into past history as

emerged: Zipa, whose capital lay in the town of Bogotá, and Zaque, with its capital at the town of Tunja.[188] These two kingdoms were fairly recent creations by the sixteenth century: their oral traditions, collected by Spanish authorities after the conquest spoke of their own expansion by conquest and annexation both of small territories and of larger domains of twenty-five to thirty villages each.[189]

The first Spanish to arrive in the area, in 1538, called them both "lord of many lords."[190] Indeed, the larger of the two, Zipa, had, according to the first Spanish survey in 1560, some 90–100 small towns and villages under its authority.[191] The elite in these kingdoms lived in large fortified towns, with elaborate dwellings that Goncalo Jiménez de Quesada, one of the conquerors, compared to paintings he had seen of ancient Troy.[192] There were several orders of these nobles: for example, the title Usaque, said to be equivalent to "duke" in Europe, whose domains were often situated along the borders. There were three such dukes in Zipa's domain: Guatavita, Ubaque, and Suba.[193]

Even the lesser lords were viewed with religious respect and reverence by their subordinates, collected tribute and labor dues, and had the power to command and to resolve disputes and ultimately the cells that made up the larger government of Zipa or Zaque. They possessed slaves, and they could order their people to labor, as happened when the Spanish held the cacique of Chia for ransom: the cacique ordered two "captains of Indians" to go for hidden gold, and they sent "those they held as slaves, and others from the pueblo." While military forces were apparently largely raised on behalf of the rulers by the various subordinates, at least some were in the command of the ruler himself, like the "Guesos" who manned frontier forts and were chosen from throughout the kingdom for their gallantry and paid by making them caciques of pueblos "which did not have legitimate heirs."[194]

THE DISINTEGRATED EMPIRES: THE MAYA: HEIRS OF MAYAPÁN

While the mini-states of southern Central America and modern-day Colombia were beginning to coalesce, the northern boundary of this region, inhabited

well, and synthetic histories that took both types of sources into consideration, such as Pedro de Aguado, *Recopiliacion historial*, written in 1582 (mod. ed. Bogota, 1906[GB]); and finally still more detailed accounts using oral traditions and documents, many of which are now lost, as well as intimate knowledge of the language and culture of a somewhat later time, such as Simón, *Noticias historiales*.

[188] For a modern survey, see Juan and Judith Villamarin, "Chiefdoms," in *Cambridge History of the Native Peoples of the Americas. Volume III, South America* (Cambridge, 1999), pp. 584–594.

[189] Villamarin and Villamarin, "Chiefdoms," in *Cambridge History*, pp. 584–594.

[190] San Martin and Lebrija, "Relación," p. 77, 84, 185.

[191] "Visita de 1560," in Hermes Tovar Pinzón, ed., *No Hay Caciques ni Señores* (Barcelona, 1988), p. 77.

[192] Jiménez de Quesada, "Epitome," in Friede, *Descubrimiento*, p. 265.

[193] Simón, *Noticias historiales*, Noticia 2, cap. 1, pp. 114–115; cap 8, p. 141; cap. 17, p. 168.

[194] Simón, *Noticias historiales*, Noticia 2, cap. 8, p. 141; cap. 14, pp. 158–160.

by the Mayan-speaking people, were heirs to a more ancient combined regime that reached back for millennia and touched the same sort of empire as the Muiscas were founding. The Maya are probably best known for their building and artistic work during the Classic period, from 200 BCE to 1000 CE, a period that had many wars and only ephemeral union, such as that of Chichén Itzá between the 860s and about 1000. Unfortunately, the monumental inscriptions that allow us to follow the Mayas in the Classical period stop around 1000.

It is unlikely that the whole of the Maya-speaking world was ever under one authority, although it does appear that a substantial section of Yucatán was united under Mayapán (1200–1441).[195] The ruins of Mayapán, although mute, suggest a capital worthy of its legendary reputation. According to the early Spanish missionary Diego de Landa's informants, Mayapán endured a civil war that ultimately tore the kingdom apart and led to the abandonment of the capital. The country subsequently broke up into sections following three great noble families: the Xius, the Cocoms, and the Chels.[196] There also were several other smaller kingdoms in the Guatemala highlands that were not a part of this political arrangement.

By the time the Spanish mapped the region in the mid- to late sixteenth century, there were some two dozen mini-states, typically centered on impressive stone buildings, some ruins of former temples or palaces, others newly constructed from their stones. These territories had carefully delineated boundaries, marked with objects and with care to include important resources, agricultural land, and so forth.[197] Their rulers claimed descent in long lineages, which would be filled out later as certificates of nobility for the Spanish, which stretched back to Mayapán. The founding ancestors were often deified, and books celebrating and elaborating their descent were the target of zealous Spanish missionaries like de Landa, who burned them and tortured their possessors.[198] These smaller entities were still ruled by an elite and performed the functions of a state, however, for according to de Landa, the lords "govern the town [*pueblo*], settling suits, ordering and adjusting the affairs of their communities [*republicas*]." At the same time, the people of the area built an elaborate house for the lord and his retainers, sowed and harvested his fields, turned over shares of hunting and wild products they gathered, and paid them much respect. Lords were always followed about

[195] Diego de Landa, *Relacion de las cosas de Yucutan* (1566), mod. ed., and French trans. ed. Brasseur de Bromburg (Paris, 1864), English translation by William Gates (Baltimore, 1937), sections 6, 9. De Landa destroyed many original Maya documents, although he preserved their content in this account.

[196] De Landa, *Relacion*, secs. 8–9. De Landa's statement that it had been 120 years since the abandonment of Mayapan is usually taken as indication that these events took place in the 1440s.

[197] Patricia McAnany, *Living with the Ancestors: Kingship and Kinship in Ancient Maya Society* (Austin, 1995), pp. 86–90.

[198] McAnany, *Ancestors*, pp. 22–31 on these lineage charters and their interest for Maya history.

by numerous retainers.[199] There was also considerable taxation and tribute, although de Landa did not dwell on it; early Spanish tribute lists, clearly drawn from the precolonial structures, mention large quantities of goods being delivered to the coffers of the political elite.[200]

However, there was not a landholding class in the sense that the European nobility held land, for de Landa was sure that all land was held in common, "and whoever occupies a place first, possesses it."[201] Labor, including service for the elite, was done in common with considerable mutual aid among the commoners.[202] The elite passed their office in the families; if no sons were available to inherit, then brothers or nephews might be called on.[203]

The Maya states were frequently at war; indeed, these wars and rivalries would aid the Spanish entry into the country. Rulers were assisted by professional captains and had "people chosen to be soldiers" whose numbers were supplemented in wartime by a draft. The armies and their leaders were supplied from their own resources, but also by public demands, so that the state held a monopoly on power, even though soldiers might be undisciplined and pillage the country even following the end of a war.[204]

The western regions of modern-day Guatemala, Honduras, El Salvador, and Nicaragua were controlled since about 900 CE by a group of Pipil-speaking (a branch of the Nahua family) mini-states, whose traditions claimed they came from the powerful Mexican empire of the Toltecs, a contention that finds some support in archaeology.[205] As in the Maya case, they claimed a unified past, although by the sixteenth century, they were divided into several mini-states, of which Cuzcatlán claimed superiority over much of the region.[206] Here, there were a number of independent mini-states, but there was a religious unity to the region with its own "Pope." The rulers included both caciques and principals within each state, and they obtained labor in the cultivation of their fields from commoners. People were required to go to war or to provide substitutes and the command of the cacique, and both secular and religious leaders were supported by the labor of the commoners and slaves.[207]

---

[199] De Landa, *Relacion*, sec. 20. McAnany, *Ancestors*, pp. 136–139 gives some idea of the volume of labor from post-conquest sources.

[200] McAnany, *Ancestors*, p. 135, based on the tribute list of Maní in 1549.

[201] However, see McAnany, *Ancestors*, pp. 84–86; 90–95 suggesting a more complicated system of holding land. In fact, de Landa actually states that cross-family cooperation was normal, which might oversimplify the actual situation.

[202] De Landa, *Relacion*, sec 20, 23.

[203] De Landa, *Relacion*, sec 24.

[204] De Landa, *Relacion*, sec. 29.

[205] Michael Smith and Frances Berdan, "Spatial Structure of the Mesoamerican World System," *The Post Classic Mesoamerican World* (Salt Lake City, 2003), pp. 21–31.

[206] A detailed history of the region based on oral tradition and perhaps documents is Francisco Antonio de Fuentes y Guzmán, *Historia de Guatemala ò Recordación Florida* (c. 1690 ed. Justo Zarragoza, 2 vols., Madrid 1882–1883 [GB]), caps. 2–3.

[207] " Relación hecha por el licenciado Palacio al rey D. Felipe II, en la que describe la provincia de Guatemala, las costumbres de los indios y otras cosas notables," March 8, 1576 *CDI* 6: 34–40. This is the earliest detailed account.

AFTER MONTE ALBÁN: OAXACA

Just as the Mayas were heirs of ancient splendor living in more modest but strat-ified societies, so on the other side of Central America, the Mixtecs of Oaxaca descended from their own illustrious past polities. Ancient Monte Albán was one of Mesoamerica's great cities, as old and nearly as important as Mexico's equivalent of Rome, Teotihuacán, and like Teotihuacán, it went through a decline. Archaeology and its inscriptions tell something of the story: beginning around 700 CE, the city of Monte Albán, which had once been the largest cen-ter in Oaxaca and perhaps ruler of an empire which had held Teotihuacán off, began declining. There was a hereditary dominant class, seated in the towns, enjoying palatial residences and served by an equally wealthy priesthood.[208] Much of their history was documented by a fourteenth-century chronicle that survived the conquest.[209] When the Spanish arrived in the region, they found two middling-sized polities, both of which had been resisting Aztec attacks since 1486, often acting in cooperation.

CAHOKIA'S REMAINS

The Mississippi Valley had known a period of substantial social and polit-ical integration in the centuries before the Europeans arrived, and as in Mesoamerica, they met only its remains. This culture took shape after about 900 CE, and was characterized by large central settlements replete with mas-sive pyramids, and clear signs of strong social differentiation in residential pat-terns, burial customs, and distribution of wealth.

Some scholars have argued that the Mississippian culture was integrated into several substantial states or even an empire. In the thirteenth century, the city of Cahokia, across the Mississippi River from modern-day Saint Louis, probably held as many as 20,000 people, living in the shadow of a vast com-plex of pyramids, one of which (Monk's Mound) was among the largest earth structures ever built. Other scholars argue that there is insufficient evidence to suggest this polity ever extended beyond several clearly related sites in the American Bottom region.[210]

In the fourteenth century, according to archaeological interpretations, Mississippian societies moved toward decentralization of authority and a

---

[208] A survey of this period is found in Joyce Marcus and Kent Flannery, "Cultural Evolution in Oaxaca: The Origins of the Zapotec and Mixtec Civilizations," *The Cambridge History of the Native Peoples of the Americas. 2.1 Mesoamerica* (ed. Ricahrd Adams and Murdo Macleod, Cambridge, 2000), pp. 394–403.

[209] The fourteenth-century chronicle is Codex Nuttal, fols 42–84, although chronological informa-tion is better understood in the early-sixteenth-century Codex Bodley. Later chronicles include the Codices Colombino and Selden. All the chronicles are published in good reproductions with commentary at www.famsi.org/research/poh./jpcodices/index.html

[210] For a discussion along with evidence, see Bruce D. Smith, "Agricultural Chiefdoms of the Eastern Woodlands," *Cambridge History of Native Peoples* vol. 1, part 1, pp. 267–292.

decline in size and structure. If Cahokia had been a center in earlier times, it was no longer that by the sixteenth century when Europeans arrived. In 1540, a northern reconnaissance party of Hernardo de Soto's expedition, the first literate witnesses to Late Mississippian culture found the area deserted around Cahokia, and archaeologists indeed argue that there was an "Empty Quarter" near Cahokia that developed as the Mississippian culture declined.[211]

If Europeans did not find an empire in the Mississippi basin, they did find a wide range of mini-states. The culture of Natchez, Louisiana, comes closest to what archaeologists consider typical of Mississippian culture, and Simon-Antoine le Page du Pratz, who lived near the Great Town of the Natchez from 1720 to 1729, described it thoroughly. It was in all probability the same polity that de Soto heard called Quigaltam when he passed in 1542, and it survived until it was destroyed by the French and their indigenous allies in 1729.[212] According to Le Page du Pratz, who interviewed high-ranking and knowledgeable Natchez, in former times their rule had extended "more than twelve days' journey from east to west and more than fifteen from south to north." At that time it "counted 500 Suns" under a single Great Sun, the title of Natchez' ruler. The empire fell, according to this account, because the sacred fire that the founder had given was allowed to go out, and had to be relit with "profane fire."[213] Internal strife and invasions had reduced the power of the Suns, and now the Great Sun of Natchez watched over a polity composed of a capital town – actually a complex of a ceremonial center with a pyramid and temple and surrounding hamlets – and eight other towns (ruled by Suns who were his brothers) with scarcely 6,000 souls.

Relative smallness of scale did not prevent eighteenth-century Natchez from having a stratified social structure that was divided into a noble and commoner class. A temple elder that le Page du Pratz interviewed explained how the polity had originated when a person descended to heaven and established their social order, creating, among other things, a rule of matrilineal descent among his daughters, and that the children of his sons should be only nobles and not succeed him. The nobles were further differentiated according to their relationships to power, so that the Great Sun and the children of his sister were all Suns, but his children and those of his brothers were of a special class called "Honored Ones"; meanwhile, other nobles' families were simply styled as nobles. A distinctive feature of the Natchez system was that the nobles were all required to marry the despised commoners, who nobles referred to as "Stinkards (*Puards*)"

---

[211] A thorough, archaeologically informed discussion of De Soto's entrada and the societies it met is found in Charles Hudson, *Knights of Spain, Warriors of the Sun: Hernando de Soto and the South's Ancient Chiefdoms* (Athens, GA, 1998), pp. 336–354 (the Mississippi portions).

[212] Karl Lorenz, "The Natchez of Southwest Mississippi," in Bonnie MacEwan, ed., *Indians of the Greater Southeast: Historical Archaeology and Ethnohistory* (Gainesville, 2000), pp. 143–150.

[213] Simon-Antoine le Page du Pratz, *Histoire de la Louisiane*...(3 vols., Paris, 1758) 2: 338–339. The English translation of 1776 is unreliable, but a modern translation by Gordon Sayre of the portions relating to the Natchez is at http://darkwing.uoregon.edu/~gsayre/LPDP.html

FIGURE 5. "Native in Summer" by Antoine le Page du Pratz. Courtesy of Special Collections, LSU Libraries, Louisiana State University.

and sacrificed in considerable numbers in noble funerals.[214] These "misalliances" lowered the status of the descendants of the elite male partners, but had no effect on the female's children – a feature of matrilineal succession.[215]

[214] Le Page du Pratz, *Histoire* 2: 334; 393–396.
[215] Sorting out exactly how Natchez kinship and succession worked has been a long-term problem in the history of the region. For an overview of this topic and a quite reasonable solution, see Lorenz, "Natchez," pp. 152–158.

If a residual Mississippian empire left its traces in the southern end of the Mississippi Valley, its traces also existed in the northern end, albeit in a less spectacular form, most notably because the northern wing ceased building the pyramids that stood out in Mississippian archaeology and at Natchez. French Jesuits, who began missionary work among the Illinois Confederacy that dominated the region around the core of ancient Cahokia in the 1670s, noted first that the region was divided into a number of small "nations" that had a sense of kinship (although not necessarily amity) among them.[216]

Each of these nations was quite stratified and their leaders possessed authority. Louis Hennepin, who traveled in the area in 1679–1680, thought the political system of the upper Mississippi Valley showed a marked contrast with the egalitarian democracies of Canada and the eastern Great Lakes region, which he knew well. Although he believed that the Illinois were "libertines" and "they have no great respect for their chiefs," he also believed that their "chiefs [*chefs*] have a more despotic authority" than those of Canada. Leaders carried a sacred fire before them – a crucial element of Mississippian society noted in Natchez traditions and practices – appointed officers, and had "valets" to serve them, and gave out "presents and gratifications at their will."[217]

Nations in the Illinois region were on the same scale as those subunits of the Mississippian culture that can be found in archaeology. The Jesuit Jacques Marquette, the first Frenchman to visit the region officially on behalf of the governor of Canada in 1673, was received ceremonially by the "Grand Captain of all the Illinois" at Peoria, his town [*Bourg*] of "fully 300 cabins."[218] When Marquette returned to Peoria in 1674 to preach, there assembled "all the chiefs of the nation with all the elders [*anciens*]," they numbered 500 between chiefs and elders, as well as "all the youth [*Jeunesse*]," which numbered more than "1,500 men" presumably men capable of fighting.[219] Hennepin thought there were even larger towns than Peoria, the town of the Grand Captain, for he noted the largest towns in the region had "four or five hundred cabins [*cabannes*] each with five or six fires [*feux*]" and each fire in turn sheltered "one or two families." Taken literally and making four people per family, these villages held somewhere between 8,000 and 24,000 people, or fully the same scale in population as Cahokia, if not in magnificence.[220] If Hennepin's observations are trustworthy, Peoria must have had a population in the 6,000–14,000 people range. Kaskaskia, a town of intermediate size, held, according to Marquette, 74 cabins (1,500–3,500 residents), and

[216] Louis Hennepin, *Nouvelle decouverte d'un tres grand paÿs situé dans l'Amerique* (Utrech, 1797), pp. 217–218.

[217] Hennepin, *Nouvelle decouverte*, pp. 218 (libertines), 306 (comparison).

[218] Jacques Marquette, "Le premier voÿage qu'a fait le P. Marquette vers le nouuelle Mexique…" 1674 in *Jesuit Relations* 59, pp. 116–125, spelling Peoria "peoüarea."

[219] Marquette, "Recit du second voyage et la mort du P. Jacques Marquette," 1675 *Jesuit Relations* 59, pp. 188–189.

[220] Hennepin, *Nouvelle decouverte*, p. 197.

elsewhere in his travels the priest found a village of 6 or 7 cabins, who had recently hived off a larger settlement to gain more food.[221] This three-order settlement pattern is remarkably similar to ones observed archaeologically in most of the Mississippian culture.

Social stratification may well have been anchored on slavery. The Illinois made many wars, even against distant neighbors to the south and west. Captains who commanded war parties were distinguished from the rest by wearing red.[222] Pierre Delliette, who lived for many years in Illinois country starting in the 1680s, described a war party sent out around 1690 in which each chief commanded a group of about twenty fighters.[223] The purpose of these war parties, according to Marquette, was to "make slaves," which they sold "at a high price" to other nations, although they probably also employed a good number themselves – in fact, Marquette was offered one himself as a gift.

When the Sieur de la Salle made the first French descent of the Mississippi in 1682, he encountered the Arkansas, who were in fact between the Illinois and the Natchez. Henri de Tonti, who traveled with de la Salle and wrote an extensive report, thought them the most "polished" people he had seen. As with the Illinois and Natchez, they maintained a sacred fire that was never allowed to go out in their major temple. The ruler met with a large group of elders from nine neighboring villages in an elaborate palace with decorated walls ten feet high.[224]

While the core of the Mississippian society was the valley of the Mississippi, archaeologists affirm that many of the features of the core region could be found along the rivers of the eastern highlands, and even the coasts of the Carolinas, Georgia, Florida, and the Gulf Coast states from the twelfth century onward. When the Spanish *entrada* led by Hernando de Soto followed a meandering route from Florida to Louisiana through Tennessee and Arkansas from 1540 to 1543, he found much of the southern part of the modern-day United States covered with a patchwork of small but highly stratified mini-states, bearing names such as Coosa, Cofitachiqui, Mabila, and Pahaca. Although not united politically, they were quite large (archaeologists seeing their total populations in the 10,000 range) and, as the archaeology suggested, highly stratified, with distinct social classes and significant differences in wealth. Although it seems unlikely that they were politically united to the core Mississippian regions in

[221] Marquette, "Premier voyage," p. 73–74, (size of Kaskaskia) Dablon, *JR* 59, 170–171 (small settlement).

[222] Marquette, "Premier voÿage," pp. 125–127; on the gift of a slave, pp. 120–121.

[223] Pierre Delliette (signed as "De Gannes"), October 20, 1721 [actually 1702] (tr. and ed. Theodore Pease and Raymond Werner as *The French Foundations, 1680–1693* in *Collections of the Illinois State Historical Library* 23 [1934]): 376–378.

[224] Henri de Tonti, "Relation de Henri de Tonty," November 14, 1684, in Pierre Margry, *Découvertes et etablissements des français dans le ouest et dans le sud de l'Amerique septentrionale* (Paris, 6 vols., 1879–1888) 1: 600–601.

the valley of the great river, they possessed many cultural traits in common, and looked to the core region as an ideological and aesthetic role model.[225]

Whatever the Spanish *entradas* saw in the sixteenth century, most of these polities were gone by the end of the seventeenth century, when the English and the French visited the areas and began to settle permanently. Of the polities named by de Soto, only Cofitachiqui was still around in 1670, when for a time it established relations with the English of Charleston. But soon this state also disappeared. Indeed, what the Europeans were witnessing as they explored much of southeastern and central North America was the transformation of stratified societies into free associations, by a process which can only be poorly understood. It was a process whose origins predated the sixteenth century and continued unabated into the eighteenth.

When the English colonized South Carolina in 1670, the people in the immediate vicinity were definitely organized into free associations, with perhaps the only connection to the Mississippian being the continuation of a tradition of sacred fires and a sense of a hereditary nobility with no real power.[226] John Lawson, traveling into South Carolina in 1700, observed that the ruler of the Santees was an exception: he was "the most Absolute Indian ruler in these parts," and Lawson noted that he could order any of his subjects killed "that hath committed any Fault that he judges worthy of so great a punishment." He went on to note that this was unusual in the area, observing that among all the others, murder was typically punished through the execution of revenge by the victim's kin, as was typical of egalitarian democracies. Lawson provided a description of this king's predecessor's tomb, in a pyramid where personal property was placed. This was in contrast to other burials in which the deceased might be buried more or less where he or she died, suggesting ultimate roots in the Mississippian culture.[227]

But this post-Mississippian culture was rare in that day. Among the nearby Waxsees, even though they were led by a "king" and "war Captain," all public business was conducted in a special house, which travelers often called "state houses," where decisions about war, trade, and other matters were made. The deliberations in these places were dominated by groups of elders. Although there was a sense of rank, Lawson thought that all decisions were reached by long deliberation, and that this was a general practice in Carolina.[228] These council houses were commonplace; Lawson regularly saw them or met in them, and his description suggests that decision making was more diffuse than the Mississippian model suggests.

---

[225] For a thorough discussion of the archaeology and its connections to the entrada, see Hudson, *Knights of Spain*, pp. 144–335.

[226] Adair, *History of American Indians*, pp. 105–108.

[227] John Lawson, *A New Voyage to Carolina...* (London, 1709 [docsouth]), p. 20–22.

[228] Lawson, *New Voyage*, pp. 37–39; for the idea that it was a general practice, compare his comments, made generally for the area he visited, on p. 195.

Timberlake, who visited the Cherokees in 1762, described their government in his day as partly aristocratic and partly democracy. Their leaders were
"chose according to their merit in war or policy at home." Decisions were
made in councils, which settled matters in deliberation, where eloquence and
powers of persuasion counted for a great deal, so that Timberlake thought
that the way to power in Cherokee society was the ability to speak in council.[229] An earlier visitor, George Chicken, went through the Cherokee towns in
1725 and noted, for example, that at the upper settlements, they met in "town
houses" where representatives met and debated public matters, the delegates
being "head men" of the place.[230] Most towns had one; Terriquo had two as
two groups had confederated in one place. While there were "kings" in his day,
the towns were not anxious to submit to royal authority, and Chicken, wishing
to deal with as few leaders as possible, headed off requests by individual towns
to meet with him. Cherokees described their governmental group themselves
as being composed of "head men and warriours" as they did in various letters
they wrote to the governor of South Carolina in 1751.[231]

Councils met in state houses – James Adair, who lived for forty years in the
region, wrote in 1775 that "every town has its state-house … where almost
every night the head men convene about public business, or the towns-people
to sing, dance and rejoice."[232] The state house of Chote was the "metropolis"
of the Cherokee country; when the "headmen of each village" assembled in it
to discuss peace with the English in 1762, according to Timberlake, it could
hold some 500 people.[233]

The power of councils greatly limited the capacity of the aristocracy to compel obedience, even in war. Timberlake observed that the political leaders he
met among the Cherokees could not punish anyone who had done wrong, but
could only deliver them to those they had wronged for punishment.[234] Social
differentiation was essentially merit-based, for when he heard enumerations
of famous leaders, Timberlake recorded that many were noted for their deeds
in war, but others primarily for their powers of persuasion and reputation for
justice.[235]

Democracy in government was also coupled with equality in goods. Adair
noted of the Chickasaws in 1775 that they had a "community of goods that

[229] Henry Timberlake, *The Memoirs of Lieut. Henry Timberlake* (London, 1765 [Göttinger
Digitalisierungszentrum]), p. 55.
[230] Samuel Cole Williams, ed., *Early Travels in the Tennessee Country, 1540–1800* (Wautaga Press,
1928), pp. 93–103.
[231] William L. McDowell, Jr., ed., *Documents Relating to Indian Affairs, 1750–1754* (Columbia,
SC, 1958), pp. 62–63; 74–76.
[232] Adair, *History of American Indians*, p. 18.
[233] Timberlake, *Memoirs*, p. 31–32.
[234] Timberlake, *Memoirs*, pp. 33, 68; elsewhere he does mention the council as having condemned
people and prepared them for death at the stake, but that women who bore the title "Beloved"
could set them free; p. 71.
[235] Timberlake, *Memoirs*, pp. 71–73.

prevailed among them, after the patriarchal model and the early Christians."[236] Cherokees, according to Timberlake, did not allow any property to pass on from one generation to another, so as "to make merit the sole means of acquiring power, honour, and riches."[237] The Cherokees used dances in which the bravest people would dance, recite their heroic deeds and then give a donation that went to relieve those suffering misfortune, or for public necessities.[238]

What political elite there was did not resolve disputes, because the only public punishment was to turn wrongdoers over to their victims for revenge. Lawson thought that the law of revenge was general in every place he visited in North or South Carolina except Santee. Timberlake heard from the Cherokees he knew that in former times they tortured their enemies for revenge, but in later years integrated them through marriage.[239] The same was true of the interior regions the English contacted in the early eighteenth centuries. The Choctaws, Creeks, Cherokees were all similarly organized, even though their ancestors can be clearly attested by archaeology as well as de Soto's reports as having once had much more stratified societies.

IMPERIAL STATES

American mini-states sometimes were united into larger entities; sometimes there is little evidence of regional unity. In only a few cases, however, there were much larger entities, imperial in scale and of long duration, that dominated as much space and as many people as the biggest polities in Europe or Africa. When the Spanish arrived in America, only two such entities – the Aztec and Inca empires – existed. Both thrived in areas that had a long history of episodic imperial integration.

THE VALLEY OF MEXICO

The heartland of the Aztec Empire was the Valley of Mexico, the highland region that had also served as the capital region for the two earlier episodes in regional integration, the empire of Teotihuacan from the first century BCE to the third century CE, and perhaps a Toltec empire from about 900 to 1200. The end of Toltec rule, if it was a unified empire, in the thirteenth century had been followed by complicated period of shifting power centers, but by the time the Spanish arrived, the imperial mantle had been taken up by three powers: the Aztec Empire, the largest and perhaps most effective, but also two other substantial polities that organized multiple subordinate mini-states, the Trascan state of Michoacán on the northwest, and the emerging, but still republican

---

[236] James Adair, *The History of the American Indians, especially those Nations adjoining to the Mississippi* (London, 1775 [AMP]), p. 17.

[237] Timberlake, *Memoirs*, p. 68.

[238] Timberlake, *Memoirs*, p. 69.

[239] Timberlake, *Memoirs*, p. 58.

kingdom of Tlaxcala on the east. The history of these struggles, which had important implications for the development of Spanish hegemony, was partly illustrated in documents, or is known from oral tradition collected soon after Spanish conquest. These codices, however, were not written narrative accounts, but rather elaborate pictographic systems that provided some information, but which had undoubtedly always been supplemented by orally transmitted elaboration, some of which was then written into historical works composed in the colonial era, such as Fernando de Alva Ixtlilxochitl's accounts of the history of the Toltecs.[240]

Although Teotihuacán might be regarded by archaeologists today as the foundation of Mesoamerica's imperial tradition, to the inhabitants of the region in the sixteenth century, that honor belonged to the Toltecs of Tollan. Ixtlilxochitl, writing in the early seventeenth century, recounts the Toltec's origin as wandering people from the north as he learned of it from oral traditions and old documents in his possession.[241] Archaeological evidence suggests that the various wandering northerners who invaded Mesoamerica were militaristic nomads, "Chichimecas," who in fact won power largely through serving as mercenaries among contending elites.[242]

The chronicles of the Aztecs show them to have originated in such a Chichimec group. After entering the service of Tezozomoc of Tepenac in 1391, they settled on the swampy land near Lake Texcoco where the Aztecs build their capital of Tenochtitlán. Through mercenary service to the Tepanacs and then as independent actors under their leader Itzcoatl (1427–1440), the Aztecs formed the Triple Alliance with two other similar lakeside towns or military garrisons, called Texcoco and Tlacopan. Under Itzcoatl's guidance, the three towns mustered their forces, conquered and subdued neighbors, and gradually built an empire, which was still growing and consolidating when Hernán Cortes arrived in 1519.

As a reflection of their origins as mercenaries, the Mexica might be thought of more as a military organization than as a wandering ethnic group, not so much the folk migrations of people as the deliberate movement of small groups of professional warriors along with their families and, no doubt, their integrated captives, voluntary recruits, and others drawn perhaps as much from

[240] The earliest known book of this sort is Codex Mendoza, the first part of which deals with history, and the second gives a tribute schedule of the Aztec Empire (and ends with an "ethnographic" description of the country). It was composed for Viceroy Mendoza at the very start of Spanish administration, but was soon followed, first by other illustrated codices, and then by written out histories.

[241] Fernando de Alva Ixtlilxochitl, *Historia de la nación chichimeca* (c. 1640, ed. Germán Vázquez Chamorro, Madrid, 2000), cap. 2. Ixtlilxochitl provides dates for the Toltec rulers in both the Christian and Mesoamerica calendar, which would place these events in the sixth century. It is possible that this represents a dynasty that grew up under Teotihuacán rule, or that the dates have been wrongly converted and the *katun* (the fifty-two-year eras in which Mesomamerican dates are given) was wrong.

[242] Michael E. Smith, "The Aztlan Migrations of the Nahuatl Chronicles: Myth or History?" *Ethnohistory* 31 (1984): 153–186.

the settled population as from their original homeland. They were organized in town wards or military subunits called *calpulli*, as these were also the basic units of their field armies. The nobility, or officer corps, were known as known as *pili*, "Precious feathers from the wings of past kings," and thus the royal house came to serve as the military and administrative elite. The commoners, on the other hand, were called *machehualli*. It should not be surprising in this background that all males were expected to undergo military training in special schools established for this purpose.[243]

According to Ross Hassig, the Aztecs were a "hegemonic empire" – a collection of territories held together by threat of force. As the Aztecs took over each territory, they allowed them to continue governing themselves under their ancient ruling families and following their own law, but required to pay tribute to the Aztecs, much as groups like the Muisca were doing in the sixteenth century. This system of government was not expensive and allowed the Aztecs to maintain a relatively small standing army, but it only allowed a low level of integration. Aztec wealth derived from demanding relatively limited tribute from a vast areas rather than intensively exploiting a smaller area. Rebellions were handled as much by mobilizing allies or other subordinate territories to use their resources as by centrally directed forces.[244]

On the other hand, the Aztec had additional resources at their command by the time Cortes arrived, which set them apart from the smaller polities of Colombia and allowed them a larger and potentially a longer-lasting empire, like the empires of Teotihuacán and Toltecs that preceded them. The most important strategy and resource came from colonists sent out by the Aztec elite into the subordinate territories. These colonies or garrisons were often located in frontier areas, but were supported by groups of permanently dependent workers, called *mayeque*. These military estates were ultimately under control of the central government and were let out as revenue assignments to units of the army and their commanders. At the same time, the Aztec leadership declared that future gains from war would be distributed based on service.

This organization created many new opportunities for the Aztec elite. They could both draw tribute from self-governing conquered territories (probably not very great) and augment it by the revenue coming from the new colonies or garrisons, rendered by the *mayeque*, recruited from the ample supplies of captives taken in their wars. At the same time, the imperial leaders managed to hold down the independence of these commanders by rotating them and making continued enjoyment of their benefits contingent on success and loyalty.[245]

Had the Aztec elite continued the policy of sowing such garrisons, as well as other similar estates in the hands of nobles and merchants throughout their

---

[243] Nigel Davies, "The Military Organization of the Aztec Empire," *Atti de XL Congresso Internazionale dglie Americanisti* (Rome, 1972), pp. 213–214.

[244] Ross Hassig, *Aztec Warfare: Imperial Expansion and Political Control* (Norman, 1988).

[245] A carefully documented description of this system is found in Ross Hassig, *Trade, Tribute, and Transportation: The Sixteenth Century Political Economy of the Valley of Mexico* (Norman, 1985), pp. 103–109.

empire, they might have achieved a much more fully integrated polity, but in the event, the Spanish arrival, large-scale revolt by allied territories, and hostile unconquered neighbors who made common cause with the Spanish put an end to the empire.

For all its incipient power, however, the Aztecs had not completed the integration of the region into their system. On the east, the independent state of Tlaxcala, itself a conglomeration of mini-states ruled by a sort of republican elite, resisted Aztec advances – their armed forces, allied with those of Cortés, would overthrow the Aztecs.[246]

Aztec empire building directed to the north met with the emerging Tarascan state (probably called Purépecha) with its capital at Tzintzuntzan (in Michoacán, Mexico). The most important information on their history came not from indigenous writing, if there was any, but a systematic collection of oral traditions, edited in Spanish by the Franciscan priest, Jeronimo de Alcalá and other collaborators, around 1540.[247] The traditions represent the state as being formed not so much by militant invading Chichimecs (as the Aztec state was), but by their alliance and cooperation with the indigenous elite of the region.[248] This military combination made a number of conquests, and by the fifteenth century, it was expanding and in open and so far successful conflict with the Aztec empire. Unlike Tlaxcala, however, the Tarascan state developed a complex bureaucracy under royal control, intertwined with a priestly elite that managed the affairs of a multiethnic state that was moving toward a single identity.[249] As described in the *Relación de Michoacán*, the critical source for its structure at the time of the arrival of the Spanish, order was maintained through a royally appointed group of bureaucrats, responsible for functional duties, collecting revenue, overseeing collective labor in the ruler's lands, ordering the population (indeed supervising just about every sort of activity), and maintaining religious requirements. These offices were created, according to the account, by the ruler named Zizíspandáquare (ruled from 1454 to 1479 and given credit for the whole organization), but they were hereditary from his time forward: "[A]ll these offices are held by hereditary succession from those

246 R. Jovita Baber, "The Construction of Empire: Politics, Law, and Community in Tlaxcala, New Spain, 1521–1640" (PhD dissertation, University of Chicago, 2005), pp. 27–65 (a brief but up-to-date survey of the institutions at the time of the Spanish contact).

247 For a careful study of the text and its relationship to history, see Cynthia Stone, *In Place of Gods and Kings: Authorship and Identity in the Relacíon de Michoacán* (Norman, 2004). Stone's work focuses on the work as one of essentially multiple authorship and relying heavily on oral tradition.

248 [Jerónimo de Acalá], "Relación de Michoacán," part 3, cap. 5, fols. 16–17v (1539), mod ed. Moisés Franco Mendoza (Michoacán, 2000) on line at http://etzakutarakua.colmich.edu.mx/proyectos/relaciondemichoacan/rm/indiceRM.asp, marking the foliation of the original MS.

249 Helen Pollard, *Tariacuri's Legacy: The Prehispanic Tarascan State* (Norman, Ok, 1993), modified in "A Model of the Tarascan State," *Mesoamerican Archaeology* 19 (2008): 217–230. For ethnic issues, see Pollard, "Ethnicity and Political Control in a Plural Society: The Tarascan State in Pre-Hispanic Mexico," in Elizabeth Brumfiel and John Fox, eds., *Factional Competition and Political Development in the New World* (Cambridge, 1994), pp. 79–88.

who had them, when one died the cançonçi [ruler] places one of his sons [*hijos*] or a brother in his place."[250]

THE INCA EMPIRE

The Inca Empire was also heir to large regional polities in the past as were the Aztecs, although the absence of written records and uncertainty of the archaeological records make the relationships unclear. Large-scale polities in the Andean region and west coastal South America may have emerged very early, perhaps as early as anywhere else in the world. The immediate past, however, were the complex and probably imperial archaeological cultures of the Middle Horizon period, which lasted from about 600 CE to 900 CE. Two complexes – Wari (traditionally spelled Huari) in the north and the ruined city of Tiwanaku (traditionally spelled Tihuanaco) in the south – were probably the nuclei of substantial empires. But all trace of them had disappeared by the time the first traditions were recorded, and there is no account of traditions leading back to them, as there was for Tollan in the Mexican highlands. Indeed, local people could offer no explanation for the ruins of Tihuanaco when Spanish travelers and administrators asked about them.

Unlike the Aztecs and other Mesoamerican cultures, the Incas did not have a system of writing, although the *quipus* (knotted strings used as a mnemonic) device helped with accounting, and perhaps even in recalling oral tradition. Hence all history of the region is known from oral traditions collected in writing in the mid- to late sixteenth century. There were many collections of traditions made in the sixteenth century, some by Spanish and some by Peruvians or mixed-race people. Most writers of tradition sought to prove points, and even institutional descriptions were sometimes colored by the purposes of the writer. For example, Pedro Sarmiento de Gamboa, who was commissioned by the Viceroy Toledo in 1571 to collect tradition and who did so diligently from a number of witnesses who swore individually to the truth of their statements, was also clearly interested in showing the Inca rule as despotic and cruel, and hence resented by subjects. Gacilasco de la Vega "The Inca" and Sarmiento's near contemporary, on the other hand, was of half-Inca descent and anxious to prove that the rule of the Incas had been benign, even exemplary. In this account, I have relied especially on the history written between 1551 and 1560 by Juan de Betzanos, who had come to Peru in 1538, married the wife of the Inca Atahualpa, and spoke Quechua fluently.[251]

Taking tradition and archaeology together, it appears that the Inca Empire began its rise in the late thirteenth or early fourteenth century in an area where there were many small mini-states, but no larger formation. Other states were vying with the emergent Inca kingdom for power, for the defining event, in the

---

[250] [Alcalá], *Relación*, part 3, cap 1, fols. 6–8v (quotation on 8–8v).
[251] Juan de Betzanos, "Summa y narración de las Yngas…" (1551), Cap. 8–32 mod. ed. and English translation Roland Hamilton and Dana Buchanan as *Narrative of the Incas* (Austin, 1996).

vision of tradition was the victory that Prince Cusi Yupanqui won over another expanding domain, Chanca. In the aftermath of the victory, Cusi Yupanqui took the name Inca Pachacutec and founded the Inca Empire, along with many of its characteristic institutions.[252] A traditional chronology places the victory over Chanca in 1438, making the Inca Empire roughly the same age as the realm of the Aztecs, and like the Aztec domain it was still expanding in the sixteenth century.

The victory that brought Yupanqui (who ruled from 1438 to 1471 in the traditional chronology) to power did not lead him to exercise absolute authority over his followers and allies, to whom he owed a great deal and whose local writ he could scarcely challenge. Indeed, the core of the Inca Empire was very much a sort of federation of relatively small mini-states that had succeeded in gathering additional resources from conquest. After defeating the Chancas, Yupanqui gathered his allies from the region to prepare them for this new burst of conquest, and they willingly did so, according to Betanzos' account, because they wished to share in the spoils.[253]

These resources were enough, however, to send the Inca ruler on a campaign of conquest that soon brought large domains under their control on all sides. He was able to increase his resources by making strategic alliances within territories he wished to annex, and then demanded taxes from them, while drawing supervisors from his core region. In his conquest of the Soras, Inca Yupanqui accepted the surrender of some mini-states, but had also imposed his own choice of rulers on some of the districts that resisted more fiercely. According to Betanzos, those rulers were fed to hungry jaguars and those who survived the jaguars were reduced to slavery; Inca Yupanqui "named certain caciques [local rulers] to be lords of those towns and provinces of the ones the tigers [jaguars] ate." He also placed supervisors drawn from his Cuzco area allies over them.[254] Huayna Capac (1493–1525), ruling as the Spanish spread out across the Caribbean, spent much of his life conquering the "Kingdom of Quito" to the north, and the civil war that broke out between his sons Atahualpa and Huascar upon his death in 1525 pitted these newly conquered lands against the ancient core of the empire around Cuzco.

The collection of conquered territories, which were constantly rebelling, according to the chronicles, had to be held together by a centrally controlled administration, funded by substantial revenues in the hands of the imperial elite. The founding monarchs built a number of such institutions. Like the Aztecs, the Inca empire (actually called Tahuantinsuyu) relied heavily on internal colonization to keep otherwise fairly disparate self-governing communities together. Attitudes about the Inca past were reflected in the history of the development

---

[252] I have accepted the testimony of de Betanzos, "Summa," following María Rostworowski de Diez Canseco, *History of the Inca Realm* (trans. Harry B. Iceland, Cambridge, 1999), pp. 23–25, and 30–36 for discounting the different version of Garcilsaco de la Vega.

[253] Betanzos, "Summa," cap. 18.

[254] Betanzos, "Summa," cap. 19.

of the *mitmaq* or internal colonization system. Sarmiento de Gamboa attributed the development of the *mitmaq* system to Pachacuti Inca Yupanqui, but it probably grew from a more ancient system of vertical colonization. Because the Peruvian highlands are located in the equatorial zones, but reach to great heights, it is possible to find micro-ecological zones ranging from tropical to arctic within a fairly small area, depending on elevation. To take advantage of this diversity, Andean villages have regularly sent out colonies of their numbers to make settlements in the various ecological zones and share their production with others in the system. The system was probably quite ancient, although much of the evidence of it is only known from colonial-era documentation.[255] However, in more recent years, archaeologists have discerned it as far back as Middle Horizon times.

It would seem, however that in the hands of Pachacuti and his successors the mitmaq system went much farther and involved many more people and fundamentally different principles than the original concept. Sarmiento de Gamboa, an unsympathetic writer who was commissioned by the Spanish governor, more or less to prove the Inca government was tyrannical, noted boldly that following his victory, Pachacuti "depopulated all the lands that were within two leagues of the city" of Cuzco, which was given to the inhabitants of the town, "sending the deprived population elsewhere." This made the population of Cuzco happy, for they "were given what cost little." In this way, Sarmiento's informants told him, "he made friends by presents taken from others."[256] Indeed, Sarmiento de Gamboa attributes the use of the system of *mitmaq* as a response to constant rebellion – a plan, "colored with some appearance of generosity, was really the worst tyranny he perpetuated." Here he carefully depopulated some regions, taking "from one 20 from another 100 more or less according to the population of each district." These were then sent to other places, attempting to match the ecology of their home regions, but far enough away from their homes that "they could not communicate with their relations or countrymen." Here they were given seeds, and power over the local people, so that they should report on plots to the nearest governor.[257]

Given its source, one might discount Sarmiento de Gamboa's claims, but Betanzos, whose chronicle does not have these polemical qualities, nevertheless describes the displacement of thousands of people following the conquest of Quito in the north. Pachacuti ordered the inhabitants of Quito and the

---

[255] This insight belongs to John V. Murra, *El mundo andino: población, medio ambiente y economía* (Lima, 2002), for its fullest development.

[256] Sarmiento de Gamboa, *Segunda parte de la Historia General llamada Yndica...* [MS 1572] (mod. ed. Buenos Aires, 1943) cap. 32. I have followed the English translation of Clements Markham, *History of the Incas* (London, 1907, reprinted New York, 1999) for quotations. Sarmiento de Gamboa's account of Yupanqui's life was drawn from the corporation (ayllu) of his descendants (see *Historia*, cap 72), which included Domingo Pascac, born in 1482 (eleven years after the Inca's death), and Juan Hualpa Yupanqui, born in 1497, and thus one generation removed from the actual events. The other informants were younger, generally born in the first decades of the sixteenth century, and thus probably two generations away.

[257] Sarmiento de Gamboa, *Historia*, cap 39.

surrounding areas to give him 15,000 people to take south with him, young married men who would be given seeds to start cultivation in the Cuzco area. Following this, he ordered other towns and provinces to repeat the process.[258] Pachacuti's successor, Topac Inca, extended the system he inherited from his father, systematizing it over the empire.[259] He gave the colonists privileges and liberties, according to Sarmiento de Gamboa, and in conquered areas continued the displacement of population, as well as moving people from mountains and forested areas to plains and to more fertile regions, precisely to prevent them from rebelling and as a means to maintain Inca domination over a large area.[260]

The empire expanded this system by sending out as *mitmaq* thousands of colonists, not just to different ecological zones, but also to different territories as a way of building estates. In this way, for example, Huayna Capac sent *mitmaqs* to colonize the province of Cochabmaba "in all parts, the natives being few and there was space for all, the land being fertile."[261] Colonists were sometimes voluntary and were given rich lands in distant areas as a reward for services, and sometimes they were groups that were being punished for rebellion or insubordination by being driven from their homelands to other regions. Sometimes, as in the case of the regions around Cajamarca, they were brought together from various other parts of the empire. In either case, they were required to keep their own customs and not to mix with the population in the areas to which they were sent. Because colonists were often rewarded with good land, and even with labor services from the inhabitants in the areas where they were planted, they found a cool reception that kept them from becoming integrated into the region of their new homes. They were thus dependent on the empire to protect them, and tended to be loyal for that reason. They were frequently planted in border areas to preserve imperial control and be a first line of defense against external enemies.

If they were sometimes privileged, however, they still produced large surpluses for the benefit of the state. In the Cochabamba valley, for example, the Incas supported some 2,000 grain houses, with the product of fields that were worked by some 25 groups serving in rotation (*mit'a* system). The original population of the area had been sent elsewhere as *mitmaq*, and the groups liable for this labor had been transplanted into the region through the same *mitmaq* system.

---

[258] De Betanzos, "Summa," Cap 26.

[259] Sarmiento de Gamboa, *Historia*, cap. 50. For his account of Tupac, Sarmeinto de Gamboa probably relied on the allyu of his descendents, who were born a generation after the Inca's death, as the oldest (Cristoval Pisac Tupac) was only born in 1522. However, he also had the testimony of Domingo Pascac, who was born during Tupac's lifetime and was about eleven years old at his death, as well as the testimony of Francisco Anti-Hualpa (or Viracocha's allyu), who was ten when Tupac died; thus both were eyewitnesses to the last years of his reign.

[260] Sarmiento de Gamboa, *Historia*, cap. 52.

[261] Sarmiento de Gamboa, *Historia*, cap. 59. The oldest of his informants were likely to have known of these events from their own recollections and not indirectly from tradition.

In addition to colonists, the Inca state set aside other areas to be worked for the benefit of the state, and these in turn generated large surpluses. Sarmiento de Gamboa also attributed much of the intensification and regularization of this to Topa Inca, noting that "Tupac Inca imposed rules and fixed the tribute they must pay, and divided it according to what each province was to contribute to the general tax."[262] Much of this surplus was deposited in storehouses that dotted the countryside and held immense quantities of material goods. Such storehouses were available to keep the army on the march, or to provide relief in case of famine.

Topa Inca not only standardized taxes, but he also created a new governmental grid to overlie the pattern of submitted mini-states and consolidated districts that his father and he had conquered. Yupanqui expanded this program and regularized it to all parts. One part of the new program was the division of the population into groups of 10, 100, 500, 1,000, and 10,000, probably as a means for allocating taxation and labor. This system was then placed in the control of a new class of administrators called *kurakas*, who were answerable only to the Inca.[263]

This positions of kuraka was not to be inherited, but was given to "the man who had the most ability and aptitude for the service." These officers were to be supported by being given estates and servants to work them, although they were not their personal property but belonged to the state, for "Curacas could not take a thing of their own authority, without express leave from the Inca." In addition to appointing *kurakas* in conquered areas and replacing the older class of rulers, Topa organized newly reduced and relocated communities to the authority of kurakas that he appointed over them.[264] At other times, they were worked by slaves or transported workers called *yanas* (who were brought individually, as opposed to the larger groups that came as *mitmaq*). Topa Inca is also credited with regularizing this class; according to Sarmiento de Gamboa's version of the tradition, when the Inca was slaughtering resisters in one province, his sister entreated him to allow them to surrender and live as her servants. Because the war was being waged in the region called Yana-yacu, they were called yanacuas.[265]

The Inca elite had other projects that cut through the whole empire and promised to increase their power. One example was the highway system, a feat of engineering that was probably as much reconstructing or connecting an existing road system as building them from scratch. Nevertheless, the highways allowed the rapid movement of large numbers of troops along them. Similarly, large storage facilities were located throughout the empire along these roads to provide pre-positioned supplies for their movement; the goods and foodstuffs

[262] Sarmiento de Gamboa, *Historia*, cap. 52.
[263] Sarmiento de Gamboa, *Historia*, cap. 50.
[264] Sarmiento de Gamboa, *Historia*, cap. 52.
[265] Sarmiento de Gamboa, *Historia*, cap. 51.

in them were also useful for famine relief, although their original purpose was probably military.

The Inca elite also endowed a new set of religious institutions, with a new priesthood devoted to new gods, or gods whose power was extended. Subject people were made to provide estates and income to the priesthood that served these deities, and although local deities were not suppressed, the royal court allowed considerable patronage and wealth for the elite.

While these various institutions put great power in the ruling elite, the Inca Empire had serious barriers to complete centralization. One of the most important was the power of the various elite families who lived near to Cuzco and had supported the Incas in their rise to power. They had been richly rewarded with lands and estates, and their network of power extended far and wide. They hoped to be able to rule alongside the Incas, or at the very least to check their power.

In addition to the Cuzco elite, the families of past members of the royal family also posed important threats to absolute centralization. The centers of power for these families were the mummified remains of their ancestor and the corporate communities that formed, ostensibly to assist in their worship. The allyus had become very strong and controlled substantial revenue, and could be the source of intrigues against the ruling family.

Expanding the empire allowed the Incas to extend their wealth and control more fully in the outer parts of the empire than at Cuzco. This tendency to form an imperial power base at the periphery came to a head following the death of Huayna Capac in 1525. He and the bulk of the regular army had been on campaign in the northern regions, where they had organized their conquests into a sort of special kingdom of Quito where rule was more straightforward and hierarchical with less necessary attention being paid to powerful families. Huayna Capac's son Atahualpa managed to claim the loyalty of this group. On the other hand, his brother Huascar won the loyalty of the elite of Cuzco, and Spaniards were able to exploit this civil war in the conquest period.

The tremendous variety of social structures of indigenous America would be an important guide to its conquest and occupation in the sixteenth century and beyond. Where there were powerful empires with taxation systems and bureaucracies, Europeans would be able to insert themselves into an existing system and make use of it to generate income for themselves. On the other hand, where there was no central authority, where decision making was fragmented, and where there was little differentiation of wealth, Europeans could not find an existing system to extract wealth to work with. In those cases, they could only use free associations as military allies, or to enslave them and make use of their labor as individuals.

PART III

THE NATURE OF ENCOUNTER AND ITS AFTERMATH

Three processes brought about three different sorts of cultural mixtures, which in turn moderated the contact of cultures in the Atlantic. These three processes were conquest, colonization, and contact. Which process developed where was very much dependent on the nature of the Atlantic societies in contact, and particularly the non-European partner to the interaction.

Conquest appears straightforward, although upon close examination it is not nearly as uncomplicated as it appears. Conquest takes place when there is a switch in sovereignty between states, so that, for example, Native American or African states surrender to a European invader. For conquest to take place, at the very least there has to be a state in existence, some person or authorized group has to have the authority to surrender and to make that declaration valid for their subjects for it to have any real force. Conquest took place largely under Spanish auspices in the Americas; in Africa, only Angola was conquered by the Portuguese and Spanish. Once conquest took place, the organization of the state was used by the conquerors to govern the population, at least initially. Only after many years might new institutions and changed circumstances alter the situation to the degree that the preexisting state apparatus was effectively replaced by something new, and in many cases the older status system survived for centuries.

Colonization took place in areas where there was no native population, for example on São Tomé Island off the coast of modern Nigeria, Barbados in the Caribbean, or Bermuda in the mid-Atlantic; or where the indigenous population could not be conquered. In places like Brazil, the eastern Caribbean, or much of North America, Native American societies were not organized into states and thus could not surrender or acknowledge a change in sovereignty. Such societies could be eliminated through enslavement, war, or disease, or they could be physically displaced, but they could not be conquered and their institutions could not be used for continuing governance. In other cases, such as in many parts of North America and even in Brazil, there were small or weak political authorities that might initially be treated as conquests and allies, but which were ultimately either displaced, enslaved, or eliminated and subsequently colonized. Therefore, in these situations, Europeans brought in a population from elsewhere. People might be brought in as free colonists, indentured workers, or slaves from Europe, Africa, or other parts of the Americas (including the surrounding Native American populations). European laws then governed the new population, modified as necessary to fit the situation.

Contact describes areas where there was no change of sovereignty, no enslavement, and little population movement. It developed in areas where Europeans met established political and social orders that they could not overcome, displace, or enslave. In this situation, Europeans were forced to coexist with another society, interacting formally and informally through diplomacy and trade. The European presence in Africa is a prime example of contact, where for centuries Europeans visited as traders or established limited extraterritorial presences in the form of forts and factories. There were contact situations in the Americas as well, although often along shifting frontiers, such as the gradually moving frontier of Euro-American advance in North America from the coast toward the Great Lakes, the Spanish frontier north of Mexico into the U.S. Southwest, or the ever-expanding frontier of the Amazon and Rio de la Plata River systems. Contact situations were also found in Brazil and along much of the north coast of South America and even in the smaller Caribbean Islands before the Euro-African population numerically overwhelmed the local population.

5

Conquest

Europeans are usually regarded as conquerors in the Atlantic World, first and foremost. The European conquest of the Canaries, the Spanish invasion of the Caribbean and then of the mainlands of the Americas, culminating in the conquest of Mexico and Peru, provide a model. The driving engine of conquest is often held to be overwhelming military superiority, with guns, horses, and steel weapons being the crucial ingredients. Indigenous peoples of the Atlantic basin, even those living in large and imposing empires in Mexico or Peru, could not stand before this military machine in this presentation, and in spite of their overwhelming numbers, they were forced to yield to the invaders. In bringing this military effort to bear, the Europeans were also aided by disease, which, while not under their control, helped soften up otherwise resistant populations and allowed a firmer and more commanding post-conquest society by demoralizing and weakening the Native American population. Diseases to which Europeans had immunity were highly fatal in American populations, producing a differential die-off that might destroy as much as 90 percent of the American population in tropical areas. This die-off not only eliminated resistance, but also made the imposition of European patterns of law and culture easier.[1]

More recent work in military history, however, has forced a modification of this position of overwhelming military superiority.[2] There is no question

---

[1] The idea that great power led to great abuses, while the characteristic of some of the contemporary sources, such as Bartolomé de las Casas, *Historia de Indias*, and especially his polemical *Brevissima relacion de la destruction de las Indias*, was particularly pronounced in considerable anti-heroic literature, such as initially Carl Sauer's carefully researched *The Early Spanish Main* (Berkeley, 1969). Such ideas especially underlay writing occasioned by the 500th anniversary of Columbus's voyages, with a strong emphasis on human rights violations, for example Kirkpatrick Sale, *The Conquest of Paradise: Christopher Columbus and the Columbian Legacy* (New York, 1990).

[2] See the important collection of essays dealing with African, Asian, and American examples, Wayne E. Lee, ed. *Empires and Indigenes: Intercultural Alliance, Imperial Expansion, and Warfare in the Early Modern World* (New York, 2011), especially 19–108 and 167–276, and Lee's own stimulating introduction, pp. 1–16.

that Europeans had developed a technology and art of war that differed from those in use in both Africa and the Americas. But this technology and art of war, while sometimes extremely useful and effective, was not adequate to allow unassisted conquest of any of the populations that Europeans met in the Age of Discovery.[3] European military technology, as we have seen, revolved around armored cavalry and fortifications on the one hand and projectile weapons designed to neutralize armored cavalry and destroy fortifications on the other.

But the innovations in weapons and tactics occasioned by the Military Revolution were not necessarily decisive in dealing with the many military challenges Europeans faced as conquerors, particularly given that from the beginning they were very seriously outnumbered and fought in ecological environments different from their homes. Armored cavalry faced serious problems in tropical regions by virtue of weight and heat factors, while the projectile weapons designed to penetrate a knight's armor had a very slow rate of discharge. Slow-firing weapons cannot allow small numbers of people to defeat larger numbers unless other factors are in play. Neither African nor American tactics were designed around use of substantial numbers of armored soldiers, so they were prepared to take a certain number of casualties from projectile weapons before closing for hand-to-hand combat, in which projectile weapons were nearly useless. Firearms sometimes had a shock effect initially, but once Atlantic armies became habituated to them, they soon learned how to use the disadvantages of their slow rate of fire, and ultimately adopted them themselves.

Cavalry had a greater impact in the Americas, where horses were unknown, but they could not have any substantial value in those parts of Africa where there was an established equestrian tradition (for example, the savanna areas of West Africa) or where horses could not survive for any significant period of time in the disease environment (the Guinea coast and Angola). There were places in the Americas, however, where climate and geography produced good cavalry country, and there the Spanish lancer was a terrifyingly effective military asset. But the Spanish could not deploy large numbers of horsemen given the difficulties of transporting mounts. Cavalry are most effective only when massed in sufficient numbers to inflict sustained casualties on fleeing infantry, and the dozens and on occasion low hundreds of mounted men in Spanish service did not meet this decisive threshold. Native Americans were reasonably quick in establishing tactical countermeasures against the horsemen after the initial encounters. Indeed, Native Americans soon became excellent horsemen themselves, and the era of cavalry superiority ended by 1600, long before many parts of the Americas were conquered.

These factors are crucial to understanding the real pattern of conquest, which was in fact the politics of alliance. Europeans made their conquests with substantial participation by Native American and African armies, who supplied

---

[3] See the important challenge to the received wisdom of Matthew Restall, *Seven Myths of the Spanish Conquest* (Oxford, 2003).

the bulk of the soldiers with whom Spanish superiority was established in the Americas or Portuguese authority in Angola. The politics of these alliances, which were as much contracts of mercenary services in the service of Native American and African aims as they were independent campaigns of conquest, shaped the way in which conquest actually took place.

The particular significance of the facts of military history in conquest go a long way to establishing the sort of cultural and political maneuvering room that various conquered peoples had in the post-conquest era. Confronting the conquerors as cooperative allies gave many Native American groups considerable leeway to shape their role in the post-conquest culture, and even those societies that were overcome militarily had advantages that derived from the status of the allied Native American rulers.

FRANCE, PORTUGAL, AND SPAIN IN THE CANARIES

In light of these concepts, the European conquest of the Canary Islands, which began in the early fifteenth century, provides both an interesting model, employed elsewhere in the Atlantic basin, and a healthy reminder that European military technologies and methods might not be able to prevail even against fighting techniques that seem remarkably primitive. Because the Canarians were organized into small states, however, Canarian leaders were able to make alliances and to surrender to Europeans in a way that some other Atlantic groups could not, and thus they were ultimately conquered or incorporated.

When the Canarians were first visited by Europeans during the early fourteenth century, they possessed no metals, and their principal means of fighting was with thick staffs enhanced by fire-hardened points, as well as by throwing stones. They did not know horses, made no watercraft, and were unable to prevent oceangoing shipping from landing on their coasts. But Canarian stone-throwing skill was remarkable, as the chroniclers Pierre Boutin and Jean le Verrier noted when describing European soldiers returning from battle in 1404 with bloody heads and arms and legs broken by stones. "Understand," they wrote, "that they throw and handle stones much better than Christians do, it seems as if they were using a crossbow when they throw them." With a well-aimed throw, a Canarian stone could break a shield "and the arm behind it."[4] A later chronicler, Abreu Galindo, described military duels in which opponents faced each other while standing on pedestals and had both to hit their

---

[4] Pierre Boutier and Jean le Verrier, *Le Canarien, ou livre de la conqueste et conuersion des Canariens...en l'an 1402*, chapter 75. There are two versions of this manuscript, one in Rouen written from two originals in 1625 (published first in a bilingual English-French edition by Richard Henry Major (London, 1872[GB]) and in French only by Gabriel Gravier (Rouen, 1874 [Gallica])). It is clearly manipulated to give a version friendly to Jean de Bettencourt in support of his family's claims, while an original one, written before 1420 and covering only events to 1405, was uncovered in the British Museum in 1899 and shows de la Salle as the driving force of conquest. A full variorum edition and Spanish translation has been made by Elias Serra Rafols and Alejandro Cioranescu (3 vols., La Laguna, 1959–1964).

opponents and avoid being hit.[5] The use of stones as projectile weapons was so entrenched that, according to another chronicler, the inhabitants of Gran Canaria still eschewed the use a crossbow as late as 1493, a century after their initial contact with European marauders.[6]

The first successful conquest of the lightly populated eastern group began in 1402 under the Norman (French) knights Jean Bettencourt and Gadifer de la Salle.[7] Others who followed used the same tactics in the century-long period of conquest.[8] The Canarian adventure established a pattern that would repeat itself over the rest of Spain's engagement in the Atlantic world, which involved military alliances as much as outright conquest.[9]

Everywhere they went, the Normans, and then the Portuguese and Spanish, used the same approach: making alliance with a local ruler, perhaps offering protection from enemies or an advantage in a war or civil war, and then using that alliance as a means of establishing their formal government and settlement in the islands. At Lanzarote, King Guardafia accepted Bettencort as king, but "as friends, not at all as subjects, and he [Bettencourt] promised to protect them against any who would do them harm," probably against other European marauders.[10] Protection was only part of the struggle, for the Normans also supported a pretender to Gaudafia's throne named Asche. After a number of political crises and maneuvers, the Normans brokered a settlement in 1404, which left Guardarfia as king but subordinate to the Normans and subject to taxation, while also enjoying the revenues of a large estate set aside for his support.[11] Guardarfia in turn offered them "all archers and soldiers" to assist

5   Abreu Galindo, a now lost Spanish manuscript of 1632 only known from its English translation by Glas as *The History of the Discovery and Conquest of the Canary Islands* (London, 1764 [Humboldt]), (a Spanish retranslation with useful notes is found in *Historia de la conquista de las siete Islas Canarias* [Santa Cruz de Teneriffe, 1977]), Book II, chapter II, pp. 67–68. In his notes Glas indicates that Abreu Galindo wrote his history from old documents found on the island in his day (Chapter III, p 14 fn.).
6   Alonso de Espinosa, *Del Origen y milagros de la Santa Imagen de nuestra Señora de Candelaria* (Seville, 1594, mod. ed. Alejandro Cioranescu, Madrid, 1958), Book 3, chapter 6, (English translation, *The Guaches of Teneriffe*, ed. and trans. Clements Markham [London, 1907 [GB], reprint 1972]), see p. 97.
7   Boutier and le Verrier, *Canarien.*
8   See Felipe Armesto-Fernández, *Before Columbus: Exploration and Colonization from the Mediterranean to the Atlantic, 1229–1492* (Philadelphia, 1992), pp. 171–173.
9   For an excellent overview of the conquest covering the complexities of inter-European diplomacy over the islands as well as the alliances with Canarians, see Armesto-Fernández, *Before Columbus,* pp. 175–212.
10 Boutier and le Verrier, *Canarien,* chapter 4. The name of the king ruling at the time does not come from this source, but from Abreu Galindo, *History,* Book I, chapter 3, pp. 11–13. European marauders were mentioned in several sources: Leonardo Torriani, "Descritione et historia del regno de l'isole Canarie," (1594), fol. 9, mod. ed. and Portuguese translation, José Manuel Azevedo e Silva, *Descrição e História do Reino das Ilhas Canárias antes ditas Afortunadas* (Lisbon, 1999), pp. 25–26, for the earlier expeditions; for later ones, see Abreu Galindo, *History,* Chapter II, pp. 9–11. This is seconded by less specific (but more contemporary) information in Boutier and Le Verrier, *Canarien,* chapter 61, noting that Spanish and other corsairs had carried off most of the people, there remaining only some 300 when the Normans arrived in 1402.
11 Boutier and Le Verrier, *Canarien,* chapters 30–34; 46.

de la Salle in the conquest of neighboring Fuerteventura, in exchange for a promise to give him some of the captives to repopulate his lands. De la Salle ordered all efforts be made to avoid killing potential workers in the battle.[12]

Guardarfia's soldiers then bolstered the Norman's conquest of Fuerteventura, where again a local rivalry and a brokered peace put the Normans in charge.[13] With the armed forces of these two smaller islands ready to assist him, in 1405, de la Salle proposed that the process could be repeated so as to create an empire by conquering other islands.[14] The campaign achieved modest results, and was badly defeated in Gran Canary.[15] In all the campaigns, the European deployed quite substantial forces, including as many as 1,000 infantry and sometimes as many as 100 armored horsemen. Yet even bolstered by Canarian allies, such attacks might not succeed. In 1443, the Portuguese attacked Gran Canaria using allies from Palma, without success.[16] In another unsuccessful attack on Gran Canaria in 1460, Portuguese commander Diogo da Silva lost so many men from his allies in Lanzarote and Fuerteventura that they claimed he ought to be charged with murder.[17] Allied Canarians fought on both sides in the war between Spanish and Portuguese conquerors at Gran Canaria in 1478–1483.[18] The final campaigns, to take Teneriffe in 1493–1497, were also marked by initial defeats, but the increasingly large participation of Canarians in the final engagements turned the tide, although even then, the leader Alonso de Lugo was successful only because the Canarian defenders could not unite against them.[19] Thus, even people who at first glance seemed primitive and

---

[12] Boutier and Le Verrier, *Canarien*, chapters 73–74; the kings' names come from Abreu Galindo, *History*, chapter IV, p. 15.

[13] Boutier and Le Verrier, *Canarien*, chapters 78–79, 87–88.

[14] Boutier and Le Verrier, *Canarien*, chapter 84.

[15] Boutier and Le Verrier, *Canarien*, chapter 85–87. The chronicle makes no mention of a settlement with Palma, and not much of one on Hierro, but concludes by noting that both were "conquered." Torriani relates that the party was received joyously, as a local prophetess had predicted they would come, and the people believed them to be gods. This allowed the party to trick many into leaving to be sold as slaves in other islands; "Descritione," fols. 88v–89v, ed. pp. 171–173.

[16] Zurara, *Chronica*, chapter 88.

[17] Torriani, "Descrittione," fols. 40v–43, ed. pp. 90–96 (on the charge of murder); Abreu Galindo, *History* Book I, Chapters XII–XIVI, pp. 43–50 (where the complaints of the local people and their refusal to continue is noted).

[18] Torriani, "Descrittione," fols. 44v–45v, ed. pp. 101–102. More details on these rivalries in Armesto-Fernández, *Before Columbus*, pp. 175–202. For later events, Hernardo de Pulgar, *Crónica de los muy altos y muy poderosos Don Fernando é Doña Isabel...* part 3, cap 18 in Cayetano Rosell, ed *Crónicas de los Reyes de Castilla* (vol. 3, Madrid, 1878 [GB]), and Torriani, "Descrittione," fols. 45v–46v, ed. pp. 104–106; and still more details on the battles and maneuvers are found in an even later source, J. Viera y Clavier, *Historia General de las Islas Canarias* (Madrid, 1772).

[19] Espinosa, *Origen y milagros*, Book 3, chapters 4–5; Pulgar, *Crónica*, part 3, cap 18; see similar statement in de Valera, cap 76, perhaps based on the same source. Espinosa, *Origen y Milagros*, Book 3, chapters 8–12. The division of the indigenous people, while noted in Espinosa, is described differently in Torriani, "Descrittione," fol 72–72v, ed. pp. 144–147, in a way that suggests greater division.

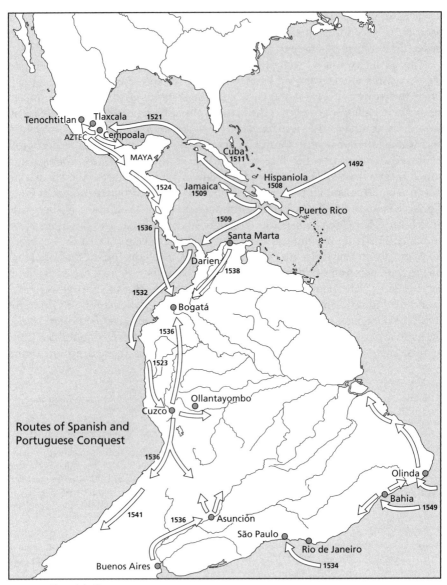

MAP 5. Spanish Conquest.

unable to resist armor, horses, and crossbows could only be defeated by the combination of European and Canarian forces.

THE SPANISH IN THE CARIBBEAN: ALLIANCE AND CONQUEST

We can see very similar politics of alliance and conquest in the earliest Spanish operations in the Caribbean. When Columbus came to the island of Hispaniola, the first American conquest, he met an ongoing military and political situation in which he was able to insert himself. Hispaniola was divided into nine distinct small states that competed with each other over territory and relative hegemony. Some had managed to subordinate the others and charged them tribute and imposed other sovereignty-limiting conditions. At some point before Columbus's arrival, one of these states, led by Caonabó and located in the center of the island, had achieved a certain level of domination.

Guaconari, whose state was the first one with which Columbus made extensive contact, was chafing under this situation and hoped that perhaps he could make an alliance with the new arrivals that could give him an opportunity to offset Canabó's advantages. He was impressed with Spanish swords and other steel products that promised some land-based military utility. He promised the Spanish an alliance and allowed Columbus to build a fort in his land and leave some Spaniards behind in the fort when the Admiral returned to Spain in 1493. When Columbus came back to Hispaniola, however, he found the settlers dead, and Guaconari claimed they had been killed in action against Canabó. Other reports, however, suggested they had fought among themselves, or had been killed by Guaconari's men in disputes over women.[20]

In spite of this inauspicious beginning, Columbus continued his alliance with Guaconari and added the support of a second cacique named Guarionex. His conquest of Hispaniola, much like the Canaries, was built on alliances and working within the local rivalries. Between 1494 and 1496, while Columbus was waging war against Canabó, his brother Bartolomé waged a similar war against the former ally Guarionex, assisted by 3,000 allied Tainos drawn from Guarionex' enemies, which forced the latter to submit and pay tribute.[21] Other Spaniards made similar alliances; Miguel Diaz married the daughter of a local ruler on the south coast of the island, and in time, that ruler supplied 3,000 soldiers for the war against Guarionex in 1498.[22] Francisco Roldán's alliance in the east, at Xaragua in 1497, however, was considered too threatening to royal control, and he was arrested by royal authorities.[23]

Unofficial Spanish ventures, little noted in the record, also established an early presence in Boriquen, now Puerto Rico. Juan Ponce de Leon and Cristobal de Sotomayor each made alliances and "exchanged names" with local caciques, then in 1511 became involved in a war between them, so that the Spanish and

[20] The differences are found in the basic accounts of Gonzalo Fernández de Oveido y Valdes, *Historia General y natural de las Indias* (3 vols., ed. Juan Perez de Tudelo Bueso, Madrid), Book 2, chapters 8 and 12; and Bartolomé de as Casas, *Historia de las Indias* (ed. Agustin Milares Carlo, 3 vols., Mexico, 1986), Book 1, Chapter 86. Chapter citations in both works allow consultation with other editions and translations. Peter Martyr, *Orbe Novo* Dec. I, cap 1, has Columbus sign "a treaty of friendship with the king."
[21] Las Casas, *Historia* Book 1, chapters 100–105; Oviedo, *Historia general* Book 3, chapters 1 and 2; and more briefly in Peter Martyr, Decade I, Book 7, all with substantial chronological divergences, that are not readily reconciled.
[22] Peter Martry, *Orbe Novo*, Decade I, Book 7 (McNutt, 79).
[23] Oviedo, *Historia General*, Book 2, chapter 13.

their allies fought each other.[24] In the process, Spanish forces from Hispaniola arrived, and the various armies deployed in the civil war ended up serving for Spain. Such private alliances pioneered Spanish expansion to Jamaica and Cuba, which, like Hispaniola and Puerto Rico, were occupied by Tainos organized in small states. Throughout the 1510s and 1520s, Spanish forces steadily advanced as these areas were brought under crown control. Eventually some Tainos from these islands would join the attacks on the Central American mainland, for Cortés brought some indigenous Cubans with him to Mexico, and Francisco de Garay used Tainos from Jamaicato assist his attack on Pánuco, also in Mexico in 1523.[25]

Almost all our sources on the Spanish conquest provide very little in the way of military details, such as noting formations or maneuvers on the battlefield. What seems certain, however, is that while the Spanish could not – or at least did not – conquer any indigenous group single-handedly, when Spanish and indigenous forces allied, they were an extremely potent military force, capable of defeating many indigenous armed forces who did not possess Spanish assistance.

THE CONQUEST OF MEXICO

Ross Hassig has analyzed Cortes's campaign in Mexico, arguing that, at least in the initial phases, he was as much a tool of Native American policy as they were of his.[26] From the point of his landing, Cortés collected alliances, first with the Totonacs of Zempoala, so that when he entered Tlaxcala, his forces already had more allies than native Spanish fighters.[27] In Tlaxcala, facing much larger armies than those of the coast, Cortés gave a demonstration of his soldiers' ability to withstand attacks, and added to this the devastating effect of employing cavalry on open ground, even though in the course of their first encounter the Tlaxcalans were already learning how to deal with cavalry by attacking the horses when they could not wound the armored Spaniards.[28] This battle, even though poorly described, shows that a typical army of conquest would have a Spanish core of infantrymen in tight formation with shields and armor, armed with artillery and muskets, and a roving group of horsemen who, being armored and mobile, could harass the enemy easily. Even still, in this

---

[24] Oviedo, *Historia General*, Pt 1, Book 16, cap. 2.

[25] Gómara, cap. 154; on Cortés's use of Cubans, see cap. 18.

[26] An excellent and concise summary of his argument is in Ross Hassig, "War, Politics, and the Conquest of Mexico," in Jeremy Black, ed., *War in the Early Modern World* (London, 1999), pp. 207–235. For a more detailed survey, see Hassig, *Mexico and the Spanish Conquest* (London, 1994).

[27] Francisco López de Gómara, *Crónica General de las Indias. Segunda parte, Conquista de Mejico* (Madrid, 1946), caps. 18, 28, 36, 38, caps. 44 (Gómara specifically mentions at least 600 allies, although his account pays relatively little attention to their activity), 45 (Allies outnumber Spaniards). Cortés mentions the participation of 700 of them in one encounter, 400 from Totonac region and Yztaemestitian; "Second Letter," ed. Pagden, pp. 58, 60.

[28] Gómara, caps. 45; Cortés, "Second Letter" ed. Pagden, p. 58.

battle, the Tlaxcalan troops managed to penetrate the allied army and "some broke in and fought the Spaniards hand to hand"; a cavalry sortie retrieved the situation, however.[29]

After several days of testing them, the Tlaxcalans decided to join Cortés in his campaign against the Aztecs. In so doing they offered to accept vassalage to Spain, and also to "pay tribute and serve him as subjects, an offer which Cortés had witnessed by notaries and interpreters."[30] According to Cortés, the Tlaxcalans offered to supply him with 100,000 soldiers to fight in his campaign, but Cortés did not accept this offer and marched to Tenochtitlán with only 4,000 allies drawn from his earlier arrangements at Tascal, Guasucingo, Churultecal, and Zempoala, although 8,000–10,000 Tlaxcalans did assist him in secondary operations.[31] The Spanish boldly entered the city in peace but, after a treacherous seizure of Emperor Montezuma, were forced to retreat with significant losses to Tlaxcala. Then Cortés realized he had to accept major help if he had any chance of success in Tenochtitlán. In the final battle against the Aztec capital, which fell to the Spanish on August 13, 1521, Cortés deployed 900 Spanish infantry and 80 cavalry, of which he suffered 50 killed. But this victory was only achieved through the intervention of the Tlaxcalan army, which Cortés's secretary Gómara put at no less than 200,000.[32]

The joint military organization pioneered in Tlaxcala became for the Spanish the instrument of the conquest of an empire in Mexico that was far larger than that of the Aztecs. The new army was often more successful than any Aztec force had been, thanks to the balance-tipping element of the Spanish infantry square, artillery, and cavalry.[33] Aztecs fought alongside Spanish once they had been defeated; already they were fighting against Tuxtepec and Coatzacoalcos in 1521.[34] Cortés's attack on Pánuco included some 40,000 Aztecs as well as a Spanish force of 300 infantry and 150 cavalry. Thanks to fighting in open country, he was speedily victorious, although many of his Aztec allies were killed, and even a good number of the Spanish were wounded.[35] Although the Spanish could now count of massive military support from allies, they continued to work on political rivalries and more alliances to further their conquests.

---

[29] Cortés, "Second Letter," ed. Pagden, p. 60; Anonymous Conqueror, "Relatione dell'alcune cose della Nuova Spangna…" c. 1520, ed. and Spanish translation in Joaquin Garcia Izcabalceta, *Coleccion de Documentos para la Historia de México* (2 vols., Mexico City, 1858 [Gallica; GB]) 1: 373–374.

[30] Gómara, caps. 53–54, 58 (quotation). Cortés, "Second Letter," ed. Pagden, p. 66, 69.

[31] Cortés, "Segunda Carta," in *Historiadores primitivos*, p. 23; Gómara, cap. 58, 65. On the role of Tlaxcala at this time, "Second Letter," ed. Pagden, p. 87.

[32] Gómara, cap. 144.

[33] A pathbreaking exploration of this theme is found in the contributions in Laura Matthrew and Michel Oudijk, eds., *Indian Conquistadores: Indigenous Allies in the Conquest of Mesoamerica* (Norman, 2007); see especially the general chapter by Oudijk and Mathew Restall, "Mesoamerican Conquistadores in the Sixteenth Century," pp. 28–64.

[34] Gómara, cap. 149.

[35] Gómara, cap. 153.

The ruler of Tehuantepec agreed to submit and pay tribute in exchange for Spanish support against his rival Tututepec in 1522.[36]

Even after the incorporation of military forces from Tlaxcala and the Aztec empire, Cortés continued to garner allies and fight on behalf of his ambitions. In the process of expansion out of the Aztec realms, the Spanish also entered into alliance with Tangáxuan II, the ruler of the Tarascan state, the Aztec's northern rivals, who, like Tlaxcala, would be natural allies of anyone opposed to them. Unlike Tlaxcala, Tarasca did not participate in the conquest of the Aztecs, but it was more than willing to use Spanish forces for its own aims. Soon after the alliance, Cristóbal de Olid attacked Culima, on the Pacific coast, with "more than 100 foot and 40 cavalry and Mechuaneses [Tarascans]."[37] In this case, the Spanish were working for the same goals of expansion as Tarascans had been for a time. The alliance turned, however, when Vasco Nuño de Guzmán installed the Tangáxuan II's ambitious adopted brother, D Pedro Cuinierángari, as "governor," formally transferring sovereignty to Spain. Cuinierángari then offered Nuño de Guzmán 8,000 soldiers to join his Tlaxcalan and Mexican allies in a long campaign to the north that also furthered earlier Tarascan ambitions.[38] In its first fifty years, the alliance resembled that of Tlaxcala, and nowhere is this more tellingly revealed than in the fact that members of the Tarascan elite married Spanish women.[39] Tarascan colonists, like Tlaxcalans, were important colonists of the north and the military arm of Spanish efforts there, vital once the silver mines were discovered.

The larger forces made available by conquest and alliance allowed the Spanish to conquer where they had failed earlier; Gonzalo de Sandoval's force of 100 infantry and 50 horsemen, augmented by 15,000 allies, succeeded in taking Pánuco when the initial assault, using only a few allies from the Caribbean, failed.[40] In fact, Cortés's lieutenants actually carried conquests that the Aztecs themselves had begun but could not carry out, but were now capable of with the added touch of Spanish cavalry and weapons.[41] Hence the Spanish-Nahua intrusion into what came to be called the Kingdom of Guatemala employed the same sorts of troops that the Aztecs had, and to that was added the component of intervening in a war between the Mayan kingdoms of Quiché and Cakchiquel, siding first with one and then with the other.[42] In these latter

[36] Gomára, cap. 150.

[37] Gómara, cap. 151, Michoacán's submission is described in cap. 148; see also Alcalá, *Relación*, part 3, cap. 23, fol. 44. See James Krippner-Martínez, *Rereading the Conquest: Power, Politics and the History of Early Colonial Michoacán, 1522–1565* (University Park, 2001) for an assertion of a more total conquest and careful critique of primary source material.

[38] Gómara, cap. 148; see also Alcalá, *Relación*, part 3, caps 20–29, fols. 39–59. On the Tarascan soldiers, see García de Pilar, "Relación de la entrada de Nuño de Guzmán," (c. 1533) in Icazbalceta, ed. *Documentos históricos* 2: 248.

[39] Delfina López del Sarralangue, *La nobleza indígena de Pátzcuaro en la época virreinal* (Mexico, 1965), pp. 171, 186, 218.

[40] Gómara, cap. 156.

[41] Laura Matthew, "Whose Conquest? Nahua, Zapoteca, and Mixteca Allies in the Conquest of Central America," in Matthrew and Oudijk, eds., *Indian Conquistadores*, pp. 104–105.

[42] Gomára, caps. 158–162; Francisco de Montero to Emperor, June 1, 1539 *CDI* 2: 212–244.

campaigns, both the Mexicans (Aztec) and Tlaxcalans were deployed in large numbers.[43] Many of them settled in Guatemala, Honduras, and Nicaragua as garrisons; colonies of those soldiers were found scattered in distinct, self-governing military colonies even in the seventeenth century.[44] Later, Tlaxcalans would also found military colonies in the north of Mexico, and their military forces were vital to the defense of the mines in that region, an area that was unstable and never securely in Spanish hands.

Similar combinations of Spanish and Mexican forces achieved the first Spanish successes in the Yucatán, although there also local forces provided a vital alliance. Francisco de Montejo's *entrada* had failed in the region in 1526–1529, and it was through making alliances with some of the rival Maya kingdoms, notably Acalan, that he achieved some success.[45]

The Spanish rule in Mexico and in Central America rested largely on the military forces raised in the conquest – these forces would still be in place, as garrisons, for example, right to the time of the War of Independence after 1811. It is not surprising, given their role in the conquest and the further development of Spanish control, that Tlaxcalan historians, like the mixed-race Diego Muñoz Camargo, produced in the half-century following the conquest celebrated the Tlaxcalans as the true conquerors of Mexico. The *Lienza de Tlaxcala*, a history of the conquest written in pictographs as well as the Nahua language written in the Latin alphabet and Spanish often shows battle scenes in which the Tlaxcalans are leading the Spanish, not just in the Aztec zone, but also in Guatemala.[46] It is not, in fact, an inaccurate depiction of the role of Tlaxcala's armed forces in the conquest. Indeed, Spain had little choice but to recognize that Tlaxcala had been indispensable in the building of New Spain as a joint partner in conquest.

These native forces were also deployed regularly against the rebellions that several of Cortés's lieutenants raised against him, and by Cortés in suppressing both them and the rising of various Native American nobles who had submitted but disliked the arrangements that submission entailed.[47] The Acalan (Maya) accounts of the conquest from their point of view, revealed in post-conquest writing, make this alliance clear, just as the Tlaxcalan accounts from Mexico do.[48]

[43] Matthew, "Whose Conquest? Nahua, Zapoteca, and Mixteca Allies in the Conquest of Central America," in Matthrew and Oudijk, eds., *Indian Conquistadores*, pp. 102–126.

[44] Espinosa, *Compendio*; For the early history (1549) of a Tlaxcalan garrison serving in Honduras, see AGI Patronato Real 58, R4, (second pagination) fols. 28–31.

[45] Matthew Restall, *Maya Conquistador* (Boston, 1998), pp. 3–23.

[46] Florine G. L. Asselbergs, "The Conquest in Images Stories of Tlaxcalteca and Quauhuquecholteca Conquistadores," and Stephanie Wood, "Nahua Christian Warriors in the Mapa de Cuauhtlantzinco, Cholula Parish," in Mathew and Oudijk, eds., *Indian Conquistadores*, pp. 65–101 and 254–316; see also Travis Kranz, "The Tlaxcalan Conquest Pictorals: The Role of Images in Influencing Policy in Sixteenth Century Mexico," (PhD dissertation, UCLA, 2001).

[47] Gómara, caps. 171–173, 179, 185.

[48] "Title of Acalan-Tixchel," in Restall, *Maya Conquistador*, pp. 58–76.

PERU

Francisco Pizarro's conquest of Peru, beginning in 1532, worked in much the same way as the conquest of Mexico a decade earlier, with extensive use of alliances, although because of the nature of the empire, it involved many more players on both the Incan and Spanish side.[49] Pizarro arrived in Peru in the final days of the devastating civil war between Huascar, ruler of the capital of Cuzco and its ancient Incan noble families, and his half-brother Atahualpa, commander of the field army in the newly conquered northern territory of Quito.[50] Pizarro almost immediately made allies among the coastal people around Tumbez, who feared his horses and hoped he would help them against Atahualpa, who had just defeated and captured Huáscar and would look for revenge on them.[51]

As in Mexico, it was through the politics of alliance that Spain won control of the empire. Pizarro, in a remarkable feat of treachery, captured Atahualpa and hoped initially that he could somehow use him as a puppet; in the end, however, Huáscar was killed and Pizarro executed Atahualpa on July 26, 1533.[52] Perhaps the only tangible benefit from this attempt to usurp Atahualpa's authority was the payment of his famous and huge ransom in gold and silver, which Pizarro hoped would draw Spanish to the country "so that enough people would come there to populate it," because "the country was large and full of many native people, and the Spanish who had come there at that point were far too few to conquer, subject and populate it" on their own.[53] It was a recognition of the limitations of his power, but even thousands of Spaniards could not do this work on their own.

The death of the two contenders effectively restarted the civil war, as Pizarro sought to locate a malleable replacement for Atahualpa, at first leaning to

[49] John F. Guilmartin, "The Cutting Edge: An Analysis of the Spanish Invasion and Overthrow of the Inca Empire (1532–1539)," in Kenneth J. Andrien and Rolena Adorno, eds., *Transatlantic Encounters: Europeans and Andeans in the Sixteenth Century* (Berkeley and Los Angeles, 1991), pp. 40–69, for an analysis of the earlier period.

[50] The narrative of events is well established in John Hemming, *The Conquest of the Incas* (New York, 1970), an accessible English account based on careful reading of the original sources. See also Carlos Sempat Assadourian, *Transiciones hacia el sistema colonial andina* (Mexico and Lima, 1994), and also Karen Spaulding, "The Crisis and Transformations of Invaded Societies: Andean Area (1500–1580)," in Frank Salomon and Stuart Schwartz, eds., *The Cambridge History of the Native Peoples of the Americas* (6 vols, in 3 parts, part III, *South America*, New York and Cambridge, 1999), pp. 904–972.

[51] Xeres, *Verdadera relación*, pp. 43–50.

[52] Here and in the rest of the chapter, I have generally followed Hemming, *Conquest*, pp. 46–120 for dates and some details, but have made my interpretations more firmly on Pedro Sancho de la Hoz, "Relatione per sua Maesta di quel che con conquisto e pacificazione...(1534)" in Gian Battista Ramusio, *Navigazione e viaggi...* (3 volumes, Rome, 1550–1606, Internet edition, http://www.liberliber.it/biblioteca/r/ramusio/. English translation by Phillip Ainsworth Means (New York, 1917). The original Spanish version of this text was lost, and Ramusio's Italian edition is the source for all modern editions and translations.

[53] Sancho de la Hoz, "Relatione," p. 2580.

Huáscar's younger brother Tupac Haullpa, and then, when he died, switching to Atahualpa's seventeen-year-old brother Manco Capac. Pizarro told Manco that he had come "with no other purpose than … to free you from the servitude" of Atahualpa's men. As he careened from supporter to supporter, Pizarro met firm opposition from Atahualpa's generals Quisquis and Rumiñavi, who opposed the Spanish march on the capital of Cuzco. Pizarro fought a number of sharp skirmishes with them, and at Vilaconga, some 2,000 soldiers from Quisquis showed Pizarro that he could not defeat them in open battle.[54]

Manco proved to be a good ally, for once they entered the capital on November 15, 1533, the new Inca responded by mobilizing 5,000 soldiers to join with 50 Spanish horsemen to attack Quisquis successfully, and then quickly followed this up by mobilizing another 10,000 soldiers who combined with 50 Spanish horse to deal Quisquis a second defeat on January 6, 1534.[55] Quisquis withdrew northward, pursued by Manco, whose forces steadily grew to 25,000 "men of war" aided by 50 Spanish horse.[56]

Even as Pizarro was fighting Quisquis, other Spanish forces were attacking Quito: one of Pizarro's captains, Sebastián de Benalcázar advanced northward from the coast, and an unauthorized expedition from Guatemala led by its governor, Pedro de Alvarado, and including 4,000 indigenous soldiers was proceeding southward but failed to reach Peru, so the war on Quito fell in the hands of Benalcázar, with a few hundred Spanish cavalry and infantry, but was bolstered by thousands of Cañari who sided with the Spanish against Quisquis who they remembered as savagely putting down an earlier rebellion.[57] As this force advanced on Quito, Rimiñavi withdrew from the city, and it was Cañarians who, in a hotly contested night battle, were instrumental in preventing a counterattack from succeeding.[58] Benalcácar was joined by reinforcements from Pizarro, some 4,000 Incan soldiers, 50 cavalry, and 30 Spanish infantry led by Diego de Almagro, which finished the campaign by 1535.[59] With Quito in Spanish hands, Spain could claim it had conquered Peru.

Most chronicles of the Peruvian campaign pay little attention to the activities of these thousands of Inca soldiers, and focus a great deal of attention on the Spanish cavalry, often naming the horsemen individually in their accounts. Yet the cavalry could not win battles by itself. In his account of the Spanish advance on Cuzco with Manco, the chronicler Cieza de León reveals the

---

[54] Sancho de la Hoz, "Relatione," pp. 2594–2596. Hemming, *Conquest*, pp. 106–110 describes this battle using a wider range of sources, and sees it as more a victory than I do, though recognizing it as a breakthrough for Incan armies facing cavalry.

[55] Sancho de la Hoz, "Relatione," p. 2598; some of these soldiers must have been raised in Jauca, which provided 4,000; Letter of Cabildo of Jauja, July 20, 1534, *Libro Primero de cabildos de Lima*, ed. Enrique Torres Saldamando (3 vols., Paris and Lima, 1888–1900) 3: 5

[56] Sancho de la Hoz, "Relatione," p. 2599.

[57] Cieza de León, *Descobrimiento y Conquista*, Parte 3, cap. 58 (some Cañari continued to keep a loyalty to Inca commanders; they were among attackers of the Spanish at Chincha, *ibid*, cap. 64.).

[58] Cieza de León, *Descobrimiento y Conquista*, Parte 3, cap. 70.

[59] Sancho de la Hoz, "Relatione," p. 2604.

limitations of the cavalry. In one engagement, a force of 60 horsemen with its allies under Hernando de Soto managed to kill 800 and wound slightly fewer Incan soldiers before becoming completely exhausted, thus suggesting that a lancer facing fleeing and terrified infantry could kill or wound about 25 before becoming too exhausted to continue. But this is a maximum, assuming all the Inca casualties were caused by Spanish lancers and not their many allies. But this rate of killing had its cost, because the Spanish surely had to engage their opponents very closely in order to inflict these casualties, thus exposing themselves to greater danger. The Incan soldiers killed five and wounded eleven of the Spanish, and also killed one horse and wounded fourteen others.[60] Given the numbers, it would seem that all the killed and wounded Spaniards had suffered from their horse being killed or wounded. If the Incan army numbered 10,000, as sources suggest, then the attacking Spanish suffered 25 percent casualties in order to inflict about 15 percent casualties.

All Spanish forces also wore armor, so they were often impervious to the projectile and cutting weapons used in America, and their steel weapons were effective against the local protective equipment. Spanish armor was particularly effective if the soldiers maintained their discipline and kept in tight formation, which European soldiers were trained to do even as they moved about. Such a formation was like a small mobile fortress on the battlefield that was very difficult for the local military to break, and Spanish artillery, crossbows, or musketry deployed within the formation provided protection for the troops, even if, given the low rate of fire, this protection was probably more psychological than practical (although artillery loaded, shotgun-style, with large amounts of small shot might be extremely effective against massed enemies).

After the occupation of Quito, one might easily say that Peru was ruled jointly by Manco and Pizarro rather than by Spain. Then, just as Cortés had sent joint armies of Aztec and Tlaxcalans to conquer domains outside the control of the Aztec Empire, so Manco and Pizarro sought to extend the Inca Empire into new lands. Manco's brother Paullo took some 12,000 Incan infantry along with 570 Spaniards under Diego Almagro and moved south into Chile, a region that had successfully resisted earlier Inca attacks.[61] At the same time, Pizarro sought once again to make Manco his puppet, but this plan backfired; Manco escaped to Ollantaytambo, raised an army, and besieged Cuzco in 1536–1537. Fortunately for Pizarro, some of his allies stood by him. The Spanish defenders still had the support of 10,000–12,000 Inca soldiers and some 80,000 porters and servants.[62] Some of these supporters were Cañari; as Pizarro, noted, they were "enemies of Manco on account of being men of Quizquiz."[63] The defenders sent out desperate pleas for reinforcements, but the

[60] Cieza de Léon, *Descobrimiento y Conquesta*, Parte 3, caps. 61–62.
[61] Garcilaso de la Vega, Pt 2, chapter 30.
[62] [Diego da Silva] "Relacion del sitio de Cuzco y principio de las guerras civiles del Perú," (1539) in *Colección de libros raros ó curiosos* 13 (1879[GB]), p. 18.
[63] Pedro Pizarro, "Relación del descubrimiento y conquista de los reinos de Perú," (1571) (Madrid, 1844 [GB]), p. 291. An English translation was published in New York, 1921[DTA].

siege was finally broken only when Paullu and Almagro returned from Chile, reinforced by another Spanish force from the coast with many Jauja allies.[64] After the siege was lifted, Manco gradually withdrew with the remains of his army to the mountains east of the country, and had transferred his government to Vilcabamba by June 1539.

During the siege of Cuzco, Manco had appealed to his brother Paullu to join him against the Spanish, but Paullu decided not to do this – had he done so, the Spanish would probably have been driven from Peru. Instead, he sought to play the same game as Manco had, and Almagro crowned him as Inca in July 1537. With a solid Inca ally, Pizarro and Almagro had their own civil war to determine who would rule for Spain, and again indigenous forces continued to provide major fighting forces.

The rivalry resolved itself in a battle at Las Salinas on April 26, 1538, to which Paullu contributed 6,000 soldiers to Almagro's 240 horsemen and 260 infantry to take on the Pizarro brothers, who had their own allies – some 15,000 Inca soldiers who had stood by them during the siege of Cuzco.[65] When Almagro's Spanish fighters lost ground in the battle, Paullu switched sides and assured both his survival and his ally's demise.[66] Pizarro gladly agreed to continue the alliance with Paullu, who was accepted as Inca until his death in 1549. Although Paullu had borne the title of Inca – or perhaps counter-Inca, given that Manco was alive through much of his reign – he gradually slipped from having the Spanish as his ally to being an ally of the Spanish. Paullu's family and a number of other elite families allied with him accepted the loss of sovereignty in exchange for concessions of land and income. Paullu assisted Goncalo Pizarro in attacking provinces that remained loyal to his brother and "did great damage to the enemy."[67] While the Spanish chronicler Cieza de León proudly recounted the role of Spanish cavalry in these actions and barely mentioned the role of Inca forces, Paullu proudly trumpeted his own role and that of his forces in a document drawn up from witnesses in 1540.[68]

Inca forces continued to be important in the inter-Spanish civil wars, as the contenders murdered each other. Manco offered the Almagrist faction, now led by Diego de Almagro's son, Diego the Younger, military support in 1542 in his opposition to the royal governor, Cristóba Vaca de Castro. Paullu also provided troops to Diego the Younger whose "help was of great importance

[64] Juan de Turuegano, November 20, 1536, quoted in Carta del Peru, 1537, Raúl Porras Barrenechea, ed., *Cartas del Peru: Colección de documentos inéditos para la Historia del Peru* (3 vols, Lima, 1959), 1: 272.

[65] Cieza de Leon, *Guerra de las Salinas*, chapter 62. The strength of Pizarro's force is given as 15,000 in "Relación del Sitio," p. 161.

[66] Cieza de Leon, *Guerra de las Salinas*, chapters 63–64; "Relación del sitio," p. 168.

[67] Cieza de Leon, *Guerra de las Salinas*, chapter 89.

[68] "Probanza fecha ad perpetuam rei memoriam ... de Pablo Inga sobre los servicos que à sua Magestad ha fecho..." (1540) *Colleción de documentos inéditos para la historia de Chile* 5 ([GB] 1889): 343 (this statement is then verified by a number of Spanish witnesses); Cieza de León, *Guerra de las Salinas*, chapter 89.

to him" because he immediately got the loyalty of the country and the forces never lacked for supplies.[69] When the Almagrists were defeated at the Battle of Chupas on September 16, 1542, Paullu's men participated on their side, at one point launching a flank attack on Vaca de Castro's advancing forces.[70] Many of Almagro's men then fled to Vilcabamba, although Paullu managed to patch up relations with the victorious Vaca de Castro.

The presence of Manco's Inca state presented a difficulty for the Spanish and Paullu, which Spanish officials sought to control, first by seeking to win vassalage from Sayri Inca, Manco's successor in 1557, promising him an estate and income if he would move to areas controlled by Spain. His son Titu Cusi Yupanqui went some distance this way, accepted baptism in 1567, but never left Vilcabamba and ultimately did not allow any Spanish control. He also made concerted military efforts against the Spanish, launching a number of military operations and seeking support from local leaders who had suffered a loss of status through the tightening Spanish grip on the political life of the country. Titu Cusi's efforts were indecisive and when he died in 1570, his brother Tupac Amaru continued the war.

This state of affairs was finally resolved by Francisco de Toledo in 1572 in a decisive attack on Vilcabamba, in which his indigenous allies provided the bulk of his forces. He called up a Spanish force of foot and cavalry numbering about 250 to launch his attack, but the Spanish force was greatly outnumbered by its "friendly Indian soldiers" (*indios amigos de guerra*) under Francisco Cayo Topa, with 1,500 soldiers "from all the provinces bordering on Cuzco, from the Cañares and mitimas [colonists]." This force was supplemented by 500 more soldiers from the Yucay Valley led by Francisco Chilche.[71] The campaign was hard fought, but eventually successful: Tupac Amaru was captured and executed in 1572. At that point, forty years after Francisco Pizarro landed at Tumbes, sovereignty over Peru had finally passed definitively into Spanish hands.

NORTHERN SOUTH AMERICA

The Spanish approach to the northern coast of South America, which they deemed "Tierra Firme" in the sixteenth century, was dominated for a long time by the sort of trade-and-raid approach that had characterized Mediterranean politics for centuries. Initially, the crown gave licenses to trade along this coast and permission to found settlements, as well as allowing the capture and enslavement of any who attacked the Spanish or refused them safe harbor or

---

[69] Agustín de Zárate, *Historia del Descobrimiento y conquista del Peru*, Book 4, cap. 14.
[70] Zárate, *Descobrimiento*, Book 4, cap. 19.
[71] Martin de Murúa, *Historia general del Peru* (ed. Manuel Ballesteros-Gaibros, 2 vols, Madrid, 1962–1964), vol. 1, cap. 79. The Cañari component was probably 400, for this number was specifically mentioned as having a tax exemption in Toledo's documents. The remainder would be drawn from the Inca army, originally commanded by Paullu, that had fought for the Spanish since 1534.

trade, but alliances were important here, too. Even here, against small polities and not empires, Spanish who fought unsupported were sometimes defeated in open battle as happened to Alonso de Hojeda near Cartagena in 1508.[72]

The Spanish founded some ephemeral settlements in the early sixteenth century, but Santa Marta (modern-day Colombia) in 1525 and Coro (Venezuela) in 1527 became the first permanent settlements.[73] Local alliances were crucial; Rodrigo de Bastidas founded Santa Marta on the lands of a cacique who voluntarily welcomed the Spanish.[74] Likewise, the cacique Manaure of Caiquetía welcomed the expedition under Juan de Amprés, who founded Santa Ana de Coro in his lands, and in recognition Caiquetia was charged no tribute – a situation that was still prevailing 200 years later in 1723.[75]

In the first few years of Spanish settlement of the coastal towns, the governors of all the towns went on expeditions into the interior, seeking to acquire gold and other valuables from those caciques in the area who agreed to support them, and attacking and enslaving those who did not. The Germans Nikolaus Federmann, Ambrosius Alfinger, and Philip von Hutten left detailed journals of some of their expeditions from Coro, which followed meandering routes, dictated by friendship or hostility of local people.[76] The chronicler Pedro de Aguado paused in his description of one such expedition made from Santa Marta by Juan de Vadillo to the land of the Pacabuyes to describe a typical friendly encounter around 1528: when the Spanish arrived and set up camp, the local people would come up organized by family groups and give "maize, yams, fish, potatoes, whatever is in the province," while greeting him with the same bowing and handshaking gesture that they used to greet their caciques. They would also turn over an acceptable amount of gold, for which he in turn gave them a silver plate as a counter-gift.[77] Sometimes the local people simply paid the Spanish off by giving a gift of gold and did not allow them on their

---

[72] Peter Martyr, *Orbe Novo*, Decade 2, Book 1 (McNutt, 103).

[73] The earlier period is best described in the sixteenth-century chronicles of Oviedo, *Historia*, Books 27–28, and Las Casas, *Historia*, Book 2; there are good modern syntheses in Sauer, *Early Spanish Main*, and Hugh Thomas, *Rivers of Gold*.

[74] Pedro de Aguado, *Recopiliacion historial* (1582, Bogota, 1906), Book 1, cap 2.

[75] Pedro de Aguado, *Historia de Venezuela* (ed. and notes, Jerónimo Bécker, 2 vols. Madrid: Editorial Maestre, 1950), Book 1, cap 1. Diego Antonio de Oviedo y Baños, *Historia de la Conquista y poblacion de la provincia de Venzuela* (Madrid, 1723; 1824 ed [GB]), English translation and notes: Jeannette Johnson Varner, *The Conquest and Settlement of Venezuela* (Berkeley, Los Angeles, and London, 1987), Book 1, cap 3 (for the observation about the exemption from any charges of tribute).

[76] Federmann, *Historia Indiana*; "Relación de la Expedición de Ambrosio Alfinger, 9 de junio de 1531, hasta el 2 de Noviembre de 1533. Escrita por Esteban Martin, Maestre de Campo de Ambrosio Alfinger," in Joaquín Gabaldón Márquez, ed, *Descubrimiento y conquista de Venezuela (Textos históricos contemporáneos y documentos fundamentales)*, 2 vols, vol. 2, *Cubagua y la Empresa de los Belzares* 2nd ed., Caracas: Fuentes para la historia colonial de Venezuela, 1988, 1st ed., 1962; Phillip von Hutten, "Zeitung aus India," in *Historisch-Literarisches Magazin* (ed. Johan Georg Meusel) 1 (1785) [http://www.ub.uni-bielefeld.de/diglib/], 51–76 (edited from a deteriorated manuscript, no longer extant).

[77] Aguado, *Recopiliacion*, Book 1, cap. 7.

lands, as happened when Santa Marta's governor Gacia de Lerma went to Tairona seeking subjects or slaves.[78]

These expeditions often enslaved dozens, if not hundreds, of those who resisted unsuccessfully, but at the same time the Spanish were sometimes heavily defeated. This was especially true when they met groups who used poisoned arrows, against which the conventional armor of the Spanish was useless. In the late 1520s, the cacique of Bondiga defeated a force from Santa Marta with poisoned arrows, disabling 25 of the 100 Spanish soldiers and forcing a retreat, while a few years later Governor de Lerma lost 70–80 men of his force of 600 in an unsuccessful attack on Buritaca, whose people used "a fine poison" on their arrows.[79] To counter these weapons, the Spanish gradually developed their own new armor, made of cotton, that completely covered horse and rider, which looked so bizarre to the newly arrived governor Alonso de Lugo (the conqueror of the last of the Canary Islands) that he "laughed at them asking why they would give away the arms that the Spanish invented for those invented by the Indians." It was, however, the experienced local settlers with their outlandish armor who rescued de Lugo's conventionally armed soldiers from annihilation.[80]

The Spanish expeditions in this region appear to have made relatively little use of allied soldiers to assist them in these operations, but this may be as much a result of Spanish tendency to tell only the story of their own people as the real absence of allies. At the same time, it appears fairly clear that many local people accepted the Spanish presence and cooperated passively in exchange for not being harassed. It is also possible, given the small size and weak centralization of the indigenous polities of the region, that the Spanish could operate without much assistance, as they came close to numerical parity with armed forces they encountered, which would be impossible in Mexico or Peru, or even Central America. There are, however, some examples of alliances. In one of his punitive expeditions, Alonso de Lugo asked the neighboring cacique Bonda to give him support and the cacique obliged with some 600 archers.[81]

The "indios amigos" and "indios de paz" who are often mentioned in texts of the time appear to have cooperated freely with the Spanish even if they were frequently mistreated, cheated, or forced into service, as was clearly revealed in an inquest into the activities of Ambrosious Alfinger, governor of Coro in the early 1530s. Spanish witnesses, who were not necessarily impartial, accused the German governor of locking Indians in various prisons and denying them food until their relatives redeemed them with gold, seizing property of "peaceful Indians," and forcing them into service.[82] Governor Lerma was also accused

---

[78] Aguado, *Recopiliacion*, Book 1, cap. 8.
[79] Aguado, *Recopiliacion*, Book 1, cap 4 (Bondiga), cap 9 (Buritaca).
[80] Aguado, *Recopiliacion*, Book 2, cap. 2; for a description of the evolved armor, see Simón, *Noticias historiales*, part 2, 2a Noticia, cap. 15.
[81] Simón, *Noticias historiales*, part 2, 2a Noticia, cap. 5, no. 4 (this entire incident is not in Aguado).
[82] Residencia of Ambrosius Alfinger by Juan de Tolosa, 1546, in Marianela Ponce de Behrens, Diana Regifo, and Letizia Vaccari de Venturini, eds., *Juicios de Residencia en la Provincia de*

of violating the peace and spoiling the relationship; according to the complaint, when he came, all was in peace and "a lone Christian could travel 40 leagues through all the land and the Indians would give him from everything that they had without doing him any harm, and today fifteen horsemen can hardly venture two and a half leagues from the port."[83] However good their treatment and acquiescence might have been, or how serious their rebellions, the service of these Native American allies was largely that of support, carrying loads and supplies, while the Spanish, for better or worse, did the actual fighting.[84]

The Spanish had to approach the Muisca regions of the interior differently than the coastal areas, as there much larger and more powerful polities existed. Inspired by rumors of rich interior kingdoms, the Spanish moved up the rivers in 1536 to the highlands of today's Colombia. One group, led by the German Nikolaus Federmann, advanced from Coro; another, led by Gonzalo Jiménez de Quesada, followed the Magdalena River up from Santa Marta. A third group led by Sebastián de Benalcázar moved northward from Quito shortly after his conquest of the region, unaware of the activities of the other two, and joined them in the conquest. The primary fighting and conquest was done by Jiménez de Quesada's group starting in 1537, the others coming late but sharing in the spoils.[85]

In the highlands, as in the coastal regions, the Spanish do not seem to have relied heavily on local people to fight, but they met considerable cooperation of local leaders and their people, who provided safe haven, foodstuffs, and many porters. The chronicler Pedro de Aguado recorded that thanks to this support, the Spanish were never without abundant food during the whole conquest.[86] The Spanish sometimes paid for local support; for example, the people of Guacheta or San Gregorio were exempted from taxes by the Spanish crown for their contribution.[87] To encourage this support, Jiménez de Quesada issued draconian orders to prevent mistreatment of the local people, even publicly hanging one Pedro Gordo for a minor theft.[88] Even though generally supportive, not

---

Venezuela (I Los Welser, Caracas, 1977), pp. 68–171. Most of his misdeeds, however, included punishing Spanish for such offenses as sleeping on guard duty, or for corruption and graft concerning the fruits of the expeditions. They suggest as much about the intensity of feeling of Spanish forced to serve under a German governor as about the mistreatment of indigenous people.

[83] "Relacion de lo que hacia en Santa Marta el gobernador Garcia Lerma," no date, *CDI* 3: 506. One of the local people's strongest complaints was about grave robbing for gold.

[84] None of the chronicles have much to say about the service of these porters, and an inattentive reader might miss it altogether, as it only comes up incidentally, for example in Aguado, *Recopiliacion*, Book 2, cap. 12 (in Jiménez de Quesada's expedition up the Magdalena River in 1536). Military forces are almost always described only by the numbers and status of fighting men.

[85] An excellent synthetic account of this phase of the Spanish conquest is in John Hemming, *The Search for Eldorado* (New York, 1986).

[86] Aguado, *Recopiliacion*, Book 3, cap. 3.

[87] Simón, *Noticias historiales*, Part II, 2 Noticia, cap. 4, no. 3.

[88] Aguado, *Recopiliacon*, Book 3, cap. 3.

all caciques supplied porters willingly: the chronicler Pedro Simón described Jiménez de Quesada's advance on the lands of one of the most powerful local rulers, called the Bogotá, with a force in which the "service Indians (*indios de servico*) [worked] half by force and half willingly."[89]

The Spanish were aided by this passive attitude – the product, no doubt, of the fact that the Bogotá of the day was regarded as an usurper who was violating tradition, centralizing authority, and raising taxes.[90] For many of the Muisca caciques, subordination to Spain was superior to submission to this usurping Bogotá, which the Spanish sources consistently called a "tyrant." The conquest was certainly not direct and immediate, for quite some time the Spanish and the Bogotá played a cat-and-mouse game of movement, harassing attacks, and negotiations.[91]

Fearing the Bogotá's strength, Jiménez de Quesada now tried to ally with the Bogotá, promising to attack the Panaches, un-submissive neighbors of Bogotá, on his behalf. When the Spanish failed to defeat them alone, the Bogotá provided them with his *guesos* or professional soldiers to assist.[92] In the end, the Panache war joined some 5,000 Muiscas that broke Panache resistance and allowed Botogá to annex the region.[93] Cooperation with the Bogotá was joined to cooperation with Tunja as well. The Spanish assisted Tunja against the neighboring region of Duitama that was harassing them "for the grievances he did to them for being devoted to us." As in the Panache war, Jiménez de Quesada called on "friendly Indians" who fought on the Spanish side and suffered losses.[94]

The tenious alliance between the Bogotá and Jiménez de Quesada was challenged when the Bogotá was killed and Sagipa, his principal general, took over instead of Chia, another contender who had worked closely with the Spanish.[95] Sagipa retained the sometimes hostile, sometimes friendly attitude toward Jiménez de Quesada, but eventually joined him to launch a second attack on the Panaches, in which Sagipa provided 12,000 soldiers. The attack was successful, and the Panaches agreed to submit to the Muiscas and to Spain. But by then Jiménez de Quesada had become close enough to Sagipa to capture, torture, and eventually kill him, then stepping into his position.[96] As in Peru, sovereign control passed to Spain, while a substantial alliance made it possible.

---

[89] Simón, *Noticias historiales*, Part II, 2 Noticia, cap. 8. Some of these porters had come all the way from Santa Marta with the force; see cap. 13.

[90] Aguado, *Recopiliacion*, Book 3, caps. 12–13.

[91] Simón, *Noticias historiales*, part 2, 2 Noticia, cap. 12.

[92] Simón, *Noticias historiales*, part 2, 2 Noticia, caps. 15–16.

[93] Simón, *Noticias historiales*, part 2, 2 Noticia, caps. 31–33.

[94] Simón, *Noticias historiales*, part 2, 2 Noticia, cap. 27; as is often the case in chronicles, the role of the "indios amigos" is scarcely mentioned in the fairly detailed account of Spanish dispositions.

[95] Simón, *Noticias historiales*, part 2, 2 Noticia, cap. 30.

[96] Simón, *Noticias historiales*, part 2, 2 Noticia, cap. 31–33.

RIO DE LA PLATA

Whereas the more famous conquests in America involved armed takeovers of existing states, the conquest of the Rio de la Plata, while it involved some violence, was much more of a conversion of an alliance into rule through marriage. Marriages eventually sealed alliance elsewhere in the Spanish world, at least in the first generation, but the nature of the marriages and resulting colony were radically different in Rio de la Plata than in other areas, as they involved a more complete merger of elites.

The first expedition to attempt conquest in the Rio de la Plata region was led by Pedro de Mendoza in 1536, and started with the founding the town of Buenos Aires at the mouth of the river. But that town, built in a dry area and with the free associations of the Charrua and Querandi as neighbors, was poorly situated and initially could not serve as a base. The Spanish attacks on these two groups, while reported as successful, were won at high cost, for the *bolas* (throwing devices of weights on the end of lines) were able to tangle the feet of the cavalry and thus neutralize them.[97] Further attacks on Buenos Aires forced the Spanish to all but abandon the place within a few years after its foundation, leaving only a token garrison.[98]

As a result of this lack of success on the coast, the Spanish moved up river, making a settlement they called Buena Esperanza peacefully among the allied Timbus. Then, in 1536, following a hot engagement with the Carios, they founded Asunción, which would become their regional center. In the aftermath of their indecisive military encounter, the Spanish made an agreement [*contract*] with the Carios according to which the latter would fight against various enemies as allies of the Spanish.[99] As the Cario were organized in small-scale mini-states, their leaders were willing to make firm alliances that they could hold. Following the alliance, joint Spanish-Cario forces began raids on the surrounding area with the aim of forcing obedience and acquiring slaves with which to build the core regions that were now developing. The Spanish and their allies made war on a second Cario leader, named Dabei, and upon storming his town, obtained his consent to serve as a military ally as well.[100]

The workings of these agreements are revealed in the account of Alvar Nuñez Cabeza de Vaca, who, arriving as governor in Asuncion in 1542, heard first various complaints from the Spanish residents, largely about taxation, and then from the Cario leaders, some about problems they had had with the Spanish, the rest almost entirely about harassing attacks by the neighboring Guaycuru and Payagua. As a result, the governor created a combined army that went out

[97] Schmidel, *Warhaffigte Bescheribung*, p. 7.
[98] Schmidel, *Wahafftigte Bescheribung*, p. 8.
[99] Schmidel, *Warhafftigte Bescheribung*, p. 13 (Timbus); 18–19 (war with the Carios and aftermath).
[100] Schmidel, *Warhafftigte Bescheribung*, pp. 30–31.

attacking the neighboring region in response to their requests.[101] The alliances were shaky at first, for when the Spanish took to fighting each other in 1543–1544, the Cario split, and some leaders attacked the Spanish and their remaining allies. The Spanish countered by making a second alliance with the Yapuris and the Guatatas, and thus were able strengthen their position.[102] Indeed, the Spanish and their Yapuri and Guatata allies undertook a lengthy expedition that netted, according to Ulrich Schmidel, the German soldier whose account is our basis for much of this history, 12,000 slaves for Asunción.[103] By 1555, Governor Domingo de Irala could report that the natives "live in peace and concord ... are every day more instructed in the Catholic faith ... with nothing of the scandals of the past" that had once led to rebellion.[104]

In the longer run, the settlement in Asunción, as well as others founded in the Rio de la Plata basin in this period, involved a joint expansion of the emerging political elite of the mini-states of the region. Their leaders clearly saw advantages in uniting with the Spanish to increase their power and to obtain slaves to augment their wealth. At the same time, they supplied the Spanish with women, indeed many women with whom the Spanish either married or at least had children.[105] Women were brought in large numbers to the various towns established in the larger region, so that women were said to outnumber men ten to one. While some of the movement of women seemed to be forced, it was also voluntary, because the women and their families resisted attempts to change it, believing that it presented opportunities to establish kinship relations and that the labor involved was neither compulsory nor arduous.[106] Because very few, if any, women arrived from Spain, by the end of the first generation – around 1560 or 1570 – the region had a Cario-Hispanic elite ruling emerging states of increased size, employing an underclass of slaves and commoners. In this region, conquest was not so much about the Spanish taking land or power

---

[101] Pero Hernandez, *The Commentaries of Alvar Nuñez Cabeza de Vaca* (Valladolid, 1555, English translation Luis Mendoza in *Conquest of the River Plate* [GB]), Cap. 19–20. Details of the sort of complaints they had, primarily disputes over women, are found in "Memoria de Hernandez," in Mariano Peliza, ed., *Historia y descurbrmiento del Rio de la Plata y Paraguay* (Buenos Aires, 1881 [GB]), pp. 167–195, which summarizes many inquests and complaints from 1538 onward.

[102] Schmidel, *Wafhafftigte Beschreibung*, pp. 42–49; see Domingos Martinez de Irala to Council of the Indies, July 24, 1555, in Peralta, *Historia*, p. 127. The accounts of this by supporters of Irala such as Schmidel, and of Cabeza de Vaca, have different visions of the chain of events and its causes. Schmidel has this as a general revolt of the Carios, but Cabeza de Vaca, *Continuation*, chapters 20–24 and 77–80, has it as simply an invasion of other Carios against those friendly to Spain or a local response to misbehavior of his opponents.

[103] Schmidel, *Warhafftigte Beschreibung*, p. 60.

[104] Irala to Council of Indies, in Peliza, *Historia*, p. 133.

[105] The role of women in the earlier period is clear enough when one considers the myriad complaints and disputes the Spanish had among themselves, and with the Cario elite, documented by partisans of Cabeza de Vaca in inquests, most of which involved relations with women.

[106] Juan del Piño Manrique, "Informe del protector de naturales del Paraguay sobre encomiendas," in Andres Lamas, ed. *Coleccion de memorias y documentos sobre la historia y jeografia de los pueblos del Rio de la Plata* (Montevideo, 1849[GB]), pp. 457–465.

from the indigenous people as participating in the strengthening of political complexity in which the elite all found advantage in maintaining ties to Spain. Both the Spanish and the Cario element (or their mixed offspring), while claiming allegiance to Spain, were not inclined to support too close ties to Spain, as witnessed by their rough expulsion of the first royal governor, Cabeza de Vaca, and the difficult relationships they continued to have with those who followed.

The settlers and their descendants, the transformed and Hispanicized Cario elite, regarded themselves as nobles; while a shoemaker might practice his art openly, as the Jesuit missionary and long-term resident Antonio Ruiz de Montoya noted in 1639, he would maintain that he had learned this trade by "some sort of magic" in order to preserve his nobility.[107] By the standards of the American colonies, the region was poor, lacking the exports that could finance a European lifestyle. One of their most important exports was yerba mate, a stimulant widely used in America, although with little market outside the continent. Vasquez de Espinosa, writing in about the 1620s, thought them terribly poor, wearing local clothes and even straw hats "since no Spanish merchandize gets here and they have no money with which to buy any."[108]

Through resettlement, the new elite established fairly large towns that were dedicated to economic pursuits and governed by representatives of the elite, all through the legal instrument of the *encomienda* (granting the rights to collect revenue), *reducción* (concentrating population) and *repartimiento* (dividing indigenous political units among Spanish conquistadors), but of a nature radically different from those in Mexico or Peru.[109] Governor Irala, establishing crown control over the colony in 1556, accepted the existence of the merged elite by granting them their holdings as encomiendas, and these, by the seventeenth century, consisted of tribute demands, primarily paid in labor by gathering mate, work that Ruiz de Montoya described as arduous and dangerous labor that he thought consumed many of the lower-class indigenous people.[110] Work in making tea or in growing cotton to make textiles contributed to revolts in the regions held in subjection by this elite, as witnessed by the revolt of the province of Calchaqui in the late sixteenth century.[111]

THE PORTUGUESE IN ANGOLA: THE AFRICAN CONQUEST

The Spanish were able to conquer, within a century of their arrival in the Caribbean, virtually every major state structure in the Americas. Only a handful

---

[107] Antonio Ruiz de Montoya, *Conquista Espiritual hecho por los Religiosos de la Compaña de Jesus en las provincial de Paraguay, Paraná, Uruguay y Tape* (Madrid, 1639, mod. ed., Bilbao, 1892 [GB]), cap. 3, p. 17.

[108] Vasquez de Espinosa, *Compendio*, p. 687 (English).

[109] The legal vagaries, mostly unenforced, or enforced only erratically, are outlined in Service, "Encomienda," pp. 242–245.

[110] Ruiz de Montoya, *Conquista*, cap 7, pp. 34–37.

[111] Ruiz de Montoya, *Conquista*, cap 8. pp. 42–43.

of holdouts remained, in the Yucatán, for example, along the back fringes of the Andes and Amazon basin or in the Mississippi Valley, and most of these were small scale and weakly centralized. But in Africa it was quite the opposite. Europeans did not have sufficient military advantages to make conquests, and indeed, could not easily even land on the coast. In striking contrast to the Americas, Europeans did not succeed in conquering even one major African polity; the closest they came to this was the taking of about one-half the territory of the Kingdom of Ndongo from which they built their colony of Angola. Even there the old rulers of Ndongo managed to hold considerable territory and were not brought into either meaningful vassalage or replaced until the mid-nineteenth and even twentieth centuries.[112]

In spite of their inability to defeat Africans even on the coast, Portuguese, like the Spanish in America, learned that they had something to contribute to African military systems in the way of armor, firearms, and other armor-penetrating projectile weapons (like crossbows). Horses, which were crucial to the Spanish conquests in the Americas, were of little help, for everywhere in Africa where horses could survive there already were equestrian cultures that could take on mounted Europeans in battle if need be.[113]

If they could not use their military technology to affect conquests, they could at least offer their services as mercenaries in African political systems. Such programs might potentially lead to conquest through the usual patterns of alliance and development of joint armies as they had in America, but in fact this rarely happened in Africa even when it seemed possible. In 1488, Bemoim, one of the rival candidates for the throne of the Kingdom of Great Jolof, appealed to Portugal to assist him in gaining the throne he claimed he had a right to. He traveled to Portugal and was given military assistance to effect his conquest, and no doubt to represent a substantial extension of Portuguese influence in his kingdom, the first step of which – conversion to Christianity – was taken in Lisbon. But upon his return, he became involved in an argument with the Portuguese captain sent to assist him. The argument increased and the Portuguese fatally wounded Bemoim with his sword, thus ending the possibilities of further advance.[114]

---

[112] For the overall story of conquest, see David Birmingham, *Trade and Conquest in Angola: The Mbundu and their Neighbours under the Influence of the Portuguese, 1483–1790* (Oxford, 1966), an old but still useful survey; a better survey of events can be found in Graziano Saccardo, *Congo e Angola con la storia dell'antica missione dei cappuccini* (3 vols, Venice, 1983–1984); more focused attention on the earlier phases can be found in Ilidio do Amaral, *O Reino do Congo, os Mbundu (ou Ambundos), o Reino dos "Angola" (ou de Angola) e a presença portuguesa de finais do século XV a meados do século XVI* (Lisbon, 1996); and *O Consulado de Paulo Dias de Novias. Angola no último quartel do século XVI e primeiro do século XVII* (Lisbon, 2000); Beatrix Heintze, *Studien zur Geschichte Angolas im 16. und 17. Jahrhundert. Ein Lesebuch* (Cologne, 1996), and Linda Heywood and John Thornton, *Central Africans, Atlantic Creoles, and the Making of the Americas* (Cambridge, 2007).

[113] For the military situation in Central Africa, see John Thornton, *Warfare in Atlantic Africa, 1500–1800* (London, 1998), pp. 99–126.

[114] The definitive reconstruction of events, along with an appendix of relevant documents, is found in Avelino Teixeira da Mota, "D. João Bemoim e a expedição portuguesa ao Senegal em 1489,"

Portuguese soldiers also entered the service of the king of Benin, probably in the late fifteenth or early sixteenth century. A letter of 1516 makes reference to the king being in the interior with all the Portuguese, making war. Benin bronzes cast in this period show Portuguese, heavily armed with swords, armor, and muskets – a fitting description of their role in Benin at the time – and Benin oral tradition recalls that Portuguese adventurers of this sort occupied a quarter in the city. But the Benin adventure did not have the formal support of the king of Portugal and resulted in neither the surrender of authority nor the imposition of tribute on Benin. It might have enriched the Portuguese who took up service, but it did not extend Portuguese authority, even nominally.[115]

Portugal's relationship with the Kingdom of Kongo involved the same sort of alliance that led to conquest in America, but again Portugal failed to make one. When Kongo's king Nzinga Nkuwu requested baptism and military assistance in 1491, King João II sent a formal military mission.[116] However, unlike Cortés in Tlaxcala or elsewhere in America, the arrangement did not include a demand for the swearing of vassalage, or the payment of tribute. Rather, this expedition, like another arranged for Kongo in 1509, only demanded payment for the military use of Portuguese soldiers.[117] In spite of occasional complaints about Portuguese misbehavior, however, Portuguese residents, whether soldiers, priests, or merchants, represented no threat to Kongo's sovereignty, and after 1553 they passed under Kongo's control.[118]

It was only when Portugal made an alliance with Ndongo in 1575 that conquest really began. Ndongo had sought Portuguese alliance in 1519 and again in 1560 without any conquest taking place, but the situation changed around 1568 when Kongo became involved in a difficult war with a mysterious group of invaders, known as Jagas, who may have been rebels within the country or an invasion by a neighbor. In the fighting, the newly enthroned king Álvaro I (1568–1587) was driven from his throne and took refuge on an island in the Congo River where he wrote to Lisbon to ask for Portuguese assistance.[119]

In exchange for military assistance by Francisco de Gouveia and 600 soldiers, Álvaro agreed to pay some tribute (which they apparently did pay for a few years), but more importantly, he allowed Portugal to establish a colony

Boletim Cultural da Guiné Portuguesa 26 (1971), pp. 63–111 (also reprinted as a separate by the Junta de Investigações do Ultramar, series separata 63)

[115] A. F. C. Ryder, *Benin and the Europeans, 1485–1897* (Harlow and Evanston, 1969) for details.

[116] Full documentation on this first mission is published in Carmen Raudulet, *O cronista Rui de Pina e a "Relação do Reino do Congo"* (Lisbon, 1992); for a reconstruction of events, see Amaral, *Reino do Congo*, pp. 21–32.

[117] Regimento a Gonçalo Roiz, 1509 in Brásio, *Monumenta* 4: 61.

[118] John Thornton, "Early Kongo-Portuguese Relations, 1483–1575: A New Interpretation" *History in Africa* 8 (1981): 183–204.

[119] Filippo Pigafetta, *Relatione del Regno de Congo et la contrade circunvizina* (Rome, 1591 [Gallica]), pp. 59–60 for the Jaga invasion; the invasion might have been a local uprising as much as the incursion of an outside people, as revealed in ANTT Inquisição de Lisboa, Processo 2522 identifying the "Jaquas" as "rebel blacks" (*negros levantados*).

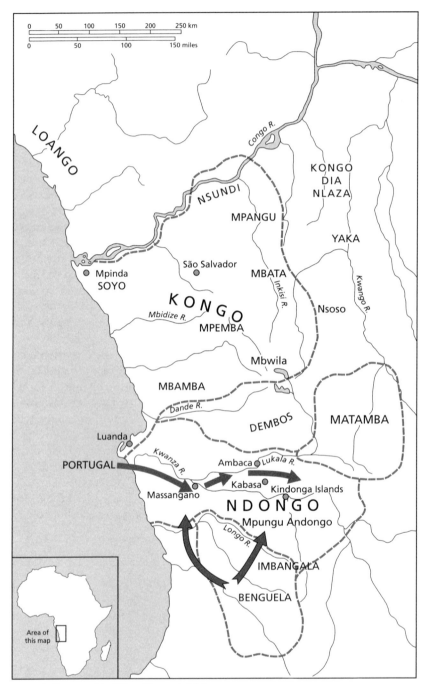

MAP 6. Portugal in West Central Africa.

in Luanda, then under his control. When he arrived in Luanda, Paulo Dias de Novais, chosen by the crown to build a colony in Angola, entered into a military alliance with Ndongo.[120] That alliance collapsed into war in 1579; Kongo, working under the agreement made in 1574 following the expulsion of the Jagas, sent an army to assist him, but it was defeated, and a desultory war between Portugal, Ndongo, and some Kongo elements continued until a peace agreement in 1599. In that period, Portugal had managed to build an alliance with some dissident Ndongo nobles that gave them some military forces and allowed them to build some forts on the Kwanza River and a small outpost in Benguela.

In spite of its limited size and control, the colony could still survive through engaging in the slave trade with its neighbors, and indeed Portuguese traders in the region built a wide-ranging network of settlements and trading communities in Kongo, Ndongo, among the Dembos between the two kingdoms, and even in the Nziko Kingdom to Kongo's east. These traders were multi-centered, as comfortable in Kongo's capital as in Luanda, the Portuguese colonial capital.[121]

The military stalemate that had reduced the Portuguese colony to a commercial outpost was broken in the early seventeenth century when Portugal entered into a new military alliance with the Imbangala, a group of bandit-soldiers who were ravaging the regions south of the colony. These soldiers, who numbered in the thousands, entered Portuguese service, allowing Luis Mendes de Vasconcellos, the governor from 1617 to 1621, to advance right into the heart of Ndongo, driving King Mbandi a Ngola to an island in the Kwanza River, while capturing more than 50,000 slaves.[122]

The Portuguese were unable to make their Imbangala alliance a vassalage arrangement, or to control them. Imbangala bands were soon pillaging Portuguese settlers as well as Portugal's enemies. While some bands supported the Portuguese, others joined Ndongo, strengthening the remaining portion of the kingdom under the vibrant Queen Ana de Sousa Njinga Mbandi and halting Portugal's advance. Portugal was able to make yet another alliance with one of Njinga's rivals Felipe Hari a Ngola, leading to a tri-cornered war between Felipe, Njinga, and Portugal (supporting Felipe) stretched into the 1650s. As expensive as the war was for Portugal, it paid for itself in the constant stream of captives through which Angola supplied both Brazil and the Spanish Indies and kept the colony viable.

[120] On this general background, see Heywood and Thornton, *Central Africans*, pp. 82–92.

[121] The extent of this network is best revealed in Inquisition texts, as many of the traders were New Christians (converted Jews) and thus under suspicion. Denunciations collected in 1596 revealed the network, as did the prosecution of Aires Fernandes, one of the leading Luanda merchants, a New Christian said to be the "sun" of the merchants, who was waiting for the Messiah. ANTT Inquisição de Lisboa, Livro 766, Visita a Angola (1596) and Processos 13087 and 13312 (case of Aires Fernandes, 1596 and Rodrigo Fernandes, 1602).

[122] Heywood and Thornton, *Central Africans*, pp.159–163.

In 1656, Portugal and Njinga made peace. They agreed on a mutual boundary, on the renunciation of Hari's claim to Njinga's throne, a status quo, and the liquidation of all independent Imbangala bands. A fragile peace, often broken by small forces on each side, prevailed and Angola became a mature colony on lines not entirely different from those in America.[123] Military operations, routinely conducted by Angola's military and its allies, continued both in the north, mostly in the lands south of the Kwanza River or in the small polities of the Dembos region, but these were as much slave raids as attempts at conquest, and certainly they added little in the way of territorial gains or submission of local rulers.[124]

EXPLOITING THE CONQUESTS

In review, the conquests of Spain in America and Portugal in Africa were grounded on the military alliances they made with a variety of local partners. The fact that no European power could conquer an area without considerable military assistance was crucial for how they would govern after conquest. Military dependence necessarily required that allied states, like Tlaxcala, would be rewarded by considerable privileges within an order that recognized Spain as a supreme leader, and that other allies, such as the nobles of Cuzco, be granted substantial incomes and exemptions as well. Spanish America was dotted, in fact, with special colonies of supporters, like Tlaxcalans, Tarascans, and other indigenous garrisons that paid no tribute and enjoyed exemptions.

Spain's need for indigenous assistance did not stop with rewarding those who had provided military support either. It would be impossible to govern even small mini-states without continuing the indigenous traditions of government. The Spanish could not import their own law for these vast populations who had no familiarity with either the language or customs of Europe. The only people capable of maintaining order and holding back complete legal and social chaos were the existing political elite and the legal and political culture that only they could understand and maintain. As a result, the Spanish always recognized indigenous rulers, usually under the rubic of natural lords (*señores naturales*), and expected them to keep order, settle disputes, and collect tributes. To reward them, "caciques," as the Spanish generally called all indigenous nobles, were given exemptions, rights to land and support, not only during the conquest period, but right through the whole colonial period.

The wealth of the conquests consisted at root in tribute payments delivered to the Spanish crown and its officials by the indigenous elite. It was these revenues, generated by the indigenous state's taxation system, that rewarded the conquerors. The most important first reward for the conquerors was to receive steady payment for their efforts. The Spanish crown or, more commonly, its representatives divided up the stream of revenue to those

[123] Heywood and Thornton, *Central Africans*, pp. 155–158.
[124] For the later period, see Birmingham, *Trade and Conquest* and Saccardo, *Congo e Angola*.

deemed worthy of reward. Typically this was handled by a revenue assignment, which went by a variety of names, but which is widely known by historians today by the common sixteenth-century term *encomienda*.[125] Although the institution had many manifestations throughout the Spanish world, its root was inevitably a temporary grant of the right to collect tribute from an indigenous state given to an individual by the Spanish crown or its designated representative.

While granting shares of tax income had its place and was the only means of extracting wealth initially, Spain also needed to allow for its settlers to have access to land for agricultural, mining, or other enterprises. The system of revenue grants could necessarily only produce income for a limited number of people, and Spanish who came to the Indies wanted to be able to own plantations and other wealth-producing institutions, so there had to be a means of accommodating those desires that did not undermine to too great an extent the concerns of the indigenous elite on which the system rested.

The Spanish began developing the encomienda system from their first activities in the Atlantic, beginning in the Canary Islands. When the Normans first conquered the Canaries, they set up a system of revenue grants, first by establishing special estates for the rulers, Guardafia on Lanzarotte and Ajose and Guise on Fuerteventura, to allow them material comfort in place of their formerly sovereign status.[126] The Normans also agreed, again as a part of the larger collaboration of conquest, not to touch the possessions of the general population.[127] But the exploitation of the Canaries would not be exhausted by tapping the rather limited surplus available to the rulers of the small islands of Fuerteventura and Lanzarotte. De la Salle also brought a good number of colonists over from Flanders and Normandy, settling each on an unoccupied parcel of land, and making further grants to the people "of quality" among them, so as to ensure that these nobles possessed sufficient land to maintain their wealth.[128] Before departing the island, he made a partition of lands, demanding one-fifth of the produce from the Europeans and guaranteeing that he would not take any of their land back for at least nine years.[129]

Nothing apparently was demanded of the Canarians, although the governor who replaced de la Salle began to make demands that were strongly resisted.[130] The failure of local records from the fifteenth century to survive and

---

[125] One of the most thorough studies of the legal system of the encomienda (and its related forms) is found in Silvio Zavala, *La encomienda Indiana* (Madrid, 1973). For a good overview in English, see James Lockhard, "Encomienda and Hacienda: The Evolution of the Great Estate in the Spanish Indies," *Hispanic American Historical Review* 49 (1969): 411–429.

[126] Boutier and Le Verrier, *Canarien*, chapters 30–34; 46 (Guardafia); 78–79, 87–88 (Ajose and Guise).

[127] For this division, see the notes on the conquest and also Abreu Galindo, *History*, Book I, chapter III, p. 13, footnote (which seems to derive from the original manuscript).

[128] Boutier and Le Verrier, *Canarien*, chapter 82.

[129] Abreu Galindo, *History*, Book I, chapter IX, p. 32.

[130] Abreu Galindo, *History*, Book I, chapter X, pp. 33–34.

the obsession of later historians with the events of the conquest have obscured how precisely income was drawn from the Canarians, if it was at all, although they undoubtedly did provide military service during the conquest of the other islands. Lands – presumably otherwise uncultivated lands, if the terms of the conquest were kept (and they well may not have been) – were granted to European settlers. The earliest clear-cut evidence of this is a land deed book from Gran Canaria in 1507, a decade after the conquest, and it covers only a fraction the land.[131]

In the century after conquest, the native Canarian population disappeared from the legal framework of the island as a distinct group, leading many to suppose that they, like the indigenous inhabitants of many parts of the Americas, died off as a result of Spanish mistreatment or disease. Bartolomé de las Casas argued a case for the end of the Canarians along the same lines he proposed for Native Americas (see discussion later in the chapter). However, a more likely reason was large-scale intermarriage, for de la Salle specifically enjoined his colonists in the fifteenth century to intermarry with the local people, according to their status. That they did so is borne out by recent research in DNA, which suggests that only about 20 percent of the seventeenth- to eighteenth-century population of one of the islands (Teneriffe) descended from European women, and most of the rest descended from groups that were present on the island long before Europeans came. At that point in the island's history, the average Canarian was slightly more than one-half of European descent, suggesting that the conquest was followed by massive intermarriage rather than mass death.[132] However, although more than half the modern population of the island descends from Canarian mothers, only about 14 percent descend from Canarian fathers, so the admixture was heavily skewed toward European males mixing with Canarian females.[133]

---

[131] Studied in depth in Fernández-Armesto, *Canaries after the Conquest*, pp. 48–68.

[132] Nicole Maca-Meyer et al., "Mitochondrial DNA Diversity in 17th–18th Century Remains from Tenerife (Canary Islands)," *American Journal of Physical Anthropology* 127 (2005): 418–426, tracing descent from mitochondrial DNA (MtDNA carried by women) and an admixture test that measures proportions of genetic material from various ancestral groups. The study identifies 18% of the MtDNA as being exclusively of European origin, and finds various North and West African roots for the others (outside of the small number of indigenous American lines). However, if one compares the haplogroups found in Maca-Meyer and others' study of ancient MtDNA from pre-conquest archaeological populations ("Ancient MtDNA Analysis and the Origin of the Guanches," *European Journal of Human Genetics* 12 [2004]: 155–162, and Rosa Fregel, Jose Pestana, et al., "The Maternal Aborigine Colonization of La Palma (Canary Islands)," *European Journal of Human Genetics* 17 [2009]: 1–11) to those in this study, it is clear that many of the haplogroups in the non-European portion of the population were already in the population before the conquest, including those of the L group, usually associated with sub-Saharan Africa.

[133] Maria Cátira Bortolini, Mark G. Thomas, Lourdes Chikhi, et al., "Ribeiro's Typology, Genomes, and Spanish Colonialism as Viewed from Gran Canaria and Colombia," *Genetics and Molecular Biology* 27 (2004): 1–8.

HISPANIOLA

The evolution of Spanish claiming income in Hispaniola is in many ways the classic example of the encomienda system, and of its abuses.[134] Its reputation stems largely from the fact that Bartolomé de las Casas and his ecclesiastical brethren used their experience on the island as a vehicle for denouncing the system as a whole, claiming that it led to the exploitation of the indigenous people and the depopulation of the island. The first laws passed to limit the encomienda also came from Hispaniola. Yet in many ways, the island was not typical, especially as the encomienda system had a relatively short life there. Columbus demanded tribute from the caciques he had conquered in 1495 in gold, cotton, and foodstuffs, which he collected that year and the next, and which he subsequently distributed to his followers.[135] The details of this distribution are lost, but it quickly developed into a system of granting the tribute collection of individual caciques to specific Spanish followers. As gold – the most desired form of tribute – was difficult to come by, Spanish encomienda holders soon located gold placers in the uninhabited interior mountains and demanded that the caciques supply them with labor instead, a task fairly easy to accomplish given that the indigenous tribute system called for subjects to work for set times in fields of their rulers; in fact, Guarionex already offered workers in lieu of paying gold as early as 1497.[136]

Columbus and his followers had considerable disputes over how the workers or caciques were to be divided up, and some Spaniards revolted against him. To overcome the revolt, in 1499, Columbus decided to make often perpetual grants of lands to the Spanish settlers to exploit for their own profit. But he made the grants within the "jurisdictions of the Indians" (*terminos y herdades de los indios*) and specified that these lands would be "worked by the Indians" (*hechas y trabajadas por los indios*). Thus, the documents establishing the grants stated that he gave "to [Spaniard] so-and-so (*fulano*) the cacique so-and-so, with so many thousand mounds of manioc (*matas y montones*)," and also that he gave "cacique so-and-so and his people to work these lands for him."[137] These terms were most appropriate for Spaniards who intended to live within the jurisdiction of a cacique, who conceded him the right to use local workers on his land, much as the cacique himself did. At least some Spaniards did exactly this; in the longer run, however, such holdings were not

---

[134] See the approach taken to the development of the encomienda in Lockhart and Schwartz, *Early Latin America*, pp. 61–121.

[135] Peter Martyr, *Orbe Novo*, Decade 1, Book 4 (McNutt, 63) (initial collection); Book 5, passim showing collection of gold, foodstuffs, and cotton. Las Casas, *Historia* Book 1, cap 105 (gives amounts of gold and cotton expected of each). That he kept and distributed the product is revealed in instructions that he received in 1497 and summarized in Carl Sauer, *Early Spanish Main*, pp.88–91.

[136] Peter Martyr, *Orbe Novo*, Decade 1, Book 7 (McNutt, 82).

[137] Las Casas, *Historia* I, cap. 160. In this section, Las Casas clearly had access to documents once in Columbus' possession or in public archives in Hispaniola, which are no longer extant.

particularly profitable, and by 1520, many of the grants were being sold off.[138] Many Spaniards, however, were more interested in working mines and chose to use the labor that the cacique supplied for working so many mounds of manioc for working the mines, either on mining land they held or lending or renting the labor out to others who held rights to mines.[139]

In the upshot of Roldán's revolt and the demonstrated gold-mining potential of Hispaniola, the crown decided to intervene by taking away Columbus's right to distribute income and using it themselves. In 1500, the king sent Francisco de Bobadilla to be governor. Bobadilla reduced the power of the settlers by restricting the terms of land grants to twenty-year terms.[140] The crown intervened further in 1502, when a new governor, Nicolas de Ovando, regranted all the lands (often favoring newcomers of high status from Spain) on shorter terms. Many of the displaced Spaniards, Licenciado Alonso de Suaso wrote in 1518, complained that their labors and blood had "prepared the table" for the newly arrived to feast.[141]

As encomienda holders changed, some attempted to move the workers physically from one holding to another; moreover, the labor demands for miners increased out of proportion to the original understanding of agricultural labor.[142] They and their caciques rejected their alliance with the Spanish, some refusing to work and other fleeing to the hills or unconquered areas.[143] Ovando launched wide-scale punitive expeditions to enforce compliance, but these apparently had only limited effect.

The flight of the formerly subject Taino population was so widespread that the crown issued the "Law of Burgos" in 1512 to regulate relations between the Spanish and the Tainos.[144] The law called for the recovery and relocation of the now largely fled indigenous population as its primary task (along with evangelization). The devastation of the Spanish economy created by the flight of the workers had such an impact that the first full accountings of the encomiendas of caciques and their workers in 1514 showed that only about 22,000 Tainos were available for labor.[145] When Jeronomite friars arrived in

---

[138] Licienciado Çuaço to Monsigneur Xevres, January 22, 1518, *CDI* 1: 332. In this case, Suaso asked to be granted such a farm, held by Xevres on Hispaniola, for provisioning his house.

[139] Las Casas, *Historia* I, cap. 160.

[140] Columbus to Prince Juan, quoted in Las Casas *Historia* Bk 1, cap 181. See also Sauer, *Early Spanish Main*, pp. 94–101.

[141] Licenciado Çuaço to Monseneur Xevres, January 22, 1518, *CDI* 1: 311.

[142] Licenciado Çuaço to Monsigneur Xevres, January 22, 1518, and Relacion de Gil Gonzalez Davila c. 1518, *CDI* 1: 307 and 332–333.

[143] Peter Martyr, *Orbe Novo*, Decade 1, book 10 (McNutt, 99); Martyr's letter, written in 1511, recapitulated the history of the grants and noted its result; see also Sauer, *Early Spanish Main*, p. 105.

[144] Ordenanzas que se hicieron en Burgos el año de 1512 para la reparticion de los indios de la isla Española, *CDI* 1: 236–241.

[145] The assessment is published in full in *CDI* 1: 50–236. This low number should not be considered in any way an assessment of the whole population as is often assumed; moreover, given that it is an assessment, it is likely that there was widespread underreporting of population and regular workers.

1517, they described the country as "depopulated" of both indigenous people and Spanish, although in this case "depopulation" probably does not mean the physical absence of people as much as the absence of available workers.[146]

The Jeronomites introduced a new element into the equation of revenue and control in the new colony – providing for the church. The encomienda, as described in 1512, put the job of supporting evangelization on the shoulders of the encomienda holders, who in turn would support priests. The religious orders, however, wished to take up this task and wanted much more independence. They proposed a more far-reaching program of regrouping all Indians into new villages of 300–400 families, along with their caciques, under clerical supervision, as they felt that their work of evangelization could only be accomplished in this way, and that the encomenderos could or would not be able to do it.[147] By 1519, in fact, they reported having regrouped some thirty villages of indigenous people in this way.[148] This program, while ostensibly aimed at making the priests more effective in their evangelization, would also give them access to a newly reorganized productive economy and guarantee them the sort of perpetual rights to income that the system of encomiendas with the laity charged with evangelization did not. It was telling that the Jeronomites apparently held a number of farms or productive properties but without encomienda workers attached, which, as they produced little profit, were being sold off quickly.[149]

However, the relocation of the rebellious population could only be done by force, and it was increasingly difficult to win battles and capture people. The demands of mining had alienated many caciques who might have served as military allies and reduced the potential coercive forces available. The cacique Enriquillo, a former ally, entered into active military resistance and fought the Spanish to a standstill between 1520 and 1534. The woes of gold mining were further complicated by widespread smallpox epidemic in 1518–1519, which took a great toll on the Taino population who had no immunities to these European diseases, and the toll was particularly heavy in areas of densest Spanish settlement.[150]

In the rapidly evolving situation on Hispaniola, some Spaniards undoubtedly used excessive force and committed atrocities against the laborers they were supplied and even against the caciques who supplied them. As these atrocities were reported to the crown and its agents, they became the basis for

---

[146] Geronimos to Charles V, January 20, 1517, *CDI* 1: 269.
[147] Memoria informatorio acerca del modo que se ha tenido en el repartimiento de indios en la isla Española... c. 1517; Geronimos to Charles V, January 20, 1517; Geronimos to Charles V, January 18, 1518, *CDI* 1: 256–257, 269–279 and 299–304.
[148] Geronimos to King, January 10, 1519, *CDI* 1: 367.
[149] Liciencado Çuaço to Monsigneur Xevres, January 22, 1518, *CDI* 1: 332.
[150] Testimony of Hernando Gorjon, April 20, 1520, in Informacion hecha a peticion de la ciudad de Santo Domingo sobre la despoblacion en que se hallaba entonces la isla Española, *CDI* 1: 397–398; for date, see Geronimos to King, January 10, 1519, *CDI* 1: 367, claiming the loss of one-third of the inhabitants of their newly founded pueblos.

a royal attack against both individual *encomenderos* and against the system of making such grants as a whole, by asserting their rights to punish those who abused the indigenous population. Monastic orders and individual priests, such as Bartolomé de las Casas, were particularly outspoken in denouncing atrocities that they laid at the feet of the practice of granting encomiendas, and their charges were sympathetically heard by crown agents who used them to win back the rights they had granted away.[151]

The Spanish crown's policies on the encomienda also created, unwittingly, what is often called the "Black Legend" of Spanish misbehavior. Given the crown's obvious interest in using its judicial powers to reverse and control encomienda grants, one must be a bit suspicious of romanticizing the idea of a Spanish "struggle for justice," and indeed even of the idea of the wholesale rottenness of the system and the atrocious behavior of the Spanish. Undoubtedly there were atrocities, but knowing the interests of those who generated our knowledge of them restricts our ability to draw too sweeping conclusions from them. Denunciations of the encomienda system, especially Las Casas's *Brevisima relacción*, were translated into northern European languages and became part of their legal claims to trade with, occupy, or even to conquer territory that Spain claimed or even held in the Caribbean. As such it entered English and Dutch colonial literature and subsequently found its way even into modern treatments of Spanish colonization.[152]

Spanish cruelty was held responsible for depopulation as well as atrocity. Las Casas, for example, argued that the encomienda holders' cruelty literally killed off the native population. The licenciate Suaso, writing in 1518, described great massacres of Indians by Ovando, and even argued that internal migrations, presumably to work in mines, caused great loss of life, reducing the population, he said, from more than a million (*un cuento*) to 11,000.[153] In describing the conquest of large islands and Mexico, Las Casas contended that the Spanish had "killed four million [*quarto cuentos*] souls, women, children, and elderly by sword and lance, and by burning alive."[154]

Modern scholars have accepted Las Casas's contention of depopulation, but have substituted death by diseases imported from Europe and Africa for the Spanish sword and lance, starting with the recorded epidemic of 1518–1519. A group of North American scholars, led by Leslie Simpson and Woodrow Borah of the "Berkeley School" compared Spanish fiscal enumerations, projections of pre-conquest populations, and other models to arrive a very high pre-contact

---

[151] A spirit of denunciation is found in all of las Casas's works, even his historical tracts such as *Historia*. But his most famous work in this genre was *Brevissima relacion de la destrucion de las Indias*, first published in 1552 and widely translated.

[152] Lewis Hanke, *The Struggle for Justice in the Conquest of America* (Philadelphia, 1949 and several reeditions). This work has been subject to a number of critiques; see notably Benjamin Keen, "The Black Legend Revisited: Assumptions and Realities," *Hispanic American Historical Review* 49 (1969): 703–719.

[153] Licenciado Çuaço to Monseneur Xevres, January 22, 1518, *CDI* 1: 307, 309–310.

[154] Las Casas, *Brevissima relacción*, p. 101.

populations and tremendous population losses, amounting to no less than 90 percent of the original population. Epidemiologists have partially supported this unprecedented loss of life by pointing out that the arrival of European and African diseases created "virgin soil" epidemics with extraordinarily high mortality.[155]

In fact, the statistical basis on which these claims are made is flawed. The Spanish did not take systematic statistics of the whole population but counted people by legal status and for specific purposes, and rarely did they include people not subject to the requirements of the encomienda system (which by the 1530s was no longer functioning as it did in 1514), and certainly not people who were not subject to Spanish authority (which included many people who had simply fled the encomiendas, or had never been under them).

Spain only actually ruled the economically useful south coast and a few hinterland locations, but by the 1530s these were already being abandoned by the elite owners.[156] It is therefore not surprising that DNA studies of Puerto Rico, whose demographic history is likely to be similar, reveals that more than 60 percent of today's population descend from indigenous females.[157] While epidemic disease probably took a toll, given that deadly massive epidemics are recorded in the documentary records, the disappearance of the indigenous population is surely exaggerated.

At the same time, the Spanish settlers, following up on their initial marriage alliances with local elites, created a new class of mixed-race elites who identified themselves largely as Spanish in those parts of Hispaniola that were not affected by the abuses of the mining system. The Spanish crown officially encouraged the Spanish to marry into Taino families.[158] The former subjects of these caciques, through becoming Christian and adopting some Spanish ways (including their language), also merged into a commoner population that was

---

[155] The classic demographic statement of decline is Sherbourne Cook and Woodrow Borah, "The Aboriginal Population of Hispaniola," in *idem, Essays in Population History* (2 vols., Berkeley and Los Angeles, 1971–1974): 376–140. The epidemiological approach is best described in Alfred Crosby, *The Columbian Exchange: The Biological and Cultural Consequences of 1492* (Westport, 2nd edition, 2003), esp. pp. 35–63. These serious writings then became the basis for more extravagant claims of genocide, especially in the early 1990s in conjunction with the Columbus Quincentenary.

[156] Lynne Guitar, "Documenting the Myth of Taino Extinction," *Kacike* (2002) (www.kacike.org/GuitarEnglish.html).

[157] Well over half the population of Puerto Rico has MtDNA pointing to an indigenous origin; J. C. Martínez-Cruzado, Gladys. Toro-Labrador, et al., "Reconstructing the Population History of Puerto Rico by means of MtDNA Phytographic Analysis," *American Journal of Physical Anthropology* 128 (2005): 131–155. The African-descended population accounts for almost 30% in Puerto Rico; it would be higher in Dominican Republic. In Cuba, indigenous MtDNA lineages account for about one-third of the population, but the proportions are surely skewed by late-eighteenth–early-nineteenth-century influx of Africans; see Isabel Mentizabel, Karla Sandoval, et al., "Genetic Origin, Admixture and Asymmetry in Maternal and Paternal Lineages in Cuba," *BMC Evolutionary Biology* 8 (2008): 213.

[158] Lynne Guitar, "No More Negotiations: Slavery and the Destabilization of Hispaniola Encomienda System" (www.kislakfoundation.org/prize/199701.html).

often not counted by the Spanish. They gradually passed almost unnoticed from being "indios" to being "Spaniards" or "mestizos" working on small holdings, growing food and tobacco, and eventually smuggling with French and English visitors.[159] In fact, what disappeared was "indios" as a legal category – as the subject of a cacique liable to perform labor – and this is easily traced in documents, from a remarkably low number 22,000 in 1514 to being all but absent in 1571.[160]

Although the debate about the granting of encomiendas was opened in Hispaniola, and royal orders and decrees establishing and modifying it were carried by later conquerors to the other islands and the mainland of Mexico and then Peru, the system never developed very far on Hispaniola itself. The mines became exhausted by the second decade of the sixteenth century, and the tendency toward managing tribute and labor through caciques, and using labor dues in particular to fuel the mining economy, was simply abandoned. The end result was that the crown effectively reassumed the encomiendas of Hispaniola in 1520, by setting the caciques and their people free (meaning free of the arrangements they formerly held with private settlers) and then calling for their resettlement along the lines envisioned by the Jeronimos, which those who still held encomiendas "felt deeply."[161]

The replacement of the old arrangements was required not just by the failure of the mining economy or even the Spanish inability to keep laborers on them. Instead, the Spanish turned to sugar production as the most likely means to become rich in Hispaniola. Sugar had produced enormous profits in the offshore islands of Africa and was also being grown on the Canaries, and it seemed likely to work just as well on Hispaniola. Some encomenderos grew sugar with the labor from their caciques in the early sixteenth century, but most would-be sugar growers simply took up unoccupied land and, instead of attempting to force the intractable Tainos to work for them, brought in slaves. The first slaves were brought in from other islands or the mainland of South America, and a substantial slave trade developed on the mainland through cooperative raiding by Spanish and indigenous forces.[162] Many more enslaved workers, however, were brought in from Africa in order "to relieve the Indians."[163] Slaves from

---

[159] For this interpretation of this period, see Lynne Guitar, "Criollos: The Birth of a Dynamic New Afro-Indo-European People and Culture on Hispaniola," *Kacike* (2000) (www.kacike.org/LynneGuitar.htm).

[160] For a critique of the methods employed, see David Henige, "On the Contact Population of Hispaniola: History as Higher Mathematics," *Hispanic American Historical Review* 38 (1978): 217–237.

[161] Licenciado Figeroa to King, November 13, 1520, *CDI* 1: 421.

[162] Relacion de Gil Gonzalez Davila, c. 1518 *CDI* 1: 334–335; Licenciado Çuaço to Xevres, *CDI* 1: 312, who claims that 13,000 out of 15,000 slaves captured on mainland South America died en route.

[163] An early reference to mixed labor forces at Acaya is Relacion de Gil Gonzalez Davila, 1518, *CDI* 1: 336; 339–340. There were repeated requests for an open slave trade (primarily from the "Islands of Portugal" or Cape Verde) in 1517–1518, championed by ecclesiastical agents; see Padres Geronimos to Cardinal Xemenes, June 24, 1517; same to Charles V, January 18, 1518,

Africa, in particular, arrived in increasing numbers in the early 1520s and soon they would turn at least the coastal areas of Hispaniola, in the words of the chronicler Oviedo, into a "second Guinea."[164]

The other great islands of the Caribbean followed a trajectory similar to that of Hispaniola, but with less attention to the issues raised by the granting of encomiendas, as they did not have gold mines. Puerto Rico, Jamaica, and Cuba all entered into the sugar-producing economy without passing through a phase of gold mining, and while each one began the production of sugar using labor dues paid by caciques, each one also turned to the politically less problematic solution of using slaves from Africa or elsewhere in the Americas as their labor force.[165] By the 1550s, it was remarked that the owners of such estates were as rich as Marquises in Spain and were very careful of who could marry their daughters because of it. As their sugar industries, which never reached the levels of sugar production in Hispaniola, also failed, the encomienda holders turned to cattle raising and agriculture, or to settle other islands like Puerto Rico, Jamaica, and Cuba, and then to the mainland of America.

ENCOMIENDA IN MEXICO AND PERU

Although the development and decline of the encomienda system in Hispaniola established important legal and social precedents, many new issues would be raised by the conquest of the large Aztec and Inca Empires. Both empires were governed on a larger scale than Hispaniola was, and both had substantial local conflicts and complexities that necessarily altered the way that tribute was extracted and distributed to the Spanish and how they had access to productive lands themselves.

Cortés conquered Mexico with the tremendous assistance of Tlaxcala, and not surprisingly he had to pay that state off with significant concessions. Spain demanded no tribute of Tlaxcala, no encomiendas were granted in its lands, its polity remained intact, governing itself through its existing institutions.[166] Aside from accepting Christianity and allowing missionaries into its lands, the Tlaxcalans were undisturbed because of their formal act of submission to Spain.

Cortés then had to divide the spoils by granting the tribute charged the defeated Aztec Empire, and the new lands added by his conquests to the south

---

CDI 1: 284; 298–299; see also the notes of the official Licenciado Suaso, Çuaço to Xevres, *CDI* 1: 326–327.

[164] Gonzalez Fernández Oviedo y Valdez, *Historia general de las Indias*...(Seville, 1535, many modern editions) Book 4, chapter 8.

[165] Justio L. del Río Moreno and Lorenzo E López y Sebastián, "La comencio azucarero en La Española en el siglo XVI. Presíon monopolística y alternativas locales," *Revista complutense de historia de América* 17 (1991): 39–78.

[166] The early history of Tlaxcala in the colonial period was outlined in Charles Gibson, *Tlaxcala in the Sixteenth Century* (Palo Alto, 1952). Many of Gibson's more somber conclusions have been challenged in R. Jovina Baber, "The Construction of Empire: Politics, Law and Community in Tlaxcala, New Spain, 1521–1640" (2 vols, PhD dissertation, University of Chicago, 2005).

to his followers, using the same encomienda revenue assignments that had been used on Hispaniola. To assist in this task, the Spanish relied on Aztec taxation schedules and documents. The Codex Mendoza, drawn up from local documents around 1535, for example, went into many pages of taxes, using the system of symbols and numbers that the Aztecs themselves used to record tribute obligations, to which Spanish notes were added.[167] The archives in Spain and Mexico contain many other similar documents, revealing tax systems, assessments, and methods of collection. Spanish officials conducted hearings with local people and officials to determine taxation levels and types as well. This revenue stream, drawn from the thirty-odd mini-states (*altepetl*) that comprised the Aztec heartland in the Valley of Mexico, was then diverted to the encomenderos, although to reward more people, some of the revenue streams (but not the taxation units) were subdivided between several encomiendas.[168]

In making encomiendas from the individual altepetls that constituted it, Cortés broke the empire up, both the central government anchored at Tenochtitlan and the provinces, stripping away intermediate levels of the Aztec government between the state and the altepetls.[169] To mollify the most powerful members of the Aztec elite, he granted two perpetual estates to the Aztec royal family, and furthermore allowed daily government to remain in the hands of the rulers of the altepetls, following scrupulously their own systems of government.[170] While the intermediate nobility of the Aztec state, provincial governors, and officials lost revenue and authority from their defeat by the Spanish-Tlaxcalan force, the local rulers lost little, at least initially, from the substitution of Spanish rule for that of the Aztecs. It is probably safe to say that the Spanish conquest was not fundamentally different from the empire-building process that the Aztecs and other Mexican hegemonies employed.

Although granting income as encomiendas was a well-established concept, the Spanish crown was not fond of it, preferring if at all possible to have their own agents control the flow of revenue. Indeed, just as Cortés was making his grants, royal agents were eliminating the encomienda in Hispaniola. Once Mexico had demonstrated its potential to generate wealth, the crown challenged Cortés' grants, threatened to take his own away, forced him in lawsuits, and passed laws limiting tenure of the encomienda holders. Often royal officials based their attack on alleged cruelties committed against the indigenous inhabitants by the encomenderos or their agents, detailed in lawsuits and investigations, providing gist for a new variant of the Black Legend already started

---

[167] Frances F. Berdan and Patricia R. Anawalt, *The Essential Codex Mendoza* (Berkeley and Los Angeles, 1997).

[168] Jason E. Lemon, "The Encomienda in Early New Spain" (PhD dissertation, Emory University, 2000), pp. 120–124, and examples following.

[169] Charles Gibson, *The Aztecs Under Spanish Rule: A History of the Indians of the Valley of Mexico, 1519–1810* (Stanford, 1964), pp. 58–78.

[170] William Sanders and Barbara Price, "The Native Aristocracy and the Evolution of the Latifundio in the Teotihuacán Valley, 1521–1917," *Ethnohistory* 50 (2003): 69–88.

FIGURE 6. "Matricula de Tributos." Courtesy of Instituto Nacional de Antropologia e Historia, Mexico.

in Hispaniola.[171] By 1555, within a generation of Cortés's catching sight of Tenochtitlan, almost all the important encomiendas had officially passed into the hands of royal officials, usually called corregidores. These officials did not hold revenue assignments, but drew salaries from the tributes of the altepetls; they also held their offices for fixed times at royal pleasure. As might be expected, corregidores often drew additional income illegally, mistreated the taxpayers, and engaged in various forms of extortions.[172]

Most of the elite Spanish who came to Mexico to govern it, or simply to capitalize on the wealth of the new conquests, lived in or around the old Aztec capital of Tenochtitlan, renamed Mexico and gradually rebuilt as a Spanish city. It soon acquired elaborate buildings, including ecclesiastical structures, government buildings, and other elements of an elite town. The discovery of silver mines in northern Mexico beginning in the early 1540s led to a flow of income that attracted even more settlers to the city and its region, and even those not directly involved in mining (a fairly small number) benefited from taxing the flow of silver (as government officials) or from supplying the miners, government, and ecclesiastical elite with supplies of food, services, and manufactured goods. This rush of Spanish settlers soon had a strongly disruptive effect on late-sixteenth-century society in the former Aztec capital and its surrounding lands, as they occupied the town and began demanding substantial economic changes.

Spanish policy insisted that settlers in the Americas live in chartered municipalities under strict royal control. Unlike so many chartered towns in Europe, the Spanish municipality in America had very little in the way of independence. The crown had the right to tax the municipalities at will, to interfere in its local legislation, and to overthrow its leaders if they did not comply with the policy of the crown. Encomienda holders lived or maintained a residence in these towns. The municipal councils (*cabildos*) in the Americas were charged with local self-government, and office holding and other forms of political participation were contingent upon being taxpayers or landowners. While they had the power to legislate for themselves and to tax to fund their decisions, the crown had the right both to overrule their decisions if they contradicted the crown's interests and to impose rules and laws if it suited its purpose.[173]

Elite immigration into New Spain also had a social demographic impact. Most of the first generation of Spanish were single men, often quite young. Most also undertook the risks of travel and war to win a sizable patrimony, with the understanding that they could raise the income and perhaps social station by so doing. Many of the first generation married indigenous women of the highest status they could attract. A survey of married Spaniards in Puebla, taken in 1534, revealed that about a quarter of the original conquerors had

---

[171] For the cruelties, Gibson, *Aztecs*, pp. 78–80.
[172] Gibson, *Aztecs*, pp. 81–97.
[173] Lockhart and Schwartz, *Early Latin America*, pp. 122–140.

married indigenous women, and more than a third (36 percent) of those who had recently arrived were married to local women.[174]

Those who were more successful would send back to Spain to obtain wives, using the wealth of their new status to underwrite marriages with socially prominent women, or at least those of higher status. It was common for Spanish nobles (even of lower status) to marry late (although they might have children by mistresses while younger); the idea was to postpone formal marriage until one was rich enough to afford the highest-possible-status wife. Because of this, Spanish valued having a Spanish-born, or later a Spanish-descended, wife and restricted their marriage choices to that group.[175]

As soon as wealth appeared, the crown opted to outlaw mixed marriage and indeed even contact between the Spanish and indigenous Mexicans. Perhaps primarily to prevent the Aztec elite and Spanish elite from combining tax breaks from both systems to engross revenue, the crown sought to keep the two entities as legally distinct as possible. They declared that Spanish America was divided into two "Republics": the "Republic of Christians" (Spanish) and the "Republic of Indians." Only the specific labor obligations of the encomienda or its subsequent wage labor process were allowed, and in some ways the system resembled, on paper at least, modern systems of social and economic segregation such as was found in Apartheid-era South Africa.[176] But the system was never close to being as closed as the South African system was, and was as much a legal fiction as reality. Its intent was to render impossible attempts to combine caciques' nobility with landowners' status and create the dreaded privileges that hampered Spanish centralization.[177]

As the presence of Spanish in the Aztec capital increased, their demand for European agricultural products formerly unknown in America also increased. Aztec tribute obligations could not easily supply beef, pork, or wheat products to the elite, and as a result, Spanish entered agriculture directly. The need to supply urban needs, plus the desire that all Spanish had for land, especially those who did not have an encomienda and thus would have to seek another source of wealth, necessarily caused pressure for a new system of taxation and supply.

Soon Spaniards, both those who held encomiendas and those who arrived later, acquired land, by a variety of means, sometimes by usurping various public categories of land recognized by the Aztecs, by buying land from either the Aztec elite or from commoners, sometime using extortion and force to make the purchases. In the 1540s and 1550s, a series of epidemics wreaked

---

[174] Francisco del Paso y Troncoso, *Epistolario de Nueva España* (Mexico, 1939–1942), pp. 137–144.

[175] Lockhart and Schwartz, *Early Latin America*, pp. 92–96.

[176] See André Gunder Frank, *Mexican Agriculture, 1521–1630: Transformation of the Mode of Production* (Cambridge, 1979).

[177] R. Douglas Cope, *The Limits of Racial Domination: Plebian Society in Colonial Mexico City, 1660–1720* (Madison, 1994). Even though Cope's research is focused on Mexico City, his general conclusions are widely applicable to regions of dense Spanish settlement.

havoc on the indigenous population, and in some cases lands were abandoned to be taken up by Spaniards. One common strategy was to regroup scattered villages into larger communities, ostensibly to aid in religious work or to reinforce villages decimated by epidemic, which in turn left much land vacant to be occupied by the Spanish who might then petition the crown to recognize their ownership.[178]

To acquire the labor necessary to work their new landholdings, the Spanish elite relied very heavily on a forced labor draft, which grew out of Aztec practices but was greatly expanded. This labor draft, called *repartimiento* in Mexico, was first applied to public works, especially flood relief, but after 1555, it came to be a regular system to supply groups of workers to the ranches and farms of the areas surrounding the city, who would work in rotation and be drawn indiscriminately from all the indigenous communities of the city through a centralized organization.[179] The repartimiento was a clumsy vehicle, and it was almost immediately superseded by those Spanish who wished to have a permanent, skilled labor force, such as the owners of textile works that were already springing up in Mexico by 1550. These owners hired individual indigenous workers for wages, and at times came to conflict with the obligations that the repartimiento placed on them. Eventually, farmers and ranchers also came to prefer wage labor with its greater permanence and predictability, and by the late sixteenth century, the repartimiento system simply could not meet the demands of farmers and textile workers for permanent or long-term laborers. The repartimiento was still used for public works, especially for draining of some portions of the lake on which Mexico was built, but after 1630, it was largely replaced by a system of wage labor.[180]

Meanwhile, the Aztec elite that had surrendered to Cortés had their own agenda for change. The Aztec hegemony was still in the process of consolidating when Cortés arrived, and old struggles for control between towns and districts reemerged in the aftermath. Town rulers found that Spanish courts might address old quarrels, dating back to the pre-Aztec days or to Aztec practices, and as a result, lawsuits to break up or rearrange the Aztec tax and government divisions went forward. Spanish lawyers aided them in this, hoping to diminish the size and political power of the rulers of the older states. Thus in many cases the older states were dismantled at least partially into more independent subunits, often either through administrative action in which an investigation would determine that custom and past history allowed the dissolution of the larger units, or through lawsuits waged in Spanish courts against the more powerful elite leaders. Spanish judges were very favorable to these developments, often found in favor of the plaintiffs.[181] In fact, these struggles

---

[178] Gibson, *Aztecs*, pp. 272–280.
[179] Gibson, *Aztecs*, pp. 224–236.
[180] Gibson, *Aztecs*, pp. 233–250.
[181] Gibson, *Aztecs*, pp.166–193; James Lockhart, *The Nahuas After the Conquest: A Social and Cultural History of the Indians of Central Mexico, Sixteenth through Eighteenth Centuries* (Palo Alto, 1992), pp. 14–58.

often generated hundreds of documents, written in Nahua and often in glyphic Nahua, frequently claimed to be of pre-conquest origin, alleging the primacy of one or another town, and presented in lawsuits.[182]

At the same time, the development of Spanish authority reduced the power of many of the former elite. Some faced super-exactions from the encomienda holders to whom they had to pay taxes, or from the corregidores who followed them. Others lost lands and followers to the epidemics, or to flight of their followers to the city or elsewhere, not to mention usurpations by Spanish landowners. The introduction of cattle disrupted indigenous agriculture, as cows and goats trampled fields and ate crops, and generally the law favored the settlers ahead of indigenous interests. Finally, the Spanish crown altered the method of succession in the old towns, replacing rule by a dynasty of rulers with collective rule by the elite, forming a town council (*cabildo*) and electing their own ruler, usually in rotation from among the old noble families, who took the Spanish title *gobernador*.[183] While in many cases the indigenous nobles were ruined by Spanish exactions, especially by forcing them to pay taxes beyond their means to raise the income, a good many others managed to acquire land, develop their own estates, and continue as successful members of a second elite, usually poorer than the Spanish one but just as proud.[184]

In the agricultural areas around the capital, landowners, many of whom had formerly been encomenderos, found ways to bind labor to them at low cost by developing a system of debt peonage. They paid low wages, but advanced money for taxes or other expenses (especially ceremonial expenses like marriages) to the Native Americans of their districts. When this money could not be repaid, the Spanish kept adding to the debt, but sought and obtained legal protection from default by demanding that no workers could leave their employ without first discharging their debts. This system, which has been compared to serfdom in medieval Europe, is often called the hacienda system, because large landed properties were typically composed of a combination of land and debt certificates that connected a surviving Native American polity and its cacique to a landholding Spaniard for generations.[185]

---

[182] Stephanie Wood, "The Social vs Legal Concept in Post-Conquest *Títulos*," *Ethnohistory* 38 (1991): 176–195; Robert Haskett, *Visions of Paradise: Primordial Titles and Mesoamerican History in Cuernovaca* (Norman, 2005); Yukitaka Inoue, "Fundación del pueblo, cristianidad y territorialidad en algunos *títulos primordolias* de Centro de México," *Cuadernos Canela* 18 (2007): 113–137 (online at www.canela.org.es).

[183] Gibson, *Aztecs*, pp. 166–193.

[184] Gibson, *Aztecs*, pp. 194–219; for a nuanced local study covering the same themes, Rebecca Horn, *Post-Conquest Coyoacan: Nahua-Spanish Relations in Central Mexico, 1519–1650* (Palo Alto, 1997).

[185] The classic description of the system is in François Chevalier, *Land and Society in Colonial Mexico: The Great Hacienda* (Berkeley and Los Angeles, 1963 [original French, 1933]). For some regional discussion of the evolution of the hacienda and its connection to the encomienda system, see Hans J. Prem, "Spanish Colonization and Indian Property in Central Mexico, 1521–1620," *Annals of the Association of American Geographers* 82 (1992): 444–459.

Historians have been mesmerized by the fate of Tenochtitlan and its surrounding communities around the old Aztec capital. All the events of that region were well documented, as the Spanish interests focused there, where the majority of them lived and where the seat of the colonial government lay. What happened in the capital region was repeated around other large towns where the Spanish settled, such as Puebla and Acapulco. But there were also vast stretches of Mexico that had few Spanish settlers, and they followed a different path, as we shall see, for these regions were less interesting to Spaniards, less disrupted by their presence and activity, and thus "poor" relative to centers of Spanish settlement.

PERU

By the time Pizarro entered Peru in 1532, the system of determining tribute and distributing it to followers in encomiendas was well established. He began to demand tribute and give out encomiendas on the coast around Tumbez even before he met Atahualpa at his treacherous encounter in Cajamarca.[186] Thanks to the precedent established in Mexico, as well as a body of law already regulating relations between the crown and its most successful conquistadores, Peru would follow the same trajectory as Mexico in its main lines.[187] Encomiendas in Peru were large, but they were better able to remain intact for longer time; moreover, the Inca elite did better at maintaining their power than was the case in central Mexico.

However, unlike Mexico, the Peruvian conquest was not straightforward. Instead of rewarding an independent state and using its army for further expansion, Pizarro had to deal with a faction of Peru's own core nobility in Cuzco, first Inca Manco before he refused to continue in 1536 and then Paullu who allied with him and gave him troops. In addition, whereas Cortés managed to control his subordinates, at least during the war against the Aztecs, Pizzaro soon found himself involved in a civil war with his followers. As the Spanish fought each other over control of Peru, encomiendas were given to supporters and taken from rebels (although often rebels worked out deals to retain their encomiendas in exchange for trading sides) frequently.

As the Spanish were struggling over encomiendas in Peru, the Spanish court was trying to abandon the whole system. A body of law had built up since the first attempts to regulate the giving of revenue assignments in Hispaniola, and ten years of experience in Mexico had taught the crown that it could exploit lucrative conquests directly. Thus, in 1542, Charles V issued the New Laws, effectively banning the encomienda in all Spanish territories, although the

---

[186] Francisco de Xeres, *Verdadera relación de la conquesta de Peru*, (Seville, 1534, mod. ed., Madrid, 1891), p. 48.
[187] For the encomienda in the conquest period, as well as other aspects of the society that quite closely resemble Mexico, see James Lockhart, *Spanish Peru, 1532–1560: A Social History* (Madison, 2nd edition, 1994).

legislation was in fact aimed at Peru in particular. The laws took the protection of the indigenous people of the Indies as its starting point, and worked from the premise, advanced by clergy like Las Casas, that the encomienda holders abused the Indians who were the source of income. The New Laws forbade the granting of new encomiendas (an issue of greatest import in Peru, as such grants were still being made and unmade in the turbulent civil strife), forbade officials from holding encomiendas (thus severing the connection between the principal wealth generating mechanism and the holding of legal authority), and ordered that existing grants revert to the crown upon the death of the holder. Income from the encomiendas was to be carefully noted and monitored by officials. It also made provision for the revoking of existing grants at any time, should the holder be found to be abusing his charges.[188]

In Mexico, the New Laws provided a legal basis for the rapid dismantling of Cortés's original encomienda grants, for there the crown had the upper hand, but in Peru, no such predominance held sway. In Peru, instead, it led to rebellion, as Gonzalo Pizarro, brother of the conqueror, led a revolt in 1544 with the purpose of ensuring that the grants remain. He expelled royal officers and settlers loyal to the crown and contemplated creating a Kingdom of Peru with himself as king. He arranged a royal wedding with Inca Paullu's family and hinted at the possibility of forming a joint kingdom ruled by Inca-Spanish nobles.

The revolt was dangerous to crown interests, and it backed off forbidding the granting of encomiendas to suppress it. In 1545, the crown sent Pedro de la Gasca to Peru to retake the region. He did so largely by reassuring those who supported the crown that they would be allowed to keep their encomiendas, and those who stayed with Pizarro would lose theirs. The strategy worked; when the royalist and rebel armies met at Jaquijaquana near Cuzco in 1547, most of the rebels changed sides and the battle was a lopsided victory for the crown.[189] As a result, Peru acquired a fairly stable population of some 500 encomenderos, holding large assignments of tribute-paying indigenous people.[190]

Viceroy Francisco de Toledo, who arrived in Peru in 1571, consolidated the system of rule, accepting the settlement of the encomiendas made in the 1560s. He apparently also hoped that he could use the opportunity of reorganization to reduce the power of the kuraka class, perhaps in ways similar to what had been done in Mexico. In his inquest into Inca history and customs commissioned by the Viceroy, Pedro Sarmiento de Gamboa found testimony that contended that the kuraka class had been created by the Inca Yupanqui as a fully

---

[188] *The New Laws of the Indies*, ed. Henry Stevens (London, 1893 [this edition includes the Spanish text]). The Spanish version is on the Web at http://www.cervantesvirtual.com/servlet/SirveObras/06922752100647273089079/p0000026.htm

[189] Hemming, *Conquest*, pp. 266–268.

[190] Peter Blakwell, "La maduración del gobierno del Perú de década 1560," *Historia Mexicana* 39 (1989): 41–70.

dependent officialdom, removable at will.[191] He noted that even though he had been informed of the "tyranny that the Incas ruled the country," Spain would recognize the "children and descendents of the Ingas" and give them something "to eat," which meant grants of land and income.[192] On the other hand, witnesses at local inquests conducted at the same time contended that the kurakas were both ancient and local. In the end, the crown could not simply reduce the old elite to the status of crown officials and accepted the local and hereditary status of the kurakas.

Much of Toledo's administrative summary involved the regularization of tribute, encomienda, service, and other matters, but also gave tax exemption to some 400 Cañares who had served in the wars, but who ordered to perform domestic security tasks, such as guarding roads.[193] More significantly, he created a new provincial system, managed to secure control of a number of encomiendas, and instituted a system of corregidors (as in Mexico) to connect the Spanish state to the indigenous nobility.[194]

In Peru, the Spanish adopted the Inca system of rotational labor, *mita*, into vast labor drafts to send to the airless mountaintop of Potosí where huge reserves of silver were discovered in 1561, or to the poisonous mercury mines of Huevelcar to extract the mercury needed to convert silver ore into a finished product. Workers in Peru were not employed only in mining. Of course, initially they needed to produce the surplus food necessary to support the mining operations. In addition, they were employed in other services such as carrying products or even in producing cash crops to feed the miners as well as the Spanish with their vast army of servants, professionals, and tradespeople who settled in the cities that the silver financed.[195]

SLAVERY, RACE MIXING, AND LABOR

From the very beginning, Spanish settlers in America needed a permanent subservient labor force for household service and for many types of agricultural and ranching activities. The system of rotational tribute labor, the taxation strategy of sixteenth-century Hispaniola, or the various rotational labor systems in use to supply mines in Mexico and Peru, did not provide for a permanent labor force or for household service. Thus the Spanish, in theory, would have to use either immigrant Spanish workers or slaves as their labor force for permanent residence. Spanish who came to America were not interested in performing menial labor such as household service, and were not much more

[191] Sarmiento de Gamboa, *Historia*, cap. 50 and 52.
[192] Francisco de Toledo to King, March 1, 1572, *Gobernantes de Perú* (ed. Roberto Levillier, 14 vols, Madrid, 1924–1926) 4: 210.
[193] Toledo to King, March 1, 1572, *Gobernates de Perú* 4: 228.
[194] Blakewell, "Maduración."
[195] Jeffrey Cole, *The Potosí Mita, 1573–1700 Compulsory Indian Labor in the Andes* (Palo Alto, 1985).

inclined to be subservient even in skilled labor. For a Spanish artisan, for example, to serve as a journeyman or laborer under a Spanish master was no better than remaining in Spain, and most expected to become masters themselves or to return home where they were on more familiar ground.[196]

Consequently, one of the most important solutions to obtaining a permanent labor force for service, for tasks requiring year-round attention and those requiring skill or training, was to employ slaves. Hispaniola society had an existing group of slaves called *naborías*, and these were enlisted in Spanish service, as were captives in wars or rebellions in the early sixteenth century. As conquest spread out from the islands, slaves were captured as well from many other places. Native American slaves were acquired initially from raiding around the Caribbean basin; for example, the Spanish soon removed virtually all the population from the Bahamas (Lucayos) islands to serve as permanent workers in Hispaniola. Later, the coasts and other islands were also raided. Sometimes this was done by roving bands of Spanish mariners; often it was done in conjunction with Native American groups. Already by the 1520s, Spanish were obtaining slaves from the north coast of South America with the assistance of Carib allies, and later still, Spanish removed the risk altogether from themselves by buying slaves on slave markets in the Caribbean, in central America, and in Venezuela.[197]

Crown policy then was to declare that war on Native Americans was only to be a "just war," usually justified by what were perceived as inhuman practices on the part of the group under attack, such as cannibalism, or just for revenge for previous attacks on Spanish colonies or subjects. This policy allowed the crown to determine who could be attacked, to tax and regulate the attacks that were authorized, and to punish or sequester the fruits of those that were not, all in the name of justice. Thus, as in the encomienda policy, the crown used its claims to promote justice as a means to limit and control the slave trade.

If the Spanish crown had scruples about the slave trade in Native Americans, it was quite willing to participate in the African slave trade, and even Las Casas, champion of the suppression of the Native American slave trade and encomienda, envisioned African slaves as replacing both the encomienda and Native American slavery, although he would later regret the position. Spain had no significant commercial ties in Africa and certainly no military ones, and the crown farmed out the right to deliver African slaves to Portuguese merchants who had the relevant access to African supplies of slaves.[198] In this way, the crown had better fiscal control and could obtain maximum revenue by supplying slaves. African slaves were expensive, and for the most part went only to rich areas, either as service workers in the cities of the mining areas or in areas

---

[196] These ideas were quite fully developed in Lockhart, *Spanish Peru*, pp. 11–109, based on the experience of Peru during the conquest period, actually before 1560. He also explored them more fully in Lockhart and Schwartz, *Early Latin America*, pp.132–142, but without the full documentation.

[197] See Sauer, *Spanish Main*, pp. 119, 154, 194 et *passim*.

[198] Enriqueta Vila Vilar, *Hispanoamerica y el comercio de esclavos* (Seville, 1977).

that produced a high-value export crop, like the sugar estates of Hispaniola (before 1580) and along the Mexican coast (after 1560 or so).

In many areas, however, no form of slave trade fully supplied the need for permanent workers, especially in places like Mexico and Peru, where a large settler community developed and the demands for service and skilled labor, and even for casual labor in an urban setting, made the needs for permanent suppressed populations necessary. There many Native Americans immigrated illegally (but with little opposition in spite of the law, which was aimed higher up the social ladder after all) to the cities, presented themselves as "mestizos" (people of mixed ancestry) or sometimes as "ladinos" (simply people who could speak Spanish and follow European cultural norms), and were ruled by Spanish rather than Native American law.[199] The mestizo class was probably at least partially real, as some Spanish did maintain sexual relations with Native Americans, although undoubtedly many pure Native Americans managed to live in cities and other places of concentrated Spanish settlement by pretending to be mixed. Spanish Cabildos passed legislation to prohibit the participation by such people in the decision-making process, on the basis that any mixed-race person must not be the product of a legal marriage, and thus bore the stain of illegitimacy. They also ensured that African slaves, or free people of African descent, could not participate in the government of cabildos on the basis that they bore a stain of slavery. Spanish census returns from Mexico and Peru in the late sixteenth century reveal the presence of large numbers – indeed a substantial majority – of "negros, mulattos and mestizos" in all the large cities.

Although born of legal necessity and social reality, the racial categories created by these manipulations took hold and eventually led to a socially inspired caste system that legal proceedings from the municipal councils tended to reinforce. In time, the racial term "white" (*blanco*) came to replace "Christian" as the designator for a European, and the system hardened.[200] To this were added additional prohibitions against the legal enfranchisement of formerly enslaved groups including those of African or mixed Native America and European descent, based on a hereditary ascription of the stains of slavery or illegitimacy, now transformed into racial categories and eventually justified by new racial ideologies in the eighteenth century.

THE POOR AREAS OF SPANISH AMERICA

The battle over the encomienda in the 1530s and 1540s, with all its drama and its supercharged air of human rights, was reserved primarily for the great empires of the Americas and had hardly any impact in the regions where smaller and divided indigenous polities created small encomiendas, held by a multitude of Spaniards. The New Laws inhibited the use of local people as slaves, and

---

[199] For the reality as practiced in Mexico, see Cope, *Racial Dominance*.
[200] The classic statement remains Magnus Mörner, *Race Mixture in the History of Latin America* (Boston, 1967).

this could have had impact on areas such as the pearl fisheries of Venezuela, where the labor force was primarily enslaved; in fact, however, it had little impact, except perhaps to Africanize the labor force. As the crown controlled the slave trade from Africa, however, this solution was more acceptable than one in which local labor was employed. In Guatemala, Panama, Oaxaca, the Yucatán, and other areas that produced few spectacularly rich products and created mini-kingdoms for Spanish settlers, there was only the most nominal attempt to suppress or retake the encomiendas. There the encomienda system hung on for very long, in some cases right through the colonial period, if not in legal name, in effective fact.

As the rich areas developed under the Spanish crown, and the encomienda gave rise to the peculiar labor system of the late sixteenth century, the poor areas that did not produce great wealth continued more or less under the original encomienda system. Yucatán, for example, while it possessed exports of value, did not generate enough wealth to make the encomienda holders there targets for either the crown's lawyers or wealthy Spanish nobles. Thus cacique and encomienda holders remained for much longer, undisturbed. Even as the legal system changed with the New Laws, the reality of the relationship remained. Thus one can find the encomienda system still flourishing in places like rural Oaxaca, Venezuela, Guatemala, and Yucatán well into the seventeenth century.

Very few Spaniards settled in Oaxaca, which remained firmly under the control of its local elites, at least initially. However, Oaxaca did produce exports for the growing city of Mexico, and even for regional markets, and Spaniards focused their attention on commercial activities that would deliver these goods to the market, rather than on the production end. Local caciques in a fairly decentralized political system sometimes managed to convert what had been public lands to their private use, and some commoners also managed to acquire land and participate in the larger economy. Even though the pressures were different from those in the Valley of Mexico or Peru, the colonial government supported a great many lawsuits and reorganizations that worked against caciques and centralized authority.[201] They awarded lesser nobles decisions in lawsuits against caciques, and this worked to destabilize the older elite. They even favored wealthier nonelites, *machuales*, who had enriched themselves in trade. As a result, Oaxaca developed a new sort of social system, ostensibly based on the Spanish chartered town, in which caciques, wealthy commoners, and other nobles participated. Virtually all the caciques disappeared, and many of the nobles who became landholders replaced them, but exercising their power through the municipal councils rather than the older state apparatus. As a result, thanks to the absence of the Spanish as landholders, Oaxaca became essentially controlled by Native Americans elites who were tied by commerce,

[201] Judith Zeitlan and Lilian Thomas, "Spanish Justice and the Indian Cacique: Disjunctive Political Systems in Sixteenth Century Tehuantepec," *Ethnohistory* 39 (1992): 285–315.

production, and taxation to the colony, who adopted Spanish social forms to their own status system, but were otherwise self-governing.[202]

The Spanish conquest of the Maya region in Yucatán was very slow; in fact, by 1546, when the first phase of conquest was over, only a ring of states along the coast had been conquered, leaving most of the interior still under Maya rule. The coexistence of the Spanish colony with a fairly powerful unconquered state system left those who lived in the conquered regions more room to maneuver. The undefeated regions became magnets for population that fled to them, a problem compounded for the Spanish by the fact that Maya rural populations had always been unsettled and moved frequently, probably for ecological as well as political reasons. In an attempt to counter this, the Spanish tried, with relatively little success, to fix the population in larger units through the process of *reducción*.

Without the pressure of wealthier Spaniards or a strong drive on the part of Spanish residents toward developing landholdings, the encomienda system was reorganized but not eliminated as the New Laws were enacted. Most of the land and production remained in the hands of the Maya states, and encomienda grantees respected their boundaries, although their populations often did not as they moved from one jurisdiction to another.

Maya political structures and forms were integrated into Spanish-style municipal councils, with the wealthy nobles holding office and rotating it every few years. At the same time, these nobles produced cash crops or rendered goods and services to the Spanish, who often resided in a handful of special towns established during the conquest. One of the most common forms of taxation was called *repartimiento*, in which the Spanish would deliver imported products in exchange for goods the Maya produced, such as unspun cotton, honey, or wax, in an uneven exchange that took much of the profit from the producer.[203]

The Maya, Lenca, and Pipil populations of the Kingdom of Guatemala had a different fate, because the Spanish were able to work gold in that area, albeit on a smaller scale than in Mexico or Peru. Labor was extracted first from among the inhabitants of the encomiendas liable for personal service, and by a good number of slaves, both indigenous and African, until the New Laws required an alteration in arrangements. Then, as in Mexico, the towns and gold-mining regions moved to taxation and paid labor, on lands that Spanish acquired by purchase, grant from vacant land, or other means.[204]

[202] William Taylor, *Landlord and Peasant in Colonial Oaxaca* (Stanford, 1972); María de los Angeles Romero [Frizzi], *Economía y vida de los españoles en la Mixteca Alta, 1510–1710* (Mexico, 1990), and also her overview chapter, "The Indigenous Population of Oaxaca from the Sixteenth Century to the Present," in *Cambridge History* 2/2, pp. 302–345.

[203] Nancy Fariss, *Maya Society under Colonial Rule: The Collective Enterprise of Survival* (Princeton, 1984).

[204] This process is thoroughly described for Honduras in Linda Newson, *The Cost of Conquest: Indian Decline in Honduras under Spanish Rule* (Boulder and London, 1986).

Other regions that were conquered and divided into encomiendas also appear to have followed similar trajectories: for example, much of the Gulf Coast of Mexico, both the lowlands and the highlands, attracted few Spanish settlers and were typically integrated into the larger regional economy as producers of consumption goods. Production was left in the hands of the elite among the Native Totonacs, while the Spanish presence was limited to commercial activity and taxation.[205]

In the Rio de la Plata region, the encomienda was not even introduced until some twenty years after the initial founding of Asunción, during which time the Spanish and Guanani elite managed to merge their families and to make use of Guarani modes of labor control in the mini-state organization of the region. The original founders of Asunción were probably granted encomiendas of the Carios who supported them, for in 1556, an aged Juan de Salazar requested of the crown that the encomienda, which once had "thousands of Indians," that was granted to him as an original settler be extended to a perpetual grant.[206] When it was introduced in 1556, the system simply accepted the existing arrangements using an encomendero class of mixed Spanish-Guarani origin. These encomiendas, called *originarios*, did not involve taxes or labor services in the sense that they did in Mexico or Peru, but rather a system of family labor.

If in Mexico mestizos were socially low, the group was not poorly regarded in the Rio de la Plata area, where mestizos held offices and were among the original founders of a number of towns. Beyond the *originarios* were outlying estates, known as *encomiendas mitayos* because, unlike the *originarios* whose inhabitants lived near to Asuncion and were more or less fixed on the estates, the *mitayos* were required to migrate to work in the town (the name deriving from Peru, where such migrant labor to the mines was an important part of the system). Here encomenderos drawn from the same Guarani-Spanish ruling group, consolidated villages and used their labor to manage production, but generally on home farms rather than in mines.[207]

ANGOLA: A RICH POOR COLONY

The Portuguese conquest of Angola was not nearly as complete as Spanish conquests were in much of America. No state fell to Portugal, although they did manage to take over some of the smaller mini-states that made up the larger kingdom of Ndongo, their principal target. The *sobas* or rulers of the mini-states were charged tribute, much as Spanish caciques were, but sobas

---

[205] For a brief overview and bibliographical study of what work has been done by historians, see Susan Deans-Smith, "Native Peoples of the Gulf Coast form the Colonial Period to the Present," in *Cambridge History of Native Peoples* 2/2: 274–301.

[206] Juan de Salazar to Council of Indies, March 20, 1556, in Peliza, ed. *Historia y descurbrimiento*, p. 201.

[207] For an overview, see Elman Service, "The Encomienda in Paraguay," *Hispanic American Historical Review* 31 (1951): 230–252.

generally rendered their services as soldiers, and later as porters for trading expeditions.

In the late sixteenth century, the collection of income from conquered sobas was through the amo system, in which a Portuguese settler was assigned a soba to support him, and an African Christian, usually from Kongo was recruited to serve as administrator.[208] But while this system had the potential to develop as the encomienda system did, in fact, there was no real exchange of labor or money.[209] Rather, Portuguese settlers, who lived interspersed with sobas' territories, acquired land through grants given by the colonial government from vacant land under the Portuguese law of *sesmaria*.[210] These lands, in turn, were worked by slaves the owners acquired as part of the participation in military ventures, or through trade with the interior kingdoms.[211] The resulting estate, called an *arimo*, was the core of settlement for Portuguese who lived in the colony.

The arimos in turn grew export crops, not usually for sale outside Africa, but to support the thousands of slaves who were concentrated in Luanda and its immediate hinterland awaiting transportation. The will of Gaspar Álvares, a successful settler, in 1623 revealed that he owned lands worked by slaves that produced grain, pigs, and cattle for the Luanda market; he also owned slaves he intended to export to Brazil or to Spanish America (for which he had bills of sale). Beyond these, Álvares also used slaves as workers in his commercial enterprises in both Kongo and the colony of Angola.[212] Surveys of agricultural production in the seventeenth century reveal thousands of sacks of grain were delivered annually to the city, using water transport routes along the Bengo and Kwanza Rivers. Smaller concentrations of landholders supported the interior forts, whose garrisons and small resident communities required food.[213]

---

[208] Fernão Guerreiro, *Relaçam Annal das Cousas que fizeram os Padres da Companhia de Jesus nas suas Missões* (4 vols., Lisbon, 1603–1611, mod. ed. A. Viegas, 3 vols, Lisbon 1930–1952) 1: 395–396. Taken from the annual letter of 1602–1603; Andrew Battel, "The Strange Adventures of Andrew Battel of Leigh in Angola…" in Samuel Purchas, *Hakluytus Posthumus, or Purchas his Pilgrimes* (London, 1625, modern edition of this chapter, E. G. Ravenstein, London 1901), pp. 64–65.

[209] For a detailed discussion of the early amo system, see Beatrix Heintze, "Die Portugiesische Besiedlungs- und Wirtschaftspolitik in Angola 1570–1607," *Aufsätze zur portugiesischen Kulturgeschichte* 17 (1981–2): 200–219.

[210] Legal aspects are visible in the earliest surviving grants of this type, given to the Jesuits, August 15, 1584, and Martim Rodrigues de Godoi, April 2, 1587, *MMA* 4: 433–439; 461–464. Many were given without papers, but orally attested, as with several given in the period between 1582 and 1858, that were later donated to the Jesuits; "Das Cousas de rais de Angolla, 1612," *MMA* 6: 91–98; Mendes de Castelo Branco, "Relação," ca. 1621, *MMA* 6: 459–460.

[211] Under terms such as those of Baltasar Bebelo de Aragão's letter of sesmaria, June 6, 1611, *MMA* 6: 8–10. A list of those later obtained by or donated to the Jesuits is found in "Das cousas de rais de Angolla, 1612," *MMA* 6: 91–98.

[212] Will of Gaspar Alvares, 1623, *MMA* 7: 89–95.

[213] Library of Congress, Portuguese MSS P-27, fol. 153, "Advertencias mais modernos e particulares … ao Reyno de Congo, e Angola," n.d. ca. 1674; for detailed geographical notes, see Cadornega, *História* 3: 5–185, for about 1680.

Angola's primary export was slaves. In the sixteenth and much of the seventeenth century, slaves were acquired first by military expeditions led by the governors of their lieutenants, but staffed by soldiers drawn from the resident Portuguese and the subordinate sobas. However, as the frontier extended inland, and as a result of military setbacks, long-range wars died down and were replaced by commercial expeditions, usually conducted by the resident Portuguese or more often their agents, called *pombeiros*. Thus a successful eighteenth-century settler would have an arimo located near Luanda or another post, and also had trading links, managed by pombeiros stretching to the slave markets of the north, east, or south.[214]

While their arimos supported them, they benefited little from the slave trade, the most lucrative part of which was under the governors, monopoly merchants based in Portugal and later in Brazil, and the crown. They were, however, often asked to abandon farms and homes to fight in wars that the governors wages in hopes of acquiring slaves. Sometimes they protested against these demands, as they did in 1660 when they refused to fight in Kisama in order to fill the governor's plantation in Brazil with slaves.[215]

Although profitable, the slave trade and related farming were not lucrative enough to allow Angolan settlers to bring in European women. As a result, as in the Americas, they ended up marrying into the families of the most powerful of the African ruling elite. Also as in those parts of America where wealth did not reach critical levels, there was a complex of family mixtures between the settlers and the sobas, creating mixed-race people on both sides of the legal divide between Portuguese and African law.

---

[214] Joseph C. Miller, *Way of Death: Merchant Capitalism and the Angolan Slave Trade, 1730–1830* (Madison, 1988), pp. 173–313.

[215] AHU Cx 7, doc. 8, Consulta of September 27, 1660; Cx. 8, doc. 8, Report of Bartholemeu Paes Bulhão, May 16, 1664.

6

Colonization

Colonization took place most commonly where Europeans could not obtain income through absorbing or conquering an existing state and its tax structure. This was clearly the case in uninhabited areas, but it was just as problematic when they faced free-association societies that leveled no taxes, but were not militarily strong or united enough to prevent some sort of establishment. It also took place where the weaker sort of states existed, not strong enough to expel the invaders but not producing enough surplus to warrant conquest. Although all the European powers that ventured into the Atlantic colonized one place or another, the Portuguese in Brazil and northern Europeans had colonization as their major form of expansion, and for them the uniform problem was dealing with unconquered free associations.

The first places the Europeans colonized were the uninhabited islands of the Atlantic, beginning with Madeira (1415) and the Azores (1437), followed by the Cape Verde Islands (1461) and culminating with the establishment of a colony on the Island of São Tomé (1485) near the Nigerian coast. The problem was how to exploit these places where there was no local population, but where soil and other resources promised some valuable return, starting with tropical hardwoods, and often going to wheat, sugar, and then to wine in the case of Madeira. The Portuguese crown typically gave these islands to their supporters with generous charters and feudal-style tenure, although they modified these as time and circumstances changed.[1]

In the earliest period, the Portuguese simply brought in European settlers – the first settlers in Madeira apparently transported workers from Europe. Some were transported from as far afield as Germany for in 1457, a German settler imported several "cultivators" (*lavradores*) to work on land he had been granted.[2] Madeira produced wheat initially, but by the 1450s, sugar was the

---

[1] A classic study, still valid for its legal dimensions, is Charles Verlinden, "Feudal and Desmenial Froms of Portuguese Colonization in the Atlantic Zone in the Fourteenth and Fifteenth Century, Especially under Henry the Navigator," in Verlinden, ed., *The Beginnings of Modern Colonization* (tr. Yvonne Frecuccero, Ithaca, 1970 [original article in French 1955]), pp. 203–240.

[2] Verlinden, "Feudal and Desmenial," p. 218.

leading crop; indeed, Madeira was one of Portugal's principal sugar-producing regions by the end of the century. European laborers were augmented briefly by slaves taken from the Canaries or purchased in Africa, although they were never enough to be a visible factor in the island's demography. But even in the 1450s, the first vines were being grown that would eventually produce Madeira's famous wines, and its most important export by the end of the sixteenth century.[3] The Azores were exploited in a similar way, primarily through the import of European workers on small properties, but they were not as successful as Madeira either in the production of sugar or wine, and instead were most valuable for the production of subsistence products to feed fleets that passed them, as the island group was a strategic outpost in the Atlantic.[4]

The Cape Verde islands, like those farther out, were uninhabited when the first Europeans came to them in the mid-fifteenth century, and like the Azores were not capable of producing much in the way of sugar, although the crop was tried there as elsewhere in the Atlantic.[5] However, in the Cape Verdes, the population derived mostly from African slaves who were brought over by the earliest settlers, rather than European peasants or free farmers. Some of the settlers may also have been free people from Africa, for some sixteenth-century Cape Verdians reported that they descended from refugees from the Senegalese kingdom of Great Jolof. The slaves of the islands produced a unique cotton cloth that was widely traded and valued throughout West Africa and eventually became one if its important exports, though primarily for the export of slaves bound for the American side of the Atlantic world.

Finally, the island of São Tomé, and its tiny neighbor Príncipe, located in the Gulf of Guinea, was by far the most successful of the sugar-producing African Atlantic islands. Sugar was established there from early times, and by the middle of the sixteenth century, the island became the leading sugar producer for Europe, yielding this distinction to Brazil only around 1600.[6] Although the initial settlement was made using the children of Jewish families taken by the Portuguese crown during a period of persecution, the vast majority of the inhabitants were drawn from African slaves taken from the adjourning coasts, especially from Benin and Kongo. Larger sugar estates developed on São Tomé than in Madeira, each like a little village, or perhaps even a small town. A number were financed directly by the crown, which, seeing the advantages of sugar production, took the risks of establishing mills. As in the Cape Verdes, some of the estates appear to have been founded or at least owned by members of the

---

[3] Vitorino Magalhães-Godinho, *Os Descobrimentos e a economia mundial* (2nd rev. ed., 4 vols, Lisbon, 1981–1983, reprinted 1991) 3: 231–240 and 4: 72–93.

[4] T. Bentley Duncan, *Atlantic Islands: Madeira, the Azores and the Cape Verdes in Seventeenth Century Commerce and Navigation* (Chicago and London, 1972). On the sugar of the Azores, see Magalhães-Godinho, *Descobrimentos* 4: 94–95.

[5] Magalhães-Godinho, *Descobrimentos* 4: 95. The islands did produce good sugar, and continued well into the sixteenth century.

[6] Magalhães-Godinho, *Descobrimentos* 4: 95–99.

African nobility. The kings of Kongo seem to have invested in some, and others may have had connection to Benin.[7]

Very few Europeans survived on the island, reputed to have such an inimical climate that Portuguese courts, chafing that Canon Law would not render the death penalty against clergy, exiled ecclesiastical malefactors deemed worthy of death to São Tomé, confident that the climate would soon work the appropriate sentence. The elite of the island, given its diverse origins, was largely either wholly African in origin or the mixed-race descendents of the early settlers, and in this way it differed from all the other plantation colonies established in the Atlantic, even as in many ways its combination of sugar, grinding mills, and slaves represented a typical or even a model of its type.

In 1709, the mixed-race faction petitioned the crown with the proposal that only they, possessing European ancestry, should be eligible to hold high positions in local government. Their African-descended rivals countered with the claim that they were equally worthy, and that descent was less important; it was their position that won royal favor.

COASTAL BRAZIL

Whereas uninhabited islands needed labor forces, the inhabited areas of America required both an adequate labor force and a way to cope with their indigenous neighbors. As these neighbors were usually free associations, they could not be made to work through the manipulation of their own forced labor and taxation systems, as the Spanish had done in their conquests. If they were to be a labor force, they had to be either persuaded to work for profit or forced to as slaves. But here the paradox was that not only were free associations difficult to engage in poorly remunerated labor, but they were also virtually impossible to conquer by military action. Hence all colonies founded in these areas had to work with indigenous people as a military threat or as military allies and to enslave them at the same time.

These problems were all evident in the Portuguese settlement in Brazil, the first example of a colony founded in an environment of free associations.[8] The issue of relations with the indigenous Tupi-speaking neighbors of the Portuguese settlements was compounded by the complicated international politics of the settlement, as other European rivals – initially Spain and France, but later also the Netherlands and England – were competing with them over settlement and trade.

---

[7] On the Kongo connection, see John Thornton, "Early Kongo-Portuguese Relations: A New Interpretation," *History in Africa* 8 (1981): 191–192.

[8] A good overview, based on up-to-date research of Brazil's sixteenth- and early-seventeenth-century history, is found in Jorge Couto, *A construção do Brasil: Ameríndios, Portugueses e Africanos do início do povamento a finais do quinhentos* (2nd ed., Lisbon, 1997); for the longer period, see also the relevant volumes (6, 7, 8) of Joel Serrão and A. H. de Oliveira Marques, gen. eds., *Nova História da expansão portuguesa* (Lisbon, 1992).

The Portuguese were creating their colony as the Spanish were engaged in conquest in the Caribbean and American mainland, while at the same time French voyagers were also exploring the Atlantic. The first Portuguese visited Brazil in a fleet under Pedro Álvares Cabral in 1500, who stopped over on his way to India following a storm. A French voyage of exploration followed in 1503, probably probing around or south of modern-day Santos. Portugal, citing the treaty of Tordesillas of 1494 in which the Pope divided the world between Spain and Portugal, insisted that Brazil belonged to them and kicked off a long-lasting rivalry with France over the trade of Brazil. Spanish sailors, visiting the southern part of the region in 1516, followed by Magellan's celebrated voyage around South America in 1520, brought Spain to the region.[9] Spain's first serious attempt to colonize the region along the Rio de la Plata and its branches that would become Argentina, Uruguay, and Paraguay took place in 1536.

Initially, European sailors did not settle at all in Brazil, but visited the coast to trade in locally produced hardwoods.[10] Free associations were engaged in a profitable trade, because the wood traders brought steel implements and sold them to the Tupi inhabitants of the coast in exchange for wood. The steel tools made it possible to cut down the massive trees, and at the same time provided the indigenous population with new and valuable implements to use in a variety of other ways.[11] For this they were willing to travel considerable distances, according to the French visitor André Thevet in the 1550s, up to 25 or even 30 kilometers bearing the heavy logs.[12] A Portuguese ship's log of 1511 gives an idea of its early scale, for the ship returned with some 5,000 pounds of wood, along with some other exotic and tropical goods that made up Brazil's exports.[13]

Portugal claimed a monopoly in this trade, and chafed at competition by merchants originating in other countries, especially France. In 1527, Portugal sent a fleet to patrol the waters off Brazil and enforce its monopoly, and it was

[9] Couto, *Construção*, pp. 199–206.

[10] The classic treatment of the Native inhabitants of Brazil and their relationship with the Portuguese is still John Hemming, *Red Gold: The Conquest of the Brazilian Indians, 1500–1760* (Cambridge, MA, 1978), but see the more nuanced treatment of John Monteiro, "The Crises and Transformations of Invaded Societies: Coastal Brazil in the Sixteenth Century," in Frank Salomon and Stuart B. Schwartz, eds., *The Cambridge History of the Native Peoples of the Americas* (6 vols, Cambridge, 1999) vol. 3, part 1, pp. 973–1074.

[11] This early economy was described in detail in Alexander Marchant, *From Barter to Slavery* (Baltimore, 1942), still a classic text, albeit one whose overall interpretation has been seriously challenged; for a recent overview, see Couto, *Construção*, pp. 281–284.

[12] André Thevet, *Les singularités de la France Antarctique, autrement nommée Amérique...*(Paris, 1558; mod. ed., Frank Lestringant, in *Le Brésil d'André Thevet* [Paris, 1997]), cap. 59, pp. 226–228; idem, *Cosmographie Universelle* (Paris, 1575; mod. ed. Suzanne Lusagnet, in *Les Français en Amérique pendant la deuxième moitié du XVIe siècle: Le Brésil et les brésiliens* [Paris, 1953]), p. 221.

[13] "Llyuro da naoo Bertoa que vay para a terra do Brazyll," in Carlos Malheiro Dias, ed., *História da colonização portuguesa do Brasil* (3 vols, Porto, 1924–1926) 2: 343–347.

soon engaged in naval battles with French and Spanish vessels. Finally, King
João III concluded that the best way to prevent French trade and limit Spanish
claims was to establish permanent bases on the coast. An initial voyage led
by Martim Afonso de Sousa planted a colony at São Vicente (near modern-
day São Paulo) in 1532 after capturing many French ships along the coast.[14]
Encouraged by this development, João III decided to establish a dozen more
posts (called donatary captaincies) all along the coast between 1534 and 1536.
To save crown funds, each donatary captain was to use his own resources
to establish a permanent colony to serve as a naval-military base against the
French and Spanish rivals. Donataries had to develop profitable enterprises to
meet these expenses and make the effort worthwhile. To encourage them, the
crown granted the donataries wide-ranging legal powers, tax exemptions, and
other privileges.[15]

Many of these captaincies either failed or did not develop. Without making
allies with a sufficiently powerful indigenous group, any colony was doomed,
as the historian João de Barros discovered when he belatedly tried to take up
his assigned donation at Maranahão around the mouth of the Amazon River, in
the heart of the domain of the Potiguars who, thanks to an earlier alliance with
French traders, killed as many as 900 colonists and soldiers that the historian
sent there in 1553.[16] Similarly, attempts to found a colony at Espirito Santo
on the coast south of Bahia were ruined by the fighters of the Cricaré in the
1560s, while the Waitacá similarly defeated Portuguese settlers and destroyed
their mills in Ilheus.[17]

As the Portuguese were struggling to build viable colonies along the coast
to counter French commerce, the French turned themselves to colonization
schemes. The most important early French attempt to colonize Brazil was made
in 1555 at the site of future Rio de Janeiro, which they dubbed "Antarctic
France." French sailors made alliances with the Tamoios. In the end, however,
their Tamoio allies were not enough to prevent Portuguese forces allied with
the Tupinambá of Bahia from destroying the settlement in 1560.

The São Vicente colony and the two captaincies of the northeast, Bahia
and Pernambuco, did make the requisite allies, and grew from posts to defend
a trade monopoly to major bases for the Portuguese penetration of Brazil.
The settlement at São Vicente moved to the town of São Paulo on the plateau
behind the coast to solidify an alliance made with four villages of Tupi who
were loyal to João Romalho, a shipwrecked sailor who had won fame and followers in the area.[18] Ramalho married Bartira, daughter of a prominent leader

[14] Couto, *Construção*, pp. 210–216.
[15] For a fuller description of the legal and technical background, see António Vasconcelos de
     Saldanha, *As Capitanias: O Regime senhorial na expansão ultramarina portuguesa* (Funchal,
     1992).
[16] Salvador, *Historia* book 2, cap. 13.
[17] Pero Rodrigues to João Alvares, 1597, *Anais de Biblioteca Nactional* 20 (1897 [BNRJ]): 255–
     256; Salvador, *Historia*, Book 4, cap. 34.
[18] Salvador, *Historia* book 2, cap. 2.

named Tebiriçá who, after demonstrating his competence as a war leader, had come to lead the federation. Ramalho then became a prominent ally of the first captain, Mem de Sá, in the 1530s, and immediately offered fighters loyal to him to defend the colony.[19] By the time the Jesuits wrote the first description of his situation in 1553, Ramalho had accumulated a large number of loyal followers and had fathered many children. Ulrich Schmidel, who visited his village (which he thought a "robber's lair") the same year, saw him as a rival to São Vicente, for he had more soldiers than the official Portuguese government and claimed to rule on his own behalf, saying he "had lived, warred, and ruled for 40 years in India [America]."[20]

Other marriages cemented the fledgling colony to its Native American supporters. Álvaro Rodrigues, another shipwrecked sailor who married a daughter of a local leader named Piquerohy, contributed to the early alliances.[21] Drawn by the success of Ramalho and Rodrigues and the potential force of an even larger alliance, other Tupi groups moved voluntarily into the area to ally with the Portuguese. Portuguese settlers who came with Mem de Sá and immediately afterward fell into the tradition of consolidating alliances with Tupi groups through marriage. Domingos Luiz Grou married a daughter of the leader of Carapucuibas who lived near Ramalho's territory, Braz Gonçalves married a daughter of the leader of Virapueiras, and Pedro Dias, a lay Jesuit, left his order to marry a second daughter of Tebriça, leader of Inhapuambuçú.[22]

Pernambuco, like São Vicente/São Paulo, was also militarily successful, thanks to the skill and tenacity of its donatary, Duarte Coelho, who founded the first settlement at Igaraçu.[23] To achieve security, Vasco Fernandes de Lucena married the daughter of a Tobajara principal, assuring their assistance.[24] His colony was almost immediately at war with the Caeté and Tupinambá who surrounded it and who had intermittent aid from French sailors anxious to ward off Portuguese control of the coast. The indigenous coalition mounted an expedition as large as 8,000 to attack the new settlements in 1549. Within a few years, 10,000 archers helped the Portuguese ward off attacks.[25] When Coelho organized a counterattack in 1569, he gathered six companies of Europeans "among whom they divided twenty thousand *negros* [in this case meaning "indians"] mostly from the heathens of the backwoods of logwood [*Gentio da matta do páu brasil*], enemies of those on the Cape," adding 35 European and

---

[19] João Ramalho's early life and even the circumstances of his being where he was in 1532 are uncertain, and clouded by detailed legends that grew up. For the basics of his contribution to the founding of São Paulo, see Manuel de Nóbrega to Simão Rodrigues, January 6, 1550; end of August 1552 and June 15, 1553, Serafim Leite, *Cartas do Brasil e mais escritos do P. Manuel da Nóbrega* (Coimbra, 1955); Tome de Sousa to King, July 1, 1553 in Dias, ed., *História* 3: 365.

[20] Schmidel, *Warhafftige Beschreibung*, p. 64.

[21] Luiz Gonzaga da Silva Leme, *Genealogia Paulistana* (9 vols, São Paulo, 1903–1905) 1: 1.

[22] Da Silva Leme, *Genealogia* 1: 15 (Grou); 22 (Gonçalves); 45 (Dias),

[23] Salvador, *Historia*, book 2, cap. 8.

[24] Salvador, *Historia*, book 2, cap. 9

[25] Salvador, *Historia*, book 2, cap. 10.

2,000 allied archers [*frecheiros*] from the island of Tamaracá. It was protected by a ring of allied Tobojara groups, and then by other indigenous groups, who, impressed by this success, joined the Portuguese.

Bahia, to the south of Pernambuco also had some success, after a bad beginning. They secured the alliance of Diogo Álvares who, like João Ramalho in São Vicente, was shipwrecked there, took the local name of Caramuru, and married Paraguaçu, the daughter of an important Tupinamba leader. Initially, he engaged in the logging trade with French shippers, and although he visited France in 1526–1528, he eventually decided to assist the first Portuguese to come to the region in 1532. Although he was unable to prevent the colony's destruction by indigenous attackers in 1545–1546, he remained steadfast in his support of Portugal.[26] Governor Mem de Sá, who came to the reestablished colony in 1549, required that the indigenous members of the alliance accept Christianity and allow missionaries in their settlements.[27] Their allies assisted in 1560 by traveling all the way to Rio de Janeiro to help defeat the French.[28]

The war against the French was almost immediately followed by an even more difficult one against the Aimoré, free associations from farther in the interior. The Aimoré began attacks on the coast in 1555 and continued them intermittently throughout the rest of the sixteenth century, making life miserable for Bahia and the whole coast south of it. The Jesuit Pero Rodrigues, writing in 1597, noted that the Aimoré had "destroyed the Captaincies of Ilheos and Porto Seguro and are already at the limits of the city [of Salvador, Bahia]." They were nomadic and "do not fight in the open field ... but make treacherous assaults from the bush with bows, arrows, and treat and wound people cruelly."[29] The immediate Aimoré threat was finally broken when Bahians made an alliance with the Potiguar of the northern regions in 1603 and brought down a force of 1,300 archers, led by Zorobabé to fight them successfully.[30]

Thanks to their strategic marriages, the early Portuguese leaders obtained military security in São Vicente/São Paulo, Bahia, and Pernambuco. But security was not enough, for the new colonies also had to be financially self-sustaining, and to that end they had to find products or exports that would pay for their efforts on behalf of Portugal. To assist in this, crown officials granted them land titles to acknowledge their status in Portuguese society, and they hoped, it seems, to build rich and profitable agricultural enterprises. Portuguese settlers quickly turned to sugar as a source of profits. Indeed, where sugar established itself in

---

[26] Salvador, *Historia*, book 2, cap 7; Álvares's early career is reported by Oviedo, *Historia*; see also Manuel de Nóbrega to Miguel de Torres, April 3, 1557, May 8, 1558, August 14, 1558 in Leite, *Cartas do Brasil*, pp. 197, 289, 302; for a study of the complex way in which he entered Brazilian historiography, see Janaína Amado, "Mythic Origins: Camararu and the Founding of Brazil," *Hispanic American Historical Review* 80 (2000): 783–811.

[27] Salvador, *Historia*, Book 3, cap. 6.

[28] Salvador, *Historia*, Book 3, cap. 8.

[29] Pero Rodrigues to João Alvares, 1597, *Anais de Biblioteca Nactional* 20 (1897 [BNRJ]): 255–256; Salvador, *Historia*, Book 4, cap. 34.

[30] Inquiry into services of Diogo Botelho, June 29, 1603, in "Correspondencia de Diogo Botelho," *Revista de Instituto Historico Geographico Brasileiro* 73 (1910); Salvador, *Historia*, Book 4.

Brazil, the settlers became rich, just as the mining settlers were the wealthy in the early Spanish Americas. Sugar had already recently demonstrated itself a very profitable crop in Madeira and in São Tomé, as well as in the Spanish colonies in the Caribbean. The first engines (mills) were constructed in 1542 and set off a "sugar fever" among other small holdings of Portugal along the coast, and by 1545, there were some twenty engines producing sugar.[31]

Duarte Coelho carried the idea to Pernambuco and quickly built a sugar mill at Iguaraçu to provide returns, with the assistance of the local people.[32] When his Tobajara allies helped him overcome the Franco-Caeté and Tupinambá alliance in 1549, Coelho divided the land among his followers, forcing the captured people to feed them until sugar mills could be constructed. The campaign extended southward to Serinham, where many more were taken as slaves.[33] The Aimoré war brought even more slaves. By 1570, Olinda and Igaraçu, the chief towns, had some 23 sugar mills, supported by 1,000 European households and many thousands of slaves taken from their defeated indigenous enemies.[34]

Jesuit missionaries, who arrived in Bahia in 1549, played a crucial role in the struggle over control and labor. As in Hispaniola, where the regular orders intervened in a privately controlled economy to ensure their success, the Jesuits couched their demands I humane terms. They argued before the crown that the colonists' wars were alienating the very indigenous people the Jesuits wanted to evangelize, and their pursuit of slavery was counterproductive both to the alliance system and the Jesuits' goals of spreading the faith. Thanks to their lobbying efforts, the crown decided in 1570 to abolish the slave trade in indigenous people, except in special cases where officials decided that war was warranted, or to rescue people in danger of being eaten by cannibals. While the policy did relatively little to stop the warfare, it tended to channel the energies of the settlers to trading (rescuing) for slaves and put warfare more firmly in the crown officials' hands.

In 1609, the crown determined that the indigenous population of Brazil should be, and remain, free. However, it also recognized that the needs for evangelization were important and so it entrusted the Jesuits to create special settlements for former indigenous slaves, for the many allied indigenous villages, and for any other indigenous groups that might want to come down ("descend") from the interior to join the colony. These settlements, called *aldeias* (villages), were to be managed by the Jesuits who would then ensure that

---

[31] A good survey, as well as a special study of the case of São Vicente, is found in Luiz Walter Coelho Filho, *A Capitania de São Jorge e a Década do Açúcar* (Salvador, 2000). In his appendix he prints a valuable Spanish survey of the Brazilian coast in which the extent of sugar production in 1544–1545 is indicated; pp. 141–143.

[32] Salvador, *Historia*, book 2, cap. 8.

[33] Salvador, *Historia*, book 3, cap. 15. It is unclear what role the 20,000 *negros* played; Salvador's terminology suggests they were slaves, and thus perhaps not combatants, but their number suggests that they had to be more than simply porters for a group of less than 1,000 Portuguese; as for the 2,000 from Tamaracá, the designation "archers" makes their role unambiguous.

[34] Pero de Magalhães de Gandavo.

the inhabitants were thoroughly instructed in the Christian religion. Many of the Jesuit aldeias were in fact a sort of military barracks, as indigenous fighters were still vital to the defense of the territories, but on the other hand, the Jesuits agreed to allow residents of the aldeias to serve as workers on sugar estates, in exchange for "fair payment" of wages. Settlers and estate owners never liked this arrangement and fought it whenever possible, and indeed many retained their indigenous slaves in spite of the law and the protestations of the priests.

In the end, the system of indigenous slavery did not last long in Bahia and Pernambuco. Sugar estate owners gladly reinvested the profit that their original indigenous laborers generated from the sugar estates in African slaves. The crown favored the African slave trade because it could tax the imported slaves, and was not troubled by the potential disruptive influence that raiding nearby Brazilian indigenous groups would entail. It would minimize the effects of the aldeia system on the labor force, as African slaves would not fall under the jurisdiction of Jesuits. It also satisfied settlers, who claimed that Africans adopted better to slavery and were more productive than indigenous slaves in any case.[35] The establishment of the colony of Angola in 1575, and the wars of Paulo Dias de Novais in the 1580s, supplied thousands of slaves directly shipped to the estates; indeed, a report of 1612 implied that Angola was the only source of slaves by then, because it was "customs and duties which they pay in Angola" that made them expensive.[36] The sugar industry soon boomed with this new labor force, which needed no Christian ministrations as the Native Americans did because they came either from Christian Africa (Kongo and parts of Angola) or because the church had allowed a mass baptism performed in Luanda harbor on-board ship to serve as a sufficient introductions to the mysteries of the faith.[37]

By the second decade of the seventeenth century, Bahia had been turned into a "New Guinea" by the surge of African workers, and Africans had all but replaced indigenous workers on the estates. As a result, the settlers relented in their pressure against the aldeia system, and not surprisingly the 1609 law declaring indigenous people as free was not much protested in all the areas where sugar was successful. The increase in wealth made possible by the import of slaves in the newly protected coastal positions and the takeoff of the sugar industry had additional social implications. Portuguese who acquired sugar "engines" (mills) as well as lands for growing sugar and labor forces of slaves, both Tupi and African initially, then later mostly African, enjoyed tremendous wealth and power, like those of nobles in Portugal.

---

[35] For the transformation in Bahia, see Stuart Schwartz, *Sugar Plantations in the Formation of Brazilian Society* (Cambridge, 1985), pp. 51–74.

[36] "Rezão de Estado do Brasil," fol. 3r, in Engel Sluiter, ed., "Report on the State of Brazil, 1612," *Hispanic American Historical Review* 29 (1949): 518–562 (original foliation marked, only Portuguese text published). See also (but mostly for Pernambuco) John Thornton, "Les États de l' Angola et la formation de Palmares (Brésil)," *Annales: Histoire, Sciences sociales* 63/4 (2008) :784–786.

[37] Heywood and Thornton, *Central Africans*, pp. 170–197 for the varieties of Christianity in Angola.

Origin and race became very important as the northeastern colonies grew rich, as genealogical records reveal. In both Bahia and Pernambuco, the earliest European settlers married indigenous women, cementing the military alliances that would guarantee security, as Jerónimo de Albuquerque, the brother-in-law of the first donatary of Pernambuco (Duarte Coelho), did not marry but had several children by Dona Maria do Espirito Santo Arcoverde "principal of the Tobajaras of Olinda."[38] But these marriages were less signicicant as the wealth of the colony increased. The two daughters born of this union, however, were both married to members of the Italian nobility who came to Pernambuco in the 1550s, while the sons became lords of sugar estates and would lead the conquest of Maranhão in the early seventeenth century.[39] As the wealth generated by owning sugar estates increased, the second-generation families married European women or Brazilian-born women of solely European ancestry from new families of noble origin that migrated from Portugal to the captaincies, drawn by the wealth. Indeed, the queen sent noble women to "marry with the rich and principal men of the country" in 1552.[40] They were so tightly intermarried by the 1640s that they had to seek special dispensations from the bishop or even the Pope to marry within the third degree of consanguinity.[41]

Although many of the earliest sugar growers were in fact noble, many non-noble groups surreptitiously ennobled themselves through the acquisition of sugar estates. They all adopted the prevailing idea among Portuguese elites that saw nobility as a closed class and excluded various non-nobles from their ranks. While in Portugal the excluded groups included those of peasant, Jewish, or Islamic roots, in Brazil the concept of purity of blood generally meant having European as opposed to African or Native American descent. Portuguese men who owned sugar mills could afford to send back to Portugal for their wives initially or from among the children of these unions later, and married into as high a social class as their new fortunes and older (somewhat malleable) lineages allowed. Planters in the northeast were notorious for the strict authority they exercised over their wives, perhaps as a part of this desire to preserve whiteness. Women were confined to the house and often were not even allowed to go out to attend mass. A popular proverb said a women should only leave the house three times in her life: first to be baptized, then to be married, and finally to be buried.[42] In fact, many elite planters sent their daughters to Portugal to be in convents rather than have them marry locally.

---

[38] António de Santa Maria Jaboatão, "Catalogo genealogico das principaes familias... 1768," in *Revista da Instituto Histórico e Geographico Brazileiro* 52/1 (1889): 42; although he wrote in the mid-eighteenth century, the author used a great many unpublished manuscripts found in Pernambuco, including parochial documents that are no longer extant, particularly in Pernambuco (in Bahia parish, registers do go back for a few places and in fragments to 1599).

[39] On these families, the Lins and Cavalcante, see Joboatão, "Catalogo genealogico," pp. 10–23 (Cavalcante) and 28–31 (Lins); on the later fate of the children, pp. 43–44.

[40] Joboatão, "Catalogo," pp. 63–64.

[41] Joboatão, "Catalogo," pp. 32–35 (Olanda and Lins families).

[42] For examples from travelers' accounts, see Charles R. Boxer, *The Golden Age of Brazil, 1695–1750, Growing Pains of a Colonial Society* (Berkeley and Los Angeles, 1962), pp. 136–137.

Already by the 1570s, this group was careful to define itself in terms of color, as "white" (*branco*) even though some – especially of the earlier group – undoubtedly had some non-European ancestry (especially Tupi) as modern genetic studies reveal.[43] At the same time, persons of mixed Tupi-Portuguese heritage born after the first generation came to fall into a category called "mamelucos," a term sufficiently new in the 1620s that Vicente do Salvador thought fit to define it for his readers in 1627.[44] A substantial number had Jewish roots, and the very active Inquisition believed they still practiced Judaism secretly. Still others had non-noble roots, especially those drawn from the merchant class and occasionally from upwardly mobile landowners (who typically grew sugarcane but could not afford to mill). This latter group, known as *lavradores da cana*, were numerous, and although not as wealthy as their peers who did own estates, *senhores de engenho*, still aspired after their lifestyle.[45]

"Whiteness" became an important element in sugar-producing Brazilian society, probably more important than simple membership in a social class defined by blood, or an income group defined by land ownership or returns from a business. Interracial sex was not uncommon in this environment, but interracial marriage was very uncommon. Le Gentil de Barbinais, a French visitor to Bahia in the early eighteenth century, was shocked to see how often the elite Portuguese lived with African-descended women, which he believed was the result of their being cared for by slaves in their youth.[46] In this way they repeated the same social strategies that had characterized Spanish men in the conquered colonies that produced rich products.

The result was the development of a neo-Portuguese society among the settlers, in which they sought as much as possible to recreate the social climate of Portugal. However, the lower orders in this climate were not peasants, but African – Afro-Brazilian slaves or bi- and tri-racial slaves and freedmen. Inevitably, skin color and racial identification became an important marker for the illegitimate offspring of the planters (both before and after their formal marriage with Portuguese partners), and Bahia and Pernambuco developed a strict caste system. European appearance, language, and customs were the markers of the elite, whereas African of indigenous appearance were the markers of the lower classes. Local legislation soon restricted the opportunities of even the mixed-race offspring who might have acquired freedom and some measure of economic independence.

Not all the captaincies were able to capitalize on sugar production to become profitable. When Schmidel visited in 1553, São Vicente was exporting sugar on the account of Erasmus Schetz.[47] The wealth generated by these mills made rich men of some of the early settlers, and they sought to use this wealth to secure a

---

[43] *Journal of Human Biology* 71 (1999): 245–299; *Human Biology* 76 (2004): 77–86.
[44] Salvador, *Historia*, Book 4, cap. 38.
[45] On the origins of the Bahia elite, see Schwartz, *Sugar Plantations*, pp. 264–275.
[46] Le Gentil de Barbinais *Nouveau Voyage au Tour du Monde* (2nd ed., 3 vols., Paris, 1728) 3: 147.
[47] Schmidel, *Warhafftige Beschreibung*, pp. 64–65.

place for themselves in their original homeland by marrying European women rather than indigenous ones. João do Prado, for example, a high-born Portuguese who made a good income during the colony's early years from the Schetz sugar mill, married Fillipa Vicente, a Portuguese woman of suitably noble origin.[48]

However, São Vicente/São Paulo did not prevail as a sugar producer, and by the end of the century the captaincy was exporting food products to the richer captaincies of the north. As a result of their failure to find sufficiently profitable export crops, Paulista (as residents of São Paulo were called) settlers failed to produce large incomes from the sale of valuable exports. Inventories show that their estates were small: in 1600, they averaged only a dozen or so slaves, although the average rose to fotty in the mid-seventeenth century when the Paulistas and their indigenous relatives and allies enjoyed great military success.[49] While slaves were important on the estates, some also held free people, like that of Fernão Dias, whose will was probated in 1605, which included fifteen slaves and five free people, or the estate of Bartolomeu Rodrigues, who left his wife eight free people in 1608.[50] Portuguese noblewomen (and indeed Portuguese women of any status) did not venture to this poor region, and as a result for most families, the many children of the original families circulated among themselves, thus preserving both the original Tupi elite and its Portuguese counterpart. A few also married their own indigenous slaves, like Pedro Afonso, who took as wife a slave he bought on the market.[51] While it was not particularly wealthy, the Paulista elite were great military leaders and they continued the tradition of raids and military expeditions against their neighbors.

As Africans replaced Tupis and other Brazilians as workers on estates, the indigenous people remained as a specialized military force, first to prevent any further effective attacks from the unconquered people farther inland, second to return runaway slaves, and third to extend Portuguese authority into the interior and fend off rival European groups. Jesuit observers noted that the allies could both keep newly arrived Africans workers in check and protect the colony: "[I]f without blacks there is no Brazil, without Indians there will be no blacks, and there will never be security."[52] In Bahia, the aldeia residents protected the Portuguese sugar engines against the raids of the unconquered neighbors, as a 1601 document reveals that they were both settled near estates and granted lands for colonization in exchange for their military service.[53] They were held to be free, but routinely petitioned the government to ensure

[48] Da Silva Leme, *Genealogia* 3: 91.

[49] John Manuel Monteiro, *Negros da terra: Índios e bandeirantes nas origins de São Paulo* (São Paulo, 1994), pp. 67–81, based on a systematic study of wills.

[50] *DAESP*, vol. 1, fol. 397, October 11, 1605 (Dias); vol 2, fol. 275, September 10, 1610 (Rodrigues).

[51] Da Silva Leme, *Genealogia* 1: 2.

[52] Cabral de Mello, *Olinda*, p. 238.

[53] APEB Livro 4, doc. 74, March 10, 1695, including this document, dated August 3, 1601, as an initial charter for the arrangement.

that this freedom was maintained against landowners who would take it away when the threat from beyond the borders was less.[54]

Tupi fighters were even more important in the life-and-death struggle over Pernambuco that broke out following the Dutch occupation of Recife in 1630. Some of the aldeia dwellers were happy to see the Dutch arrive and deserted to them, but a good many remained loyal to the Portuguese and assisted in the eventual expulsion of Dutch forces from Pernambuco from 1644 to 1654. During the course of the war, one of the Tupi leaders, known as Camarão, became a sort of overall commander of indigenous forces allied to Portugal, and in the aftermath, his office, which was hereditary in his family, formed a sort of high command for the captaincy's indigenous people.

The Dutch war created a second problem for Pernambuco, which was the development of a large African state in the immediate interior of the whole captaincy in the area called Palmares. Thousands of slaves had run away during the war, and the state, which had tens of thousands of inhabitants and a unified leadership, represented a constant threat to the sugar mills, raiding them regularly and providing safe haven for others who wished to flee. Indigenous allies provided the vital manpower for the Portuguese to meet this threat as well. The governors of Pernambuco sought to sow aldeias of loyal Tupis in the area of Palmares to break up the state as garrisons to be left in the region to discourage the formation of runaway communities, as the case with twenty-five families of the aldeia of Ananazes in Serinhaem in 1668.[55] As the war progressed, planting aldeias of allied indigenous people became a regular part of the advance. When Bandeirante-Tapuya forces stormed the capital of Palmares in 1694, they left a number of soldiers as well as aldeias under their own command to ensure that a large runaway settlement did not develop again and to take action against the smaller runaway settlements that remained. As late as 1750, these aldeias were still there with their own command.. The struggle with Palmares occupied much of the remainder of the seventeenth century (its capital fell to the Portuguese-Tupi forces, including those brought up from the São Paulo area by Domingos Jorge Velho, a mixed-race leader, in 1694).

The war had also stirred up the interior indigenous people, commonly called Tapuya by the Portuguese, from a Tupi word that simply means "enemy." The Dutch had cultivated relations with them as a part of their war effort, and they did not stop their attacks following the war, although they were gradually brought into alliance. Conscious of the importance of maintaining its alliances and heading off trouble, the governors of Pernambuco assiduously cultivated peaceful defensive relations with the Tapuya and other indigenous groups after

---

[54] APEB, Livro 4, doc. 74, March 10, 1695. The many attached documents include records of service of various of the aldeias, along with certificates to various "Capitães de Indios."

[55] AUC VI, 3ª, I-1–31Disposizões, fol. 49, no. 16, March 23, 1668; also serving as scouts and as a main force (300 out of 900) fol. 62, nos. 54 and 63, both December 24, 1661; as a garrison, fol 93v, no. 144, August 23, 1663; again fol. 157, no. 114, November 11, 1664.

the war.[56] It is indicative of the situation that when, in 1661, a group of some 600 Tapuya of the "nation of João Duim" agreed to come to Pernambuco and settle in an aldeia named Capibaribe, they were placed under the command of one of Camarão's officers and given a priest, Father João Duarte do Sacramento, to minister to them.[57]

As in Pernambuco, the soldiers of Bahian aldeias were also assigned to capture runaway slaves or to attack their settlements in wooded and desolate places. The estate records of the Jesuit holdings in Bahia, for example, note in the 1590s and onward that runaways were regularly returned by "Indians," often for cash. Thus in 1722–1723, allied indigenous soldiers were to attack mocambos, or runaway settlements, one of which had several hundred residents, so as to avoid the development of larger and more dangerous agglomerations "as had been done in Pernambuco."[58]

The alliance was not always stable, for grievances might lead to small-scale revolts as it did when, in 1698, a group living on the estate of two widows expelled the Jesuits, forcing a lengthy inquest into the situation.[59] Sometimes landowners pushed in on lands designated for the aldeias; the inhabitants of the aldeia de Santo Antonio de Jaguaripe complained in 1726 that a powerful neighboring landowner, Joseph de Argollo Menezes, was taking their land and reassigning it to a variety of people.[60] But landowners might also make private alliances with indigenous groups. In the early eighteenth century, Joseph Figueira managed to build up his estate near the town of Ilheus and, with the assistance of "wild Indians" who were "his friends," defied the efforts of authorities to arrest him for various misdeeds he was alleged to have done.[61]

On occasion, indigenous soldiers could play a role within the colonial politics. In the early eighteenth century, strong tensions developed in Pernambuco between the local resident sugar producers of Olinda and the merchants who operated through Recife (who were called "mascates" as a term of disparagement). In 1711, as a result of disputes over precedence, taxation, and judicial conduct, the producers revolted and expelled the governor, in what was called the "War of the Mascates" (*Guerra dos Mascates*). The rebels from the sugar estates mobilized an army consisting of their slaves and a significant army of Paulistas who had come to Pernambuco to fight the runaway slaves who had formed a powerful kingdom at Palmares. This force was enough to allow them

---

[56] Arquivo da Universidade de Coimbra [AUC] VI, 3ª, I-1–31Disposizões dos Governador de Pernambuco, fol. 14v, no. 29, May 4, 1654.

[57] AUC VI, 3ª, I-1–31Disposizões, fol. 60, no. 49, September 22, 1668; fol. 61, Order to João Duarte do Sacramento and to the Prelados of the convents, September 1 and 25, 1668, on fol. 62, no. 53, September 12, 1661; local landholders were engaged to assist them with food until a harvest came in.

[58] APEB, Livo 17, doc. 6, February 2, 1723.

[59] APEB, Livro 5, doc 18, January 20, 1698. I have been unable to follow the outcome as the document is very faded.

[60] APEB, Livro 20, doc. 42, January 17, 1726.

[61] APEB Livro 20, doc. 60, January 19, 1726.

to capture Recife and to terrorize the merchants of the town. But the Mascates recovered, and attacked the city again, supported by royal soldiers including the indigenous troops (under the command of Camarão) and the company of Afro-Brazilian soldiers, raised in the war against the Dutch, called Henriques in honor of their original commander, António Henriques. These forces, combined with locally raised irregular units known as Tumbacundés, were able to rout the rebels and reestablish authority.

While the Northeast expanded under the ultimate guidance of the powerful captaincies of Pernambuco and Bahia, the South consisted of only the much poorer but equally bellicose province of São Paulo. The expeditions of the Paulistas, often also called *bandeirantes* (flag bearers, from the flags that identified them), were directed against enemies of the Portuguese crown, like the Spanish territories along the Rio de la Plata and farther in the interior, or simply against nearby and rival Tupi groups. Many were also searching for deposits of valuable minerals, always hoping to reproduce Spain's spectacular success at Potosí. Sometimes their expeditions employed hundreds and even thousands of their slaves, clients, and families and might last for years.[62] They assisted the crown in the wars against the Dutch in the 1640s, and then in the 1680s and 1690s helped colonize the Rio São Francisco region south of Bahia; finally, a group under Domingos Jorge Velho was commissioned to attack and colonize the large state built by African runaway slaves in Palmares in the hinterland of Pernambuco in 1691, earning a parcel of land grants in the former kingdom's capital after they stormed it in 1694.

While the Paulistas' success in war made them famous throughout Brazil, it was probably the search for wealth that motivated them more. Many of their expeditions into the interior were to seek mineral wealth, as the profits of sugar had eluded them and favored the Northeast. It was, however, the discovery of gold in what would become the province of Minas Gerais that gave them their biggest opportunity to become truly rich. A Paulista backwoodsman, Manuel de Borbo Gato, was said to have discovered significant deposits of gold in the Rio das Velhas area some time around 1685 and worked the deposits secretly, but by 1695, word of the discovery had leaked out, prompting a rash of prospectors to the region, and soon other strikes were made in Rio das Mortes and Rio Doce.[63]

The Paulistas staked out claims, but were soon joined by hordes of people from all walks of life from every part of Brazil, and by the end of the century from Europe as well. The Paulistas scornfully called the newcomers "Emboabas," a perjorative term of uncertain origin and definition, and felt sure, given their local control, private armies of Carijó slaves, and retainers, that they could evict the Emboabas. But the crown was also concerned that the land would fall from their hands, either to the Paulistas or perhaps to French or

---

[62] Paulistas and bandeirantes have a long and celebratory tradition in Brazilian historiography, especially in the massive work of Affonso de Escragnolle de Taunay, *História Geral das Bandeiras Paulistas escripta á vista de avultada documentção...* (10 vols., São Paulo, 1924–1949).

[63] A good general account of the events of this period is in Boxer, *Golden Age*, pp. 35–41.

Spanish interests (as the French did attack Rio de Janeiro in 1710).[64] Moreover, well-connected residents of the long-wealthy northern captaincies of Bahia and Pernambuco began to arrive, adding their weight to the crown's interests.

The struggle over the mines led to what was subsequently called the War of the Emboabas (1708–1709) in which the intruders generally came out on top, in spite of their apparent disadvantages, particularly as the Paulistas could not present a united front, and the crown was prepared to throw virtually unlimited weight into the efforts to retain the region under its control.[65] The most prosperous and successful of the Paulistas joined the top ranks of Minas society, but many of the less successful ended up once again conducting missions into the interior searching for more mines and another chance.

Initially, the Paulistas used their own Carijó slaves as workers on the mines, and even in the early eighteenth century, indigenous people accounted for about 15 percent of the labor forces, at least in some of the mines.[66] But by far the largest labor forces were brought in from Africa, as the slave trade diverted from the sugar plantations of Bahia and Pernambuco to Rio de Janeiro, the easiest port of call for slave ships bringing workers to the mines. The earliest miners often lived with or had children by these African slaves, as is revealed in the books of parish visits, such as one recorded for Sabará in 1734 in which virtually the only major sin reported was "concubinage" or even "illicit communication" in which a settler confessed to living publicly and scandalously with one of his slaves – some even confessing to "second lapses."[67] As the region became wealthier, the insistence on legitimate marriage to women of European descent became more prominent. The wealth generated by the mines soon promoted a copy of the sort of society found in Bahia or Pernambuco, although the fairly large number of mixed-race people of means, the descendant of these early unions, prevented the full exclusion of such people from municipal office.[68] Whereas the Paulistas had often been mixed-race and Tupi-speaking, the northeastern concepts of racial purity and strict caste marriages prevailed among the successful miners, most of whom brought the ideas with them from either Portugal or the Northeast of Brazil.

Their failure in the War of the Emboabas led the disappointed Paulistas and others who had not been as successful in mining to push the mining frontier farther to the west. By 1730, new mines of gold and diamonds had been found in Cuyabá and then in the Mato Grosso, the densely wooded land in the center of Brazil.[69] But there, the transition from Paulista-controlled mining camp

---

[64] On the French attack on Rio de Janeiro, see Boxer, *Golden Age*, pp. 84–105.

[65] Boxer, *Golden Age*, pp. 61–83.

[66] Renato Pinto Venâncio, "Os últimos Carijós: Escravidão indígena em Minas Gerais: 1711–25," *Revista Brasileira de História* 17 (1997): 1–15.

[67] Arquivo da Cúria, Belo Horizonte, Paroquia de Sabará, Visitas Pastorais, Visitador Lourenço J. de Q. Coimbra, 1734.

[68] Boxer, *Golden Age*, pp. 164–167.

[69] José Barbosa de Sá, "Relação das povoaçoens do Cuyabá e Mato Grosso de seos príncipios thé os prezentes tempos" (August 15, 1775) in *ABNRJ* 23 (1901–1904): 5–58.

with indigenous labor to control by high-born Portuguese or northeastern-ers and an African labor force was speeded up. Once strikes were made, the established miners of Minas Gerais quickly moved in. The Paulista cycle began again, although no more major strikes were made. The far-western extension of modern-day Brazil was, however, largely the work of the Paulistas and their search for mineral wealth.

As in Bahia and Pernambuco, the indigenous people became a military force, whose primary mission was to expand the frontier and fight the unconquered Native Americans surrounding them, as well as to maintain order by fighting against any runaways. Royal orders made it clear that although the Jesuits and other religious orders were in charge of their administration, they were to be considered free and could not be used for any work, but were primarily in the royal service.[70] This work was clearly to fight, for an order of 1714 required that "dispersed" Indians of the mining district be gathered in an aldeia to combat "the invasions of various runaway negros and highway robbers who descend on the roads and pillage and rob passers-by."[71] This policy was to be an exten-sion of those in other provinces, where the work of rounding up runaways was entrusted to the office of *capitão de mato* (captain of the woods), who with some regular soldiers and the various aldeia inhabitants would respond to the challenge of the growing number of runaway communities.[72] African slaves brought in to mine often ran away and formed *quilombos* (runaway settlements), some of considerable size. From there they raided the neighboring estates and mines or provided a safe haven and magnet for others who would run away. Consequently, the indigenous people were most often dispatched to attack the runaway communities and to settle in the area.

At the same time, the port of Rio de Janeiro, once a sleepy coastal town with a few sugar estates and a handful of planters, was transformed. As the easiest port to export the mineral wealth of the newly discovered mines, Rio was so changed that it soon outstripped even the older sugar-estates-fed towns of the north, eventually replacing Salvador (in Bahia) as the capital of Brazil in 1763.

NORTHERN EUROPEANS IN NORTH AMERICA, THE CARIBBEAN, AND SOUTH AMERICA

The northern European colonies in America, settled on lands that were domi-nated by free associations to the same degree that Brazil was, showed a similar evolution but with some interesting twists. The northerners were only modestly successful in either enslaving indigenous people or conquering the mini-states of eastern and southern North America or northern South America. This feature

---

[70] APM, Secção Colonial, cod. 4, fol. 61, King to Governor, April 8, 1713; fols. 82–84, King to Governor, April 7, 1714 (and referring to a letter of September 14, 1713).

[71] APM, Secção Colonial, cod. 4, fols. 95–97, November 4, 1714.

[72] APM, Secção Colonial, cod. 4, fols. 178–179, January 12, 1719.

immediately sets them apart from the colonizing ventures of Portugal in Brazil or the conquests that either the Spanish or Portuguese made in areas with mini-states, and where the indigenous inhabitants played a vital and integral role in the life of the colonies. As a result, northern Europeans had to bring a labor force in as colonists, either free settlers and indentured servants from their homelands; or enslaved people, who came overwhelmingly from Africa. There were different mixes of colonists in various parts of the Americas, depending largely on the success that the colonists had with finding exports that could produce high incomes. Where they found such exports, African slaves tended to dominate, and government tended to be oligarchic and concepts of racial purity carefully guarded; where this situation did not prevail, the labor force tended to be free colonists or indentured servants and government leaned more toward democratic models.

France was the first of the northerners to try colonial ventures in America; in addition to the Rio de Janeiro colony, which Portuguese destroyed, they also tried to build a colony on the Carolina coast of North America in 1562, which was annihilated by the Spanish from Florida in 1566. Both colonies were as much strategic bases to develop trade, along the lines of trading factories, as they were intended to be settlements with colonists who hoped to produce goods for a market.

When the Dutch and English began their own moves to colonize the Americas, it was very much linked to their military aims in the larger war against Spain, which heated up following the Anglo-Dutch alliance of 1580 and lasted until a series of truces in 1607–1609. Colonial ventures were seen as strategic bases, planted in areas that were close to those areas of South America where the Portuguese or Spanish did not have colonies – the coast north of Pernambuco, Brazil, south of Venezuela, and the unconquered islands of the eastern Caribbean. Another wing concentrated on North America, virtually untouched by Spain except for ephemeral colonies in Florida.

Colonization was often pioneered by privateers, particularly during the wars between various northern European countries and Spain in the first half of the seventeenth century. The early privateers were merchants who equipped their own warships to attack Spanish shipping in order to win compensation for losses they had suffered earlier from Spanish seizures.[73] While privateers were not themselves particularly interested in colonization, the home governments that commissioned them saw the establishment of American bases as a valuable means of promoting this informal sort of war.

Sir Walter Raleigh's colony of Virginia (actually constructed in North Carolina) in 1585 was a military base that was supported almost entirely from Europe, but it was an expensive failure in the long run, and was abandoned in

---

[73] K. R. Andrews, *Trade, Plunder, and Settlement: Maritime Enterprise and the Genesis of the British Empire* (Cambridge, 1984) for a full examination; for the Dutch, see Cornelis Goslinga, *The Dutch in the Caribbean and in the Guianas, 1680–1791* (Amsterdam, 1991); also see Heywood and Thornton, *Central Africans*, chapter 1.

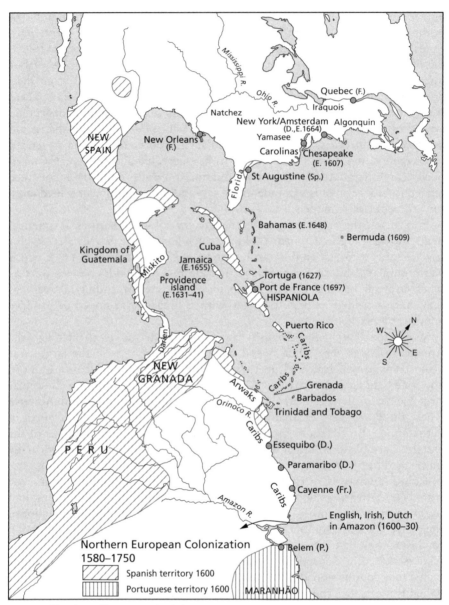

MAP 7. Northern European Activity.

1590. Dutch attempts to build colonies on the "Wild Coast" around the mouth
of the Amazon were equally conceived to assist in their plans to take Brazil,
and met with similar fates in the short term. But the early military phase had
shown northern Europeans that there were also commercial possibilities in the
Americas, and when a new wave of war and colonies began following the end

of the truce (1621) between England, Spain, and the Netherlands, a new sort of colony developed.

While the Truce put a damper on the idea of colony as naval base, the information that the privateers, who were also often from merchant families or had mercantile connections, gathered led to a new, more peaceful set of colonies during the truce. Here the idea was to build commercially successful ventures that might eventually turn into military bases again, and on a stronger footing, when war broke out again, as all believed it surely would when the truce expires. The start of the Thirty Years' War in 1618 put an end to all doubt concerning the utility of American bases in any case.

The Virginia colony, established at Jamestown in 1607, represented an important step in the colonization of North America, although it had been preceded by an unsuccessful venture in Maine in 1602. Unlike Raleigh's settlement at Roanoke, Virginia was planned to exploit commercial possibilities with the Native American inhabitants, in sassafras and then in tobacco. Both Virginia and its twin island settlement of Bermuda were to be bases for military and naval operations and commercial colonies supported by agricultural labor in export products; in the end, however, Bermuda was the naval and privateering base and Virginia continued as a commercially successful settlement.

Commercial prospects for many colonies also depended on trading with the indigenous people, particularly for valuable and exotic furs. Beavers, who roamed the woods from Pennsylvania northward, were particularly valuable, but deerskins could also fetch a good price. Some Europeans and their American-born descendants made a living hunting and trapping, but the majority of these valuable exports were obtained through trade with Native Americans.

France's colonization of Canada, following the founding of Québec in 1609, relied initially on trading beaver skins with the inhabitants of the St. Lawrence River valley. Given the somewhat precarious military situation, the French crown wanted to have a sufficient body of Europeans on the ground to hold it, envisioning that colonists could grow wheat and other subsistence crops for export to French cities. The French crown made grants, called *siegneuies*, of large stretches of territory to powerful colonists starting in 1628, and grantees, called *seigneurs*, in turn brought in indentured workers, called *habitans* to live on their lands. Most *habitans*, upon gaining formal freedom, remained on the lands of their lords as rent-paying peasants, or alternatively sought to enter the fur trade on their own. Relatively few French women came to Canada in the seventeenth century, and a good many of the men returned to France, or ended up in informal relations with Huron women, producing a substantial mixed-race population. French colonists in the Saint Lawrence valley grew food crops successfully for the European market while still exploiting trade in furs with the Hurons. As the colony stabilized, its families became famous in demographic history for its extraordinary population growth, marked by very high birthrates and much higher completed family sizes than in France.

A Dutch merchant consortium established a trading base at Fort Orange (later to be renamed Albany) on the Hudson River in 1614. The success of the Hudson River trade, and the merchant consortium's desire to keep the profits of it in their own hands, led to the establishment of a second base at the mouth of the Hudson on Manhattan Island by the West India Company in 1626, named New Amsterdam (and eventually renamed New York by the English). The colony was to become self-supporting through growing foodstuffs and some limited exports (tobacco was deemed a potential export crop), and to secure the region against foreign competitors while giving the company a base.

In all these areas, however, the northern European settlers were unable to secure the sort of armies of enslaved or closely allied indigenous people that the Portuguese used so effectively in Brazil. Initially they sought to create alliances with their Algonquian neighbors, and this included key intermarriages with the local elite – for example, John Rolfe's celebrated union with Pocahontas – but this did not result in the union of English and Native American that characterized the Rio de la Plata or Amazon areas for Spain and Portugal.

In New France, the early colonists made a close alliance with the Huron who lived near their principal settlement at Québec, which put them at odds with the Huron's long-standing enemies, the Iroquois to their south. However, the French mission villages around Québec, populated primarily by Hurons who were either captured or more often induced to stay there, were not quite the secure fighters that the Portuguese *aldeias* had been in northeastern Brazil, and one can hardly imagine armies of Hurons conquering and settling the Mississippi Valley and Great Lakes as the Tupi allies of Portugal did in northeast Brazil or the Amazon. Similarly, the French traders were quite unlike the Portuguese *bandeirantes* of São Paulo who they resembled in many other ways (especially in being mixed-race, or *métis*) in that they had neither plantations of enslaved Native people nor loyal armies of Tupi warriors to support them.

The Dutch then fell into the alliance with the Iroquois, enemies of the pro-French Hurons, an alliance forged as soon as Fort Orange was settled, and passed on to the English when they took over New Netherland in 1664 and renamed it New York. As both groups were free associations, the alliances were potentially insecure, although both held for a long time.[74] In any case, the Hurons suffered horribly for their alliance, for after 1648, the Iroquois carried thousands of them off in a series of devastating attacks on the French positions, but one can hardly say that Dutch interests (or English after 1664) were directly enhanced by these wars. At the same time, unlike the Portuguese settlements in São Paulo, the intermarriage was confined primarily to nonelite settlers in both places whose economic interests in the fur trade were more important than their political or military interests.

---

[74] Francis Jennings, *The Ambiguous Iroquois Empire: The Covenant Chain Confederation of Indian Tribes with English Colonies* (Norton, 1990); and Daniel K Richter and James Merrill, eds., *Beyond the Covenant Chain: The Iroquois and their Neighbors in Indian North America, 1600–1800* (State College, 2003).

The coastal regions, dominated by the weak mini-states of the Algonquian-speaking people, were somewhat different, but still followed a pattern that varied from that of Iberians a century earlier. The Plymouth and Massachusetts Bay colonies, founded in 1620 and 1630, respectively, also made alliances with the local leaders, notably with the Massachusetts sachem, Massasoit. As they branched out to the south, they found themselves also allied with the sachems of Narragansett, and eventually became embroiled in local conflict with the Pequot, as English and Dutch interests also clashed. The Pequot War of 1637, in which an English force and a large Narragansett allied army destroyed the main Pequot town and killed or enslaved most of its inhabitants, was an important development of that political arrangement.[75]

Although these were mini-states, and the English presence could conceivably have given them a start, the English did very little intermarriage and sought rather to isolate the indigenous people from their settlements – for example, encouraging their allies to accept Christianity and become settled in what were called "praying towns," in effect keeping them at arms' distance. The difference between, for example, the Spanish approach to the Rio de la Plata basin, where widespread intermarriage followed by a settlement that turned mini-states into encomiendas, and the settlement of New England was probably a result of immigration demographics. In Paraguay, Spanish males came and allied themselves to the local communities; in New England, religious dissidents came as whole families, indentured servants soon obtained wives, and the colonization movement created a momentum that pressed indigenous people out. The reaction, King Philip's War, in 1675 only heightened this difference.[76]

The New England settlers, however, found that their access to furs was limited by stiff competition from their neighbors, and the soil, while rich enough to allow subsistence farming, hardly allowed much in the way of exports. Fortunately, New Englanders could fish the rich banks off their coast and farther north. Fish and whale products formed the bulk of New England's exports from 1650 onward, and much of the rest came from shipping services New Englanders provided to other colonies – even delivering products to Europe – the result of a shipbuilding industry, itself an offshoot of their specialization in fishing.[77]

In Virginia, where the colonists met the powerful Powhatan confederacy and made an alliance with its ruler, there was an early move in several locations toward intermarriage alliances on the lines of Paraguay or São Paulo. John Rolfe's celebrated marriage to Pocahantas is the best known of several such key unions. But the war of 1622 and the subsequent war of 1644 made that alliance problematic, again probably because of the demography of settlement.

[75] Alfred A. Cave, *The Pequot War* (Boston, 1996).

[76] James Drake, *King Philip's War: Civil War in New England, 1675–1676* (Boston, 1999), which interprets the war less as a clash of civilizations than of factions with both indigenous and European members.

[77] John McCusker and Russell Menard, *The Economy of British America, 1607–1789* (Chapel Hill, 1991), pp. 91–116.

Even in Virginia, enough whole families of European origin formed to make the British settlers' demographic push drive the indigenous people back and even out rather than forming closer alliances. Alliance politics in most of British America was a matter for the frontier, away from the growing settlements, and not the core region beyond the earliest years of its infancy.

RICH AND POOR IN THE COLONIES OF THE NORTHERN EUROPEANS

The economic and demographic fate of the northern European colonies was largely determined by their capacity to develop high-value exports, and those that did soon developed a highly stratified society with a significant number, if not a majority, of African population, while those that did not developed a much more democratic, largely European-descended population who came either as free settlers or indentured servants. Although high-value exports varied, the most significant was sugar, as revolutionary in the seventeenth-century Caribbean as it had been in Brazil a century earlier.

The Caribbean settlements were roughly contemporary with the North American ones. Here they faced the Caribs, organized as free associations, and had to face Spanish rivalry. The Spanish had long-standing alliances with the Arawaks in the northern part of South America, and the Portuguese could deploy their Tupi allies against northern European settlements to their north. But the Spanish were still engaged in a long-standing war against the Caribs of the Lesser Antilles, who had raided Puerto Rico, in particular through the whole sixteenth century and beyond.

Northern Europeans sought to use Spanish-Carib hostility to their advantage, as French privateers did as early as 1534.[78] Walter Raleigh, in carrying the war into the Caribbean, actively sought alliances with the Native people of Trinidad, and winning them temporarily into an alliance was able to strike at the Spanish on the nearby mainland, forcing Spain to make stronger alliances on Trinidad itself, including creating a settlement there. As more northern Europeans came into the Caribbean and sought to build colonies in the early seventeenth century, the Spanish struck back. Spanish and indigenous forces destroyed English colonies in Grenada in 1609, and several times on Tobago. In all, John Scott, an early English chronicler of the events, noted some fourteen failed attempts by various European groups to found a colony in Guiana, and three in Trinidad.[79] Not surprisingly, unoccupied Barbados became an important starting point in 1625, along with St. Christopher (St. Kitts), where both French and English established outposts while negotiating with the Caribs,

---

[78] Manuel Lando to Emperor, July 2, 1534, in Murga, *Historia documental.*
[79] BM Sloane MS 3662, John Scott, fols. 45v–46v; 39v–40v (this manuscript is partially published, with its original foliation marked, in Harlow, ed., *Colonizing Expeditions*, which also publishes relevant primary documents on English colonization).

who occupied the middle of the island. The French also founded early colonies in Martinique and Guadeloupe in the 1620s, and Grenada in the 1640s.

Further south, English, French, and Dutch colonies looked actively to a Native American alliance as a way to garner local support against the Spanish, and supplied them with weapons along the way. The survival of colonies in the Amazon, the Guianas, and Surinam depended on making good alliances with the various Arawak or Carib groups in the vicinity. At the same time, Caribs provided all their European visitors with tobacco that they grew for export, helping in this way defray the costs of the colonies.[80]

Dutch settlers founded a number of short-lived colonies in the Amazon and along what they called the "Wild Coast" (modern-day Guiana) from 1605. In these efforts they were often thwarted by the Caribs operating in alliance with the Spanish. When the Dutch founded a colony in Tobago in 1627 with the idea of growing tobacco and sugar, a Carib-Spanish attack largely destroyed the fledgling colony a decade later. Survivors of the Tobago colony made their way down to the Wild Coast and in 1637 created a colony in Essiquibo, the root of what would become Guiana. By the early 1660s, they had converted to sugar, made a series of alliances with the neighboring Caribs, and started a successful colonial venture.

The northern Europeans needed to engage in agricultural pursuits to make the Caribbean colonies pay, for unlike the situation in North America, there were no high-value commodities, like furs, that could be acquired by trade. In the Caribbean, however, producing sugar was the way out, as they had to look no farther than the concentrated wealth of Bahia and Pernambuco to see its effects. Both English and Dutch colonists were already trying to grow and mill sugar in the Amazon in the 1620s, but the Portuguese campaigns against them in 1623–1625 put an end to this promising experiment, rendering the Amazon too dangerous for continued sugar exploitation. Unlike the early English and French Caribbean colonies, the Dutch started growing sugar immediately on Tobago. They were exporting sugar in significant quantities from the island by 1628, a start that was cut short, however, by the Spanish-Arawak invasion of 1637.[81]

As promising as these early ventures were, the Dutch West India Company's efforts were directed more toward securing the already sugar-producing colony of Brazil than starting out on their own, which they achieved with the conquest of Pernambuco in 1630. However, the Dutch did not envision themselves becoming sugar planters in Brazil, and were primarily content to allow the Portuguese planters to continue their production, the Dutch only creating a monopoly on the purchase of their exports. Eventually, some of the Dutch

---

[80] Andrews, *Trade, Plunder*, pp. 280–303.
[81] Early Tobago exports are cited in reports of the Zeeland Chamber, OWIC 20, f. 145 (export of twenty chests of sugar) in 1628, f. 241v (green ginger), f. 257 (tobacco) in 1630; a Spanish translation of a captured Dutch document of 1633 reveals they were growing tobacco, cotton, ginger, and sugarcane; BL MS Add 36321, fol. 188v.

settlers in Brazil did begin planting, only to be expelled with their colleagues (and with a good number of Portuguese Jews, who had abandoned their nominal Christianity under Dutch occupation), most taking refuge in the nearby settlements in Essiquibo where they joined the Tobago settlers who had founded the colony.

Lacking either conquered or enslaved Native people, the northern European colonies had to rely on indentured laborers from their homelands as their principal labor force to grow tobacco, which from very early on brought enough profit to make colonies from Canada to the Caribbean viable, if not rich. Potential indentured servants agreed to a contract in Europe so that they could labor in America. Promising them that they could become landowners and independent farmers growing an export crop, the planters agreed to transport them to America in exchange for three to seven years of labor, depending on how much the would-be settlers could pay for their passage.

While the use of indentured servants was the most important source of workers for all the northern Europeans, religious dissidents who were willing to immigrate to the Atlantic regions in exchange for the right to practice their own brand of Christianity provided an important additional thread. Unlike the colonists elsewhere in the lands settled by northern Europeans, religious dissenters were not looking for strategic bases, did not have an interest in carrying on a war against Spain, and indeed, were not particularly interested in developing highly profitable export crops. Puritans, Calvinists, and other religious dissenters in England, who were from moderately prosperous families, might not have been drawn to America by economic promises alone, but were lured their by religious freedom. The Plymouth Colony and Massachusetts Bay colony had exactly this sort of motivation, although even there, the settlers had to promise some sort of revenue-earning product to pay their way – which they supplied by trading with Native American neighbors and, like the French *habitans* in Canada, by planting food crops that could stand the long Atlantic transportation to European markets (and later to American ones).

It remained for Barbados to become the first successful sugar colony in the southern Caribbean. Barbadian settlers did not try to grow sugar immediately, in spite of their connections to the Amazon region, from which they obtained even some Native American slaves. Instead they focused initially on tobacco, and then switched over to cotton in the late 1630s, using indentured labor.[82] Neither crop brought much wealth, but it did produce a colony with a large number of smallholders, as indentured servants earned their freedom and set themselves up as independent farmers. Much of the land was held in small parcels, growing cotton and tobacco for sale but raising hogs, turkeys, and a wide variety of other stocks for what was clearly a substantial local subsistence

---

[82] Barbados National Archives [BNA], Recopied Deed Books [RC] contains a list of early indentures and deeds from about 1641. The deeds are often sold for commodity prices, stated in tobacco or cotton. The lists in the 1640s usually state the price in cotton.

economy.[83] They only began to grow sugar around 1641, when the first mention of a plantation sold to grow sugarcane is mentioned in the records.[84]

A handful of the wealthiest planters invested in sugar estates, and soon generated enough income that they could obtain African slaves, as indentured workers would not serve as the permanent labor force they hoped to have. Although British shipping had been visiting Africa since the late sixteenth century, they did not purchase slaves there. Instead, what African slaves came to the Americas were captured by privateers from Portuguese shipping delivering captives to markets in Brazil or the Spanish territories. Bermuda became a privateering base, and the first slave captured by privateers arrived in 1617.[85] However, although the slave population was numerous enough that Bermuda became the first colony to issue regulations concerning them and to worry about the possibility of revolt, the majority of the settlers were still indentured servants.[86]

The Rich family, earls of Warwick and a leading family engaged in privateering, had strong roots in Bermuda, and in 1634 moved their naval headquarters to Providence Island, off the coast of Central America.[87] From the start, the Riches sought to populate the island with indentured servants from England, but their privateering ventures continued as well, as they were issued a number of letters of marque in 1635 and 1636.[88] Their efforts produced a large number of African slaves who rapidly became numerous enough to create concerns about the general security of the island and drastic measures, including orders that their numbers never be more than half the population.[89] Nevertheless,

---

[83] See the many deeds in BNA, RC 3/1 fols. 155–202 and *passim*, where land parcels are most commonly 20–30 acres with a few for 50, and inventories include a few servants, although many are mentioned without servants. These documents are sale documents and not probated wills, so they only reflect property being sold.

[84] BNA, RC 3/1 fol. 293, Indenture, June 1, 1641, Capt. Francis Stecke, Capt. Reynold Allen, and Capt. David Dix.

[85] Already by 1615, the Spanish were complaining that English privateers based in Bermuda had taken more ships than all the earlier privateers; ARA St Gen 6900, April 22, 1615, letter from Spanish Ambassador, Diego Sarmiento de Ocuña, Conde de Gondomar. The comings and goings of privateers in early Bermuda were noted in the chronicle of an early governor, Nathaniel Butler, *The Historye of the Bermudaes or Summer Islands* (ed. J. Henry Lefroy, London: Hakluyt Society, 1882), pp. 84–86, 144–146, 242–246 (the editor wrongly attributed the work to John Smith).

[86] African slaves were numerous enough in 1619 to draw attention of an early Dutch visitor, a castaway named Pieter Barentszoon, Nicholas van Wassenaer; 12 Deel (1626), fol. 39v; on their regulation, see Bermuda Colonial Records [BCR] Vol. A, p 35v, "An Act to restrayne the insolencies of the Negroes" 1623, transcribed in J. H. Lefroy, ed., *Memorials of the Discovery and Early Settlement of the Bermudas or Somers Islands, 1515–1685* (London, 1877, 3rd ed., Toronto: University of Toronto Press, 1981) 1: 308–309.

[87] An excellent study of the Providence Island experiment is found in Karen Ordahl Kupperman, *Providence Island, 1630–41: The Other Puritan Colony* (Cambridge, 1993).

[88] These letters, including instructions for capturing slaves, among their targets, are found in PRO CO 124/1, Book of Entries of the Governor and Company of Adventurers for the Plantation of the Island of Providence, Insructions to various captains, fol. 95–95v, 104, and *passim*.

[89] For example, PRO CO 124/2, fols. 124–25v, from letter to the Swallow, July 3, 1638.

they were, in fact, a majority by the time the colony was taken over by Spanish forces in 1641.

Slave raiding, especially in the Amazon and Surinam, provided another stream of slaves even though Africans taken from Portuguese vessels made up as much as 15–20 percent of the labor force on the English colonies of northern South America. Barbados obtained a supply of slaves from the Amazon. These colonies managed to obtain meaningful numbers of slaves, either Native Americans or Africans taken by force from Portuguese vessels, but their numbers did not pass beyond 15 percent of the labor force, and in Barbados they were probably no more than 5 percent.[90] The remaining labor force was brought as indentured servants from Europe.

Both the wealth generated by sugar and the desirability of slaves rather than servants as a labor force made acquiring large numbers of slaves by purchase attractive. The *Star* of London owned by an African trader named Samuel Crispe brought the first boatload of Africans acquired by purchase at Calabar to Barbados in 1642.[91] A sizable slave trade grew up, servicing this group of planters, and by 1645, Barbados was receiving multiple boatloads of Africans, purchased straight from the African coast.

Only a handful of wealthy planters obtained these slaves; even though Richard Ligon's lively description of the island as he saw it in 1648 recorded nearly 100 slaves on the estate where he lived, bills of sale from the 1640s show a large number of small farms changing hands, and a smattering of African slaves working alongside English servants.[92] Slave labor was not initially confined to Africans or Native Americans, either. In the 1650s, Barbados received a surge of English prisoners of war, openly called "slaves," who served lifetime indentures as punishment imposed by courts martial for participation in the Scotch rebellion; these workers ceased to come, however, with the restoration of peace. In was thus only in the last half of the 1650s that Barbados began massive importations of slaves, tens of thousands coming in by the end of the decade. Barbados inventories show only a handful of African slaves even in 1650, but by 1655, slaves were forming the majority of workers on probated estates and indentures.[93] By 1670, the overwhelming majority of the settlers in the island were Africans; Lord Willoughby claimed that 70,000 out of the 75,000 inhabitants were African slaves, and the sugar plantation economy reigned.[94]

What happened in Barbados was repeated very quickly in the other English colonies – St. Christopher (now called St. Kitts), Antigua, and then

[90] Heywood and Thornton, *Central Africans*, pp. 254–262.
[91] BNA, RC 3/1, fol. 202–203 (last of February 1642).
[92] Richard Ligon, *A Trve and Exact History of the Island of Barbados* (London: Humphrey Morely, 1657).
[93] This process can be traced in BNA, RC 3/1. In the 1640s, though some estates did have slaves, the vast majority were in fact English workers serving time.
[94] BL Egerton, 2395, fol. 490, Lord Willoughby's interest in the island of Barbados, March 17, 1670.

Jamaica, taken from the Spanish in 1655. The French colonies of Martinique, Guadeloupe, and their portion of St. Kitts also experienced a sugar revolution that paralleled that of Barbados. France also began trading in slaves in 1639, and French companies were soon delivering their own flood to their colonies once the sugar revolution took hold in the 1650s. As these island colonies boomed, the parents of the sugar revolution in South America prospered as well, for all three northern European colonial powers – France, England, and the Netherlands – built colonies on adjacent land in the Guianas and Surinam. By 1660, they were sufficiently successful to be receiving whole boatloads of slaves to feed sugar's constant need for more workers.

Rapid growth in the slave trade paralleled the sugar revolution, as the planters' wealth made it worthwhile to freight whole ships in Africa to carry to the concentrated markets in the Americas. The Company of Merchant Adventurers into Africa, chartered from older English companies that dealt with other African commodities, was given the monopoly to carry slaves to the new rich colonies, and this was in turn absorbed into the Royal African Company in 1672. By the start of the eighteenth century, the English company, along with private merchants, drove the largest slave trade from Africa of any European nation.

In parallel with the English trade, the Dutch West India Company began purchasing slaves in Africa in 1638 to supply their colony in Pernambuco, Brazil, and in 1641 they captured Luanda, Angola, and its immediate hinterland from the Portuguese. Their hopes that they could control the vast central African slave trade, which formed a huge share of the whole trade to America, were dashed when they were unable either to dislodge the Portuguese from their interior positions or control the trade, as Portuguese merchants continued to export most of Angola's pre-invasion trade to the parts of Brazil still held by Portugal (primarily Bahia). However, once the Angola venture was finished by a successful Portuguese counterattack in 1648, the Dutch company maintained its slave trading along the central African coast north of Angola and in West Africa, continuing it even after Brazil was lost. When Company went bankrupt, it was reorganized as the Second West India Company, no longer a privateering venture but founded on the slave and sugar trades.

The transformation that the sugar revolution created not only affected the established players in the northern European colonial ventures. In the 1630s, dissatisfied Dutch merchants, chafing at the monopoly powers of the Dutch West India Company, persuaded rulers in Denmark and Sweden to form their own West India Companies. The Swedish Company, founded by Willem Usselinx in 1635, was initially conceived as a project to purchase copper in West Africa, but soon changed into a company that would create a naval base in North America (Delaware), raid Spanish shipping in the Caribbean, and grow tobacco while trading with Native Americans. It was successful in this venture, although the colony in North America was taken over by the Dutch. But in 1664, the company changed its nature, now dedicated to trading gold on the Gold Coast, purchasing slaves from the nearby African sellers, and founding an island colony to grow sugar.

Other Northern European powers that joined the quest for American colonies following the sugar revolution proceeded directly to the sugar and slave connection. When the Duke of Courland (modern-day Latvia) decided to found his own colony on Tobago (abandoned by earlier Dutch settlers in 1637), he first ensured that the company establish a trading post in Africa (on the Gambia River) so that slaves could be delivered to the island once the first colonists arrived in 1654. The Brandenburg Company, Prussia's own attempt at exploiting the possibilities of the sugar revolution, set up its African posts, also on the Gold Coast, to take advantage of whatever gold trade there might be, and acquired its own Caribbean island.

Plantation slavery was challenged by powerful slave revolts. Slave revolts rarely aimed at overthrowing slavery; most such plans were only revealed by slaves under torture who had been denounced as plotting. Rather, they usually sought to separate from slave society and build their own communities either independently or in conjunction with indigenous people. Hostile Caribs sheltered runaways and used them in their wars against French settlers in St. Christopher, Martinique, and Guadeloupe; in fact, the return of such runaways was a major point in negotiations between French and Caribs.[95] In French Grenada, the handful of African slaves brought in by the settlers in 1649 decided to escape to the Caribs who occupied the rest of the island and were quite hostile to the French settlers. But they soon found themselves mistreated and enslaved, and many sought to return.[96] When the French managed a successful war against the Caribs in Martinique, they demanded the return of runaways in their treaty of 1660, a standard part of negotiations of those days.[97] Given the instability of such indigenous-African alliances, many African runaways opted to form their own communities. Indeed, the French islands had a number of communities of all-African runaways long after the defeat of the Caribs who had originally harbored them and then agreed to return them.[98]

English colonies did not have as many alliances of runaway slaves and indigenous people; for example, when they took over Jamaica in 1655, they found no distinct indigenous community, but they did find several groups of well-established runaway slaves, who they called Maroons, soon augmented by slaves who fled English estates. From the 1660s through the 1690s, as thousands of new African slaves were imported to boost the sugar industry, Jamaica experienced a series of violent revolts, led especially by slaves from the Akan region (usually called Coromantees in English documents). The object of these

[95] Jean Baptiste du Tertre, *Histoire general des Antilles habitués par les François* (4 vols., Paris, 1667; Facsimile reprint, Paris, 1973) 1: 502–503; 467–468.
[96] [Bénigne Bresson], *Histoire de l'isle de Grenade en Amérique*, fols. 80v–83, (mod. ed. Jacques Petitjean Roget, Montreal, 1975; for the identity of the anonymous author, see pp. 26–35).
[97] Du Tertre, *Histoire* 1: 468–469, 521, 544, 575–576.
[98] Du Tertre, *Histoire* 1: 457–459, 502–503, 521, 544, 575–577.

revolts, as in the case of so many others, was to break free of the plantation zone and seek refuge in the mountains. After years of unsuccessful attempts to break them militarily, the English opted to recognize them, opening treaty negotiations in 1739.[99]

In the treaties, the colonial government allowed Maroons to become self-governing entities under their own leaders, but also insisted that they allow a white resident in their community, that they return any further runaways (and help capture runaways in general), and that they serve to defend the island should the need arise. Such treaties were common, as we can see, in the case of the Jamaican Maroons, it probably is anchored in military traditions of the Akan who built the community. Although there were a good many in Jamaica who doubted the wisdom of enlisting the Maroons into the British system of defense, the Maroon leaders honored their treaties, supplying decisive assistance to the British during the revolt of 1760–1766, called Tackey's War. Thistlewood's diary often noted the return of runaways by Maroons, as well as a regular trade that planters had with them.

Many of the rebels, or at least the leaders among them, were veterans of African wars; indeed, perhaps the majority of rebels and a large percentage of all slaves were ultimately captured in war and thus had military experience.[100] This experience may have given them the boldness and confidence that made large-scale armed breakouts possible. This confidence also made them willing to raid the colonial society, often to secure women or just for pillage. Military factors may have played a role in the most widespread revolts, for example the Saint John's revolt of 1739 in the Virgin Islands, in which almost all the island fell into the hands of the rebels, or Tackey's War in Jamaica, in which rebels occupied five parishes. Often these revolts, which may actually have aimed at securing the whole island, were ethnically specific. Tackey's War, for example, was quite specifically among and for Akan slaves, to the point where plans to keep other Africans in slavery may have been part of the program. It is interesting to note that at the height of the war, Thistlewood opted to distribute weapons to his slaves for use against the rebels should they attack the estate. Clearly, the forces of collaboration and rebellion were in complex interaction.

In most of the northern half of North America, a "poor" economy developed, much like that of São Paulo or Maranhão in Brazil. Unable to earn high profits, the colonies had to rely on non-slave labor forces. The Chesapeake colonies, Virginia and Maryland, unlike their Caribbean counterparts, did not enjoy much access to African slaves, although privateers brought in a handful beginning in 1619. Nor were they successful in obtaining workers either as free people or slaves from the Algonquian-speaking mini-states whose lands they first colonized.

---

[99] For the history of the Jamaica maroons, see Mavis Campbell, *The Maroons of Jamaica, 1655–1796: A History of Resistance, Collaboration and Betrayal* (Trenton, 1990).

[100] John Thornton, "War, the State, and Religious Norms in Coromantee Thought," in Robert Blair St. George, ed., *Possible Pasts: Becoming Colonial in America* (Ithaca, 2000), pp. 181–200.

But unlike Brazil, where the various Native American groups provided the labor, in North America, the population was augmented by increasing settlement of free migrants as servants or as settled religious dissidents. Especially among the religious dissidents that settled most thickly in New England and Pennsylvania, whole families came and soon established replicas of English and German towns along the coast, and then in the interior. They were self-reproducing, and indeed the low population density and generally healthier conditions in America, compared to Europe, led to very high fertility. They had no need to intermarry with Native Americans as the Paulistas had in Brazil, and had their own yeoman group of free settlers by the 1650s. Only a handful of people who made their living from trade were prepared to live among the Natives, and they willingly took Indian brides to cement trading alliances. The mixed-race frontiersmen were crucial to the development of commerce, but it was the agricultural immigrants who eventually dictated policy and shaped the colony.

In the southern half of North America, however, the colonizers discovered "rich" products in the form of tobacco and then especially rice and indigo, which caused a radically different development. By the 1630s, the Chesapeake colonies of Virginia and Maryland had succeeded in producing the best tobacco for the European market. One by one, other colonies either abandoned production or cut it back, and the Virginians enjoyed a boom. While profitable from the outset, tobacco did not generate enough income to bring in large numbers of slaves until the very end of the seventeenth century, when prices for slaves and quantities available had risen to meet demands from the explosion of sugar production in the Caribbean.

The growth of the slave trade, fueled by the sugar revolution in the Caribbean, soon brought enough enslaved Africans to the English that slaves became more readily available in the more successful colonies of North America. Virginia received its first slaves from occasional privateers, but in 1655, the first large cargo purchased in Calabar and Allada by a Dutch factor arrived, much of which was acquired by one of the wealthier tobacco growers, Edmond Scarbough, from New Amsterdam. Following the severing of the Dutch link in 1664, Virginia acquired its slaves from the English Caribbean where the thousands of slaves unloaded in Barbados, Jamaica, and the smaller islands provided a market at lower prices that Virginians could afford.[101] By the early eighteenth century, the wealthier tobacco growers of the Chesapeake region generated enough demand to obtain whole cargoes of slaves from Africa. The tobacco boom fueled more immigration until the middle of the eighteenth century, when a self-sustaining slave population made further trade less attractive.[102]

---

[101] Heywood and Thornton, *Central Africans*, pp. 44–48.
[102] Alan Kulikoff, *Tobacco and Slaves: The Development of Southern Cultures in the Chesapeake, 1680–1800* (Chapel Hill, 1988).

Further south, along the coast of the Carolinas, the cultivation of rice and indigo yielded the magic of high profits, and a region that was sparsely inhabited and employed indentured workers, prisoners from Europe, and Native American slaves was suddenly converted in the 1710s to a major slave importer. Poorer Barbadians pushed off the island by the growth of plantations and the arrival of slaves settled on the coast of South Carolina in 1670, and also began obtaining slaves initially from their former home. As indigo and rice generated large incomes, South Carolina had enough wealth to participate in the direct African trade, like Virginia, in the early eighteenth century. By the 1750s, the population of the Carolinas was more than half African, the densest concentration of both wealth and African slaves in North America.[103]

As was the case in Brazil, the vagaries of economic success produced radically different societies in the colonies of the Northern Europeans. The poor colonies, primarily in North America, never generated sufficient incomes to participate in the slave trade to any significant degree, but, unlike the Paulistas of southern Brazil, also never managed to enslave the Native Americans. As a result, they developed through the immigration of religious dissidents and indentured servants. In many respects, the French settlements along the St. Lawrence River in Canada, Dutch colonies on the Hudson, and the New England and Mid-Atlantic colonies of England were largely European in their background. Because the free immigrants either came with their families (the usual situation of the religious dissidents) or eventually created families from Europeans, and because they had an almost explosive demographic capacity, the poor colonies of the northern Europeans were the most European of all American colonies. At the same time, their relative poverty meant that the wealthier among them, while still socially preeminent, never came to dominate government and society the way the prosperous colonists did in the Caribbean or in Brazil. In New England, a remarkably democratic tradition of local government grew up, with higher levels of political participation than one met in Europe. The Middle Colonies and the St. Lawrence valley, though more under the control of the wealthier among the colonists, also shared a higher degree of political participation than one met elsewhere in the Americas.

In the island colonies, the wealth of sugar production made for strong parallels with the situation in the rich Brazilian north. The slave trade brought in a black working class; in Barbados, the majority European yeoman class that predominated in the 1640s mostly left the island, either returning to England or heading to North America, especially South Carolina – a pattern paralleled on a smaller scale in the other islands settled before the sugar revolution. In Jamaica, following the English takeover in 1655, the rush of Africans began almost immediately as sugar thrived, and a group of small freeholders of European ancestry never developed – a situation paralleled almost exactly in

---

[103] For early South Carolina, see Peter Wood, *Black Majority: Negroes in South Carolina from 1670 to the Stono Rebellion* (Norton, 1974).

the French portion of Hispaniola, which they called Saint Domingue (modern-day Haiti), taken over in 1697.

Thus, in these colonies, governmental forms tended to be elected assemblies, but the participation was restricted by wealth and color, leaving the franchise in the hands of a tiny percentage of the wealthiest people, all of European descent. In both Jamaica and Barbados, the richest of England's sugar islands, there was an assembly, and as in Brazil, concepts of racial purity and the immigration of European women, drawn by the wealth, led to strong caste divisions. In mid-eighteenth-century Jamaica, this racial hierarchy was very strong; even poor whites of few talents could count on complete support by their wealthier peers, a solidarity reinforced by frequent visits and hospitality among themselves. The situation also created a sense of determined independence and liberty among the white population making them very unruly.[104]

There were strong barriers against interracial marriage, although hardly any against sexual relations with slaves. Thomas Thistlewood, whose huge diary covers from 1750 through 1786, shows him to have had sex 3,852 times with 138 slave women, yet he fathered only a few children, who he favored greatly.[105] For all this, and his sadistic cruelty to the slaves under his control, Thistlewood had a strong relationship, much like a marriage, with Phibbah, a slave of one of his neighbors.[106] Thistlewood's comments and observations about his white neighbors suggest that he was not atypical in most regards from other white Jamaicans.[107]

The planters on all the Caribbean islands were greatly outnumbered by the slaves, and yet they managed a brutal regime of labor and punishment, which so diminished fertility and increased mortality that only large supplies of newly arrived Africans kept their numbers up.[108] They maintained their authority in

---

[104] For an excellent study of white Jamaican society and its attitudes toward race, anchored on Thomas Thistlewood's diary, see Trevor Burnard, *Mastery, Tyranny and Desire* (Chapel Hill, 2004).

[105] Burnard, *Mastery*, p. 156.

[106] Burnard, *Mastery*; Douglas Hall, *In Miserable Slavery* (with extensive quotations from Thistlewood's diary). Thistlewood met her while an overseer on one estate, and tried to buy or lease her when he left the estate, but was refused; on June 23, 1757, she gave him "a gold ring to keep for her sake."

[107] The diary, housed in the Lincolnshire Record Office, Monson Deposit 31, has been much commented on, although most commentators have used the excerpts given in Hall, *Miserable Slavery* (and to a lesser extent Burnard, *Mastery*) to understand him. Thanks to Trevor Burnard, who gave me a transcript of the diary, I was able to consult it directly myself at length. From my observation, it was primarily a systematic diary of his daily health, sexual activity, and social rounds, and less systematically other events. Although it has accounting elements in it, such as inventories of slaves, notices of their off-days, and some records of payments and receipts, it is not a business record as such. It was undoubtedly not intended as a "mirror to his soul," but rather as a record of a limited set of events, and can reveal relatively little about his personality.

[108] Amanda Thornton, "Coerced Care: Thomas Thistlewood's Account of Medical Practice on Enslaved Populations in Colonial Jamaica, 1751–1786," *Slavery and Abolition* 32 (2011): 535–559 (Thistlewood's diary is sufficiently detailed that it is possible to calculate an exact infant mortality rate – in this case, for example, 417‰).

the face of such odds with difficulty; Thistlewood regularly had physical fights, more or less one on one with his slaves, who were frequently insolent and often ran away, although many simply took time off and returned. Yet he, and other planters, managed to maintain this situation. In part they did so by allowing privileges to some slaves who assisted them in maintaining order – Thistlewood, for example, had a relationship with Lincoln, one of his slaves, that resembled a partnership, and Lincoln helped greatly in maintaining order. It was not uncommon for Thistlewood to send one group of slaves out to look for others, or for his slaves to catch runaways of other people.[109] Indeed, his watchman, Daniel, once arrested two runaways from another estate, taking them to a jail.[110]

In addition, savage punishment, intended to be a form of terrorism, also helped, at times, even including attempts to manipulate slave owner's conceptions of religion or African religion in this effort.[111] At the same time, masters often overlooked what might seem serious offenses.[112] Moreover, although Thistlewood records giving beatings to his slaves for a wide range of offenses, such as eating cane, quarrelling with each other, eating dirt, and the like, he also attended trials that were held against slaves accused of offenses, and in one case, the slave with whom he had a ferocious fight was acquitted.[113] Finally, in Jamaica at least, slaves were sometimes paid for services, and were allowed time off to tend their own gardens and sold the produce on the market. While Edward Long's assertion that slaves controlled 20 percent of the money in Jamaica may have been an exaggeration, it was probably true that by allowing the slaves both space and time away from the rigors of plantation labor, and allowing them to form families or at least partnerships, masters made violence and running away less attractive. In this case, it is not surprising that when Nancy and Maria were late coming to the fields in 1786, Thistlewood did not beat them, but fined them each "one bit."[114]

---

[109] Thistlewood diary, June 23, 1751 (sends a runaway back to master with a slave escort); October 4, 1751, a neighbor's slaves capture and return one of his (and other entries October 2–10); Februrary 11, 1752, June 12, 1752; February 26, 1754; April 1, 1755; April 16, 1757; May 16, 20–25, 1757.

[110] Thistlewood diary, May 12, 1757; see also June 7, 1757, Cyrus delivers runaway; August 1, 1757, a runaway delivered to him by a slave from another estate; April 26, 1786, his slaves capture others.

[111] Vincent Brown, "Spiritual Terror and Sacred Authority in Jamaican Slave Society," *Slavery and Abolition* 24 (2003): 24–53; and *The Reapers' Garden: Death and Power in the World of Atlantic Slavery* (Cambridge, MA, 2008).

[112] Thistlewood had a reputation for toughness; hence one of the slaves said of him, "He not for play," and he concocted terrible punishments like "Derby dose" in which one slave would defecate into the mouth of another. Yet his diary does not record punishments of this drastic sort frequently (my impression gained by reading the diary, but not quantified).

[113] Thistlewood diary, July 26, 1786.

[114] Thistlewood diary, September 25, 1786. At about this same time he was routinely paying women he had sex with two bits.

The collaboration between slaves and masters, which made continued exploitation of the labor force possible, created a remarkably stratified slave society. In Saint Domingue, France's richest sugar colony and the largest Caribbean concentration of slaves, Girod de Chantran, a Swiss visitor of the 1780s, compared the plantations to the palace of the Ottoman Empire, with finely graded positions of power and authority.[115] Jamaican slaves who were well established often used others slaves to do their work and indeed even to work for them.

On the North American mainland – the Chesapeake colonies and the Carolinas – the pattern was different. While tobacco, rice, and indigo produced enough wealth to bring in African slaves, the greater space available and the need for provisioning allowed the former indentured servants to remain and create a livelihood. Thus, the African-descended population remained either a minority, as in Virginia, or barely a majority (reaching about 60 percent by the mid-eighteenth century), as in South Carolina. Political and social forms produced a more lively legislative process, as the poorer class of whites managed to retain some say in politics, and often their influence was considerable on issues close to them as a class, such as western expansion to acquire more land and policy with regards to Native Americans.

The economic development of Virginia and, to a lesser degree, the Carolinas resembled northeast Brazil following the decline of sugar in the 1670s, in that smaller landowners, growing either food crops or tobacco, managed to create an economy of mixed small and large landholders with a mixed production. But whereas in Brazil, racial barriers decreased in the interior and "Indian," African, and European residents intermarried, in Virginia, the caste-based racial barriers remained, in large measure because the demographic nature of the earlier settlement, the explosive growth of European-descended settlers, their inability to force or entice the bulk of the Native American population of the interior to join the colony, and the relatively small number of African slaves compared to the European population contributed to the differences in racial attitudes in the two regions.

As the European-descended population in all these colonies was substantial and geographically quite concentrated (the slaveholding households declined in size and landholding as one moved inland from the coastal areas), they were able to sustain themselves demographically by intermarriage within their group. The poorer group tended to have attitudes of racial purity resembling those of their social betters, so that intermarriage between the poorer free population and African slaves (or freedmen) was limited in both law and practice. The slaves on the plantations tended to be concentrated in villages (or quarters) that were self-contained and restricted, creating a world of impoverished Africans and their descendants. However, in North America, unlike the Caribbean, the African population became self-sustaining and, by 1750, in Virginia at least, rapidly growing, thus creating another difference with the

---

[115] Girod de Chantrans, *Voyage d'un Suisse dans les colonies d'Amérique* [Neufchatel, 1785, mod ed. Pierre Pluchon, Paris, 1980), p. 124.

Caribbean, where African-born slaves were often the majority even in the late eighteenth century.

Colonization was only simple in uninhabited places, such as São Tomé or Barbados; in those that were inhabited by free associations, there were multiple complexities, particularly concerning military affairs and acquiring labor forces. Nevertheless, Europeans managed to create the requisite military alliances to assure their capacity to occupy territory, and then to acquire the laboring population to make colonies pay. The crucial determinant, however, was the return that export crops could bring – where there was a rich crop like sugar, the resulting colony was highly stratified, usually with an African underclass, and racially exculsive. Where there was not a rich product, the class differences and racial distinctions tended to be less, and government was often quite democractic. The strongest differences took place in those areas where Europeans arrived in family groups, particularly in North America, for there, even in a democratic environment, racial differences were emphasized; but in places where immigration was male only, racial differences were considerably less, even though slavery was sometimes more pronounced, as in São Paulo.

7

Contact

In some areas of the Atlantic world, there was no effective conquest or colonization of one region by another, or at least the processes were sufficiently drawn out that frontiers developed. Such situations took place when Europeans established stable trading relationships with existing polities, as they did all along the African coast, except the conquest of Angola and colonization of South Africa. In the Americas, contact situations developed where unconquered Native Americans defined a frontier with colonists or conquerors, and where at times the two groups interpenetrated each other fairly deeply. In these environments, there were fascinating possibilities for cultural and political exchange between equal partners.

THE AFRICAN COAST

On the coast of most of Atlantic Africa, Europeans and Africans came into extended contact, but there was no change of sovereignty. Europeans discovered in the fifteenth century that there was not going to be any conquest and what colonization there was would have to be restricted to the uninhabited offshore islands of the Cape Verde group or São Tomé. Elsewhere on the coast, Europeans came as transient visitors or perhaps as invited guests, tolerated and accepted as long as they conformed to local norms. This general situation was only violated in Angola after 1575 and South Africa after 1652, where Europeans were able to make limited conquests and establish colonies.

European trade with Africa was of two sorts: shipboard trade and factory trade. In shipboard trade, Europeans made no permanent settlement or base on the coast, but traded either directly from their vessels' decks or docked the vessels to be temporary trading posts. Factory trade, on the other hand, involved the European traders establishing a permanent post on the coast, which would conduct continuous trade with the surrounding African communities, and hold it until ships arrived. These ships would then not have to stay for long stretches on the coast.

Shipboard trading was the norm on several stretches of the African coast, for example, the Ivory Coast, much of the Niger Delta, and the coast east and south of there down to Loango. The Ivory Coast is the most extreme example of this: even though Europeans traded regularly with the coast and purchased a great store of items ranging from ivory to "Kwakwa" cloth for export or sale elsewhere in Africa, they never established any stations. Instead, trade was usually conducted from anchored ships off the coast, and Africans only came out to visit the ships in their own watercraft. In an environment of fleeting and often virtually anonymous relationships, trading was cautious and suspicion was prevalent. Europeans knew little of the life and politics of the region, Africans probably knew just as little about the Europeans, and documentation of any sort is very limited.

Shipboard trading was somewhat better established in the Niger Delta region. Ships could only trade effectively by going up into the river and creek network and creating a shipboard base. However, they did visit the land and formed fairly stable long-term relationships with the leading authorities and traders of the larger towns such as Elem Kalabari (New Calabar) and Bonny, or in the nearby Cross River with the political and commercial elite of Old Calabar.[1] The volume of trade from this region was substantial, especially the slave trade, and ships lingered for substantial periods, even up to months on the coast taking in their cargos. Alexander Falconbridge, a ship's surgeon who visited the region several times in the 1770s, noted that upon arriving in Bonny or New Calabar, "it is customary for them to unbend the sails, strike the yards, and begin to build what they denominate a *house*" on the ship, by placing a latticework over several yards that were stretched between the masts. The latticework was then covered with rush mats from the shore, and the area divided by a "barracado" from the rest of the ship (which was also supplied with inward-facing blunderbusses and light artillery to put down "the insurrections that now and then happen." The quarters for the slaves were further subdivided in order that slaves could be separated by sex during the time they were held between the first purchases and the ship's final departure.[2] The king of Calabar (or Bonny) and his noblemen, who Falconbridge reported were known as "parliament men" because they served as royal advisors, visited the ship, engaged in trade on their own terms, and then allowed free trading between the visiting ship and the ordinary merchants. Falconbridge believed that it generally took three months to receive the whole cargo of slaves, who came "sometimes in small and sometimes in larger numbers."[3]

[1] Alexander X. Byrd, *Captives & Voyagers: Black Migrants across the Eighteenth-Century British Atlantic World* (Baton Rouge, 2008), Part 1. This is a good introduction to the trading life of the region.

[2] Alexander Falconbridge, *An Account of the Slave Trade on the Coast of Africa* (London, 1788 [GB]), pp. 5–7.

[3] Falconbridge, *Account*, pp. 8–9.

While shipboard trading may have been commercially viable, it clearly limited the kinds of noncommercial interactions that might take place. Once a ship left the region, it took all its personnel who had survived the stay, and many would never return, but some made regular voyages and were well known to the African traders. Antera Duke, who was a literate African trader in the town of Old Calabar, kept a diary in the local variety of English of his transactions between 1785 and 1788.[4] It is fairly clear that whereas he had little knowledge of some captains who arrived in the port, others he knew better, and he also noted some social gatherings and meetings between African traders and the captains.[5] While there was often long-range continuity between the Europeans as a group and Africans as a group, more intimate relationships were limited. Europeans did not seek to influence African culture around them or to recreate anything of their home in the African environment that they regarded as hostile and uninviting. The African traders, however, did make some important adjustments – at the very least, learning to read and write in their own form of English, and on occasion sending their own children to Europe to study.[6]

If shipboard trading with its fleeting relationships characterized one element of life on the African coast, factory trading represented another. In factory trading, the Europeans established a permanent presence on or near the African coast. There were two variants of settlement trading. The first, used exclusively by Portugal, was the establishment of a base on an offshore island, and then sending out traders to reside for longer or shorter times on the coast. The second variant, employed by other Europeans, was to establish a factory on the coast, where a small commercial community under the control of a company would reside, sometimes in a fort and with a garrison, year round.

When the Portuguese were established in West Africa, they constructed a colony in the previously uninhabited Cape Verde islands, and brought slaves from the mainland to settle. In addition, at least a few members of elite groups from Africa (especially the Senegal region) also found their way to the islands. The Cape Verdes became the center for Portuguese activity, with a governor and, after 1534, even a bishop. Commerce between the coast and the islands, a relatively short sail away, was thus like a factory and its hinterland, but not exactly so. Many traders from the island moved to the coast, and there they settled and made their own arrangements with local powers. Settling on the mainland allowed them to avoid certain levels of taxation and control that living in the Cape Verdes did not, and not surprisingly many of the Portuguese who

---

[4] Published in Daryll Forde, *Efik Traders of Old Calabar* (Oxford, 1956). A new interpretation of the diary and a retranslation is in Stephen Behrendt, A. H. Latham, David Northrup, and A. J. H. Latham, *The Diary of Antera Duke, an Eighteenth-Century African Slave Trader* (Oxford, 2010).

[5] Duke Diary, April 30, 1785, inviting all the captains to come ashore; May 26, 1785, a group of three traders "Drisht whit men" (dressed in European clothes) to visit the ships.

[6] For a fuller version of this trans-Atlantic dimension of Niger Delta traders, see Randy Sparks, *The Two Princes of Calabar: An Eighteenth Century Atlantic Odyssey* (Cambridge, MA, 2004).

settled on the mainland were from outsider groups, such as New Christians who were abundant there even in the early sixteenth century.

These settlers, who were both unofficial and illegal in the eyes of the Portuguese government, were known as *lançados* or *tangosmaos* in the Portuguese sources. *Lançados*, or anyone wishing to trade in the region south of roughly the Gambia River, had to make arrangements with local power holders. In the sixteenth century, this involved a local institution in which a "master of a house [*senhor de pousada*]," after exchanging pleasantries with a trader "who came to stay some time," would order all his wives [*mulheres*] to appear, from whom he would order the visitor "to choose the one who seems to him the best."[7] The woman he chose would then serve him "in all manner of service." Such a woman was called *cabondo* in the local language.[8] In the longer run, the arrangement was seen as something akin to a marriage, for it was understood that he would clothe her and "take no other women," or he would forfeit his goods. However, unlike African traders whose children by the cabondo were "considered children of the master of the house, like other children … if one happens to be begotten by a white [*branco*, but probably anyone with Portuguese affiliations], they give it to the father who takes it away."[9]

These unions created a new class of people on the coast, although they were integrated into the same communities, "relying on the good word and protection of their hosts." Because of this reliance they were vulnerable and sometimes ill-treated or robbed by local people. Some kings, such as Matsamba, the mid-sixteenth century ruler of Cazamansa, did look out for their interests. In a celebrated case, Matsamba protected a Portuguese from a wrongful accusation of rape, no doubt orchestrated by a local man and his wife to win possession of the European's goods.[10] But for every Matsamba there were others who were less sympathetic or more inclined to milk the commercial community, so that

---

[7] António Álvares de Almada, "Tratado breve dos rios de Guiné" (1594) in *MMA*² 4: 347–348 (an annotated English translation by P. E. H. Hair is found at http://digital.library.wisc.edu/1711.dl/AfricaFocus.Almada01 with notes at …Almada02). I have altered Hair's translation in the use of the verb *mandar*, which implies a more coercive arrangement here than in Hair's version, "demands that the guest should choose." The Portuguese term "mulher" is used for the women offered to the *lançado*, which can mean simply "woman" but also "wife," so it is unclear as to whether the host offered one of his own polygamous wives, or simply a woman under his care and charge. Likewise the status of the woman, as a wife or something else, remains ambiguous. The visitor in the text is rendered singular, Brásio's edition emends to make this visitor a plural.

[8] BSGL, Manuel Álvares, "Etiopia Menor," (c 1609), fols. 62–62v (English translation by P. E. H. Hair at http://digital.library.wisc.edu/1711.dl/AfricaFocus.Alvares01). This description includes most of the same details found in Álvares de Almada.

[9] Álvares de Almada, "Tratado Breve," *MMA*² 3: 348. Hair translates in the singular in these later passages, implying that this is the work of the lord of the house, whereas in the Portuguese the verbs are plural here, suggesting a custom of the country and not of the master himself.

[10] André Donelha, "Descrição da Serra Leoa e dos Rios de Guiné do Cabo Verde" (1625), published, along with an English and French translation by Avelino Teixeira da Mota and P. E. H. Hair (Lisbon, 1977), fol 32v (original manuscript marked in edition and translations).

the goods of *lançados* were routinely confiscated when they died, unless they took refuge at sea when ill, thus being under Portuguese jurisdiction.[11]

Not surprisingly, where there was a sufficient concentration of *lançados*, as around the mouth of the Rio Grande, they banded together. In 1589, Manuel Lopes Cardoso, a Cape Verde-based trader, persuaded the local ruler named Chapala to allow him to build a fort at Cacheu to protect against French and English corsairs then active on the coast. Once built, this fort and another at Bissau became a refuge and center for *lançados* in the area, and as that became obvious, African leaders retaliated in 1590, attacking the fort unsuccessfully, thanks, not surprisingly, to the information supplied by two "black *ladina* [able to speak Portuguese] women of their own land," in all probability drawn from that class of women involved in the traders' business and lives.[12] The fort remained, and even though the traders continued to be harassed in their business, at least their property was respected.[13]

Local circumstances made a big difference, for according to the Cape Verdian trader Manuel Álvares de Almada, writing at the end of the sixteenth century, in the area of the Beafadas farther south, traders managed to live comfortably and well protected by powerful local families, and when a fort was built at Porto da Cruz to protect them, they found conditions more confrontational, so that they were saved some difficulties but added others.[14] But if the fort protected the *lançados* from the demands of their hosts, it also placed them more fully under Portuguese jurisdiction from Cape Verde, and there was thus constant tension between Portuguese control, local African demands, and that of the emerging Luso-African community. In this process, some *lançados* moved away from the fortified settlements to seek better arrangements all along the coast to Sierra Leone, along the coast of Senegambia.

While these West African trading stations provided bases and had some influence on the coast, Central Africa had a different history. Here the Portuguese had a complicated relationship with the Kingdom of Kongo and eventually also founded a conquest colony in Angola.[15] In some ways the establishment of a Portuguese community in Kongo paralleled that in the West African areas under the factory system. But from the beginning of the period of contact, Portuguese resided in Mbanza Kongo, Kongo's capital far in the interior, although they also took up residence at the coastal port of Mpinda at the mouth of the Congo River. By the 1590s, there were Portuguese resident at other points in Kongo,

---

[11] Álvares de Almada, "Tratado Breve," *MMA*² 3: 299 (integration), 334 (taking refuge in ships).
[12] Álvares de Almada, "Tratade Breve," *MMA*² 3: 300. While the term *ladina* generally refers to language ability, it also has a cultural component, Hair renders the term "half civilized," which seems to me a more negative connotation.
[13] BSGL, Álvares, "Etiopia Menor," fols. 16v–17v; (writing some twenty years later about the events and the following period); Álvares de Almada, "Tratado Breve," *MMA*² 3: 300 (written more or less at the time of the events).
[14] Álvares de Almada, "Tratado Breve," *MMA*² 3: 329–330.
[15] For a fuller treatment of the Portuguese in Angola before 1660, see Linda Heywood and John Thornton, *Central Africans, Atlantic Creoles, and the Making of the Americas* (Cambridge, 2007), Chapters 2–3.

such as Mbumbi in Mbamba province, Ngongo Mbata in Mbata, and Okango on Kongo's eastern frontier.[16] Still, the center of most business ventures was at Mbanza Kongo (São Salvador after 1570). The Portuguese community had become self-governing under a captain appointed by the King of Kongo after 1553. They took up government and military service in Kongo and held offices and titles. Some married into the royal family and other elite families and were involved in many plots along with their royal patrons.[17] Others were priests and helped organize and teach in Kongo's Western schools. Their mixed-race offspring were bilingual and bicultural, but in a country whose own elite was in many ways parallel to them. This community came under pressure as the Portuguese in Angola called on them to join Angola following the foundation of that colony in 1575.[18] They resisted, but in the aftermath of the Angolan wars against Kongo from 1622, many were massacred by the general population.[19] Another large massacre followed the Kongolese defeat at the Battle of Mbwila in 1665, and after that date, most Portuguese were based in Luanda, handling their operations in Kongo through their own agents, or *pombeiros*.

The colony of Angola formed a more conventional, if much larger, settlement-trading post and was the prime base for Portuguese commerce in all of Central Africa. It amounted to the port of Luanda and the courses of two rivers, the Bengo to the north and the Kwanza to the south, including its affluent the Lukala, and an isolated seacoast port at Benguela to the south. Within this zone the Portuguese exercised the authority of their conquest, using a mixture of military forces, mostly raised by their subordinate sobas, allied Imbangala bands, and some regular soldiers, as already noted. Beyond this zone, however, Angola bounded on independent African states: Kongo to the north, a group of smaller semi-independent states (who had sworn vassalage to Portugal, but only sometimes obeyed them), to the east Matamba-Ndongo, the kingdom built by Queen Njinga from the unconquered portions of Ndongo, and the kingdom constructed in the 1630s by the Imbangala band of Kasanje. South across the Kwanza were a group of small kingdoms that also maintained their independence: Hako, Libolo, and the Kisama states.

Portugal's relations with these areas was through regulated trading posts, called *ferias*, where an agent (*capitão mor*) resided and where trade was supposed to be conducted. Small Portuguese communities, most residents of which

[16] ANTT Inquisição de Lisboa, Livro 877, "Visita ad Angola," fols. 26v, 62v, 64, 84v, 89. The purpose of this Inquisition investigation was primarily to determine the location of "New Christians" (converted Jews) in Angola, but it also outlines the locations of many trading posts not mentioned in other documents.

[17] John Thornton, "Early Kongo-Portuguese Relations, 1483–1575: A New Interpretation," *History in Africa* 8 (1981): 183–204.

[18] For example, Domingos de Abreu de Brito, "Svmario e Descripção do Reyno de Angola" (1591), in Alfredo de Albuquerque Felner, ed. *Um Inquérito à vida administrativa e economica de Angola e do Brasil* (Coimbra, 1931), recommended severe punishment for disloyal Portuguese in Kongo in 1591.

[19] Mateus Cardoso to Fr. Rodrigues, 1624, *MMA* 7: 294; Nationaal Archief Nederland, Staten Generaal, vol. 5157, Session of October 27, 1623.

were racially mixed, made considerable compromises to live in the two worlds of central Africa. Some had intermarried with the surrounding elite – for example, Matamba's ruling elite was married into the Portuguese subjects of eastern Angola. The rulers of the independent states were reluctant to allow the Portuguese to pass beyond these trading posts. When Manuel Correia Leitão was sent by the commercially minded governor António Álvares da Cunha to explore the land beyond Angola's eastern regions in 1755–1756, he was uniformly blocked by the ruling powers, and gained what little knowledge he could of the lands further east, which was just then coming under the domination of the emerging Lunda Empire, by interviewing slaves and travelers from the interior.[20]

It was not until the end of the eighteenth century that this impasse was broken, as Portuguese traders spread out from Benguela on the south, establishing themselves in the larger kingdoms of the central African highlands in the 1770s (after a major war) and eventually penetrating into the interior so far as to cross from Angola to the other side of Africa. It was not long after this that a Lunda diplomatic expedition arrived with great fanfare in Luanda. Thus, the penetration of Portuguese goods and traders from Angola's neighbors, some of whom had been influenced by the Portuguese communities there, brought some European cultural knowledge and news in the heart of Central Africa.

Elsewhere, outside of Central Africa, the European settlement was less involved in African politics and confined largely to factories to facilitate trade, especially the gold trade, and most originated in the efforts of the northern Europeans. The earliest permanent factories were established by the Portuguese on the inhospitable coast of the Sahara at Arguin (1469) and then at São Jorge da Mina (1482), popularly called Mina or Elmina (as it is called today). Both these early posts were established in areas that would handle gold trading, and the later Senegal posts established by the Portuguese and then by the Dutch and French also had this objective. The post established by the English in the Gambia River in the mid-seventeenth century was originally designed to protect gold trading. The plethora of trading forts established in the seventeenth and eighteenth centuries on the Gold Coast by English, Dutch, Swedish, and Danish companies also began their lives as gold-trading centers.

Factory trading was generally regarded as a superior means of conducting business, especially for the large trading companies. Thus, it was not uncommon for European concerns or groups of merchants to seek to create a factory in an area otherwise dominated by shipboard trade. The Portuguese had a trading post at Ughoton to serve their interests in the Benin trade, but abandoned

---

[20] Correia Leitão's report was published in 1937; an updated edition of the original and English translation was subsequently published by Jan Vansina and Eva Sebastyén, "Angola's Eastern Hinterland in the 1750's: A Text Edition and Translation of Manoel Correia Leitão 'Voyage' (1755–56)," *History in Africa* 26 (1999): 299–364; for traveling troubles, see fols. 6–7v, 9, and 12. A statement by local people about the geography of the interior from this mission is found in Arquivo da Universidade de Coimbra, VI-3ª-I-2-14, Colecção Condes de Cunha, no. 198, Declaraçao dos potentados…1756.

it in the mid-sixteenth century as trading patterns shifted. The Dutch returned to this idea in 1716 and for a few years maintained their own post at Ughoton, but it was also abandoned in the shifting politics of civil-war-era Benin.[21]

The English built a short-lived trading post at Cabinda in 1718, but this was destroyed by the local authorities in 1723. The Portuguese attempted a more elaborate scheme to build a fort at Cabinda and to use it as a base to monopolize trade on the coast in 1783. This program, with its monopolistic intentions could never find local favor, and it, like the less ambitious English plan, was defeated when the ruler of Ngoyo attacked and destroyed it.[22]

France created one of the most ambitious attempts to set up a network of trading posts in the interior when they began in the early eighteenth century to establish a chain of trading posts and centers along the Senegal River, and thus deep into West Africa. The idea was to monopolize trade not only along the Senegal coast, but even in the Gambia, and if possible to control the gold fields of Bambuhu along the Falémé River.[23] As in the coastal holdings, French officials of the Company of Senegal negotiated with local political authorities at various places along the river to gain permission to build trading posts. Two rulers in northern Bambuhu, for example, accepted the construction of French forts in their lands in 1726 and 1728 as they thought it might provide them with protection against Fulbe armies from nearby Xasso, which every year "forced them to take refuge among the crags of the mountains to save their lives." But such permission was tempered by the fear (at least partially justified) that the French hoped to take control of the mines.[24] The French then organized regular fleets of riverboats to go from their main headquarters on the coast to these posts. The system was not successful in the long run, and by the end of the century it had been abandoned.

Copious records from the Dutch fort at Elmina give us an idea of the sort of society that grew up in the shadow of this trading post and settlement.[25] In the early eighteenth century, Elmina counted about 250–300 European-born employees in its population, of which some 60 percent were salaried soldiers of the garrison. These appointments were temporary, and many employees returned to Europe, short the roughly one in five who died in any given year. Life for most of the Europeans was fairly boring; much of their time when not working was taken up with drinking. Although many might retrun to Europe,

[21] The history of this post can be found in J. F. C. Ryder, *Benin and the Europeans, 1485–1897* (London, 1969).

[22] Both these schemes are described in Phyllis Martin, *The External Trade of the Loango Coast* (Oxford, 1972).

[23] André Delcourt, *La France et les éstablissments français au Sénégal entre 1713 et 1763* (Dakar, 1952).

[24] Claude Boucard, "Relation du Bambouc par Claude Boucard (1729)" ed. Philip Curtin and Jean Boulègue, *Bulletin de l'Institute foundamentale de l'Afrique Noire* 36 (1974): 252–255.

[25] A good study is Harvey Feinberg, *Africans and Europeans in West Africa: Elminas and Dutchmen on the Gold Coast during the Eighteenth Century* (Philadelphia, 1989).

a good number had relationships with local women, as their wills reveal, for not a few left goods to "my black woman" (*negerin*).

Under the circumstances, it is not surprising that the soldiers left more than just goods, for a small community of mixed-race people, mostly the descendants of these informal liaisons, surrounded the fort; its residents were normally also employed for a salary. In fact, some 800 to 1,000 people were listed on payrolls as working for a salary, mostly mulattoes whose names show both Dutch and Akan elements. In addition, some 300 company slaves augmented this African and African-descended workforce. Most of the free people were settled in Elmina's African town, which in the eighteenth century comprised some 1,000 houses, most built of stone. Its market served the fort and the town, for records show that the company did not plant its own crops, but purchased these supplies from the town, and as the slave trade grew, so did the demand for foodstuffs. Relations between the town and the community were managed by the Makelaar, an official who had connections to both the fort and the larger African world.

The population around these forts was composed of people from many backgrounds, including free peasants living in the vicinity or who had moved there, slaves brought in by the factory that remained in its service, and people of higher status, either existing political authorities or people of noble background who moved to the factories. There were also African women who served as wives and as concubines of the factors, their servants, or the soldiers. Some were of fairly high status, providing a link between the European trading community and the African commercial and political elite.

Surely the most famous of these higher-status women were the *signares* of Senegambia, women who served as a sort of circulating wives and trading partners of the various European factors.[26] Gorée, the French trading post situated on an island off the coast of Senegal, had some 200 residents in the eighteenth century, of which about one-half to two-thirds were mixed race, along with some 1,500 African settlers who came there to trade or settle and an equal number of slaves.[27] The Signares would be married to Frenchmen who came to serve fairly short terms in the factory, and then when the first factor left, they would take up the same relationship with the next one, in sequence.[28] But according to Joseph Alexandre le Brasseur, who lived on the coast in the

---

[26] For an overview of their history, see George Brooks, *Eurafricans in Western Africa: Commerce, Social Status, Gender and Religious Observance from the Sixteenth to the Eighteenth Century* (Athens, OH, and Oxford, 2003), pp. 122–160, 250–316; a more detailed study by the same author, "The Signares of St. Louis and Gorée: Women Entrepreneurs in Eighteenth Century Senegal," in Nancy Hafkin and Edna Bay, eds., *Women in Africa: Studies in Social and Economic Change* (Stanford, 1976), pp. 19–44.

[27] Charles Becker and Victor Martin, eds., "Mémoire inédit de Doumet (1769): Le Kayor et les pays voisins au cours de la seconde moitié du XVIIIe siècle," *BIFAN* series B, 36 (1974) editor's n. 10, pp. 50–51 citing a variety of statistical sources.

[28] For a classic description, from Senegal in the second half of the eighteenth century, see M. Doumet, "Mémoires historiques sur les different parties de l'Afrique dépendant de l'isle de Gorée..." in Charles Becker and V. Martin, "Mémoire inédit de Doumet," 45 and *passim*.

1770s, they insisted that their "concubinage ... have all the characteristics of marriages approved by the Church." In fact, they had public celebrations of them, and no one would be mistress to a man "no matter how rich" if he did not publically acknowledge them.[29] Indeed, those who followed their husbands to France, as occurred at times, were ruined by the experience and had to return empty-handed to Gorée, and so for the most part they insisted on being public concubines and refused to marry, or at least to marry officially (while still insisting on ceremonial recognition of their status). Their interest in the slave trade gave them trans-Atlantic interests, and the Senegal group was particularly attached to Cayenne (in modern-day Guiana), where many of the slaves went. Their fashions, a combination of local and European fabrics and designs, pioneered the "traditional" fashions of elite women in Senegal today, and their commitment to being sensual rather than domestic led Le Brasseur to describe them as having a "sweetness that goes so far as indolence."[30] Most signares had substantial numbers of personal slaves, which they lent to the factory from time to time, but their larger commercial connections to the African society in the interior, even though they identified themselves as Christians in a larger Muslim society, gave them real commercial connections, and not surprisingly they did not always follow the rules or even the interests of the French company.[31]

Women involved in this sort of practice in areas where the English had a factory were often called "wives of the coast." They were not people of low status, but were from the equivalent ranks of African society, and they developed trading networks with their kin and connections. They shared this local knowledge with their husbands, while at the same time benefiting from their relationships with the traders. It was probably true that trade along this coast could not take place without them.

Not all trading posts, even fortified ones, originated in the gold trade. The English post at Bence Island in the Sherbro region of Sierra Leone, or the several posts created on the "Slave Coast" near or in Whydah and its surrounding areas, were never gold-trading centers. These were mostly company forts, established in the hope that by having a presence in the area, factors could buy the many products that Africans sold, including slaves, more effectively by having a permanent buyer on the coast.

In Upper Guinea, trading factories were private concerns of merchants who settled among the Africans.[32] When Dutch merchants began trading along the

---

[29] Joseph Alexandre Le Brasseur, "Details historiques et politiques, mémoire inédit de J. A. Le Brasseur," ed. Charles Becker and Victor Martin *BIFAN* series B, 39 (1977), p. 110 (Le Brasseur's note D).

[30] Le Brasseur, "Details historiques," p. 110 (Le Brasseur's note D).

[31] Doumet, "Mémoire," pp. 32, 34; Le Brasseur, "Details historiques," p. 110.

[32] George Brooks, *Eurafricans in Western Africa: Commerce, Social Status, Gender and Religious Observance from the Sixteenth to Eighteenth Centuries* (Bloomington, 2003). For an earlier, pioneering effort, see Walter Rodney, *A History of the Upper Guinea Coast, 1545–1800* (Oxford, 1970). For a more detailed look a the Guinea Bissau region, see Philip Havik, *Silences*

1. *Negresse esclave.*   3. *Marabou ou Prêtre du Pays.*
2. *Signare de l'Isle S.t Louis.*   4. *Negre armé en Guerre.*

FIGURE 7. "Signare de l'Isle St Louis" print from *L'Affrique et le peupie affriquain*, 1789. Courtesy of Manuscripts, Archives and Rare Books Division, Schomburg Center for Research in Black Culture, The New York Public Library, Astor, Lenox and Tilden Foundations.

coast, they found the whole of it in the hands of "the Portuguese" as they called the Luso-African settlers. These Portuguese, most of whom were descended from *lançados* settled there from Cape Verde in the sixteenth and seventeenth centuries, were like the Portuguese elsewhere on the coast – of mixed race and not particularly loyal to Portugal. Richard Jobson, an early English visitor of 1620, noted that "they call themselves *Portingales*, and some few of them seeme the same, others of them are *Molatoes*, betweene blacke and white, but the most part as blacke as the naturall inhabitants" – the result of at least three generations of intermarriage with Africans. The ones he noted along the Gambia lived scattered over the country in groups of two or three, married or "keepe with them the country blackewomen," as noted earlier (although there was a group still living in the forts of the late sixteenth century). They spoke Portuguese, considered themselves Christian, and took it "a great disdaine, be they never to blacke, to be called a *Negro*." Those living on the Gambia, unlike perhaps the colleagues in the forts, could easily expect their goods to be expropriated by local kings upon their death.[33]

These northern Europeans threatened Portuguese trade, at least as it was seen in Cape Verde and in the forts, and so they tried to prevent it. By the late seventeenth century, the *lançados'* descendants exercised much more influence and political power than previously, when they were at the mercy of their African hosts. Ambrósio Gomes, for example, was noted in 1671 as the richest man in Guinea with "a multitude of slaves" and, in a change from the past, "much feared by the neighboring kings, and who makes war and peace." Nor did he fear Portugal, for he was rich and powerful enough to be chosen as an interim governor of Cacheu.[34] After his death in 1679, his wife, Bibiana Vaz, herself a well-connected trader, inherited his wealth and in some degree leadership of the *lançado* community against the attempts of Portugal to limit their trade. In 1684, she and other conspirators arrested the Portuguese official, José Gonçalves Doliveira, who had been charged with creating a government monopoly, and then established a short-lived "republic" run by the *lançados*.[35]

Just as Bibiana Vaz dominated the coast in the seventeenth century, José Lopes de Moura dominated Sierra Leone in the mid-eighteenth century. Like his predecessors, Lopes de Moura was more interested in free trade with anyone than any national loyalty. And he, like others, found that by playing in local African politics, he could inherit positions of authority in the local African states, where in many ways a more logical loyalty lay. Facing competition from

and Soundbites: The Gendered Dynamics of Trade and Brokerage in the Pre-Colonial Guinea Bissau Region (Münster, Hamburg, Berlin, Vienna, and London, 2004).

[33] Richard Jobson, *The Golden Trade of a Discovery of the River Gambra and the Golden Trade of the Aethiopians* (London, 1623 [EEB; 1904 ed.GB]), pp. 28–30 (see also a fully annotated modern edition, edited by D. P. Gamble and P. E. H. Hair, *The Discovery of the River Gambra (1623)* [London, 1999]).

[34] AHU Cx 2, July 20, 1671, quoted in Havik, *Silences and Soundbites*, p. 163.

[35] Havik, *Silences and Soundbites*, pp. 162–173. This is often told: see Rodney, *Upper Guinea Coast*, pp. 209–212; Brooks, *Eurafricans*, pp. 148–150.

European trading companies, for example, he managed to ruin the English factory in Sierra Leone in 1728.

English traders who arrived in Africa in the late seventeenth century became established in the region around the Sherbro River in southern Sierra Leone, where there was no preexisting Portuguese presence. Zachary Rogers and John Tucker, for example, arrived there with the English Company of Merchant Adventurers in 1665, and were joined by Thomas Corker, a trader for the Merchant Adventurers' successor company, the Royal Africa Company, in 1684. All these traders married immediately into local elite families from the African polities of the region, and then more or less forced the company to hire them as local agents in the 1690s.

Thus this coast also became, like the Portuguese-influenced region farther north, a domain of mixed-race families with strong commercial and political connections.[36] Henry Tucker (also known as King Hal), a powerful trader of the mid-eighteenth century, had, according to the slave trader Nicholas Owens, "been in England, Spain, and Portugall, and is master of the English tongue." He had some "6 or 7 wives," and his slaves and free dependents had built a town near his home so that "his riches set him above the kings and his numerous people above being surprised in war."[37]

James Cleveland was another powerful merchant whose roots probably went back to an earlier settler-trader in Sierra Leone. When Robert Bostock, a Liverpool slave trader, sent his ship *Jimmy* to Sierra Leone in 1787, he advised the skipper, Peter Berme, to save goods worth forty slaves for "Mr Cleveland" with whom he had an indenture, and to acquaint him with his every move; for all that, however, he was never to entrust any goods to "any of the natives," for if he did, "you would never see them again."[38] Cleveland could supply "gromutas (grumetes)" or local sailors, to assist in manning small craft, and was the best person to ask advice about trading conditions, as Bostock asked him to advise one of his new captains on such matters.[39] In addition to slaves, Cleveland also dealt in gum and ivory and had various credit arrangements in the Caribbean.[40] Bostock wrote him a number of formal letters praising him and asking after his health and that of his family, bemoaning that he had not heard from the coastal trader. He was sufficiently attentive of his trading partner that he noted, "I have sent you 8 ruffled shirts of my own daughters making marked with your name on and beg you except of and hope they will fit you."[41] Clearly Cleveland was an important person for all traders on the coast. In the

---

[36] Rodney, *Upper Guinea Coast*, pp. 216–221; Brooks, *Eurafricans*, pp. 293–305.

[37] Nicholas Owens, "Journal" ed. E. Martin, *Nicholas Owens: Journal of a Slave Dealer* (London, 1930), p. 76.

[38] LRO TUO 387 MD 54, Robert Bostock to Capt. Peter Berme Liverpool, July 2, 1787.

[39] LRO TUO 387 MD 54, Bostock to Cleveland, Liverpool, June 19, 1788 (the first of two letters of the same date).

[40] LRO TUO 387 MD 54, Bostock to Steven Bowers, June 19, 1788; same to Mr. Cleveland, June 19, 1788 (three letters, same date) and August 10, 1788.

[41] LRO TUO 387 MD 54, Bostock to Mr. Cleveland, Liverpool June 19, 1788 and several others of the same tenor following.

1790s, his forces often raided neighbors to collect debts, and as a result of this and accepting pledges against debts, he was able to deport a good number of people in the slave trade. Because much of local politics, with its tiny mini-states, was controlled by the Poro Society, it is not surprising that Cleveland managed to get control over its senior membership.[42]

FRONTIERS WITH FREE ASSOCIATIONS IN THE AMERICAS

Europeans barely made any inroads into Africa before the late nineteenth century, and they also had failed to occupy a great deal of the Americas. North Americans are well aware, for example, that the "winning of the West" was largely a product of the second half of the nineteenth century, and Argentines are equally conscious that the Pampas were outside Spanish control at the end of the colonial period. In today's Brazil, the Mato Grosso provides a backdrop for their own version of the saga. In fact, the frontier was deeper and less clear in earlier times, so that the maps that adorn schoolbooks even today often exaggerate the extent of European control over the Americas, representing in many cases colonial claims rather than real occupation.

On the frontier, not only did European colonization constantly, albeit sometimes slowly, encroach on areas occupied by Native American societies, but the nature of Native American society in the areas played a role as well. In Africa, the Europeans came up against state-organized societies that they could not conquer; in America, the Spanish and Portuguese conquered most state-organized societies very early, except in the mini-states of the Maya interior and along the Orinoco and Amazon Rivers. Generally, once the initial resistance of state societies was overcome or incorporated, whether it was the Aztec or Inca Empires, the Carjió in southern Brazil, or Powhatan in the Chesapeake, and Massasoit in New England, European expansion met free associations.

Free associations presented formidable problems to the European attempts at conquest. Their decentralized decision-making process and lack of enforcement meant that they could not simply surrender, nor could their leaders be co-opted as might happen with even fairly decentralized states. If defeated, they often chose to retreat. In addition, they had a very egalitarian distribution of wealth that, because it lacked concentration, did not need to be defended. This made their mobility all the more effective as a means of resisting. Early and effective resistance gave free associations time to learn about the weapons and arts of war that Europeans brought to the Americas, to adopt to them, and to master them themselves. If Spanish cavalry was devastatingly effective against massed armies of Incas or Aztecs, by the 1580s, the Spanish were facing skilled equestrian fighters in Northwest Mexico and Chile who had ample stocks of horses and rode as well as any Spaniard. Guns and powder were soon acquired and mastered by the Iroquois, Caribs, and other free associations. In the end, the

---

[42] Rodney, *Upper Guinea Coast*, pp. 218–219.

Europeans and their colonists had little more to rely on than their own high birthrates and their capacity to plow in thousands of new settlers from Europe, Africa, and other parts of the Americas to create a relentlessly dense occupation of land to expand their horizons.

Unlike the African states, free associations did not attempt to prevent Europeans or their American colonists from entering their lands. Free associations, by their nature, were not intent on defending territory, and whereas they might attack war parties that entered their lands, they welcomed traders. French traders from Canada penetrated deeply into the heart of the continent in the late seventeenth century, using the Great Lakes and Mississippi Valley as corridors. Small groups of them settled along the river, joining others who moved up the Mississippi from the south following the founding of the colony of Louisiana in the early eighteenth century. The Brazilian bandeirantes, albeit often with more hostile intentions, likewise made great voyages into the South American interior, typically in search of gold and diamonds, but also in search of slaves.

Different settler groups dealt with the American frontier in widely differing ways, in part dictated by the nature of the societies they dealt with – that is, whether they were free associations or smaller mini-states – but also by the demographics and background of the Europeans themselves. Generally, the Iberians – Spanish and Portuguese – approached them through two strategies: the first was to enslave as many as possible through wars and then to maintain them as subordinate laborers and fighters; the second was to use ecclesiastical institutions to "reduce" them (as the Spanish called the process) or make them "descend" (go down the rivers to settlements) as the Portuguese of Brazil and the Amazon called it. In both cases, missionaries of many different orders tried to organize them into allied communities that would then provide labor services or military assistance.

In most cases, the frontier societies that resulted were not rich enough to attract many European women, and as a result, the settler pioneers usually intermarried with those among the allies they deemed to be elite, creating mixed-race families that tended to define themselves as "white," Spanish, or Portuguese and intermarry within their group. At the same time, they never ceased creating a second mixed-race community of illegitimate offspring, the children of slaves, concubines, and sometimes wives of nonelite Europeans who continued to marry into the indigenous world. Often in time and particularly with Christianity and racial mixture, many indigenous people living within the settler world were simply defined as residents.

The northern Europeans, however, generally eschewed this strategy. English, Scandinavian, Dutch, and French colonists often did bring women with them, either in the initial settlement phase or soon after, even if the colonies were not particularly rich. This was particularly true of colonies, such as those of New England, that were settled by religious dissidents. As a result, although they did make alliances with the indigenous people, and often these were quite stable, they tended to create separate and racially pure settlement communities.

European settlers were constantly reinforced from Europe and managed incredibly high fertility, leading to considerable demographic growth, which put the settlers into often bloody competition with their Native American neighbors.

In Spanish and Portuguese areas, the frontier tended to produce a vast mixed-race population in various proportions African, indigenous, and European in origin (depending on the exact migration patterns), in which "Indians" were separate legally and under missionary supervision. In the English and French colonies of North America, the tendency was to create strongly divided "Indian" and colonial societies often culturally at odds and frequently focusing on racial purity. Of course, even in the English and particularly in the French colonies, there were frontiersmen, traders who penetrated into the free-association world, who found themselves required to intermarry, although the offspring of these unions were often disparaged once the settlement frontier reached them.

We can distinguish several large frontier zones in the Americas during the period before 1825. There was the frontier north of the Spanish conquest of Mexico, extending from the northern boundaries of the former Aztec Empire into the U.S. Southwest, and east almost to the Mississippi River. That frontier bordered on the one created by English and French colonization of the east coast of North America as it expanded into the Mississippi Valley. Next there was the great Caribbean sphere, scene of the first colonial occupations, but still incompletely occupied in 1800, including many of the islands of the Caribbean, but also sections of the coast of Venezuela, New Granada, and the Spanish Kingdom of Guatemala (Central America), which only really occupied the half bordering on the Pacific. The Caribbean zone also reached along the coast of South America to the Orinoco Basin. Another frontier zone was formed in the hinterland of northeastern Brazil, slowly occupied as the coast was settled. The frontier extended northward into the Amazon Basin, and then south from there following the tributaries of the Amazon to include the eastern parts of Peru and Bolivia. A final frontier zone centered on the southern cone of South America in the great grassy Pampas of Argentina, the southern portions of Chile, and the Mato Grosso of Brazil.

REDUCTIONS AND THE FRONTIER: IBERIAN STRATEGIES IN NORTHERN MEXICO

As the Spanish conquered Mexico and began expanding beyond the borders of the Aztec Empire, they soon encountered the people they called, following Aztec usage, Chichimecas. The name Chichimeca itself was probably pejorative, and related to Aztec and Spanish beliefs that people who lived in small communities, went naked (as they did), and ate virtually any food were hopeless barbarians. Such organization was, of course, typical of free associations, most of whom lived in small, seasonal, and scattered settlements the Spanish called *rancherías*.

Nuño de Guzmán led an army of 500 Spanish and 1,000 allied Tlaxcalans and Tarascans through the region in the 1530s claiming conquest, but with little tangible result. It was only after the silver mines at Zacatecas were discovered in 1546, and a resulting silver rush that would bring thousands of Spaniards and their Tlaxcalan and Tarascan allies to open mines, that occupation counted. Other silver strikes in the northern region soon followed, and the Spanish enterprise in New Spain suddenly became doubly important to the Spanish crown. Indeed, the nature of New Spain itself was, as we have already seen, underwritten by the wealth that poured from these mines.[43]

Many Spanish settlers entered the region, populating the mines, arranging workers for them, and growing foodstuffs and raising cattle to provision them. They were not necessarily interested, however, in controlling the whole area, and this region, unlike Mexico itself, did not have a preexisting state apparatus that would organize the area and provide a coherent political unit. Instead, the miners simply took up as much land as they needed to dig and provision the mines, founding settlements scattered throughout the region. Many of the permanent population of the mining towns and adjacent farms were brought up from the Mexican heartland, peasants from Tlaxcala and Tarasca, allies of the Spanish in their conquests now transplanted to the northern frontier. They usually settled as soldier-farmers in the vicinity of the newly founded Spanish towns; here, as in the conquests elsewhere, the "Indian friends," as they were often called, formed the bulk of fighting forces.

The haphazard settlement pattern of the Spanish in these northern regions was possible because free associations did not necessarily oppose settlement of strangers within their realms. In spite of the arrangements that Guzmán made in his rapid-fire armed tour of the region in the 1530s, no free association would feel bound by such arrangements, and beginning in 1551, Chichimecas began attacking the miners and especially their supply trains. But silver, desperately needed to fuel Spanish ambitions in the Low Countries and elsewhere, was too valuable and strategically important to abandon, and as a result the Chichimeca attacks led to what was termed the Chichimeca War, a war of low levels of intensity but continuing on and off for half a century until around 1600.[44] Operations in this war usually involved retaliatory raids on the population deemed responsible for attacks on Spanish settlements or wagon trains, but it also included considerable enslavement of the targeted population.

In the first phases of the war, the Spanish tried to adopt terror tactics that they called "war of fire and blood [*fuego y sangre*]." Some Spanish policy makers even considered it appropriate in the defense of their mines to exterminate the Chichimecas, and priests were willing to bend Biblical norms to support

---

[43] Peter Gerhard, *The Northern Frontier of New Spain* (Princeton, 1982), for a detailed history of Spanish exploration and settlement in the region.

[44] The classic and still useful study of the Chichimeca war is Philip Wayne Powell, *Soldiers, Indians, and Silver: The Northward Advance of New Spain, 1550–1600* (Berkeley and Los Angeles, 1952). Powell published a substantial collection of documents: *War and Peace on the North Mexican Frontier: A Documentary Record* (Madrid, 1971).

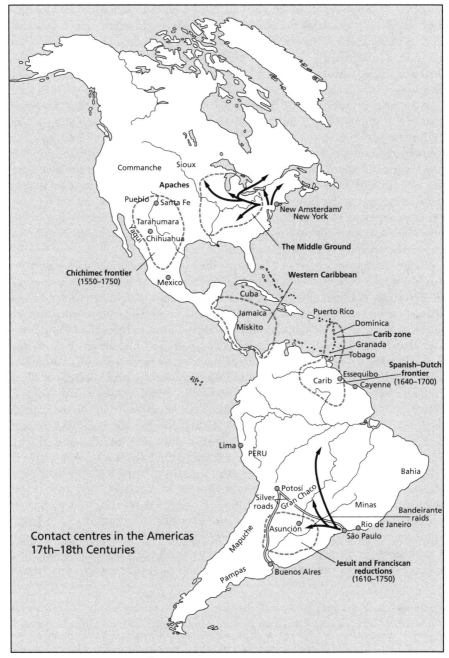

MAP 8. Contact Zones in the Americas.

genocide.[45] Whatever their intentions, however, extermination was simply beyond Spanish means as the Chichimecas proved sufficiently adept militarily to deal the Spanish many small defeats. In the 1580s, Spain's difficulties were compounded when the northern peoples had all acquired horses and guns, thus becoming fearsome mounted raiders, depriving the Spanish of their initial advantages in weapons, horses, and armor.[46]

Now at a disadvantage in mounted warfare, the Spanish abandoned any idea of extermination and shifted to defending the mines and their supply lines with their available resources. They built forts (*presidios*) in key locations and detailed military units to accompany the wagon trains that brought supplies northward and silver south to Mexico. While this approach had some success, the Spanish authorities finally decided that the most cost-effective way to stop the raiding was to buy the Chichimecas off with ample gifts, including agricultural implements. A bureaucracy was created, and the functioning of the systematic gift giving is well revealed in the records that this entity kept in the late sixteenth and early seventeenth centuries.[47]

Given the nature of free associations that were typically at war with their neighbors, the policy of supplying Chichimeca groups with goods amounted to mercenary contracts in which Spain's closest allies would help defend them against enemies farther away. To effect the alliances, military officers arranged the formal surrender or submission of groups who were then placed under the administration of priests, Franciscans in the south (in Chichimeca country) and Jesuits for the most part in the north as the frontier crept northwestward.

Both religious orders accepted administration of the new subjects or allies under an extension of an older policy with different purposes called "congregation" or "reduction," which would become a key concept in use by Spanish missionaries not only in Mexico but in all their frontier societies. The concept had first been elaborated during the turbulent discussion of how to deal with the *encomienda* system in Hispaniola that led to the Law of Burgos in 1512. In Hispaniola, reductions were considered as a means to bring back the local population that had fled to the hills in response to the unexpected and unwelcome change in tribute structure demanded by the early miners. The Law of Burgos and subsequent legislation developed the idea of "reducing" the population by having them settle in larger communities under religious supervision. Such a settlement gave the religious orders a place in the new colonial system and access to labor and income as well as fulfilling the larger crown objective of

---

[45] Stafford Poole, "War by Fire and Blood: the Church and the Chichimecas, 1585," *The Americas* 22 (1965): 115–137.

[46] On the spread of horses in the region, see Powell, *Soldiers*, pp. 50, 175; Jack Forbes, *Apaches, Navaho, and Spaniard* (Norman, 1960, 2nd ed., 1994), pp. 34–40; Thomas Frank Schilz and Donald Worcester, "The Spread of Firearms among the Indian Tribes on the Northern Frontier of New Spain," *American Indian Quarterly* 11 (1987): 1–10.

[47] The records are kept in AGI Contaduria 851 (a file of more than 3,000 pages) and studied in Philip Wayne Powell, "Peacemaking on North America's First Frontier," *The Americas* 16 (1960): 225–233 (the accounts and documentation are discussed in Appendix), pp. 249–250.

asserting its control over the colony through operating judicially to end abuses, which priests could do both by offering religious instruction and protection.

Indeed, the idea that the indigenous people of the Americas should be congregated and then placed in the care of the religious establishment became a staple of Spanish policy in their subsequent mainland conquests. It would be applied in Mexico and Peru to move and resettle indigenous people in order to make room for new Spanish landholdings, to accommodate population losses from epidemic diseases, and to provide a place for the religious orders in the government of these rich, core areas. As in the islands, the Church's role (and particularly that of the religious orders) was to be that of protector and educator of the indigenous population.

In northwestern Mexico, the policy underwent another shift, for the Jesuits were now interested in centralizing a population that had never been centralized in order to convert them, to introduce them to more intensive agriculture, and by that to make them more useful to the Spanish settlers. Hopefully in their eyes, reduction would give Chichimecas a stake in a different lifestyle – the town with chapel and priest, fixed in place and in contrast with the shifting, tiny, and difficult-to-control *ranchería*.

As this strategy was worked out in the Chichimeca area, it was immediately applied as further explorations north of that zone revealed yet more silver mines, initiating a new rush to establish posts in the distant north. The pattern of Spanish settlers, military convoys, and Tlaxcalan and Trascan settlers continued there, but from the very start negotiations with various groups began, and Jesuits reduced the population of those willing or coerced to join the Spanish effort. In theory, the inhabitants of the reductions would grow cash crops to sell to the mines for a fair price and could be recruited to work there for a fair wage. However, the desire on the part of miners to enjoy the labor of the reduced indigenous people soon provoked abuse and revolt.

Northern groups like the Tepehuanes and Tarahumara attacked Spanish settlers in the same way as the Chichimeca had in the sixteenth century, raiding supply and export systems and settlements. To prevent this, the authorities organized convoys and built forts as they had in the Chichimeca region.[48] Hostilities after 1600 in the northwest followed a form not seen in the Chichimeca War – larger regional groupings attacked the Spanish simultaneously under united leadership. These leaders were typically prophetic, perhaps the only sort of large-scale leadership that free associations could accept, and may have been influenced by the religious tone introduced by Jesuit missionaries seeking to create alliances and maintain subjects.[49]

---

[48] For example, see the military service records of Jerónimo Velásquez Dávila, 1617 and Miguel de Barassa, 1618, in Hackett, ed. *Historical Documents Relating to New Mexico, Nueva Vizcaya and Approaches Thereto to 1773* (3 vols., Washington, DC, 1926) 2: 97–101 (Spanish and English on facing pages).

[49] On the Tarahumara region, see Roberto Mario Salmón, "Tarahumara Resistance to Mission Congregation in Northern New Spain," *Ethnohistory* 24 (1977): 379–393.

An early episode of sporadic warfare was intensified in the region of the Acaxees, for example, when an unnamed prophetic leader emerged, perhaps around 1602, to coordinate it, claiming to be a bishop who also "baptized, said mass, married them and taught them a new creed and prayers." Francisco de Urdiñola, the Spanish leader in the area, took vigorous action, in this case extending the conciliatory program, making reductions (he consolidated seventy "pueblos and rancherias" into twenty-four, resettling them on flatlands and giving them to the Jesuits), and capturing and punishing the self-proclaimed bishop.[50] A far more dangerous war, the Tepehuan Revolt of 1616–1623, was led by another prophet named Quautlatas, who claimed to have received messages from a stone "idol" that spoke to him, promising victory and the destruction of Spanish ships that might bring more settlers. The Jesuits were their first targets, and most of the priests who had led the reductions of the region were killed. But Spanish settlers, mostly ranchers or farmers who supplied the mines at Parral and Durango, were also killed, and the region was won back only through extended punitive expeditions.[51]

Similar wars followed periodically as mining towns extended farther north into Sinaloa, with the same ultimate results. In 1648 and again in 1650 and 1652, the Tarahumaras revolted in a weaker but similar pattern of attacks with religious leadership, this time often former converts embittered and ferociously anti-missionary and anti-Spanish, directed against the priests and settlers.

While settlers valued the reduced population for their labor, and certainly slave labor or salaried labor taken from the reductions was important, reductions were also an important means of recruiting allies. Initially, the allies were brought from the south, from Tlaxcala or Trasca, but in the northern regions and following the Chichimeca War, they tended to be voluntary allies from the region. Throughout this period, the Spanish were always served by "Indian friends" or allies – a memorial of 1693 notes that "the soldiers absolutely cannot take the field without a number of Indian friends," while also specifying that the salaries of eight Spanish soldiers ought to be applied to giving pay to forty such indigenous fighters.[52] In the 1670s, the mining frontier advanced a bit more, followed by successful missionary work and reductions, expropriations and exploitation, and a large revolt in 1690. A new war began in 1696–1698 in which Spanish forces and a good but unspecified number of allied indigenous people captured and resettled several thousand of the inhabitants of the immediate neighborhood, placing them under ecclesiastical jurisdiction and thus pacifying them. The idea in general was to reduce attacks on settlements and roads by following "the hostiles to their dwelling places until they are conquered."[53]

---

[50] Francisco de Urdiñola to King, March 31, 1604, in Hackett, *Historical Documents* 2: 89–90.
[51] "A brief and succinct account of the events of the war with the Tepehuanes ... from November 15, 1616 to May 16, 1618," in Hackett, ed. *Historical Documents*, 2: 101–115.
[52] Report of Joseph Francisco Marín, June 15, 1694, in Hackett, ed., *Historical Documents* 2: 375–377.
[53] "Reply of the fiscal concerning various questions relating to the war with the hostile Indians of the kingdom of El Parral..." April 1, 1698 in Hackett, ed., *Historical Documents* 2: 420–436.

Military reduction was vital the farther north the frontier went. Most of the people of the Opata region in Mexico's Sonora province, for example, joined Jesuit reductions in the early and mid-seventeenth century and accepted their new economic system. While the Jesuits may well have seen the expansion of Christianity into this region as a worthy enough objective, it also had military implications, for Spanish needed the Opatas to fight for them as much as to work after 1694 when horse-riding nomads, the Apaches and the Seris, provided a serious challenge to the northern frontier. Opatas were instrumental in the Spanish defenses, although they revolted in 1696 when they forced the Spanish to abandon a fort they had garrisoned in their lands; they accepted a long-term alliance with Spain later. While the revolts were suppressed and Spanish interests protected, the hills throughout the north contained thousands, perhaps the majority of the population, who were not reduced. They created something of a counter society, sometimes working in the missions, sometimes returning to their *rancherías* and to their older, but now modified, beliefs, very often continuing to raid convoys and harass settlements of both the Spanish and their numerous allies. In the complicated world of Northwest Mexico, the Spanish were sometimes mediators in disputes that might rage in the interior and sometimes threaten the life of Spanish miners and ranchers, as for example the settlement of a dispute on the verge of causing a war in the 1690s between the Conchos and the Tarahumaras.[54]

In the long run, Spanish survival depended on winning over at least enough of the local population as military allies to secure the supply routes. One important part of this strategy was the digging of wells and the introduction of new animals, which made it possible for the population in the region to alter their lifestyles and receive important material benefits. Jesuits were able to dig deeper and more permanent wells than the indigenous people had. In fact, Father Eusebio Kino, a tireless Jesuit missionary who worked in the region near the present-day U.S. border in the late seventeenth and early eighteenth century, generally expressed his mission successes by noting the digging of wells and the introduction of stock.[55] He was also acutely aware that another important consequence of the reduction was developing allies who could defend the settlements against the Apaches and other raiding nomadic groups.[56]

In good years, the water was adequate to support the traditional small, scattered *rancherías*, but during drought they endured severe suffering. The Jesuit reductions offered relief from this sort of drought and thus proved very attractive. Likewise, the possibility of engaging in market production using the new animals, or selling surpluses of grain from irrigated land, was also very attractive. But the discipline of the mission and the demands for labor, which

[54] Marín Report in Hackett, ed., *Historical Documents* 2: 373–374.
[55] Report and Relation of Father Eusebio Kino, 1710, publications of the Wisconsin Historical Society, online at www.americanjourneys.org, translated from "Favores celestiales de Jesus y Maria SS^ma Apostol de las Yndias," part V, cap 2, pp. 440, 444, cap. 4.
[56] Kino, "Report," cap. 3.

missionaries often acquiesced to, made some aspects of live on the mission difficult. Thus, when better weather returned, many people left the reductions and returned to life in rancherías, which Franciscans thought of as leaving the Christian fold. This cycle of resistance and revival continued on a small scale for the rest of the colonial period. Indeed, the mountains of the region even today hold Tarahumaras who have never accepted Christianity or outside rule.[57]

The Yaquis and their near neighbors, the Mayos, of the coastal region of Northwest Mexico had a different history. Their communities were settled in better-watered regions, and they welcomed Jesuit reduction when the latter came in 1614–1617, reorganizing them from some eighty small communities scattered along the rivers to just eight larger ones. Jesuit priests introduced European livestock and greatly improved irrigation, which allowed these larger communities not only to be self-sufficient, but also to export surpluses to the Spanish economy. As there were no Spanish settlers, the Yaquis and Mayos lived peacefully in the new economy, but as Spanish settlers and miners began operating nearby in the 1680s, the cycle of demands began, culminating in the Yaqui Revolt of 1740. But the Yaquis and Mayos were never as much threatened as the people farther inland, and their revolts, while hostile to Spanish government and even the Jesuits, were more thoroughly Christian than those of the Tarahumara. In the aftermath, the Spanish government established a harsher routine with more obligatory labor in the mines and farms nearby, and in 1772 the whole group was required, for the first time, to pay taxes. This they resolutely refused to do so and the colonial government was not strong enough to enforce the rule, Yaquis and Mayos would not be taxed until the 1830s.

The region of the Pueblos in modern-day New Mexico, the northernmost extreme of Spanish expansion in the region, was different again from that in the mining region. In 1598, Juan de Oñate, at the head of a large military and colonial mission, obtained the voluntary submission of all the large compact villages of the Rio Grande Valley. Franciscans rather than Jesuits were assigned the task of evangelizing the people, and Spanish settlers were rewarded with encomiendas to extract labor from various villages to work farms they planned to establish. The colony began producing exportable food and manufacturing surpluses, but there was friction between the missionaries and the civilian settlers over questions of taxation and labor. Both missionaries and settlers used labor from Pueblos to work their lands, sometimes employing harsh and abusive methods, and frequently did not provide satisfactory compensation to the workers in question.

Pueblos had accepted Spanish as military protectors, but they had proven unequal to Apache and Commanche raiders, who, mounted and drawn to the valley by an increasing number of targets, made life miserable for the residents. The Spanish military forces also found it expedient to enslave captives in these

---

[57] A good overview of this region is Edward Spicer, *Cycles of Conquest: The Impact of Spain, Mexico, and the United States on the Indians of the Southwest, 1533–1960* (Tucson, 1962), pp. 25–39.

wars, and indeed to provoke them, in a short-range search for more easily exploitable slave labor, but in the long run only provoked more violent and effective counterraids. This combination of forces caused the Pueblos to revolt in 1680, a massive and successful revolt that annihilated the Spanish and missionary presence in a part of the valley. The resistance took religious form, in the guise of a revitalized indigenous religion followed by Christian coverts, and rejecting religious teaching.

The victorious Pueblos, however, had no central plan and were thus even less able to stop Apache raiding or to prevent the Spanish from returning to rule, so that after sporadic fighting and considerable out-migration, the Spanish reestablished control in 1696. One of the effects of the war, however, was the capture and sale of thousands of horses from Spanish lands in New Mexico to other people to the north, helping promote the spread of horse riding to the Great Plains of North America.

When French traders entered the Mississippi valley, they encountered indigenous people riding horses; de la Salle met mounted Plains nomads in 1678 wearing leather armor.[58] Furthermore, within a few decades, muskets were diffused into this region by both French and Spanish traders, and the armor was eliminated as being useless against a specially redesigned musket with a short barrel for use as a cavalry weapon.

The social transformation of the Great Plains in the eighteenth century by the combination of horse and musket had such a remarkable effect that it is sometimes called the Equestrian Revolution. The great regional beneficiaries of this were loosely called Sioux (in the northwestern parts of the zone), Apache (in the southwestern part, bordering on the Spanish territories), and Comanche (in the Western zone from the Rocky Mountains), as each of these groups, a confederation of loosely allied bands, attacked and sometimes absorbed neighbors, in the process gradually becoming predominant in their region. Although retaining their essential organization as free associations, the societies of the Plains became more stratified as the most successful fighters achieved considerable personal wealth and could obtain multiple wives – like Carib canoe owners.[59] But the archetypical Native American of the Plains, the Indian warrior with his feathered bonnet, horse, and firearm – for many Americans the very symbol of Indians – was a creature of the Atlantic world, with full contact with the economy of the Atlantic if not either Europeans or Africans.

Much of the transformation took place before the arrival of literate witnesses and can only vaguely be reconstructed, but some flavor can be gleaned through the remarkable annals that the Sioux maintained. These historical records, called "Winter Counts," were illustrated by a detailed picture for each year (counted from first snowfall to last snowfall) depicting the most important

---

[58] Sieur de Tonty, "Memoir Sent in 1693 on the Discovery of the Mississippi…" in Louise Phelps Kellog, ed., *Early Narratives of the Northwest* (New York, 1917), p. 320.

[59] Pekka Hämäläinen, "The Rise and Fall of Plains Indian Horse Cultures," *The Journal of American History* 90 (2003): 833–862.

event of the year. Some of them reach back into the early eighteenth century and record wars or raids, successful hunts, unusual climatological events, and the like. Oral traditions explaining the pictures accompanied them, and special people were designated to keep them.[60]

In Mexico, the Apache provided a constant system of raiding against virtually all the Spanish positions, at times even forcing the abandonment of remote locations and farms. Spanish authorities were ultimately powerless to prevent the constant attacks and they became a part of frontier life for both Spanish settlers and their many allies, both from the south and among reduced inhabitants. They kept the Apaches in check largely in the same way they had the Chichimecas, by buying them off through subsidies and hoping to make enough alliances with some groups to fend off raids by others – a delicate balance that had to be constantly adjusted.

AN EQUESTRIAN FRONTIER: THE SOUTHERN CONE
OF SOUTH AMERICA

South of the reductions, and of the southern expansion of Spain into the Inca Empire (which is actually Chile today), there was a different situation.[61] Initially the Spanish made a rapid penetration, as they had in northwest Mexico. They enjoyed considerable success in the areas that had already been under Inca control, and founded Santiago, the capital of what was to be called the Kingdom of Chile, in 1541. In 1550, Pedro de Valdiva invaded the core region of Mapuche country, with 200 Spanish cavalry, 300 indigenous fighters from the northern region, and a much larger force of soldiers and servants (*yanaconas*) from the Inca heartland.[62] The Mapuche, however, had an effective means of mobilizing large numbers of soldiers to fight against the Spanish, although the tens of thousands reported in the earliest Spanish reports are almost certainly exaggerated. The first resistance was led by Ainavillo, who the Mapuche had elected toque, or general, and was singularly unsuccessful, largely because the Mapuche had no effective way to deal with cavalry.[63]

---

[60] The Brulé Dakota Sioux count keeper Baptiste Good's count is notable for this great length. He wrote it on cloth using older manuscript materials but including the oral narrative in writing. The classic account of the Winter Count was written by a cavalry officer, Garrick Mallery, "Picture Writing of the American Indians," *Tenth Annual Report of the Bureau of Ethnology* (Smithsonian Institution, Washington, DC, 1888–1889), whole issue. The most important of the Lakota ones are illustrated and explained in full color at the Smithsonian's Web site, "Lakota Winter Counts," http://wintercounts.si.edu

[61] Alvaro Jara, *Guerra y Sociedad en Chile. La transformación de la guerra de Arauco y la esclavitud de los indios* (Santiago, 1981); see also Pierre Blancpain, *Les Araucans et la frontière dans l'histoire du Chili des origines au XIXème siècle* (Frankfurt, 1990).

[62] For a careful study of the role of indigenous allies in these and later Spanish operations, Andrea Ruiz Esquide, *Los indios amigos en la frontera araucana* (Santiago, 1993).

[63] In addition to the eleven letters written to various people by Valdiva himself, published *Cartas de Pedro de Valdivia : que tratan del descubrimiento y conquista de Chile* (ed. Jose Toribio Medina, Madird, 1929), there are a number of chronicles of these early operations: Jerónimo de

By 1553, Valdiva had founded six more towns along the Chilean coast, and began working a gold mine, using subject Mapuche labor. However, the Mapuche did not tolerate this situation long and resisted under two new toques, named Caupolicán and Lautaro, who had been captured and served Valdiva as a groom. Lautaro had learned enough about the Spanish cavalry to create tactics to neutralize some of their effectiveness, and, as vice toque, led successful attacks and managed to capture Valdiva himself.[64] Even though Mapuche had learned enough from their first encounters with the Spanish to fight them successfully at times, the Spanish forces managed to move deeply into their territory, constructing forts and founding towns that were often later abandoned or destroyed.

Although there were periods of peace, the Mapuche were never content with the occupation of their territory. Beginning in 1598, Mapuche leaders struck back again and in what was called "the destruction of the seven cities" they forced the abandonment of all the Spanish foundations south of the Biobio River by 1604. The Spanish continued to hold on to enough territory to prevent Dutch or English privateers from making an alliance with the Mapuche, and their fears were more than realized when the Dutch seized Valdivia in 1643.[65] The continual wars also frequently resulted in the capture of slaves by otherwise ill-paid Spanish soldiers, even if territorial gains were not made.[66]

Undoubtedly the cause of the greater Mapuche success in the later sixteenth and early seventeenth centuries was related not only to their developing effective anti-cavalry tactics, but to their learning cavalry skills themselves.[67] The Jesuit priest Alonso de Ovalle, who knew the Mapuche in the early seventeenth century, described how youth who showed ability were moved into riding "and are very expert at it," forming, in his view, a sort of nobility, who fought especially with lances.[68] In the heat of battle, according to Ovalle's near contemporary Diego de Rosales, they could take the "reins in their mouth, and guide the

Vivar, *Crónica y relación copioso de los Reinos de Chile* (Santiago, 1958, but written c. 1558); Alonso de Góngora Marmolejo, *Historia de Todas las Cosas que han Acaecido en el Reino de Chile y de los que lo han gobernado* (written c. 1575, published Santiago, 1850 [GB]); Pedro Mariño de Lobera, *Crónica del Reino de Chile* (ed. and corrected by Bartolomé de Escobar, c 1600, published Santiago, 1865 [GB]).

[64] Vivar, *Crónica*, cap. 115; Góngora Marmolejo, *Historia*, cap 14; Mariño de Lobera, *Crónica*, Part 3, cap. 41–43 (with substantially more detail but written later).

[65] Margarita Gascón, *Naturaleza e Imperio. Araucanía, Patagonia, Pampas, 1598–1740* (Buenos Aires, 2007); *idem*, "The Defense of the Spanish Empire and the Agency of Nature: Araucanía, Patagonia and Pampas during the Seventeenth Century" (University of New Mexico, LII Research Paper 46 (2008), http://hdl.handle.net/1928/6910).

[66] Sergio Villalobos, *Vida fronteriza en la Araucanía. El mito de la Guerra Arauco* (Santiago, 1995), pp. 89–101.

[67] Guillaume Boccara, *Guerre et ethnogènese mapuche dans le Chili colonial: l'invention du soi* (Paris, 1998), and "Etnogénesis mapuche. Resistencia y restructuración entre los indígenas del centro-sur de Chile (siglo XVI–XVIII)," *Hispanic American Historical Review* 79 (1999): 425–461.

[68] Ovalle, *Historia*, pp. 85–87.

horse from side to side," freeing both hands for "furious lance throws, rising in their stirrups and using the strength of all their body." In fact, in Rosales's inventory of their weapons, he did not note firearms, as they relied more on their lances, heavy clubs, poison-tipped arrows, and other weapons.[69] These skills, and their continued ability to put aside their internal feuds, so typical of free associations, to fight a unified war when the Spanish threatened, made them unconquerable.

At the same time, these traits, born in battle, also made them successful against neighbors, and soon the Araucanian system had spread to the east, across the mountains and into modern-day Argentina and Brazil in the South American equivalent of the North American Equestrian Revolution. These horses, as well as cattle who escaped from Spanish ranches along that corridor, went wild and formed vast herds in the southern grasslands that were ideal for their propagation.

As a result, virtually all the free associations, many of which had lived primarily by hunting and limited small-scale agriculture, were turned into predatory nomadic cavalry.[70] In the Gran Chaco and Mato Grosso regions of Argentina, Paraguay, and southern Brazil, the people away from the mini-states of the rivers were nomadic foragers living as free associations. Initially the Spanish-Guarani alliance created in the 1530s put them at a serious disadvantage as the Spanish cavalry greatly upset the military balance that had characterized the region from ancient times. They were forced on the defensive and took shelter, according to Jesuit Martin Dobrizhoffer, "where they could not be attacked, defended by trenches and impenetrable woods."[71] But that balance shifted at some point in the seventeenth century. Dobrizhoffer, who recorded the history of these groups during his residence from 1749 to 1767, but particularly the Abipones, related that "a centenarian," told him how they managed to overcome their disadvantages by stealing some horses, in fact as many as 100,000 in 50 years (and up to 4,000 in a single raid), then gradually learning to ride them and transformed themselves into formidable equestrian nomads. There, with the aid of their allies and neighbors, the Macobios and Tobas, they waged ceaseless war against the Spanish and the Guananis, both those in the towns under secular administration and those in the missions. By 1718, roads that had once been safe were impassable.[72]

[69] Rosales, *Historia general*, p. 118–119.
[70] Salvador Canals Frau, *Las poblaciones indígenas de la Argentina* (Buenos Aires, 1973); José Miranda Borelli, *Etnohistoria del Chaco* (Resistencia, 1978).
[71] Martin Dobrizhoffer, *Historia de Abiponibus, equestri bellicosaque Paraquariae natione...* (3 vols., Vienna, 1784 [GB]), 3: 3–6. This book was translated into German by R. Keil as *Geschichte der Abiponer, einer berittenen und kriegerischen Nation in Paraguay...* [GB] at the same time and place as it was published in Latin, and Dobrizhoffer perhaps authorized or assisted in the translation as German was his native language (although this is not noted in the text). An English translation appeared in 1822 [GB], but is marred by omissions of some passages.
[72] Dobrizhoffer, *Historia*, 3: 9–15.

As Dobrizhoffer described it, they remained as free associations after this revolution. They were organized by "troops" (*turmas*), and ruled by "caciques," who possessed no peacetime power or authority, but were followed in war. Caciques, or "captains," a term that Dobrizhoffer noted had been naturalized into their language from Spanish, led them. Captains were in some degree hereditary, but more often less qualified heirs were passed up in favor of more qualified members of the same family, or at times even unrelated but worthy leaders. They were not distinguished from their followers by dress, deportment, or material goods and, like the Caribs, tended to recruit and maintain followers for any raid or other endeavor by holding drinking parties (where the captains might in fact be reviled and even beaten should their followers disagree with them). Not only were caciques unable to extract any tribute from their followers, but the followers were not bound to particular captains by oaths or any real sense of loyalty, readily abandoning one for another who might be more successful. Even women could hold the office, presumably not for their warrior capacities but for their sagacity.[73]

The Spanish found themselves in near perpetual war with these equestrian nomads, trying at times to "reduce" them to village life and place them under ecclesiastical supervision so as to prevent raids, although at other times the idea of exterminating them through the war of "fire and blood" was entertained.[74] In fact, the Spanish lacked the capacity to do this. In a tour of inspection of the region of Tucumán that bordered the Abipones and their allies in 1749, the Spanish colonel Juan Victorino Martínez de Tineo found some 7,223 soldiers, mostly "poorly armed" who had to act both as a defensive shield against their mobile opponents, and an aggressive force to carry war against them.[75] While this represented a numerical superiority against the Abipones who, according to Dobrizhoffer, numbered no more than 5,000 of which only 1,000 could be effective, a number that might not be more than tripled by including their immediate allies, the area was vast and the initiative almost always lay with the indigenous people whose lifestyle made them so mobile and possessing nothing they needed to defend.[76]

The solution that the Spanish provided for the southern equestrian raiders was the same as elsewhere: to persuade them to enter into reductions, abandon nomadism, and become Christians. Dobrizhoffer, hardly an unbiased reporter on this as he proudly describes his success, thought that the foundation of Jesuit settlements had ended the war.

[73] Dobrizhoffer, *Historia*, 2: 109–118.
[74] An overview with detailed documentation Alberto José Gullón Abao, *La frontera del Chaco en la Gobernación del Tucumán, 1750–1810* (UCA, 1993).
[75] AHN Madrid, Consejos 20375, exp. 1, Caja 2, Pieza 2, "Diario de Juan Victorino Martínez de Tineo, coronel, gobernador de Tucumán, sobre las expediciones militares al Chaco realizadas durante su mandato, años 1749–1754," [PARES] fol. 9.
[76] Dobrizhoffer, *Historia*, 2: 106; on their mobile lifestyle, 118–134.

While the Spanish battled with various indigenous groups, a new interstitial group developed. The traveler Carrio de la Vandera, crossing from Montevideo to Peru in the 1770s, described what he called the *gauderios* (better known by the later term *gauchos*), who followed a seminomadic life, riding horses and living off cattle that were more or less wild, both near Montevideo and throughout Tucumán. They lived, he believed, wastefully, killing animals solely to eat certain choice cuts, and indulging in incredible quantities of meat. Their culture borrowed a great deal from the indigenous people – for example, the use of bolos to entangle the hooves of animals and horses and the use of the lance as a weapon of choice.[77]

THE CARIBBEAN FRONTIER: THE CENTRAL BASIN

The Caribbean basin formed a vast intercommunicating zone even before the arrival of Columbus. Early Spanish explorers met watercraft from all the islands of the Caribbean, trading vessels from the Mayan-speaking Yucatán and the coast of Central America – today's Colombia and Venezuela – and even from the Orinoco River basin as they explored the region. It is probably safe to say that the Caribs themselves, located in the center of the zone and with a strong maritime tradition, formed its unity. When Columbus entered the Caribbean, his first contacts on Hispaniola complained to him of Carib raids, and at the same time Caribs were raiding and had settlements not only along the coast of northern South America, but were beginning to attack upstream along the Orinoco River Valley. In time, Carib raiders would even reach the northern branches of the Amazon.[78]

The Caribs were fearsome to Europeans, thanks to their naval skills, and their capacity to organize, at least temporarily, fairly large numbers of people. Columbus's original understanding with Guaconagari in Hispaniola included both a war against his rivals on the island and protection against the Caribs who were raiding his lands. If Spain made conquests in Hispaniola, they had much less luck in the islands to the south. Not only did attacks on the Carib islands fail, but they often were costly failures. Caribs raided Puerto Rico so persistently in the early to mid-sixteenth century that they may have played a crucial role in the slow start of the sugar industry on that island, as the records of the city council of the island's capital of San Juan show.[79] Spaniards were

---

[77] Alonso Carrió de la Vandera, *El lazarillo de ciegos caminantes* (ed. Antonio Lorente Medina, Barcelona, 1985 [Biblioteca Ayacucho]), pp. 22, 96.

[78] Douglas Peck, "Prehistoric Seafaring Explorations by the Taino and Caribs in the Antillies and the Maya from the northern Yucatan," online at http://www.newworldexplorersinc.org/PrhstNWE.pdf

[79] King to Juan Ceron y Miguel Diaz, November 9, 1511 (many raids), Capitulation to Juan Ponce de Leon, November 27, 1514 (take fleet to attack Caribs); Baltasar Castro to Emperor, November 16, 1520 (5 canoes with 150 Caribs attack); Licenciado la Gama to King, November 19, 1529 (8 canoes attack); Council minutes, October 23, 1530 (11 canoes attack); Cabildo to Diego Ramos y Sebastian Rodrigues to King, May 10 and 14, 1546 (constant attacks), among

killed and their forces decimated by "flecheros" (archers) whose weapons were very effective, much as African seaborne archers had thwarted Portuguese raiding on the African coast a half a century earlier.[80]

In spite of the Carib offensive, the Spanish managed to establish footholds in the pearl fisheries of Cumaná (Venezuela), primarily by engaging in alliance politics, which also allowed them to acquire slaves in the crucial early sixteenth century when Hispaniola caciques were withdrawing their workers from the Spanish mines.[81] Girolamo Benzoni, visiting northern South America around Cumaná and the Gulf of Paría between 1541 and 1556, noted the complexities of these alliances with "lords of peace" (*signori di pace*), in which slaves were taken but no significant change in sovereignty took place.[82]

Starting in the late sixteenth century, English, French, and Dutch – and then Danish and Swedish – settlers founded colonies in the Carib islands, with varying degrees of success. As we have seen, these settlements were initially to support privateering efforts in the wars against Spain, and capitalized to some extent on alliances with the Caribs. Numbers and determination allowed the northern Europeans to expand their colonization, and as the sugar revolution took hold in the mid-seventeenth century, the Caribs abandoned the islands where Europeans had the most success, withdrawing to Dominica, St. Vincent, and St. Lucia by the end of the seventeenth century. These islands managed to hold off attacks for much longer, and it was not until the late eighteenth century that the remaining Carib islands fell more or less effectively under European control.

NEW FORCES IN THE CENTRAL BASIN: BUCCANEERS AND RUNAWAYS

Almost as soon as Europeans began to settle, they brought slaves from Africa to assist them, and eventually to become the main labor force, especially in areas where plantation crops like sugar were grown. Given the harsh conditions of the sugar estates, many of these African slaves sought their freedom by running away. If conditions favored it, runaways sought shelter among indigenous people, as did the earliest runaways in Hispaniola, for Africans were reported among the ranks of the cacique Enriquillo's followers who fought the Spanish in the 1520s.[83]

many others, printed in Vicent Murga, ed., *Historia documental de Pureto Ric. I El conejo o Cabildo de la Cuidad de S Juan de Puerto Rico (1527–50)* (Rio Piedras, 1956).

[80] Sauer, *Early Spanish Main* is still the best recounting of this period. See also Hugh Thomas, *Rivers of Gold: The Rise of the Spanish Empire from Columbus to Magellan* (New York, 2005), with much more emphasis on the Spanish end of the story.

[81] Sauer, *Early Spanish Main*, pp. 161–177.

[82] Girolamo Benzoni, *La historia del Mondo Novo* (new edition, Venice, 1572[Gallica]), fols. 4–7.

[83] Carlos Esteban Dieve, *La Esclavitud del negro en Santo Domingo* (2 vols., Santo Domingo, 1980) 2: 440–442.

However, at times the indigenous people were not inclined to accept run-aways, or even actively participated in returning them. In such cases, those Africans who wished to run away had no choice but to form their own com-munities. After a revolt, like a breakout from the plantations of Espaniola in 1522, the rebels formed several *maniels* or slave runaway communities that dotted the interior of that island by the 1540s, and made so much trouble for the authorities that the latter launched concerted campaigns to wipe them out, albeit not entirely successfully.[84] Similarly, slaves being brought to Venezuela in 1550, and armed to assist the Spanish, "decided to follow their own desires … and live among the Indians," so they deserted en masse, forming a runaway community.[85]

Where runaway communities had coastal access, they might participate in smuggling or support privateer and pirate voyages. The runaways were partic-ularly active on Hispaniola and made regular contact with visiting smugglers or privateers from France, England, and the Netherlands. In 1611, for exam-ple, English vessels visited a community at Rio Coro in Hispaniola, where the inhabitants traded hides that they hunted, rode and bred horses, and were pre-pared to defend themselves against any Spanish attack.[86]

Settlers dealt with the runaway communities by military attacks, but if these failed, they frequently made arrangements to recognize the independence of the communities in exchange for aid in war and agreements to assist in return-ing other runaways. In 1612, after years of seeking to extirpate the runaways near Vera Cruz in a community led by a man known as Yanga, the Spanish decided to recognize the community as an independent self-governing entity in exchange for their agreeing to assist in returning other runaways. Such a pattern would persist, and indeed was found all over the Caribbean zone. The recognition of a group of maroon communities around the city of Cartagena in 1693 represented another example of recognizing the independence of run-aways, and indeed the heritage of this treaty is still found in the Colombian town of Palenque, heir to the 1693 treaty.[87]

Runaway communities were often founded in the wake of slave revolts, and these were in turn often the work of African ex-soldiers, packed into estates and reorganized to fight.[88] They fled, but were pursued and had to fight to defend

[84] Dieve, *Esclavitud* 2: 445–454. Many of the original documents are quoted and published in Cipriano de Utrera, *Historia Militar de Santo Domingo (Documentos y Noticias)* (3 vols., Ciudad Trujillo, n. d. [1950]), especially 1: 383–400.

[85] Antonio de Herrera y Tordesillas, *Historia general de los hechos de los castellanos en las isles y tierra firme del Mar Océano* (mod. ed., 17 vols., Madrid, 1934–1957), Decade 8, book 6, chap-ter 12.

[86] AGI SD 54, fols. 3v–9v Declaraziones de Agustin Brito y Guillermo Pereyra, frances, March 25, 1611; see AGI SD 54, Diego Gomez de Sandoval to King, SD, October 10, 1611 for one such attack..

[87] Roberto Arrazola, *Palenque. primer pueblo libre de America: historia de las sublevaciones de los esclavos de Cartagena* (Cartagena, 1970).

[88] Thornton, *Warfare*, pp. 127–148.

PACIFICATION *with the* MAROON NEGROES.

FIGURE 8. "Pacification with the Maroon Negroes." Print after the original painting by Agostino Brunias in Bryan Edwards's *History Civil and Commercial of the British West Indies*, London, 1801. Courtesy of the John Carter Brown Library at Brown University.

themselves, often for years until they won the right to self-government from the colonial authorities. The military background goes a long way to explaining their success in keeping themselves independent. It also made them inclined to develop hierarchical structures in line with military ranks. For example, in

1634, the runaways of Limón, near Cartagena, were moving toward a more hierarchical structure, including holding others as slaves.[89]

As the sugar economy took off, so did the importation of slaves and their flight to wherever they might go. French settlers in Grenada, for example, found that many of their slaves fled to the Caribs, and sought to recover them by treaty. Some of the runaways were so sufficiently discouraged by their treatment by the Caribs that they opted to return to their former masters.[90] Caribs on unconquered and unoccupied islands accepted runaway slaves throughout the seventeenth century from colonies of all the European powers.[91] St. Vincent in particular became a haven for runaways, many of whom did so by commandeering coastal vessels to make their way to the island. In addition, the runaway population of the island was reinforced in 1675 by the survivors of a shipwrecked slave ship, who landed first on nearby Bequia and then transferred to St. Vincent.[92] The African runaways and shipwreck survivors were so numerous on St. Vincent that they and their descendants became a significant biological component of the population, the "Black Caribs" as the English called them (they called themselves Garífuna), because they remained primarily Carib in language and culture.[93]

In some other islands, such as Barbados, there were few opportunities to run away thanks to the absence of either wasteland or welcoming indigenous people. A few plots to rebel were uncovered, but there the problem of running away, at least massive running away, was less of concern to masters. Not so in Jamaica, where runaways from the 1670s onward formed fairly large communities in the interior mountains.[94] For much of the early eighteenth century, small-scale wars were waged between the settlers and the runaway slaves, many of whom used African military experience to good measure. Indeed, the fact that so many were from the Gold Coast, and that they used the sort of military tactics that were typical of that region, reinforces the idea that ex-soldiers played an important role in the development of runaway communities.[95]

---

[89] John Thornton, "Les États de l'Angola et la formation de Palmares (Brésil)," *Annales: Histoire, Sciences sociales* 63/4 (2008): 796–797. The story of Limón has been told in some detail in the various publications of Kathryn McKnight, "Confounded Rituals: Spanish Colonial and Angolan "Maroon" Executions in Cartagena de Indias (1624)," *Journal of Colonialism and Colonial History* 5 (2004): 1–53.

[90] Bresson, *Histoire*, fols. 79–81.

[91] N.A.T. Hall, "Maritime Maroons: 'Grand Marronage' from the Danish West Indies," *William and Mary Quarterly* 42 (1985): 476–498; Hilary Beckles, "From Land to Sea: Runaway Barbados Slaves and Servants, 1630–1700," *Slavery and Abolition* 6 (1985): 79–94.

[92] William Young, *An Account of the Black Charibs in the Island of St. Vincent...* (London, 1795), pp. 6–10.

[93] Nancie Gonzalez, "From Cannibals to Mercenaries: Black Carib Militarism, 1600–1840," *Journal of Anthropological Research* 46 (1990): 25–39, and idem, *Sojourners of the Caribbean: Ethnogenesis and Ethnohistory of the Garifuna* (Champaign-Urbana, 1988).

[94] Long, *History of Jamaica* 2: 340–347.

[95] John Thornton, "The Coromantees: An African Nation in the Americas," *Journal of Caribbean History* 32 (1998): 161–178, and "War, the State and Religious Norms in 'Coromantee' Thought:

Finally, in 1739 and 1740, the English settlers, unable to dislodge the Maroons, treated with them, granting the runaways some independence and self-government (but with a European supervisor) and commissioning their leaders into the English military as captains. They agreed to return additional runaways should they seek shelter among them, and to assist the English government in war should the island be attacked.[96] The value of the treaty was demonstrated in 1760, when a large slave rebellion, known as Tackey's War, broke out, and its forces were sufficiently strong to defeat the colonial militia. Eventually five parishes were temporarily under Tackey's command. But the Maroons, summoned into the fight, were able to fight Tackey to a standstill and returned some control to the colonial authorities, who finished the job of suppressing the revolt by bringing a substantial number of English troops.[97]

As sugar took off, privateering moved toward piracy. While privateers operated within a legal system established for the taking of enemy prizes and regulated by courts, such as the English High Court of Admiralty, and operated only in wartime, some privateers broke their national allegiances and became pirates, taking ships at any time and for their own profit. Pirates, frequently called buccaneers in the Caribbean, had multiple origins; one original group lived on the north coast of Hispaniola. Descendents of Spanish smallholders, probably of mixed race with a good smattering of runaway slaves, many of the early bucaneers made a living by smuggling, especially selling hides from the large herds of wild cattle that lived there. Already in 1600, Spanish officials complained of the north coast, where "the local people" [*los naturales de la tierra*] helped the "enemies" trade on the coast and provided lookouts for the ships.[98] The business had become sufficiently troublesome that the Spanish authorities began discussing, as early as 1603, the idea of removing the entire population from the region, and indeed did move many people so as to limit smuggling, although naysayers in the island objected that the scheme would only make the least subordinate elements on the island more capable of living in the region.[99] Similarly, in nearby Jamaica, colonists were ordered in the same year to remove their "cowboys [*baqueros*] and slaves" from some areas so that the crowd of smuggling ships could not be served.[100]

This uncontrolled population became the *boucaniers* of French parlance. In addition to smuggling, they became pirates, building long dugout canoes that

---

The Ideology of an African American Nation," in Robert Blair St. George, ed., *Possible Pasts: Becoming Colonial in Early America* (Ithaca and London, 2000), pp. 181–200.

[96] Mavis Campbell, *The Maroons of Jamaica, 1655–1796* (Trenton, 1988).

[97] Long, *History of Jamaica* 2: 447–472.

[98] Museo Naval, Navarete Coll, vol. 23, doc 14, Parecer que dio D Francisco Coloma sobre el discourso que se dio en le Consejo Real de las Yndias por D Luis Faxardo ... Ano de 1600.

[99] AGI SD 1, Consejo de Indias to King, April 22, 1603; Memorial of Cabildo of SD, August 25, 1604, in Rodriguez Demorizi, *Relaciones historicas* 2: 257. See K. R. Andrews, *The Spanish Caribbean: Trade and Plunder 1520–1630* (New Haven and London, 1978) for a larger view.

[100] AGI SD 100, Melgarejo to king, Jamaica, June 13, 1603.

they used to prey on Spanish coastal vessels, capturing them and eventually graduating to larger ships. In 1625, French privateers attacked Hispaniola, united with Maroons and buccaneers, and then fled to the island of Tortuga, a rocky, easily defended island off the coast. In 1631, some sixty of these French made a contract with the Dutch West India Company to place themselves under its protection.[101] By 1632, there were some 300 people in Tortuga, including newly arriving French and Dutch settlers.[102]

The English Providence Island Company, chartered in 1629 to carry on privateering against the Spanish, subsequently made Tortuga its own base. The Spanish reacted to the establishment of this base by attacking it several times. French, English, and Dutch privateers and merchants did business with them, smuggling in Africans to serve as workers producing tobacco. After the Spanish attacks, Tortuga fell under the control of a renegade Frenchman who rebuilt it as a free piracy capital.[103] But at the same time, it remained a center for production, growing tobacco, among other things, and importing indentured servants and taking many African slaves from among their prize ships.

During episodes of war, this uncontrolled group of freebooters found mercenary service in the navies of England and France as privateers, and some were invited to settle in the larger colonies, as for example the group that Governor Henry Morgan of Jamaica allowed to establish themselves at Port Royal.[104] Because they were from lower social orders, English officials could officially distance themselves from their activities while at the same time promoting them.

In many ways, buccaneer society came to be characterized as a militantly organized free association. Members of the larger buccaneer group called themselves the Brotherhood of the Coast and established their own rules. Alexander Esquemelin, a French man who had been an indentured servant in Tortuga and had run away to be a buccaneer, became their chronicler, and provided the best description of them and their organization.[105]

Life on buccaneering ships was different from that of the earlier generation of privateers or even merchant ships. In these vessels, sailors were common wage workers, or worked for "shares" of the final profits. Discipline was harsh

---

[101] de Vries, *English* 16. It was overrun in 1635 by the Spanish; he saved some Englishmen there at the time; p. 124.

[102] AGI Santa Fe 39, fol. 2, Francisco de Murga to King, Cartagena, May 30, 1632.

[103] A[lexander] O. Exquemelin, *De Americaensche Zee-Roovers* (Amsterdam, 1678 [Gallica]), pp. 3–8. The German translation of 1679 [LofC] alone is faithful, the Spanish edition of 1681[LoC] has many errors, all taken in by the English translation of 1684 [LoC] (which calls the author John Esquemeling) with errors of its own (hence my decision to cite the original). The French translation of 1686 in turn incorporates a great deal of material from other sources, to the extent that it is almost a new work. Later editions of the French and English translations also include histories of more pirates. The first full edition of the last original English in modern times is *A History of the Buccaneers of America* (Boston, 1856 [GB]).

[104] Exquemelin, *Zee-Roovers*, part 2 is in fact a paen of Henry Morgan, as well as a full account of his adventures.

[105] Exquemelin, *Zee-Roovers*, pp. 35–37.

and a strict hierarchy of decision making and accounting was observed.[106] However, in buccaneer ships, they were governed by rules that had various names, among which were the "Jamaica Rules" that divided all prizes taken strictly by shares, leaving extra shares for those in command positions or those who distinguished themselves in action. Captains and officers were elected and could be removed by a vote of the crew (although thanks to their maritime skill, such captains and officers tended to be from the same social origins as the leaders of regular ships). For the servants and former slaves (as many as one-third or even more of the buccaneers were former slaves from Maroon communities, or who ran away to the ships), life among the buccaneers was a radical break from tradition and an opportunity to participate in a profitable venture, which might bring them returns many times what they could earn as a regular sailor. Not surprisingly, buccaneers had little trouble recruiting new crew members from among the crews of their prizes.[107]

Recent historiography has focused heavily on the democratic and even revolutionary elements of the buccaneers, including allegations that the pirate ships had high levels of homosexuality, or that the pirate tradition focused on defining masculinity.[108] While pirates certainly did sign oaths and agree to rules (a wide variety were in circulation), there was a constant contestation, even in the midst of voyages, between the officers and the crews over discipline, with each group seeking to use any occasion possible to challenge or change them.

William Dampier's early-eighteenth-century voyages, for example, were characterized by battles over what he called the Jamaica Discipline (the exact terms of which were not well defined).[109] In another case, Roberts's long cruise of the Caribbean, which ended with his death off the coast of Africa in 1721, was a similar battle between Roberts and his men.[110] Pirate ships under the democratic rules were certainly better places for nautical labor than naval or merchant vessels, but their overall purpose was still theft, sometimes sanctioned by a letter of marque, but often not. Firsthand accounts of life among the buccaneers, such as Exquemelin's famous history, reveal clearly that innocent people were robbed, tortured, and brutally killed by buccaneers.[111] They might sell slaves at the same time that they integrated slaves into their crews.[112]

---

[106] The point is amply demonstrated in Marcus Rediker, *Villians of All Nations: Atlantic Pirates in the Golden Age* (Boston, 2004).

[107] Rediker, *Villians*.

[108] Barry Burg, *Sodomy and the Pirate Tradition: English Sea-Rovers in the Seventeenth Century Caribbean* (New York, 1995); Hans Turley, *Rum, Sodomy, and the Lash: Piracy, Sexuality, and Masculine Identity* (New York, 1999).

[109] Peter Earle, *The Pirate Wars* (London, 2005), p. 103.

[110] Charles Johnson, *A General History of the Pyrates from their Rise and Settlement on the Island of Providence to the Present Time* (2 vols., London, 1724–1728). This book is organized by biography, and Johnson is probably a pseudonym for another writer (Daniel Defoe is often proposed); here see vol. 1, pp. 258–315.

[111] Exquemelin, *Zee-Roovers*, pp. 47–74 (the history of Lollonois).

[112] Kenneth Kinkor, "From the Seas: Black Men under the Black Flag," *American Visions* 10 (1995): 26–29; Arne Bialuschewski, "Black People under the Black Flag: Piracy and the

Buccaneering was as much participation in a democratic criminal gang as it was making a statement against class oppression.[113]

In fact, pirates were all of these things, a group that on the whole defies consistent categorization. There seems little doubt that among themselves pirates could be democratic and might even reflect the sort of revolutionary ideas that one might expect from a largely working-class group.

Eventually, some Caribbean-based pirates shifted their operations to the Indian Ocean, particularly Madagascar. According to Charles Johnson, whose history of the pirates was published in 1724, one group, led by John Mission, founded a settlement in Madagascar, which they called Libertalia, and which was ruled by the same combination of election and meritocracy that was typical of the ships themselves.[114] As political power of individual groups was limited in Madagascar, the pirates forged alliances with local groups in exchange for mercenary service. While serving this way, they captured or were given slaves that they in turn sold into the Atlantic slave trade on English and American ships.[115]

THE CARIBBEAN FRONTIER'S WESTERN END: CENTRAL AMERICA

As sugar-driven growth continued in the Caribbean, and the Caribs gradually abandoned many islands, the frontier moved westward toward the coast of Central America. Buccaneers and runaway slaves both played a vital role in the western Caribbean, for there they encountered many communities that were independent of any outside control. Spain had not been very successful in conquering the Caribbean coast of Central America in a zone from western New Granada to the southern edge of the Yucatán peninsula.

The Spanish laid claim to Central America largely through the conquests of Alvarado in the 1520s and 1530s when they established the Kingdom of Guatemala, which included not only Guatemala, but also Honduras, Nicaragua, today's El Salvador, Costa Rica, and Chiapas (in Mexico today). This kingdom was a conglomeration of Maya, Lenca, Pipil, and other mini-state societies that lived mostly on the Pacific side of the isthmus. But on the Caribbean coast (or the Atlantic coast, as Spanish-speaking writers often call it), they had much less success. In Costa Rica, the problems were in the provinces of Talamanca and Borua, dominated by mini-states that were in constant war with each other, and, even more frustrating, reputed to have substantial gold mines.[116] In spite of numerous expeditions into the region,

Slave Trade on the West Coast of Africa (1718–1723)," *Slavery and Abolition* 29 (2008): 461–75.

[113] The position taken, for example, in Earle, *Pirate Wars*.

[114] Johnson, *Pyrates*, 2: 33–48.

[115] Arne Bialuschewski, "Pirates, Slavers, and the Indigenous Population in Madagascar, c 1690–1715," *International Journal of African Historical Studies* 38 (2005): 401–425.

[116] "Memorial para el Rey nuestro Señor de la descripción y la calidades de la provincial de Costa Rica" (1610), in Léon Fernández, ed *Colección de documentos para la historia de Costa Rica* (10 vols, Paris, 1881–1907 [GB]) 5: 156–157.

permanent Spanish settlement was only achieved in the Central Valley of the highlands of Costa Rica (where there was no gold) around the city of Cartago, founded following the expedition of Juan Vázquez de Coronado in 1562, and the Nicoya peninsula on the Pacific side. In 1605, Spanish authorities established the town of Santiago de Talamanca to create a base for working the gold mines, but it was wiped out and occupied by the Talamancans in 1610, never to be reoccupied by Spain.[117]

Having Atlantic ports for the export of Peruvian and Guatemalan gold and silver was too important for the Spanish not to establish some coastal presence. The Spanish had built towns along the coast, and some flourished, but often the coast just a few miles on was effectively out of Spanish control. For the Peruvian exports, the Spanish focused on Panamá, the narrowest part of the isthmus, and soon built the town of Panamá on the Pacific side. But it was difficult to subdue any of the indigenous people in the area, and they perpetually threatened the road to Nombre de Dios and then Portobello, the Atlantic-side ports. Vasquez de Espinosa, describing the situation in Panama in the early seventeenth century, noted that Darien had been given over to *indios de guerra*, as had all of Veragua save the Pacific coast.[118]

In this setting, the use of indigenous labor to move supplies and gold was out of the question, so Panamá used African slaves as the core of their transport sector. A report by Alonso Criado de Castilla in 1575 noted that 1,600 Africans employed "for service" resided in the city itself, and a further 400 were guiding the mule trains that carried the silver across the isthmus, while another 500 engaged in farming and other support activities, making them by far the majority of the population under Spanish control. Those indigenous communities that were listed in the report were "free," meaning that they did not pay tribute or were not granted to encomenderos; they were economically integrated through selling cattle they raised for export.[119]

With this large concentration of Africans and their constant movement, it is not surprising that many ran away; by the 1540s, there were a substantial number in various mountain regions. Soon the group in Darién had become a sort of small polity, led by one Bayano until his capture in 1558, which even then included at least one subordinate settlement.[120] The success the Spanish enjoyed against Bayano did not stop marronage. Statistics in Criado de Castilla's 1575 report showed that more than half of all the African-descended

---

[117] Juan Carlos Solárzano Fonseca, "Rebelions y sublevaciones de los indígenas contra la dominación española en las areas períficas de Costa Rica," *Anuario de estudios centroamericanos* 22 (1996): 125–147.

[118] Vasquez de Espinosa, *Compendio*, nos. 898, 905.

[119] Alonso Criado de Castilla, "Summary Description of the Kingdom of Tierra Firme" (May 7, 1575), in Pedro Pérez de Zéleson, et al., eds., *Costa Rica-Panama Arbitration: Documents annexed to the Case of Costa Rica* (4 vols,. Roslyn, 1913[GB]) 1: 182–183.

[120] Pedro de Aguado, *Historia de Venezuela* (1581), cap. 9, books, 9–13. The subordinate community is in chapter 11.

population in Panamá was living in the mountains, and had made their own king.[121]

These free Africans were not at all averse to entering into alliances with the English, and in fact became one of the earliest allied groups of privateers in the sixteenth century. In 1572, Francis Drake's men went to a town of the Panama Maroons not far from Nombre de Dios, the port from which the silver fleet carried its precious cargo to Europe, a neat settlement of 50–60 households, but noted that it was subordinate to a king in a "citie," which could raise 1,700 fighting men. In fact, according to Philip Nichols, Drake's chronicler, there were two kings, one north and the other south of Nombre de Dios.[122]

The government of Panamá worked tirelessly to either expunge or co-opt the Maroon communities. Eventually, through a combination of force and nego-tiation, they brought the maroons over to their side by the 1590s.[123] Vasquez de Espinosa noted of them in the 1620s, that they were free with "a Spanish captain" and that among their tasks was bringing in runaway slaves.[124]

In addition to failing to subdue the indigenous free associations of the coast, the Spanish also failed to complete the conquest of the Maya region. They established reasonable control of the coastal lowlands of northern Yucatán after 1540, but the interior of Yucatán remained independent under the Itza kingdom, as were the coastal regions on the south and southeast side of Yucatán. Starting in 1544, the Domincans sought to bring this region into alli-ance, establishing a province that was nominally loyal to Spain at Verapaz. In their report on the area in 1574, Dominican priests noted both that the area contained tributaries (which Spanish officials had enumerated) and also that no Spaniard actually lived in the area.[125] Without Spanish settlers, the region was run more or less by indigenous ruling class, although Spanish officials might dictate some laws and regulations, as Martin Tovilla claimed he did in 1635.[126]

Meanwhile, the Maya towns of the Caribbean coast were scarcely con-quered at all. Cristóbal Dolid, a rebel follower of Cortés, entered the region and "made peace with" a number of large interior towns (of which he named five and noted the existence of others) "without any risk" as the caciques joined

---

[121] Criado de Castilla, "Summary Description," in Pérez de Zéleson, et al., eds., *Costa Rica-Panama Arbitration: Documents* 1: 183.

[122] Philip Nichols, *Sir Francis Drake Reuiued...* (London, 1628), pp. 7, 51–57.

[123] For a good summary, Ruth Pike, "Black Rebels: The Cimarrons of Sixteenth Century Panama," *The Americas* 64 (2007): 243–266.

[124] Vasquez de Espinosa, *Compendio*, no. 896.

[125] Report of the Province of Verapaz by the Monks of Saint Dominic of Cobán, Friar Francisco Prior of Viana, Friar Lucas Gallego, and Friar Guillermo Cadena, December 7, 1574, in Lawrence Feldman, ed. and trans., *Lost Shores, Forgotten Peoples: Spanish Explorations of the South East Maya Lowlands* (Durham and London, 2000), pp. 8–16; the absence of Spaniards is noted on p. 7, and of Spanish settlements on p. 16.

[126] Martin Tovilla, Book 1, cap 22, in Feldman, *Lost Shores*, pp. 85–94. Given the nature of the Spanish presence, these regulations, while revealing the structure of governance and problems, could probably not be enforced.

them peacefully. Others who followed made similar peace arrangements and received food and sometimes other commodities.[127] Spanish explorers and conquerors, in addition to struggling against each other, established coastal forts at Puerto de Caballos (today's Puerto Cortés) as well as at inland indigenous towns like Naco and San Pedro Sula, but these were not particularly well inhabited just a few years later. A report on the coast noted that San Pedro Sula had briefly had a gold rush and its people had become rich, but by 1586 it was all but abandoned, and indeed Spanish control elsewhere had declined. The coastal towns were populated, but in fact much of the interior was "land of war" and completely unconquered.[128]

The origin of all these settlements appear to have been alliances made with local rulers, hence the references to "indios de paz" who invite the Spanish to come in, ally with them, raise military forces in their defense, and share revenue with them through the local encomienda system. Strife, which the Spanish often viewed as "rebellion" given the legal vision of "indios de paz" as subjects, might be rivalries between existing political units, or true rebellions against tributary demands.[129] In some ways, then, much of today's Guatemala, Honduras, and Nicaragua were mining frontiers as those of northwest Mexico, except that their neighbors were sometimes stratified mini-states as well as free associations. Not surprisingly, when conquistadors failed to bring the region under Spanish control, missionaries followed, throughout the early seventeenth century, but with a notable lack of success.[130]

Runaway slaves figured into the mix along with the semi-independent Maya towns. Silver was mined on the Pacific side of the Kingdom of Guatemala, so slaves were needed to transport the metal to Puerto de Caballos or Trujillo, the Atlantic ports that were almost all that Spain held in the north. As in Panamá, the slaves ran away. Thomas Gage, an Englishman who served as bishop of Guatemala in the 1630s, recorded that some 300 runaways formed a community and pillaged pack trains carrying goods down the Caribbean coast of Honduras to Puerto de Caballos.[131] While the group was considered dangerous, it did not apparently have contact with foreign shipping.

John Cockburn, whose ship was taken by pirates and marooned on the coast of Honduras in 1730, traveled south along the Guatemala-Honduras border, giving a good feel for the wild mixture of settlements in the region. He met a pirate gang of "men of almost all nations," including several African-descended

---

[127] Testimony de Francisco de Muñana, Diego de Dueñas, Rodriguo de Vargas, May 15, 1525, in "Relacíon" of Pedro Moreno, CDI 14: 247, 252, 258; each of these witnesses gave a different list of named caciques, thirteen in all.

[128] Antonio de Ciudad Real, *Relacíon breve y verdadera de algunos cosas de las muchas que sucidieron al Padre Fray Alonso Ponce* (2 vols., Madrid, 1872–1875 [GB]) 1: 345–351.

[129] Francisco de Montero to Emperor, June 1, 1539 CDI 2: 212–244.

[130] Jesús Maria García Añoveros "Los franciscanos en el Reino de Guatemala, siglo XVII," *Hispania sacra* 45 (1993): 521–554.

[131] Thomas Gage, *The English-American, his travail by land and sea...* (London, 1648 [GB]), pp. 130–131.

people, near Puerto de Caballos and several times encountered Afro-Jamaicans who considered themselves English enough to assist him. He proceeded inland and found the majority of the population was indigenous, although a few mulattoes could be seen. At San Pedro Sula, he met a real Spanish official who planned to send him to the regional capital of Comayagua to be dealt with (probably by imprisonment in the mines, which were under Spanish control).[132] The indigenous population near Santa Cruz was also under Spanish authority, telling him they had to pay tribute in gold that they panned from rivers themselves. However, Cockburn's party also passed two other "Indian towns," one named Candiliero and the other unnamed, that appeared to be self-governing under their own "governors" or kings (but they could at least speak some Spanish) and were probably complex societies belonging to the Maya zone.[133] He eventually passed into the more closely controlled districts of the Pacific side of Central America, and even though he met quite a number of mixed-race people, he had very few encounters with Spaniards, and none outside the few of the towns until he reached the Spanish centers beyond Tegucigalpa.

Eastern Honduras and Nicaragua did not have large Maya towns and were beyond the silver export routes that led further east to Trujillo. Two indigenous provinces, Taguzgalpa and Tologalpa, covered the region in the sixteenth century, and the Spanish sent both military and ecclesiastical missions there to conquer or, lacking that, to reduce them in the sixteenth and early seventeenth centuries, but none had any success.[134] Although the area was inhabited by a number of different indigenous groups, one of the core districts was the Kingdom of the Miskito in Taguzgalpa, where both outside contacts and self-liberated slaves played an important role.[135]

Privateers who followed in the wake of Drake's raid on Panamá worked in the Miskito region. The Providence Island Company founded its main base in the western Caribbean on Providence Island in 1630, primarily to attack Spanish shipping coming from Cartagena and Panamá, and to take advantage of allies on the coast of Nicaragua in particular. There they could penetrate up the broad rivers all the way to the mountainous interior, where the Spanish had their conquests and mines.[136]

The Company found a useful ally in the Miskito and around 1640 they brought the son of a "king" of the Miskito to England, who was alleged to have sworn vassalage to England. Subsequent kings, Oldman and his son Jeremy

---

[132] John Cockburn, *A Journey Overland from the Gulf of Honduras to the Great South Sea* (London, 1735 [GB]), pp. 16 (coastal pirates), 25 (San Pedro Sula), 28 and 29 (Negros from Jamaica), 37 (indigenous paying tribute with panned gold).

[133] Cockburn, *Journey*, pp. 22, 45.

[134] Jesús Maria García Añoveros, "Presencia franciscana en la Taguzgalpa y la Tologalpa (la Mosquitia)" *Mesoamerica* 15 (1988): 50–52.

[135] On the social organization of the region, see Thomas Cuddy, Political *Identity and Archaeology in Northeast Honduras* (Boulder, 2007), pp. 6–16, 73–74, 140–144.

[136] Troy Floyd, *The Anglo-Spanish Struggle for Mosquitia* (Albuquerque, 1967), pp. 17–25.

who was ruling at the end of the seventeenth century, were commissioned as well to look out for "straggling Englishmen" in order to aid them.[137]

But it was not just an English connection that defined the Miskito Kingdom. In the mid-seventeenth century, the Miskito received a group of African slaves who had taken over their ship and, in an attempt to sail it back to Africa, ran aground near Cape Gracias a Dios on the Nicaraguan-Honduran border.[138] Accounts of their fate varied: Exquemelin, the first to report on them, thought they were enslaved by the Miskito, although they were already gaining freedom when he visited in 1671.[139] The French privateer Raveneau de Lussan, who stopped there in 1688, heard a milder account, that the survivors of the shipwreck had been hospitably received and were granted an area in which to settle, then intermarried with the local people.[140] However that may be, the self-liberated Africans intermarried with the Miskito to form the Mosquitos-Zambos, as the Spanish called them from the term for mixed African indigenous people.[141]

An English pirate known only as "M. W." described the coast of Nicaragua and a part of Honduras in 1699 as inhabited by some indigenous groups ("wild Indians" in his terminology), of which he mentioned several but only named the Alboawinneys and Oldwawas, as well as a few more or less independent indigenous settlements along the coast before turning to the Miskito. If the Miskito formed a kingdom, it straggled along the coast, and had only very loose control of the region; there were several settlements of ex-buccaneers, a few independent indigenous villages, and some titled Miskitos.[142] He also noted the Spanish-held port of Trujillo was growing and exporting sasparilla and cocoa (which they illegally sold to passing English, Dutch, and French ships), and a second Spanish town at the mouth of the Wanks River, as well as a number of interior towns where Spanish control was stronger, notably Segovia, which buccaneers sacked a few years earlier. Spanish missionaries had penetrated some distance into the interior behind Trujillo but they had not succeeded in making

---

[137] Michael Olien, "The Miskito Kings and the Line of Succession," *Journal of Anthropological Research* 39 (1983): 201–203 has worked out the details.

[138] Benito Garret y Arlovi to King, November 30, 1711, in Manuel de Peralta, ed., *Costa Rica y Costa de Mosquitos. Documentos para la historia de la jurisdicción territorial de Costa Rica y Colombia* (Paris, 1898 [GB]), pp. 57–58. In addition to accounts from the indigenous side given him by missionaries who worked around Segovia and Chontales, Garret y Arlovi also interviewed an ancient African (*negro*) named Juan Ramón.

[139] Exquemelin, *Zee-Roovers*, p. 150.

[140] Raveneau de Lussan, *Journal du voyage fait a la Mer de Sud avec les Filibustiers de l'Amerique* (Paris, 1690 [Gallica]), p. 265. There is an unreliable English translation, 1930.

[141] Olien, "Miskito Kings," p. 202–203; Karl Offen, "The Sambu and Tawira Miskito: The Colonial Origins and Geography of Intra-Miskitu Differentiation in Eastern Nicaragua and Honduras," *Ethnohistory* 49 (2002): 334–342.

[142] M. W., "The Mosqueto Indian and his Golden River," in Awnsham Churchill, *A Collection of Voyages and Travels, some now printed from original manuscripts for the first time…* (6 vols., London, 1732) 6: 285–288; additional comments confirming this account can be found in Ambosio de Santaella y Melgarejo to Crown, October 3, 1716, English translation in *Costa Rica-Panama Arbitration* (4 vols., Rosselyn, 1913) 4: 221–223.

any significant conversions or alliances; other missionaries from Guatemala had also come to the coast, and some had been murdered.[143]

Foundationally, the Miskitos seemed to be a free association. Exquemelin described the Miskitos of Cape Gracias a Dios near the Honduras-Nicaragua border in 1671 as "maintain[ing] themselves as a little republic, and they recognize no overlordship [*Opperhoost*] such as lord or king over them."[144] "M. W." wrote of them that "the plain dictates of natural or moral honesty are the law of these people" they having no courts, judiciary, or officials. Although he named a number of "captains" and a "king," he was careful to note that they "are in quality all equal, neither king nor captains of families bearing any more command that the meanest," except in time of war when they would submit to authority. Political equality was coupled with economic freedom: "on no account did they pay any taxes, rents or do any sort of services, but have all the country in common."[145]

At some point in the early eighteenth century, the Zambos acquired the office of king, for while M. W. reported that Jeremy, the king in 1699, was indigenous, Carlos de Casolara, an ex-slave who had lived on the coast between 1703 and 1728, said the king in his time was a "mulatto" and lived "mixed with the Indians."[146] It was perhaps this phase that led the bishop of Nicaragua, Benito Garret y Arvoli, who took up office in 1708, to present the rise of the Africans as a violent usurpation in which the "negroes vanquished the caribes" who then withdrew into the interior, allowing the victorious Africans to take the indigenous women as wives. A visiting Englishman, Nathaniel Uring, gave a similar description of a Zambo takeover as he heard it in 1711.[147]

As they gained power and control within the Miskito Kingdom, the Zambos also conducted a series of fearsome raids up and down the coast of Central America in the eighteenth century, capturing slaves by the thousands to retain in their own households and also to sell to English traders.[148] The English, in turn, recognized their kings, often crowning them in Jamaica, and supplied them with weapons and purchased their slaves.[149] In addition, the English provided diplomatic support and Mosquito leaders allowed Englishmen to settle

[143] García Añoveros, "Presencia franciscana," pp. 50–52.

[144] Exquemelin, *Zee-Roovers*, p. 150.

[145] M. W., "Mosqueto Indian," p. 293.

[146] M. W., "Mosqueto Indian," pp. 287–288; Flor de Oro Sorazano and Germán Rivero Vargas, eds., "Declaracion de Carlos Cazarola, negro esclavo bozal, 1737," *Wani* 10 (1991): 86.

[147] Garret y Arlovi to King, November 30, 1711, in Peralta, ed., *Costa Rica y Costa de Mosquitos*, pp. 57–58; Nathaniel Uring, *Travels and Adventures of Captain Uring* (London, 1722 [GB]), p. 227.

[148] Mary Helms, "Moskito Slaving and Culture Contact: Ethnicity and Opportunity in an Expanding Population," *Journal of Anthropological Research* 39 (1983): 179–197.

[149] Philip Dennis and Michael Olien, "Kingship among the Miskito," *American Ethnologist* 11 (1984): 718–737, and Michael Olien, "General, Governor and Admiral: Three Miskito Lines of Succession," *Ethnohistory* 45 (1998): 277–318.

in substantial numbers their midst after 1740.[150] In 1746, the English placed a "superintendent" in the region, who had, however, little or no control over the Miskito; he did have control over the more than 1,000 English settlers.[151]

English settlers in the Miskito Kingdom subsequently acquired land, granted to them by the kings in official documents, and brought in slaves to establish plantations growing sugar, indigo, and other tropical products.[152] In doing so they became probably the only European-directed slave economy in the Atlantic under the authority and protection of an indigenous polity.

At the other end of the zone, the English also built a colony on the coast of Yucatán, the Bay Colony, the eventual Belize. Loggers founded the town and soon brought in slaves to assist in the labor, harvesting logwood (a dye source) and mahogany for a booming market.[153] This colony was the northern anchor of British influence, just as the Mosquito Shore, protected from Spanish interference by the Zambos, was the southern end. The Miskitos provided important military protection to the settlement at Belize as well as protecting English interests in their own territory, so that a detachment of "settlers and Indians from the Mosquito Shore" assisted the English of Belize in an attack on Balacar (Yucatán) in 1779.[154] It was only at the end of the eighteenth century that the Spanish were able to force the English from the Mosquito Shore, but they were no more able to colonize it against Miskito resistance than they had in the seventeenth century.[155] The Miskito would remain outside of foreign control until the late nineteenth century.

THE CARIBBEAN FRONTIER'S SOUTHERN END: ORINOCO VALLEY

The greater Caribbean ultimately abutted the coast of South America, from the Guianas to the Orinoco River. Spanish explorers were visiting the small mini-states of the Llanos of the Upper Orinoco soon after they established themselves in Bogotá in the later 1530s. They were drawn by stories of fabulous wealth associated with a mysterious kingdom that lay in the Guiana

---

[150] For a good account of these encounters, but which overplays the role of the English in transforming Miskito society, see Germán Romero Vargas, *Las sociedades Atlántico del Nicaragua en los siglos XVII y XVIII* (Managua, 1995).

[151] For the diplomatic aspects, see Troy Floyd, *The Anglo-Spanish Struggle for Mosquitia* (Albuquerque, 1967); for a well-documented history that gives the English a role of dominance, see German Romero Vargas, *Las sociedades del Atlántico de Nicaragua en los siglos XVII y XVIII* (Managua, 1995), a position my reading of the record does not support.

[152] Romero Vargas, *Sociedades*, pp. 105–110, provides many examples of land grants and slave holdings culled from the archives in Belize and London.

[153] On the mahogany trade, see Jennifer Anderson, "Nature's Currency: The Atlantic Mahogany Trade, 1720–1830," PhD dissertation, New York University, 2007.

[154] Governor Dalling to Lord George Germaine, August 28, 1779, in John Alder Burdon, ed., *Archives of British Honduras* (3 vols., London, 1931–35), 1: 126.

[155] An excellent overview of the English settlement in Belize is found in O. Nigel Bolland, *The Formation of a Colonial Society: Belize from Conquest to Crown Colony* (Baltimore and London, 1977).

Highlands, called Manoa. The ruler was said to be "Eldorado" or the "Golden One," who annually dipped himself in a lake and emerged covered in gold. However, following the failure of the early attempts, the Spanish gradually abandoned this adventure.[156]

Walter Raleigh, an early English privateer, having read the earlier literature on Eldorado, began visiting the eastern end of the Orinoco with the aim of both thwarting the Spanish and winning the gold for himself and for England. Raleigh, as well as a number of Dutch, Irish, and French groups, also pursued the more prosaic trade in tobacco, hammocks, and dyewoods with the local people of the region, most of whom spoke Carib or Arawak languages and had an extensive network of trade and war that stretched from the coast along the Amazon-Orinoco watersheds, Trinidad, and the southern islands of the Caribbean, such as Grenada and Dominica. The Spanish governor Antonio de Berrio decided to meet this threat by establishing a presence on the island of Trinidad and at Santo Tomé at the mouth of the Orinoco River in 1593–1597.

The earliest northern European exploration of the lower Orinoco roughly coincided with the emergence of a powerful southern wing of Carib expansion. In 1596 the Caribs of the Caribbean and the Arawaks of the Orinoco began a large war, ostensibly to determine "which of the two nations was the most noble," although the Caribs had been launching constant small raids on the Arawaks for some time before this great war. The Caribs under Tocaurama raised 120 pirogues, the Arawaks under Aramaya, their "General," only 60. After much maneuvering through the tangled mouths of the Orinoco, the two fleets met at the Guainí River, in which the Arawaks, despite their inferior numbers, were victorious.[157] The victory, while celebrated and remembered for years afterward, did not prevent Carib penetration of the Orinoco in the longer run.

Northern European entry into the Orinoco thus led to a double war, between Spain and the northern European on the one side and between Caribs and Arawaks on the other. The Spanish threw their support to the Arawaks, masking an alliance by calling those around Santo Tomé their subjects under a regime of encomienda. Given that the same groups were often held to be in "rebellion," however, they were really more like voluntary allies.[158] On the other side, thanks to the Carib-Arawak war, the Caribs formed their own alliance with the Dutch who, initially established on Tobago in the 1620s, were driven from there by a Spanish-Arawak force to Essequibo in the Surinam-Guiana region of mainland South America in 1637. From that base and others nearby, they formed a tight alliance with the Caribs, similar to that of the

---

[156] For a good overview of the efforts to find El Dorado, see John Hemming, *The Search for El Dorado* (Boston, 1978).

[157] Antonio Vázquez de Espinosa, "Compendio y Descripcion de las Indias Occidentales," ed. and trans. Charles Upson Clark (Washington, DC, 1942 [English], 1944 [Spanish]), no. 181–182; for the earlier raiding, see no. 177.

[158] Vázquez de Espinosa, "Compendio," no. 182. See, for example, the survey of the Arawakan groups living around Santo Tomé around 1620; nos. 169–170, 175.

Spanish with the Arawaks. The Caribs, in turn, developed an extensive trading network during the course of the seventeenth century, which stretched along the Orinoco valley and the hinterland of the Guianas.[159] Carib raiding was accompanied by the capture of many people as slaves, some of which were sold to the Dutch as a first labor force for sugar plantations, and later as a non-plantation labor force. In addition, the Caribs integrated a good number of the slaves into their own societies.

The Spanish intended to cement their alliances through their customary use of missionary reductions, starting from the post at Santo Tomé near the mouth of the Orinoco. The Capuchins, who arrived largely from the northern coastal areas of Venezuela, had a hard going at first, but as the Dutch became more interested in the sugar production of their colonies and could obtain reliable supplies of African slaves, their need to press farther and farther into the interior to reduce the risk of attacks on their coastal positions lessened. The Dutch and English settlers on the coast of South America gradually developed an economy based largely on sugar production, but always supplemented by trade with the various indigenous groups, who also protected them, especially from the Spanish. Indeed, a Spanish report of 1662 notes the presence of 1,000 settlers along this coast, with 400 closely allied Caribs, and "a greater number of negroes, founding a new Brazil."[160]

Spanish missionaries and settlers began moving into the Llanos of the upper (western) Orinoco in the late seventeenth century, aiming to thwart Carib-Dutch expansion, occupy this region, and continue the search for El Dorado. Missionaries formed alliances with the more significant of the mini-states, most notably the Saliva, Maipuri, and Achagua.[161] Missionaries were not well accepted at first, but as Carib raiders penetrated deeper and deeper into the Orinoco and raided the Llanos region regularly between 1729 and 1744, formerly reluctant indigenous leaders looked to the Spanish for assistance and accepted missionaries and Christianity.[162] The Spanish seized this opportunity and made the necessary alliances to secure the Orinoco Valley for Spain after 1750.

SLAVERY, A RUNAWAY'S KINGDOM AND REDUCTIONS IN NORTHEAST BRAZIL

As the Spanish developed the reduction as a military- and labor-supplying means to deal with frontier societies in northern Mexico, the Portuguese hit

---

[159] For Carib developments in the period, see Neil Whitehead, *Lords of the Tiger Spirit: A History of the Caribs in Colonial Venezuela and Guyana, 1498–1820* (Dodrech, 1998).

[160] Pedro de Viedma to the King, March 20, 1662, Boundary Dispute, doc. 85, http://www.guyana.org/Western, p. 177.

[161] The contemporary chroniclers of these missions were Joseph Gumilla, *El Orinoco illustrado y defindido...* (2 vols, Madrid, 1745 [GB]), esp. vol. 1; and Filippo Salvadore Gilij, *Saggio de storia Americana* (3 vols., Rome 1780–82 [GB]).

[162] Gumilla, *Orinoco Ilustrado*, part 2, caps. 9–12.

on a similar system in their colonization of Brazil. The Brazilian interior that stretched inland from the thin line of settlements in the sugar-producing north-eastern captaincies of Bahia and Pernambuco presented another great frontier area, occupied by unconquered indigenous people who were soon joined by various groups of African runaway slaves. Portugal sought to control this situation through many of the same means the Spanish used – by recruiting indigenous groups to fight for them (and reinforce the groups that had already been integrated during the earlier conquest period), to expand the colony, and to recover the runaway Africans.

After its initial founding and colonization through the sugar industry, Brazil faced the dangers from the interior. The Portuguese occupation of the coast north of Pernambuco, Maranhão, and ultimately the Amazon valley was to forestall advances of northern Europeans in the region in the early seventeenth century. Although the initial settlers were not directly interested in attacking Brazil, the potential military threat drove the Portuguese to move to the north.

Portugal had the benefit of an existing group of allies, who provided them with the skilled military manpower necessary for their task. In 1597, Manoel de Mascarenhas Homem led 178 Portuguese "foot and horse" along with 820 archers from Pernambuco and Paraíba against the Potiguar and French in Rio Grande. This campaign was augmented the following year by 84 Europeans and 350 Tupi.[163] To maintain this pressure, Pero de Sousa's led an expedition to Paraiba with 75 Portuguese and 200 Tupi in 1603.[164]

The French heightened the threat when they occupied Maranhão in 1612 and allied with local Tupinambá; some 1,200 of them accompanied 40 French soldiers and 10 sailors to attack the Camarapin, the inhabitants of the island of Marajó.[165] But Portugal had more allies. In a report of 1612, an anonymous author noted that in Pernambuco they still had to endure "the aldeias of free Indians" as "they aid in conquering and populating the coast up to the Rio Grande [ie to the north]." The aldeia of Dobeiuasu in Itamarca, he noted, could raise 5,000 archers, although they avoided whites.[166] When the Portuguese under Jerónimo de Albuquerque attacked the French fort, its commander had 400 French soldiers and 2,000 allied Tupinambá.[167]

The Dutch and English soon posed their own threat, particularly in the Amazon after about 1610.[168] In 1623, when Pedro Teixeira led a force to attack English and Dutch in the Amazon, his 70 Portuguese soldiers were

---

[163] Salvador, *Historia*, Book 4, caps. 31–32.
[164] Salvador, *Historia*, Book 4, cap. 38.
[165] Evereux, *Voyage*, fols. 25–25v.
[166] "Rezão de Estado," fols. 95v and 103v.
[167] Testimony of Noel de la Mota, and Antonio Landuzeo, November 20, 1614, in "Interrogatorio do prisoneiros francezes do combate de Guaxenduba," in *Anais da Biblioteca Nacional de Rio de Janeiro* 26 (1904): 265, 272 (fifty more French soliders were sick and did not fight).
[168] A good description of the English and Irish efforts as well as Portuguese responses, and translations of many of the key documents, are found in Joyce Lorimer, *English and Irish Settlements on the Amazon, 1550–1646* (London: 1989).

accompanied by 1,000 Tupi allies, and a subsequent expedition against Dutch settlers counted 50 Portuguese soldiers and 300 allied Tupis.[169] But this was a small affair compared to the Dutch invasion of Pernambuco launched by sea in 1630, a direct attack on the coast with thousands of soldiers. The Dutch only occupied the coast, unable to expel the Portuguese. The English, encouraged by the fall of Pernambuco, began serious attempts to colonize the mouth of the Amazon, where they landed 500 settlers in 1630. Soon they had persuaded a good number of local people to join them and even provoked a revolt against Portugal by other groups that had formerly been allied. Portugal opposed this with a mighty force of some 5,000 allied Tupinamba, assisted by 240 Portuguese in 127 canoes in 1632, eventually driving the English out and punishing their Tapuya allies.[170]

The English failure in the Amazon was in part because they could not muster enough indigenous allies, and the same problem ultimately undermined Dutch efforts as well, even though they realized the significance of such alliances and sought vigorously to obtain them. They had some success, for in 1637, a force of 350 Dutch soldiers and 650 Tapuyas attacked and captured the post of Seara.[171]

In spite of their attempts to do so, however, the Dutch were unable to persuade enough of the allied Tupinambá to abandon Portugal, or win over the Tapuyas, who were enemies of the Portuguese, to defend their colony. The Portuguese continued activities in the north of their holdings as the Dutch threat mounted, and the largest expedition, led by Teixeira into the Amazon, took place in 1638 when he led an initial force of 70 Portuguese soldiers and 200 Tupi in 17 boats, which eventually grew to 900 Tupis in a total of 45 canoes.[172] Even though the Dutch had a substantial military force from Europe, their defeat at the hands of a Portuguese-Tupi force drove them from Brazil in 1654.[173] In the aftermath of the war, the indigenous forces of Pernambuco were gathered for military purposes into a command under António Felipe Camarão, the leader of the Portugal's indigenous Brazilian forces during the war.

As in the Caribbean, the essential indigenous-Portuguese relationship on the frontier was complicated by the presence of runaway African communities. Sugar estate records show regular flight of their African slaves "to the Indians."[174] In the 1580s, some of the Tupi *santidades* (religious meetings) near Bahia included "negros de guiné" as well as Tupi, who may have provided

[169] Bernardo Pereira de Berredo, *Annaes historicos do estado de Maranhão* (Lisbon, 1749, 3rd ed., 2 vols., Florence, 1905 [GB]) Book 6, no. 504, 2: 197; Book 6, no. 531, 1: 208.

[170] Pereira Berredo, *Annaes*, Book 8, no. 599, 612–622, 1: 239–240, 244–248.

[171] Pereira Berredo, *Annaes*, Book 9, no. 671, 1: 268.

[172] Pereira Berredo, *Annaes* Book 9, no. 669, 1: 267.

[173] Military aspects and the indigenous policies of both parties are detailed in Cabral de Mello, *Olinda*.

[174] "Livro de Contas do Engenho Sergipe do Conde," in Instituto de Açúcar e Alcool, *Documentos para a história do Açúcar* (3 vols., Rio de Janeiro, 1953–1956) 2: 87, 144, 157, 222.

the first haven for runaways who would later build whole communities in the interior.[175]

When runaway settlements, typically called by the Kikongo/Kimbumdu term *mukambu* (*mocambo* as the Portuguese wrote it), were first reported in "Palmares" a wooded mountain range in the hinterland of Pernambuco in 1612, they were already giving authorities a good deal of trouble.[176] But over the course of the next decades, they grew very large, perhaps as the result of remarkable circumstances. One important aspect was the unique ethnic composition of Pernambuco slaves in the early to mid-seventeenth century, drawn from either the Kingdom of Kongo or its neighboring Kingdom of Ndongo as the Portuguese wars against them (or civil wars within them) came to supply virtually the entire slave trade to Brazil.[177] The languages and cultures of these two regions were very similar, and moreover both had strong influences of both the Portuguese language and culture reaching back to Kongo's engagement with Portugal in the late fifteenth century. A report of 1612 makes it clear that by that time, people called "negros de guiné" in Brazil were in fact from Angola.[178]

The community in Palmares, which stretched along the mountainous interior of Pernambuco, became a substantial threat to the colony, both because it raided the plantations and because its existence allowed more slaves to run away. When the Dutch took over Pernambuco in 1630, thousands of slaves deserted the plantations and took to the existing communities in Palmares. Attacks by runaways on the plantations eventually drew the Dutch into war against Palmares. Dutch descriptions in the early and mid-1640s spoke of two "forests" in which there were both scattered settlements and fortified towns (as well as caves where people could hide) containing, 6,000 and 15,000 persons, respectively, or probably a good quarter of all people of African descent in Pernambuco.[179] One abandoned settlement described by the Dutch officer Jan Blaer in 1645 had 220 houses, which local people said housed 500 males, which suggested a population in the range of 1,500, and the community was in fact a group of related settlements ruled by a "king."[180]

[175] Alida C. Metcalf, "Millenarian Slaves? The Santidade de Jaguaripe and Slave Resistance in the Americans," *American Historical Review* 104 (1999): 1531–1559.

[176] "Rezão do Estado do Brasil" (1612), ed. Engel Sluiter, "Report on the State of Brazil," in *Hispanic American Historical Review* 39 (1949): 553. The area of Palmares is now in Alagoas State, following the nineteenth-century dismantling of Pernambuco.

[177] John K. Thornton, "Les États de l'Angola et la formation de Palmares (Brésil)," *Annales: Histoire, Sciences sociales* 63/4 (2008): 769–797.

[178] "Rezão do Estado," ed. Sluiter, p. 523. There are no comprehensive records of the imports to Brazil during this time, and so one must work by extension from the records of imports into the Spanish Caribbean, for which the standard analysis in Enriqueta Vila Vilar, Quadro IV.

[179] G. Piso and G. Marcgrave, *Historia Naturalis Brasiliae* (Batavia, 1648) Book 8, chapter 1, p. 261; Casparis Barlaei *Rerum per octennivm in Brasilia* (Amsterdam, 1647), pp. 242–243 (both incorporated into Johan Nieuhof, *Gedenkwaerdige Brasilianse Zee- en Lantreise* [Amsterdam, 1682]).

[180] NAN OWIC 60, Portuguese translation, sometimes defective, in "Diario da viagem do capitão João Blaer aos palmares em 1645," *Revista do Instituto Archeologicao e Geographico Pernambucano* 10 (1902): 91–93.

By the 1670s, Great and Little Palmares had combined into a single state known as Angola Janga, with fifteen main settlements and a host of smaller ones, under a single king named Ngana Zamba.[181] The main town had 1,500 houses (this would imply nearly 5,000 people); the second-largest one had some 800. Ngana Zamba lived in a palace of multiple houses, and people addressed him as "majesty" while clapping their hands in greeting, a typical central African sign of respect. In addition to the supreme king, and a second king ruling in another town, there were other "potentates and major chiefs [*cabos*]" who ruled the lesser settlements, as well as "ministers of justice." As expected in a still heavily central African polity, there was a church with a priest, "who serves as a parish priest," providing regular church services, reflecting no doubt the Christian background of Angolans in general.[182] Given that the trade of Brazil in this period was probably even more exclusively with Angola than before the Dutch invasion, relative ethnic homogeneity was probably still its main characteristic.

Many settlers within Brazil sought to coexist with Palmares rather than attack it. Already in 1664 the governor of Pernambuco proposed establishing a general pardon and integration of Palmares into Brazil, but his overtures were rejected, and one of the local leaders who accepted a Portuguese offer was executed by officials sent from the capital.[183] In 1678–1679, there were active negotiations to bring about a regularization of the state's relations with Brazil, but they were halted when a local coup brought down Ngana Zamba.[184] At last, the colonial government brought up Paulista troops under Domingos Jorge Velho who, with great loss and effort, stormed the capital of Palmares in 1694 and affected the scattering of its settlements.[185] Although runaways returned to the Palmares region, they lived in smaller, scattered settlements without the sort of central direction that characterized Palmares at its height.[186] While runaways and their settlements remained a problem for Pernambuco settlers, the threat of a counterstate was allayed.

THE AMAZON FRONTIER

The ultimate consequences of the war against the Dutch in Pernambuco was further expansion into the Amazon, to rid it of northern European rivals and

---

[181] Thornton, "L'états d'Angola," 776–780.

[182] "Relação das guerras feitas aos Palmares..." in *Revista do Instituto de Historia e Geographia do Brazil* 22 (1859): 307–309.

[183] AUC 31, Dispozições I, fol 93v, Francisco de Britto Freyre note, August 23, 1663; the treaty had been made very shortly before, as de Britto Freyre mentioned it on April 17, fol. 91, no. 31.

[184] Bando de Sargento Mor, March 26, 1680, in Edison Carneiro, *O Quilombo do Palmares, 1630–95* (São Paulo, 1947), pp. 228–229.

[185] Requerimento of Domingos George Velho. c. 1694 in Ernesto Eannes, *As guerras nos Palmares: Subsitios para a sua historia.* vol. 1, *Domingos Jorge Velho e 'A Troia Negra 1687–1700* (only volume, São Paulo, 1938), pp. 315–343.

[186] Thornton, "États d'Angola."

forestall any further operations there on their part, ultimately confining them to the Guiana region.[187] The Spanish proved a more difficult group. Portuguese advances in the Amazon in the seventeenth century pressed farther into the interior, eventually meeting the Spanish positions in the regions just west of the Andes in the eighteenth century. When a force from Maranhão led by Pedro Teixeira reached Peru in 1638, for example, the officials there became alarmed, even though at the moment the Portuguese and Spanish crowns were still united. He left a marker on the river bank where, in his opinion, the division of the world made by the Pope in 1494 delineated the border of Portuguese and Spanish possessions.

The Portuguese brought their own military forces with them, in the form of Tupi allies from Pernambuco. These sizable forces allowed them greater leeway in negotiating with local allies, as they did indeed in taking Maranhão. The Portuguese leaders of these forces, at least those who intended to stay in the area, married local women, probably of the nobility of the area, and their children were thus all mixed race. In time, of course, this mixed-race aristocracy that regarded itself as Portuguese by virtue of their origin in the male line, their religion, and to some extent their language (even though they often spoke Tupi as much as Portuguese), became a closed society that intermarried among themselves. It is notable that even today, after considerable European migration in the nineteenth and twentieth centuries, more than 50 percent of the population in northern Brazil that is classified as "white" (*branco*), descends on their female side from indigenous women.[188]

The Portuguese invasion fitted into the existing pattern of interstate warfare and enslavement in the Amazon. It had long been dominated by mini-states and thus possessed the sort of small-scale aristocracy that the Spanish had joined in Paraguay, and these were ready for alliances of one or another sort. Likewise, the mini-states thrived on capturing slaves and building up their core regions with these forced laborers. Petty empires of conglomerated mini-states built around a particularly effective leader might have had important local impacts, and thus the larger "kingdoms" through which early Spanish travelers passed on both the Amazon and Orinoco were such agglomerations. But they were in all probability unstable, as archaeologists have been able to provide evidence of regional powers with enough influence to make substantial differences in settlement patterns as far back as the eleventh and twelfth centuries. The Portuguese were simply the most successful users of these strategies.

[187] Joyce Lorimer, *English and Irish Settlements on the River Amazon, 1550–1646* (London, 1989) for a full discussion of the Amazon in this period as well as a large selection of original documents in English translation.

[188] Juliana Alves-Silva, Magda da Silva Santos, Pedro E. M. Guimarães, et al., "The Ancestry of Brazilian MtDNA Lineages," *American Journal of Human Genetics* 67 (2000): 454–455; by contrast, a similar study revealed that no white Brazilians had indigenous ancestry on their paternal side; D. Carvalho-Silva, F. Santos, J. Rocha, S. Pena, "The Phylogeography of Brazilian Y-Chromosome Lineages", *The American Journal of Human Genetics* 68 (2001): 284–285.

The Portuguese, like the Amazonian people into whose territory they expanded, achieved a leisure class lifestyle by capturing slaves and employing them as laborers, both to provide personal service and agricultural work.[189] The luxury goods they needed to demonstrate an elite lifestyle were imported thanks to exporting tobacco and other agricultural products. To acquire slaves, they continued the process already in place – making raids (*entradas*) into the interior along the rivers, using their Tupi military forces, and augmenting them from local slaves and allies they made along the way. In this way Francisco de Potflis claimed the right to enslave at least sixty houses of Tapuyas for his sugar mill in 1721.[190] These raids captured and enslaved people who were then divided among the raiding parties and provided their labor force. In addition to raids, the settlers also took merchant voyages (*entradas de resgate*) into the river, in this case buying slaves to carry back to their estates.

The Portuguese built towns, first Belém (1616) and then at Manaus (1669), by agglomerating captives and allies around their settlements. The enslavement of Amazonians was coupled with another institution – "descending." Often Tupi groups would "descend" the river to the Portuguese settlements to join military alliances, and sometimes also to provide labor. Thus, when the Dutch threat seemed to loom, the crown opted for 400 Indians to fill out the ranks to fight them and their Carib allies.[191] When the Portuguese built a fort at the Rio Branco in 1777, they intended to use descended indigenous people as part of the force to defend it.[192]

However, the crown and the church were not content with this process and placed important conditions on it. First of all, they forbade slave raids that were conducted simply to acquire slaves, and required all wars be justified by priests. Furthermore, they required that the priests be in charge of the indigenous groups, ostensibly to ensure their instruction in Christianity. On this basis the Jesuit order, as well as a number of other ecclesiastical bodies, created an elaborate body of law governing warfare and enslavement, while ensuring that these religious bodies possessed access to laborers in their mission villages (*aldeias*). Historians have tended to see the struggle between the settlers and the priests in terms defined by the eloquent Jesuit spokesperson, Father António Vieira, who worked on the Amazon in the 1650s. Vieira, a master of the Portuguese language and a multitalented statesman as well, presented the case as settler slave traders and raiders against Jesuit evangelists.[193]

---

[189] The best account of Portuguese activities on the Amazon is probably David Sweet's still unpublished dissertation, "A Rich Realm of Nature Destroyed: The Middle Amazon Valley, 1640–1750" (University of Wisconsin, 1974). Also see Hemming, *Red Gold*, and *Amazon Frontier: The Defeat of the Brazilian Indians* (London, 1987), and more recently, *The Tree of Rivers: The Story of the Amazon* (London, 2008).

[190] AHU Pará Doc 36905, Bernardo Pereira de Berredo to King João V, August 10, 1721

[191] Royal Order to João da Maya da Gama, February 17, 1724, in Nabuco, ed. *Limites*, 1: 35.

[192] AHU Pará doc. 42714, João Pereira Caldas to Martinho de Melo e Castro, June 12, 1777.

[193] Hemming, *Red Gold*, is probably the most sophisticated historian to adopt this position completely, but it is found in much of the historiography, considering the nature of our sources, which mostly come from documents of complaint and legal suits.

Lawsuits and complaints about slave trading and raiding often form the basis of our information about the contending parties, and indeed conflicts of interest abounded. A royal inspector, Calisto da Cunha Valadares, sent to suppress those "whites who have been going to the interior (*sertão*) making slaves" in 1737, was subsequently denounced for having ties with slave expeditions himself, and was in fact killed by the would-be victims of one such raid.[194] In 1732, a Carmelite priest Jozeph de Payva complained that a "tropa de rescate" going to buy slaves in the interior led by Gregorio de Morais Rego with Father Lucas Xavier, a Jesuit as its chaplain, had failed to live up to its "obligations under the law" by illegally enslaving people who were not at war with Portugal, including Christians who were already in missionary villages (*aldeado*), who would be taken to Maranhão, there to be divided among the residents "to work their lands, collect fruit and increase their industry, and be useful in commerce."[195]

Another lawsuit of 1738 reveals further dynamics. The case began when the government of the city of Belém, which was in a "bad state because of the shortage of slaves it needed for its agriculture and services" in 1737, asked a well-known and respected landowner, Lourenço Belfort, to finance a slave-buying expedition to "the interior of the Amazon," there being no money in the treasury to finance it. They applied to the Junta de Missões, the clerical body charged with certifying such expeditions, and it issued strict instructions to him to avoid war, even if attacked, although the expedition could take slaves during defensive action, but only "on the day of battle" and not later, either for vengeance or to follow up. It also provided for supervision of expenses and accounting for all the slaves. He was to avoid a repetition of an expedition of 1728, which had terrorized the "principals" or leaders of the independent villages that had hitherto been at peace with Portugal, but had now fled into the woods. According to his detailed diary, Belfort gathered his forces, but was thwarted in recruiting indigenous fighters from the missionary-controlled village of Santo Angelo, as the missionary in charge claimed there had been an insurrection recently and he could not spare the men. Nevertheless, he managed to complete his mission successfully with the loss of two men killed along the way.[196]

The crown preferred descents to either slave raids or purchases of captives. The people who descended were supposed to be protected by the crown and the missionaries and paid salaries for their work.[197] In 1734, Manoel do Couto,

---

[194] BL Add MSS 37043, fols 108–108v, King to the Ouividor Geral of Pará, May 21, 1737; also fol.s. 111–111v Royal letter, March 17, 1738, on the passage of canoes with weapons for slave raiding.

[195] BL, Add MSS 37043, fols. 56–57v, Complaint of Fr. Jozeph de Payva Real, March 12, 1732 (copy of 1901).

[196] BL, Add MSS 27043, João de Abreu de Castelbranco, Governor of the Maranhão, to the King, September 5, 1738, with numerous attachments in the form of sworn testimony.

[197] An example of the rules is found in Royal Order to Christovão da Costa Freire, March 9, 1718, in Joaquim Nabuco, ed., *Limites entre le Brésil et la Guyane anglaise. Annexes du premier memoire. Documents portugais* (2 vols., no place, 1903[GB]), 1: 28–29.

a Jesuit, organized a trip into the interior of Para to descend "60 houses of Indians" on behalf of his father who needed them to cultivate his fields, particularly to grow cocoa on land he had been granted. The priest would in turn be their administrator, meaning that it would be a private village created for the purpose of forming a labor force, for which the rules stipulated that salaries would be paid.[198] Such grants were common at the time, as other documents reveal.[199]

Thus when the leaders of Belem sent Lourenço Belfort to go to trade in slaves in 1737, it enjoined him to encourage any indigenous people he met to "descend" peacefully to the Portuguese area.[200] As they were engaged with mini-states rather than free associations, these negotiations took the form of striking bargains with elites among the indigenous people who agreed to move the people they commanded to come down to the mission areas, and in turn have their leadership roles confirmed. João de Couto Fonseca noted that the "principal" with whom he was in negotiation in 1735, named Ipô, was surrounded by his "relatives and vassals."[201] A royal order of 1702 noted that it was customary to recognize these elites, for example by giving the "principals" and "those they regard among themselves as knights (*cavalleiros*)" special insignia (and designating them with military ranks such as sergeant and merinho mor), but it balked at going so far as to pay them salaries, as the public expenses could not cover it.[202] On the other hand, at least one principal petitioned for a knighthood in the Order of Christ for his service to Portugal.[203] Some indigenous people even held Portuguese titles, as the "indio" Baltazar da Silva in 1765.[204]

We can see the workings of the elites' decision to descend from a report of 1727, in which the missionary Francisco de São Manços described how two principals, Mascolmim, son of Boniatá and a principal of the village of Calarapari, and Mascotu, daughter of Huzá and a principal of the village of Popunhari, descended the Nhanmondás River and settled "to their content" at the mission of Nhamundâs. There they found "good land" in "abundance for their agricultural works" and now wished to found new villages under the spiritual guidance of the missionaries of Piedade. They were members of the "nation" of Paracuató, which in this context appears to be a mini-state rather than an ethnic group, which had ten named villages "and many others" all living under the leadership of Teumigé of the village of Moxotorei. As these

[198] BL Add MSS 37043, fols.159–161, Manoel de Couto Statement, April 1, 1734.
[199] AHU Pará, docs. 37075 for the descent of 200 houses, Nicolau Ferreira da Costa to King João V, September 8, 1725; 37153 João da Maia da Gama to King. João V, September 10, 1726 (to take up a descent of fifty houses granted to his dead father).
[200] BL, Add MSS 37048, fol. 130v, Instructions to Lourenço Belfort, October 21, 1737, cap. 13.
[201] BL Add MSS 37043, fol. 165v, Statement of João de Couto Fonseca, June 11, 1735.
[202] Royal letter to Manuel Rollim de Moura, October 27, 1702, in Nabuco, ed., *Limites*, 1: 23–24.
[203] AHU Pará, Doc. 5310 Requerimento de Silvestre Francisco de Mendonça Furtado January 17, 1767.
[204] AHU Pará, doc. 41880, Decree of King José I, September 12, 1769.

were relatives of the contented principals, Father Francisco hoped that they too would descend in time and engaged in protracted negotiations with Teumigé and his subordinates to complete the process. These indigenous people were often cultivating or gathering various wild spices, such as cacao and cloves, which could be exported for profit and might benefit from marketing access that the missionaries supplied.[205] In fact, it was common practice for nations to relocate in stages, as Antonio da Rocha Machado noted in his petition of 1735 to bring the remainder of a nation he had persuaded to descend earlier.[206]

By relocating they might be better placed to export their goods and they, as catechists and lay leaders in the missions, remained in control of their followers. Royal officials appointed principals, in this way continuing and maintaining power that might be more tenuous under other systems of succession, as when Inácio Coelho of the Aruwã nation petitioned for the title of principal for the village of São José do Igarapé Grande in 1755.[207] While the missionaries ran the religious life, the older elite ran the economic and social life as far as it did not touch the strictures of Christian morality as defined by the missionaries.

The literature of complaint often suggests that there was trickery employed to bring the indigenous leaders down and to enslave them. But leaders had means to flee; as noted, they rarely brought everyone at once and waited to see how things were before bringing the rest. Of course, they often had the option to flee, or even to revolt, which usually meant fleeing, though often after considerable disruption. Such a disruption upset a good part of the Amazon in 1747.[208] Another similar revolt upset its eastern end in 1756, and there were certainly others that were small enough in scale to miss recording.

International and interregional politics also played a role in creating and maintaining alliances. The Carib invasion of the Orinoco basin also affected the Amazon in the late sixteenth century, especially after the Caribs allied with Dutch settlers in Essequibo in the 1630s. The raids from the Orinoco put great pressure on the Spanish, forcing them to move down the rivers from the Andean highlands, eventually sending missionaries to reduce the inhabitants. This in turn led to their conflict with the Portuguese and their allies. By the end of the seventeenth century, Spanish and Portuguese missionaries were competing for the loyalty of the indigenous leaders in Cambebe, where Teixeira's marker was placed.[209]

---

[205] "Relação que Frei Francisco de S. Manços, Religioso da Provincia da Piedade e Missionario na aldeia de Nhamondás faz ao Rei de sua viagem ao Rio de Trombetas..." January 6, 1728, in Nabuco, ed., *Limites*, 1: 39–40; 47–48 (for additional negotiations with the head of the nation, Teumigé, for his own descent).

[206] BL Add MSS 37043, fol. 163v, Petition of Antonio da Rocha Machado, April 13, 1735.

[207] AHU Pará, doc. 39837, solicitation of Inácio Coelho, prior to March 15, 1755.

[208] AHU Pará, doc. Doc 39125, Francisco Xavier de Mendonça Furtado to King José, November 13, 1747.

[209] Antonio Miranda letter, May 25, 1695; Antonio de Albuquerque Coelho de Carvalho to King, July 20, 1697, in Nabuco, ed., *Limites* 1: 8–11; 14–15.

Thus, missionaries became the leading edge of Spanish occupation from the middle of the seventeenth century, although this was particularly pronounced in the eighteenth century as the missionaries and their indigneioius allies increasingly threatened Portuguese interests. In the 1750s, Portuguese outposts on the middle Amazon began receiving reports of Dutch and Carib attacks along the Negro River, and made decisions, like the Spanish, to move their own outposts northward along the Negro and into the headwaters of the Orinoco, where they found themselves bumping up against Spanish patrols.[210] As elsewhere, expansion was driven not just by economic opportunity or evangelistic fervor, but by the politics of protection of borders and the indigenous people beyond those borders, who might pose threats to either Spain or Portugal.

RIO SÃO FRANCISCO

While the struggle over Palmares effectively closed the interior frontier of Pernambuco for the seventeenth century, settlers did penetrate into the frontier behind Bahia. Sugar estates declined in this period, but the northern captaincies also became targets for new economic growth. Tobacco and food crops, not much grown before the late seventeenth century, provided economic solvency, but usually in the hands of much smaller proprietors.[211] Although the sugar engine with its associated lands did not disappear from the north, the small-holding producer of tobacco and food crops became more important. Settlers of modest means arrived from Portugal, and they were joined by freed slaves of African and Native American descent, of former residents of aleidais and mixed-race people of all sorts. Brazilian territorial interests, formerly confined to hugging the coast, now looked inward, and landholding moved toward the interior mountains. The valley of the São Francisco River proved to be useful for cattle raising, and these products, in turn, were vital to the sugar industry. Cattle ranching to supply both the coastal and international markets with meat and hides attracted middling-level settlers from all over Brazil who could not own a sugar engine or enjoy great wealth. The movement into the area was spearheaded by cattle barons who were granted vast lands in which to raise their cattle, and who raised and used their personal resources to develop and exploit them. In the process, the indigenous free associations, often called Cariri, and Portuguese ranchers conflicted over hunting of cattle and the role of cattle in disrupting Cariri agriculture.

The penetration in the north is described well by the Capuchin priest Martin de Nantes. According to him, around 1671, an important landowner named Antonio de Oliveira "looking for pasturage for his cattle" found a group of

[210] An excellent history of the Carib role in the region is Neil Whitehead, *Lords of the Tiger Spirit: A History of the Caribs in Colonial Venezuela and Guyana, 1498–1820* (Dordrecht and Providence, 1988).

[211] B. J. Barickman, *A Bahian Counterpoint: Sugar, Tobacco, Cassava and Slavery in the Recôncavo, 1780–1860* (Stanford, 1998) for Bahia, and Castillo for Pernambuco.

indigenous people on the banks of the Paraíba River. They obligingly let him bring his cattle there and he in turn found a Capuchin priest, Father Theodore in Pernambuco, to teach them, and then accompanied by the captain and ten or twelve mamelucos – "his friends" – he set both himself and the priest up on the place.[212] The relationship, however, was far from idyllic, for Cariris found the cattle harmful to their crops, and soon hostilities broke out.

These problems eventually led to what the Portuguese called the War of the Barbarians.[213] It was bloodthirsty and indeed even genocidal, as free associations waged small-scale war against the cattle ranchers and their allies. In instructions given by the governor of Pernambuco to his commander in 1688, he was enjoined not to "give any quarter to the barbarians" or to hold back in order to preserve them to be slaves, but "to slaughter them and continue until you finally destroy them."[214]

However much the governors led wars against the indigenous people of the interior, it was primarily private forces of the ranchers that played an important role. In 1709, for example, we learn that to protect a peace arrangement, authorities in Bahia refused Colonel Garcia d'Avila Pereira, a Bahian landowner, permission to make war on the neighboring and presumably unconquered indigenous people.[215] In all likelihood Colonel d'Avila Pereira may have used allied indigenous fighters to wage this war; in any case, he recruited new Indians to settle on his land in 1722, and was waging war with legal permission at that time.[216] Over the course of the eighteenth century, in a process that is poorly documented, the cattle ranch with a mixed-race (but largely indigenous in origin) labor force replaced the small, scattered villages of free associations.

GRAN CHACO

The Portuguese entered the lands of the Matto Grosso, in modern-day southcentral Brazil, in search of minerals, a continuation of their discoveries in Minas Gerais. The initial explorers were bandeirantes from São Paulo, at first raiding the Guarani who had been reduced by Jesuits along the rivers of Paraguay. However, after the Paulistas had discovered gold in Minas Gerais, and deprived of it by the "Emboabas" in the early eighteenth century, their expansion continued in search of another Minas Gerais. Indeed they found it, in the midst

---

[212] De Nantes, *Relation*, p. 2.

[213] Pedro Puntoni, *A Guerra dos Bárbaros: Povos Indígenas e a Colonização do Sertão Nordeste do Brasil, 1650–1720* (Sao Paulo, 2002); see also Hemming, *Red Gold*, pp. 345–376.

[214] Mathias da Cunha to Antonio Albuquerque da Camara, March 14, 1688, *DH* 10: 277–278. In this case they were spared as the expedition failed; see same to Bishop of Pernambuco, September 29, 1688, *DH* 10: 306.

[215] APEB, Livro 8, doc. 711, Garcia d'Avila Pereira, September 12, 1709, and the response, doc. 712, June 16, 1709.

[216] APEB Livro 17, doc 25, Petition of Col Garcia de Avila Pereira, April 20, 1722; in 1721, he had requested munitions to conduct a war against another indigenous group; Livro 19, doc 108, February 5, 1721.

of the Matto Grosso at the Cuiabá and nearby Coxipó Rivers, around 1718. Soon there was a gold rush, and by 1726, the newly founded town of had some 7,000 residents. This population included Portuguese and Paulistas as had the towns of Minas Gerais, and, like the mining district to the east, many African slaves – nearly half (2,600) the town's residents in 1726 were Africans.[217]

As happened in northern New Spain, the Portuguese and Paulista miners and their African and Carijó slaves soon met problems with the free associations through whose lands they traveled and into whose midst they settled. On the one hand, there were the Paiaguá, who lived on the banks of the rivers that penetrated the region, and who raided the new arrivals constantly. On the other hand, there were the Guiacurú, equestrian nomads, lancers, and raiders like the Toba, Abipone, and others to their south. In 1736, the two groups made an alliance that pestered the miners incessantly. Major campaigns were launched, villages raided and destroyed, but the Portuguese settlers were unable to make an effective defense.

In many ways the struggle over Paraguay and the larger watershed of the Rio de la Plata mirrored the conflict in the Amazon, as in both regions it matched settlers who had entered into mini-states and established an agricultural regime that was denounced by Jesuit priests. In Paraguay, however, the conflict between priest and settler was also an international one, between Spanish Jesuits and Portuguese bandeirantes, along with Spanish encomenderos.

We have already noted the presence of the development of the encomienda in Paraguay in describing its conquest in the sixteenth century. Spanish Jesuits who came to Paraguay in 1607 founded their first reduction, "after a year of incredible labor," in 1611. This reduction, San Ignacio, was among free associations who lived scattered in "forests, mountains and valleys and in hidden arroyos" in groups of "three, four, or six houses alone."[218] As we have already noted, Spanish penetration of the Rio de la Plata region resulted in the foundation of a strong alliance with the Guaraní around Asunción, and the development of a merger of the Guaraní (or Cario) elite with the Spanish soldiers through intermarriage. Jesuits believed that the labor system established by this elite was driving the indigenous people away from the church and leading to revolts like that of Calchaqui.[219] In addition to pressing for reforms in the system, the Jesuits also sought to establish a countersystem, primarily by working among communities that had not fallen under the control of Paraguay or Brazil, raiding from its base at São Paulo. The Spanish crown entrusted the

[217] A chronicle of events dated August 15, 1775 but making use of long-lost original documents, by Joseph Barbosa de Sa, "Relação dos povaçoens de Cuyabá e Mato groso de seos principios thé os prezentes tempos," *Anais da Biblioteca Nacional de Rio de Janeiro* 23 (1901), pp. 6 (first settlers) "both Paulistas and emboabas" et seq. A worthwhile summary of these events is found in Boxer, *Golden Age*, pp. 254–270, based largely on this, but also on other sources.

[218] Antonio Riuz de Montoya, *Conquista Espiritual hecha por los Religiosos de la Compañia de Jesus en las provincias del Paraguay, Paraná, Uruguay y Tape* (Madrid, 1639, mod. ed. Bilbao, 1892 [GB]), chapter 5, p. 29.

[219] Ruiz de Montoya, *Conquista*, chapters 7–8, pp. 35–44.

Jesuits with protecting this region, which they did in ways that differed substantially in details from the settlers in Asunción.

Many Guaraní communities opted to swear allegiance to Spain and accept Jesuit leadership in the confused period that followed the invasions of the bandeirantes, because the Jesuits could offer them protection from the bandeirantes. At the same time, the Jesuits, who denounced the *encomieda mitayo* system being practiced from Asunción-based Spanish-Guaraní mestizos as being exploitative prevented the expansion of this system into the region of Paraguay and organized their own province there.[220] As the pressure on these settlements increased in the early seventeenth century, the Jesuits provided arms and military direction, which made the settlements much more attractive and thus created a generation used to Jesuit discipline. In areas closer to the Spanish towns and settlers, Jesuits and settlers were often involved in conflicts over the management of these new and productive units.

The combination of the preference for people from free associations for liberty and that of the Jesuits for order produced the peculiar social structure of the reductions, a sort of seventeenth-century socialism in which resources were pooled and doled out according to the needs of the community, while a small committee dominated by a Jesuit priest and his closest associations made community decisions that were paternalistic but not democratic. Jesuit reductions, which numbered thirty-two in the late seventeenth century, were nominally run by the Fathers of the Company, but actually managed by the *curas*, their catechists. Family groups were assigned land in individual plots to meet their own subsistence needs, which they worked individually, as well as working up to three months a year on communal fields, the product of which was sometimes sold on the market and sometimes supplied the community. Profits were managed by the Jesuits for the benefit of the community. The system has sometimes been seen as a sort of benevolent communism and even a utopian society, and at other times an oppressive theocracy.[221]

NORTH AMERICA: THE "MIDDLE GROUND"

As English, Dutch, and French settlers established themselves along the east coast of North America and the St. Lawrence Valley, they pushed out the inhabitants of the mini-states that dotted the coast, or enfolded them within their frontier. Beyond the initial frontier, however, was the land of free associations, dominated by the Iroquoian-speaking Iroquois and Hurons and west of them Algonquian-speaking groups. In the mid-seventeenth century, the Iroquois underwent an explosive expansion. The League to which the Iroquois belonged provided a loosely organized but effective means of allowing the

---

[220] Ruiz de Montoya, *Conquista*, chapter 8, p. 40–42.
[221] See John Crocitti, "The Internal Economic Organization of the Jesuits among the Guarnai," *The International Social Science Review* (2002) for a vision from the later part of the period.

Iroquois to avoid internal conflicts and deflect their aggressions outward.[222] Whether they were provoked by a search for beaver skins to sell to Europeans, or whether they were engaging in Mourning Wars caused by conflicts internal to the region, they created a relentless expansion.[223] The possession of European firearms probably also contributed to their irresistible success.[224] Iroquois war parties smashed the Huron League and then turned west and to some degree south, moving through western Pennsylvania, to the circum-Great Lakes region. Jesuit missionaries witnessed the mini-states of the Illinois and their neighbors (including the ruins of the ancient city of Cahokia) in the 1680s just as Iroquois raids were crashing into them.

Refugees from the Iroquois campaigns often formed mixed groups, new "tribes" like the Shawnees or Trois-Rivières whose members spoke multiple languages and came from several different cultures. This disrupted space formed what Richard White has called aptly the "Middle Ground" – a region that was fully engaged with the settler world, for many of the refugees of the great Iroquois wars formed a triangle of defensive positions centered on the modern states of Michigan, Illinois, and Wisconsin.[225] Many "nations" inhabited this space; Bacqueville de La Potherie, who wrote of the region in the early eighteenth century, saw it as well populated, with each town (*bourgade*) located near the others. But they had come to peace with each other, in spite of "some wars."[226] To promote their defensive interests, they swore a nominal allegiance to France, as a way to counter Iroquois expansion. By 1701, when the Iroquois advance ran out of steam, "republics" of highly mixed groups under fluid leadership began to reoccupy the Ohio Valley, vacated by the people fleeing Iroquois expansion.[227] The Iroquois themselves, having absorbed thousands of captives, lost much of their ethnic identity.

Europeans and their American-born descendants made deep geographical penetrations into Native American societies and found that they could be accepted into the sort of society that was prepared to receive strangers. This created a series of Euro-American mixtures: the "squaw men" of the English frontier in North America, of the Franco-Huron *couriers de bois* who pioneered the French fur trade deep into North American – as far as the Mississippi Valley in the late seventeenth century.

[222] On the expansion, see Daniel Barr, *Unconquered: the Iroquois League at war in colonial America* (Greenwood, 2006), pp. 37–94.

[223] For a review, and the an interpretation based on cultural rather than economic movitations, see Brandão, *Fyre Shall Burn No More.*

[224] On the impact of European weapons and tactics, see Wayne E. Lee, "The Military Revolution of Native North America: Firearms, Forts, and Polities," in Lee, ed. *Empires and Indigenes*, pp. 49–79.

[225] Richard White, *The Middle Ground: Indians, Empires and Republics in the Great Lakes Region, 1650–1815* (Cambridge, 1991).

[226] Claude Charles le Roy, Sieur de Bacqueville de la Potherie, *Histoire de l'Amerique Septentrionale…* (4 vols., Paris, 1722), 2: 49.

[227] White, *Middle Ground*, pp. 1–49.

Most of these frontiersmen got their start in the fur trade, where they bought furs from Native American trappers and sold them to patrons from Europe. They were successful in interposing themselves as middlemen in this trade, and the companies that nominally employed them sought in vain to control their activities and engross their profits. While the first generation of these frontiersmen were European and very occasionally African, their descendants were mostly of mixed race, because the traders never generated enough profit to bring over European wives, and their frontier life did not lend itself to European-style marriages in any case. They were bilingual and often bicultural as well – perfect middlemen.[228]

French traders advanced into the Mississippi River system in the late seventeenth century, the celebrated voyages of the Sieur de la Salle, Jacques Marquette, and Louis Jolliet in the 1680s following earlier voyages of trade. The French subsequently consolidated their presence in the system by establishing small settlements in the Illinois country and then in Louisiana, first at Biloxi (now in Mississippi) in 1699 and later at other points near the mouth and the lower course of the Mississippi. The Louisiana settlement was in part to establish a presence on the Mississippi trade corridor and also to deter Spanish advances from Texas and Florida.[229] They also needed to deal with the English from Charleston, South Carolina (founded in 1670), who were advancing commercially at least into the Lower South in the early eighteenth century.

As French-speaking trappers and traders penetrated the Mississippi River system, Euro-American settlers were at the same time advancing up to the Ohio River, which lead to constant friction with the inhabitants of the area. These settlers, primarily from Virginia, who first dominated Kentucky and then moved into western Pennsylvania and the Ohio valley, adopted and imitated much of the wood lore and techniques of the Algonquians and Iroquois, and in many respects resembled them socially as well. They lived in compact, often fortified settlements, hunted deer for the skins (and also beavers to a lesser extent), and sought revenge as the best means of settling disputes. No single polity could claim control of the area, for the free associations could form leagues of a very tenuous sort, but certainly not enforce their power on anyone else, while neither France nor England (operating through the Iroquois) could demand the sort of obedience they hoped for in an area so far from their operational homeland, where they had to proceed with Native American support in war. The Virginians, for their part, operated far enough to the west that the authorities of Virginia could exercise no serious control over them, but among them many were "Indian haters" who would form no league with Algonquians or any other Native people, and yet were more at peace with each other.[230]

[228] White, *Middle Ground*, pp. 94–141.
[229] "Mémoire de la Coste de Floride et d'une partie du Mexique," (c. 1699) in Margry, *Establissments* 4: 308–323.
[230] White, *Middle Ground*, pp. 368–396.

Farther west lay undisrupted societies that were not yet in the state of flux that characterized the eastern regions, but from which groups like the Fox or the Sioux might intervene in Algonquian affairs.

This situation of flux and negotiation ended as the Virginians, and then other Anglo-American settlers, moved in toward the end of the eighteenth century. Indian hating as an ideology, plus their ultimate alliance to the stronger and more populous regions farther east, gave them an insuperable advantage in the disjointed politics of the "Middle Ground." Making no alliances, they were in perpetual war with the Native people, punctuated only by truces.[231] Initially, the indigenous societies of the Middle Ground were able to play off French and English ambitions against each other, but when France was defeated in the Seven Years' War (1756–1763), the English won a monopoly of diplomatic relations and sought to use it to their advantage.[232] The settler advance of the late eighteenth century could be temporarily held back, for the Algonquians, recognizing the unity of their foes, organized higher levels of unity themselves, sometimes defeating the Anglo-American settlers and backwoodsmen.[233] For all that, in the end, they were increasingly forced back and had to accept defeat or immigrate farther west, where the process would repeat itself until there was nowhere left to retreat.

THE LOWER SOUTH

The indigenous people of the Lower South were undergoing a major transformation as these European groups descended on them in the early eighteenth century. When Spanish explorers crossed the Lower South in the sixteenth century, they found Late Mississippian mini-states dominating the scene, as de Soto's adventures of the 1540s revealed. But the social organization that French, English, and later Spanish knew was far more egalitarian. How this transformation took place is still a mystery, for the evidence, locked in archaeology, is ambiguous. Many scholars look to the transformation as taking place as a result of European actions, either the early Spanish entradas, or the development of the substantial slave trade that followed the English occupation of South Carolina in 1670, as well as other ecological and epidemiological catastrophes the followed. Robbie Ethridge has described the phenomena as a "shatter zone" in which societies were broken and transformed into weaker and more vulnerable polities.[234] While this interpretation certainly has weight,

[231] Daniel K. Richter, *Facing East from Indian Country: A Native History of Early America* (Cambridge, MA, 2001). pp. 189–236.

[232] Francis Jennings, *Ambiguous Iroquois Empire*, pp. 275–309; White, *Middle Ground*, pp. 413–470.

[233] Gregory Evans Dowd, *A Spirited Resistance*, for an account of these attempts and unity and their problems.

[234] For an examination of the idea of fundamental transformation, see Robbie Ethridge and Charles Hudson, eds., *The Transformation of the Southeastern Indians, 1540–1760* (Jackson, 2002); Eric Browne, *The Westo Indians: Indian Slave Traders of the Early Colonial South* (Tuscaloosa, 2005), pp. 4–8.

one cannot entirely ignore the possibility of internally generated issues, or that for the average inhabitant of the Mississippian world, decentralized societies might have offered attractive possibilities of equality and justice, if counterbalanced by warfare. This region had experienced previous cycles of instability, and in any case the start of the transformation of the larger Mississippian culture predated the Spanish arrival. Whatever the cause, however, the Creeks, Choctaws, and other groups were more like free associations in their social organization as described in the eighteenth century than like mini-states.

From the late seventeenth century onward, indigenous rivalries interlaced with those of Europeans: the Spanish in Florida (including the southern part of modern-day Georgia), the French in Alabama and Louisiana, and the English in South Carolina all had concluded alliances with indigenous people, both to thwart hostile intentions of their European rivals and to capture Native Americans to serve as slaves in their growing economies. In the late seventeenth and early eighteenth centuries, most armed forces undertaking warfare on behalf of European objectives involved many more indigenous than European fighters.

Warfare and enslavement probably played a role in this transformation, and all Europeans took advantage of this, particularly the English from Charleston. The English of South Carolina engaged in a lively slave trade with the Caribbean from early in the days of the colony, typically by purchasing the captives taken by their Native American allies in local wars.[235] The cause of these wars is not easy to determine; for example, an inquest into a war between the Cherokees and Yuchi in 1710, investigated by a commission in 1714, was told by some that slave traders incited the war, but by others that the governor of South Carolina sent a paper ordering it, and yet others claimed that there was a long-standing grievance between the two groups.[236] When d'Iberville arrived at Biloxi to make a foundation in 1700, he learned that the English were accompanying a Chickasaw party "and they make war on all the other nations to carry away as many slaves as they can, which they [the English] buy and do a great commerce in, which has ruined all the Savage nations."[237]

One result, as farther north, was the breaking of some groups, and consolidation of others. Le Page du Pratz, surveying the ethnic situation around Louisiana around 1750, observed that hospitality often allowed nations to ally, or to be accepted within another nation. If a nation with 2,000 warriors were to pursue another with only 500, but if the weaker group were to be accepted in alliance with a group allied with the stronger nation, it would abandon its

---

[235] Alan Galley, *The Indian Slave Trade: The Rise of the English Empire in the American South 1670–1717* (New Haven, 2002).

[236] W. L. McDowell, ed., *Journals of the Commissioners of the Indian Trade, September 20, 1710–August 29, 1718* (Columbia, 1955), 53–56. The testimony includes several Native Americans and some traders. The board of trade was interested in discrediting private merchants and traders, and held that traders incited wars that disturbed their trade.

[237] "Journal du voyage du chevalier d'Iberville sur le vasseau de Roi la *Renommé*, em 1699..." in Margry, *Etablissments* 4: 406. Later the group passed five villages destroyed by the wars; p. 407.

pursuit by reason of the rule of hospitality.[238] This situation had produced a large group of mixed and refugee nations.

In any case, the French and the English made alliances a keystone of not only their attempts to engross the lucrative trade in deerskins, but also to prevent the strategic plans of their rivals (and among the English this was often rivalries between North and South Carolinas, or Virginia). But it also involved the complex politics of the local groups as well. The Yamasee War of 1715–1716, for example, involved a confederation of former English allies against South Carolina, and was broken when the Cherokees, who had initially cooperated with their longtime rivals, changed sides. While the Iroquois explosion shaped the history of the Midwest, the rivalry between the Cherokee and the Creeks, shadowing that between the French and the English dominated the south.

---

[238] Le Page du Pratz, *Histoire de la Louisiane* 2: 244.

PART IV

CULTURE TRANSITION AND CHANGE

The Atlantic World was a great mixer of cultures. People from four continents met in a broad variety of settings and circumstances and exchanged a wide range of cultural ideas and practices. In addition to the changes induced by inter-action, many Atlantic people also moved from familiar home environments to ones that were quite unfamiliar, and in the process were forced to make adapta-tions that shaped a new worldview. Others – most Europeans, some Africans, and many Native Americans – remained at home and accepted input from outsiders.

Cultural change is erratic in any case, arising from the inner workings of a society as well as from interaction, all stimulated further by movement and envi-ronmental change. We can divide cultural elements into a number of categories as a means of understanding this change. There are some elements of culture that are "hard" – that is, they are difficult to change, and typically break before they are much altered. Language is the best example of a hard cultural element that changes very slowly and is ill-suited for much cultural exchange. On the other hand, there are elements of culture that are "soft," which can change rap-idly and are very open to absorbing new ideas and elements. Aesthetics, such as art and music, are the most malleable and open cultural element. In between these two extremes lies religion, worldview, and philosophy, which people are often committed to for ideological reasons, but which are nevertheless subject to change if it can be managed within the rules of the system.

While hardness or softness are important first elements to consider in study-ing cultural change in the Atlantic world, there are other considerations as well. One of these is the degree to which population transfer occurs in such a way as to preserve communities. For example, the controlled movement of freeborn families, voluntarily transferring themselves from western England to New England in the seventeenth century, was likely to preserve a great deal of the existing culture, with change taking place mostly as a result of the new environment, economic transformations following the movement, and the interaction with Native Americans.

On the other hand, the transfer of millions of Africans to America during the slave trade did very little to preserve community. Africans became slaves through the disruption of war, rarely traveled as families, and were often set-tled into environments where they were forced to live in close proximity with people of quite different cultures. Furthermore, they were subject to a harsh social regime that sometimes actively sought to modify their culture and other times limited cultural activities by rules designed to prevent revolt or enhance work performance. Clearly the two groups would have different cultural pro-cesses and different degrees of influence.

Of course, there were groups that did not move at all. Many indigenous people of the Americas, even when conquered, remained fixed in their ancestral communities, Europeans for the most part did not leave their home continent, and a great many Africans received influences from abroad while remaining at home. For these people change took place in different ways within a community that had all the possibilities of retaining its past, even though it was still, to a greater or lesser degree, obliged or invited to adjust to new cultural elements.

Moreover, there is also a question of power, coercion, and culture change. Scholars today have noted that many elements of culture are shaped by relations between social classes, political power, and ethnic domination, where these ele-ments play an important role. A good number of scholars have argued, as Arnold Bauer has recently done in a carefully documented and presented study, that in the conquest societies of Latin America, the Spanish sought to distance them-selves from the indigenous peoples and thus resisted whatever temptation there might be to eat their food, use their ceramics, dress in their manner, or share in their artistic culture. Slaveholders in the Caribbean, Brazil, or North America are likewise sometimes held to have been engaged in a program of deculturation, and survival or continuation of African culture can be seen as an act of resistance. As we have seen, there were many areas of cultural interaction – for example, in the contact zones, where no such program of cultural maintenance or domination was possible. Moreover, it is worth noting that in conquered areas, the Europeans had to maintain long-standing alliances with many various indigenous people; indeed, the significance of these alliances, as we shall see, was important even at the end of the colonial period. Even in the slave colonies, especially ones like the Caribbean regions, Europeans needed the cooperation of a significant number of the slaves themselves to maintain their authority.

More significant still, any act of deculturation requires considerable effort and expense, and while Europeans, particularly those of the higher elite, wished to show their status in terms that would be recognized by their European peers, their primary goal in their relations with the lower classes was to extract labor and ensure security, to which deculturation was a casually considered and inconsistently applied idea. The Spanish, for example, were anxious to use at least some of their power in conquest to change the religion of the people they conquered; masters at times wanted to alter the culture of the slaves they owned. The element of forced cultural change must therefore join the more benign internal mechanisms of change or the type of changes that took place with people exchanging ideas and items through their encounter.

8

Transfer and Retention in Language

Languages are hard cultural elements because they are complex systems of representation that take a long time to learn and rely on a high degree of uniformity to work. Language occupies a significant portion of the brain's stored memory, and research indicates that it is most efficiently and effectively learned before one is twelve years old. Even good speakers who learn a language after twelve store the new language in a different way in the brain than those who learn it earlier, suggesting that language acquisition is more complex than learning many other skills. Furthermore, learning a new language later in life is difficult and rarely completely mastered. Even though most people are capable of learning new languages even when they are quite old, they are unlikely to speak the new languages with native levels of proficiency.[1] Language change rarely takes place, therefore, within one generation, for the effort of replacement is very large and not very productive. People may learn a new language and speak it every day, but they are unlikely to forget their original language, and in most cases will revert to it when circumstances permit.

Language change takes place, rather, between generations, when children are acquiring their language for the first time. Children can acquire more than one language at a time and still achieve native levels of proficiency, so it is possible for children in a multilingual setting to become multilingual themselves and communicate freely in both or even more languages. If there are strong pressures to speak just one of the several languages, however, they may abandon their own multilingualism with their children, thus making a new generation that is monolingual. A model of three-generation complete change (immigrant speakers of one language, bilingual children, and monolingual grandchildren

---

[1] K. H. S. Kim, N. R. Relkin, N., R. de La Paz., and K.-M. Lee, "Localization of Cortical Areas Activated by Native and Second Languages with Functional Magnetic Resonance Imaging (fMRI)," *Proceedings of the International Society for Magnetic Resonance Imaging* 1 (1996), 283; D. Perani, E. Paulesu, N. S. Galles, et al., "The bilingual brain. Proficiency and age of acquisition of the second language," *Brain* 121 (1998): 1841–1852.

in a different language) thus makes sense, and is widely observed in immigrant communities in modern days.

RETENTION AND LOSS AND EUROPEAN SETTLERS

The colonization of North America forms a good model for the survival of language in a setting of immigration. There was a distinctive pattern among European immigrants to North America, especially to the "poor" regions north of the Chesapeake where there were relatively few African slaves, and where the Native American population was displaced rather than ruled. David Hackett Fisher, in an important study of cultural continuity and change among English settlers in North America, points out that it is possible to argue that not only did the English who came to America in the seventeenth and eighteenth centuries preserve English as their language (no surprise), but even that they retained local dialects from their home districts. This was because, as Fisher argued, immigration from England was remarkably homogeneous, and thus not only language and dialect were preserved, but large elements of other aspects of culture from family structure and life ways to architecture and even food. In making this argument, he revived an older historiographic tradition known as Germ theory (which has nothing to do with disease) that argues that American culture derived from more or less undisturbed English culture transferred as a block across the ocean.

Fisher's argument relies heavily on the concepts of cultural conservatism and defines four regions that transferred not only language but many other folkways. These regions were: the New Englanders who immigrated from eastern regions of England; the colonists of the Chesapeake Bay region who arrived from the southern part of England; people of the Delaware River valley who traveled from the Midlands regions; and finally the Scotch-Irish from the Scotch and Irish borderlands, who settled the vast western region of the Appalachian highlands.[2]

Fisher's approach has been sharply criticized on a variety of fronts, especially that it seems to give too much credit to the founders of the regions and pays too little attention to non-English settlers (especially to Germans in the Delaware Valley, Dutch in New York, and Africans in Virginia), but there is something to be said for one of its underlying concepts. That is, that European immigration, at least to poor North America, did link fairly distinctive European cultures to American regions through patterns of immigration. Furthermore, even though these patterns sometimes involved different gender rates (for example, in some areas, men arrived in large numbers and were only followed by women) in the longer run, they tended to produce large, multi-settlement communities of people from similar cultural and linguistic backgrounds from a restricted European source.

---

[2] David Hackett Fisher, *Albion's Seed: Four British Folkways in British America* (Oxford, 1989), pp. 9–12, methodological considerations, 57–62 (Massachusetts), 256–264 (Chesapeake), 470–475 (Delaware Valley), 652–655 (Backcountry [Appalachian]).

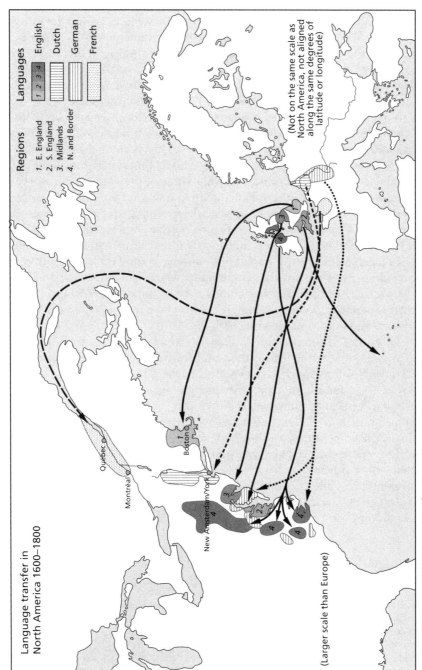

Language transfer in
North America 1600–1800

Regions
1. E. England
2. S. England
3. Midlands
4. N. and Border

Languages
1 2 3 4 English
Dutch
German
French

(Not on the same scale as
North America, not aligned
along the same degrees of
latitude or longitude)

(Larger scale than Europe)

Québec

Montréal

Boston

New Amsterdam/York

MAP 9. European Languages in the Americas.

The English colonization of North America was paralleled by the French colonization of the Saint Lawrence valley in Canada between 1608 and the British takeover in 1763 when Canada had some 80,000 inhabitants of European descent.[3] Like the Chesapeake group in English North America, this was composed of fairly wealthy members of the lesser nobility or some better-placed merchants and the lower classes following as indentured servants, typically from the same home areas in the north of France. The crown made generous grants to the elite settlers, called, using feudal terminology, *seigneuries*, whose recipients were then obligated to build mills, establish householders to farm the land, and provide for some public services. The commoners, called *habitants*, were essentially indentured servants.[4] Males considerably outnumbered females, almost two to one at first, but while some of the French who worked as fur traders lived outside the valley and often married the Native American daughters of their trading partners, most of the *habitants* settled on farmsteads in the valley and married women of French heritage, and in this way transported French culture more or less intact to their new Canadian home. A small group of French colonists also settled in Louisiana in the early eighteenth century, providing a nucleus for that community, which had somewhat less that 10,000 by the end of their domain in 1803.[5] A few hundred Frenchmen along with their slaves also occupied "Illinois country" (at their two settlements of Cahokia and Kaskaskia) in the same period.[6]

Not long after the founding of French Canada, the Dutch West India Company began the settlement of thousands of people from the Netherlands in the Hudson Valley and East Jersey during the period between 1614 and 1664.[7] The West India Company also provided generous land grants to its wealthier backers, called *patroons*, and they also arranged for settlement from their home areas. Not all the commoners who entered the colony were Dutch; Isaac Jogues, a Jesuit who wrote a description of the colony in 1646, reported that no less that eighteen languages were spoken in the colony (presumably including non-European ones).[8] While many came from German-speaking parts of the Rhine Valley or from the Baltic region and speaking Scandinavian languages, Dutch was generally the language of daily life, and the non-Dutch speakers did not form communities of their own, but lived among the Dutch.

---

[3] Population data is summarized in the Census of Canada; see http://www.statcan.gc.ca/pub/98–187-x/4151287-eng.htm#2

[4] Richard C. Harris, *The Seigneurial System in Early Canada: A Geographical Study* (Madison and Québec, 1966); for a more dynamic study, see Louise Duchêne, "L'évolution du régime seigneurial au Canada aux XVIIᵉ et XVIIIᵉ siècles," *Recherches Sociographiques* 12 (1971): 143–183.

[5] Marcel Giraud, *A History of French Louisiana* (tr. Brian Pierce, 5 vols., Baton Rouge, 1991 [French original, 1966]).

[6] Carl Ekberg, *French Roots in the Illinois Country: The Mississippi Frontier in Colonial Times* (Champaign-Urbana, 2000).

[7] Jaap Jacobs, *New Netherland: A Dutch Colony In Seventeenth-Century America* (Leiden, 2005).

[8] Isaac Jogues, "Nouum Belgium" (August 3, 1646), *JR* 28: 106–107.

Dutch immigration did not stop even when the English took over the colony and renamed it New York in 1664, when the population was around 9,000, although it did slow appreciably.

In 1655, the Dutch West India Company absorbed the colony founded by the Swedish West India Company in Delaware (New Sweden), whose own settlers were Swedish with a substantial number of Finnish colonists as well. The Dutch governor at the time, Pieter Stuyvesant, allowed them to continue as a self-governing community, called the Swedish Nation, under the domination of the West India Company, an arrangement that was only terminated when the English took over and granted William Penn control over this region.[9] Penn then put an end to the legal status of the Swedish Nation in 1681, although this did not stop immigration from Sweden (including Finland) for some time to come.

In each of these cases, the settlers were originally promoted by organizations that used the primary language of the government's home country as their official language. However, in addition to these Europeans, the colonial period witnessed large-scale settlement by Germans in North America, even though no German state or chartered company sponsored a colony there. From the very beginning Germans came to colonies where other languages were the governmental tongues and the language of official business as well as that of a number of the other settlers. Although, as noted already, Germans came to New Netherlands under Dutch sponsorship, they did not form separate communities in that region. However, when William Penn founded Philadelphia in 1688, he consciously sponsored significant German colonization, and this group came more or less as a block, as if the colony were their own. A smaller group also settled in South Carolina, where at least for a time, they also formed a block of German-speakers in an English colony. Subsequent migrations took these Germans, many of whom came to America to seek religious liberty and came from a wide variety of Pietist churches (Brethren, Moravians, Amish, and Mennonite) but were also accompanied by many Lutheran Germans who spread beyond their primary core east of Philadelphia, to eastern and central Maryland and ultimately also into Ohio.[10]

What all these groups had in common was that they came in sufficient numbers from sufficiently homogeneous backgrounds that they formed whole communities – not just villages but groups of interlocked and networked villages that allowed them to retain and preserve their original culture. Even the German settlers typically founded all-German communities, and even tended

---

[9] Amandus Johnson, *Swedish Settlements on the Delaware* (2 vols., 1911). In spite of its age, this study, which focuses in detail on the European immigration, is still the best study of the colony, based on a careful reading of a wide range of original sources.

[10] For a good overview of settlements and motivations, see Aaron Spencer Fogelman, *Hopeful Journeys: German Immigration, Settlement and Political Culture in Colonial America, 1717–1775* (Philadelphia, 1996); see also A. G. Roeber, *Palatines, Liberty, and Property: German Lutherans in Colonial British America* (Baltimore, 1993) and Marianne S. Wokeck, *Trade in Strangers: The Beginnings of Mass Migration to North America* (State College, 1999).

to concentrate from the same German subregions; it was not unusual for one group of settlers to send letters back to Europe to encourage others from their home area to follow. At other times, Germans, upon arriving in Philadelphia, would search for compatible communities of Germans in the counties lying to the west until they found one that suited them.[11]

However, in the case of all of the later settlers just cited here, they were subsequently encapsulated in colonies that were ruled by people who spoke other languages, and in all cases here, the other language was English. English-speakers took over New Amsterdam (New York) in 1664, New France (Canada) in 1763, and Louisiana in 1803. In the case of the Germans in Pennsylvania, South Carolina, and Maryland, English-speakers ruled the colony from the very beginning of the colonial movement.

The change in sovereignty might have made little difference initially. In each case the English agreed to respect local law and custom and in general inter-fere little with the daily life and local government of the communities of the Hudson Valley, St. Lawrence, Pennsylvania, or Louisiana. For the most part, the English governments honored these promises, thus creating a European multicultural contact.

The first generation of settlers in encapsulated communities would not give up their language, of course, because they arrived as adults and were unlikely to be able to learn English at the same level of comfort they enjoyed in German, Dutch, Swedish, or Finnish. But their children, like the children of many immi-grant communities in many other times and places, had the opportunity in their language-learning years to take up the dominant language. Thus, in the-ory at least, the language could take the three-generations-to-extinction path, as children might become bilingual in their parents' language and English, and their children would be monolingual in English. However, in the encapsulated communities, the transition from bilingual to monolingual in English was greatly slowed and even halted when the community was large enough that people could marry and conduct the vast majority of their business with others of their language group. In many areas, the original language was retained this way for a very long time, and only in the Hudson Valley was it lost completely by everyone. The loss of Dutch in the Hudson is an interesting study for it reveals patterns that will apply not only in the other areas, but also to other groups, such as Native Americans and Africans.

The long-term preservation of Dutch relied on two things: (1) the size and integration of the Dutch-speaking community, so that people would normally interact and intermarry others who spoke their language; and (2) the degree to which community members were isolated from regular interaction with English-speakers. In the case of the Dutch in the Hudson Valley, these condi-tions were met through the eighteenth century, but rapidly lost later. Initially, the Dutch peasants lived on large farms that produced surpluses for interna-tional sale. Sales from New York went to faraway places, including Europe and

[11] Fogelman, *Hopeful Journeys*, pp. 69–99.

the Caribbean, and Dutch merchants often managed a great deal of it, in spite of laws passed from time to time in England to restrict the colonial trade to English territories and English merchants.[12] These farming communities produced much of what they consumed in their own communities. Thus, when Peter Kalm visited New York and Pennsylvania in 1748–1749, he noted that most of the Dutch in the Hudson valley spoke Dutch among themselves, even though many must have been living in the third generation and even at the start of the fourth generation since the colony became English. In Albany, the heart of the rural Dutch settlement, it was the dominant language; only the soldiers of the garrison were English-speakers.[13]

While the retention of Dutch, perhaps even as the only language, by small farmers in the Hudson Valley might be expected from the size of the community, matters were different for the elite. They had a large international business, and a need to communicate with their English neighbors and business partners, and thus quickly took up English. Many of the more prominent Dutch farmers and merchants deliberately sent their children to English-language schools in order that they acquire native proficiency in English. Within a generation of the political change, the Dutch elite was bilingual, using English in their business dealings but Dutch with their farm workers and small farming neighbors. Daily interaction was the key. Kalm noted that Dutch was starting to yield to English even among nonelites in towns where there was a great deal of interaction, such as on rural Staten Island where the Dutch and English had settled among each other, and while the older generation spoke mostly Dutch in Kalm's day (though they might understand English), the children were much more inclined to speak English and indeed took affront, as Kalm heard it, at being called Dutchmen.[14]

As English settlement along the Hudson increased, however, more and more small farmers found themselves living close to English neighbors, and even farm workers and members of the lower class found work in English businesses. The situation that Kalm observed in Staten Island gradually came to the fore in these later years. Consequently, their need to speak at least rudimentary English increased, and this in turn put a premium on their ensuring that their children, the group most fit and capable of learning a new language at native levels of proficiency, learned English while young. As more and more people became bilingual, the need to retain Dutch was lost. A sizable number of people found that they could dispense with Dutch as a second language, either because they had no Dutch-speaking partners or because their Dutch-speaking partners could manage in English. As a result of this, and increasing English-language education as compulsory schooling developed in the valley, Dutch

---

[12] This international commerce is studied in detail in Claudia Schnurmann, *Atlantische Welten: Engländer und Niederländer im amerianisch-atlantischen Raum, 1648–1713* (Cologne, 1998).

[13] Peter Kalm, *Travels into North America* (tr. John Reinhold Forster, 2nd ed., 2 vols., London, 1773) 2: 100–101.

[14] Kalm, *Travels* 1: 183, 210–211.

was lost and by 1850 was spoken by only a handful of elderly people, often even then as a second language.

German might have suffered a similar fate in Pennsylvania, had it not been for unusual circumstances. Like the Dutch, the Germans had to deal with their English neighbors and business partners in an export-oriented economy, and like them also they found more English interpenetration with their communities as settlement density increased in their most thickly populated areas. In the late eighteenth century, most Germans, like their Dutch cousins farther north, had become bilingual in English and German. Also like the Dutch, many of the Germans eventually abandoned German entirely in favor of English.

The Amish and Mennonite communities formed a partial exception to this rule. They came from communities that had been isolated and persecuted in Germany and Switzerland, and had become intensely reclusive as a matter of practical necessity, which in turn had become internalized in their theology. They turned away from all but minimum interactions with their English-speaking neighbors, and chose to develop far more inward-looking communities, building their own schools and refusing to participate in the affairs of the larger community beyond the minimum. As a result, the "Pennsylvania Dutch" came to be known not only for their habits of rejecting many modern innovations and practicing an extreme cultural conservatism – dressing, for example, in clothing of the early eighteenth century until the present day – but also by retaining German as their home language and the language of religious worship. In this way a small segment of the German community retained its language (along with other elements of German culture) in an environment that would otherwise have led to its rapid assimilation along the lines of the Dutch in the Hudson Valley.

The encapsulated French in the Saint Lawrence form a variant pattern, for despite being under English control since 1763, French continues in the region to this day, and is, if anything, increasing rather than declining in usage. The English, there as in the Hudson, made generous concessions to the French residents on legal, religious, and linguistic grounds. The French-speaking community in Québec was large enough, both in its numbers and its territorial extent, and internally integrated enough that English never became the dominant language, and French was retained comfortably into the twenty-first century. As English made incursions in the twentieth century, it was met with an emotional defense of the French language that continues to shape Canadian politics to the present day.

The exigencies of commerce and community might not always decide the language factor in favor of the colonial language. In the Danish West Indies, for example, the administration and the settlers were essentially from different linguistic worlds. The island colonies had been founded for Denmark, as so many other such colonies had, by Dutch capital on the move. Although Danes were among the earliest settlers on the islands, the bulk of the settlers came from Dutch- and English-speaking areas. Much of the island's commerce, including a good deal of the slave trade, was handled by English and Dutch concerns, and therefore it was an advantage to keep those languages in the mix. The first newspapers published in these islands were in English and Dutch, and the two languages survived very well for a long time, even though all official correspondence (after the early years) was in Danish. Even the colonial language of the slaves was not Danish, but a creole with Dutch and English elements. More widespread use of Danish only came with mass educational systems in the nineteenth century, and when the islands passed over to U.S. administration in 1917, Danish was soon replaced by English.

The island of Aruba forms a distinctly different pattern. It was originally inhabited by Caqueitos whose closest relatives lived in nearby Venezuela; the Spanish removed the original inhabitants in the sixteenth century, but later on replaced them with more people of the same background. In 1636, the Dutch West India company occupied the islands in order to protect the strategic and more productive island of Curaçao from potential Spanish attack. When the Dutch pirate Exquemelin visited the island around 1671, he reported an interesting situation in which a small Dutch garrison ("a sergeant who acts as governor and 15 soldiers") occupied one settlement, while the rest of the island "is inhabited by Indians who speak Spanish, and in matters of religion remain under the Spanish," who sent a priest to the island to maintain them in the faith.[15] This situation remained more or less stable over the intervening years, especially as the West India Company discouraged any further settlement on the island, which thus remained essentially in the hands of Spanish-speaking indigenous people. In the later eighteenth century, settlers did arrive, primarily from Curaçao, where a local creole language today known as Papiamento, also based on Spanish and Portuguese, had developed. Aruban Papiamento thus became the ordinary language of the population, although Dutch was always the official language, and the situation remains so up to the present day.[16]

LANGUAGES AT HOME: THE FATE OF AFRICAN AND AMERICAN LANGUAGES IN CONQUESTS

If the development of a speech community was critical to the survival of a language or its loss, clearly those people who were conquered or lived in the zones of contact continued speaking their original languages. Thus, Nahua, the language of the Aztecs, or Quechua, the speech of the Incas, were continued by the vast majority of the population in areas that fell to Spanish conquest. Their further retention, however, followed many of the same rules that governed the European languages arriving in North America. When business dealings and multilingual settlement favored it, people would become bilingual, sometimes eventually abandoning their ancestral languages.

---

[15] Exquemelin, *Zee-rovers*, p. 94. The English translation (p. 112) is very misleading, leaving out sections and mistranslating others.

[16] See Jan Hartog, *History of Aruba* (1953), for the linguistic history.

From very early on, the cacique class in both New Spain and Peru learned Spanish and soon had their children educated to native levels of proficiency in it. Those that remained in rural areas with few Spanish settlers and links might need to retain native proficiency in their original languages as well, to communicate with their subjects. Likewise, those thousands of indigenous people who left rural areas to live in Spanish towns needed to learn rudimentary Spanish to survive, and their children were inclined just as rapidly to learn it as their first, and perhaps, if they had severed their ties to their home areas, their only language. In such settings, social pressures actually favored complete language change in two rather than three generations.

Spanish policy and economic reality tended to reinforce the linguistic isolation of rural Native Americans, by restricting Spanish settlement and creating fairly large zones that were locally autonomous and thus had little need to communicate with Spanish-speaking people beyond the elite level. The distinction between rich areas where there were many Spanish settlers concentrated in blocks, and poor areas where there were few, if any, Spaniards and they were not so concentrated is crucial. It is not surprising that in some rural communities, records were kept in the local languages such as Nahua, various Mayan languages, and Mixtec. This was not only true in the Nahua or Mayan-speaking areas that had a tradition of literacy and records keeping (although they changed the system of writing from a glyphic to an alphabetic system), but it was also true in Peru, where there was no tradition of literacy. Quechua became a written language and some amount of records keeping was done in it during the colonial period.

In areas where local languages survived in situations of conquest, however, they did undergo changes. James Lockhart has investigated these changes for a number of American languages and revealed a consistent pattern for all of them that may have wider implications. In the first stage of contact, he noted in his classic study of Nahua, the language first provided interpretations within Nahua vocabulary for a number of words from Spanish for what were to them exotic items, such as horses, steel, firearms, and a number of new plants and animals. These were awkward words that combined Nahua roots to create new words. The first phase did not last long, however, and the Spanish versions of the words were borrowed into Nahua, after being modified to fit Nahua phonology and grammatical requirements.

The first phase, then, essentially amounted to borrowing nouns that name items the Aztecs had never seen before, like steel or horses. But this phase was followed, after about half a century, by a new phase in which more Spanish words, especially nouns but often also verbs, were borrowed, to describe not only new material items, but also terms of constant interaction, such as terms for trading, tax paying, and religious duties that had Nahua equivalents. In a final stage, in the eighteenth century, the language borrowed widely from Spanish all parts of speech and a wide range of interactions. Lockhart followed this detailed study up with a briefer one in which he sought, quite successfully, to show that a similar pattern had been followed in Quechua and Maya.[17]

At the same time that these Native languages were undergoing change, they were also expanding in scope and breadth. Missionaries used Nahua in Mexico and Quechua in Peru in their catechisms, and were likely to use them in as many areas as possible, baring the necessary linguistic work to produce materials in many minor American languages. Many communities that had not spoken these languages found it to their advantage to learn them and to educate their children in them. As a result, they became simplified in the way that linguas franca often do, and were spoken much more widely than they ever had been in the precolonial period.

In some rural areas, the isolation was sufficiently strong that the Spanish who lived there underwent pressure to change languages. The Maya areas provide an excellent example. Unlike Mexico and Peru, the Maya region of Central America did not develop the sort of export products that would attract large numbers of European settlers. Those that did come, mostly encomienda holders from the era of conquest (which proceeded very slowly in any case, lasting until the 1690s), were unable to attract European females to marry them. As a result, the Spanish population rapidly became racially mixed as Spanish settlers married into the Maya cacique class, and then their children married among themselves. Only priests and a handful of top officials were biologically European, and they usually did not remain in the region more than their term of service, or did not leave children behind them.

As a result, many of the settlers, forced to deal with native workers and peasants in a stable encomienda system, found advantages in being bilingual. Children of the original Spanish settlers were thus not only racially mixed but were usually bilingual, learning their Mayan from their mothers. Indeed, Spanish officials often complained that the local landowners spoke much better Mayan than Spanish, or argued that they could not understand them. Testimony from the eighteenth century made it clear that virtually all business conducted orally was done in Maya, Spanish being reserved for written discourse, and even there, a good deal of literature in Maya does exist from this period. They were also concerned about local officials holding meetings of town councils and keeping records in a language that they could not understand.[18]

A similar situation arose in southern Brazil and Paraguay, where, although there was a conquest, the lack of a revenue-generating export product kept European women out. The settlers of São Paulo married women or took concubines from among the local Tupi-speaking elite population, whose subjects served as the labor force on their estates and the armed forces in their military

---

[17] James Lockhart, *The Nahuas after the Conquest: A Social and Cultural History of the Indians of Central* Mexico (Stanford, 1992).

[18] On the language situation, see Nancy Farriss, *Maya Society Under Colonial Rule: The Collective Enterprise of Survival* (Princeton, 1984), pp. 97–114; for detailed study of the Maya literature, see Matthew Restall, *Maya Conquistador* (Boston, 1998).

expeditions. Like the Spanish settlers of the Yucatán, the Paulistas became bilingual, learning Tupi as their first language from their mothers and Portuguese mostly for conducting business. Fernão Cardim, writing about Brazil in 1570, noted that while all the Portuguese who came to Brazil and had dealings with the indigenous people learned to speak Tupi, "the children of the Portuguese born here, both men and women, speak it better than Portuguese, especially in the Captaincy of São Vicente [of which São Paulo was the most important settlement]."[19] A visitor in 1610 noted that the population of São Paulo was "mostly mamelucos [mixed-race descendants of Portuguese and Carijos] and rarely Portuguese."[20] The Jesuit missionary Antonio Vieira observed in the 1680s that Tupi was still the language of most homes in São Paulo, and the children only learned Portuguese in school.[21] Domingos Jorge Velho, the famous Paulista who brought his private army up to the northeast to fight against the Tapuya, the runaway state of Palmares, and clear the region for cattle raising in 1685, had to bring an interpreter with him, as no one could understand his Portuguese, a distant second language to him.[22] Jesuits taught Tupi in the missions, and at least some Tupi learned to write in it. When the Dutch invaded Brazil in 1630, some of the Tupi-speaking subjects went over to them, while others remained loyal to Portugal. Felipe Camarão, a famous Tupi leader, wrote a series of letters in 1645 to Pedro (Pieter) Poti, another leader who had taken up the Dutch cause, berating him for his decision and threatening him, to which Poti replied in kind. The letters, written in Tupi and preserved in the Dutch archives, are a remarkable testimony to the extent to which Tupi had become a written language.[23]

The Spanish who settled in Asunción, the root of the colony of Rio de la Plata (modern-day Uruguay, Paraguay, and Argentina), intermarried so quickly into the indigenous Cario ruling class, and were joined by so few Spanish women, that they can be regarded as much Cario as Spanish culturally. Spanish took a back seat to Guarani, a language so closely related to the Tupi of Brazil that a common lingua franca, called "lingua geral" (general language), grew up as an amalgam of several of the dialects. The Jesuits taught lingua geral in their schools, and it became a written language in which a certain amount of local records were kept. A visiting inspector, sent in 1744 to investigate the impact of a law requiring the speaking of Spanish in all the colonies, reported "the customs and language of the Spaniards born here, as well as that of the Negroes

[19] Cardim, *Tratados*, p. 170–171.
[20] Jacomé Monteiro, "Relação da provincial do Brasil," in Serafim Leite *Historia da Compania de Jesus no Brasil* (10 vols., Lisbon, 1938–1950) 8: 395.
[21] Antonio Vieira, 1694, quoted in Cheryl Jensen, "Tupi-Granarí," in R. M. W. Dixon and Alexandra Aikhenvald, eds. *The Amazonian Languages* (Cambridge, 1999) p. 127, n. 5.
[22] Bishop of Pernambuco to Junta das Missões, May 18, 1697, in Erneso Eannes, *As guerras nos Palmares* (Lisbon, 1938), p. 353.
[23] The letters were published and translated in Pedro Souto Maior, *Fastos Pernambucano* (Rio de Janeiro, 1913), pp. 149–153.

and mulattoes, of which there are many, is that of the Indians, with few differences." A Jesuit resident observed the same thing: everywhere Guaraní was spoken in lieu of Spanish, and in rural areas "no one knows another language other
than that of the Indians."[24] The Scotch merchant James Robertson, ascending
the Paraná River in 1811, noted that upon reaching Corrientes, Guaraní had
superseded Spanish and "excepting the better classes of men, few speak that
language [Spanish] with either fluency or propriety." The women barely spoke
it at all, preferring Guaraní "in which they are very eloquent."[25]

The province of Tucumán between Paraguay and Peru was largely the land
of Quechua, this having replaced local languages slowly, but Spanish seemed to
have flourished, for Carrio de la Vandera, crossing it in the 1770s, noted that the
women "speak Quechua when dealing with their children, but speak Castillian
without any throwbacks [*resabio*], something which I have not encountered
in the people of New Spain and much less those of Peru."[26] Perhaps this was
a reflection of the presence of many humble Spaniards among the population and the majority status of mixed-race gauchos among the population,
where mixed-race and Spanish fathers dealt with mothers who still spoke the
local language at home. The population, therefore, was still likely to remain
bilingual.

While Tucumán had settled into bilingualism, others areas had not yet made
that transition. Filippo Salvador Gilij, a Jesuit with a good ear for languages,
noted that polylingualism was common in the mid-eighteenth-century, Orinoco
valley because of the linguistic proximity of the various local languages, and
thought Spanish was difficult for them, being "of such a different character
of that of the Indians." He had seen examples of several children of different
languages speaking together, each talking in their own language, but all understanding the others.[27] Humboldt also saw the problems of learning Spanish
when he passed from Venezuela into the *llanos* of the Orinoco valley in the
early nineteenth century; he discovered that the porters who accompanied
him could not actually speak Spanish well enough to conduct a conversation.
Spanish priests in the area told him that they did not speak local languages and
that the local people often misunderstood them when they preached in Spanish,
mistaking *Inferno* (Hell) for *invierno* (winter). Just as the Jesuit Gilij believed,
and perhaps repeating local folk wisdom, the German traveler thought that
the local language was so different from Spanish that it was all but impossible
for the people to learn this new language. The region had been disturbed and
the mission reductions were still new, so that multiple languages prevailed,

[24] Both quoted in Barbara Ganson, *The Guaraní under Spanish Rule in the Rio de la Plata*
(Stanford, 2003), p. 80.
[25] John and William Parish Robertson, *Letters on Paraguay: An Account of Four Years' Residence
in that Republic* (2 vols., London, 1838 [GB]) 1: 255.
[26] Carrio de la Vandera, *Lazarillo ciego*, p. 97.
[27] Filippo Salvador Gilij *Saggi di storia Americana...* (4 vols., Rome, 1782 [GB]), vol. 3, Book 2,
cap 1, p. 38.

although three were becoming prevalent.[28] Spanish settlers had come to the area in some numbers, and perhaps in time it would transition to be more like Tucumán.

Across the Atlantic in Angola, conquest also did not bring European women and resulted in the rapid mestization of the settler class. Children, even of wealthy settlers, were typically educated linguistically by their mothers, who themselves rarely had the opportunity to use languages other than Kimbundu at home, thus reinforcing bilingualism at best. Portuguese who came to Angola in the seventeenth century became landowners and military officers, employing thousands of slaves or local workers on their estates.[29] Their contact with Portuguese was largely through international commerce and government, so that those who lived in rural areas had little need of Portuguese, but considerable need of local African languages. Although all records were kept in Portuguese, by the eighteenth century, most settlers spoke Kimbundu, the local African language, in their homes. A series of mid-eighteenth-century governors denounced this situation, charging that council meetings were conducted in a language they could not understand. They proposed outlawing the speaking of Kimbundu through a variety of wild and wholly unworkable schemes, to no avail.

In Angola, as in the Maya region, the language problem worked as it did in all areas where a colonial language did not replace the local one. One might expect language change in Kimbundu to parallel those in Nahua or Quechua, but in many ways it did not. First of all, Kimbundu was not itself a written language. Even though it was used as a language in catechisms written in the 1620s, there are no other Kimbundu texts or administrative documents extant. When orders and proclamations were made in Portuguese Angola, often they were to be read, in "abundo" and Portuguese, but if the Kimbundu text was ever written out, no version has survived. Instead, it seems most likely that it was simply translated on the spot and spoken orally, much the way sermons often were in both Kongo and Angola.

We are thus at a loss to determine the degree to which Portuguese penetrated Kimbundu. Kimbundu is documented only in the catechism of the mid-seventeenth century, a grammar of 1697 (actually written in Brazil), and a long and poorly constructed dictionary of the late eighteenth century.[30] The catechism

---

[28] Humboldt, *Personal Narrative* 2: 173, 239, 244, 246–249, 253–254.

[29] For a worthwhile overview of the status of Kimbundu in Luanda, see Jan Vansina, "Portuguese vs Kimbundu: Language Use in the Colony of Angola (1575–c. 1845)," *Bulletin des Séances de l' Académie des Sciences d'Outre-Mer* 47 (2001–2003): 267–281.

[30] The catechism was composed sometime around 1626 by the bilingual Mbundu, Dionisio de Faria Baretto, and published by the Jesuit (born in São Salvador, Kongo) António do Couto, as *Gentio de Angola Sufficiemente Instruido* (Lisbon, 1652). There was also a grammar composed in Brazil in 1697; Pedro Dias, *A Arte de Lingua de Angola* (Lisbon, 1697, although the first license to publish was issued in Bahia, Brazil, suggesting that it was composed there), and the dictionary was completed by the Capuchin priest Bernardo Maria da Cannecati [Cannecatiim], *Diccionario da lingua bunda ou angolense* (Lisbon, 1804).

reveals little Portuguese linguistic influence, even in religious terminology, although the modern form of the language (documented in the late nineteenth century) does show considerable linguistic borrowing from Portuguese.[31]

Angolan documentation reveals another dimension of this situation. In local archives maintained by *sobas* in Angola, documents were written in Portuguese.[32] The Portuguese language of these texts appears in many ways like a reverse of the second-stage Native American language as described by Lockhart. That is, there is widespread borrowing of nouns and sometimes verbs from Kimbundu, a much higher percentage than would be found in official correspondence, even that originating in the rural and backwater areas of the colony. Fernão de Sousa, governor from 1624 to 1630, kept a register of incoming correspondence from local officials (some of the few documents that have survived from Angola) and these are full of extensive borrowings from Kimbundu, both nouns and verbs.[33] The writing of António de Oliveira Cadornega, chronicler of the Angolan wars, who arrived in 1639 and finished his chronicle in 1681, also showed widespread influence from Kimbundu in nouns and verbs.[34] An eighteenth-century archive of documents written by the rulers of Caxinga, a Portuguese ally just north of Angola's core region, also shows a deeper penetration of Kimbundu, even in grammar, especially with regards to word order and emphasis.[35] These sobas, while subordinate to Angola, were in a twilight zone of sovereignty, more responsible for their own affairs than any cacique in America, yet still officially a part of the Portuguese world.

Kikongo, a neighboring and related language, has a similar history. Kongo was not conquered, but the Kongo elite were literate only in Portuguese and often spoke the language. Nevertheless, the few linguistic materials we have

[31] For example, Heli Chatelain, *Folktales of Angola* (Philadeliphia, 1894 [GB]), which contains numerous texts. I was struck in listening to oral traditions at N'dalatando, Angola, in August 2004 and Malange, Angola, in July, 2008, by the degree to which the language was penetrated by Portuguese.

[32] An important collection of these documents from the archives of the soba of Caculo Cacahenda with its earliest documents from the mid-seventeenth century is Ana Paula Tavares and Catarina Madeira Santos, eds., *Africae Monumenta. A Apropriação da Escrita pelos Africanos* (in progress, vol. 1, Lisbon 2002). Eva Sebastyén, a Hungarian researcher, obtained documents from several rural archives in 1988. I have had the opportunity to examine some of these documents as well.

[33] Fernão de Sousa's correspondence has been published by Beatrix Heintze, ed., *Fontes para a história de Angola do século XVII* (2 vols., Lisbon, 1985–1988); see especially his letter to his children, which includes close summaries and quotations from local correspondence; 1: 215–362.

[34] António de Oliveira Cadornega, *História geral das guerras angolanas* (mod. ed., Matias Delgado, 3 vols., 1940–1942, reprinted 1972).

[35] Archives of the Soba of Caxinga, Cuanza Norte, Angola, declarations of Antonio Andreza Mendez, October 27, 176?; Antonio de Cristovão, December 11, 1774; Antonio Francisco Capelle Candalla, no date but roughly 1775 (these documents were obtained by Sebastyén in the late 1980s, and copies shared with the author). Many of these local archives are full of documents that were nineteenth-century forgeries of earlier documents, simply to establish land claims as Portuguese administration tightened. This particular set appears to be authentically eighteenth-century on the basis of paleography.

from that language, which include a catechism of 1624, a fairly extensive dictionary of 1648 (and smaller ones in the eighteenth century), and a short sermon, also of 1648, show very little Portuguese influence, primarily in terms that related to new items of material culture. In short, neither Kongo nor Kimbundu seem to have passed the second stage of Lockhart's model, possibly reflecting the greater cultural independence of the African conquests and contact situations.

Kongo, while not in any way a colony of Portugal, used Portuguese as its official language, and there are a fairly large number of Portuguese language official documents surviving from the seventeenth and fewer but still some from the eighteenth centuries. These, too, show influence from Kikongo, to some degree in phonology and vocabulary (in the form of loan words, mostly nouns) and also in grammar. Thus, Kongolese Portuguese has elements of a creole language in it, as well as those of a second-stage language.

LINGUAS FRANCA IN THE MIDDLE GROUND

One last instance of linguistic change needs to be noted. This was the remarkable linguistic problems that the Native Peoples of northeastern North America faced in the late seventeenth and eighteenth centuries. The problem was not entirely that of contact through conquest, for these regions were free associations not under alien rule. They were, however, very much in deep contact with European languages, because during the course of the seventeenth century, and especially in the eighteenth century, they ceased production of many common-use items and imported these from the world economy. Edge tools and textiles, for example, were virtually all made outside of their domain, though they might be modified for aesthetic purposes within the Native American world. Furthermore, because they were free associations, trade tended to be decentralized and individualized, without as many intermediaries as one might find in societies with a more developed class structure. Consequently, Native Americans had more contact with outside languages in this area than they would in agricultural centers of Mexico or Peru.

This situation was exacerbated by the extreme social disruption that followed the Beaver Wars or Mourning Wars after 1648. The rapid expansion of the Iroquois westward during this period broke up many communities, forcing multilingual refugee communities to form in what is today the U.S. Midwest. In addition, as the Iroquois, so successful in war, integrated more and more captives and adopted people who spoke other languages into their community, it proved harder and harder to assimilate them linguistically. At times, Iroquois-speakers were outnumbered in their own communities.

For many of the new refugee communities, there was no single dominant language and no dominant group; rather there were connections of convenience and security. Here the situation came to resemble that of the slave communities of other parts of the Americas, where there was an immediate need for a lingua franca. Of course, in the earlier stages of this linguistic confusion, the lingua franca was either Iroquois or Algonquian, the languages of the most active groups in the area. The Baron de Lahontan described two "mother languages" he observed in the late seventeenth and early eighteenth centuries, which "differ from each other as little as French and Norman." These were Huron (the French term for the language that included Iroquois) and Algonquian, which were "sufficient for a person to pass through Canada, which I close with the banks of the Mississippi River," even though there were "an infinity of others which few Europeans can understand even up to the present."[36] As to the "infinity of other" languages, as Louis Hennepin traveled down the Mississippi with the Sieur de la Salle in 1674 on the eve of the Iroquois breakthrough into the area, he noted that every particular nation had its own language and there was no lingua franca; each little nation would send one of its members to live in the villages of their allies to serve as ambassador and linguist.[37]

But the use of a lingua franca developed quickly, for Pierre François Xavier de Charlevoix, passing through the same regions in 1721–1722, remarked on the same development, adding a third language –Sioux – to the mix, spoken farther to the west and relating to the spread of the more intense interactions in a larger zone, as well as the continuing disruption of warfare and refugee flight.[38] It was in these languages, the most widely understood, that traders needed to communicate with local people. Native peoples began speaking creolized French (and in some cases English) as their trading relations with people speaking these languages as their native tongue increased.

As English settlers moved into their areas, however, this pattern changed. Unlike the French, who came into the frontier areas and beyond in very small numbers as itinerant traders, the English (and after the Revolution, citizens of the United States) came as farming settlers, who augmented their agriculture with trading and hunting hide-bearing animals. Their denser presence and cultural proclivities, which were not as oriented toward assimilation into Native American society as the French had been, made English a language with more force on the ground. Moravian missionaries, who penetrated into the Ohio country in the 1750s and 1760s, often noted the presence of English, and at times communicated with indigenous people in that language, as they were understood in it, and less so in the specific Native American languages they had already learned.

As the development of colonies in Louisiana, Florida, and South Carolina created a new "Middle Ground" in the southeast, a similar situation arose with the expansion of the Muskogee language. Expansion and raiding by Chicksaws and Chocktaws, like the raiding of the Iroquois farther north, gave Muskogee

---

[36] Le Baron de Lahontan, *Memoires de l'Amerique Septentrionale...* (2 vols., The Hague, 1703 [GB]) 2: 197–199.

[37] Louis Hennepin, *A New Discovery of a Vast Country in America...* (Chicago, 1903 [GB]) Cap. 42, 1: 215.

[38] Pierre François Xavier de Charlevoix, *Journal of a Voyage to North America Undertakne by Order of the French King* (2 vols., London, 1761 [GB]) 1: 288.

its impetus. When William Batran traveled into the interior behind Charleston in the mid-eighteenth century, he noted that "the Muscogulge tongue is now the national or sovereign language; those of the Chicasaws, Chactaws, and even the remains of the Natches, if we are to credit the Creeks and traders, being dialects of the Muscogulge: and probably, when the Natches were sovereigns, they called their own the national tongue, and the Creeks, Chicasaws, &c. only dialects of theirs. It is uncertain which is really the mother tongue."[39]

The Equestrian Revolution brought about radical change in the Great Plains further west. Álvar Nuñez Cabeza de Vaca, who was shipwrecked in Florida in 1542 and ended up wandering for many years in what is today Texas and surrounding states, noted that even in those days, people who did not speak each other's languages communicated in a complex sign language. Cabeza de Vaca used it himself, for even though he knew six local languages, he still needed it in some places.[40] As the horse greatly increased mobility and the great consolidations and migrations took place, people of many different language groups were thrown together, perhaps with even more fluidity and diversity than in the Middle Ground of the Great Lakes region. The sign language thus became more and more valuable, and many nineteenth-century travelers noted its existence as well. The people of this region may have used Sioux as a lingua franca to some extent, as French observers noted. But this was also supplemented by the sign language, which drew attention from so many travelers in the region in the nineteenth century. Garreck Mallery, a U.S. Army interpreter who worked with Plains groups in 1876–1879, made a detailed study of this language, which remains a classic treatment to this day. Although the Plains sign language could not express everything that a language could, it was a remarkably efficient means of communication.[41]

Similar situations also brought about a remarkable expansion of the Tupi language. The Portuguese and Spanish policy of placing indigenous allies under the tutelage of Jesuits created a situation in which the priests, in order to simplify their use of the language in instruction, both religious and for higher studies, created a number of works in a standardized form of the language, which could then be spoken throughout the entire Tupi zone, which stretched from Pernambuco in the north to the Spanish colonies in the Rio de la Plata basin in the south. The movement of Tupi allies from one place to another helped maintain this standardization as did their contacts with the Portuguese even where they had not agreed to settle on aldeias.

---

[39] Bartram, William, 1739–1822, _Travels through North and South Carolina, Georgia, East and West Florida_ (Philadelphia, 1791), p. 368.

[40] For an assessment of this and other early sources on sign language, see Susan Wurtzberg and Lyle Campbell, "North American Indian Sign Language: Evidence of Its Existence before European Contact," _International Journal of American Linguistics_ 61 (1995): 153–167.

[41] Garrick Mallery, "Sign Language among North American Indians Compared with That among Other Peoples and Deaf-Mutes," _First Annual Report of the Bureau of Ethnology to the Secretary of the Smithsonian Institution_ (Washington, DC, 1879–1880).

The Portuguese subsequently transplanted thousands of Tupi-speaking soldiers in the Amazon when they decided to occupy it to forestall colonization by Dutch, English, or French rivals in the early seventeenth century. As the Portuguese began the conquest of the Amazon basin, a region that was originally multilingual, Tupi emerged as a lingua franca, spoken by people who were considered Portuguese (but of mixed race and culture) as well as the allied Tupis. In time, the uniformity of Tupi, though transformed into a sort of creole language, changed into a new dialect, but one that became the normal language throughout the whole basin.[42]

THE END OF AFRICAN LANGUAGES IN AMERICA

The logic of retention and loss of European and American languages also applies to the failure of African languages to assert themselves anywhere in the Americas. The primary reason for this was that in many cases (Brazil being a notable exception), Africans did not settle in blocks, but rather in multilingual communities from the very beginning. It was the enforced multilingualism of slave communities, rather than any policies or efforts of slave masters, that ended African languages, even though some slave owners, in an effort to enhance security and control, adopted strategies to limit the speaking of African languages on their estates.

Africans brought to the Americas as slaves usually lived at the intersections of two very different sorts of communities. The first community was what might be called the "nation" and the second one was the estate. A national community was formed by all the slaves in a given colony or area that spoke the same language or lingua franca from Africa. There is not always an exact fit between these languages and those spoken in Africa, probably because it was in the social interest of the slaves to build the largest possible linguistic community. The estate, on the other hand, was the residential unit of most Africans (in urban areas, the concentration of the town made it like an estate). Estates were usually multilingual, with Africans from several language groups present.

Africans who were newly arrived in the Americas undoubtedly craved social contact with other people with whom they could have comfortable conversations, and as such were naturally drawn to those who spoke their native language. If such were not to be found, they tried to do the next best thing, which was to find those who did not speak their native language, but at least one that they knew from home, such as a lingua franca. Barring that, they had to accept social and cultural isolation until they could learn one or another of the languages around them. Most Africans, however, came into places where there were around them people with whom they could speak.

Members of language communities that were not well represented in the Americas might have to speak another African language, perhaps a lingua

---

[42] M. Kittya Lee, "Conversing in Colony: The Brasílica and Vulgar in Portuguese America, 1500–1759," PhD dissertation, Johns Hopkins University, 2005.

franca from their home territory, instead of their home language. Thus the people who spoke a language known in English-speaking America as "Ibo" had adopted one of the several dialects and languages spoken in the central Niger Delta as a medium of communication in America. Likewise, many speakers of Gã from the eastern region of modern Ghana probably spoke "Coromantee" (Akan or Twi) in America as they were a small community and Akan was spoken as a lingua franca in their homeland. Mandinka may also have served as an American lingua franca for people from some parts of Senegambia, even though they spoke Serer or another West Atlantic language at home. A study by Bonaventure Yai of the "language of Mina" as it was recorded in Brazil in the mid-eighteenth century reveals the basic structure of Ewe (spoken today in the Republic of Bénin) but with several dialects and even other languages also found in some of its vocabulary, suggesting that it was a new and probably American-based creole.

National unity was important to Africans in America, especially where there were many nations. John Taylor, who visited Jamaica in 1687, observed that slaves were brought from Cape Coast, Caramantine (both towns on the Gold Coast), Gambia, Angola, Popo (the Slave Coast), and Madagascar, and even here he failed to note other regions that were shipping slaves to the English colonies.[43] He noted that on their days off, the slaves would go out in "great companys, goeing to visit their countrymen in other plantations, where according to their own countrey fashion they feast, dance and sing."[44] In testimony about an alleged plot hatched by slaves in Antigua in 1739, witnesses recalled that during social events, some of the people present drank toasts to a particular nation. Court "drank to the Coromantees in Coromantee," and Oliver declared that he "Ebo blood and never failed." [45] Marriage registers in Brazil, Mexico, and other Catholic and Iberian counties note that often people chose marriage partners from within their nation, no doubt because they wished the comfort of speaking their native language at home, and because cultural expectations of marriage from Africa could be shared.

In urban areas, the national units might be virtually institutionalized. Africans often marched by nations in the many religious festivals in Iberian countries, and often the nation had a formally elected king. In Pernambuco, Brazil, for example, the king of the city of Recife was called the "King of Congo" and presumably was elected from among the people of that "nation" (or more likely from among Central Africans).[46] Suchou de Rennefort, a French traveler,

---

[43] John Taylor MS, in David Buisseret, ed., *Jamaica in 1687: The Taylor Manuscript at the National Library of Jamaica* (Kingston, Jamaica, 2008), p. 546 (pagination of the original manuscript, as marked in the edition)

[44] Taylor manuscript, p. 540; 542, for holiday celebrations.

[45] NAUK, CO9/10 fols. 67, 77, Antigua Minutes of Council, November 1, 1736 – January 31, 1738, "Negro's Conspiracy."

[46] On the earlier history of the King of Congo in Recife, see Marcelo Mac Cord, *O Rosário de D. Antônio: Irmandades negras, alianças e conflitos na história social do Recife, 1848–1872* (Recife, 2005), especially pp. 61–93.

FIGURE 9. King and his Suite, detail depicting the musicians (w/c on paper). By Carlos Julião (1740–1811) Biblioteca Nacional, Rio de Janeiro, Brazil/ Giraudon/ The Bridgeman Art Library.

witnessed the African-descended population of Pernambuco, celebrating their feast on Sunday, December 10, 1666. As he watched, some 400 men and 100 women celebrated Mass, after which they "elected a king and queen" and then paraded through the streets "singing, dancing and reciting verses which they have composed." The slaves dressed up in the clothes of their masters and mistresses, including gold jewelry, and the celebration cost, by his estimation, 100 écus. The king and his officers went about with "a sword and dagger at their side" and did not work for a week.[47] Although Suchou did not specifically say the king and queen were of Congo, a century later, the king of Congo was a regular office, which was recognized by official documents, and he had, moreover, the right to recognize kings over other nations in Recife.[48]

Le Gentil de la Bordinais, a French traveler visiting Lima in 1715–1716, observed that the Africans were divided into "tribes" and that each had a king

[47] Souchu de Rennefort, *Histoire des Indes Orientaless* (Paris, 1688), pp. 207–209.
[48] Marcelo McCord, "Identidades Étnicas, Irmandade do Rosário e Rei do Congo: socialibilidades cotidianas recifenses—século XIX," *Campos* 4 (2003): 51–66.

who dispensed justice and in other ways saw to the order of the nation. When the king died, he was given an elaborate funeral. The city government actually paid the owner of a slave for his services if he was made king.[49] In many cities one or another lay confraternity organized among the African and African-descended population might supply a king, and many of the fraternities were organized on national lines.

At times, it may have been possible for something like a single African language dominance to take place, and this situation was particularly marked in Brazil and in some parts of Spanish America. In the first four decades of the seventeenth century, the vast majority of the Africans crossing to the Americas to Spanish and Portuguese colonies came from West Central Africa, and of that group most spoke Kimbundu, although a significant minority also spoke the closely related Kikongo.[50] They formed what might be called the "Angolan Wave." Not surprisingly, Jesuit missionaries in Bahia and Pernambuco were moving toward using Kimbundu as a language for their instructions; for example, Jesuits were composing treatises and learning Kimbundu in the late sixteenth century. Pedro Claver, another Jesuit working in Cartagena, learned to speak Kimbundu, and the catechism in Kikongo produced in 1624 was already being printed in Lima for use among Africans in that city. An early grammar of Kimbundu was printed for use in Brazil in 1697. Equally strong, but much less visible, Kimbundu- and Kikongo-speakers completely dominated the imported Africans in all the French, English, and Dutch colonies that formed in the Americas during the same period, for their slave population was derived virtually entirely from the trade passing from Angola to the Spanish Indies.[51]

Pernambuco probably remained the most Angolan of all the Portuguese captaincies in Brazil, and probably in all the Americas. Statistically, as far as we can tell, an overwhelmingly large percentage of the slaves coming to that region were from West Central Africa, perhaps because the captains held the contract for Angola in the first half of the seventeenth century. According to statistics compiled by the Dutch from customs records, all the slaves brought to Pernambuco in the period between 1620 and 1623 were from Angola, a situation that may well have prevailed both before and after this statistical run. Although the Dutch did introduce non-Angolan slaves (primarily from the Niger Delta region and from Allada) during the 1640s, the predominantly central African importation continued following their expulsion, thanks to the fact that the heroes of the war against the Dutch were rewarded by making them governors of Angola after the Portuguese recovered the captaincy in 1654. Suchou de Rennefort believed that all the Africans in Pernambuco "are carried from Angolle" when he visited in 1666.[52] Although Pernambuco

---

[49] Le Gentil de la Barbinais, *Nouveau voyage autour du monde* (3 vols., Amsterdam, 1728 [Gallica]) 1: 114–115.

[50] Linda Heywood and John Thornton, *Central Africans, Atlantic Creoles and the Making of the Americas, 1585–1660* (Cambridge, 2007).

[51] Examined in detail in Heywood and Thornton, *Central Africans*, pp. 38–42.

[52] Souchu de Rennefort, *Histoire*, p. 207.

did have somewhat more diverse slave origins in the eighteenth century, especially from "Mina," the Portuguese term for the region around the kingdom
of Dahomey in West Africa, in 1702, the elite of Bahia managed to persuade
royal authorities to grant them a lion's share of the Mina trade, restricting
Pernambuco to only three to four ships a year.[53] This was further reduced, for
a mid-eighteenth-century report noted that Pernambuco sent only one ship a
year to Mina as opposed to twelve to sixteen from Bahia.[54] Seventy nine percent of the slaves entering Pernambuco between 1750 and 1758 were from
Angola, according to another report.[55] The situation became even more pronounced once a trading company was established, for of the nearly 25,000
slaves brought into Pernambuco (and remaining there, not being reexported
immediately to the southern mines) between 1761 and 1770, 87 percent were
from Angola.[56] In this situation it seems quite likely that Kimbundu was the
lingua franca among the Africans of the region and, given its large predominance, is likely to have been carried forward from one generation to the next,
although almost certainly coexisting with Portuguese, because slaves needed to
communicate in the colonial language as well.

Elsewhere in Brazil the situation was also remarkable. Once the "Angolan
Wave" faltered in the late seventeenth century, Angolans were joined by slaves
who came very largely from the Mina Coast, a fairly restricted region on West
Africa surrounding the Kingdom of Dahomey. By the early eighteenth century,
Minas were close to the majority of imports in Bahia and Rio de Janeiro, the
slave port that served the growing mining districts of Minas Gerais. A collection of inventories from the archives of Bahia reveal that in the two decades
spanning from 1740 to 1760, almost three-quarters of the slaves were listed as
being from Mina, and the number was only slightly less (about 70 percent) for
the 1780–1790 period.[57] Virtually all the rest were from Angola.

Two African languages were predominant in Minas Gerais: the language of
Angola and the language of Mina. Pedro de Almeyda, who governed Minas
Gerais early in the mining boom, instructed Jesuit priests to learn both of these
languages, because "the negros from Angola and Mina come already as adults"
and could not, he believed, master Portuguese. Priests were mastering these
two just as they had the "lingua geral" for work with the Tupi-speakers.[58]
More than 60 percent of the slaves observed in inventories from the mid-
eighteenth century claimed Mina as their ultimate home, the remainder being

---

53 APEB Livro 13, doc. 30, March 29, 1718; Livro 14 contains rules dating from 1702 on the shipping of tobacco and the trade of Bahia and Pernambuco.
54 IHGB, DL 33.3 "Diversas memórias d'África," fol. 12.
55 IHGB, Arq 1.2.17, no. 13, fols. 103v–104; 149v–150.
56 IHBG, Arq 1.2.11, fols. 41–41v "Do Estado de decadencia em que de achavão as Capitanias
de Pernambuco no tempo de commercio livre, e do augmento que tiverão com a fundação da
Companhia" (1777).
57 These data are drawn from the study of Carlos Ott, "A procedência étnica nos escravos Bahianos
no século XVIII," *Clio* 1/14 (1993): 33–59, inventory data on 35–41.
58 APM Secção Colonial, cod. 4, fols. 713v–716, Pedro de Almeida, October 4, 1719.

from Angola. The "lingua geral" of Mina became well established in Minas Gerais; in fact, in 1741, Antonio da Costa Peixoto published a phrase book in this language intended to allow masters more easily to communicate with their slaves – a strong suggestion that the language had become a lingua franca in wide use.[59]

But this remarkable Brazilian situation was not generalized, and where the Angolan wave may have had considerable impact all over the Americas, the subsequent history of the slave trade broke up the linguistic dominance of single groups. By the 1640s, English, Dutch, and French merchants were acquiring thousands of slaves from several points in West Africa, especially from the region around Allada (what would be the Mina homeland for Brazilians) and Calabar (the Niger Delta), and soon also from Senegambia. By the 1720s, slaves that came to English and French colonies in the Caribbean represented every region of Africa engaged in the slave trade. As the right to carry slaves to Spanish colonies passed into Dutch and then into English hands, Africans arriving in the Spanish Americas came from the same widely varying cultures that populated the Caribbean islands. Venezuela's exploding cacao production, which took off in the late seventeenth century, brought Africans, delivered by Dutch and English ships both legally and especially illegally, from the whole of Atlantic Africa. In all these areas, therefore, Africans lived in multilingual and multicultural settings, even when they lived, as they often did, in the company of other enslaved Africans.

In these areas, the multilingual setting was the estate – the normal residence pattern for rural slaves – or the town. The estate was the place of their work and where they made their homes. Countless estate inventories from every corner of the Americas show that whereas most estates that had more than a dozen workers or so had some blocks from the same nation, they were mostly from several – and on larger ones, sometimes from a half-dozen – different nations.[60] In testimony about the 1739 Antigua plot, witnesses noted hearing toasts being drunk to estates and plantations, and Oliver drank to the "Windward [estate] people," bewailing the fact that the life there had "gone down" when one of his friends left for town.[61] This sort of attachment to a property had its violent side as well. Thomas Thistlewood's diaries reveal the degree of antagonism that might exist between the enslaved residents of neighboring estates: Thistlewood's workers were often robbed by slaves from neighboring estates, and his residents as well sometimes robbed, arrested, and shot at those from

[59] Antônio da Costa Peixoto, *Obra Nova da lingua geral de Mina* (Lisbon, 1741, new edition), Yeda Pessoa de Castro, as *A lingua mina-jeje no Brasil: um falar africana em Ouro Preto do século XVIII* (Belo Horizonte, 2002); see also Olabiyi Yai, "Texts of Enslavement: Fon and Yoruba Vocabularies from the Eighteenth and Nineteenth Centuries in Brazil," in Paul Lovejoy, ed., *Identity in the Shadow of Slavery* (London, 2000), pp. 102–112.

[60] John Thornton, *Africa and Africans in the Making of the Atlantic World, 1500–1800* (2nd ed., Cambridge, 1998), pp. 192–204.

[61] NAUK CO 9/10, "Negros Conspiracy," fol. 77.

other estates they perceived as trespassing. Such incidents were common: for example, in March 1764, Thistlewood and a substantial number of slaves got into a shooting incident over fishing rights with the slaves of his neighbor, George Williams; a month later, he and his slaves arrested and beat the slaves of William Ricketts who had robbed them of fish, causing Ricketts to issue a threat against Thistlewood.[62]

The multiethnic estate naturally created a situation like that faced by the Dutch in English New York, only in much less space and with little room for an exclusive community. They would live in a situation in which they themselves would prefer to speak their own language at home and with their friends, but their children would be in a position to learn two or more languages as native speakers. If the children came from a home in which both parents spoke the same language – and research on marriage patterns in baptismal, marriage, and estate records in Latin countries where names usually included an ethnic indicator suggests that Africans chose to marry within their own nation as much as 75 percent of the time – they were likely to learn that language at home. Outside, however, they would have to learn another language to communicate with other children with different national backgrounds.

By default, the other language, in which second-generation slaves would become bilingual, was the colonial language, a creole with a European base language. It was essential for all slaves to learn at least a rudimentary form of this language in any case, for it was the language of their masters and the language of command. While few masters were willing to teach the language formally, they expected it to be learned, and we can see from such evidence as runaway slave advertisements that most long-serving Africans acquired some proficiency in it. But their children would have acquired this language with native proficiency.

John Taylor summed up the process nicely as he observed it in Jamaica. After noting the wide range of African origins on the island, "all these spake each a severall language, which the other dost not understand." But "in all plantations these Negroas are mix't one with another, and all sone learn to spake broaken English, by which means they are capable to understand their work." Taylor, believing that ethnic hatreds and rivalries arising from this linguistic diversity (and imagining that they lay close together and fought each other), supposed that rebellions were kept in bay by it, but he was afraid for the future. "As for their children" he wrote, "they learn not only their mother tung, but to spake English also," so that "'tis to be doubted in the next age the Crebolian Negroas will be propagated to a generall insurrection."[63]

The creole languages spoken in the Americas, like Taylor's "broaken English" of Jamaica, may well have originated on the coast of Africa, where a sizable number of people learned the languages of their trading partners in order to facilitate their business, and had already gone through many transformations

---

[62] Thistlewood Diaries, March 18, 1764, April 13–14, 1764; see also February 22, 1761.
[63] Taylor manuscript, p. 547.

before he observed it in 1687. The first Portuguese-based coastal trading language developed very early in the history of the contact; already in the sixteenth century, Portuguese playwrights were imitating it, and it is clear that at that point African slaves in Portugal also spoke the same language. This language, called a creole, involved a vocabulary drawn from one or another European language, but a different grammar.[64] Creole grammar has been the subject of considerable debate, some authorities maintaining that it is a basic grammar common to many African languages, while others maintaining that it is a fundamental minimal human grammar, varied enough to represent all human needs, but as minimally simple as needed. It is fairly clear that it does not conform to the rules of any particular African grammar, so it seems more likely that it does represent a very regular grammatical system that allows the learner to focus on vocabulary and yet have a language that was comprehensible to a native speaker of the colonial language. In any case, the African creole languages are quite similar to those in America, and it seems likely that the original "instructors" of colonial languages were those who had first mastered it on the coast of Africa. Then, finding themselves enslaved in America, they became the teachers of others who were learning the language for the first time.

For second-generation children of African ancestry, there was little incentive to teach their own children the African language that they may have used as children. Of course, they often used it in communicating with relatives, friends, or newcomers of that nation, but for the interactions with the masters and with slaves of other nations, the colonial language would make the most sense. Given that virtually everyone would have to be able to at least understand the colonial language, the process of linguistic change would be even more rapid than it was in Dutch-speaking New York after the English takeover, where the persistence of a local community might make bilingualism attractive for longer.

Most cases of the survival of African languages in the Americas that are reported in the twentieth century relate to special circumstances not unlike those of Pennsylvania Dutch. Linguists have been fascinated by the presence of American-born people of African descent speaking African languages, especially Yoruba and Kikongo, even in the twentieth century. In the first case, the origins of such communities are from the last years of the slave trade, or the brief period of "voluntary" migration in which Africans – often freed recaptives taken at the end of the slave trade – were transported, often as family groups, to the Americas. They had more freedom over their place of settlement than did Africans who came as slaves, and could thus form more homogenous communities. Finally, in the case of linguistic survival for several generations (usually by people who are bilingual), the African language is encapsulated

---

[64] For the early history of the creole of Guinea and its use in Portugal, see Thornton, *Africa and Africans*, pp. 213–216.

in the activities of a religious community that uses the language as the one of ritual and of secrecy.

Perhaps the best example of the automatic way in which multiculturalism led to the loss of African languages is the case of Saint Domingue/Haiti. At the time of its revolution in 1791, about three-quarters of the population were African-born and thus native speakers of African languages. We must assume that at least a significant percentage even of those who were not born in Africa were bilingual in an African language and creole French. Furthermore, of this large group of slaves proficient in African languages, those speaking Kikongo must have been a significant group; perhaps as many as one-third of the population, especially in the northern parts of the island, were Kikongophones. Beyond this, the conditions of the Revolution often caused large blocks of slaves to run away from their estates and to form bands. Often such bands were organized along national blocks and tended to settle into discrete areas, thus creating a potential speech community. Finally, the Revolution ended control by the slave masters and any linguistic or security policies they may have had. And yet by the end of the nineteenth century, there was virtually no one on the island, certainly no large community, who spoke Kikongo. Everywhere, creole French, undoubtedly because it was widely known as a lingua franca, became the effective language of local government and commerce, and linked all the diverse linguistic communities of Haiti.

Creole forms of the colonial languages that emerged as a stable element quite soon on most American settings were themselves to some extent eroded as some slaves, especially the upward-mobile or freemen, sought to speak more standardized forms of the language. But the creole had a powerful effect in its own right on the language even of the master class. George Washington, who took his only voyage out of North America to Barbados in 1755, noted with some disdain that the Barbadian elite spoke in the same way as did their slaves. Creole speech was often regarded as comic. While traveling in Brazil in 1717, Le Gentil de la Barbinais witnessed a play in which in one scene, a nun presented an account of gallantries and lovers in the court of the Viceroy in the "corrupt Portuguese" of a slave, a touch the players hoped would amuse their audience.[65]

The preservation of a community was therefore vital for the transmission of the first element of culture – that of language. As long as communities held together and had more need to speak one language than another, they would continue to speak it, but if they were broken up, or needed to know a new language for frequent conversation, they abandoned their own language for a new one. Thus, the conditions of colonization, the dynamics of rule, and the vagaries of commerce all conspired to preserve or break languages.

---

[65] Le Gentil de la Barbinais, *Nouveau voyage autour du monde* (3 vols., Amsterdam, 1728) 3: 151.

9

Aesthetic Change

If languages survived or broke in the Americas depending on the survival and maintenance of speech communities, the same rules did not apply to aesthetics. Unlike languages, which are "hard" and difficult to change quickly, aesthetic principles are "soft" and can be changed much quicker. If aesthetic standards change between cultures, and indeed between social classes or fractions within a given culture, the idea of the creation of beauty and the idea that there is such a thing as beauty is universal. Recent research in neuroaesthetics suggests that all humans have a capacity to appreciate beauty, and aesthetic reactions to natural phenomena and deliberate human creations have measurable physiological manifestations.[1] Indeed, the appearance of artistic representations, which began at least 100,000 years ago in Africa, is widely held as one of the clear markers of the brain reorganization that signals the emergence of our species from others.[2]

If all humans can experience physiologically measurable responses to aesthetic production, it is also clear that cultural elements play a determining role in the specificity of the reaction. It is also clear that art, music, or decoration can be appreciated without the long process required for a child to learn language. Aesthetic elements can be mixed, resorted or redeployed, but languages cannot – no one would understand a person who mixes vocabulary and grammar from multiple languages in the same sentence. Whereas native proficiency in languages is really only acquired in childhood, people can easily learn to appreciate new aesthetics at any point in their lifetime. If a multilingual

---

[1] Here I rely on the pioneering work of Berlyne, *Aesthetics and Psychobiology* (East Newark, 1971) and more recent work such as I. Rentschler, B. Herzberger and B. Epstein, *Beauty and the Brain: Biological Aspects of Aesthetics* (Basel, 1988); D. W. Zaidel, *Neuropsychology of Art: Neurological, Cognative and Evolutionary Perspectives* (Hove, 2005). An excellent overview of recent work is Martin Skov and Oshin Vartanian, eds. *Neuroaesthetics* (Baywood, 2009).

[2] Christopher Henshilwood, Francesco d'Errico, and Ian Watts, "Engraved Ochres from the Middle Stone Levels at Blombos Cave, South Africa," *Journal of Human Evolution* 57 (2009): 27–47.

sentence would be gibberish, a performance or object that drew simultaneously on several cultures might easily be appreciated by everyone.

The nature of material production leads to different levels of aesthetics. Humans have always decorated their material items by adding features that have no functional utility but are perceived by their users as satisfying an aesthetic sense that characterized humanity as a whole – a point proved by the fact that the "Human Revolution" in archaeology is accompanied by a profusion of decorations, paintings, and depictions of what may be aesthetic activity. The quality of some of the earliest human artistic works strongly suggests that they were executed by talented people who had a good eye for color, form, and movement, and these special talents must have been a part of the human package that defined our species.

However, when the technology of production requires widespread deployment of many people as producers, many items cannot rely on the talent and skills of special producers. This is revealed in the decorations that one might find on daily-use objects like pottery or the textiles of daily clothing. Given the wide distribution of ceramics and, in the preindustrial world, the large number of only moderately skilled producers necessary to produce them, these decorations were usually fairly standardized and simple. They reflect cultural differences and provide some limited insight into aesthetic ideas at a mass level. Their production and particularly their level of artistic production is fairly low, and it is precisely because they are so standard that archaeologists can readily tell when and where a piece of pottery is made, even from a fragment.

But ceramics, like textiles, have a second level of artistry, and those items typically are made for social or economic elites. It is possible to make ceramic material that is perceived as finer than regular ware, or to produce cloth and clothing that is similarly better. These differences are not necessarily functional, but they are artistic. Not only is elite pottery of finer material, but its decoration is more varied and requires more skill and artistic talent to produce. Owners of such pottery use it to display their status, and the uniqueness of an artistic piece marks that status. Whereas overall design and decoration may well continue to be standardized, these items are far more distinctive in any culture than the ordinary ware, and what is more significant, social elites are more likely to mix cultures, importing rare and expensive wares and displaying a variety of cultural products.

Pottery, as a commodity produced by large numbers of people, requires little special talent, although the fine pieces made for the elite are the work of far more specialized and talented producers. What is visible in pottery is even more visible in other aspects of expressive culture, such as music or fine visual art. These types of items are actually produced by only a segment of the society, usually with special skills or talent, while its appreciation is manifested by the whole population.

Neither music nor art is functional and therefore requires no particular design. Furthermore, the nature of its dissemination allows for a very few people to produce it for a much larger audience than would be possible with concrete material items like pottery. People can and do discern quality in music, not so much in the nature of the instruments or other material considerations as in the nature of the actual sound or physical movements. Here, particularly in music or art, virtuosity is important. Talented and skilled individuals create and contribute far more to musical culture, even at the level that the mass of ordinary people consume, than they do in the production of material goods. Furthermore, fine musical production is often a public product consumed by all at all levels of society in a way that a material object cannot be. In many ways, therefore, music in particular is an aesthetic product that most freely expresses cultural change, differences, and convergences.

MASS MATERIAL CULTURE: POTTERY

Thanks to its durability and the minor aesthetic element of decoration, pottery is often the standard-bearer of culture and culture change. Since the transition from foraging to farming, humans all over the world have made ceramic vessels to eat and drink from, to cook their food, and store oil or grain. Thus, ceramics are functional, but also bear important cultural and status messages in their shapes and decorations.

Ceramic material is formed when clay becomes hardened through drying. Sun-dried clay can retain fluids, but not for long. If it is heated to a high enough temperature, minerals within clay (and all pottery must be made from clay that contains minerals, and not just any earth substance) turn to glass and both become durable and will not dissolve in water. It is this feature, which can be attained from simple fires (not special, very hot fires), that allows ceramic to hold water and thus become useful. Earthenware is the simplest and least expensive ceramic material, generated when clay is heated to about 500° C (which can be achieved in a large open fire). For earthenware heated to these low temperatures (low-fired), it is often necessary to apply glaze (a special type of clay that turns more fully into glass) to the pottery to make it entirely leak proof, although even unglazed low-fired pottery can still be functional.

If utility were all that is required of pottery, no one would ever produce anything other than low-fired earthenware. But in ancient times, people discovered that by generating much higher temperatures, or by applying artistic treatments, they could produce ceramic material that was more aesthetically pleasing, and also more expensive. As societies became complex and differentiated in wealth and social status, production of more expensive and beautiful ceramics developed as a means of displaying this wealth.

The most ancient pottery was handcrafted, which meant that the clay was shaped by hand, often using the method of coiling, where rolled-out strings of clay were coiled around a base and then the seams in the coils worked out. To achieve more artistically pleasing results, however, early potters sometimes employed a potter's wheel, which allowed greater control over thickness, uniformity, symmetry, and shape. As it required skill to use, it also increased cost. Price was further increased by the invention of ever more complex decorating techniques, which allowed figures to be added to them, multipart pieces with handles, spouts, necks, and other treatments, engraving, multicoloring, and the like, which could both be technically interesting and engage artistic fancies. Artistically decorated pottery of high-grade ceramic thrown on a wheel could be fantastically expensive, even if no better at holding liquids than the peasant's sturdy, crooked, low-fired, handcrafted earthenware.[3]

ELITE POTTERY TRADITIONS

In the emerging Atlantic world, elite cultural traditions often met in situations of contact and conquest. The rapidity with which cultures met often meant that strikingly different aesthetic traditions were brought suddenly into contact. Studies of this interaction at the elite level have shown that in general, elites tended to both preserve their own distinctive wares and to exchange them with other elites. This was true even in situations of conquest, where the elite of Europe often took political precedence over the elite of America.

In Iberia, for example, wheel-made high-fired earthenware glazed with a special tin-based glaze called majolica was the mainstay of the elite. It was not as notable for its ceramic material as for its varied glazing and the artistic treatment that the surface decoration received. Majolica originated in the Middle East and passed to the Iberian Peninsula in the twelfth century, and it continued to be elaborated in Spain and Portugal without as much devotion to producing higher levels of ceramic material.

Whereas the Iberian elite focused its attention on majolica as the elite ware of choice, northern Europeans were far more interested in developing the features of high-fired ceramic materials (especially porcelain) and less with the decoration. Porcelain was first made in East Asia, and northern Europeans devoted considerable attention to imitating it, first with stoneware – a high-fired ceramic with some of the characteristics of porcelain – and finally by direct imitation.[4]

Production of distinctive elite pottery was not restricted to Europe. The Mississippian culture, North America's most complex, also had strong differentiated pottery, as revealed in excavations at Moundsville that showed both high skills employed in pottery made in elite precincts of the site and superior ceramic material.[5] In the polities of the Amazon basin, fine elite ceramics passed through exchange networks, and are today recovered by archaeologists.[6] One

[3] William Barnett and John Hoopes (eds.), *The Emergence of Pottery: Innovation and Technology in Ancient Societies* (Washington, DC, 1995) is an archaeologically focused study of early pottery making.

[4] The long and complicated story is told in William Burton's classic account, *A General History of Porcelain* (2 vols., London, 1921, reprinted 2009, 2010). For the story of Meissen porcelain, see vol. 2, pp. 140–148.

[5] Vernon James Knight, "Characterizing Elite Midden Deposits at Moundville," *American Antiquity* 69 (2004): 304–321.

[6] Michael Heckenberger, "Amazonian Mosaics: Identity, Interaction, and Integration in the Tropical Forest," *Handbook of American Archaeology* (New York, 2008): 941–961.

of the striking ceramic productions of the Marajó island polities at the mouth of the Amazon was elaborate funeral urns, of varying size and decoration (as well as artistic skill) that set the elite off from commoners.[7] The Incas made a special, high-quality elite pottery that was largely distributed through the state, in contrast to locally made wares.[8] In Mexico, potters frequently mass-produced standard forms, and elite centers routinely had attached groups of specialists who produced fine ware with artistic decoration.[9]

The elites of Africa, who also consumed aesthetically differentiated pottery, were not concerned with producing the higher-fired ceramics, but they did not hesitate to consume them. Excavations at Savi, the capital of the Kingdom of Whydah that was destroyed by the army of Dahomey in 1727, revealed that while the nonelite population used low-fired utilitarian earthenware pottery that was usually undecorated, the elite also had imported a wide range of ceramics, including high-fired Dutch, French, Iberian, and English pottery and Chinese porcelains.[10] Müller, describing Fetu on the Gold Coast in the mid-seventeenth century, observed a very limited material culture in ceramics, mostly a pot for cooking and a dish for eating. But on the other hand, he thought that the elite "possess more utensils and more precious," although the precious items he described appear to have been imported items such silver spoons or silver dishes.[11] Research on the ground has generally confirmed this. At Elmina, a commercial town that grew up around the Dutch fort, a very sizable proportion of the ceramics was imported, and as at Whydah, included high-fired stoneware as well as Chinese porcelain.[12]

As the Spanish colonized America, they were anxious to maintain the aesthetic traditions of their homeland, even as they also recognized the elite ware

---

[7] Denise Schaan, "Into the Labyrinths of Marajoara Pottery: Status and Cultural Identity in Prehistoric Amazonia," in Colin McEwan, Cristiana Barreto, and Eduardo Neves, eds., *Unknown Amazon: Culture in Nature in Ancient Brazil* (London, 2001), pp. 108–133.

[8] Tamara Bray, "Inka Pottery as Culinary Equipment: Food, Feasting, and Gender in Imperial State Design," *Latin American Antiquity* 14 (2003): 3–28; Francis Hayashida, "State, Technology and State Production: Inka Pottery Production in the Leche Valley, Peru," *Latin American Antiquity* 10 (1999): 337–352; Cathy Costin and Melissa Hagstrom, "Standardization, Labor Investment, Skill and the Organization of Ceramic Production in Late Prehispanic Highland Peru," *American Antiquity* 60 (1995): 627–628.

[9] Deborah Nichols, Elizabeth Brumfiel, Hector Neff, et al., "Neutrons, Markets, Cities and Empires: A 1000-Year Prospective on Ceramic Production and Distribution in Postclassic Basin of Mexico," *Journal of Anthropological Archaeology* 21 (2002): 25–82; Elizabeth Brumfiel, "Elite and Utilitarian Crafts in the Aztec State," in Brumfiel and T. K. Earle, eds., *Specialization, Change and Complex Societies* (Cambridge, 1987), pp. 102–118; Robert Santley, Philip Arnold, and Christopher Pool, "The Ceramics Production System at Matacapan, Veracruz, Mexico," *Journal of Field Archaeology* 16 (1989): 107–132.

[10] Kenneth Kelly, "Transformation and Continuity in Savi, a West African Trade Town: An Archaeological Investigation of Culture Change on the Coast of Bénin in the 17th and 18th Century" (PhD dissertation, UCLA, 1995), pp. 141–157, 175–180.

[11] Müller, *Afrikansche*, pp. 147–148.

[12] Christopher DeCorse, "Culture Contact, Continuity and Change on the Gold Coast, AD 1400–1900," *African Archaeological Review* 10 (1992): 182–183, 189–190.

of their new subjects, as for example in Mexico, where the Spanish majolica with its bright glazes met elite Aztec Redware and Black-on-Orange ware. We know that the Europeans not only imported majolica after the conquest, but took considerable trouble to create their own centers of manufacture of it, for example, in Puebla, Panamá, and Mexico, which did a fine business supplying other Spanish centers with this particularly Iberian aesthetic. The American pottery centers employed indigenous workers, often under Spanish masters. In the mid-eighteenth century, even more local centers emerged – for example, Peru did not make its own majolica until the eighteenth century.[13]

The emergence of a far-flung network of majolica production and consumption has led some scholars to argue that Spanish disdain for conquered people had an aesthetic as well as economic and social dimension, in that they turned their backs on older, American traditions in ceramics.[14] But careful study has revealed this not to be true. Archaeologists have demonstrated that Nahua potters in Mexico continued to produce Redware and Black-on-Orange Ware for many years after the conquest. Studies of consumption among elite Spanish households show that while they insisted on majolica in their homes and supported local production of the pottery, they kept and displayed both majolica and Redware and Black-on-Orange ware in their houses.[15]

While the Spanish crown may have insisted on a legal separation of Spaniard and Indian, these views were not necessarily shared at the level of daily life or aesthetics. Spanish ware was also consumed by indigenous people, at a level commensurate with their wealth, and the potters of both traditions tended to maintain their own patterns of decoration without incorporating much of the other tradition.[16] In short, producers generally were conservative in their output, but consumers accepted products from both traditions, depending on their means, so that elites had both Aztec- and Spanish-style ware.

In Mexico, where there had been conquest, and where there were a large number of elite Spanish settlers concentrated in the city, the two traditions maintained themselves at the elite level. Things worked out differently in other areas, where conquest was not as dramatic and where the Spanish community was smaller, poorer, and less capable of maintaining ethnic aloofness. Thus, in Hispaniola after the early sixteenth century, or outposts like Florida, imported pottery, even from Mexican producers, was rare and virtually all the pottery

[13] Florence Lister and Robert Lister, *Andalusian Ceramics in Spain and New Spain: A Cultural Register from the Third Century BC to 1700* (Tucson, 1987); John Goggin, *Spanish Majolica in the New World: Types of the Sixteenth to Eighteenth Century* (New Haven, 1968).

[14] For example, see the recent work of Arnold Bauer, *Goods, Power, History: Latin America's Material Culture* (New York, 2001).

[15] Enrique Rodríguez-Alegría, "Eating Like an Indian: Negotiating Social Relations in the Spanish Colonies," *Current Anthropology* 46 (2005): 552–573, who has also argued that this indicates they ate with indigenous elites, although the replies to the article published at the end strongly and sometimes convincingly contest this.

[16] Thomas Charlton, "Contemporary Central Mexican Ceramics: A View from the Past," *Man* 11 (1976): 517–525.

in question was from indigenous sources. Kathleen Deagan, whose archaeological work has informed the use of pottery in these sites, argues that racial mixture, so common in poorer colonial areas, led to cooking pottery tending to be indigenous as the women in these mixed marriages (or more often, female concubines or servants) used pottery in their own tradition. On the other hand, pottery used in tableware, where status is more openly revealed, showed a higher frequency of majolica, albeit from a wide variety of sources, both American and European, undoubtedly a reflection of the limited wealth and opportunities of such regions.[17] However, it should also be noted that in many of these areas the level of social differentiation in the mini-states of the region did not produce such elaborate elite pottery. Spanish settlers on the far northern reaches of New Spain routinely consumed locally made indigenous pottery that largely followed and developed designs that date back to prehistoric times; indeed, the European-descended and mixed-race inhabitants of the area around modern day Tucson, Arizona, used it substantially until the arrival of the railroad in 1880.[18]

Whereas the pottery traditions of Spanish America reflected the meeting of elite cultures, those of the northern Europeans were different, if for no other reason than the northern Europeans did not make conquests of socially and aesthetically stratified American cultures, and could only produce their own elite pottery. Even though English potters at Jamestown tried to produce elite pottery as early as 1625, archaeological remains reveal that most colonists who consumed elite pottery were content to import it from a wide range of sources, even before the passage of the Navigation Acts in 1651 forbade the production of elite goods by Americans.[19] Dutch potters made a bit more progress in local production, even after they were subject to English law in 1664. An "extraordinary potter" was reported at Renslaerwick in 1653, and Dirck Claesen was established as a potter in New Amsterdam (New York) in 1657, where high-quality whiteware was being made in 1684 and stoneware in 1730 at Corselius pottery on Potbaker's Hill in Lower Manhattan (New York).

[17] Kathleen Deagan, *Spanish Saint Augustine: The Development of a Colonial Creole Community* (New York, 1983) and "Colonial Origins and Colonial Transformations in Spanish America," *Historical Archaeology* 37 (2002): 3–13. For a critique of generalizing the relationships that Deagan discovered first at St. Augustine, Florida (the "St. Augustine pattern"), to the rest of Latin America (as well as an analytical summary and bibliography of her other work), see Barbara Voss, "Gender, Race and Labor in the Archaeology of the Spanish Colonial Americas," *Current Anthropology* 49 (2008): 861–875 and comments to p. 887 by many of the current researchers on these topics.

[18] James Heidke, "Native American Pottery," in J. Homer Thiel and Jonathan Mabry, eds., *Rio Nuevo Archaeology, 2000–2003: Investigations at the San Augustín Mission and Mission Gardens, Tucson Presidio, Tucson Pressed Brick Company and Clearwater Site* (Tucson, 2006, online at http://www.cdarc.org/pdf/rn/rio_nuevo_ch07.pdf), no pagination.

[19] Beverly Staube, "The Colonial Potters of Tidewater, Virginia," *Journal of Early Southern Decorative Arts* 21 (1995): 1–40; Robert Hunter, "The Green Spring Planter," *Early American Life* 20 (1999); Thomas Davidson, Jamestown-Yorktown Foundation, personal communication, on the archaeological work.

It was only in the eighteenth century that Anglo–North American potters began producing elite ceramics locally, in fact, playing a key role in the development of the English ceramic industry. Anthony Dutché of Philadelphia appears to have been making a prototype porcelain using local clay that may well have been at the root of the first English porcelain production in 1744.[20]

Northern Europeans who established themselves in the Caribbean also met an environment where there was no indigenous elite pottery, and where for the most part the Carib inhabitants were displaced and not conquered. There too, limited evidence shows that local production of pottery managed to re-create elite styles. Habitation Loyola, a successful Jesuit-run sugar plantation in Cayenne (modern-day Guyane), shows that French Americans produced fine pottery locally, for the debris found there by archaeologists included imported fine stoneware and Chinese porcelain, but the Jesuits also manufactured their own pottery, using a staff of fourteen slaves who produced earthenware both for use on the estate and for export within the region.[21]

NONELITE POTTERY

Whereas elites might mix pottery traditions, nonelites also produced and consumed pottery, which tended to be more utilitarian than beautiful, but which still gives insight into aesthetic change. Lower-class people, slaves, and indentured servants rarely consumed imported pottery – they made it themselves. In general, archaeologists who investigate this pottery have called it "Colono-Ware," which meant locally produced, handcrafted, low-fired earthenware.[22] The term originated from what was deemed mysterious pottery, which seemed to fit no particular tradition, that showed up around colonial settlements (first in North America but later throughout the Americas).[23] At first it was ascribed to local Native Americans, but it showed little connection to any Native American tradition, so it was then ascribed to African slaves and their descendents.

However, Colono-Ware in North America and in Caribbean sites associated with slaves does not match African decorative patterns very well either.[24]

[20] Bradford Rauschenberg, "Andrew Duché: A Potter 'a Little Too Much Addicted to Politics,'" *Journal of Early Southern Decorative Arts* 17 (1991): 1–101; William Ross Hamilton Ramsay, "Bow First Patent Porcelain: New Discoveries in Science and Art (William Cookworthy)," *Magazine Antiques*, September 1, 2006.

[21] Nathalie Crouteau, "L'habitation de Loyala: Une rare exemple de prospérité en Guyane Français," *Journal of Caribbean Archaeology* Special Issue (2004).

[22] Lourdes Dominguez, *Arqueologia colonial Cubana* (Havana, 1995); Manuel Garcia-Arévalo, "Transculturation in Contact Period and Contemporary Hispaniola," in David Hurst Thompson, ed., *Columbian Consequences* (2 vols., Washington, DC, 1990) 2: 297–314.

[23] For a detailed history of Colono-Ware and its archaeological interpretation, see James Deetz, *Flowerdew Hundred: The Archaeology of a Virginia Plantation, 1619–1865* (Charlottesville and London, 1993), pp. 78–90. See also the classic work of Leland Ferguson, *Uncommon Ground: Archaeology of Early African America, 1650–1800* (Washington, DC, 1992), pp. 96–107.

[24] A good survey of Caribbean archaeology with a critical assessment of attempts to link it to specific African cultures is Mark Hauser and Christopher DeCorse, "Low-Fired Earthenwares in

Many of the vessel types and forms imitated European pottery, and indeed it also had affinities with the low-fired, handcrafted earthenware that was widely produced by humble makers in Europe, and in addition to being produced by African slaves they were also found in Native American communities.[25] In short, Colono-Ware is largely a new creation, not directly imitative of any one tradition, but a sort of highly mixed and eclectic set of functional wares.

The Colono-Ware of Africans and their American descendants is particularly interesting, given the multicultural nature of African settlement in the Americas; as we have noted with regards to language communities, it might not be surprising that no African tradition would be uniquely presented in their pottery. Perhaps the most African component of the Colono-Ware made by Africans and their descendants in America was not their ceramic material or decoration, but their shape. The forms of pots are important artistically and thus a part of their aesthetic, but pots are also functional, and the shape must reflect how the users intend to employ them – for cooking, eating, and the like. In South Carolina archaeological sites, Colono-Ware was made in types of pots that represented the sort of shapes and designs that were used in most African cultures, reflecting their ideas of cooking techniques, but this tendency was less pronounced in Virginia, where there was also a tradition of imitating European designs.[26]

Colono-Ware seems to have been the pottery of the poorest people, minimal pottery for people with little time to make pots. Excavations at Seville Plantation in Jamaica revealed that even among slaves there were elites, however. Four Afro-Jamaicans who were buried in the mid-eighteenth century were probably among the slave elite: one at least seems to have been a skilled worker, a carpenter, another was a woman who may have had healing or spiritual roles; all were buried in coffins suggesting a certain distinctiveness. The fill around their coffins was mostly delftware, a glazed earthenware from Holland, and even one fragment of stoneware, or moderately expensive higher-quality European pottery. While the fill may be simply broken pottery that was at hand, the fact that so much was of European manufacture and the possibility that it was deliberately broken suggests that those slaves who enjoyed a somewhat better standard of living consumed more imported pottery than their poorer peers.[27] Lacking skilled potters capable of producing more aesthetically pleasing pottery of their own traditions, they turned to European elite pottery.

The study of Caribbean pottery is particularly instructive, because on many of the islands there is a sharp break between the pottery produced by indigenous people and that of the sugar estate; moreover, given the low number of Europeans on the islands, virtually any production must have been in the

the African Diaspora: Problems and Prospects," *International Journal of Historical Archaeology* 7 (2003): 67–98.

[25] Edward Heite, "Colono: Also a European Pottery Tradition?" (published on the Web at http://heite.org/pdf/Colono-1).

[26] Deetz, *Flowerdew*, pp. 90–91.

[27] Douglas Armstrong and Mark Fleischman, "House-Yard Burials of Enslaved Laborers in Eighteenth Century Jamaica," *International Journal of Historical Archaeology* 7 (2003): 33–65.

hands of the slaves.[28] Colono-Ware was probably made in fairly limited contexts in North America, but in Jamaica, it was the daily ware of practically everyone. There was an elaborate marketing system of all sorts in Jamaica, much of the production for it, including pottery, was in the hands of slaves, and in fact, during the eighteenth century, the ware became close to standardized and its production centered in a few specialized locations.[29] In Jamaica, for example, there is not a clear distinction in pottery remains from the Great House at Drax Hall plantation and that consumed in the slave quarters, and although the quality distribution varies, European-made pottery is found on both sites.[30] As elsewhere, the locally produced earthenware of Jamaica (often called Yabba) has no clear parallels in Africa or in Europe, as with the North American Colono-Ware, with many decorative patterns (but mostly none at all), and again as in North America, the most African element of it is that the most common designs were created to accommodate cooking techniques that are used widely in Africa, such as the use of three stones to balance a pot on the fire.[31]

But this sort of creole aesthetic might not apply to everything. At about the same time that Colono-Ware and separate slave quarters appear on North American sites in Virginia and South Carolina, the inhabitants of these areas also made ceramic pipe stems. Pipe stems were being produced in Virginia since early times, and other were imported from Europe; initially most were undecorated white clay items. In the last part of the seventeenth century, however, a certain number, usually under 10 percent, were decorated in a new design quite different from the design of the other pipe bowls and stems. Here decorative motifs point strongly to similar designs in the southeastern part of modern-day Nigeria, the area served by the Niger River and its related streams and rivers.[32] Distribution of the decorated pipes often correlates with slave quarters. Shipping records also point to Niger Delta district, often served by the port of Calabar, as the source for a significant number of Virginians from Africa, although not by any means all of them. At points, however, this region did supply as many as half of the imports of people, and thus it might not be surprising that their pipe designs would be important in the aesthetic decorations of pipes. The pattern of imports of people to the Chesapeake region during this period is also unique; people from the Niger River Region were not brought in significant numbers to South Carolina, and not surprisingly perhaps, these design features are not found in that area.[33] The distinctive pattern did not last, however, and by the eighteenth century, this decorative pattern was no longer

---

[28] Hauser and DeCorse, "Low-Fired Earthenware," pp. 86–88.
[29] Mark Hauser, "Between Urban and Rural: Organization and Distribution of Local Pottery in Eighteenth Century Jamaica," in Akinwumi Ogundiran and Toyin Falola, eds., *Archaeology of Atlantic Africa and the African Diaspora* (Bloomington, 2009), pp. 292–310.
[30] Hauser and DeCorse, "Low-Fired Earthenware," p. 79.
[31] Hauser and DeCorse, "Low-Fired Earthenware," p. 88.
[32] Deetz, *Flowerdew*, pp. 91–102, including a useful presentation of earlier interpretations.
[33] Deetz, *Flowerdew*, p. 101.

in use. Possibly a small group of talented producers from one area had created a fashion that was widely followed, but disappeared with them.

The interactions of different cultural traditions in lower-class sites is revealed most clearly when one considers contexts outside the slave societies outside the Anglophone world. Excavations in the interior mining districts of Brazil, settled by the Portuguese and their African slaves in the eighteenth century, reveals widespread Colono-Ware made locally probably by African slaves. While decoration patterns there use some motifs that are found in Africa, the decoration of this pottery is not from any single African tradition, and moreover employs a wide range of forms. Some of the pottery is decorated with painted red slip, which does occur in Africa, but not much in the regions from which the slaves were drawn; instead it seems to be drawn from indigenous traditions of the area, and it is often found in European settlements. Thus, it would seem that potters, who were African born, combined European, indigenous, and African techniques and aesthetics to create something quite new, even if the pottery itself – low-fired earthenware – was not particularly elaborate or artistic in its intentions.[34]

The question of pottery is more complex when dealing with the independent free associations of the contact zones. By the nature of free associations, there were not great concentrations of wealth and thus no particular reason to develop an elite pottery. But at the same time, in North America at least, the considerable export capacity that Native Americans controlled allowed them to purchase a wide range of commodities, particularly because they were able to meet their basic subsistence needs through their own labor. A wide range of European consumer goods thus found their way into indigenous homes, purchased through the proceeds of the hunt and trading. In the years following 1760, a number of these goods substituted for ceramic products, as, for example, metal pots replaced pottery cooking pots. Study of the grave goods of Native North Americans has shown that imports from Europe joined and often almost completely replaced local equivalents, although they were not always used the same way (for example, thimbles were often reused as bells). Ceramics held out fairly well, in that some low-fired and locally made earthenware continued to be made and used in the eighteenth and early nineteenth centuries.[35]

The Evolution of Fashion: Cloth, Clothing, and Exchange in the Atlantic: The European settlers

Clothing and textiles have a functional use, just as ceramics do, and within the physical and practical requirements of keeping heat in and moisture out,

---

[34] Marcos André Torres de Souza and Luís Cláudio Pereira Symanski, "Slave Communities and Pottery Variability in Western Brazil: The Plantations of Chapada dos Guimarães," *International Journal of Historical Archaeology* 13 (2009): 513–548.

[35] George Irving Quimby, *Indian Culture and European Trade Goods: The Archaeology of the Historic Period in the Western Great Lakes Region* (Madison, 1966), the classic study summarizing a great deal of early archaeology; for advances since this work, see Patricia Rubbertone, "The Historical Archaeology of Native Americans," *Annual Review of Anthropology* 29 (2000): 425–446.

or cooling the skin and keeping off the sun, aesthetics play a big role in determining how this task is accomplished. In his classic overview of world fashion,
Fernand Braudel argued that fashion changes most for the richer classes, and
where there is political stability, it changes less.[36] In the Atlantic world, as one
might expect, there was considerable evolution of fashion as cultures met and
moved from place to place.

In Europe, the biggest elite fashion change was the movement from the
dark-colored and Spanish-inspired outfits popular in the sixteenth and seventeenth centuries to ones with more color that originated in France, which was
the eighteenth-century center of fashion (as indeed it would remain for a long
time). The trend was resisted in Spain, but by 1670, it had yielded. Within this
larger shift, there was considerable variety of hats and hat types with broad or
narrow brims, collar styles, either large or small, placement of buckles, bodice
styles, sleeve lengths, and the like.[37]

In the American colonies, there was a tendency for the elite, at least, to follow closely and imitate the fashions of their metropolitan country. Yet at times,
the empire went faster than the motherland, for the elites of the Spanish colonies abandoned black sooner and with more of a vengeance than in Spain itself.
The French traveler, Amadée Frézier, visiting Spanish Peru in 1716, was himself
a bit intimidated by the fervor and color of this Spanish colony.[38] Brazil also
took to what might be considered extremes; French travelers like the Gentil de
la Barbinais, from a fashion conscious and self-styled leading center of tasteful
dress, found the Brazilian elites altogether too gaudy and their dress somewhat
too lewd for his taste.[39]

Religion often helped shape fashion, although not so much in Catholic
Brazil or Spanish America, in spite of the strong hold that the church had
on many aspects of social life. Rather it was in Protestant areas, and especially those settled by religious dissidents, that religion dictated dress. Puritan
Englishmen, settled in New England, despite their reputation and indeed their
own remarks about the frivolity of fashion, seemed to have been quite comfortable wearing many of the latest English and continental styles, albeit not so
colorfully, having a preference for what they called "sadd colours" of gray and
muted dark tones, and for less extreme variations in styles of cuff or hat.[40] But
not always: Quaker settlers in the Delaware Valley and Pennsylvania sought to
dress "plainly" as a part of their religion, and many of the German colonists of
Pennsylvania, at least some of them, most notably the Amish and some of the

---

[36] Fernand Braudel, *Civilization and Capitalism, 15th to 18th Century, vol. I. The Structures of
Everyday Life: The Limits of the Possible* (3 vols., trans. Siân Reynolds, New York, 1981), pp.
311–315.

[37] Braudel, *Capitalism and Material Life* 1: 317–321.

[38] Amadée Frézier, *Relation de la voyage au mer du Sud* (Paris, 1716), p. 237.

[39] Le Gentil de la Barbinais, *Nouveau voyage* 3: 145–148.

[40] David Hackett Fisher, *Albion's Seed: Four British Folkways in America* (Oxford, 1989), pp.
139–146.

Mennonites, would eventually try deliberately to wear clothing of an earlier epoch and to enforce a close adherence to those bygone fashions.[41]

These strictures did not trouble the settlers of the Chesapeake who generally wore the fashionable clothing of the gentle-born of England and changed it as often, whereas workers tended to dress more or less as the rural peasants of England had.[42] In the West Indies, English or French, the wealth produced by sugar allowed the elite to enjoy all the fashionable clothing found in their home countries, even more than in the wealthiest of the North American colonies. Indeed sometimes this wealth reached a proportion where the propertied class resided in Europe, leaving management to people of lesser status.

AFRICAN FASHION: A CONTACT ZONE

Africa provides a different model for changing fashion. As a contact area, Africa was not settled from outside the region and had no particular reason to alter its clothing patterns or development, but in fact the continent did change quite a bit. Already in the seventeenth century, African elites were adding coats and hats from Europe to their wardrobe, which became a complex mixture of African fabrics and designs and European accessories. Most Africans retained the robes and knee-length skirt-type lower garments that tradition had held, but many elites added upper garments that had not been a part of the older tradition, except in Muslim lands. King Nzinga Nkuwu of Kongo received Portuguese visitors in 1491 bare-chested, whereas Garcia II received a visiting Dutch delegation in 1641 wearing Spanish boots and loose-fitting trousers, with a European coat, his only purely African item being his *mpu* or hat of authority. But the Kongo elite would only dress in this way on the most formal of occasions and to meet Europeans, for they preserved the netted shirt, *nkutu*, as an item of fashion right through the eighteenth century. Even the dignified Antonio Manuel, Kongo's ambassador to Rome in 1608, is depicted wearing one in a bust of him carved shortly after his death by the noted Italian sculptor Francesco Caporali.[43]

Rulers and elites in West Africa often wore whole suits of European clothing when receiving Europeans, though typically wearing more African clothing or mixtures at other times. When John Atkins visited the lands around Sierra Leone in 1721, a local Christian ruler, Senhor Joseph, received him "in European dress (Gown, slippers, Cap, etc.)"; elsewhere on the Malaguetta Coast, another petty ruler, John, wore a sailor's coat and an old hat, but also was distinguished by the number of rings on his toes. By far the most common dress in the region, at least of the lower classes, was a "Tomy, or Arse-clout."[44]

---

[41] Fisher, *Albion's Seed*, pp. 544–552.
[42] Fisher, *Albion's Seed*, pp. 354–360.
[43] Heywood and Thornton, *Central Africans*, p. 218.
[44] John Atkins, *A Voyage to Guinea, Brazil and the West Indies...* (2nd ed., London, 1726), pp. 55, 58, 60.

FIGURE 10. Agostino Brunias print, "Villagers Merry-Making in the Island of St. Vincent with dancers and musicians, a landscape with huts on a hill, ca. 1775." Courtesy of the National Library of Jamaica.

At the Sestos, the same things applied: Pedro the local ruler's dress was "very antick ... a red Bays gown checkered with patches of other colors, like a Jack pudding," while his nobles were "naked."[45] Not all elite Africans necessarily followed in the line: the "consa," or serial wife, of the Gold Coast factor dressed entirely in "country fashion" in spite of her considerable attachments to the European world.[46] Her situation was particularly remarkable, because the famous signares of Senegal had pioneered their own fashions that appeared as roughly a halfway mark between the country dress and European clothing.

The treatment of African women's hair showed a remarkable evolution during this time, for observers along the coast in the fifteenth and early sixteenth centuries noted that women went bareheaded, and fashion dictated that hair be patterned by wearing it generally short and cutting it to different lengths, or braiding and plaiting it, perhaps working shells or other decorations into it. This could produce a wide variety of hairstyles, the Dutch traveler Pieter de Marees showed no less than sixteen different styles for Benin in 1602.[47] Yet,

[45] Atkins, *Voyage*, p. 64.
[46] Atkins, *Voyage*, p. 95.
[47] De Marees, *Beschrijvinge*, pl. 18 (unpaginated).

at least in coastal areas where there was a Christian population of mixed race, women quickly took to covering their heads with scarves, perhaps as a stricture of Christianity, just as both Christian and Muslim women in Africa covered the top parts of their bodies following conversion. In Kongo, a Christian kingdom, such dress was the norm, while in the Kimbundu-speaking region to its south, a very similar region in other cultural ways, women continued going bare-breasted until well into the eighteenth century, save for the colonial areas around Luanda, where fashion followed the Kongolese pattern more closely.

It was this coastal or Christian costume that slaves took across the Atlantic with them, rather than purely African styles.[48] Many slaves, of course, were dressed by their masters in clothing that was designed to be cheap as much as it was to represent any fashion, but generally modeled on what the European working poor wore. Jean-Baptiste Labat, making sartorial suggestions to a would-be French sugar planter in the early-eighteenth-century Caribbean with 120 slaves, suggested two simple shirt-and-pants suits for men and shirt-and-skirt outfits for women, while noting that many planters skimped on even this simple outfit.[49] But even if they were slaves, Africans and their descendants did not accept this as the end of their clothing, for by one route or another many managed to equip themselves with more elaborate costumes, at least for feasts and dances. Labat himself describes this more elaborate costume, which resembles, at least as much as a verbal description can tell us, the dress of the Christian coastal West or Central African for women and a variation of European male garb for men.

INDIGENOUS AMERICA

Indigenous Americans interacted with Europe extensively, sometimes as conquered people, but even in conquered areas, with class-driven clothing, and at other times as independent people in contact zones. In Peru, the striking drawings of Felipe Huaman Poma de Ayala, done around 1615, record clothing of both the traditional Inca lords and commoners, and then show the panoply of changes that took place after the conquest. In his drawings of early kings, Poma de Ayala showed them wearing a knee-length tunic, variously decorated with designs that indicated lineage or rank. They wore sandals on their feet, fringed bands around their knees, and cloaks over their shoulders, along with various headpieces.[50] Officials in the same set of drawings were similarly attired, again with the primary differences being in the nature of their

---

[48] Thornton, *Africa and Africans*, pp. 231–234.

[49] Labat, *Voyage*, 3: 443–444.

[50] Kongelige Biblioteket, Copenhagen, GKS 2232 4°, Juan Felipe Huamán Poma de Ayala, "El Primer Nveva Corónica i buen gobierno," 1615, digital facsimile, transcription, edition and notes by Rolena Adorno and John Murra, http://www.kb.dk/permalink/2006/poma/info/en/frontpage.htm. An abridged English translation: David Frye, *First New Chronicle and Good Government, Abridged* (Indianapolis, 2006). The kings are displayed between pp. 53 and 110 of the manuscript.

headwear and the designs on the tunics.[51] Commoner males, in turn, were shown in the same basic clothing, but with less decoration and without the knee bands.[52] Women for their part dressed similarly to the men, except that they wore full-length dresses whose sleeves were more decorated that males' and cloaks closed with a pin. Like men, the elite women had complex designs on the fronts or bottoms of their dresses and wore sandals. They sometimes wore their hair long and free, but usually had a veil that covered the hair but not the face.[53]

The Spanish conquest of Peru had already had an impact on the clothing by Poma de Ayala's time in the early seventeenth century, a generation later. In the second part of the chronicle, which illustrates life in the post-conquest period, the commoners' clothing was more or less unchanged. On the other hand, the indigenous elite had witnessed a varied integration of European fashions. The highest levels of the elite – for example, the senior lords of Cusco and immediate descendants of the Incas – were dressed more or less completely as Spaniards, wearing shoes (not sandals), coats, pantaloons, and cloaks with round-topped bowler hats, just as their Spanish compatriots, who Poma de Ayala also illustrated.[54] However, the outfit of Cones Paniura, the chief overseer of 500 Indians, consists of a short tunic decorated in designs reminiscent of the Inca elite's tunic and pantaloons that include a set of tassles that seem to incorporate the knee bands of the past, but has shoes and not sandals.[55] Inca elements increase as one moves down the status ladder; Chira of Muchuia has more Inca design in his clothing, and Poma of Chipau, a mitmaq in charge of five tributaries, is more or less dressed as a member of the pre-conquest Inca elite, as are a number of other low-ranking *kurakas* and officials.[56]

Women showed a similar evolution, so that the queen had more or less fully Spanish clothing, except that her dress incorporated a typically Incan design.[57] Women were in the end less likely to be fully Spanish, for a picture showing a "good Christian" principal and his wife shows him dressed in mostly Spanish clothing while she wears a much more Peruvian outfit with a cloak clasped by a pin, much as her ancestors had.[58] Interestingly enough, Poma de Ayala thought that clothing should be differentiated by status, and his illustration of a local lord and Spanish official on this point belies the varied dress of his officials in

---

[51] Poma de Ayala, "Corónica," pp. 115 and 149–167, except for the foreign captains shown on pp. 149 and 167.

[52] Commoners appear in Poma de Ayala, "Corónica," pp. 153, 196–202.

[53] Poma de Ayala, "Corónica," pp. 120–130, showing queens, and 173–215, showing noble females and some commoners.

[54] Poma de Ayala, "Corónica," pp. 753–759.

[55] Poma de Ayala, "Corónica," p. 761; see also the Indian officials on pp. 778, 781, and 790 (a great drunkard and "enemy of the Spanish" is not so in his dress).

[56] Poma de Ayala, "Corónica," 761–765 (incorporating increasingly more Incan elements), 769 (Poma of Chipao); see also pp. 806–820.

[57] Poma de Ayala, "Corónica," pp. 771, 773.

[58] Poma de Ayala, "Corónica," p. 775.

FIGURE 11. "De Sambaygo y Mulata, Calpamulato," oil on canvas ca. 1770, by Buenaventura José Guiol. Photographer: Carlos Germán Rojas. Image courtesy of Colección Patricia Phelps de Cisneros.

earlier pictures.[59] On the other hand, lower-class people who had not remained in Inca society, such as mestizos or Africans and their descendants, wore clothing more or less entirely like what Spanish people of equivalent status or class might wear.[60]

Indigenous Mexican illustrated chronicles give us a good vision of the life in the Aztec empire and its Tlaxcalan neighbor. The Codex Mendoza shows that Aztec men wore a loincloth as their basic clothing in the pre-conquest scenes, over which was placed a cloak, tied at the shoulders, with both sides open that reached down to the ankles in both front and back. Workingmen, however, usually dispensed with the cloak, whereas the elite apparently had their cloaks colored and probably of finer material. Women for their part wore an ankle-length skirt and placed a smock that reached from their shoulders to below the waist on top of it.[61] Elites, such as officials of the Aztec state, wore the same clothing, but it was often colored and vividly decorated, and frequently included feathered and other elaborate headgear.[62] Military officers, on the other hand, wore two-piece suits with long sleeves for the top part and

[59] Poma de Ayala, "Corónica," p. 800.
[60] Poma de Ayala, "Corónica," pp. 499, 509.
[61] Codex Mendoza, fols. 60 and 61, which shows the raising of children of both sexes. The coloring of cloaks is not a feature of the Codex Mendoza illustrations but does appear in many of the paintings in the Florentine Codex; see also Codex Magliabechiano, p. 155.
[62] Codex Mendoza, fol 65.

tight trousers on the bottom, unlike the common clothing; they were colored and often made of finer materials or feathers, although the rank and file do not appear to have worn any special clothing.[63]

People of the Mixtec region around Oaxaca dressed much as their Nahua-speaking neighbors of the Aztec empire, as is illustrated in a number of their own codices. As they yielded to the Spanish, most of the elite continued in office, but fairly quickly added Spanish items to their clothing. A mid-sixteenth-century codex, Codex Yanhuitlan, shows a cacique of the region, Don Domingos, wearing a Spanish shirt and trousers, but a traditional cloak.[64]

As in Peru, this inventory of Mesoamerican clothing changed through contact with the Spanish. In the eighteenth century, artists in both Mexico and Peru (but particularly in Mexico) began to produce remarkable illustrations, called "casta paintings," which were intended to depict the various cross-breedings that the mixture of Native Americans, Africans, and Europeans had produced.[65] While the paintings are interesting for what they reveal about concepts of various mixed-race classes, they are also wonderful sources for the clothing and objects of everyday life. The "indios" of the various pictures are dressed more or less identically to the ordinary people of the codices, but once one moves up the class scale, or includes people of mixed ancestry (of which casta paintings, by their nature, focus on), they wear a bewildering variety and combination of clothing. What casta paintings cannot reveal, however, is the dress of the indigenous elite, the landholders, inhabitants of privileged towns and districts (like Tlaxcala), and the like. While it is possible that the indigenous elite may have continued some traditions in these depictions of castas that had some indigenous ancestry, it cannot be clearly seen.

While we might not be surprised to see a sartorial Hispanicization of the indigenous elite in those conquered areas where the elite continued to be wealthy, intermarried with the Spanish, and played an active role in higher society, we would not be surprised to see the continuation of more traditional dress by lower orders, including the lower orders of the indigenous elite. Elsewhere in the Americas, however, there is less differentiation and the interactions are more complex. In much of South America, indigenous people remained unconquered, but not out of touch with the Spanish and Portuguese, and some were integrated into the colonial societies as slaves. In these areas, however,

---

[63] Codex Mendoza, fols. 64 and 67; for the rank and file, see Florentine Codex, fol. 3v; other scenes of warfare, such as fol. 34, shows all fighters wearing the colored suits. See also the battle scenes in Lienzo de Tlaxcala, fol. 79. Tlaxcalan elite soldiers dressed in clothing similar to that of the Aztecs; Lienzo de Tlaxcala, fol. 316.

[64] Codex Yanhuitlan, plate XVI, published in Kevin Terracino, *The Mixtecs of Colonial Oaxaca: Ñudzahui History, Sixteenth through Eighteenth Centuries* (Stanford, 2001), p. 33.

[65] Ilona Katzew, *Casta Painting: Images of Race in Eighteenth-Century Mexico* (New Haven, 2004). There are numerous collections of these paintings on line, for example http://www.nuestrosranchos.com/en/castas, http://recorri2.com/portal/index.php/es/contenido-carga-78/41-historia/272-castas-de-la-nueva-espa.html

missionaries had very often introduced new clothing, either in the reductions they organized or by simple influence.

Throughout much of the continent outside of the Andes, in fact, fashion was not expressed in textiles at all, for nudity or near-nudity was most common among everyone in the basins of the great eastern rivers, and in fact wearing any clothing at all was the clearest evidence of cultural exchange. In the aldeas of Brazil, where the religious orders did much to dictate fashion to the rank-and-file dwellers, they were not permitted to be naked, but neither did the missionaries dress them as Europeans. Instead, the people in the reductions wore simple calf-length pants (for males) and a form-fitting version for women, who covered their chests with a second piece of cloth, while males went bare-chested. On the other hand, mixed-race people, such as mamelucos (Native American–European), often wore a tunic that covered the shoulders and had sleeves and reached down to the knees, along with leggings or bare legs. This might be supplemented by an additional top cloth, as Albert Eckhout's dramatic painting of a mid-seventeenth-century mameluco soldier reveals.

A Portuguese account of a series military-religious missions between 1768 and 1774 to the Tibagi River region in the interior of São Paulo in the modern state of Pará, Brazil, shows how ideally clothing fit into the missionary concept. The Cainguangues, who inhabited the region, are shown in the initial scene in a series of prints illustrating the expedition with the males standing naked, with only a leaf over their private parts (but, the author explains, "really without the leaf … which is painted there for decency"), and the woman wearing a two-part skirt that covers her from the waist down. However, next to these figures the man is shown wearing a shirt, which still does not cover his genitals, while the woman is shown with clothes that "leave her very content and satisfied," which is a skirt and blouse in matching floral pattern. The remaining prints show the whole rather complicated pattern of gift giving, in which desirable clothes play an important role, in the complex process of persuasion, treachery, and settlement that characterized this particular campaign and the process in general.[66]

As with the Portuguese aldeas in Brazil, so Spanish-controlled South America beyond the Andes was notable for its lack of textile clothing. Although Martin Dobritzhoffer, a Jesuit working in the Chaco region, scolded Europeans for thinking that all savages went naked, he promptly noted that the Paraquariis did. And if they were not naked, their clothing was still very limited. The Abipones, the group with whom he had most contact, were modest, as their Jesuit champion explained, wearing a linen garment thrown over the shoulder, but rode more or less naked (and clearly were not concerned about being naked, in battle or while working).[67] However, Abipones were not averse to

---

[66] The prints are published in Glória Kok, *O sertão itinerante: Expedições da Capitania de São Paulo no Século XVIII* (São Paulo, 2003), pp. 170–189.

[67] Dobritzhoffer, *Historia* 2: 135–137.

FIGURE 12. "The Mexican Indians' Method of Hunting," from 'Hacia alla y para aca' (color litho) by Florian Baucke (1719–1789). Museo de America, Madrid, Spain. Image courtesy of The Bridgeman Art Library.

wearing Spanish hats on occasion, just as they admired and acquired Spanish riding equipment.[68]

Florian Baucke, another Jesuit missionary to the Chaco region in the mid-eighteenth century (1749–1967), described the life of the nearby Mocovi people, who are shown in his striking and naïve watercolors as usually going about naked. A scene of men rounding up horses, for example, shows no clothing at all, whereas another of women gathering honey from trees shows them wearing a simple skirt (the colors suggest it was a textile skirt). His own verbal descriptions suggest clothing and attitudes toward it similar to those of Dobritzhoffer, although he also notes the use of leather armor for fighting.[69]

The nakedness of the Abipone and their neighbors was shared, in pre-contact times, even with the stratified societies of the Guarani. When Ulrich Schmidel visited the Paraguay region around 1536, he met the local king, a man with considerable jurisdiction and power and who possessed, among other things, a silver crown. But the king was as naked as the rest of his people,

[68] Dobritzhoffer, *Historia* 2: 138.
[69] Published in Etta Becker-Donner, ed., *Zwettler-Codex 420 von P. Florian Baucke: S. J., hin und her hin süsse, und vergnügt, her bitter und betrübe* (2 vols., Vienna, 1959–1966) 2: 460–461, 590 (armor) see also plates XXXIII, XXXVIII, LXII (armor), and XX, XXI, XXVII, LXV.

and his adornment was restricted to blue body paint, jewelry, and other bodily decorations and modifications. This was not for shortage of cloth; the women, Schmidel learned, made fine cotton mantles, which they slept on at night or wore over their shoulders against cold weather.[70]

As the eighteenth century drew to a close, the independent indigenous inhabitants of the Pampa lost some of their strength to the increasing settlement of Europeans, mestizos, and mulatos from the coastal towns and Peru. These groups, gauderios or gauchos, usually of mixed ancestry, preserved a good deal of the independence of the Abipones and others they replaced, but did not take up their clothing. Carrió de la Vandera, crossing their lands in 1771–1773, noted that while they still employed the bolo, that most indigenous of weapons, along with the lance, they wore clothes that, while he thought them poor, being only a simple poncho (and presumably trousers as well), were primarily of European origin.[71] The gaucho style even spread to the wealthier inhabitants of the region, albeit with expensive modifications. James Robertson, a Scotch traveler along the Paraná River in 1811–1812, noted immediately that the wearing of poncho, broad-brimmed hat, and tight-fitting trousers appeared as soon as one left Buenos Aires, where more European fashion prevailed.[72] Indeed, he met Francisco Candioti, a wealthy landowner in Santa Fe, the "prince of the Gauchos," who had his gaucho equipment tailored of the finest material in Peru, but whose pattern was distinctively regional.[73]

In the Orinoco and Amazon, the situation was similar in spite of its social classes and more complex government. Gonzalo Pizarro, upon entering the Amazon headwaters from Peru in 1539, noted all the inhabitants went naked, thanks, he believed to the inconvenience of wearing clothes in such a hot climate.[74] Indeed, Acuña, describing the situation in 1638, believed that this was characteristic of the inhabitants of the whole of the river, for although they grew cotton, they did not use it to make clothes.[75] A notable exception to this general rule was found in the province of Omagua, one of the largest and most powerful of the mini-states in the region, where, Acuña noted by 1638, the people were all "decently clothed" and even made their own cotton cloth. The priest believed that they had learned this from the Spanish by intermediacy of people who shared a border with them and the mission villages.[76] This may well not have been the case, however, for in the same area, Carvajal noted the people were "greatly bejeweled with gold and clothes" (*ropa*) when he visited the area in 1540, before there was any missionary presence.[77]

---

[70] Schmidel, *Wahrhafftige Beschreibung*, pp. 35–36.
[71] Carrió de la Vandera, *Lazarillo*, pp. 22–23.
[72] J. P. and W. P. Robertson, *Letters on Paraguay, Comprising a Record of Four Years Residence in that Republic* (2 vols., London, 1838) 1: 183–186.
[73] Robertson, *Letters* 1: 208–211.
[74] Garcilaso de la Vega, *Commentarios* 2nd part, Bk 3, cap 2.
[75] Cristoval de Acuña, *Nueve descobrimiento del gran rio de las Amazonas* (Madrid, 1641[GB]), no. 39, fol. 18.
[76] Acuña, *Descibrimiento*, no. 51, fol 24v.
[77] Carvajal, *Descubrimiento*, p. 25.

Whatever the case was on the upper Amazon, missionaries did make a point of seeking to clothe the naked indigenous people anywhere in the Americas they found them. The Spanish Jesuit Joseph Gumilla noted that in the Orinoco basin before contact, men wore only a skimpy loincloth, and women a short skirt that left the top bare, but focused their decoration on body paint, without which, the priest believed, they would consider themselves naked. In describing many encounters with previously un-contacted indigenous groups in the late seventeenth century, Gumilla compared the event to Adam and Eve's discovery of shame, in which dressed Indians from the mission were objects of curiosity at first, but gradually, due to an awakening sense of shame, the newly contacted Native Americans wished for clothing.[78] Perhaps it was a missionary's wishful thinking, but also the integration for those who were brought into colonial society.

When Alexander von Humboldt crossed northern South America from Cumaná along the Orinoco and then east to Peru in 1800, he noted that the Chaymas, the most numerous inhabitants of the country, still went completely naked or nearly so. The German traveler thought that they had an "insuperable aversion to clothing." In mission villages, they wore a sort of tunic that left much of the body naked, and which they took off in the frequent times that it rained. Humboldt in fact noted that the clothing was little changed from descriptions he had read in writings of the earliest visitors in the sixteenth century, aside from the small additions insisted on, not always very successfully, by the priests. Elsewhere in the Orinoco region, where the missionaries had made no impression, clothing was more or less absent.[79]

While nudity or near-nudity might be practical fashion in lowland South America, the temperate climate of North America would not allow the same level of undress, and thus textile fashion was likely to have an impact. North Americans had considerable access to the world market, thanks to their collective control over the production and export of valuable products such as deer and beaver skins, or their capacity to sell their military service in exchange for imported commodities. Thus, they fit into the world economy as specialized producers who earned a sizable return from their production. As a result, and despite their own – and often historians' – insistence that this "dependency" made them poor, in fact they were moderately wealthy, albeit, like all specialists, subject to depletion of their resources or price swings.

Jean Lescarbot, writing the first detailed description of the inhabitants of today's Canada, noted that the men wore a leather undergarment around their private parts, and kept heavy fur robes over themselves in colder weather. Women's underclothing covered a bit more, but they too wore fur robes in the cold. To keep their lower extremities warm, they wore leggings and moccasins (*mekezin* in his orthography) to keep their feet warm. However, even in

---

[78] Joseph Gumilla, *El Orinoco Illustrada y defindido...* (2nd augmented ed [1st ed, 1740 (GB)]), 2 vols., Madrid, 1745 [GB]) 1: 136–139.

[79] Alexander von Humboldt, *Personal Narrative of Travels to the Equinoctial Regions of the New Continent during the Years 1799–1804* (4 vols., tr. Helen Williams, London, 1818) 3: 230–232.

his day, in 1603, they were purchasing French hats with their trading furs.[80] William Wood, writing in 1634, described a very similar outfit for the various Algonquian groups of New England, with a simple breechclout, leggings, and moccasins, and including fur cloaks for cold weather. As in Canada, Wood's neighbors were already trading, buying coarse blankets with their furs to augment their clothes, but as he said, "they love not to be imprisoned in our *English* fashion."[81] Andriaen van der Donck, noting similar dress in the people living around New Netherland in 1634, was also quick to note that they were rapidly acquiring duffels from Europe and replacing leather breechclouts (*Clot-lap*) with them.[82] At about the same time, Roger Williams observed that English and other European cloth was fast becoming important for making the clothing, such as breechclouts and women's undergarments, that lay closest to the skin.

This tendency, noted early, continued, so that eighteenth-century pictures and descriptions continue to show the same basic clothing arrangements – that is, breechclout, leggings, and cape or robe, depending on weather – but they were ever more rapidly replaced with imported fabrics. Father Louis Hennepin, traveling in the Great Lakes region and southward near the headwaters of the Mississippi in the 1680s, described the clothing of the local people in his day: some dressed in skins, the older tradition, but those who "have commerce with Europeans wear a shirt, a coat with a hood, and a strip of cloth that hangs down in front and back and is fastened to a belt." More, when the spring hunt was finished, there were those who bought French body coats, shoes, and hats that they wore "out of respect for the French." They continued with the leggings and moccasins, although some leggings may well have been cloth rather than leather. They might also augment their old-fashioned fur robes with blankets, which they held in place with their hands.[83] A French portrait, executed in 1717, shows a "Neppesingue" dressed in cloth but with the same combination of clothing, except for not wearing leggings.[84] His dress is almost identical to the four Iroquois kings who visited England in 1710, although one of them, Theyanoguin, designated "emperor" by the English, wears European shoes and pants.[85] On ceremonial occasions, or when visiting abroad, Native American leaders might don European clothing, as Pocahontas did during her visit (and portrait) in England in 1616.[86] Military uniforms, or at least the coats of them, and even more items of European clothing might be worn frequently as the occasion merited.

---

[80] Marc Lescarbot, *History of New France* (bilingual edition, 3 vols., Toronto, 1914), 3: 131–133 (French 372–373).

[81] William Wood, *New England's Prospect* (London, 1634), p. 48.

[82] Van der Donck, *Beschrijvinge*, pp. 56–57.

[83] Hennipin, *Nouveau voyage*, pp. 181–182.

[84] Bibliothèque Nationale de Paris, "Sauvage Nepisingue en Canada 1717." Online at http://gallica2.bnf.fr/ark:/12148/btv1b78043626

[85] Paintings by John Verelst, now in the National Library and Archives of Canada.

[86] Engraving by Simon de Passe published in *The generall historie of Virginia, New-England, and the Summer Isles* (London, 1624).

In more southerly areas, where climate was generally mild, Algonquian-speaking people were typically represented as wearing simply a one-piece garment that covered the lower body to the waist for both males and females. John White's striking paintings of today's North Carolina in the late sixteenth century shows this costume very well.[87] Georg Friedrich von Recke, whose visit to Georgia in 1726 left a vividly illustrated sketch book that shows a wide variety of clothing, includes the same garment, but also adds, for many, nice illustrations of the leggings that covered from the mid-thigh to the ankle, attested for the residents of New England and Canada, and also included a cloak worn over the shoulders for colder weather, again as in the north.[88] Similar pictures adorn Simon le Page du Pratz's early-eighteenth-century illustrations of the life of the Natchez of today's Louisiana and their neighbors.[89]

But the southern and warmer end of the spectrum of Native Americans underwent the same sort of transformation that Hennepin noted in the late seventeenth century. When Timberlake visited the Cherokees in 1762, he noted that most of them wore the same clothing, more or less, as the Europeans did, but that the elders "still remember and praise the ancient days" when they wore "a bit of skin about their middles, moccasins, a mantle of buffalo skin for the winter, and a lighter one of feathers for the summer."[90]

Native American ideas of decoration and clothing customs had its own impact on the clothing of Europeans who settled in their midst, for the eighteenth-century frontiersman often added many Native American items to his clothing (women did not follow suit with quite the same vigor), so that at times, they could hardly be differentiated from the Native Americans who they often hated and killed at every opportunity.

VIRTUOSITY: PRODUCER AND CONSUMER IN MUSIC AND FINE ARTS

Ceramics and fashions were mostly produced by a large number of producers and consumed widely as well. By contrast, performance aesthetics, especially music, involved a different dynamic, primarily because of the role of individual artists in producing music for whole communities. Unlike the potter or the clothier, the highly skilled artist, the virtuoso, is the key to musical change (and other fine art forms as well). But also unlike clothiers or potters, musicians

---

[87] The paintings and engravings drawn from them by Theodor de Bry can be found online at http://www.virtualjamestown.org/images/white_debry_html/jamestown.html

[88] Philip von Reck, *Von Reck's Voyage: Drawings and Journal of Philip Georg Friedrich von Reck* (mod. ed. and tr. Kristian Hvidt, with Joseph Ewan, George F. Jones, and William C. Sturtevant, Savannah, 1980). The illustrations are also online at http://base.kb.dk/manus_pub/cv/manus/ManusIntro.xsql?nnoc=manus_pub&p_ManusId=22&p_Lang=alt

[89] Le Page du Pratz, *Histoire de la Louisiane*, illustrations numbered 33 (2: 300, summer dress), 34 (2: 309 winter dress), and 35 (2: 314 woman and girl) as displayed on Gallica at http://gallica.bnf.fr/ark:/12148/btv1b2300740h.planchecontact.r=le+page+du+pratz.f28.langEN

[90] Timberlake, *Memoirs*, p. 51.

FIGURE 13. Alexander De Batz, "Desseins de Sauvages de Plusieurs Nations, 1785."
Courtesy of the Peabody Museum of Archaeology and Ethnology, Harvard University,
41–72–10/20.

and their audiences influence each other, mutually forming what I am calling a
patronage community.

The patronage community starts with the virtuoso artist. While it may be
true that anyone can sing and clap their hands, not everyone can play a musical
instrument, and archaeology has established that people have been augmenting
their own voices and bodies with instruments since prehistoric times.[91] Musical
instruments are ubiquitous in human cultures, but both archaeological work
and recorded observation make it clear that only a small number of people in
any given culture actually play them. Most households did not possess a musical instrument and therefore from very early times, musicians were specialists
supported by the community effort of their audiences, even if they still had to
engage in other labor to support themselves.

Musical instruments are difficult to master, and some people master them
far better than others. This complete mastery, virtuosity, is an important aspect
of aesthetic production and gives it a special character. Neuroaesthetics contends that humans possess a sense of aesthetics that is physically manifested,

---

[91] See, for example, Zubrow Cross and F. Cowan, "Musical Behaviours and the Archaeological
Record: A Preliminary Study," in J. Mathieu, ed., *British Experimental Archaeology* (2002), pp.
25–34, where bone flutes dating to at least 36,000 years ago are documented; see also Stephen
Mithen, *Singing Neanderthals: The Origins of Music, Language, Mind, and Body* (Cambridge,
MA, 2005).

and thus making a distinction between good and bad production is a common human characteristic. However, scientific investigation of aesthetic reactions has not produced a universal aesthetic, so it is also quite clear that there are culturally determined tastes that also define this quality.[92] Given this characteristic, those people, virtuosos, who are able to produce aesthetically pleasing work within a particular tradition are widely recognized and thus granted meaningful support in exchange for their production. This may take the form of leisure to practice their art, or simply the form of respect or attention. In complex societies, with social classes and centralized government, those who possessed incomes and wealth have supported musicians as clients, but even in simpler, more egalitarian societies, communities have patronized musicians.

In this way, musicians cultivate patronage communities of varying size and wealth to support their work – some might win a handsome living by creating music for a small number of wealthy patrons, others from a larger number of poorer patrons – but in each case, the musicians' primary task was to create musical forms and innovations that would induce the community to provide the necessary support.[93]

These patronage communities reflect a particular performer-audience relationship that shapes aesthetic production in music. Virtuosity is unproductive to musicians if their final product does not please their patronage community. Therefore, musicians shape their playing and their creations to fit their perceptions of the aesthetic sense of their patronage communities, whether it is a wealthy government official or landowner, the owners of a tavern or theater frequented by commoners, or even the democratic considerations of a free association or peasant villagers. At the same time, the efforts of the musicians to create pleasing music for their patronage community often shapes and changes what audiences expect, and this complex interrelationship between producer and consumer induces changes in culture and creative development.

The particular role of individual virtuosos in shaping and changing music means that cultural influence is not necessarily dependent on demography. That is, a small subgroup can influence a much larger group even if it is not from the same demographic group – ethnic minorities might be able to become musical creators in a way that linguistics minorities never could be, for language is much more dependent on demography than aesthetic culture is. One could imagine a talented individual single-handedly changing a whole culture's music, as indeed happens in more recent and better documented times.

---

[92] See the mixed results reported in Skov and Vartanian, *Neuroaesthetics*.

[93] My concept of a patronage community was born from reading various works of Pierre Bourdieu, notably *Distinction: A Social Critique of the Judgment of Taste* (tr. Richard Nice, Cambridge, MA, 1984 [original French, 1979]), esp. pp. 97–256 and *The Rules of Art: Genesis and Structure of the Literary Field* (tr. Susan Emanuel, Stanford, 1995 [original French 1992]). However, my own vision of the structure of patronage differs sufficiently from Bourdieu's (which is anchored on stable European societies, especially following the nineteenth century) that I have not employed either his terminology or many elements of this theory.

Much of musical culture in the early modern world was quite fixed and changed only slowly. Large group participation was important, and songs and music typically accommodated the limited vocal range of most untrained people. Musicians were probably more numerous in the whole population than they would be as technology such as recording changed the face of musical production. It was probably the virtuosos both among the poorer classes and the elite who drove change in styles, and when cultures came into contact, it was also the virtuosos who pioneered the changes that led to new music in the Atlantic world.

PATRONAGE IN THE DEVELOPMENT OF CLASSICAL AND FOLK TRADITIONS IN EUROPE

Patronage communities formed by wealthy elites were an important element in the development of virtuosity as well as the movement of aesthetic traditions in Europe. The Church patronized artists and musicians for much of the European Middle Ages and early modern period, creating a large class of specialized performers, schools of music, and other support for the talents of the most adept performers. When the medieval church decided to promote the Gregorian Chant as a sort of official music for the Mass, and even created a system to annotate it to ensure standardization of some of its features, they also created a continent-wide patronage community that shaped musical taste. A few laypeople, often of the nobility, also supported musicians such as the medieval troubadours or German minisänger. [94]

Medieval and early modern nobles regularly studied music and took lessons from masters, which also produced additional opportunities for virtuosos to enhance their own training and skills while maintaining professional status. Although the nobles did not necessarily become performers, and certainly not professionals themselves, they did develop a much higher appreciation for music than those without any formal training in music. [95] The widespread participation in music by the primary supporters of virtuosos led to greater demands for excellence in both performance and creativity.

By the early modern period, patronage had created a Europe-wide network of musicians who traveled from patron to patron and developed both a sense of local tradition and a pan-European tradition. For example, thanks to determined patronage by the Dukes of Burgundy in the late fourteenth century, musicians from all over Europe flocked to the Dukes' holdings in the lower Rhine valley to study and to perform. As a result, they developed musical styles that appealed to a wide range of European elites, and musicians from the Low Countries (usually called the Franco-Flemish School) often found patronage in the courts of powerful noble families in Italy. The Medicis in various places, the Sforza in Milan, and the Este in Ferrara all employed Franco-Dutch musicians,

---

[94] Harold Gleason and Warren Becker, *Music in the Middle Ages and the Renaissance* (Bloomington, 1981).

[95] Here Bourdieu's concept of cultural capital is relevant; see *Distinction*, pp. 226–256.

as did the church chapels throughout Europe.[96] Printing music in the period also allowed the members of an ever-larger community of specialized musicians to share ideas and test their audiences. The focus on virtuosity produced "stars" – musicians whose fame was widespread, such as Josquin Desprez (1440–1521) or Giovanni Pierluigi da Palestrina (1525–1594), and whose compositions and styles influenced others in the way that allowed single virtuosos to exert disproportionate influence on musical culture.[97]

In the fifteenth century, travel and interconnections between musicians and masters had thus created something of a pan-European elite patronage community. A certain break in this uniformity took place with the reformation in the church, and as a result, regional traditions developed, as courts and church bodies associated with them developed their own styles and cultivated their own artists. Italy and Germany, France, England, and Iberia all developed distinctive styles, but artists continued to travel and perform in other regions, so that the consciousness of regional difference was counterbalanced by performances of multiple European traditions in each locality, and the continuing publication of increasingly comprehensive systems of writing music down. Thus, in England, local composers like Thomas Tallis produced modified English versions of music that was originally created on the continent, and Thomas Morley wrote and modified music borrowed from Italian sources, especially madrigals.[98]

The Baroque period of the seventeenth century and the Classical period that followed, while producing music with different aesthetic characteristics, were still founded on the combination of virtuoso players and singers and a patronage community composed of ecclesiastical elites and nobles. In the Baroque, the highly skilled and professional characteristics of what was called Art Music were intensified, so that composers like Antonio Vivaldi, Johann Sebastian Bach, Georg Frederic Händel, and Henry Purcell were renowned throughout Europe, and indeed, thanks to colonization movement in the Atlantic region, in the Americas as well.[99] In the Classical period, regional cultures and "schools," such as the Mannheim school made famous by Johann Sebastian Bach (1685–1750), continued, but the idea of a pan-European tradition was well established.

The Bach family was a good example of the way in which professionalization and training worked, for the world-famous Johann Sebastian and his various predecessors and descendants worked and studied in many places, primarily in southern Germany.[100] Wolfgang Amadeus Mozart (1756–1791), another scion of a musical family, traveled widely in Germany, Bohemia (Prague), and Italy to

96 Allan Atlas, ed., *Renaissance Music: Music in Western Europe, 1400–1600* (New York, 1998).

97 David Fallows, *Josquin* (Turnhout, 2009); R. J. Stove, *Prince of Music: Palestrina and His World* (Sydney, 1990).

98 Suzanne Lord and David Brinkman, *Music from the Age of Shakespeare: A Cultural History* (Westport, 2003), xix, 69–70, 195–197 and *passim*.

99 Claude V. Palisca, *La Musique Baroque* (Paris, 1994).

100 Percy Young, *The Bachs, 1500–1850* (London, 1970); Christopher Wolff et al., eds., *The New Grove Bach Family* (New York, 1983).

study and perform, stayed for a time in London (1764–1765), and was patronized by both laypeople and the church.[101] The Classical tradition included both religious music and secular music, as both religious and secular patronage communities demanded music appropriate or in accordance with their tastes. Patronage of such music was a sign of nobility, but the performances of many, especially the religious musicians, were public and often attended by fairly large numbers of people from many walks of life.

Artistic production often followed patronage across the Atlantic as well as in Europe, and in general, where wealth was concentrated, Americans tended to follow European models and even to patronize European artists. In Brazil, as in other Iberian Catholic countries, the Church played a major role in patronage of art and music, not just for the church itself, but for the ubiquitous lay confraternities, the major social organization for people of all varying social and economic statuses. Studies of confraternities' finances reveal that the bulk of their expenses were for sumptuous (or at least as sumptuous as possible) displays of cultural production, including patronizing musicians.[102] Confraternities demonstrated their wealth and cultural sophistication in the frequent processions organized on feast days of the church, where dancing and music were particularly noted and the highest fashion was displayed for all to see. François Froger, a French world traveler, witnessed one such festival in Bahia in 1697, and was greatly impressed by the huge popular turnout and stately grandeur of part of the event, but shocked by what he saw as "lewd postures" of the dancers.[103]

In addition to the confraternities, artistic performance of a more or less strictly European sort was available through the church, which often formed the gatekeeper of a patronage community that might include the masses of ordinary people. Le Gentil de la Barbinais, a globe-trotting French traveler, witnessed a play put on in 1717 by the Brazilian nuns of Salvador, in which, he claimed, each spent a year preparing a musical number and acting a play, which was much too scandalous for his taste, involving a love affair between a noble gentleman and a nun.[104] Later, he attended another festival, dedicated to São Gonçalo de Amarante, where there was "an astonishing multitude of people dancing to the sound of their guitars," and he found it incredible "in a church to see priests, women, monks, knights, and slaves dancing and leaping pell-mell."[105]

[101] Ruth Halliwell, *The Mozart Family: Four Lives in a Social Context* (Oxford, 1998).
[102] Fritz Teixeira de Sales, *Associações Religiosos no Ciclo de Ouro* (2 vols., Belo Horizonte, 1963) 1: 82–84.
[103] François Froger, *Relation du Voyage de Mr. de Gennes au Detroit de Magellan* (Paris, 1698), p. 131.
[104] Le Gentil de la Barbinais, *Nouveau voyage au tour du Monde…* (3 vols., Amsterdam, 1728) 3: 149–152. The gentle-born author thought the musicianship of these nuns to be inferior, perhaps because it contained some creole elements, but more likely because it did not match his idea of the European standard.
[105] Le Gentil de la Barbinais, *Nouveau voyage* 3: 156.

In Spanish America, transplanted Spaniards – and soon afterward locally trained indigenous people – performed and then composed European-style music.[106] The town of Puebla in Mexico emerged in the seventeenth century as a cultural center and, judging by the collections of music housed in its cathedral archive, included a large number of pieces originally written and composed in Europe. However, the collection also includes a number of locally born composers, whose work, while not musically much different from the work of the European masters such as Mozart or Händel, demonstrated that local production of European-style music advanced there, at least in the category of sacred music.[107]

Given the role of the church, it is not surprising that they patronized musicians who could produce European-style music. From the beginning of the conquest in Mexico, priests trained indigenous Mexicans in European musical styles, and choirs and chapel bands proliferated all over the region. Increasingly, local composers introduced and modified European music to American audiences, without necessarily departing from the conventions of Europe, as for example, the locally born composer Manuel de Sumaya, who brought Baroque music to Mexico.[108] The church undoubtedly played a role in the continuing presence of elite European music in Peru as well, where the cathedral chapter of Cuzco and other largely European musical centers performed classical European music and songs.[109] Important roles were also played by the monastic orders and nunneries, where musical performance, typically of European music, or perhaps local music in European style, was an important part of their life. The fact that talented yet youthful nuns were often brought into the chapter for considerably lower fees than other nuns suggests that virtuosity was at least a partial factor in choosing musicians.[110]

The Brazilian elite patronized music patterned after Portuguese and other European systems, and some of the African or Afro-Brazilian musicians with talent were shunted into this sort of production. Brazil produced a number of African-descended and mixed-race composers and musicians whose work fit into European artistic music, patronized by the elite. Some of these bands were mentioned as being popular in the eighteenth century, and composers like Jerônimo de Souza Pereira and the noted harpist and professor of music Felipe Benício Barboza were noted for their talent and skill.[111]

---

[106] For an overview, see John Ogasapian, *American History through Music: Colonial and Revolutionary Eras* (Westport, 2004), pp. 11–28.

[107] Alice R. Catalyne, "Music of the Sixteenth to Eighteenth Centuries in the Cathedral of Puebla, Mexico," *Annuario* 2 (1966): 75–90.

[108] Michael Dean, "Renaissance and Baroque Characteristics in Four Choral Villancicos of Manuel de Suymaya: Analysis and Performance Editions (Mexico)" (PhD dissertation, Texas Technical University, 2002).

[109] Geoffrey Baker, "Music at Corpus Christi in Colonial Cuzco," *Early Music* 32 (2004): 360–363.

[110] Geoffrey Baker, "Music in the Convents and Monasteries of Colonial Cuzco," *Latin American Music Review* 24 (2003): 1–41.

[111] Claver Filho, "A Mão do Negro na Música Erudita Brasileira," in Araújo, *Mão Afro-Brasilica*, pp. 306–309.

North America followed much the same pattern, where the larger cities like Williamsburg, New York, Philadelphia, and Boston hosted artists and musicians who followed European models closely, while Europeans regularly visited or resided for a greater or lesser time in America. Singing and dancing masters could be found in all the major towns, and balls and theater engagements usually featured music in which the European-trained performers were most welcome.[112] Benjamin Franklin noted that the best American artists usually went to Europe, seeking patronage.[113] "Music," he noted, "is a new art with us,"[114] reflecting the widespread idea among American elites that there was little that America could offer in terms of creative production, that it could only be content with importing, or imitating, European models, both English and, especially in Pennsylvania, German. Even farther down the class ladder, among the middle classes, it was England that set the cultural model, helped by the printing of music, the importation of instruments, and even the productions of locally born artists and musicians – who often sought training in Europe.

FOLK MUSIC AND MUSICIANS

As the wealthy courts and churches patronized the highly trained and specialized musicians, lower ranks in European society patronized what is sometimes called folk or popular music.[115] Knowing how popular music originated or was propagated has always proved a difficult task – the music was rarely written down, and in general life among the common people was only recorded when members of the literate elite decided it was interesting to them. Nevertheless, enough evidence exists to suggest that the creative portion of it, as opposed to performance or participation was probably in the hands of a relatively few talented and committed musicians, whose creative work was then imitated by others, so that the virtuoso ruled in the folk tradition as well as the elite.

Folk musicians might be professional or semiprofessional, but often performances involved at least some group performance; for example, all would sing a song led by a musician with an instrument, or perhaps with a recognized good singing voice. Minstrels, a generic term for such itinerant performers, might seek their fortune in any place, and in 1321, they formed a guild in Paris, which lasted until its suppression in 1776.[116] The German medieval tradition

---

[112] Kate Van Winkel Keller, *Dance and its Music in America, 1528–1789* (Pendragon Press, 2007), for an excellent overview using original sources.

[113] Benjamin Franklin to Ingenhousz, May 16, 1763, A. H. Symth, ed., *Benjamin Franklin, Writings* (New York, 1905) 9: 41.

[114] Benjamin Franklin, December 11, 1763, Smyth, *Franklin, Writings* 4: 209.

[115] The definition and significance of popular versus elite culture has been much debated, especially following Peter Burke's important piece *Popular Culture in Early Modern Europe* (London, 1978). Burke's contention that a strong divergence took place along class lines in popular culture since 1700 has been debated and criticized.

[116] Edmond Kerchever Chambers, *The Medieval Stage* (2 vols., Oxford, 1903 [reprinted New York, 1966]), Appendix F, 2: 258–259.

had developed into *Meistersingers*, who also founded guilds with a system of training singers and poets that resembled that of artisan guilds with apprentices and journeymen, culminating with masters (*Meister*). People were drawn into the guilds largely through demonstrated talent rather than social position; for example, Hans Sachs, one of the greatest of the Meistersingers, was a shoemaker by trade.[117] They created musical rules both for composition and performance and had competitions. They performed publically on holidays in churches and in public squares. In any case, there were a host of commoner musicians, who often doubled as actors, poets, entertainers, tricksters, and even tooth-pullers. Living an itinerant life, they represented the professional element in popular music.[118]

The life of musicians whose music catered to the common people, a large but generally poor patronage community, was often difficult, although for the best it might be quite comfortable. The early-seventeenth-century Spanish novelist Agustín de Rojas Villandrando created an imaginary dialogue in which various groups of performers are defined in a series of questions and answers, which shows how close the coordination was between the actors/singers and their commoner patronage communities who ultimately supported them well or poorly.[119] Talent and creativity were important in determining the performers' success.

A significant difference between the elite-sponsored tradition and the folk tradition lay in the process of creation and change. No one can be sure who composed popular folk tunes, going back to the enthusiasm for folk traditions that overtook European intellectuals in the late eighteenth century; according to some commentators, they have been the spontaneous creation of people. Others argue that the composition went back to elites from the higher ranks of the nobility or clergy, and then worked its way down the social scale to commoners. While understanding popular creativity in terms of social class is not irrelevant, the real distinction is between some undefined spontaneous creation and creation by virtuosos, whatever their rank or formal training, as the elite music was, but with the names of the creators unknown.[120] It is thus better to focus on that group of creators as something in itself, whose long-term success may depend in some measure on their social position, but whose contribution to the overall creativity may in fact be quite independent of class or status, and governed by the preferences of their patronage community.

The absence of written annotation and large-scale performances tended to keep folk tunes standardized, but most of what we know about it shows that musicians must have shared their musical repertory widely (albeit with some

---

[117] Wilhelm Berger, *Hans Sachs: Schuhmacher und Poet* (Frankfurt am Main, 1994).

[118] Burke, *Popular Culture*, pp. 42–47; 92–102, 106.

[119] Agustín de Rojas Villandrando, *El Viaje entretenido* (Madrid, 1604, mod. ed., Manuel Cañete, 3 vols., Madrid 1901[GB]) 1: 149–152.

[120] On the question of authorship, and the spontaneous, natural, "whole people" concept versus one of composition, see Burke, *Popular Culture*, pp. 20–22; 24–29; 58–64.

linguistic and regional divisions to be sure).[121] Folk musicians, if the practice recorded at the end of the eighteenth century is a guide, showed their virtuosity by improvising their play, much as a modern jazz musician might modify and embellish a standard popular song, rather than composing new music.[122] In the sixteenth century, folk music began being printed and distributed, at first as lyrics to be sung to popular and well-known tunes, but later in musical annotation borrowed from the systems developed by the higher levels of the elite. This in turn allowed for the development of composition and dissemination of songs by musicians who could read and reproduce the music, and its alteration in conjunction with the common people who patronized them. From the point of view of a historian of music, the advent of written music is the first concrete evidence of the music being created, even if creators are often still elusive. Changes that are visible in the music itself – the notes being played, the instruments in use, the flourishes and decorations, and most significantly the influences of one musician on another – can only really be traced through the study of recorded music.

THE ANGLO-AMERICAN FOLK BALLAD – CULTURAL STABILITY IN MIGRATION

While wealthy colonial Americans patronized work that imitated and extended European models, even the humble might continue to reproduce European models in the folk tradition. The same sort of forces that shaped languages, but with considerably more openness, conditioned musical change. Thus, for example, one would expect that when communities moved as whole blocks from one section of the Atlantic to another, they would bring their musicians and their music more or less unchanged along with them. Germans migrating to Pennsylvania faithfully reproduced the music of their motherland in the new setting, and maintained enough contact over time that they updated their repertory. Germany's higher "art music" also traveled to America, and not just to German communities, as German musicians often won favor in England, which regarded German musicians and artists as superior to their own. But even the average German immigrant carried his native music with him.

The same was true of English immigrants who flocked to North America. Ethnomusicologists are aware that the Anglo-American folk ballads performed in the United States in the twentieth century had clearly demonstrable roots in English and Scottish folk ballads recorded as far back as the seventeenth century, including the same instrumentation, tunes, and even lyrics as their European forebears. In short, patterns of English music crossed the Atlantic in the same way that the English language did.

While the English ballads, many of which were printed in the seventeenth century and beyond, provided a model, often Americans performing them

---

[121] Burke, *Popular Culture*, pp. 29–58.
[122] Burke, *Popular Culture*, pp. 124–130.

would localize their content and change them to reflect situations of American life. Through comparison of this body of material, which began with the systematic collection of Francis Child at the end of the nineteenth century, scholars have revealed striking continuities between European and American folk ballads.[123]

Furthermore, given the patterns of migration, musicians and their patrons crossed simultaneously and to the degree that they formed culturally self-sustaining communities, they preserved and continued the older musical traditions, while developing them internally. At the same time that English music crossed the Atlantic, so too did Dutch and German music and, like its English counterpart, established itself in the communities to which it migrated. But unlike languages, musical communities did not have to die out, and indeed did not. German and Dutch musicians might learn to play for English audiences, and although they would not share exactly the same aesthetic in music, the musicians sought mightily to find common ground, taking what they could from their own tradition and highlighting those elements that seemed pleasing to English ears, while perhaps downplaying that which was less pleasant so as to maximize their patronage community. At the same time, all musicians borrowed from other traditions and mixed them in the way that seemed most pleasant to their audiences. In short, music quickly became mixed, and it is not surprising that the most easily illustrated direct carryover, the Anglo-American folk ballads, tended to be found in regions that were the most isolated, needing to be "discovered" in the twentieth century.

In fact, German and Dutch musicians might have found their task easier because musicians were already blending traditions – in fact, constantly doing so – in Europe. German airs and Dutch tunes were heard in England, and the reverse was also true. Although the world of the sixteenth through eighteenth century did not have modern mass communication or recording of music, musicians themselves were mobile enough that musical styles might be freely exchanged in nearby areas.

THE MUSIC OF INDIGENOUS AMERICANS

Movement of people from Europe to America in large blocks – a particular feature of North American colonization – continued European musical culture in the Atlantic, just as the movement of linguistic communities tended to preserve languages. For the indigenous population of the Americas, remaining in place would clearly have the tendency to retain the musical culture of the past and to continue it in the future. For the indigenous people, the issue was change in musical form from contact with Europeans, and the potential to have their aesthetic sensibilities influence those of the Europeans (and, as we shall see, Africans) who came to their shores.

---

[123] Francis J. Child, *The English and Scottish Popular Ballads* (10 vols., Boston, 1882–1898).

Given the many and varied social relationships created between indigenous Americans and Europeans, it is not surprising that the nature of this interaction varied widely and by region. In some of America, powerful local indigenous elites patronized music just as the European elite did, but in other areas – free associations or mini-states with minimal concentrations of wealth – there was a musical tradition that resembled more closely that of folk music in Europe, with semiprofessional musicians patronized by communities.

At the same time, patterns of contact, colonization, and conquest made for variable relations between European musicians and indigenous American audiences: in some areas, the European and American elites joined to patronize new music brought from Europe; in others, colonized, enslaved, or conquered Native Americans lived under the supervision and influence of the European masters and colonizers. Then again, America had a vast contact zone in which there was the opportunity for considerable leeway for performers to shape musical tastes of all the parties engaged in aesthetic interaction.

Patronage played an important role in the powerful pre-contact American empires. The Aztec elite, both religious and private persons, patronized musicians at the time of the Spanish arrival. Gerónimo de Mendieta noted, for example, that "each lord had in his house a chapel with composer-singers of dances and songs, and these were thought to be ingenious in knowing how to compose the songs in their manner of meter and the couplets that they had. Ordinarily they sang and danced in the principal festivities that were held every twenty days, and also on other less principal occasions." While this noble patronage was no doubt important, the real locus of musical contact was certainly at the level of religion. In Aztec Mexico, music was heavily patronized by religious organizations, and descriptions of music suggest that priests played an important musical role, in that the music that accompanied ceremonies was often played by priests.[124] The patronage of the temple was thus the crucial element in music, especially because so much of what the temple performed was public music for festivals and other occasions.

Bernardo de Sagahún recorded songs that were given to him by older priests when he was compiling his linguistic work, and the resulting work, *Cantares mexicanos*, while not annotated so that the melodic elements can be recovered, was annotated to illustrate drum patterns.[125] In addition to a variety of percussion instruments intended to carry the song, the Aztec priests played a variety of wind instruments.

---

[124] Gerónimo de Mendieta, *Historia eclesiastica indiana* (ed. Joaquín García Icazbalceta, Mexico City, 1870 [GB]), Bk 2, Cap. 31.

[125] John Bierhorst, ed. and trans., *Cantares Mexicanos: Songs of the Aztecs* (Stanford, 1985). The English translation of the text, presented also in the original Spanish, is sometimes held to take too great liberties with the language; see James Lockhart, "Care, Ingenuity, and Irresponsibility: The Bierhorst Edition of the Cantares Mexicanos," in *idem, Nahuas and Spaniards: Postconquest Central Mexican History and Philology* (Stanford, 1991), pp. 141–145.

FIGURE 14. "Aztec musicians" from the *Florentine Codex*. Ms. Med. Palat. 218, c. 262v., courtesy of Biblioteca Medicea Laurenziana, Firenze.

The Inca elite also patronized musicians for their public festivals, in which there was ample music and dance. Andean cultures in general had an ancient tradition of flute making and playing, including complex multi-tube flutes.[126] Playing these well required considerable skill and practice, in spite of Bernabé Cobo's contention, that anyone picked up the instrument and with only one lesson of practice was considered a master – a reflection of this Jesuit's surely exaggerated vision of seventeenth-century rural music rather than the music of the court.[127]

Even in mini-states where rulers exercised relatively little authority or had fairly small domains, they patronized musicians. Ulrich Schmidel, traveling with the Mendonza expedition into the Rio de la Plata basin in 1536, met the king of the Xarayas (in modern-day Paraguay), who came with his musicians playing on instruments that resembled oboes (*schameyen*). The king had the musicians play for him "at table" and the "men and most beautiful women must

---

[126] Robert M Stevenson, *Music in Aztec and Inca Territory* (Berkeley and Los Angeles, 1976), pp. 241–273.

[127] Bernabé Cobo, *Historia del Nuevo Mondo* (ed. Marcos Jiménez de la Espada, 4 vols, Seville, 1890–93 [GB]), Bk 14, cap. 17, 4: 228–229.

dance for him," which Schmidel and his companions thought "wonderful."[128] Gumilla, among the earliest to evangelize the upper Orinoco basin in the 1730s, described a wide range of musical instruments but generally in the form of flutes played at the elaborate funeral for one of the "magnates" of the Saliva nation, accompanied by solemn dancing.[129] He spent an entire chapter in his book on the region, describing the sonic qualities of a very large military drum of the area.[130] In North America, the ruler of a mini-state in coastal modern Georgia entertained the Spanish expedition of Pedro Menéndez de Avilés in 1564 with his own dancers and musicians.[131]

While these elites may have patronized virtuoso musicians – and our limited sources are not sufficient to be sure – the free associations probably had only the mass of people as a patronage group to support virtuosity. European assessments of the music of indigenous North America were generally unflattering, finding it monotonous and little ornamented with instruments. This may simply be the cultural shock of encountering another musical tradition, but it may also be a reflection of the sort of musical culture that develops where there is little opportunity for patronage by powerful elites, and where for that reason virtuosos are less likely to have a wide impact.

Marc Lescarbot, who served as a chronicler to Samuel de Champlain's voyages to Canada in the early seventeenth century, took an interest in the local musical traditions. He noted, for example, that the French explorer, upon landing, was met by a large group of people singing, among whom pipers were playing a sort of reed flute.[132] Lescarbot even went on to record the words to some of the songs, and attempted to render the music by placing the notes (in the form of "do, re, me, fa, so, la, ti, do") in his book. This song, which had religious content, was performed by a religious leader, who may have been a virtuoso performer himself.[133]

The relatively limited role of virtuosos may explain why Paul Le Jeune, an early Jesuit missionary, thought the music of the Montagnais he heard in 1634 was simply spontaneous. They sang, he said, on almost any occasion, and often their songs were monotonous, involving the same words repeated endlessly for long periods. People sometimes asked Le Jeune to sing in his own music, which they compared to the warbling of birds; when they heard a group of Europeans singing, they thought the multipart performance a confusion of voices. Le Jeune, like Lescarbot, thought that religious leaders exercised some direction in music, because he believed that the drum, managed by a "sorcerer," led performances

[128] Schmidel, *Wafhafftigte Beschreibung*, p. 35 (this assumes that Schmidel's spelling is his version of *schalmei*, an archaic German word for oboe).

[129] Gumilla, *Orinoco Illustrado* 1: 217–218.

[130] Gumilla, *Orinoco Illustrado* 2: 121–131.

[131] Bartolomé Barrientos, "Vida y hechos de D Pero Menéndez de Avilés, cavallero de la hordem de Sanctiago, adelantando de la Florida," in Genaro García, ed., *Dos antiguas relaciones de la Florida* (Mexico, 1902 [GB]), pp. 93–94.

[132] Lescarbot, *New France* 2: 325 (French 558).

[133] Lescarbot, *New France* 3: 105–108 (French 360–362).

most of the time.[134] Father Giuseppe Bressani, writing in 1653, thought that the Hurons did not teach music as an art – that is, in a professional way – at all, but rather took to it spontaneously.[135]

We should probably not push the idea of an absence of professional musicians too far, for hints in the early reports suggest that at least musical instruments were played by specialists, even if most daily-life singing was more or less the spontaneous rendering of simple, well-known melodies. Jesuits Claude Pijart and Charles Raymbaut witnessed a large group of people, gathering from many miles around at the home of the Nipissiriniens in 1642, in which the assembled crowd – which they estimated at some 2,000 – danced a three-part "ballet" accompanied by a drum and singing. This particular gathering had special musicians present, apparently, for they arose following one of the parts.[136] That there were at least some professional musicians who traveled from place to place to play is revealed in a letter of Paul Raugeneau in 1648 in which he told how Christian converts drove away a musician who had come from another village to play for a feast at their village, because he insisted on adding a section considered heathen to the celebration.[137] During one early visit to the Upper Iroquois in 1655, the missionaries Joseph Chaumont and Claude Dablon were regaled with music and singing in their praise in the local special style, and which was led by musicians who provided a rhythmic interlude.[138]

Farther south in North America, where free associations still ruled in the back country of the Carolinas, Timberlake noted the professionalization of Cherokee musicians during his stay in their country in 1762. In describing a warriors' dance in which a collection for the poor was taken up, he observed that "the stock thus raised, after paying the musicians, is divided among the poor."[139] William Bartram, his near-contemporary, noted that in the Cherokee communal meeting houses there was a special seating area for musicians, both singers and instrumental performers, who played for communal events such

[134] Paul le Jeune, "Relation de ce qui s'est passé en la Nouvelle France, en l'année 1634," *JR* 6: 185–191; 279.

[135] Giuseppe Bressani, "Breve relatione d'alcvne missioni de' PP. della Compagnia di Giesù nella Nuoua Francia" (1653), *JR* 38: 263.

[136] "Relation de ce qui s'est passé en la Nouvelle France, en l'année 1642," *JR* 23: 159–161 (i.e., 155–159).

[137] J. M Chaumonot to Superior, June 1, 1649, in Paul Ragueneau, "Relation 1647–1648," *JR* 34: 101.

[138] Jean de Quens, "Relation de ce qui s'est Passé en la Mission des Peres de la Compagnie de Iesus, au Païs de la Nouvelle France, és Années 1655 & 1656," *JR* 42: 67–69. Robert Stevenson, "Written Sources for Indian Music to 1882," *Ethnomusicology* 17 (1973): 32, n. 74 contends that the comment that the airs had "nothing of the savage in them" (*qui n'auoient rien du sauuage*) and their subsequent praise of aspects of the music suggests that they had absorbed some European musical influences, which makes a bit too much of the phrasing, as it might simply represent faint praise of music he found more pleasing than other indigenous music.

[139] Timberlake, *Memoirs*, p. 69.

as ballgames.[140] The U.S. explorers Lewis and Clark visited the Sioux in 1804, leaving a description of the free associations of the Great Plains. There they were seated in a large council house and described an orchestra, composed of several instrumentalists and a number of vocalists, that played for a ceremonial occasion.[141]

European music was introduced to the indigenous people of America from the very early days of contact. For example, Samuel de Champlain's explorers to Canada at the start of the seventeenth century, upon being greeted by indigenous flute players, played their own music in return.[142] Indeed, when the Spanish expedition under Pedro Menéndes de Avilés overwhelmed the French colony in Georgia in 1564, he invited a nearby ruler to dine with him and each had their own musicians play during the meal.[143]

These initial contacts and many others often brought about a sharing of musical culture, perhaps in a competitive way. As Europeans moved in more permanently, either as conquerors, settlers, or trading partners, the interactions increased and changed direction. Where Europeans conquered, as in Mexico and Peru, they often used their music as a cultural bridge to assist in evangelization. Not surprisingly, the Church played a crucial role not only in patronizing the creation of elite music for Europeans settled in America, but also in bridging to local elites and eventually to even commoners among their new subjects.

In Mexico, the church took over the functions of the priests from the Aztecs because it perceived them as both the targets of evangelization and the creators of the most important Aztec music. Ecclesiastically supervised music was from the start a mixture of traditions. For one thing, the priests introduced string instruments, and in addition they moved from a five-tone to a sixteen-tone scale, which produced music that they, at least, thought was less monotonous than that of their Aztec converts. Apparently the Aztec laity also came to accept and even to embrace this music.

In Cuzco, the capital of Inca Peru, even under the Spanish, great festivals like that of Corpus Christi typically featured indigenous music, in which musicians from the surrounding parishes performed music using their own instruments, and often carefully differentiated their songs and styles to accommodate regional differences. Such performances were already being organized in the mid-sixteenth century, and two centuries later, colorful performances by indigenous musicians, dancers, and marchers continued to be an important feature of the procession. However, the crossing of musical frontiers began

---

[140] William Bartram, *Travels through North and South Carolina, Georgia, and East and West Florida* (Philadelphia, 1791), pp. 298–299.

[141] Meriwether Lewis, *History of the Expedition under the Command of Lewis and Clark, To the Sources of the Missouri River, thence across the Rocky Mountains and down the Columbia River to the Pacific Ocean, performed during the Years 1804–5–6, by Order of the Government of the United States* (ed. Elliot Cowes, New York, 1893 [1814]), pp. 135–137.

[142] Lescarbot, *New France* 1: 325 (French 558).

[143] Barrientos, "Pero Menéndez de Avilés," pp. 93–94.

early as well. Spanish priests adopted an Incan victory song, for example, Christianized and perhaps with some changes in music, in 1551.[144] However, for the Inca elite, taking on Spanish culture was part of their own strategy for retaining their power and wealth. By the seventeenth century at least, indigenous musicians attached to some of these confraternities were playing European instruments in lieu of local instruments, and indeed, musical historian Geoffrey Baker has proposed that they deliberately adopted a great deal of European musical culture as a means of establishing, especially for the well-born Cuzco elite, that they shared in the heritage of the Spanish as much as in their own past.[145]

Although the great processions organized by the main churches were important, perhaps the greatest exchange took place in the religious confraternities, which helped organize local life, and which frequently employed musicians. The Jesuits of Cuzco, as in other cities, trained indigenous people to play European instruments, and perhaps also in European music, for certainly Jesuit-trained indigenous musicians were hired often to play in festivals with musical numbers performed for the Spanish elite of the city.[146] While in these performances they played European-style polyphonic music, they must also have found employment in local venues where the music probably incorporated the indigenous musical sensibilities but undoubtedly also mixed European and Andean musical traditions and instruments.

The archives of many Latin American cathedrals contain sheets of local popular music as well as the European musical traditions. Some of these productions were intended to represent indigenous music, or more likely, to include elements taken from indigenous traditions into European musical systems, and thus transformed to be a new American music.

For the Spanish who wished to use music as a tool in evangelization, musical virtuosity was perhaps of great significance. When approaching the relatively small mini-states and free associations, they felt that by introducing the complexities of European music of the Baroque they might win hearts through creating and controlling virtuosity, especially in cultures where it was not well developed because of lack of patronage.

This tendency is well illustrated in the Spanish conquest into the lands of the Chichimecs north of Mexico, where settlers were confined to a handful of silver-mining towns and a desperate war was waged against the free associations over control. In this area, as we have seen, the role of missionaries in reducing the indigenous people and thus winning military allies to protect the mines was of first-line significance. Unable to defeat the local people militarily, they hoped the Franciscans and other religious orders would at least neutralize them. While the Franciscans had some military support, their primary task would be attempted largely through persuasion.

---

[144] Baker, "Corpus Christi," pp. 355–357.
[145] Baker, "Corpus Christi," pp. 364–366.
[146] Baker, "Convents and Monasteries," pp. 13 and n. 77.

We know relatively little about the earlier periods, but Franciscan strategies seem to have been to create a musical form, European in origin, that might accommodate mass singing by untrained local people, but would be led by virtuosos who they trained. In New Mexico in the early seventeenth century, for example, Franciscans taught local people who they thought had talent to sing European songs and use European instruments. In fact, the region boasted an organ as early as 1609. Our extant documentation for the mission focuses almost entirely on European music, and performances were judged generally on how well a metropolitan European standard had been met. While the musicians may not have literally been able to perform for the king in Madrid, as some elated missionaries claimed, they probably did produce a music that had virtuosity not found in the preexisting culture and with that pioneered the acceptance of the music. Nevertheless, the local styles persisted – indeed they can still be found today – as well as some blended music that lay outside older documentation but is clear in the modern music of the region.[147]

Spanish penetration farther into northwest Mexico (including today's California and Arizona) in the late seventeenth and early eighteenth centuries continued the strategy developed farther south and in New Mexico. Here, Jesuits took the lead, but clearly used the same methods as the Franciscans had in the southern zone. Again the strategy was the development of European musical styles, played on European instruments by indigenous people that the missionaries trained. Ignaz Pfefferkorn, one of the Jesuits, particularly noted how well his own singers and players might match up with the best in Europe. On the other hand, Pfefferkorn also noted that many of the local people made their own instruments in European style and taught others to sing. His off-handed comment that sometimes these singers missed the notes or sounded off tune suggests that they had subtly caused their own music to enter into syncretism – again in the region in modern time, music with indigenous roots was still being played and performed, certainly suggesting the potentials for such mixtures.[148]

Spanish missionaries were generally not very appreciative of the local musical culture, and perhaps thought that their own music was sufficiently attractive that they did not need to bother much with local musical traditions. But at times, especially when the indigenous religious leaders were themselves musicians or their activities had musical or dancing as part of their authority, missionaries might seek to suppress local music. In eighteenth-century Texas, Franciscans tried to introduce Spanish dances as a way of competing with the local dance (and musical) tradition called *mitote*. While the people took to the

[147] John Koegel, "Spanish and French Mission Music in Colonial North America," *Journal of the Royal Musical Association* 126 (2001): 15–22.
[148] Koegel, "Mission Music," pp. 22–31 (see especially pp. 24–26, quoting Ignaz Pfefferkorn, *Sonora: Description of a Province* [ed. and trans. Theodor Treutlein, Albuquerque, 1949], pp. 246–247, 269, 289).

Spanish dances, they also continued the mitote as well, in spite of the fact that missionaries regarded the dance and music as non- and even anti-Christian.[149]

Exactly what music was played by the well-trained missionary musicians is difficult to discern. The names of the tunes are recorded, but often no musical scores have survived. We know from the surviving corpus of cathedral music from Mexico, as noted earlier, that purity of European form was important in the province's capital and among its European or European-descended elite (and their indigenous elite counterparts). The discovery of more humble missionary music in the old missions of Alta California (modern-day California) shows that there was a divergence in music from Europe to America. Whether it was an adaptation of the missionaries (many were not Spanish) to the type of performance that could be expected in the sparsely inhabited and poor regions, or whether it was a compromise with local traditions is still very much up in the air. There is little doubt, however, that the mission music from California, and probably from the Mexican missions from which it derived, was simpler and more direct, easier to memorize, and more likely to be accepted by humble singers than the complex music of the Baroque and early Classical period being performed in the cathedrals.[150]

The cathedral archives of Spanish America also hold collections of music that are explicitly labeled as being in the style of African music or of indigenous music; for example, the archives of Puebla hold music called "tlaxcalteca" from the nearby, semi-independent vassal of Spain. While scholars disagree as to how closely these musical scores fit what original indigenous or African music was, it is clear that they are not simply European music composed in America but contain original elements drawn from the musical repertory of those cultures. Indeed, they would be examples of what the result of the meeting of the two traditions might sound like.

The idea of developing musical virtuosity as a means of winning the local people was not confined to Spanish missionaries in Mexico. The Paraguay missions used a similar approach in an equally difficult situation. While the Guarani elite had more or less joined with Spanish invaders to create the Guarani-speaking mixed-race Spaniards of the towns and encomiendas, the missionaries worked in other Guarani areas to develop musical virtuosity. Anton Sepp, a Tyrolian Jesuit with considerable musical training, arrived in Paraguay in 1693 intent on introducing the reductions to the best in European music. He brought a range of musical instruments with him and, from his accounts and those of other Jesuits, trained the local people who showed talent in the building of instruments and in performing on them.

---

[149] Koegel, "Mission Music," pp. 33–34.

[150] C. H. Russell, "Serra and Sacred Song at the Founding of California's First Missions," *Musical Quarterly* (2009); Grayson Wagstaff, "Franciscan Mission Music in California, 1770–1830: Chant, Liturgical and Polyphonic Traditions," *Journal of the Royal Musical Association* 126 (2001): 54–82.

The result was that European art music, perhaps with some variations to accommodate the group singing common in the missions, was introduced to the region on a large scale and with a radically different patronage community. The repertory included sacred music, but also a number of operas; some were in Spanish, but for many of the songs the words were in local languages. In 1712, Domenico Zipoli, a notable European musician who would have probably had a significant career in Italy had he remained there, had a spiritual awakening and joined the Jesuits, later volunteering for service in Paraguay. His music was soon renowned in Paraguay, and dozens of manuscripts found in mission archives bear his name, sometimes, perhaps apocryphally. In many cases, European music was simply performed in indigenous languages; in some cases, newly composed music, using the European canon, was composed for the missions. While most of the music found in the archives in Bolivia (the only place where a significant corpus remains) is attributed to Jesuit authors, it is quite possible that local people composed some as well.[151]

In the lands lying around and north of the missions, however, another form of music, anchored perhaps in Spanish folk music, was being performed by the gauchos, whose songs greatly interested Carroio de la Vandera during his eighteenth-century journey through Tucumán on his way from Buenos Aires to Peru. The gauchos were not elites, even though mostly of mixed race and in many ways culturally they identified with Spain. They played European instruments and sang songs of love and honor, particularly on guitars. Their themes were Christian but not particularly driven by the Church, and the music was sufficiently pleasing to Carrio de la Vandera that it probably had more European than indigenous elements.[152] James Robertson was rowed down the Paraná River from Asunción to Buenos Aires in 1812 by Payaguas, hired but hardly subject to the colonial authorities, who regaled him with their music, which they played, however, on guitars – an imported instrument – and perhaps not too differently from the music of the Gauchos.[153]

Humboldt believed that the Salivas of the Orinoco made complex musical instruments in pre-contact times, but that the Jesuits introduced European instruments as well as their singing styles and musical tastes. Even many years after the Jesuit expulsion the music remained, and he was surprised to find them singing European songs and playing a variety of European instruments.[154]

It was not just Spanish missionaries that used music to win and hold converts, for it was similarly employed by French Jesuits in North America. They did not follow their Paraguayan brethren in introducing the elite European musical tradition, but they still looked to Europe for the model, translating

---

[151] George Buelow, *A History of Baroque Music* (Bloomington, 2004), pp. 405–408.
[152] Carrio de la Vandera, *Lazarillo ciego*, pp. 90–93.
[153] Robertson, *Letters* 1: 351.
[154] Humboldt, *Personal Narrative* 4: 547.

lyrics into local languages for their proselytes. In the annual letter of 1644, Jesuits reported that the Hurons said their prayers more fervently once they had been set to music.[155] Undoubtedly the most famous of these early translated hymns was the "Huron Carol" attributed to either Jean de Brébeuf or Paul Ragueneau, composed with Huron lyrics to the French carol "Une Jeune pucelle" around 1645 – today one of Canada's national songs.[156]

In their extension of the mission to the Onondaga in 1657, Jesuits encouraged local people to come for musical and dancing exchanges, sparing "neither the drums nor the musical instruments," the French singing in "savage" style and the Onondaga in French style.[157] Louys André, in his mission to the Nippisiens in 1670–1671, found preaching did little to win people over, but that playing a musical instrument and singing persuaded them to join in and thus to learn Christian precepts.[158] Hurons around Québec, settled in Jesuit villages, also performed more purely European music, forming, according to a visiting Frenchman, a second choir at church masses, singing harmoniously and probably along the lines of European church music.[159]

Indeed, the Jesuits used their own musical abilities and the interest that indigenous people all over Canada had in their music as a means of pursuing evangelical ends aggressively. In 1671, Claude Allouez and Louis André created hymns in indigenous languages, which they set to French airs in their mission at the Bay des Puans, and then, finding that the people enjoyed the music, recruited bands of small children who sang songs directed at what the Jesuits thought of as religious errors, which were tolerated because of the youth of the singers and perhaps the appeal of the songs.[160] Heni Nouvel, writing in 1672, said that the singing of French schoolchildren inspired the Huron children to take up singing hymns in their own languages everywhere they went, scorning the music of their ancestors.[161] Reading Jesuit accounts, one might think that the entire indigenous musical tradition was being replaced, but this was hardly the case, given that it has survived even to the present day.

This sort of musical virtuosity was not the monopoly of Jesuits, or even Catholics. The Moravians, who, after arriving in 1740, played a crucial role in missionary work and cultural exchange in what would become Pennsylvania

---

[155] "Relation de ce qui s'est passé en la Nouvelle France, en l'année 1644–45," *JR* 28: 33.

[156] Ernest Myrand, *Noëls anciens de la Nouvelle-France: étude historique* (Québec, 1899), pp. 30–34. There is no seventeenth-century copy of the hymn or reference to it in contemporary literature, but the tune and words were recovered apparently from the traditional memory of Hurons only in the late eighteenth century by Etienne-Thomas Girault de Villeneuve, who died in 1794. The translation into French was made for Myrand by Paul Tsaenhohi, a Huron notary.

[157] Paul Ragueneau to Procurator, in "Relation de ce qvi s'est passé en la Novvelle France, és années 1657–1658," *JR* 44: 23.

[158] "Relation de ce qui s'est passé..." (1670–1671), *JR* 55: 132 (i.e., 134).

[159] Lettre d'un François Captif chez les Agnieronnons, à un sien Amy, des Trois Riuieres, c. 1660 *JR* 47: 97.

[160] Claude Dabon, "Relation..." (1671–1672), *JR* 56: 133–135.

[161] Henri Nouvel, "Relation de ce qui s'est passé de plus remarquable aux missions des Pères de La Compagnie de Jesvs en la Nouuelle France, Les années 1672. et 1673," *JR* 57: 61–63.

and Ohio, believed strongly in singing and music, in large part because their theology stressed mystical conversion that music assisted. For all Moravians, "Singistunden," or singing sessions, were part of every community. Within five years of starting their presence in Pennsylvania, "our musicians had composed a pretty cantata in English … the first that has been composed in Bethlehem." That same year, the church diary noted that "the Indians could now sing some of the nicest hymns in their own language, which Br. Büttner had translated for them."[162]

AFRICAN MUSICIANS AND THE AMERICAN TRADITION

If we can see the continuities in European music as played and consumed by both elite and nonelite migrants, and the continuation of indigenous musical culture in place, it is more difficult to explain the remarkable conquest of the musical world of the whole Western hemisphere by music of African origin. Africans came as slaves, and if that was not enough, their culture was often disparaged and despised by the classes of Europeans most likely to own them. Yet in spite of these problems, African musicians and their descendants would create world-conquering musical styles whose global dimensions are quite visible today. It is a paradox that reminds us that aesthetic success where virtuosity is involved does not have to rely on either demography or prestige. Rather, by being placed in an environment of extreme multiculturality, African musicians were forced to forge a music that appealed to a widely diverse set of audiences. Ironically, the same forces that ended the speaking of African languages in America gave the musical triumph to the same people.

We know nothing of what sixteenth- or seventeenth-century African music sounded like, but we know from descriptions of instruments and from illustrations that Africans used many percussion instruments and that their music was probably very rhythmic, in all likelihood polyrhythmic, as it is today. It seems likely as well that it employed "blue notes" or generally did not accept the same scale divisions as in Europe, making it recognizably distinctive. This difference probably helped define the varying reactions that visiting Europeans had to African music: some, like Giovanni Antonio Cavazzi, an Italian missionary preaching in Angola, thought it sounded like the "cries of the damned in Hell," whereas others, such as the German Johan Nieman, visiting the Gold Coast in 1684, found it pleasing.[163] Among those who did not generally like the music, there were those who did enjoy the sound or playing of this or that instrument, or this or that element, even if they thought the whole assemblage was discordant, disharmonic (probably a reaction to blue notes), or chaotic (a response, perhaps to polyrhythms).

---

[162] MAB, Bethlehem Diary (Bethlehem Digital History Project, http://bdhp.moravian.edu/home/home.html, entries from February 25, 1745 (singing in indigenous languages)).

[163] Johan Nieman to Brandenburg Company, March 8, 1684, in Jones, *Brandenburg Sources*, p. 88.

As in Europe, many African musicians were the subject of patronage by wealthier people. The sixteenth-century Dutch traveler Pieter de Marees's description of the Gold Coast at the start of the seventeenth century reveals the presence of special bands playing for the elite – an observation elaborated on by the seventeenth-century visitor Johann Wilhelm Müller, who also noted that each officer in an army brought his musicians when mobilized.[164] In eighteenth-century Dahomey, the royal band was captured in one unfortunate war and had to be redeemed for a high price, suggesting that the court there also cultivated virtuosity.

We can also be sure that at least in some areas African music was influenced from beyond the local community, often through religion. In Islamic West Africa, for example, instruments were often shared with North Africa, and no doubt the presence of Islamic ideas may have shaped the way these instruments were played. Similarly, the prestige of Middle Easterners or North Africans in the Islamic world of the Sudan could have influenced the importation of musicians and their music through patronage by the Sudanese elite. The Sudanese world was the land of the *griot*, a specialist musician whose skills and products were valued by courts and elite families. Griots were expected to perform and to compose heroic music both to educate the nobility and to acknowledge and celebrate the activities of former heroes or contemporary rulers. The cultivation of the griots and their links to Islam and its music may have created a classical tradition of considerable reach in the larger Sudan region.

When Europeans reached Africa, they sometimes encountered the patronage tradition themselves. The Jesuit missionary Baltasar Barreira, living in Sierra Leone in 1607, related a story of a young German horn player, employed on a Dutch privateering ship, who was captured by Africans on the Ilha de Idolos and presented to the king of Fatema in whose jurisdiction the islands lay. The king, impressed by the German's virtuosity with his horn, employed him in his court to spice up his own orchestra, and even called on him to teach other young men, some from neighboring areas, who came to study with him. It is hardly surprising that the horn player was indifferent to the pleas of the Jesuit to attend mass and leave his non-Christian environment, for he was comfortable with the new patronage community and prestige his new position gave him.[165] The incident reveals not only the idea of a regional classical tradition supported by the elite, but also the role of training and the development of virtuosity among the class of musicians in a region of fairly small states outside of the Islamic tradition.

No ethnomusicologist has followed up to determine if horn playing in Sierra Leone was permanently altered by this nameless young German, but the combination of virtuosity and patronage make it possible that it was. It might not always work, for the Jesuit priest Jean Baptiste Labat, commenting on the memoires of the Chevalier des Marchais, thought it strange that French

---

[164] Pieter de Marees, *Beschrijvinge*, p. 87b; Müller, *Afrikansche*, pp. 104, 137.
[165] Fernão Guerreiro, *Relaçam annual das cousas que fizermam os Pades da Companhia d Iesus...* (Lisbon, 1611), Book 4, chapter 4, fol. 234v.

merchants residing in Whydah had not succeeded in introducing French music there, in spite of what he felt would be a good opportunity.[166] It seems more likely that such a combination did indeed make a difference in West Central Africa, where patronage and religion combined.

When the Kingdom of Kongo converted to Christianity, it took European church music along with other elements of the religion. Diego de Santissimo Santo, a Carmelite priest who visited Kongo in 1583–1584, noted that there were already present in Kongo a number of choirs that performed what he considered excellent Christian music, and one man he encountered could "sing to the organ," meaning polyphonically, the multipart harmony characteristic of Baroque music.[167] This music in all likelihood corresponded quite closely to European musical ideas and thus might have seemed, at least initially, alien to the African population with its very different ideas of music, but one that was at least predisposed to accept that in Christian contexts this was appropriate music.

In 1619, the Jesuits established a mission in Kongo and, as elsewhere in the world, they sought to develop African musicians and virtuosos who would perform in the European tradition. They organized choirs to perform Christian music, more or less in European style and often with European instruments. By 1625, they believed that their new singing had replaced all the original music. They did not stop with that; they maintained that this music kept wild animals from attacking livestock around the city, and when they temporarily stopped their songs, the wild animals returned, only to stop once the singing resumed.[168] While the Jesuits certainly did not replace the local music (and the animals were probably not charmed for long), they did continue the tradition of European-themed church music already in place in the sixteenth century. Capuchin priests visiting the coastal province of Soyo in 1645 observed 500 schoolchildren ages 8 to 15 traveling around singing Christian hymns in their own language.[169] Most traveling missionaries noted that Christian hymns were being sung in all parts of the country, with or without missionary supervision, often in areas that had not seen a European or a missionary in a generation. The tradition continued unabated even when missionary worked dropped off in the mid-eighteenth century, for the "mixed mission" that worked in Kongo in 1781–1788 could still find whole communities, which had gone many years without missionaries singing hymns.

Jesuits played an even more important role in the evangelization of Angola, as they were among the founders of the colony in 1575. By the early seventeenth century, there were Jesuit-organized choirs performing not only in the

---

[166] Jean Baptiste Labat, *Voyage du Chevalier des Marchais en Guinée, isles voisines et a Cayenne fait en 1725, 1726 & 1727...* (3 vols., Paris, 1730) 2: 250.
[167] Diego de Santissimo Sacramento, December 2, 1584, *MMA* 3; 296; *idem*, "Relaçion del viage que hiçe[n]... fols. 117–118v," *MMA* 4: 361–365, 367.
[168] Antonio Franco, *Synopsis Annalium 1625*, no. 14, p. 245.
[169] Serafino da Cortona to the Provincial of Order, March 20, 1648, *MMA* 10: 99.

Portuguese cities like Luanda, but even in rural areas.[170] When they celebrated the anniversary of their hero saint, Francisco Xavier, in 1620, Jesuit-organized choirs of Mbundu singers probably performed European-style music, if Jesuit practice elsewhere is a guide.[171] When Njinga Mbande, sister of the king of Ndongo and its future queen, entered the Portuguese capital of Luanda in 1622, she was greeted with bands playing music "both abbondo [Mbundu] and European."[172] Pedro Tavares, a Jesuit who worked tirelessly among the Africans under Portuguese authority along the Bengo River north of Luanda on the Kongo-Angola border, organized choirs to assist him and to sing the appropriate hymns. At the marriage of a prominent local leader in 1632, both African and Europeans played for the couple.[173]

If some of the priests tried hard to maintain a purely European sound to religious singing, their work was quickly undermined, for African instruments at least, and probably their musical aesthetic also, entered into the performance of religious music. When Njinga became queen of Ndongo and Matamba, she allowed missionaries to preach in her country after 1656 and returned to Christian worship herself; marimbas were being played in her religious services, no doubt with an impact on the nature of the music performed.[174] An eighteenth-century Capuchin guide for workers in Kongo noted the progress that this sort of synthesis of European and African music had made in Christian music: in describing a rural mass, it noted that those who were "capable of singing" sang along with it, while "many instruments of country use accompanied the song, which through their diversity could not create concord and produced a confused harmony." An accompanying illustration shows that in fact two marimbas, two African-style side-blown horns, two thumb pianos, and a drum were accompanying the priest, who probably found the music much less pleasing than the parishioners did, whose taste, rather than his, was being accommodated.[175]

It is not clear how important this new synthesis of music in central Africa was in forming the Christian religious music of Africans in America. Certainly thousands of Kongos poured every year into the slave trade, bound for every part of America. All carried in their heads, or at least their tastes, both European music from the church and their own continuing musical tradition, and most likely a synthesis of the two.

---

[170] Baltasar Barreira to General, May 15, 1593, *MMA* 15: 332.

[171] "Relação das Festas que a Residencia de Angolla fez..." (1620), in Alfonso de Albuquerque Felner, ed., *Angola: Apontamentos sobre a ocupação e início do Estabelecimento dos Portugueses no Congo, Angola e Benguela* (Coimbra, 1933), pp. 531–541.

[172] MSS Araldi, Cavazzi, "Descrittione evangelica," vol. A, Book 2, p. 24.

[173] ARSI Lus 55, fol. 100, Pedro Tavares account, 1635.

[174] Antonio Gaeta da Napoli, *La Meravigliosa Conversione della Regina Singa...* (Naples, 1668), p. 290.

[175] Biblioteca Civica, Torino, MS 457, "Missione in practica." (ca. 1750) fol. 7, online at http://www.comune.torino.it/cultura/biblioteche/iniziative_mostre/mostre/missione/prefazione.html

The case of African music in the Americas shows how a combination of patronage and a tendency for talented individual musicians to mix and alter music created a profoundly new and appealing music that eventually conquered almost every corner of the continents. Not only were some elements of African music retained in the Americas, but African-inspired music also became ubiquitous in the Americas, quite independent of the size of the African-descended community. It should be recalled, however, that African musicians did not generally come in communities, and the distribution of musicians into estates did not promote homogeneity either. Ironically, however, these very factors that made it impossible for African languages to survive gave African musicians the ability to project their musical vision into a much larger and more diverse audience because it forced them to create something new and broadly pleasing.

As in the case of speakers of African languages, first-generation Africans tried to maintain their own aesthetic sense in music. "National" music accompanied the development of "national" languages among African who were willing to travel and undergo some risk to be with others who shared their specific heritage, even if the circumstances did not permit it. Slaves in the French Caribbean observed by Charles de Rochefort in the 1640s and 1650s made their own instruments and gathered whenever possible to play music, sing, and dance.[176] Other writers noted that these gatherings were often by "country" (*terre*), suggesting an interest in their own African regional music.[177] Africans brought at least the design of some musical instruments from their homelands to the Americas, such as the banjo, the marimba, or the berimbau, and they adopted European instruments and made them their own, as they did with the violin (fiddle).

Nor was this national sentiment just confined to estates or rural areas. National sentiment and sociability took place in urban settings as well. Le Gentil de Barbinais, passing through Lima at the end of 1715 and early 1716, noted that the several African national groups in the city each had their own king, and when he died, the members of his nation assembled, "the men in a hall where they danced and got drunk, the women in another where they wept for the dead and did sad dances around his body." They sang his praises "and accompanied their voices with instruments as barbarous as their music and poetry," and no doubt drawn from the national tradition.[178] The Brazilian-born poet Gregorio de Mattos commonly commented on the urban music of Bahia where he lived in the late seventeenth century. At one point he mentioned seven dances popular in his home, whose names frequently reveal an African origin, such as Pandulungu, Guandu, and Cubango – with these specific names suggesting an origin in Angola. Another musical form, the arromba, was performed by priests, including the one who had previously been a Canon

---

[176] Charles de Rochefort, *Historie naturelle et morale des illes Antilles de Amerique* (Rotterdam, 1658), pp. 321–322.
[177] Du Tertre, *Histoire* (4 vols., Paris, (1667–1671)) 2: 526–528.
[178] Le Gentil de Barbinais, *Nouveau voyage*, 1: 115.

in the church in Angola, in a musical procession in Minas Gerais in 1738.[179] A celebrated description of Bahia in the eighteenth century by Luis dos Santos Velhena devoted a short chapter to the very visible gatherings of Africans with the "playing of many and horrible drums, dancing shamefully." They too danced by nations, "singing heathen songs, speaking diverse languages," just as there were "diverse nations that compose the slaves coming from the coast of Africa."[180]

If meeting by nations helped preserve a musical heritage for Africans in America, their residence on estates pushed them to cross cultures. The estates on which African musicians lived were profoundly multicultural, no matter how much people may have sought to recreate their national culture in America. In the first instance, there were usually Africans from more than one nation, and hence more than one musical culture, just as there was usually more than one language on any estate or any city. Musicians who served only patronage community of the estate or a nation thus would be more successful if they could find ways to blend these national musical traditions together in order to create satisfying sounds that would be appealing to all the various musical cultures on the estates, thus expanding the patronage community and its potential to support the musician.

Although slavery did not permit much concentration of wealth, slave societies managed to create patronage communities that could cultivate virtuosity. Celebrations that de Rochefort witnessed on St. Christopher (St. Kitts) in the mid-seventeenth century involved pooling of resources and sharing them out among the musicians.[181] Jean Baptiste Labat, writing about the same areas half a century later, noted that "they [the slaves] have among them those who play the violin very well, and who earn money by playing in assemblies and at the festivities of their marriages." From his description, the instrument in question seemed more like a banjo than a violin. Although Labat thought their playing not as good as that of Spanish and Italian peasants playing guitars, there is no question that their playing satisfied their patronage community and that they had, as Labat admitted, virtuosity.[182]

A remarkable study by Richard Rath reveals how musicians might increase the reach of their patronage community by blending national musics in Jamaica in the late seventeenth century, through the example of one preserved musical session.[183] The session was observed and recorded by Hans Sloane in 1688, in which he witnessed a celebration with music and dancing, and obtained a score of the music that was played from a certain Mr. Baptiste. As Rath points out,

---

[179] Rogério Budasz, "Black Guitar Players in Early African-Iberian Music in Portugal and Brazil," *Early Music* 35 (2007), p. 6.

[180] Luís dos Santos Vilhena, "Recopilação de noticias soteropolitanas e Brasílicas..." in Braz do Amaral, ed., *A Bahia no Século XVIII* (3 vols., Bahia, 1969) 1: 134.

[181] Rochefort, *Historie naturelle* 2: 321.

[182] Labat, *Nouveau voyage*, 4: 159.

[183] Richard Rath, "African Music in Seventeenth Century Jamaica: Cultural Transit and Transmission," *William and Mary Quarterly* 50 (1993): 700–726.

although Baptiste employed Western symbols and conventions, he used them to show a number of features that ethnomusicologists would regard as diagnostic of African music, such as the use of microtones and syncopation. Rath further demonstrates that the patterns of the use of progressions is very similar to musical traditions still living in Africa, thus proving that African musicians had transported the music of their homelands to America. One of the pieces, labeled "Kromanti," included lyrics that were recognizably in the Akan language, and indeed were to a song whose variants are still played today. The words of the piece labeled "Angola" were not readily decipherable, but appear to represent a Central African language.

Another level of analysis reveals an even more interesting result. The three musical pieces that Sloane recorded are each labeled by "nation" – one is "Papa," another "Kromanti," and a third "Angola" – reflecting, generally, central and west Africa. Apparently these three diverse musical styles were played at a single celebration, and one could well imagine that Africans were routinely exposed to the music of other African cultures at such events. The possibilities of such exposure were exploited by the musicians, always anxious to build as large a patronage community as possible and please as many as possible, by combining elements of multiple traditions into a single piece of music.

Indeed, two of the pieces reveal exactly this strategy. In the piece labeled "Angola," there are two registers for two players. The upper register contains elements that are quite distinctly Akan and not found much in Angola, whereas the lower one has mostly Angolan elements. In "Kromanti," a different and more profound transformation appears to have taken place. This piece, for a single player, incorporates elements from both Angolan and Akan traditions, suggesting that its musician had created a real fusion of musical styles.[184] That the anonymous musician was playing it apparently successfully to a large gathering suggests that he had probably succeeded in building a larger and more diverse patronage community than he might have done by sticking to one tradition, and this would undoubtedly lay the foundations for further developments along the lines he was pioneering. No doubt, other African musicians, even though they told European and American observers that they were playing the music of this or that nation, were actually extending the range of their musical culture, and building a wider and richer patronage community was probably their motive.

Naturally, if they could, African musicians would be anxious to extend their patronage community to masters, with their much greater resources, and to shape a music that would win their hearts. In a play of 1580 by the Portuguese dramatist Antonio Ribeiro Chiado, for example, an African guitar player in Portugal is forced to give up his seat because he was a slave, but immediately was given it back thanks to the virtuosity of his playing, which induced those

---

[184] Rath's original work is expanded in his *How Early America Sounded* (Ithaca, 2003), pp. 68–77. Further observations and a sample of his reconstruction of these two pieces can also be found online at http://way.net/waymusic/?p=13 (accessed January 16, 2008).

assembled to call him "the black Orpheus."[185] Talent could thus trump status, if it was great enough, and winning approval of the masters would surely help improve both status and finances.

When Richard Ligon visited Barbados in the mid-seventeenth century, a few years before Sloane's visit to Jamaica, he met an African musician named Macow on the estate. This slave played music on a variety of instruments for his fellows at various occasions, but his skill was such that he interested Ligon as well. Ligon proclaimed him a talented musician, and although the English visitor was not able to present scores of Macow's performances as Sloane was to do with the Jamaican musicians a quarter-century later, he did note that Macow was prepared to play for whites. Indeed, Ligon even taught him to play the theorbo, a European instrument.[186] Labat, as well, would sometimes play the violin for his slaves at their dances and entertainments in the last years of the century. While he did not say what music he played, it seems likely that he played European music but necessarily had to accommodate the nature of the dance.[187]

Those virtuosos who combined music successfully could enjoy renown and more lucrative patronage. A slave who could play an instrument, like the Maryland slave in 1749 who "can sound a Trumpet play on the fiddle," might be dressed better and priced higher than a regular field hand.[188] No doubt the possibility of better treatment and the opportunity to further their own passions for music spurred slaves with musical interests and abilities to appeal to masters' tastes. American masters, too, on occasion sought to influence their slaves and to implant some of the European musical culture. A remarkable number of African slave and free violinists are recorded in various sources in Charleston, South Carolina, often in the employ of dancing masters.[189] While these violinists might well have played European music for their employers, they may well have introduced further elements of that music to the African music of their fellow slaves.

When the French traveler François Pyrard de Laval visited Bahia in 1607, he learned that the former governor of Angola, probably João Furtado de Mendonça, had employed another Frenchman from Provence, a musician and accomplished player of several instruments, to create a band on his large sugar estate to play "constantly." He had organized some twenty to thirty people both to sing and to play musical instruments, presumably in European, perhaps in French and Portuguese, style.[190] In those days, the vast majority of slaves arriving in Brazil were from Angola or Kongo, and perhaps the efforts

[185] Budasz, "Black Guitar Players," p. 4.
[186] Richard Ligon, *A Trve and Exact History of Barbados* (London, 1656), pp. 48–49.
[187] Labat, *Nouveau voyage*, 4: 159.
[188] Elizabeth Donnan, *Documents Illustrative of the History of the Slave Trade to America* (New York, 1969) 4: 32.
[189] Keller, *Dance and Its Music*, pp. 107–117.
[190] François Pyrard de Laval, *Voyage de Pyrard de Laval aux Indes orientales (1601–1611)* (mod. ed. Xavier de Castro, Paris, 1998) 2: 818.

of Jesuit music instructors in Angola influenced the band's proclivities as well as the efforts of their Provençal director. On the other hand, a musical group formed by the Jesuits in Cartagena a few years later had Africans from several different nations, as well as a healthy serving of Angolans, and it also played probably fairly orthodox Christian music.[191]

As with music so with dance, as indeed the two go together, albeit without the same necessary emphasis on creative virtuosity. There was certainly dancing that required skill, and those with the most of it were admired in Africa. In central Africa, for example, military dancing, called *sanga* in Kikongo, was a means of training in and maintaining the skills necessary for hand-to-hand fighting, and involved dancing with weapons in hand. Even when muskets had replaced swords and lances, the dances continued to be performed, much the same way that close-order drill has been maintained in modern armies long after automatic weapons rendered such formations suicidal. Virtuosity was important, for Queen Njinga, though of advanced age, performed one such dance before her army as the Capuchin missionary Cavazzi watched. He was amazed at her flexibility and agility and commenting on it was told, "I am already old, when I was a young girl, I yielded nothing to any Jaga in speed of foot or skill of hand."[192]

If such dancing passed to America, it might be found in the martial types of dancing that one meets in occasional accounts of stick fighting, or the mysterious dancing and kicking master whose owner in eighteenth-century South Carolina was saddened when he ran away. Indeed, the unusual fighting from an upside-down position characteristic of Brazil and known as capoeira probably originated from a very similar tradition of the central highlands of Angola, brought, in all likelihood, in the late eighteenth and early nineteenth centuries when Benguela slaves were regularly traded across the Atlantic to Brazil.[193]

The Jesuit priest Jean Baptiste Labat provides a valuable notice on dancing as he observed it in the French Caribbean at the close of the seventeenth century. Each nation had their own dances: he mentions and describes dances done by "Mines" (Gold Coast), Senegalese and Cape Verdians, and Congos. His description of the Kongo dance matches, interestingly enough, a Kongolese dance that was detailed first by Cavazzi in the 1660s and then at the end of the century by Capuchin missionaries, which was called the "royal dance" and involved singing praises of someone while dancing more or less in place. The missionaries thought the dance solemn and graceful, but Labat, who knew it in the Antilles, though he also found it tasteful, thought it "little diverting."[194]

---

[191] Biblioteca Nacional de Colombia, Inquest into the life of Pedro Claver, 1658, fol. 175, testimony of Diego Falupo.

[192] Cavazzi, *Istorica Descrizione* Book 6, para. 31.

[193] Thomas Desch-Obi, *Fighting for Honor: The History of African Martial Art Traditions in the Atlantic World* (Columbia, SC, 2008).

[194] African descriptions: Cavazzi, *Istorica Descrizione* Book 1, para. 334; Marcellino d'Atri, "Gionate apostoliche," pp. 336–337; Luca da Caltanisetta, "Viaggio," fols. 60–60v; Labat, *Nouveau voyage* 4: 158.

But Labat, like the slaves he owned and knew, devoted the most attention to the *calenda*. This was a dance that originated in Allada, but had already passed from Africans to European-Americans as it was also done by the Spanish "who learned it from the Negroes, and it is danced in that way in all the Americas in the same way as by the Negroes." The dance was so popular among Spanish creoles that it made up, according to Labat, "their whole diversion being performed even in the churches, in their processions and even the religious scarcely forget to dance it on Christmas night on a theatre raised in their choir, whose grillwork is open, so that the people can be part of the joy that these good souls witness by the birth of the savior." The dance was performed in rows of men facing women, but special space was reserved for the best to dance separately and the whole was often witnessed by spectators. This dance, though unlike the military affairs of central Africa, seems also to have required some virtuosity and perhaps won its creativity that way. Labat, because he thought some of its individual movements lascivious, tried to ban it, as did public authorities in the French West Indies (though they were concerned more with the security threat of the large assemblies that the dance drew), but the passion that Africans had for it was too much for regulation; it was, Labat said "quite beyond the imagination; the old, the young and right down to children, whoever has the strength to sustain it. It seems as though they danced it in the wombs of their mothers." [195]

Named African dances also passed from Angola, in particular, into Brazil. One text says, "I am the paracombé from Angola." [196] Some of the dances had religious overtones in their African setting – for example, the dance called *calundu* in Angola and Brazil. Calundus were the names of the dances, and also, in Brazil at least, of the gathering at which these were performed. In Brazil, Catharina de Angola was denounced and repented for holding calundas, which "presumed that the said dances invoked the demons." [197] But the music had an appeal that reached beyond its original audience, perhaps because of musical changes. When Nuno Marques Pereira heard music played on a variety of African and European instruments for a calundu in early eighteenth century, it kept him awake and made him think such music must have been played in Hell. But the landlord [*morador*] with whom he was staying, now quite acculturated to this music, thought "there was no better sound to sleep quietly with." [198]

[195] Jean-Baptiste Labat, *Nouveau voyage aux isles de l'Amerique* (4 vols., Paris, 1722) 4 : 154–160 (under the year of 1698).

[196] Quoted in Rogério Budasz, *A Música no tempo de Gregório de Mattos: Música ibérica e afro-brasilica na Bahia dos séculos XVII e XVIII* (Curitiba, 2004), p. 30 (Portuguese version on p. 31). Budasz provides scores of music for these dances in this book, drawn from an early-eighteenth-century manuscript held today in the University Library of Coimbra, Portugal.

[197] Arquivo da Cúria Metropolitana, Belo Horizonte, Paroquia de Sabará, Visitas Pastorais, 1734, fol. 53v, 23 March (calando, denounced for superstition and demonism).

[198] Quoted in Budasz, *Música*, pp. 12–13 (with slight modification of translation).

Much of Central African dancing contains hip movements that Europeans perceived as lascivious or obscene, and this may well account for the hostility with which the church received them. The "cãozinho" (little dog) included a movement called *umbrigada* in Portuguese, which involved touching the navel and was regarded as sensuous to the point of scandal.[199] Mexican priests thought the same thing; Juan Jose Solorzano, noted a dance called "Congo" in Acapulco in 1777, years after the arrival of new Africans had stopped, which he denounced to the Inquisition as "shameful [*dishonesto*] and provocative."[200] James Sweet has documented the transit of the calundu from an essentially sacred dance in Angola to a secular one in Brazil, then its transformation in Brazil to a dance in which both African- and European-descended people participated, and eventually its transition, again as a social dance, to Portugal, finally making a new transit back to Brazil.[201]

Aesthetics, especially, the type performed by virtuosi, was the real mixing bowl of cultures in the Atlantic World. The opportunities created by the soft nature of aesthetics to allow mixtures and new forms to emerge from very different old ones made the aesthetic culture of the Americas dynamic. It is perhaps the ultimate explanation for the continued success of the culture of the Americas in the formation of world culture in the modern world.

[199] Budasz, *Música*, pp. 28–29.

[200] Archivio General de la Nación, Mexico, Inquisición, 1159, fol. 304, December 15, 1777, online at http://www.agn.gob.mx/guiageneral/Imagenes/index1.php?CodigoReferencia=MX09017A GNCL01FO006INSE002INUI1159&Tipo=H

[201] James Sweet, "The Evolution of Ritual in the African Diaspora: Central African Kilundu in Brazil, St. Domingue and the United States, Seventeenth to Nineteenth Centuries," in Michael Gomez, ed., *Diasporic Africa: A Reader* (New York, 2006), pp. 64–80.

10

Religious Stability and Change

Religion forms a middle ground in culture and culture change. On the one hand, it is potentially as exchangeable and flexible as aesthetic principles, but on the other it often demands rigorous loyalty, and thus changes relatively little. We have noted, with regards to language change, how German Amish and Mennonites in Pennsylvania held on to German as their language because of the strictures of religion.

The period from about 1500 to the early nineteenth century was one of great religious turmoil throughout the Atlantic basin, but particularly in Christianity. In Europe, the Reformation tore the existing church order to pieces, and in its aftermath, intense theological debate coupled with emotionally charged religious war called long-held beliefs into doubt. Religious fundamentalists, both Protestant and Catholic, went to war with long-standing customs and practices.

The spread of Christianity from Europe to the Americas and, to a lesser extent, Africa is one of the singular features of the development of the Atlantic world, so that one could say that for much of the Atlantic, Christianity had become its religion, replacing or at least absorbing many others by 1800. Only in Africa was Christianity's impact limited to a narrow wedge of Central Africa where the Kingdom of Kongo and the Portuguese colony of Angola were its adherents. Outside this larger area, only the Kingdom of Warri in the Niger Delta area (modern-day Nigeria) and scattered communities in West Africa, around Bissau (modern-day Guinea-Bissau) and in the immediate vicinity of the trading posts of various European colonies in Senegal, Sierra Leone, the Gold Coast (modern-day Ghana), and the Slave Coast (modern-day Togo, Republic of Benin, and western Nigeria) were part of a Christian community. Even as Christianity was spreading in Africa, at times, particularly in the Senegambian and Sierra Leone regions, Islam was also expanding, and the Christian coastal community met an emerging and increasingly militant Islamic wave moving south and west.

THEOLOGICAL UNDERPINNINGS

Throughout this period, therefore, religions were in active interaction throughout the Atlantic world. What all religions, whether in Africa, America, or Europe, had in common was a belief in the Other World, a normally invisible sphere that coexisted with but dominated This World, which is the material world we all live in. This World was governed in part by the laws of nature concerning perception, movement, and events that were predictable and reasonably well known, but the Other World both governed these laws and was not bound by them. However, because the Other World was normally imperceptible to the five senses, its existence was only known indirectly to humans.

To know about the Other World, humans received revelations, messages from the Other World of one or another kind, that exposed some aspect of its structure, history, or the intentions of the forces and actors that inhabited it. Some revelations were extensive, comprehensive, and complex, such as the large body about the Other World contained in the origin stories of the Jewish and Christian bibles, or similar passages in the Qu'ran, but other revelations were very limited and even personal, such as the flash of confirmation that a believer might have from an answered prayer, or the outcome of the successful performance of a ritual.

Revelations might be received in a variety of ways, both direct and indirect. A common form was divination, a process whereby someone in This World would generate a random event while asking the Other World to influence the event in such a way as to convey a message or answer a question. Other methods included prophecy, in which an especially talented person received messages personally through seeing visions, hearing voices, or having dreams that provided information either at the prophet's request or as a spontaneous decision on the part of the Other World to choose someone to be a prophet. The Prophet Muhammad, for example, according to Muslim tradition, did not choose or even want to be a prophet and only acceded to covey's God's messages when the Angel Gabriel demanded it and his wife Khadija encouraged him. Certainly a dramatic form of prophecy was when a person was possessed by an entity from the Other World, which took over his or her body and spoke using its medium's vocal capacity. Such prophets appeared regularly in Africa and among Africans displaced by the slave trade to the Americas.

Because revelation was a limited process, and the potential rewards from abuse were sizable, religious traditions usually insisted on some verification of the messages received or claimed to be received by prophets, diviners, or others who communicated with the Other World. Such verifications were generally miracles, which might be dramatic actions contrary to the laws of This World, such as healing incurable disease, raising the dead, predicting the future, or obtaining knowledge that might be unattainable with the normal five senses or everyday living experience. Most of the time, simple verification at a later time of the message such as an answered prayer, the unfolding of predicted events, or success in healing constituted miracles.

Revelations, once verified, can then be arranged between two ideal and extreme types: discontinuous and continuous. Discontinuous revelation was typically extensive and contained a great deal of information, usually delivered to the whole community of believers, but occurred fairly rarely. Once delivered, it was transmitted from one generation to the next, either through oral tradition or the composition and preservation of written texts. Holy Scriptures such as the Jewish or Christian bibles, the Talmud, and the Qur'an were all texts that incorporated discontinuous revelations, and the works were valued because they were held to provide information of lasting significance and from which a framework of action could be constructed.

Continuous revelations were perceived by any number and types of people, happened frequently, and not uncommonly were of limited value to the large community except when the contents of many were studied to detect larger patterns. Continuous revelation might not be the basis for a general religious framework, most often simply confirming or conforming to the larger picture developed from discontinuous revelations. But at the same time it might also be a source of innovation in religion. The divinations of fortune tellers, readings of astrologers, statements of possessed spirit mediums, spontaneous apparitions of Other-Worldly entities and the like were initially part of a tradition of continuous revelation, although sometimes, if the receiver's messages were deemed of general importance, they might be incorporated into discontinuous revelation. Continuous revelation relies primarily on a constant flow of revelation to renew and revise religious belief, usually to individuals.

Religion itself was assembled by verifying, sorting, analyzing, and interpreting revelations, and those who constructed religion proceeded in a way not unlike a scientist interpreting data. Theological strife typically revolved around questions of the authenticity of discontinuous revelations, the validity of continuous revelations, or the logical patterns of gathering and sorting revelations. Religions varied by the degree to which set bodies of people were charged with the task of regularizing revelations, and how much that power could be exercised generally. In highly stratified societies, such as Europe, priests were secure in their positions and their determinations on the matter of religion accepted and even violently enforced by the coercive mechanisms of the state against those who doubted. But in such societies, religious dispute might join political and social fractures, creating wars of religion that wracked Europe for much of the early modern period. At other times, and particularly in societies that were not stratified, such as American free associations that had little institutional authority, priesthood was always precarious, as indeed it could be even in some stratified societies, as it was in many African societies.[1]

---

[1] For a fuller discussion of these terms with special reference to African religions and Christianity, see John Thornton, *Africa and Africans in the Making of the Atlantic World, 1400–1800* (2nd ed., Cambridge, 1998), pp. 235–253.

CONTINUITY AND CHANGE IN CHRISTIANITY

The period of European expansion intersected with massive religious upheaval and change in European religion. The Reformation, with its origin in Luther's questioning of Church doctrine in 1517, took off just two years before Cortés's men advanced on Tenochtitlán, and the Counter-Reformation or Catholic Reformation dates from the Council of Trent, which began its meetings in 1545, as rival Spanish and Inca factions were deciding the fate of Peru. The Reformation precipitated or contributed to widespread warfare between rival interpreters of its message and those who denied it altogether, and was still a vital force in the Thirty Years War (1618–1648), when English and Dutch privateers were singing hymns as they raided Spanish and Portuguese vessels and founded colonies in America.

While the leaders of the Reformation and their Catholic opponents were largely concerned with the proper interpretation of discontinuous revelation, in debates in which rival biblical verses and interpretations were hurled at each other, new forms of continuous revelation emerged. The late seventeenth and eighteenth centuries brought about both a more skeptical attitude toward religious affairs in some circles and the emergence of continuous revelation through a mystical reaffirmation in others.

In general theological terms, all the Western churches during the Reformation were conflicted about the authority of discontinuous revelation and its implications for who had the right to interpret them. In addition, all the churches of the Reformation and post-Reformation era continued to wrestle with the proper balance between discontinuous and continuous revelation. These vexing struggles joined with politics to generate or at least justify wars and revolutions, and they were carried abroad both by colonists and by missionaries to the Atlantic world.

For Christians, the Bible was the single most important source of discontinuous revelation. The Bible was a record of a series of revelations, starting with the Five Books of Moses, which God was said to have revealed to Moses, and followed by other texts of revelation to prophets. The Christian Bible started with accounts of Jesus' life and revelations and was followed by a series of letters and histories that also recorded divinely inspired teaching. Christians also accepted additional revelations attested in Church histories, or by other writers deemed to be divinely inspired.

This body of scripture was complex and at times contradictory, and by the fifteenth century, the task of safeguarding, disseminating, and interpreting them was in the hands of what the medieval church called the Magisterium. The Magisterium was self-selected, in that it was primarily ordained priests and monks, led by bishops and the Pope, which occasionally met in larger Church councils in times of schism or deep-seated disputes to resolve its internal divisions. The Magisterium created, on the basis of this chain of revelation, a distillation of faith, best demonstrated in the books of catechism intended to provide a minimal version of Christian belief as a guide to priests wishing to teach. One of the most famous, the *Opus tripartitum*, was published by Jean Gerson, the chancellor of the University of Paris, in the early fifteenth century, though it only won fame in the sixteenth century, as the Reformation made the need for a clear definitions of faith more pressing.[2]

Although the Reformation is rightly associated with Martin Luther and the dramatic events that his dispute with church authorities set forth, the roots of it go much deeper, perhaps well into the thirteenth century.[3] For some time, the elite of the Church had been defining and redefining, studying and modifying the body of writing that was deemed revelation. They were concerned about its original meaning in the dead languages in which it was written, and whether the process of copying manuscripts had corrupted the text. To help in the grasping of meaning, some church leaders were translating the Bible into contemporary languages, like John Wycliffe in England, to render the texts more fully comprehensible to those who knew Latin but were not versed in Greek or Hebrew.[4]

There was considerable debate in the process of this ongoing discussion among the religious elite, even though most accepted that the church needed to return to its original roots by closer study of its scripture. The reform movement (of which Luther's Protestant reformation was only a part) was essentially a fundamentalist movement, seeking to restore what its intellectuals believed was the pure theology of Jesus, the Apostles, and the early Church. The Catholic Reformation used many of the same ideas that Luther did, in fact. What distinguished the Protestant Reformation from the later Catholic Reformation (or Counter-Reformation), put in place by the Council of Trent in 1560, was a fairly legalistic dispute over the authority of the Papacy and the Magisterium.

Martin Luther's "Ninety-Five Theses" posted on the church door in Wittenburg, a university town in Saxony, invited his fellow intellectuals to debate a series of ideas that challenged the Pope's capacity and authority to affect events in Purgatory, to forgive sins, or to possess access to leftover merit of saints, but not the question of the position of the Pope as head of the church or inspired by the Holy Spirit.[5] The key reformers – Martin Luther, Huldrych Zwingli, or Jean Calvin, to name only the best known – argued that anyone could interpret scripture (discontinuous revelation), not just those who made up the Magesterium; as Luther wrote in "The Babylonian Captivity of the

---

[2] Johannes de Gerson, *Opus tripartitum de praeceptis decalogi de confessione et de arte moriendi* (Paris, 1505 [Gallica]).

[3] For a "deep roots" interpretation, see Pierre Chaunu, *Les temps des Réformes* (Paris, 1975), who claims that it began in 1277 (pp. 95–142).

[4] Wycliffe did not translate the Bible from the original languages, but only offered an English translation of Jerome's Latin translation.

[5] Martin Luther, "Disputatio pro Declaratione Virtutis Indulgentiarum," in *D. Martin Luthers Werke: Kritische Gesammtausgabe* (127 vols., Weimar, 1883 [http://luther.chadwyck.co.uk/]) 1: 231–238. An English translation is in Jaroslav Pelikan and Helmut T. Lehmann, eds., *Luther's Works* (55 vols., St. Louis and Philadelphia, 1955–1986) (henceforth abbreviated *LW*).

Church" in 1520, "all of us who are Christians are priests. There are indeed priests who we call ministers who are elected from among us, who do everything in our name."[6] More specifically he challenged the idea that the Magisterium could define discontinuous revelation, calling it an "accursed lie that the Pope is the arbiter of Scripture or that the Church has authority over Scripture."[7] Zwingli, for his part, argued that it was absurd to think "that the Church gives Scripture its authority, has power over Scripture, can change Scripture."[8]

Reformers argued that the post-biblical literature the Church regarded as authentic was not a record of revelation, because parts of it contradicted other parts and sometimes apparently the Bible, and therefore all Church practice had to be tested against the Bible, and lacking a basis there, should be rejected. Luther contended, in referring to Church Councils where the Magisterium met to resolve deep-seated disputes, that "when anything contrary to Scripture is decreed in a council, we ought to believe Scripture rather than the Council."[9] Reformers used the absence of biblical precedence to challenge the idea that only sacraments delivered by an ordained priest could ensure salvation, or that the saints that the Church urged people to revere did not have the power to deliver messages or intercede in Heaven. In the more immediate present, they agreed that the Pope could not authorize indulgences to get the condemned out of Purgatory or Hell.

While they might agree that the Church could neither condemn nor promise humanity's salvation, the reformers disagreed on what was required to be saved. Luther believed that only faith could do it, and not simply receiving the sacraments from ordained priests – faith alone was sufficient. Calvin, on the other hand, while rejecting the saving power of sacraments as his German colleague had done, argued that certain special "elect" were preordained (*predistinari*) by God to be saved, as it was "plainly owing to the mere pleasure of God that salvation is spontaneously offered to some, while others have no access to it."[10] Some of Zwingli's followers, latching on to the question of the sacrament of baptism, founded many Anabaptist groups who held that one could only be baptized after attaining knowledge of the religion, and hence only as adults. All agreed that it was not simply through obedience to the Church or taking in the sacraments, or even living a good life (doing "good works"), that would lead to salvation. These theological divergences came to be important, and Calvinist and Lutheran branches (and later subbranches) defined two broad Reformation approaches that were debated theologically, as well as fought over politically, in the years that followed.

---

⁶ "De captivitate Babilonica ecclesiae" (1520), *LW* 6: 564.
⁷ Lectures on Galatians 1.8, *LW* 26.57.
⁸ Quoted in context in Cameron, *Reformation*, p. 137.
⁹ *LW* 32.81.
¹⁰ Jean Calvin, *Institutio Christianae Religionis* (Geneva, 1559, mod. ed. August Thurlock, Berlin, 1834 [GB]) (a 1599 English translation by Henry Beveridge is online at http://www.ccel.org/ccel/calvin/institutes.html, Book 3, chapter 21, n. 1 (the larger argument runs from chapters 21 to 25)).

The reformers' contentions had the effect of undermining not only Church authority, but any authority. Luther was troubled by the idea that anyone could interpret Scripture, even when translated in vernacular languages. As Luther evolved from theologian to leader, his work moved back to limiting authority to selected individuals, or recreating the Magisterium in a new form, especially in the face of the challenges of free interpretation. The German Peasant War, while not entirely motivated by individual interpretation of the Scriptures, was nevertheless ground for religiously inspired leadership that drew on Luther's ideas, and Luther devoted an entire tract to denouncing it and its religious dimensions.[11] Some early leaders in the Anabaptist movement adopted strongly Millenarian positions, arguing that the end of time was near and that Apostolic doctrines of absolute freedom and communal goods combined with the belief that true Christians could not and should not serve states, which led those with anarchist leanings to challenge all authority.[12] When John of Leiden seized the German town of Münster and declared communism, including the sharing of wives and husbands, leading to its violent suppression in 1525, authorities moved to suppress Anabaptism everywhere in Europe.[13]

To meet the challenge posed by radical interpretation of scripture, Luther fell back on continuous revelation to the religious elite. Luther argued that the interpretation of the Bible must also be guided by the Holy Spirit, so that continuous and discontinuous revelation worked together. "If God does not open and explain Holy Writ, no one can understand it; it will remain a closed book, enveloped in darkness."[14]

For his part, Calvin wrote that "that those who are inwardly taught by the Holy Spirit acquiesce implicitly in Scripture."[15] He created a comprehensive vision of Christianity in his *Institutes of the Christian Religion*, which included a good deal of post-Biblical literature in his commentary, and many of his most important points were actually drawn from the writing of the Church Father, St. Augustine.[16] For example, he tried to show that Augustine did not put the authority of the Church above the Gospels, or that people were inherently sinful.[17] This post-Biblical element, as well as careful interpretation of Biblical passages, led Calvin to create his own vision of a tightly governed society in which the saints, as he called those preordained to be saved, had to monopolize the interpretation of scripture.

As a result of the intersection of differing opinions about the interpretation of Scripture, political authorities, and the opposition of Catholic rulers to the

---

[11] "Wider die räuberischen und mörderischen Rotten der Bauern," in *LW* 18: 344–361. Other writings of the same period showing his concern for discipline and obedience, including references to Müntzer's revolt, are found on pp. 279–401.

[12] Norman Cohn, *The Pursuit of the Millennium* (3rd ed., Oxford, 1970), pp. 223–280.

[13] George H. Willimas, *The Radical Reformation* (3rd ed., St. Louis, 1992 [1st ed., 1962]).

[14] *LW* 13.17.

[15] Calvin, *Institutio*, Book I, chapter 7, n. 5.

[16] Calvin, *Institutio*, pp. 40–45.

[17] *Institutio* 2.5 (inherently sinful), 7.3 (church and Gospel).

expansion of Protestant ideas, Europe became divided into religious blocs. The initial wars, waged largely in Germany, resulted in the Peace of Augsburg in 1555, which established that rulers would choose the appropriate religious path for their countries following the formula "*cujus region, ejus religio*" or "as the ruler goes, so go the followers." The Peace of Augsburg did not include Calvinists, however, and assertions of their strength and reactions against it would lead to the emergence of Calvinist polities in Switzerland and the Lower Rhine Valley, as well as the establishment of strong Calvinist communities in France, Bohemia, and elsewhere in Eastern Europe.

As Lutherans, Catholics, and Calvinists divided Europe among them, the Anabaptists' share declined rapidly. A profoundly quietist form of Anabaptism, called Mennonite after their leader Menno Simms, developed in the southern Rhine Valley and Switzerland and won toleration by stressing detachment from the world and from interest in government.[18] The Mennonites, as well as their offshoot, the Amish, spread to the Low Countries and then to Prussia (where Mennonites from the Netherlands were valued for their water management skills), its Rhine Valley territories, and England.

While the intellectual elite of the church was planning reform, the theology of much of Europe was quite at odds with the thinking of the elite. If Christians believed the basic story of God's creation and the importance of Jesus, they had added a great deal by continuous revelation. Other-Worldly figures, usually saints, continuously revealed themselves through miracles, often healing miracles, and most believers thought that devotion to these beings through prayer and pilgrimage to shrines built at the sites of the more spectacular miracles were what counted in their religious lives.[19] After concluding a careful survey of religious practice in late medieval and early modern Flanders, historian Jacques Toussaert concluded that the people were 80 percent Christian in self-conception (*morale*), 15 percent in understanding Church dogma, and only 5 percent in attending to sacraments.[20] Some historians have argued that this popular Christianity followed a class or status divide, with the poor and rural following a more "magical" life of devotion to saints, miracles, and healing and the elite following a bookish Christian ethos, but in fact, the elite often was as much connected to the continuously revealed Christianity as their subordinates.[21]

When scholars in the nineteenth century discovered this medieval Christianity through documentary research or the investigation of still continuing vestiges of it, they thought it an ancient paganism maintained through the years, or

---

[18] William R. Estep, *The Anabaptist Story: An Introduction to Sixteenth-Century Anabaptism* (3rd ed. Grand Rapids, 1996 [1st ed., 1963]).

[19] Stephen Wilson, *The Magical Universe: Everyday Ritual and Magic in Pre-Modern Europe* (London and New York, 2000). Wilson adopts a very wide definition of magic in this work.

[20] Jacques Toussaert, *Le sentiment religieux en Flandre à la fin du Môyen-Age* (Paris, 1960), pp. 66–67.

[21] John Van Engen, "The Christian Middle Ages as a Historiographical Problem," *American Historical Review* 91 (1986): 519–552, and the substantial literature cited therein.

even an ancient and partially hidden anti-Christian movement.[22] But this is only occasionally true, as many miracle stories reveal that most of the specific and local manifestations of Christianity in Medieval Europe were the result of continuous revelation that had taken place since the conversion of the region to Christianity. It was integral to and grew out of a Christian milieu.

The real division was between the fundamentalist reforming elite of the Church and most of the rest of the population, including a good many priests. Although the roots of the reform movement were probably always in the leaders of the church's thinking, they had not managed to convey it to the rest of Christendom. Indeed, Christians did not gather in churches regularly; they did not pay as much attention to question of sacraments or salvation and regarded priests primarily as a channel of continuous revelation.

To make their reforms work, the elite had to take aim at continuous revelation. Continuous revelation promised authentic revelation that might be received by anyone, under any circumstances, even more than Biblical reading did. The messages and information contained in such revelation might change or contradict teaching, even though most continuous revelation was personal and not theological in content. The pre-Reformation Church recognized the validity in theory of messages occasionally delivered to people by apparitions of the Virgin Mary and other saints, and the basic principle of continuous revelation was so widely accepted that it would be impossible to eliminate it.[23]

The church elite had never been happy about continuous revelation, and worked to limit it, although they were primarily content to ensure only that they approved of its practices and were free to contradict them when they wished.[24] Continuous revelation could be theologically dangerous, and the Church often punished and persecuted those whose revelations failed to conform to doctrine, or contradicted important elements of it, or threatened in other ways the power that it held. In 1500, for example, an unnamed craftsman from Gand was burned at the stake for revelations given to him by his "good angel" who told him that he did not need to pay attention to "the church, the Mass, or the sacraments." His executioners found him to be "apparently devout" and "a man of good conscience," but did not spare him for all of that.[25]

---

[22] For an influential nineteenth-century view, see Jules Michelet, *La Sorcière* (Paris, 1852), English translation as *Satanism and Witchcraft: A Study in Medieval Superstition* (London, 1883), and Margaret Murray, *The Witch-Cult in Western Europe* (London, 1921). Modern views include Jacques Delumeau, *Catholicism between Luther and Voltaire* (Philadelphia, 1977 [original French, 1971]), making the argument even for later periods; see also Carlo Ginsburg, *Ecstasies: Deciphering the Witches' Sabbath* (London, 1990). For Post-Refromation ideas about pagan survivals and "non-Christian" elements in folk religion, see Keith Thomas, *Religion and the Decline of Magic* (London, 1971); for an opposing view, see Van Engen, "The Christian Middle Ages," and works cited there.

[23] William Christian, *Apparitions in Late Medieval and Renaissance Spain* (Princeton, 1981), for a regional study with general application.

[24] Jonathan Sumption, *Pilgrimage: An Image of Medieval Religion* (London, 1975), pp. 50–55.

[25] *Corpus documentorum inquisitionis haereticarae pravitatis Neerlandicae* (5 vols., ed. Paul Fredrecq, Ghent and the Hague, 1889–1902) 1: 493.

One of the more dangerous fruits of continuous revelation was Ritual Magic, a set of beliefs posed by largely intellectual Europeans from about the late fourteenth century.[26] The core concept of Ritual Magic was the belief that God had given King Solomon power over the demons, and that Solomon used them to assist him in performing wondrous works. Solomon was alleged to have written a book, *The Key of Solomon*, where he provided instructions for how demons might be enslaved for the benefit of mankind, and copies of the book began to appear and were disseminated widely in Europe in the fourteenth and fifteenth century.[27] Ritual Magicians considered themselves devout Christians and believed that their activities would only work if they followed Christian practice, in which case it was blessed by God and supported by angels and saints.[28]

Late medieval theologians rejected this argument, Solomon's power, and the *Key of Solomon* as nothing more than a diabolic trick to ensnare the believers. Their response to the Magicians, and particularly to the role of demons and the Devil, would guide a great deal of the Reformation. In 1487. Heinrich Kramer (aka Institoris) and Jakob Spenger published *Malleus Maleficarum*, which set out basic ideas about the power of demons and linked them specifically to witchcraft.[29] Church thinkers argued that the Devil had the power to perform miracles and, in effect, to make revelations of his own. The suspicion of magic carried over from Catholic to Protestant. In a sermon preached at Epiphany in 1522, devoted to the three Magi Kings who visited Jesus at his birth, Luther called them "wise men" in the tradition that Europeans understood meant that they were people "who know a great deal about the secret arts," which is sometimes "accomplished by the black arts and the help of the devil." The "miraculous deeds" of such people were not "altogether done by the devil's cunning" but rather "by a combination of natural forces and the power of the devil."[30]

---

[26] There were a number of *grimoires*, or books of magic, in circulation in the late Medieval times claiming to be copies of much older texts. Most such texts only are known in copies made in the fifteenth century or later, and can probably be safely said to have been made relatively briefly before that, though surely using a wide range of earlier sources and ideas.

[27] *The Key of Solomon (Clavicula Salomonis)* ed. S. Liddell MacGregor Mathers, (London, 1888, revised with some passages restored that Mathers omitted, J. H. Peterson, 2005). The apparatus in this edition, as in many others, is intended as a guide to practitioners, but is scholarly nevertheless.

[28] The *Key* is not the only *grimoire* or book of magic; in fact there were a number in circulation in the Renaissance period. The oldest attestable one is the *Liber Juratus* (known in English as the *Sworne Book of Honorius*), mentioned in the twelfth century, with the oldest extant manuscripts being from the fifteenth century; see the critical edition at http://www.esotericarchives.com/juratus/juratus.htm

[29] Heinrich Kramer and Jakob Spenger, *Malleus Malificarum maleficas, & earum haeresim, ut phramea potentissima conterens* (first published 1487; see the 1580 edition at http://digital.library.cornell.edu/cgi/t/text/text-idx?c=witch;idno=wito60). An English translation was made by Montague Summers in 1928 and revised in 1948 (online at http://www.malleusmaleficarum.org).

[30] Martin Luther, Sermon for Epiphany, Matthew 2: 1–12, 1522, in *The Sermons of Martin Luther* (8 vols., Grand Rapids, 1983) 1: 325–326.

The Spanish inquisitor Pedro Ciruelo applied the idea of diabolic revelations more generally in an influential tract, *Tratado en que se repruevan todas las supersticiones y hecherizias (Tract Reproving all Superstitions and Witchcraft)*, first published in 1530. In it, he laid out a number of folk beliefs, seemingly innocent in themselves, which were held to be diabolic practices by virtue of seeking "vain" solutions to problems. That is, if a person tried to solve a problem by invoking supernatural agency instead of, say, herbal remedies or other natural strategies, they would not be heard by God, but would be heard by the Devil. The Devil then could and would perform the necessary miracles to convince the unwary of the efficacy of what they were doing. Thus anyone doing this sort of supernatural meddling without clerical oversight and guidance was making an "implicit" pact with the Devil, even if they did not make the sort of "explicit" ones that Spenger and Kramer wrote about. This would include any form of fortune telling, by astrology, geomancy, divination as well as other activities in which supplications, even to saints, might be condemned.[31]

Because a pact, even if only implicit, with the Devil was witchcraft, all non-ordained mediators with the Other World were witches and thus punishable by death.[32] While these widely ranging practices – and a equally wide range of beliefs in spirits, angels, and other supernatural agents – were not necessarily associated with each other, and certainly not with either Europe's pre-Christian religion or other religious traditions, they were all lumped together by the Church as "superstitions," and ultimately as witchcraft.

In some cases, reformers applied Diabolism to the lay religion with its saints and healers. A sixteenth-century preacher in Béthune, northern France, told his flock that if one seeks the "hammer of St Eloi" (a healing saint) to cure an illness, "you are idolaters, and if it happens that you should be cured, it is not at all the hammer of St Eloi that cures you, it is the Devil." Anticipating Protestant complaints against Catholic practice, he went on to denounce such things as carrying Brevets and lighting candles in honor of "Saint this or that," or "Saint I don't know which," which in his opinion was all "idolatry" and "devilries" because they revealed a lack of confidence in the straightforward aid of God.[33]

The full application of this theology was manifested in the witch crazes of the sixteenth and seventeenth centuries, for which *Malleus Maleficarum* became the handbook, being reprinted and republished dozens of times. Luther

---

[31] Pedro Ciruelo, *Tratado en qve se reprvevan todas las svpersticiones y hecherizias* (rev. ed., Pedro Antonio Iofreu, Barcelona, 1628 [GB]). Jofreu's additions were in the form of a commentary, so the text was still current through the mid-seventeenth century. English translation by Eugene Maio and D'Orsay Pierson, *Pedro Ciruelo's A Treatise Reproving Superstitions and All Forms of Witchcraft...* (Cranberry, NJ, 1977).

[32] Norman Cohen, *Europe's Inner Demons: An Inquiry into the Great Witch Hunt* (rev. ed., Chicago, 2000 [original, 1975]), pp. 168–170.

[33] Bibliothèque Municipale de Lille, MS 131, quoted in Robert Muchembled, "Sorcellerie, culture populaire, et christianme au XVIe siècle en Flandre et en Artois," *Annales: Histoire, Sciences Sociales* 38 (1973): 273.

commented specifically on the killing of witches, especially women, for his most specific comment was in the context of women's alleged susceptibility to Satan, which was in fact a central theme of *Malleus Maleficarum*.[34] Thousands of people were interrogated, often tortured, and frequently killed in sometimes horrible ways in what was originally and ultimately an attempt to control continuous revelation and reduce it to approved forms with predictable results that left fundamental Church doctrines intact. The witch craze affected both Catholic and Protestant regions of Europe, although the form of its suppression varied.[35]

The concept of diabolism followed European immigrants to the New World. In the Catholic Iberian countries, branches of the Inquisition were soon investigating claims of witchcraft rooted in the tradition of Diabolism, and indeed including a great many of the same practices that were now deemed illicit in Europe.[36] France did relatively little work of this sort in its colonies, in part because it lacked the Inquisition and its traditions, but also because France itself ceased its own determined pursuit of witches in the seventeenth century, when the colonization movement was just beginning.

In Protestant English territories, there was also little pursuit of witches, save for the famous but somewhat isolated Salem witchcraft trials in the late seventeenth century. Although this American witch craze was neither as long-lasting nor as devastating as its European precursors, it did fit as a late variation into Demonism.[37] Demonism as a theology would also play a critical role in Christianity's spread to other religious traditions in the Atlantic world, as missionaries spread out to make them Christian, as we shall see.

Despite having the weapon of Diabolism to challenge continuous revelation, neither the Catholic Church nor its Protestant rivals either denied that some such revelation was possible or that it could be beneficial. The process of continuous revelation in the post-Reformation world is best presented in Spain, thanks to a systematic study of village and urban religion in the late sixteenth century ordered by Philip II as part of a general survey of his kingdom and empire. Part of the extensive questionnaire sent out to each village in the realm inquired about the churches, local customs, or feast days. Although the inquest

---

[34] Sermon, March 11, 1526, *LW* 16: 551; the witch craze as being specifically targeted at controlling women found considerable interest in the feminist movement; see Anne Llewellyn Barstow, *Witchcraze: A New History of the European Witch-Hunts* (New York, 1994) for a serious treatment of this issue.

[35] Brian Levack, *The Witch-Hunt in Early Modern Europe* (2nd ed., London and New York, 1995).

[36] See as an example, Laura de Mello e Souza, *The Devil in the Land of the Southern Cross: Witchcraft, Slavery and Popular Religion in Colonial Brazil* (Austin, 2004).

[37] There is a vast bibliography on this topic: see Mary Beth Norton, *In the Devil's Snare: The Salem Witchcraft Crisis of 1692* (New York, 2002); John Demos, *Entertaining Satan: Witchcraft and the Culture of Early New England* (New York, 1982); Carol F. Karlsen, *The Devil in the Shape of a Woman: Witchcraft in Colonial New England* (New York, 1987). For a collection of original documents, see Bernard Rosenthal et al., ed., *Records of the Salem Witch-Hunt* (New York, 2009).

was done after the Council of Trent, the practices it revealed and accepted were probably continuations of activity that had been going on since the Middle Ages. Often, as it turned out, striking events, disasters, and unusual weather patterns were sometimes held to be revelations, and churches were built or abstinences ordered because of them, as they were thought to be revelations of this or that element of the Other World, and elaborate methods were devised to divine the saints to whom to dedicate churches.[38]

Although Spain is well documented in this regard, similar sorts of revelation were reported all over Europe. The English Calvinist traveler and divine John Lauder, traveling in France in 1665, for example, noted that the people of Orléans had a feast day dedicated to God. They decided to do this when "the Virgin appeared to a certain Godly woman" and complained "that she had 4 dayes in the year for hir, and God had only the Sabbath," which the people took as admonition to pay more attention to him, and hence they held a festival for him.[39]

CHRISTIANITY AS A MISSIONARY RELIGION

As we have seen, European Christianity and sometimes its disputations entered into the Atlantic world through the migrations of Europeans to Africa and America. But the religion also spread along with and frequently outside of the flow of migration through evangelism to the non-European inhabitants of the Atlantic world. Although Christianity has always been an evangelical religion, its attitude toward followers of other religions has varied. In the late medieval background to European expansion, especially in southern Europe, opinions of other religious traditions, especially Judaism and Islam, varied according to currents in theological and political thought.

On the one hand, there was a school of thought that argued a position that the founding revelations of other religions originated with the Devil, extending the logic of Diabolism from the struggle against the Ritual Magicians and popular Christianity to other traditions. For them, other religions could not be tolerated, and converting their followers was a battle against the Devil himself, a battle in which no compromise was possible. Others, while accepting the general tenets of Diabolism, did not believe that it applied to the other religions in question, and that their religious practice must have had some divine inspiration in them and that Christianization might be little more than critical alterations that required little change in religious life.[40] Politics paralleled these theological positions, with the more rigorous definitions of other religions following situations where there was political domination and

---

[38] William Christian, *Local Religion in Sixteenth Century Spain* (Princeton, 1981), pp. 38–39.
[39] *Journals of John Lauder of Fountainhall...* ed. Donald Crawford (Edinburgh, 1900 [Gallica]), p. 11.
[40] James Muldoon, *Popes, Lawyers, and Infidels: The Church and the Non-Christian World, 1250–1550* (Liverpool, 1991).

more permissive ones where evangelization could not count on the powers of state.

Initially, the other religions that were most troubling, as closest at hand and sharing theological concepts, were Judaism and Islam. All traditions accepted the basic concept that discontinuous revelations, sent by God and subsequently recorded in writing, were the basis for religions life; likewise all accepted the identity of the God who sent messages to all three faiths. For Christians the problem was that the Jews had refused to accept the revelation given by Jesus, and the Muslims, while accepting Jesus as a source of revelation, added additional revelations presented to Muhammad, which Christians and Jews did not accept.

A theory that had gained prominence in the Middle Ages was that the Jews had obstinately refused to accept Jesus because they had been beguiled by the Devil.[41] A similar theory was applied to Muslims to the degree that Christian theorists argued that Muhammad had received his revelations from the Devil, thus converting Islam into a Diabolic religion.

Franciscan priests were the first to seek the conversion of people met in the course of Atlantic exploration, in the Canary islands.[42] Already in 1351, before the conquest of any of the islands, the Papacy approved a bishop to be seated at Telde on the Grand Canary Island to cover evangelization. We know that missionary priests were working in the islands, but have little information about their actual labors or their missionary techniques. We also have little information about their level of success, and the chronicles of European wars and conquests in the Canaries do not mention much about an indigenous, pre-conquest conversion.[43]

Part of the conquest of the first Canary Islands, Lanzarotte and Fuertaventura by Robert de la Salle in 1404, was the Normans' insistence that the island leaders be baptized as a part of their homage, perhaps operating under the assumption that swearing oaths of loyalty would not be effective unless all parties were Christian. In any case, the chronicle of the expedition records in detail the catechism used for the conversion. This catechism was not a program for the extirpation of Canarian religion, about which it had nothing to say, but rather a statement of the history of the world from a Christian perspective, primarily to inform the Canarians of the existence and teaching of Jesus. Its core philosophy recalls the sin of Adam and the rescue made possible by Christ, about

---

[41] For a full development of the theory and its applications, see Joshua Trachtenberg, *The Devil and the Jews: The Medieval Conception of the Jew and Its Relation to Modern Anti-Semitism* (Philadelphia, 1943, 2nd ed., 1983).

[42] J. Vincke, "Comienzes de las misiones cristianos en las islas Canarias," *Hispania Sacra* 12 (1959): 193–207; see also Marina Mitjá, "Abandò de las Illes Canaries per Joan I d'Aragò," *Annuario de Estudos Atlanticos* 8 (1962): 325–353 (including a dossier of documents, pp. 340–353); Juan Alvarez Delgado, "Primera conquista y christianización de la Gomera," *Annuario de Estudos Atlanticos* 6 (1960): 445–492.

[43] Antonio Rumeu y Armas, *El Obisbado de Telde* (Madrid, 1960).

whom it offers very little information, save in a summary of the Nicene Creed, but it made no call for renunciation of any Canarian belief.[44]

While ignoring the existing religion may have had the necessary results for forming alliances, the real conversion – convincing the local people of the truth of the Christian gospel – required an act of continuous revelation. Such an act is detailed by the mid-sixteenth-century historian-priest Alonso de Espinosa, who gave credit to Our Lady of Candelaria as being the medium for the conversion of the Canarians. Espinosa's account of the conversion of the Canaries, especially Gran Canaria where he worked, reveals a more complex process of conversion than the simple retelling of the Christian story that characterized the haphazard evangelization of the first conquests. Instead, Espinosa describes a process that can be classed as co-revelation.

Co-revelation is the occurrence of an event that is recognized as a revelation by believers from two different religious traditions. That is, each accepts the revelation as genuine and a source of religious knowledge. It is a vehicle that allows the merger of religions through the juncture of the revelation. According to Espinosa, around 1400, before the first Christian missions came to the Canaries, two shepherd boys discovered a statue along the beach when it startled their sheep.[45] When they tried to throw stones or cut the statue, their weapons turned on them. Frightened and curious, they returned to their village and sought guidance from the local ruler of Guimar, who upon seeing the statue declared that it was a holy thing.[46] They decided to transport it to the village, and when they touched it, the two shepherds found their wound miraculously healed.[47] There they placed it in the king's house, although eventually it was moved to a cave near his house where it was the object of devotion.

Some years later, a Canarian who had been captured by European marauders, carried to Spain, and baptized came to Guimar and immediately recognized the statue as that of the Virgin Mary. He organized a cult and placed the image in a grotto near the beach (Canarians often kept religious items in caves). Subsequently many people reported hearing angelic voices and seeing processions of angels in the night, and even found drippings of angelic wax that miraculously appeared each year, just in time for the Purification ceremony, helpful because there was no natural source of wax on the island.[48] De Espinosa inserted a document of 1497 into his text in which the first Spanish governor certified these miraculous events.[49] With this introduction, the

---

[44] Reproduced in *Le Canarien*, chapters 47–52.

[45] Alonso de Espinosa, *Del Origen y Milagros de la Santa Imagen de nuesta Señora de Candelaria…* (Seville, 1594) Book 2, cap. 1, and cap. 3 (an English translation by Clements Markham as *The Guanches of Tenerife*, published London, 1907, reprinted 1972 [GB]). He claims to have used oral tradition and picture writing known to the natives as the basis for his claim.

[46] Espinosa considered the image to be the work of angels, and discounted theories that it came from a shipwreck or was abandoned by sailors, *Origen* Book 2, cap. 4.

[47] Espinosa, *Origen*, Book 2, cap. 2.

[48] Espinosa, *Origen*, Book 2, caps. 7–9.

[49] Espinosa, *Origen*, Book 2, cap. 10.

Christian faith had spread even before the Christians, and moreover to other islands, for the inhabitants of Lançarote had come and stolen the image, until plagues – sent by God, they believed – forced them to return it.[50] Not to be outdone, other islands subsequently reported their own miraculous images, in imitation of the most famous one of Guimar.[51] In fact, the earliest notarial and church documentation from the large islands of Teneriffe and Gran Canaria reveals that Virgin Mary was much revered in the Canaries, because most identifiable Canarians in these records mention her in their documents.[52]

This whole tale is an excellent example of co-revelation, which was particularly relevant in Africa because there religious knowledge was largely based on continuous revelation. Although local practice and cosmology varied widely, Atlantic Africa did not recognize the idea of recorded discontinuous revelation in holy books of one or another kind. Indeed, most of Africa did not write at all, and those who did were Muslims writing in Arabic, and thus fitting under a different rubric. The Kingdom of Kongo, which became Portugal's and the Catholic Church's most successful and durable voluntary conversion of people who could not be conquered by force or made to convert, shows how important the role of continuous revelation was in validating co-revelations that created the African vision of Christianity.[53]

Unlike the Canaries, where conversion took place long before the recording of the circumstances, and oral tradition filled the gap, the conversion of the king of Kongo is described in contemporary documents, as is its co-revelation. When the Portuguese first arrived in Kongo in 1483, they exchanged hostages with the kingdom, leaving five Portuguese and taking five Kongolese with them back to Portugal. These Kongolese were then returned home in 1488, after having first learned of Christianity, and from their descriptions, as well as those of the Portuguese who remained behind, King Nzinga a Nkuwu decided to explore Christianity and asked for missionaries to come.

The missionaries came in 1491, and it was during this visit that they recorded the co-revelations, which were set to writing as soon as they returned to Portugal.[54] According to this report, following his baptism the king was pondering the Christian message and called the court together to discuss it. As the members were assembling, two of them reported having a dream of a beautiful woman urging the king to convert. Two people dreaming the same dream simultaneously was regarded as a miraculous event, so

---

[50] Espinosa, *Origen*, Book 2, caps. 11–12.
[51] Espinosa, *Origen*, Book 2, cap. 14.
[52] Felipe Fernández-Armesto, *The Canary Islands after the Conquest*, pp. 180–199.
[53] Thornton, *Africa and Africans*, pp.254–260.
[54] An inquest was made of six of the ranking Portuguese upon their return. Although now lost, it was the basis for an account that the royal chronicler Rui de Pina wrote in about 1492 and incorporated into his chronicle of João II in 1515. Both the 1492 (known only in a contemporary Italian translation) and 1515 version (in Portuguese) are published in Carmen M. Radulet, *O Cronista Rui de Pina e a "Relação do Reino do Congo" Manuscrito inédito do "Códice Riccardiano 1910"* (Lisbon, 1992).

the king took special note of their dreams, while the Christian priests present explained that the woman in the dream was the Virgin. As this was transpiring, a third latecomer burst in and announced that he had found a stone, perfectly shaped like a cross, on the banks of the river while coming to court. The priests, in examining the stone and observing that it was shaped as if man-made, yet was a natural object, declared it a miracle.[55] For Kongolese, bodies of water form a boundary between this world and the other world, and hence the discovery of an object there is particularly auspicious and revelatory.[56] Thus, the co-revelation was confirmed, and the stone was placed in the first church built in Kongo, where it was still to be seen in the mid-seventeenth century.[57]

This revelation of 1491 was joined by another a few years later, when King Afonso was fighting against his brother for the throne of Kongo in 1509. Afonso, who described the war as a struggle between him, a Christian, and his brother who opposed Christianity, also related that his success was a result of divine intervention. According to his report, his opponents had been routed when a troop of the Heavenly Host, led by Saint James, appeared in the sky and caused his pagan opponents to flee in panic.[58] The symbols of this miracle were subsequently incorporated into Kongo's coat of arms, which was employed on all official documents and symbols until the end of the nineteenth century.[59]

The process of co-revelation resulted in a merging of theologies to create a Kongolese version of Christianity. Afonso I, the real founder of Kongo's Christian synthesis, developed this version of the religion by consulting with Portuguese priests and sending his own people to study in Europe, including

---

[55] Rui de Pina, "Chronica del Rei D. Joham II," cap.62 ed. from the 1492 and 1515 recensions in Radulet, *Cronista*, pp. 125–126, 150.

[56] At least in modern Kongo cosmology, for an attempt to understand this religious system from older sources, see John Thornton, "Religion and Ceremonial Life in the Kongo and Mbundu Areas, 1500–1700," in Linda M. Heywood, ed., *Central Africans and Cultural Transformations in the American Diaspora* (Cambridge, 2002), pp. 71–90.

[57] [Mateus Cardoso], "Historia de Reino de Congo," ed. António Brásio, *História do Reino deo Congo (Ms 8080 da Biblioteca Nacional de Lisboa)* (Lisbon, 1969) cap. 21, fols. 28–28v.

[58] First described in Afonso's now lost letter to the king of Portugal in 1509, but probably the source for three letters written for him in 1512, addressed to his subjects, the lords of his kingdom, and the Pope, 1512, all three published in Brásio, *Monumenta* 1: 256–271. Two important early-sixteenth-century accounts are probably based on the original letter; Martin Fernandez de Enciso, *Suma de Geographia* (Seville, 1519), np (text is unpaginated); and João de Barros, *Decadas de Asia* (Lisbon, 1552), Decada I, Book 3, chapter 10 (see text reproduced in Brásio, *Monumenta* 1: 144–145).

[59] See Afonso's description of the coat of arms and its connection to the miracle; Afonso to his Lords, 1512 in Brásio, *Monumenta* 1: 258. A contemporary book of arms, the "Livro de António Godinho," illustrates them; see black-and-white photograph facing p. 432. A color photograph appears in Luiz Felipe de Alencastro, *O Trato dos Viventes: Formação do Brasil no Atlântico Sul* (São Paulo, 2000), figure 7. A beautifully framed reproduction of Godinho's version is hanging in the Museu Real in Mbanza Kongo today, which also owns an original stamp for making the seal on letters.

his son Henrique who was ordained as a priest and then consecrated as a bishop in 1518. This team, including both Europeans and educated Kongolese, then created the basic outlines of what would remain Kongo's version of Catholicism.[60]

Kongo differed from the Canaries, as indeed it did from the Americas, in that conversion did not take place in the process of conquest, or follow conquest, and no doubt this fact contributed to the liberal, open theology that developed there. In unconquered Kongo, Afonso and the kings who followed him were much more in charge of the organization of the church and the theological content of the resulting Christianity.

When translating Christian terms into Kikongo, writers and thinkers in both Kongo and Portugal employed terms drawn from Kongo's own religious terminology. In the catechism used for teaching Christianity in Kongo, published in 1624, God is referred to as *Nzambi a Mpungu*, the ancient Kikongo name for the creator of the universe; priests are *nganga*, a name of the traditional intermediaries with Kongo's original Other-Worldly entities. The term *nkisi*, which referred in the traditional religion to an Other-Worldly force that had entered into a material object and converted it into a power object, was used by the translators to mean "holy," so that a church was known as *nzo wakisi*, "holy house," or a house filled with Other-Worldly power.[61]

The Portuguese priests who were sent to Kongo to assist in its conversion were greatly impressed by Afonso, regarding him as an "angel sent from heaven" who "knew the lives of the saints better even than we did," according to Rui d'Aguiar, Portuguese confessor and theological leader of the European side of the group. This open-ended approach to religion allowed even quite fundamental differences in theology to be glossed over. In Kongo's traditional religion, the dead were translated to the Other World, which allowed them to remain in the immediate vicinity where they lived but now transformed into ancestors, the subject of cult activity in daily life. Christianity had a different view of the fate of the dead, who went off to the Other World (Heaven or Hell) for reward or punishment, but had little impact in the lives of their descendants. By focusing energy on the dead and All Saint's Day, Kongolese Christians could honor their ancestors and visit their graves while still staying within the Church.[62]

In addition to blending elements of Kongolese theology into the practice of Christianity in Kongo, they nationalized it. Kongo's most important holiday, Saint James Day (July 25), while technically dedicated to a European saint, was actually a celebration of Afonso's victory over his brother in 1509. When Portuguese soldiers facing a Kongolese army at Mbumbi in 1622 challenged

---

[60] John Thornton, "Perspectives on African Christianity," in Vera Hyatt and Rex Nettleford, eds., *Race, Discourse, and the Origin of the Americas* (Washington, DC, 1994).

[61] Thornton, "Perspectives on African Christianity," pp. 169–198. I have employed modern orthography for these Kikongo terms, but pluralized according to English rules.

[62] Thornton, "Afro-Christian Syncretism," pp. 172–186.

their invocation of Saint James, the Kongolese replied that their Saint James was black.[63]

During Afonso's reign, when Christianity was not well established, the Portuguese crown encouraged the new Christianity and supported Afonso's attempt to head the church by backing the elevation of Afonso's son Henrique to the priesthood and his ordination as a bishop in 1518.[64] However, following Henrique's death, the Portuguese crown sought to control the church by placing it under the bishop of São Tomé, who they controlled. Kongo tried to regain control and in 1596 managed to get their capital São Salvador to be the seat of a bishop, but Portugal won the right to appoint him. In the following years, Kongo rulers isolated the bishops and in the end they simply retreated to Angola, leaving Kongo on its own.[65] Thanks to this setback, the Portuguese bishops were reluctant to ordain any Kongolese as priests, leaving the country frequently bereft of clergy.

Unable to control the bishops, Kongo organized its church around its laity; they were responsible for continuing the church in the absence of ordained clergy. These lay ministers, usually called "school masters" (*mestres de escola*), were drawn from the nobility, educated within Kongo's own school system, and conducted regular religious services.[66] By 1570 at the latest, according to the priest Francisco de Medeiros, the mestres, "who were natives of the country," had managed to teach everyone "humble and great," so there was no need for outsiders to teach.[67] To augment this organization, and to allow for the performance of the sacraments by ordained clergy, Kongo's rulers eventually brought Capuchin missionaries to the country, beginning in 1645.[68]

The Capuchins were the first order to bring the Counter-Reformation to Kongo, and although other orders had noted Kongo's interesting mix of local religious concepts and Christianity, the Capuchins denounced the mixture as "superstitions" and linked them with Diabolic influences. They set out to clean the country of all elements of Christianity not found in their vision, just as they were doing in Europe at the time.[69] Although the Capuchins organized idol burnings, they had only lukewarm support for their efforts from the state and, without any coercive power of their own, were forced to accept Kongo Christianity as it was practiced.[70]

---

[63] Cadornega, *História geral*, 1: 105.

[64] For his biography, see François Bontinck, "Ndoadidiki *Ne-Kinu* a Mubemba, premier évêque du Kongo (c. 1495–1531)," *Revue Africaine de Théologie* 3 (1979): 149–169.

[65] Saccardo, *Congo e Angola* 1: 112–116; 131–136; 187–188.

[66] Heywood and Thornton, *Central Africans*, p. 66.

[67] ANTT Inquisição de Lisboa, Processo 2522, fol. 144, Testimony of Francisco de Medeiros, 1584.

[68] The history of the origin of the Capuchin mission is found in Saccardo, *Congo e Angola* 1: 193–194; 335–342; see also John Thornton, "The Development of an African Catholic Church in the Kingdom of Kongo, 1491–1750," *Journal of African History* 25 (1984): 147–167.

[69] Thornton, "African Catholic Church," pp. 149–150.

[70] Richard Gray, "*Come vero principe catolico*: The Capuchines and the Rulers of Soyo in the Late Seventeenth Century," *Africa* 53 (1983): 39–54 on their most successful efforts in Soyo in the late eighteenth century.

FIGURE 15. Njinga's Baptism. Source: Ezio Bassani, "Un Cappuccino nell'Africa nera del seicento. I disegni de Manoscritti Araldi del Padre Givanni Antonio Cavazzi da Montecuccolo," *Quaderni Poro* 4 (1987).

The independence of the Kongo church, and the preaching of the Capuchins that often injured Kongolese pride, produced its own dissention. In 1704, D Beatriz Kimpa Vita, who claimed to be an incarnation of Saint Anthony and to visit Heaven every weekend (and thus to have very solid revealed knowledge), upbraided Capuchin missionaries for denying that there were black (or Kongolese) saints. Beatriz maintained that Jesus had been born in Kongo and that the Virgin Mary and Saint Francis were also Kongolese. While Beatriz's mission was not successful in transforming Kongo's church, and the elite opted for Catholic orthodoxy a second time, her preaching certainly hit a chord among the Kongolese population.[71] In the following century, Kongolese artists made a plethora of religious objects depicting Christ as a Kongolese, with African features and a loincloth decorated with unmistakable Kongolese motifs. Many other elements of Kongolese theological iconography were also incorporated into these crucifixes.[72]

[71] For Beatriz and her movement, John Thornton, *The Kongolese Saint Anthony: Dona Beatriz Kimpa Vita and the Antonian Movement, 1684–1706* (Cambridge, 1998).
[72] An important study of this iconography is found in Cécile Fromont, "Under the Sign of the Cross in the Kingdom of Kongo: Shaping Images and Moulding Faith in Early Modern Central

Kongo also developed a tradition of evangelization; Afonso had put a priest of his own in the kingdom of Ndongo in 1526, when a Portuguese mission there failed. Diogo I (ruled 1545–1561) sent chapel boys to evangelize the Mbundu regions to its south as well as Loango to the north. The Kongo pattern of theology was carried to Angola, when Kongo soldiers and Kongo priests and catechists joined Paulo Dias de Novais in the conquest of Angola.[73] When the first catechismal literature in Kimbundu was produced in 1628, it translated theology along the same lines as in Kongo, and in the church in Angola, local practices were similar to those of Kongo. For example, the catechism referred to God as Nzambi, a local term for God, and also, by using terms such as "unzambi" (a qualitative form of nzambi) to mean divinity, the catechism absorbed much of the same sense of existing religion as had been used in Kongo.[74] Moreover, in Mbundu religion, the local deities left taboos for their followers, called in Kimbundu *kijila*, a term that the catechism used to mean "commandments" even in the Ten Commandments.[75]

It was common for Jesuit priests like Pedro Tavares, one of the most active, to pull down the large shrines to territorial deities (*kiteke*) and replace them with crosses.[76] As in Kongo, sometimes these were accompanied by miracles or co-revelations, such as the ending of droughts. The cult of the dead was reflected in *ntambu* – extensive funeral rites that incorporated Christian elements, but were at times denounced as being covers of more traditional rites.[77] However, unlike Kongo, the church in Angola was always closely associated with Portuguese colonial rule, and met with more resistance. An occasional flurry of piety was likely to come from independent neighboring countries, such as Queen Njinga's independent state in Matamba following her reconversion in 1654, or the rule of her pious successor (probably baptized during this time), Verónica I (ruled 1681–1721).

While there may have been a contentious relationship between Angolans and the Church, African practices were incorporated into the Christianity of the region even as practiced by the Portuguese living there. Portuguese residents of Angola frequently took up some of the African rituals. Lorenzo da Lucca, a

Africa," (PhD dissertation, Harvard University, 2008); see also John Thornton, "Black Jesus: Christian Art in Eighteenth Century Kongo," paper presented at the Round Table, "A Cidade de disenterrar para presevar," Mbanza Kongo (Angola), September, 2007 (forthcoming with acts of the conference).

73 Heywood and Thornton, *Central Africans*, pp. 98–108.
74 António de Couto (ed.), *Gentio de Angola sufficiemente instruido nos mysterios de nossa sancta Fé, obra posthuma composta pello Padre Francisco Pacconio da Companhia de Jesu redusida... pello Antonio de Couto...* (Lisbon, 1642) Dialogue I, 14 (Nzambi as God, both as the Father, the Son, and the Holy Spirit); II, 12 (where *unzambi* is used to mean immortal soul). The history of Paconio's mastery of Kimbundu and preparation of the catechims is detailed in the introduction to Bontinck and Nsasi, *Catéchisme*, pp. 39–40. Unlike the Kikongo catchism, which was a translation of a well-known Portuguese catechism, the Kimbundu one seems to have been made specially for use in Angola.
75 Couto, *Gentio* I, 8v; (use of *kijila* as commandment in Ten Commandments).
76 Heywood and Thornton, *Central Africans*, pp. 185–196.
77 Thornton, "Religion and Ceremonial Life," pp. 86–90.

Capuchin priest, complained in 1716 that "white ladies" of the city of Luanda were regularly visiting traditional healers when they were sick, and used the Bulongo ordeal to determine guilt, the efficacy of such procedures being in effect a continuous revelation.[78] A fine example of the role of revelation in such local practices is documented in the case of Portuguese ("white") soldiers at the garrison of Cambambe, who made a Mandinga, or protective charm, using a mixture of Christian and Mbundu elements, and then tested it by putting it on a dog and shooting the dog, whose survival provided the requisite miracle.[79]

Several eighteenth-century governors denounced the practice of white Angolans, as well as baptized and presumably Christian blacks, following such practices as celebrations of Quicumbi and tambe (a funeral rite), as well as seeking cures from religious practitioners or mixing them into Christian practice, but in fact, the practices were, in the eyes of those who used them, certified by efficacy.[80] Even though the Portuguese had success in the conquest and evangelization of Angola, they were not particularly successful in eliminating even the open practice of non-Christian religions. A memorial of 1820, for example, explicitly lists a number of illicit practices concerning marriages, female menstrual confinement, and burials, as well as the names and locations of notable "idols" or local shrines.[81]

The Kongo church was the most successful of Portugal's conversions in Africa, but it was not the only one. Portuguese missionaries also converted the king of Warri, a small state in modern-day southwestern Nigeria, to Christianity around 1590, and also enjoyed some temporary but generations-long success among the small states of modern-day Sierra Leone in the early seventeenth century. We know less about these other conversions, but it is likely that they also involved co-revelations. In Sierra Leone, for example, former African priests joined European clergy in shaping the new theology, although we possess too little information to go beyond this information.[82] When priests sought to create a catechism for Allada in 1658, they focused on ideas that would come from co-revelation, most notably using *Vodu* as the term for God and *Lisa* as a term for Jesus. In Allada's theology, Vodu is a general term for deity, and Lisa is the name for one-half of a dual-divinity Godhead.[83] In all these cases, the absence of a coercive European presence allowed the establishment of a religious tradition that incorporated Christianity into an

---

[78] ANTT Inquisição de Lisboa, Cadernos de Promotor, Livro 279, fols. 39–40.
[79] ANTT Inquisição de Lisboa, Processo 5744, Vicente de Morais, 1716.
[80] AIGHB Lata 214, Pasta 5, "Dedução dos factos do Bispo de Malaca e do Barão de Moçamedes, Governador de Angola," (c. 1792). See in this regard, Linda M. Heywood, "Portuguese into African: The Eighteenth Century Central African Background to Atlantic Creole Cultures," in Heywood, ed., *Central Africans and Cultural Transformations*, pp. 91–116 (especially 108–111).
[81] AIHGB Lata 347, pasta 30, fols. 21v–22v, Felix Bellamo Fabiano, "Rellação do Estado effectivo dos Sobas, e Quilambas que comtem a Jurisdição deste Prezidio das Pedras de Pungo andongo, e das forças que cada qual em, e Capazes de por em Armas. Feita ao 10 de Janeiro de 1820."
[82] Thornton, "Perspectives," pp. 186–189.
[83] Thornton, "Trail of Voodoo," p. 267.

existing religious system with the outcome sometimes being recognizable as Christian, sometimes not.

Perhaps the most common outcome was the incorporation of a few Christian elements into local religion. For example, the Bishop of São Tomé was surprised to learn that people from Calabar, in the delta of the Niger River, asked him to know which was the greater saint, "Jesus Joseph" or "Antonio," as they had salvaged figureheads of such figures from wrecked Portuguese vessels and determined that these items had spiritual significance and power – enough that they fastened them to their own ships. Their understanding of Christianity might also have been enhanced by their proximity to the Christian kingdom of Warri.

It is probably correct to say that the new form of Christianity that emerged in those parts of Africa that regarded themselves as Christian (Kongo, Angola, Warri, and at times Sierra Leone) was a successful merging of the various religious traditions, but also that it had a limited impact in Africa outside of the core areas of the conversion. However, the impact of African Christianity, and perhaps especially its Central African component, would have a disproportionate impact in the Americas where thousands of African Christians were carried off as slaves.

INDIGENOUS AMERICANS CONFRONT THE MISSIONARIES

The year after the first Portuguese missionaries planted Christianity in Kongo, and set up what would become a fruitful conversion for central Africa, Columbus landed in Hispaniola and soon was converting Tainos, as a part of building alliances and accepting submission. Ramón Pané, the priest responsible for the this work, used methods remarkably similar to those used in the Canaries by teaching them the Christian story as a part of the general story of mankind, and they accepted this and proceeded to learn Christian prayers and songs.[84]

But this work was helped by co-revelations. Pané reported miracles; for example, when Guarionex ordered some Christian images left in a chapel destroyed, the people charged with doing so buried them instead, saying, "Now your fruit will be good." But a man digging later in the fields discovered that some yams had grown up very quickly where the images were buried, and in the shape of a cross. The idea that burying sacred objects in fields promoted their fertility was a part of the Tainos' own beliefs, attested by archaeology and other accounts, so it is no surprise that even Guarionex's own mother, who

---

[84] Ramón Pané, *An Account of the Antiquities of the Indians* (ed. and trans. to Spanish by José Juan Arrom, trans. to English by Susan Griswold, Durham, 1999), cap. 26. The original account was composed, according to Arrom, in 1498, but is only known through notes in other sources, and an Italian translation of a Spanish copy was inserted in Fernando Colombo's account of his father's life (Alfonso de Ulloa, *Historie del S. D. Fernando Colombo...* (Venice, 1571), cap. 61). This English translation, which incorporates material from several sources in various languages, is thus no less reliable than any other version now available.

Pané described as the "worst woman I have known in those parts," declared the event a "miracle [that] has been wrought by God where the images were found." Pané concurred, calling the chapter of his treatise that covered this event, "Concerning what happened to the images and the miracle God worked to show his power."[85] Co-revelations that had brought conversions in the Canaries and Kongo might also work in America.

The population of Hispaniola, like that of the Canaries, either died out or was assimilated into the Spanish population by the mid-sixteenth century, and so the concept of Diabolism that played such a role in reform did not really come to play. Columbus argued that the *zemis* found throughout the island and clearly images used in religious worship were not works of the Devil, but were simply acts of trickery on the part of power-hungry caciques, and Pané for his part also held back from defining zemis as idols or of being charged by the Devil.[86] Only Bartolomé de las Casas, writing just before the Council of Trent, saw anything Diabolic in the zemis, though he thought it was limited.[87]

THE GREAT EMPIRES: MEXICO AND PERU

The Aztec Empire and its neighboring Mesoamerican cultures formed a large intercommunicating religious zone, sharing iconography, mythology, and religious ideas from the southern extension of the Maya zone in Honduras and Nicaragua to the northern end of the Aztec and Tarascan empires in northwest Mexico. In all these regions, there was a permanent, professional priesthood that relied heavily on discontinuous revelation, frequently in written form. Many of the sacred scriptures of the various regional versions of religion were destroyed in the Spanish conquest, though a few have survived, and between these and the Spanish descriptions (which often tried to be as neutral in presentation as possible given the religious convictions of the Spanish recorders), we can gain a fairly detailed vision of what they believed.

In these countries as in the islands, the initial work was one of rapid Christianization without much recourse to theological issues. Shortly after Cortés managed to win the submission or alliance of the people of the central plateau of Mexico, he asked the crown to send him Franciscan missionaries to engage in converting these new vassals and allies.[88] In 1523, "The Twelve" (a dozen priests, numbering, significantly enough, as the Apostles) arrived in

---

[85] Pané, *Antiquities*, caps. 25 and 26; see also Arrom's note, p. 36 n. 155 on the religious significance in Taino society.

[86] Fernando Colombo, *Historie*, cap. 62, trans. in Arrom's edition of Pané's *Antiquities*, pp. 44–45; Pané, *Antiquities*, caps. 14–20.

[87] Bartolomé de las Casas, *Apologetica de las Indias* (mod. ed. Juan Pérez Tudelo y Bueso, Madrid, 1958), cap. 164.

[88] Hernán Cortés to King, *Cartas de relación* (ed. M. Alcalá, 10th ed., Mexico City, 1978), pp. 203–204.

Mexico to begin the work. They baptized tirelessly, sometimes using their own saliva for holy water when baptismal water lacked, and performed the sacrament, by their count, millions of times.[89] These Franciscans were members of regular teaching orders that also included, as time went on, Dominicans, Augustinians, and Jesuits. All these orders turned to providing a careful, theologically nuanced catechism once the phase of mass baptism was over. Although the tutelage of the Mexicans by regular clergy was initially envisioned to take place in a few years, and their jurisdiction over the "Indians" returned to the secular clergy, in fact it would last until the end of the eighteenth century.

One of the tasks that the clergy put to themselves was to study the discontinuous revelation of Mexican religion to determine its origin. Because no earlier conversion (Canaries, the Caribbean islands, or Kongo) had discontinuous revelations, this was a new task. The original priests who came to Mexico, most notably Toribio de Motolinía, writing in the late 1530s and early 1540s, provided an initial interpretation of the Mexican religion, based on their experience and reading the books of the Aztecs.[90] In his vision, the great founder of Aztec society, Quetzalcoatl, was an "honest and temperate man" who never married and lived "chastely" introducing natural law, fasting, and the Aztec system of self-sacrifice system of drawing blood from various parts of the body. This sacrifice, contended Toribio de Motolinía, the best known of the Franciscans, was "not to serve the Devil, but as penitence against the wickedness of language and hearing."

While Motolinía and his colleagues found admirable elements in an ancient deity, they ended up affirming that much of Aztec religion, including the forms of self-sacrifice practiced in his day, was the work of the Devil for his own ends.[91] Having thus decided that while the original Aztec religion may have been divinely inspired, it was now effectively in the Devil's hands, they decided to extirpate the outward signs of the old religion. At their urging, Cortés issued an order that they should destroy it, beginning in Texcoco in 1525, "where they had the most and largest teocallis [Nahua for temple] or temples of the Devil," which Motolinía described as "the first battle made against the Devil."[92] Andrés

---

[89] Toribio Motolinia, "Historia de los Indios de Nueva España," in Joaquín García Icazbalceta, ed., *Documentos para la Historia de Mexico* (2 vols., Mexico, 1858–1866) vol. 1, Tratado Primero. It is still worthwhile to read Robert Ricard's classic treatment of the evangelization, *The Spiritual Conquest of Mexico: an essay on the apostolate and the evangelizing methods of the mendicant orders in New Spain, 1523–1572* (tr. Lesley Byrd Simpson Berkeley and Los Angeles, 1966, first French ed., 1933).

[90] Motolinía, "Historia" does not exist as a single manuscript, but the version compiled by Icazbalceta comes from multiple sources and gives several "present year" statements within it – for example, 1536 and 1540.

[91] Motolinía, "Historia," Epistolo Proemial (1541); for Diabolic elements in practice as they witnessed it, see Tratado 1, caps. 2 and 3; on further background on the European concepts of Diabolism as well as its application in Spanish territories in the New World, see Fernando Cervantes, *The Devil in the New World: The Impact of Diabolism in New Spain* (New Haven, 1994).

[92] Motolinía, "Historia," Tratado 1, cap. 3.

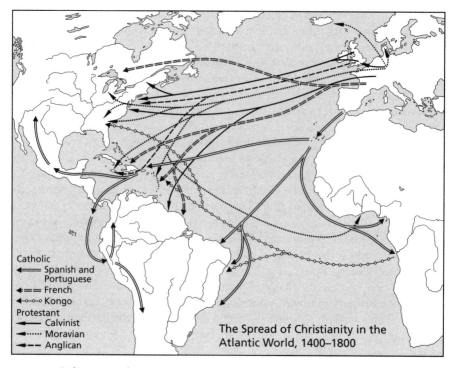

Catholic
◀══ Spanish and Portuguese
◀═══ French
◀-○-○ Kongo
Protestant
◀─── Calvinist
◀······ Moravian
◀─── Anglican

The Spread of Christianity in the Atlantic World, 1400–1800

MAP 10. Religions in the Americas.

de Olmos, using the examples of witchcraft literature from Europe to further the idea of a Diabolic religion, supported the idea of complete extirpation in his decisive treatise on Aztec religion in 1553.[93]

Motolinía's first decision was elaborated on and deepened in the following years by more extensive study of Aztec scripture, aided by the Aztec clergy who had become Christians. In fact, Motolinía believed that as a fortuitous working of the will of God – a sort of miracle – many priests who resisted conversion had died, leaving only the Christian helpers behind.[94] Led by Bernardo de Sahagún, the priests and their lay assistants compiled a massive collection of religious, cultural, and historical data and rewrote it an alphabetic system for representing Nahua, and then in Spanish translation.[95] This body, and

[93] Andrés de Olmos, *Tratado de hechcírias y sorteligios* (ed. and trans into French Georges Baudot, Mexico, 1979).

[94] Motolinía, "Historia," Tratado 1, cap. 2.

[95] Bernardino de Sahagún, *Florentine Codex: General History of the Things of New Spain* (trans. Arthur J. O. Anderson and Charles E. Dibble, 13 parts, Salt Lake City and Santa Fe, 1950–1985), an excellent edition in Aztec orthography and Nahua with English translation (see also *Historia general de las cosas de la Nueva España*, ed. Angel María Garibay K., Mexico City, 1981, for the Spanish version).

FIGURE 16. "Quetzalcoatl" from *Codex Magliabechiano*. By kind permission of the Ministero per i Beni e le Attività Culturali della Repubblica Italiana/Biblioteca Nazionale Centrale di Firenze.

other "painted books" or "pictures," provided the primary source from which European priests decided how to deal with Mexican religion.[96]

The Dominican Diego Durán began a synthesis of their thoughts in the 1570s, by arguing that the indigenous people of the Americas were in fact a lost tribe of Israel, and suggested that they therefore had a sort of Old Testament basis including religious ideas and practices that he thought had Jewish origins.[97] He continued by contending that the god Topiltzin (another name for Quetzalcoatl), recognized by the earliest priests as a positive character, was in fact Saint Thomas the Apostle. In this version, when Jesus sent his Apostles out to spread the message, he sent Saint Thomas east to "India" and eventually to America. There, as Topiltzin, he had introduced Christianity (and hence a sort of New Testament), including adult baptism, which Durán found in America in the same form as in the early

[96] The oldest of these is probably Codex Borbonicus, which is primarily glyphic in nature but has short glosses written in Nahua.

[97] Diego Durán, *Historia de las Indias de Nueva España yIslas de Tierra Firme* [1579 and 1581] (mod. ed., 2 vols, Mexico, 1866–1880 [GB], English translation by Doris Heyden [Norman, OK, 1994]), cap. 1. This text was only discovered in the nineteenth century, but was frequently cited in other works and its ideas were well known.

Church.[98] Then, drawing on the Aztec scriptures, Durán asserted that tales
of Quetzalcoatl's humiliation and overthrow by his enemies represented
a victory by the Devil and hence the Diabolic religion that reigned at the
time of the Spanish arrival. From the Spanish point of view, then, one could
reconcile the idea that God would not have left Americans without any revelation of their own, with their conviction that the Devil had nevertheless
taken over religious life as the Spanish met it in Mexico.

If the co-revelation they found in their interpretation of Mexican sacred
literature satisfied the Spanish priests, it had a slightly different impact on the
religious elite of Mexico. There is no reason to believe from their writing that
they were not prepared to accept the convergence of revelation, and this may
well have shaped their general acceptance of the new religion (and they continued to play a part in it through their service in the church). Like the Spanish
they engaged in some historical speculation to reach similar ends.

The Codex Rámirez, a very early but post-conquest chronicle, written in
Nahua and perhaps by an indigenous author, related that a variety of auguries
and omens, interpreted more or less correctly by Aztec priests, preceded the
Spanish arrival, and led the Emperor Montezuma to declare that the Spanish
were his gods.[99] Thus, the account describes continuous revelations, within
the indigenous system of revelation, and thus forming a co-revelation for the
Spanish arrival.[100] According, for example, to the early-seventeenth-century
mixed-race historian Fernando de Alva Ixtilxóchitl, the Aztecs believed that
Quetzalcoatl, before leaving for exile after his overthrow, announced he would
return, and along with reports of his physical appearance as fair-skinned and
bearded, the Spanish arrival coincided with this.[101] This idea was striking
enough that it was presented in slightly variant forms by other writers of the
time, including the Spanish priest Bernardino de Sahagún and the mixed-race
historian Hernando Alvarado Tezozomoc, along with more stories about auguries and predictions concerning the Spanish that preceded their arrival, placing
the event in cosmic terms.[102]

Most indigenous people thus came to understand these convergences of
revelations as meaning that the Christian revelation was an extension and

---

[98] Durán, *Historia*, caps. 79, 86.

[99] [Attributed to Juan de Tovar] "Relacion del Origen de los Indios que habitan este Nueva España
segun sus historias," [c. 1587] in Manuel Orozco y Berra, ed., *Cronica Mexicana* (Mexico,
1878[GB]) pp. 77–80. Widely called the Codex Ramírez after an early owner, many scholars
believe that this employed an even earlier text (Crónica X) written in Nahua "pictures" by an
early convert, which was also the source of several later descriptions of Aztec religious history.

[100] Camilla Townshend, "Burying the White Gods: New Perspectives on the Conquest of Mexico,"
American Historical Review 108 (2003): 659–687, on a thorough refutation that this particular myth was held in pre-conquest Mexico.

[101] Fernando de Alva Ixlilxóchitl, "Historia de la nación Chichimeca," [written between 1610 and
1640] in Alfredo Chavero, ed., *Obras Historicas de D. Fernando de Alva Ixlilxóchitl* (2 vols.,
Mexico, 1891–1892 [GB]), vol. 2, caps. 1 and 80.

[102] Bernardino de Sahagún, *Historia General* and Hernando de Alvarado Tezozómoc, "Crónica
Mexicana" (1598), in Orozco y Berra, ed., *Cronica Mexicana*, caps. 105, 108.

expansion of their own religion, and thus had little difficulty adding Christianity to their existing tradition. The priests, determined to extirpate the diabolic religion, saw this as backsliding, and many scholars have seen it as resistance to forced conversion. In Spain's ally Tlaxcala, where there was no Spanish coercive power, the local religious leaders simply placed images of "Jesus Christ crucified and his blessed mother" among their images. Motolinía thought that the Tlaxcalans believed "as if they had a hundred gods, and wanted a hundred and one." While the priests pressed them to break the images and to grind them to make cement to build the churches, they managed to preserve their essence within the church.[103] Even in the conquered areas, as the priests dedicated churches, the Nahua people managed to include symbols of the old religion, and continued in the worship of the old deities at night, or in forests, or elsewhere, even as they sang Christian hymns and accepted baptism and other signs of devotion.[104]

The regular priests, drinking in the notion of extirpation of Diabolic religion, tried their best to stop the practice of co-devotion and mistook it for resistance. In the battle against associating Christianity with Mexican religion, they decided only to use Latin or Spanish terms in their Nahua catechism for religiously significant concepts, rather than adopt a Nahua term and create a co-revelation, as in fact was being done at exactly the same time in Kongo.

Complete extirpation of Mexican religion would have required considerable coercion, and the lay authorities, who would have had to support it, were lukewarm or reluctant to expend resources on such a radical solution. The first bishop of New Spain, Juan de Zumárraga, who came in 1528, was also authorized by the crown to bring the Inquisition with him and was, indeed, licensed to be an inquisitor. The Inquisition tried remarkably few cases involving indigenous people for idolatry or other religious offenses (only 19 out of 152 cases tried between 1522 and 1543 involved indigenous people), considering the extent and pervasiveness of joint worship.[105] Those who were tried, such as the celebrated case of Carlos Ometochtzin, the ruler of Texcoco in 1539, were tried as much for potential rebellion as for religious reasons, even though claims were made (resolutely denied by many testants) of his worshipping other deities or renouncing Christianity.[106]

---

[103] Motolinía, "Historia," Tratado 1, cap. 3.

[104] Motolinía, "Historia," Tratado 1, cap. 4.

[105] As tallied by J. Jorge Klor de Alva, "Colonizing Souls: The Failure of the Indian Inquisition and the Rise of Penitential Discipline," in Mary Elisabeth Perry and Ana Cruz, eds., *Cultural Encounters: The Impact of the Inquisition in Spain and the New World* (Berkeley and Los Angeles, 1991), pp. 6–7. Klor de Alva's explanation of the failure of the Inquisition differs somewhat from my own.

[106] His process was published by Luis González Obregón, *Processo inquisitorial del cacique de Tetzcoco don Carlos Moetochtzin (Chichimecatecotl)* (Mexico, 1910; reprinted Austin, 1980); see the discussion of the politics of the case in Martin Leinhard, *Disidentes, rebeldes, insurgentes: resistencia indígena y negra en América Latina : ensayos de historia testimonial* (Madrid, 2008), pp. 29–50.

In the end, in 1571, the crown forbade using the Inquisition to enforce the suppression of the Devil, arguing that the indigenous people were too new in the faith to be treated severely, but also surely because the coercive mechanisms to apply inquisitional techniques widely were lacking. The Mexican Inquisition did try a modest number cases of Indians accused of various forms of "idolatry" all understood to be a form of Devil worship in subsequent years, but they were rare and had little larger impact.[107] There would be no massive and violent repression in America as there had been in the witch craze in Europe. As a result, the synthesis of revelations that characterized the early years of the colony continued more or less unabated.

The continuation of a co-revealed synthesis of Christianity and local religion was well demonstrated in denunciations of idolatry published, for example, by Hernando Ruiz de Alarcón in the 1620s and Jacinto de la Serna in the 1650s.[108] While both these writers wrote vigorously about what they saw as a diabolic synthesis of religions, they did so only in limited areas, and they met with lukewarm responses by state officials and other interested and influential parties.

New continuous revelation also played a role in creating a transformed religious system. As an example, a legendary story from Sula written in the late seventeenth century related that when the Spanish first came, the town council decided they had to have a patron saint. As it happened, two of the councilors dreamed simultaneously of Santiago, and thus a miraculous choice had been made.[109] The apparition of the Virgin of Guadeloupe, recorded only in the mid-seventeenth century, was the most important continuous revelation, however, especially for the many indigenous people who lived and worked in cities and towns, away from the traditional authorities and missionaries.[110] The Virgin of Guadeloupe, according to the accounts published in the mid-seventeenth century, appeared to an Indian in 1531, shortly after the conquest. The appearance of the Virgin was not strictly speaking a co-revelation, although in some ways she can be equated with pre-conquest practices; rather she was a new continuous revelation. What was significant about the Virgin of Guadeloupe was that she had the physical appearance of a Mexican, and thus became the patron saint of the mixed-race or acculturated native population

---

[107] For some samples from across the colonial period, see Serge Gruzinski, *Man-Gods*.

[108] Hernando Ruiz de Alarcón, *Tratado de las supersticiones y custumbres gentilicas que hoy viven entre los indios naturales de este Nueva España* (Madrid, 1629, mod. ed. Francisco del Paso y Trancoso, Mexico, 1953), online at http://www.cervantesvirtual.com/servlet/SirveObras/03693951900225939732268/index.htm; Jacinto de la Serna, *Manual de ministros de los Indios para el concimiento de sus idolatrias y el extirpacion dellas* (1650, mod. ed. Madrid, 1892 [GB]).

[109] Lockhard, *Nahuas under Spanish Rule*, p. 236.

[110] The earliest known references to the apparition of the Virgin come from Miguel Sánchez, *Imagen de la Virgen Maria, Madre de Dios de Guadelupe...* (Mexico, 1648), mod. ed. Ernesto de la Torre Villar and Ramiro Navarro de Anda, eds., *Testimonios histórico guadeloupanos* (Mexico City, 1982), pp. 152–281.

of Mexico.[111] Her cult spread rapidly after the publication of the story of her apparition, in Spanish and Nahuatl of Luis Laso de la Vega's *Huei tlamahuiçoltica* in 1649.[112]

The Mexican religious synthesis became the central paradigm for Christianization as the Spanish conquest turned south, occupying Central America, including Oaxaca and the Yucatán. In both areas, soldiers recruited from the Aztec heartland and Tlaxcalans provided the military muscle to achieve victories for Spain, and they served as go-betweens in the interpretation of the religion. In Oaxaca, therefore, it was from the Nahua catechists and ecclesiastical helpers that the Catholic faith originated. We have considerably less literature on the process of co-revelation that might have accompanied the "spiritual conquest" of Oaxaca, although it probably involved the process of co-revelation and the growth of co-devotion. An early and celebrated Inquisition case against the rulers of Yanhuitlan and Coatlan in, respectively, 1545 and 1547, like similar cases in Mexico, was partly about factional struggle and partially about secret worship of older deities, and the Inquisition's interest may well have been piqued as much by the threat of rebellion or civil war as by true religious resistance.[113]

In any case, the Church in Oaxaca would eventually come to terms with local religion. The catechism in the local language published in 1595 made substantial concessions to indigenous concepts, first of all by employing local terms for a number of theological concepts, and also by employing imagery that merged Mary, the mother of Jesus, with local deities. In short, it was co-revelation by means of language and imagery, subtle and unspoken but nevertheless real. In Oaxaca, even more than in Mexico, the priests, whatever their views of extirpation of idolatry might have been, were completely unable to compel the abolition of the existing religious system and were seemingly content with a subtle co-revelation of words and images.

If the Spanish capacity to hold Mexico slackened the enthusiasm that priests had to extirpate idolatry, it was not clearly revealed in the Yucatán, where the Spanish managed to build a base at Mérida but failed to displace the major kingdoms of the interior lowlands until the late seventeenth century. Still, the priests managed to win mass conversion among the people they did gain control of. As in Mexico, the Maya people appear to have approached the new religion as an addition to their existing one, and thus continued to worship their old deities.

---

[111] Stafford Poole, *Our Lady of Guadeloupe: The Origins and Sources of a Mexican National Symbol, 1531–1797* (Tuscon, 1995), which demonstrates that the legend probably did not play a role in the original conversion of Nahuas to Christianity, but was very significant to the mixed-race Mexicans of the sixteenth century.

[112] For a modern, annotated bilingual Nahuatl and English edition, see Lisa Sousa, Stafford Poole, and James Lockhart, eds., *The Story of Guadeloupe: Luis Lasco de la Vega's Huei tlamahuiçoltica of 1649* (Palo Alto, 1998).

[113] This case is presented in full in Kevin Terraciano, *The Mixtecs of Colonial Oaxaca: Ñudzahui history, Sixteenth through Eighteenth Centuries* (Stanford, 2001), pp. 274–310.

In 1562, in response to reports of hidden idolatry, the Franciscan superior, Diego de Landa, proceeded vigorously to suppress it. He thus began what would become a spirited attack on Mayan idolatry, which he held to be diabolically inspired. Even at the time of the denunciations, the circumstances suggested that secular rivalries among both indigenous people and various Spanish factions played a role in the process, and some Spanish encomenderos vigorously denounced de Landa's efforts. De Landa and his assistants, for their part, engaged in ruthless interrogations, often employing torture. As the inquest became more heated and brutal, communities were soon turning in more and more people, and the stories of idolatry became more and more convoluted and elaborate. For some, this was all evidence that the priests had taken some isolated incidents and, by overreacting and especially conducting the kind of inquests that they did, soon ensured that a large plot would reveal itself. Others have taken the results more literally and argued that the Maya were in fact resisting Christianization, subtly but effectively. As in Mexico, however, the secular authorities, including the elite Spanish residents, turned against the expensive and divisive actions of the priest and he was forced to desist.[114]

Christianity's primary mode of entry into the Yucatán, however, was not through a direct attack on the local religion, but rather through Christian miracles and co-revelations associated with saints, especially the Virgin Mary. In his systematic history of the spiritual conquest of Yucatán, written in 1633, Bernardo de Lizana described the creation of Marian cult centers in all the major centers the Spanish controlled. In each case the new centers were built on or near older divine centers, which de Lizana carefully named and described, more or less in competition with them (or perhaps, to local people, sharing co-revelational space with them). Attentive to stories of miracles, he recorded those that had an impact on the faith of those who witnessed or heard of them. In his account of the most famous of the Virgins, the Virgin of Izamal, Lizana noted a number of miraculous healings, both of Spaniards and of Mayas, as well as the initial miracle, the inexplicable continuation of the cult's meager food supply for its adherents during a long famine.[115]

However, de Landa's initial attacks on Maya religion had had its impact. In addition to hiding idols and practicing their older religion more discretely, Mayas, who had the longest tradition of literacy (and the most fully developed writing system) in Mesoamerica, also recorded their underlying theology and mythology. As the Spanish introduced alphabetic writing to replace the older hieroglyphic, Maya elites re-recorded their older precious materials in this new writing system, recognizing, perhaps that the new system would replace the older one, which

---

[114] For a full description of the inquisitorial procedure of de Landa, see Inga Clendinnen, *Ambivalent Conquests*, pp. 72–112. Also see her article, "Disciplining the Indians: Franciscan Ideology and Missionary Violence in Sixteenth-Century Yucután," *Past and Present* 94 (1982): 27–48.

[115] Bernardo de Lizana, *Historia y Devocionario de la Sacratissima Virgen* in *Historia de Yucatán. Devocionaria de Nra Sra de Itzmal y Conquista Espiritual de Yucután* (mod. ed. 2 vols., 1892–93), Part 1, caps. 4–13 (a spiritual geography) and Part 2 (a description of miracles).

would then become unreadable (as indeed happened). It was only in the late seventeenth century, when the priest Francisco Ximénez learned of this hidden writing, that it came to light. Ximénez recovered, recorded, and translated a local book, called the *Popol Vuh*, probably written while de Landa and his associates were gathering and destroying Maya religious literature in the 1550s.

The *Popol Vuh* related Maya mythohistory at length, and by presenting a linguistically sophisticated exposition of Maya religious concepts, Ximénez thought he could assist in planting Christianity.[116] The text, at least as presented by Ximénez, was produced from fear its content would be lost, but was also explicitly done by Christian Mayas. Elements of the history clearly relate to the Book of Genesis, but most of its content seems indisputably of Maya origin.[117] It is quite possible then that it represented an attempt by the Maya elite to reconcile at least the cosmology of the Maya with Christian cosmology – a task that made much more sense to the Mayas that it did to the Spanish priests. Indeed, in his prologue, Ximénez notes that "at the beginning … it says things that conform well to the Holy Scripture and Catholic Faith," but that later it descends into "a thousands lies."[118] Later still, a series of other books, possibly of nearly as ancient a pedigree, called books of *Chilam Balam*, were found in other Maya cities, and these were presented in much the same way in the eighteenth and nineteenth centuries.[119]

In the early eighteenth century, Chiapas experienced a series of new continuous revelations, in which persons, sometimes *ladino*, claimed special communication with Catholic saints and became immediate objects of great local devotion. The religious movement took on political implications and culminated in an outright rebellion at Caucuc in 1713.[120] These revelations, although new and not particularly associated with cultic centers as the earlier ones had been, were in many ways a continuation of the process of saintly revelation. In 1761, Jacinto Canek combined some of these elements in his claim to restore Maya kingship, both crowning himself with the crown from the head of an image of the Virgin of Gaudeloupe and predicting that his reign was to be found in the *Chilam Balam*.[121]

---

[116] For a detailed study of the *Popul Vuh* and Ximenez in their historical context, see John Woodruff, "The 'Most Futile and Vain Works' in Father Francisco Ximénez: Rethinking the Context of Popul Vuh" (PhD dissertation, University of Alabama, 2009).

[117] Newberry Library, MS Ayer 515, Francisco Ximénez, "Empiezan las historias del origen de los indios de esta provincial de Guatemala," fols. 1–5 (commonly known as Popul Vuh), online at http://library.osu.edu/sites/popolwuj/folios_eng/PWfolio_i_r_en.php, with K'iche, English, and Spanish transcriptions and translations.

[118] Newberry Library, MS Ayer MS, Ximénez, "Empiezan," fol. iir.

[119] Ralph Roys, ed. and trans., *The Book of Chiliam Balam of Chumayel* (Washington, DC, 1933). Eight other such books are also known.

[120] Victoria Bricker, *The Indian Christ, the Indian King: The Historical Substrate of Maya Myth and Ritual* (Austin, 1981), pp. 55–69.

[121] Bricker, *Indian Christ*, pp. 70–76; Robert Patch, "La rebelión de Jacinto Canek en Yucatán: Una nueva interpretación," *Desacatos* 13 (2003): 46–59, online at http://redalyc.uaemex.mx/redalyc/pdf/139/13901304.pdf

THE CHURCH IN PERU

The situation in Peru was different from Mexico, in that a written scriptural tradition did not exist, but there was nevertheless a strong religious and cosmological mythology that was caught up in the origins of the Inca state, and which was widely reported in early sources, both those of European visitors and of the mixed Inca-Spanish elite. At the same time, however, the pattern of religious interaction and change was very similar in both regions: both found indigenous and Spanish religious elites coming to terms with co-revelation of older discontinuous revelation, and wrestled with the question of Diabolic revelation.[122]

Unlike Mexico, where a fairly rapid and straightforward political conquest took place, in Peru, both conquest and evangelization were slower, more complicated, and involved more twists and turns of power and faith. We know very little about what Spanish priests taught during the first twenty-five or thirty years of the conquest period, although we do know that they engaged in mass baptisms. But at the same time, we know that the Incan religious elite was busy reconciling what they were taught with their own revelationary history, as was passed down either in the form of memory aides of knotted string (*quipus* or *khipus*) or strictly by memory, with Christian ideas. Juan de Santacruz Pachacuti Yamqui, writing in 1613, related stories that firmly connected the ancient Andeans to the Bible, which he said he had been told by his grandfather and others of his grandfather's generation (i.e., perhaps current in the mid-sixteenth century).

In Santacruz Pachacuti Yamqui's version of ancient wisdom, a sudden cry from the devils, which he called *hapiñuñus*, "we are defeated!" announced to them that Jesus had been crucified and they disappeared from the country. This was followed by the appearance of a bearded man called Tonapa or Tonapaca Viracochanpachayachicachan, dressed in white, of whom Santacruz asked, "would this man not have been the glorious Apostle Saint Thomas?" Making it clear that he thought Tonapa was Saint Thomas, Santacruz Pachacuti Yamqui recorded stories at some length of the apostle's teaching, and of various relics and reminders of his passages found in Peru in his days, including a notched staff that were said to contain the seven precepts of the Church. While most people did not listen to Saint Thomas, the Inca Manco Capac, the eventual founder of the empire, did and preserved his memory, which was passed on from there. He also noted that the third ruler, Maytacapac, predicted that the Gospels would come and ordered the idols and *huacas* (burial places where the spirits of the dead might be consulted) burned, and although the monotheistic religion introduced by the Apostle and continued by the wisest of the Incas continued, Diabolic incursions did take place up until the Spanish arrived.[123]

---

[122] Jeffery Klaiber, "The Posthumous Christianization of the Inca Empire in Colonial Peru," *Journal of the History of Ideas* 37 (1976): 507–520 presents a good overview of the various writers.

[123] Joan de Santacruz Pachacuti Yamqui, "Relacion de Antigüedades deste Reyno del Pirú," in Márcos Jiménez de la Espada, ed., *Tres relaciones del antigüedades peruanas* (Madrid, 1879), pp. 231–255.

Another convergence story, written in Quechua using the Latin alphabet by someone from Huarochiri around 1600, and edited by Francisco de Avila, retold a local story of a great flood, and adding "when the Oceans overflowed," said, "We Christians believe it refers to the time of the [Biblical] flood." [124] Thus, Andeans were prepared to accept and incorporate the ideas a great deluge and of a wandering Saint Thomas, just as the Mexicans had done, and to find what they thought were ample proofs of their imperfect but significant pre-Spanish Christian identity. Indeed, while they believed that there were Diabolic elements in Peruvian religion as practiced in the pre-conquest period, they also felt that purification required little real effort and the basic religion was a base to build from.

However the creation of a synthesis was also complicated by the religious politics of the conquest period, and particularly by the Taki Onqoy in 1560, when the country was still divided between Tupac Amaru and the Spanish and their collaborators from Cuzco. According to a report by the priest Luis de Olivera, the leaders of this religious movement held that at one time in the past, the *huacas* had conquered God (the Spanish diety), but that the Spanish, by destroying the *huacas*, had reversed that earlier victory. Now, the Taki Onqoy contended, the situation was to be reversed again, and the *huacas* destroyed by the Spanish would be brought back to life.

The people who had allied themselves with God by baptism were now to realign themselves to the *huacas* and to drive the Spanish out. The *huacas*, however, had changed, for instead of going back to the mountains or springs as was customary, they were now residing in people, taking them over by possession, and these possessed believers were presenting continuous revelation.[125] Olivera presented the case as being fundamentally anti-Spanish, and allied with Tupac Amaru's party, even to the point of not allowing adherents to eat Spanish food or use Spanish materials. Other documents, however, show that Christian saints as well as the *huacas* possessed believers.[126] One witness, interrogated in 1570, noted that a number of women had saints' names, "in order to be revered as saints," and they were perhaps possessed by saints themselves.[127]

---

[124] Frank Salomon and Urioste, *The Huarochiri Manuscript: A Testament of Ancient Andean Religion* (Austin, 1991); Avila's account was published in 1646 as *Tratado de los evangelios que nuestra Madre la Yglesia nos propone...* (Lima, 1648); no modern edition of this text is available, I have used the English translation in Markham, ed. and trans., *Narratives*, pp. 121–147 (cited by chapter). Compare manuscript's chapter 3.34 to Avila's chapter 4.

[125] This letter is quoted in Cristoval de Molina, "Fabulas y mitos," in Urbano and Duviols, *Relacion*, pp. 129–132; an English translation is in Clements Markham, ed. and trans., *Narratives of the Rites and Laws of the Yncas* (London, 1883), pp. 59–63.

[126] On the many and varied interpretations that modern historians have given to the Taki Onqoy, see Jeremy Mumford, "The Taki Onqoy and the Andean Nation: Sources and Interpretations," *Latin American Research Review* 33 (1998): 150–165.

[127] "Informaciones de Cristobal de Albornoz," in Luis Milliones and Pedro Guibovich, eds., *El retorno de las huacas: Estudios y documentos sobre el Taki Onqoy, siglo XVI* (Lima, 1990), pp. 88 and 99.

The Taki Onqoy probably played a substantial role in the attitude that the most active Spanish clergy had to Peruvian religion. Between 1560 and 1575, priests compiled stories about the Peruvian past and Inca religion, and discovered the convergences with Biblical authority that local people had probably already been making, but found what they considered more compelling evidence of Diabolic intervention. Juan de San Pedro, writing in 1560, for example, noted that Incas believed in a divine Trinity, but contended the Devil "told them this most false Trinity."[128] Likewise, both he and Cristobal de Molina, who wrote in 1575, believed that local stories showed evidence of Christians visiting Peru in ancient times, and leaving artifacts of their visits and preaching, before they were killed off by diabolically inspired enemies. They even dismissed stories, like those of Santacruz Pachacuti Yamqui of the Inca Yupanqui instituting what seemed to be a Christian religion, as simply inventions of the Devil to fool them.[129]

It would take longer for the elite Counter-Reformation-inspired Spanish and mixed-race Andean regular priests, like the Jesuit Blas Valera, to accept this much history, and they focused more on the corrupting nature of Diabolic influence in the religion as it was practiced in Peru at the time of the conquest. This was even true of Gacilasco de la Vega, the most erudite of the mixed-race apologists, who reported the sort of ideas that Santacruz Pachacuti Yamqui wrote about, but tended on the whole to dismiss them.[130] They persisted in believing that it was necessary, as their colleagues in Mexico did, that there was little or nothing to save in the old religion.

However, the religious synthesis proceeded anyway, whether the regular priests liked it or not. As in Mexico, the idea of extirpation was too radical and too expensive to carry out in full, and so manifested itself as occasional enthusiasms for rooting out the old religion after finding its syncretic practice among their Christian indigenous parishioners. The desire to engage in extirpations, even campaigns of extirpation, was possible because the normal religion of people in the Andes was this blending of reworked and reunderstood discontinuous revelation of Andean and European origin along with a continued belief that the *huacas* were more or less a part of the religion and there was no reason to supplant them.

Thus the *huacas* were always to be found, and priests to serve them were rarely lacking. If an inquisitor decided to root out idolatry, there was no shortage of evidence of its existence, as treatises and testimony taken by the "Visitas de Idolataria" regularly revealed. From time to time, an enthusiastic inquisitor,

---

[128] [Juan de San Pedro], "Relacion de la Religion y Ritos del Peru...," in *CDI* 3: 1–58, this quotation on p. 14. A more modern edition is Lucila Castro de Trelles, ed., *Relación de la religion y ritos del Peru* (Lima, 1992).

[129] [de San Pedro], "Relacion," in *CDI* 3: 22–24, and 51–53; Cristoval de Molina, "Relacion de los ritos y fabulas de los incas," *CDHC* 1: 1–103; for a more recent critical edition, see Enrique Urbano and Pierre Duviols, *Relacion de las Fabulas y ritos de los Incas* (Madrid, 1989).

[130] Klaiber, "Posthumous Christianization," pp. 518–520.

sometimes for personal reasons or because of other political concerns, would pursue idolatry (as the continuing Andean religious practices were usually called), and witnesses would be interrogated, sometimes tortured, evidence would be collected, and a group of perpetuators would be punished.[131] The scope and scale of these investigations was relatively small, even if intense; there was nothing in Peru even vaguely resembling the massive work of the witch craze in Europe, and not surprisingly, the synthesis set down in the early colonial period remains to the present day.

NEW GRANADA

The Spanish conquest of the New Kingdom of Granada, completed by 1540, followed in many ways the patterns established in Mexico and Peru. Although the highlands of today's Colombia had not reached a full political integration at the time that Jiménez de Quesada led his men up from the coast, they had the sort of religious life that was characteristic of Mexico or Peru. There was, for example, a more or less permanent priesthood (which the Spanish called *jeques*), trained at what Pedro Símon, an early-seventeenth-century Jesuit chronicler, called a "university" where they studied for as much as a dozen years, and were then posted in the country.[132] At the same time, however, they served in dozens of local cults, anchored on sanctuaries, the origin legends of which the thoughtful Jesuit noted and recorded.

Jeques should probably be counted as not being a particularly precarious priesthood in light of this long training, but nevertheless, they operated in the Other World, and at times sought revelations, especially through chewing strong tobacco, which gave them interpretable dreams. They were called on to heal the sick, and in this their actions could be considered miraculous, although at the same time their professionalization protected them from criticism should they fail.[133]

In any case, they were identified by the Spanish priests from the very beginning as working with the Devil, and they were the principal enemies to be extirpated, along with the shrines they served, as a means of eliminating witchcraft.[134] It was helpful, from the Spanish perspective, to take this position, because many of these shrines were also repositories of vast treasures of emeralds, gold, and fine cloth. Indeed, the search for and looting of these sanctuaries was one of the early goals of the conquistadors, and Símon notes a story of an old encomendero, aging and short of gold, who persuaded one of

---

[131] For an excellent survey of the "Middle Period" work of extirpators, as well as a good survey, drawn from their testimony and that of their witnesses on daily religious life, see Kenneth Mills, *Idolatry and its Enemies: Colonial Andean Religion and Extirpation, 1640–1750* (Princeton, 1997).

[132] Símon, *Noticias historiales*, Noticia 4, cap. 5, no. 1. Símon gives the correct Chibcha name as "Ogque," which the Spanish could not pronounce and thus rendered it as "jeque."

[133] Símon, *Noticias historiales*, Noticia 4, cap. 5, no. 3. The tobacco "revealed the Devil."

[134] Símon, *Noticias historiales*, Noticia 4, cap. 5, no. 4 (extirpation in the Savanna of Bogotá).

his indigenous servants to reveal such a treasury to him, which she eventually did. The encomendero, working with a priest (who carried holy water, because the place needed exorcism before looting), enriched himself with the spoils of the sanctuary.[135]

If the clergy identified the jeques as agents of the Devil – and in some cases, where such power was wielded by local political leaders, that the Devil himself was in charge – they were also prepared to locate a divine presence in the region.[136] Símon tells of local legends that describe the arrival, around 150 CE, of a "preacher" with a long beard dressed in what might pass for Biblical clothing, who taught new values and laws, and who left among other things a tradition of reverence for the cross and the idea of a Trinity. But in the aftermath of his passing out of the region, the Devil had intervened in the form of a variety of local deities who persuaded the people to adopt the religious customs and beliefs they held at the time of the Spanish arrival.[137] While Símon does not explicitly identify the preacher as the Apostle Thomas, it is clear that he or another apostle was intended.

Given that Símon was writing in the seventeenth century, it is unclear whether these stories were simply his reinterpretation of local religious lore or whether the stories that were emerging for him to hear were in fact local creations, fed perhaps by similar interpretations and reinterpretations emanating from Peru and perhaps grasped by local catechists or others in a position to reshape their own views and present them to the priests. It is possible, therefore, that like the indigenous religious leaders in Mexico and Peru, they created a joint cosmology that allowed the continuation of the old religion and the addition of Christianity.

Jesuits brought the ideas from the highlands of New Granada into the Llanos of the Upper Orinoco in the early seventeenth century, but it took a long time for their mission to have success – in fact, not until the eighteenth century. Gumilla, the earliest chronicler of this mission, as well as his successor Filippo Salvador Gilij, followed in the footsteps of other Jesuits, first by confirming that the groups of the region all believed in a universal creator god and the Deluge. Indeed, Gumilla was pleased to see that they regarded the sun simply as fire and not as a god.[138] Likewise, while they all believed in a Devil figure, both Jesuits were disinclined to see an organized Diabolic cult, for as Gumilla wrote, "God did not permit any of these people to give him any cult

---

[135] Símon, *Noticias historiales*, Noticia 4, caps. 4 and 13 (story of the encomendero and the priest).

[136] Símon, *Noticias historiales*, Noticia 4, cap. 14, nos. 1–2.

[137] Símon, *Noticias historiales*, Noticia 4, cap. 3, nos. 1–4; cap. 11 no 3. The date of the preacher's arrival is given at 4.3.2 using the local time reckoning – "20 ages [edades], each of which has 70 years" (1,400 years, which would then be 150 CE counting the end date as 1550).

[138] Gumilla, *Orinoco Ilustrado*, vol. 2, cap 1, pp. 9 (Deluge), 10–12 (universal creator god, and sun as fire). Filippo Salvador Gilij, who followed Gumilla, extended and deepened Gumilla's conclusions, *Saggi di storia Americana...* (4 vols., Rome, 1782) vol. 3, Book 1, caps. 1–2 (idea of God broken down by nation); on the Deluge, cap. 4.

or adoration at all," and in his reflection on Orinocan religion, Gilij thought it "admirable that God did not wish the Orinocans to be subjected to diabolic lies, even though allowing them to be idolatrous."[139] Although he recognized that they had among them healers, he was disinclined to think they did their art by Diabolic plot, and in short to evangelize these people required no more than instruction on Christianity without any great effort of extirpation, and former healers became evangelists of a sort.[140] Even the miraculous healing, source of co-revelations that the Jesuits might claim seemed rather dim, indeed most of Gumilla's examples were drawn from people who expired upon receiving baptism.[141] Gilij notes more miracles, however as an aid in conversion.

CONVERTING FREE ASSOCIATIONS

Much of the Spanish contact with indigenous American religions took place in the stratified world of the great empires, and even their initial experience was anchored in the mini-states of the Caribbean. But all the expanding European powers and their missionaries also encountered free associations, from the first contacts with the Caribs through the expansion into the Great Plains of North America or the Choco and Pampas of Argentina and Brazil. In these areas, the religious concepts of the indigenous people varied widely and often differed substantially from the empires where so much of Spanish policy was made, and at the same time, the nature of interaction made many religious options unworkable.

On the other hand, those missionaries who could not conquer Native American people had necessarily to deal with them on their own terms, with the result that the religion in question would be accepted through revelation and valued quite differently than priests expected. The Spanish did not deal systematically with free associations until their engagement with the Chichimeca in the late sixteenth century, and it was the Portuguese in Brazil who first dealt with free associations in the Tupi regions around their colonies.

Tupi religion was fairly free-flowing, as one might expect in a society with few figures or institutions that had authority. Religious knowledge came largely from priests called *pagés*. The pagés received revelations, sometimes through visions, sometimes through possession, and using this knowledge they taught what cosmology people accepted, healed the sick, and dealt with social problems. Thus, according to the Jesuit Pero Correia in 1551, a pagé "regarded himself as a saint" and persuaded the others that he was inhabited by spirits who "allowed him to know everything." The people did not "think that God gave

---

[139] Gumilla, *Orinoco Ilustrado* vol. 2, cap. 3, p. 29; Gilij, *Saggio* vol. 3, Book 1, cap. 3, pp. 14–17 (he does note that some distant heathens might make offerings during their dances to a diabolic figure); cap. 7, p. 27 (quotation).

[140] Gumilla, *Orinoco Ilustrado*, vol. 2, cap. 4; Gilij thought that what cult they gave the devil was motivated by fear rather than adoration; *Saggio* Vol. 3, Book 1 cap. 7, p. 30.

[141] Gumilla, *Orinoco Ilustrado*, vol. 2, cap. 2.

them life or death and what they wanted but their saints."[142] Occasionally, a particularly well-regarded pagé would organize a large gathering in which people would come for many miles. Women would come and confess their sins and ask for pardon. The pagé put a mask called *cabaça* (calabash in Portuguese) on his face and would then be possessed by the spirit appropriate to the mask and spoke in its voice.[143] The Jesuits, who described Tupi religion in detail in the 1550s, called such gatherings "*santidades*," but also recognized the Tupi word for them – *caríba*.[144]

Although the earliest years of Portuguese presence in Brazil are poorly documented, it is fairly clear that their first converts were among the indigenous people who decided to ally with them to defend their settlements. The "principals," as the Portuguese called their leaders, and perhaps many of their followers were baptized as a part of this process, and Jesuits then tried to deepen and develop their faith and to cleanse it of what the Jesuits regarded as Diabolic elements.[145] Initially, in fact, the Jesuits devoted themselves to teaching the children in the settlements of the military allies reading, writing, and Portuguese, while introducing Christianity to the children and to prevent them from following the beliefs of their parents.[146]

Manuel de Nóbrega, writing just a few months after the Jesuits arrived in 1549, declared that the Tupi had no religion or organized cult, which was to say that there was not systematically transmitted discontinuous revelation. He and his colleagues, however, did describe a religious life, and they used its concepts to shape their own presentation of Christianity, in much the same way as they did in Kongo. They decided that the Tupi deity of thunder, Tupana, was the closest thing they had to God, and immediately began using it as a translation for "God" in catechismal literature – a considerable divergence from Spanish thinking that concluded that all divinities of the ancient Mexican or Peruvian past were manifestations of the Devil.[147] They also used the name of an evil figure in Tupi religious thought to mean the Devil. Furthermore, although Diabolic language was often used to describe the activities of the pagés, Fernão Cardim, who worked in Brazil from 1584 to 1601, observed

---

[142] Pero Correia to João Nunes Barreto, June 20, 1551, in Serafim Leite, *Cartas dos Primeiros Jesuitas no Brasil 1538–53* (3 vols., São Paulo, 1954–1957) 1: 225.

[143] Manuel de Nóbrega, "Informação das terras do Brasil," 1549, in Leite, *Cartas* 1: 150.

[144] Pero Correia to João Nunes Barreto, June 20, 1551, in Leite, *Cartas* 1: 225; the Tupi term is found in Fernão Cardim, "Treatie of Brazil," in Samuel Purchas, *Purchas his Pilgrimes* (4 vols., London, 1626, mod. ed., London, 1905), vol. 4, book 7, pp. 1289–1290. Although the original was in Portuguese, Purchas obtained his copy in 1601 and is the most complete. A Portuguese translation, augmented by another early copy in Portuguese was published in Rio de Janeiro, 1881.

[145] Cristina Pompa, *Religião como tradução: Missionários, Tupi e Tapuia no Brasil colonial* (Bauru, 2003), a serious and careful study that effectively addresses issues raised by several generations of previous scholars.

[146] De Nóbrega, "Infromação," in Leite, *Cartas*, 1: 149.

[147] De Nóbrega, "Informação," in Leite, *Cartas* 1: 150.

that although they had sorcerers, they did not worship them but only went to them to cure sickness.[148]

Saint Thomas provided a bridge between religions in Brazil as it had in Mexico or Peru. Indeed, the story of Saint Thomas's visit to America, which would become widespread elsewhere in Catholic America, began in Brazil. According to a German newspaper report in 1514, Nuno Manuel and Cristovão de Haro, officers on a Portuguese ship that stopped for food in Germany, reported that the Brazilians had "knowledge of Saint Thomas." According to this report, when the sailors saw a cross on a stone and "they spoke of Saint Thomas, [the local people] said that he was the small god, but there was another god who was greater," which the Portuguese connected to Saint Thomas on his way to India.[149] De Nóbrega was already elaborating on the story in 1549, and took a trip to see the footprints of Saint Thomas, which he said, "according to their ancestors," was called Zomé. Others also added that he had left these prints while passing Brazil on his way to India, but promised to return some day.[150] By 1552, Vicente Rodrigues was leading processions to these footprints, and built a chapel there.[151]

The Jesuits had long theological discussions and answered questions about what Christianity was, and at the same time did their best to place themselves as a new type of pagé. For the Jesuits, the principal religious struggle was to eliminate or replace the pagés with themselves, while the pagés struck back by accusing the Jesuits of using magical means to harm the converts.[152] Leonardo Nunes went to villages in the early morning, "because it was still the custom of their principales or pagés in whom they believe a great deal to preach then."[153] They preached in the midst of santidades, as de Nóbrega did in 1551, telling them that he was "the true santidade," and that "the bishop was the Pajé-graçu which is to say the great father."[154] They competed with the pagés in performing miracles such as healing the sick; indeed, in 1552, Vicente Rodrigues believed that "many sicknesses were cured, thanks to the prayers of the fathers" in Bahia.[155] Jesuits established their own santidades, without necessarily intending to, as when they founded their mission at Piratininga near São Paulo in the early 1550s. One Tupi leader came "three hundred thousand miles" to be with the Jesuits, claiming that his inspiration was a dream he had of his dead son who had been baptized.[156]

---

[148] Cardim, "Treatie" in Purchas, *Pilgrimes* vol. 4, book 7, p. 1290.

[149] "Copia der Newen eytung aus Presilg lant," printed in Augsburg, n.d. (but Nuno and Cristovão de Haro visited Brazil in 1514 and the ship came to Hamburg on October 12), fol. 2a in Emil Weller, ed., *Die ersten Deutschen Zeitungen* (Tübingen, 1872 [GB]). This text was republished with a Portuguese translation in 1922.

[150] De Nóbrega, "Informação," in Leite, *Cartas* 1: 151; many of these same elements were also reported in Vicente do Salvador, *História*, Bk 2, cap. 7.

[151] Vicente Rodrigues to Religious of Coimbra, September 17, 1552, in Leite, *Cartas* 1: 377.

[152] De Nóbrega, "Informação," in Leite, *Cartas* 1: 150.

[153] Pero Correia, in Leite, *Cartas*, 1: 220.

[154] Francisco Pires, 1551, in Leite, *Cartas*, 1: 386.

[155] Vicente Rodrigues to Simão Rodrigues, May 1552, Leite, *Cartas* 1: 320–321.

[156] Quadrennial Letter, May–September 1554, Leite, *Cartas* 1.

Meanwhile, the traditional santidade began to take on distinctly Christian elements. In 1580, the Inquisition investigated one such gathering at Jaguaripe, near Sergipe in Bahia. While it contained most of the elements of the older ceremony, its leader, a former Jesuit student named Antonio, included crosses and rosaries as well as Christian prayers in his ceremony. He claimed to incorporate the legendary Tupi ancestor Tamandaré and to be the "true Pope," and thus appointed bishops and saints.[157] In 1585, the Governor of Bahia suppressed the santidade, but numerous other *santidades* of this sort appeared in later times elsewhere in Brazil; Jesuits reported at least one more santidade in the early seventeenth century, which incorporated many Christian elements.[158]

Meanwhile, at the southern end of the Tupi-speaking world, religious life proceeded somewhat differently. Although the Tupi-speakers of the region around São Paulo and the Rio de la Plata basin were organized in mini-states rather than egalitarian democracies, their religious life was not much different. They had no more established priesthood or discontinuous revelation than did their linguistic cousins farther north. There, too, were pagés and santidades as in Brazil. In fact, merging cosmologies began even before the conquest: the first Franciscans to the coast, in 1537, met a prophet named Etiguara (which means "poet" in Tupi), "who spoke in two hundred languages by the Spirit of Prophecy: saying that shortly some True Christians, brothers of Saint Thomas would come to baptize them." He had appeared four years earlier and already had disciples, and gave them songs to sing and rules to follow, including monogamy and eschewing cannibalism. His disciples "preached the Catholic Faith openly." In this way, he combined the Saint Thomas story with the role of the pagé, and to the Franciscans these were "great marvels which the Lord worked."[159]

The earliest Spanish efforts accompanied the first colonization in the greater Rio de la Plata River system, centered in Asunción under Franciscan auspices after 1538. The allied inhabitants around Asunción were soon considered Christian, although very little in the way of religious description was left. A memorial of 1556 speaks of problems with marriage and administrative issues rather than with anything theological.[160]

---

[157] The santidade is known primarily through several inquisition documents, and is often interpreted as an anticolonial statement because it involved refugees from Portuguese-controlled areas; see Rodolfo Vainfas, *A heresia dos Índios: Catolicismo e rebeldia no Brasil Colonial* (São Paulo, 1995), which uses the full range of documentation.

[158] Fernão Guerreiro, *Relaçam* (1609, mod. ed. 1929), p. 381.

[159] Bernardo de Armentia to Juan Bernal Díaz de Lugo, May 1, 1538 quoted in Juan de Torquemada, *Los veintiún libros rituales i monarchia Indiana con el origen y guerras de los Indios Occidentales, de sus poblaciones, descubrimientos, conquista, conversión y otras cosas maravillosas de la misma tierra* (3 vols., Madrid, 1726 [1st ed. 1615]), Book 15, cap. 48.

[160] Martin Gonzalez, Clerigo to King, June 27, 1556, in Blas Garay, ed., *Colección de documentos relativos à la historia de América, particularmente à la historia de Paraguay* (Asunción, 1899), pp. 252–258.

Nevertheless, Christian ideas spread and were propagated by Tupi-speaking prophets far afield. Just as there were Christian santidades in Brazil, so the Chiriguanos, living at the headwaters of the Rio de la Plata system and next to Peru, had their own prophet. The Viceroy of Peru, Francisco de Toledo received emissaries of one such prophet in 1573, and following an inquiry made in Chriguano country he learned that the prophet named Santiago dressed in long white clothes and claimed to have been sent by Jesus. He carried small crosses with which he healed people and was preceded by a large one that no one touched, but which moved by itself. His teaching advised them to be good, to mine silver, to be friendly with the Spanish, marry monogamously, and avoid killing or eating people. The viceroy was impressed and anxious to discover if these things were true miracles or not. There were a few Spaniards resident in the country and at least one Christian African woman who gave testimony.[161]

This period of poorly documented but apparently successful mission activity was followed by the arrival of the Jesuits at the beginning of the seventeenth century. They had little to do in Asunción or its vicinity, and soon were drawn to the Paraná River valley, a region that was previously hostile to the Spanish and their allies, but, thanks to bandeirante raiding from São Paulo, was looking for a Spanish alliance.

Thus, the Jesuits were invited to enter the country on behalf of local leaders who found alliance more inviting than earlier. The going was hardly easy, for the Jesuits found both general cooperation and considerable resistance. These lands were mini-states, under the leadership of caciques who had considerable authority. Many caciques claimed spiritual powers to intervene in health, weather, and fortune, as well as the existing class of religious leaders, who also engaged largely in continuous revelation for the same issues.

The Jesuits essentially entered this spiritual universe as another player, using their own abilities to produce continuous revelation. They did not doubt the capacity of the local spiritual leaders to obtain continuous revelation, but the Jesuits were adamant in ascribing it to Diabolic contracts, either explicit or implicit. Antonio Ruiz de Montoya, an early Jesuit and chronicler of the mission, described Taubici, the ruler of a town near the Jesuit reduction of Loreto, as "a great Magus and witch [*hechizero*], a familiar of the Devil." He learned of coming events through his consultations with the Devil, and had other powers from the same source.[162] Elsewhere, the ruler was "desirous to hear matters of his salvation" but was challenged by a "minister, preacher of lies who went in mission from place to place [*pueblo a pueblo*]," who claimed that he was "God, Creator of heaven and earth and men" and that he controlled health, weather, and the fertility of the soil.[163]

[161] A study with translations of all the relevant documents in is Jack Dabbs, "A Messiah among the Chiriguanos," *Southwestern Journal of Anthropology* 9 (1953): 15–58.
[162] Ruiz de Montoya, *Conquista Espirtual*, cap. 9, pp. 45–46.
[163] Ruiz de Montoya, *Conquista Espiritual*, cap. 9, pp. 47–48.

At the same time, however, the Jesuits of Paraguay believed that the Guaraní knew the True God, called Tupan, and that they had a story of the Flood. However, they did not make any sacrifices to the True God, but only acknowledged his existence. As elsewhere, Ruiz de Montoya ascribed this knowledge to the preaching of Saint Thomas the Apostle who, he believed, had visited here, just as his Portuguese coreligionists believed he had visited Bahia half a century earlier.[164] When the Jesuits entered a district of the same region, they were met with wild enthusiasm in which the local people said that Zomé, who had visited them in ancient times, had taught the same doctrine under the same cross. The Jesuits fully believed this account, added that the "elders, magi and witches had usurped the teaching, making it their own," and adding other signs of the Apostle in Brazil and Peru. It was enough to invoke his teaching, they believed, to win cooperation from the people and overthrow their religious competitors.[165]

Revelations and co-revelations furthered the work of spiritual conquest. Ruiz de Montoya noted a series of spiritual dreams by prominent Guaraní people in which entities associated with Christianity appeared to sometimes reluctant leaders. These dreams were sometimes accompanied by miraculous healings and other verifications.[166] The most dramatic one followed the death of a "good Indian" who had been a Christian for a long time, and who a few hours afterward arose from the dead. He reported having been accosted by a demon who declared that his soul was lost for a sin he had neglected to confess. Finally, he reported to the astonished Jesuit and a large crowd of people, Saint Peter appeared to him, along with two angels – his own guardian angel and another called Saint Miguel.[167] Other cases, equally astonishing, assisted the work of conversion, according to the Jesuits.[168]

As elsewhere, Christian revelations happened outside of Jesuit control and often counter to Jesuit beliefs. The Fathers at San Ignacio were troubled, for example, by a powerful local ruler named Miguel Artaguaye who "baptized and married." Deciding to "pretend to be a priest," he dressed in clerical garb, but with feathers, and said Mass, and finally denounced the priests in the same anti-Diabolic language that they might typically use to denounce a local religious leader.[169]

By the middle of the seventeenth century, the Jesuits had established their string of reductions and were generally content with the results of their efforts. Not long afterward, however, they began new missions into the Gran Choco, controlled by a variety of free associations that, having become equestrian, were now both formidable raiders and ripe targets for peace by evangelization

---

[164] Ruiz de Montoya, *Conquista Espiritual*, cap. 10, pp. 50 (True God); 53 (Flood).
[165] Ruiz de Montoya, *Conquista Espiritual*, caps. 21–16, pp. 94–116.
[166] Ruiz de Montoya, *Conquista Espiritual*, cap. 15, pp. 68–72.
[167] Ruiz de Montoya, *Conquista Espiritual*, cap. 17, pp. 75–76.
[168] Ruiz de Montoya, *Conquista Espiritual*, cap. 18, pp. 80–85.
[169] Ruiz de Montoya, *Conquista Espiritual*, cap. 11, pp. 56–57.

efforts of the Jesuits. There, according to Martin Dobritzhoffer, the people had no concept of God, but instead worshipped the Devil, who they conceived as their "grandfather." Having thus claimed that they, unlike the Guarani and other Tupi-speaking groups, possessed no conception of God, the missionaries proceeded simultaneously to introduce the concept of God in Spanish and to denounce other religious activity as Devil worship.[170] The principal characters in this cult were the healers and spiritual guides who Dobritzhoffer defined as "magicians" and, although doubting that they performed any of their miracles through Diabolic intervention, still made them to be the main enemy of evangelization.[171] Indeed, the Jesuits primarily directed their attention to teaching Christian law and extirpating the old religious leaders – tasks that Dobritzhoffer, at least, thought were easily accomplished.[172]

NORTHWEST MEXICO

Christianity came to the lands north of the Aztec empire through the larger strategy of alliance the Spanish employed to protect their interests in silver mining in Sinaloa and Sonora and beyond, in which they attempted to persuade groups to join them, and along the way to accept baptism and join the Church. The Jesuits, who provided the spiritual end of this strategy, had their best initial success among the indigenous people of Sinaloa who had allied with the Spanish, and their earliest baptisms were the spouses of Spanish settlers and their children or orphans.

Beyond this they moved into a world of free associations or very weak ministates where religion was not so formally constituted as in Peru or Mexico, and in both of which continuous revelation was the norm. For this reason, Andrés Pérez de Ribas, a Jesuit who helped lead the spread of Christianity, wrote that they had no religion, believed in no higher God, "not even a false one," and thus, ironically, had no idolatry. But he was also quick to establish a diabolic presence among them in the form of wise men, healers, and others who did indeed contact the Other World.

Religious life in the region was dominated by individual priests whose power and prestige were largely based on the perceptions of their followers that they had genuine connections with the Other World. One Zuaque leader named Taxicora, who flourished around 1605, was believed to have levitated a horse, and he challenged the Jesuits to do the same.[173] For him,

---

[170] Dobritzhoffer, *Historia*, vol. 2, cap. 8.
[171] Dobritzhoffer, *Historia*, vol. 2, cap. 9 never gives the term in the local language, but conveniently defined it (see p. 79) as from Classical sources, *Magi* (Persian), *Chaldaei* (Assyrian), *Philosophi* (Greek), *Prophetae*, and *Brachmanes*, and others, and in modern languages as *Zauber*, *Hexenmeister* (German), *Hechizero* (Spanish). In Latin, he calls them *praestigatoribus*, and in the German translation of his book (p. 90), he uses usually *Zauber*, so I have made his term to be "magician."
[172] Dobritzhoffer, *Historia*, vol. 3, caps. 11 and 12 (similar great success with the Macobios).
[173] Pérez de Ribas, *Triunfos*, Book 2, cap 27, p. 102.

these "sorcerers" were the enemy of religion, luring people who were without a fixed doctrine (or thus a discontinuous revelation) to them (or back to them) when the priests came.[174] They were quite sure that the religious leaders they fought against did indeed have supernatural powers, but they attributed them to the Devil. Indeed, Pérez de Ribas' account is replete with stories of the Devil appearing to people and of sorcerers consorting with the Devil, taking his advice, and the like. But they also did not engage in the extirpation campaigns that characterized Mexico and Peru; the situation was far too insecure and the alliances too shaky for such action. As Pérez de Ribas noted, they proceeded "slowly and cautiously" as they "uprooted the weed that had grown among the unripened wheat."[175]

The Jesuits, for their part, attempted to play the same role as those they denounced, and whenever possible to work miracles as their counterparts did. To read their stories, by Pérez de Ribas or others, is to believe that they did indeed work miracles. Certainly working miracles was crucial, for whole groups would switch sides when a flood or an epidemic seemed to suggest that the Other World did not favor the Jesuits, and likewise, they benefited if they were perceived as being helpful against such calamities. An earthquake, for example, convinced the Zuaques to approach the Jesuits to join the church, while a drought was ended, the Jesuits believed, when the people prayed to the Virgin Mary.[176] On the other hand, when the Jesuits destroyed a stone image that was said to cause crops to grow well, an unexpected storm blew in, undermining their efforts.[177]

These miracles of revelation were the primary way in which they won people over, on an almost individual basis but usually through the conversion of prominent religious leaders.[178] One convert was made to renounce all pacts he had made with the Devil upon his conversion. In another case, a converted healer continued to be troubled when the Devil visibly appeared to him and told him to go back to his old ways. Pérez de Ribas was able to ward off this Diabolic apparition by supplying the convert with an image of the Virgin.[179] In Tepehuanes in 1608, a young woman, formerly a curer (using, the Jesuit said, "herbs and witchcraft"), healed the wife of a Spanish settler by

---

[174] Andrés Pérez de Ribas, *Triunfos de nuestra santa fe entre gentes las mas barbaras y fierasdel nuevo orbe* (Madrid, 1645, mod. ed., Mexico, 1944). English trans. by Daniel T. Reff, *History of the triumphs of our holy faith amongst the most barbarous and fierce peoples of the New World* (Tucson, AZ, 1999 [marking the pagination of the 1645 ed.]), Book 1, cap 5, pp. 16–19; his comments on government are in Cap 3, pp. 11–12.

[175] Pérez de Ribas, *Triunfos*, Book 2, cap. 23, p. 94.

[176] Pérez de Ribas, *Triunfos*, Book 2, cap. 6, p. 47 (earthquake); Book 2, cap. 18, p. 80 (Virgin delivers from drought).

[177] Pérez de Ribas, *Triunfo*, Book 2, Cap 11, p. 60.

[178] Pérez de Ribas, *Trunfos*, Book 3, caps. 22–23, pp. 191–197 (in the Tehueco region), is particularly replete with examples.

[179] Pérez de Ribas, *Triunfo*, Book 2, Cap 30, p. 112.

laying hands on her and saying the name of Jesus and Mary – an interesting co-revelation.[180]

As elsewhere, Christian entities began to appear in indigenous revelations. At San Felipe in 1590, local people changed the ceremony to adopt orphans, altering the iconography from figures of their original religion to a man, woman, and child, which they explained to the Jesuits represented God, Mary, and Jesus. The Jesuits praised this effort and accepted it theologically, but they also transformed it further by moving it into the church.[181]

Co-revelation and co-devotion even played a role in anti-Spanish warfare. The Tepehuan war of 1616–1618, which the Spanish called a rebellion, was led by a charismatic leader, named Quautlatas, who had also accepted parts of the Christian revelation and had lived among the Christians. He took on the role of priest, just as the Jesuits had in their own way taken on the same role with regards to the local people. Quautlatas announced that a crucifix in his possession was his God, but that God was angry with the Spanish for he had assigned them their part of the world and they violated his law by coming to Mexico. He also declared himself a bishop and conducted baptisms, marriages, and other sacraments, while he and his followers regularly desecrated Christian images in the many towns they attacked.[182] A second important leader, Francisco Gogoxito, was a former Christian who served primarily as a military leader but publicly accepted Quautlatas's revelations and desecrated images.[183]

The tendency toward the more powerful and influential religious leaders creating syncretic movements is revealed even more clearly in the Pueblo War of 1680–1696. Franciscan missionaries were charged with the conversion of the New Mexico mission that included a series of independent and weakly centralized mini-states running along the Rio Grande centered on Santa Fe. The Franciscans in New Mexico, like their Jesuit compatriots in Sinaloa and Sonora, believed that the local religion was led by people who had made pacts with the Devil or were allowing Diabolic revelations to rule their lives. Communal religious activities, particularly the religious meetings of the kivas (*estufas*) and the masked dance of the kachinas, were thus held to be inspired by the Devil. Perhaps this developed religious life with clear religious-political leadership made the Franciscans more inclined to extirpation than the Jesuits were, but their pressing to suppress them backfired. Moves to forbid katchina and to close the kivas, as well as to round up, punish, and even execute religious lead-

---

[180] Javier Alegre, *Historia de la Compañía de Jesus en la Nueva-España*, ed. Carlos Maria Bustamante (3 vols., Mexico, 1842 [GB]) 2: 5.

[181] Pérez de Ribas, *Triunfos*, Book 2, cap. 3, pp. 40–41.

[182] Pérez de Ribas, *Trunfos*, Book 10, cap 13, pp. 598–599; and Cap 35, p. 639, quoting a letter of José de Lomas and giving his name; Cap 18, p. 605 (desecration) and 607 (killing priests). The revolt itself is described in great detail here, covering cap. 13–36, pp. 598–641; see also Francisco de Urdiñola to King, March 31, 1604, in Hackett, *Historical Documents* 2: 89–90.

[183] Pérez de Ribas, *Triunfos*, Cap 31, pp. 633–634.

ers were pursued with varying degrees of rigor for a generation, before it broke into a revolt.[184]

The conspiracy and subsequent revolt was led by several leaders from different towns, but Popé was the most prominent and their collective leader. Popé claimed to have religious knowledge from the apparition of three Other-Worldly entities who appeared to him and told him to be rid of the Spanish and the priests, to renounce all things Spanish and Christian including baptism (and to wash the baptismal water away with a special bath), to destroy and desecrate all images and churches, and to kill the Spanish and priests. Unlike the Tepehuan movement earlier, there was no compromise with or incorporation of Christian elements in Popé's revelation.[185]

The Pueblo Revolt showed, perhaps, the futility of the extirpation strategy of the Franciscans, given their weakness and incapacity to call on repressive forces systematically. In any case, in northwest Mexico, as elsewhere in the Iberian world, the eighteenth century witnessed a drawing back from the militant attitude of the sixteenth and seventeenth centuries. When Father Eusebio Kino expanded the mission of northwest Mexico into the present-day United States at the end of the seventeenth century, his diary rarely mentioned any encounters with the Devil, miraculous works or theological battles. Instead, his work was far more political, relying on introducing farming, digging wells, or raising livestock.[186] The Inquisition in Mexico and elsewhere became less concerned with religious crimes as well, focusing much more or moral crimes such as bigamy or homosexual behavior, both for the non-European people under its jurisdiction and for the Spanish and creoles.

NORTH AMERICA: FRANCE'S MISSIONS

French Jesuits and Recollets, who began intensive evangelization of the Hurons and Algonquian-speaking people in Canada in the early seventeenth century, found that initially they were very well received. They believed that they were

---

[184] Declaration of Diego Lopez Sambrano, December 22, 1581, in Charles W. Hackett, ed. and trans., *The Revolt of the Pueblo Indians of New Mexico and Otermin's Attempted Reconquest, 1680–82* (2 vols., Albuquerque, 1942), 2: 298–302; also Opinion of Fray Francisco de Ayeta, December 23, 1681, pp. 308–310.

[185] Information on Popé and his movement comes virtually entirely from testimony of indigenous people captured in 1681, published in the original Spanish with a detailed linguistic and historical commentary in Barbara de Marco, "Voices from the Archives I: Testimony of the Pueblo Indians on the 1680 Pueblo Revolt," *Romance Philology* 53 (2000): 375–448 (marking the folios of the original text) and in English translation in Hackett, ed. *Revolt* 2: 232–236, fols. 55v–57v (testimony of Juan, an Indian, December 18, 1681); 239–240, fols. 58–58v (testimony of Joseph, a *ladino*, December 19, 1681); 246–249, fols. 60v–61v (testimony of Pedro Naranja, from Queres, December 19, 1681); 250–252, fols. 62v–63v (testimony of Juan and Francisco Lorenzo, December 20, 1681).

[186] Report and Relation of Father Eusebio Kino, 1710, publications of the Wisconsin Historical Society, online at http://www.americanjourneys.org, translated from "Favores celestiales de Jesus y Maria SS^ma Apostol de las Yndias," part V, cap 2, pp. 440, 444, cap. 4.

making rapid progress in their mission, and met little or no resistance to their efforts. However, Jesuit goals, like those of Spanish and Portuguese missions elsewhere in America, focused on first reducing the Hurons, Algonquians, and other groups to "civilized" living, which meant being very much like French peasants – living in fixed villages, farming, and accepting authority.[187] But it was not long before they became aware that the people with whom they were dealing were completely averse to ecclesiastical discipline, failing to abandon their old religion and, moreover, to follow the commands of the church. Failure of the Jesuits to persuade Hurons, who became their principal targets, to live the way they wanted them to caused the priests to travel deeper into Huronia (as they called the Huron region) and seek to create Christian villages that would be like the villages of other Hurons, but with Christian morals (and with Jesuit leadership of a flexible but religious and authoritarian nature). They felt satisfied that these villages would be successful, even though the numbers of people so concentrated were small. Consequently, the Jesuits also created "flying missions" in which they would travel to unconverted regions and seek either to spread a Christian message or to persuade the leaders to set up Christian villages under their guidance.

When Iroquois attacks hammered the Christian villages in the 1640s and then created waves of refugees in the following years, the Christian village concept was altered but not changed. Huron villages became multicultural, but retained their Christian character. At the same time, French overall strategy shifted away from attempting to settle the interior to trading with unconquered people. In this environment, the Jesuits working with traders and their own catechists made further inroads into the people living in a fairly large area that was the field of the fur traders. By 1700, Jesuit villages and other inspired by them were found throughout the future province of Ontario and much of the upper Midwest of the future United States.

The Jesuits' targets relied heavily on continuous revelation for their religious beliefs. The Jesuit priest Jean de Brébeuf, writing in 1636 about the Hurons near the emerging colonial town of Québec, noted the presence of revelation of various sorts. When he asked how people knew of the afterlife, he was told that "it was ... persons brought back to life, who made the report." He then went on to relate stories involving people who sought the land of the dead, and had the dead appear to them and guide them in various ways.[188] Dreams were also vital to Hurons: "they look upon their dreams as ordinances and irrevocable decrees," wrote de Brébeuf, because the dream is "the oracle that all these poor Peoples consult and listen to, the prophet which predicts to them future events, the Cassandra which warns them of misfortunes that threaten them." However,

---

[187] A good overview of the Jesuit mission and general French policy is in James Axtell, *The Invasion Within: The Contest of Cultures in Colonial North America* (Oxford, 1986).

[188] Paul le Jeune, *Relation de ce qui s'est passé en la Nouvelle France, en l'année 1636* (Paris, 1637), part II, Iean de Brebevf, "Relation de ce que s'est passé dans le Pays des Hvrons en l'annee 1636," pp. 101–107, *JR* 10: 146–157.

not every dream was considered a revelation. Some dreams were simply held to have been "vain"; even those whose dreams were regarded as important "do not give heed to their dreams indifferently they recognize some as being false and some true – the latter being quite rare."[189]

There were also gifted men, whom the Jesuits called "Jugglers," who claimed special knowledge of the Other World or possessed powers to influence it. Typically they performed cures for the sick or predicted the future and were judged effective or ineffective based on their success in these endeavors. Such people sometimes discovered their power in dreams, and the belief in the veracity of them was the impetus for both their entering the field and being accepted.[190] Brébeuf was hostile to the idea that these people might have genuine revelation; others thought the power was surely diabolic. Joseph Lafitau, who lived among the Mohawks in the early eighteenth century, was sufficiently impressed by the spiritual leaders to describe them as "prophets" in the sense of the Old Testament prophets.[191]

Hurons and other indigenous groups that accepted Christian ideas typically did so through revelations and miracles, and such stories are regularly reported in Jesuit sources. It was common in the theology of Hurons that people would acquire guardian spirits, usually though a revelationary experience, such as a dream or vision. Most people would, in fact, actively seek such an experience, often through isolation and fasting, in what is called a "vision quest" in which a guardian spirit would appear to the seeker and form a lifelong relationship. Jerome Lalemont described the quest and its results dramatically in his report of 1642, of a person whose guardian was an old man who predicted his life course and appeared to him periodically.[192] In pre-contact times, and throughout the period, such spirits often took the form of animal familiars, but with Jesuit teaching, it was much more common for them to be Christian saints, and particularly the Virgin Mary.[193] In fact, it is probably safe to say that visions of the Virgin were the most frequent route to conversion because this formed a co-revelation.[194]

---

[189] De Brebuf, "Relation ... 1636," pp. 117–118, *JR* 10: 168–171. For a full and interesting account of dreams and out-of-body experiences as a part of Huron religion and reported by the Jesuits, see Robert Moss, "Missionaries and Magicians: The Jesuit Encounter with Native American Shamans on New England's Colonial Frontier," in Peter Benes, *The Wonders of the Invisible World, 1600–1900* (Dublin, 1992) pp. 17–33.

[190] De Brebeuf, "Relation ... 1636," pp. 133–139, *JR* 10: 192–201, as one might expect with a priest, the story seems absurd and the actors appear as lunatics rather than guided by religious impulses, but the context supposes that what happened in these cases took place with more sincerity in other occasions.

[191] Joseph François Lafitau, *Moeurs des sauvages ameriquains compares aux moeurs des premiers temps* (2 vols., Paris, 1724) 1: 121–125.

[192] Jerome Lalemont, "Relation de 1642," in *JR* 23: 155–159 (English translation on facing pages).

[193] Lalemont, "Relation de 1639," in *JR* 17: 153–155.

[194] William Hart, "'The Kindness of the Blessed Virgin:' Faith, succor, and the Cult of Mary Among Christian Hurons and Iroquois in Seventeenth Century New France," in Nicholas Griffiths and

The Jesuits recognized the vision and dream experiences of both the religious elite and the ordinary people as revelations, but they valued them differently. Although they often denounced the indigenous prophets and seers as Diabolic, in large measure because they did not produce Christian messages, and their route to the other world was not under Church authority, they did accept the process as revelatory. For example, Lafitau compared the experience of a revelation through a dream to that of Old Testament dreams and prophecies.[195] If the experiences had a Christian outcome, however, they usually accepted them as co-revelations.

SPIRITUAL CRISIS AND RENEWAL IN EUROPE: 1650–1800

As Protestant and Catholic religious elites in Post-Reformation Europe debated the value of this or that revelation, or the interpretation of revelations in general, or the role of revelation in the task of interpreting the hard parts of Scripture, they also created a spirit of doubt. Who could be sure which revelation was true or false? How could we be sure that any revelations, especially ancient ones, were properly recorded? For those who found guidance from the Holy Spirit as a means of verifying doubts about difficult places in the Scripture, how could one be sure the inner voice of the Holy Spirit was not actually the Devil himself?

The pressure of these doubts among the elite sometimes led to a turning away from the idea of revelation at all, and in fact found satisfaction in the growing rationalist, materialist, or scientific outlook, which denied miracles and revelation and found God in the workings of the mind or in nature.[196] Given the turmoil in England in the seventeenth century, it is not surprising that Deism, which was founded on the idea that reason alone and not revelation was the foundation of religion, would emerge there.[197] Famous philosophers such as Thomas Hobbes and John Locke laid its foundations in the mid-seventeenth century. Matthew Tindal's *Christianity as Old as Creation*, published in 1730, might be said to be the culmination of the earlier ideas, a sort of textbook of Deism. Tindal held that God had given a rule to people and it could be observed in nature without revelation, by "the use of those faculties, by which men are distinguished from brutes, is the only means they have to

Fernando Cervantes, eds., *Spiritual Encounters: Interactions between Christianity and Native Religions in Colonial America* (Nebraska, 1999), pp. 65–90.

[195] Lafitau, *Moeurs* 1: 108–167. This whole chapter is a philosophical excursion into comparative ethnography using ancient and various other world religions as a starting point, and working with concepts like those of revelation.

[196] Richard Popkin, *The History of Scepticism from Savonarola to Bayle* (New York and Oxford, 2003, a revised and expanded third edition of a work with varying titles, first published in 1964).

[197] For a good survey of Deism in the larger Enlightenment, see Jonathan Israel, *Radical Enlightenment: Philosophy and the Making of Modernity, 1650–1750* (Oxford, 2002), esp. pp. 157–328.

discern whether there is a God; and whether he concerns himself with human affairs, or has given them any laws; and what those laws are?"[198]

Tindal argued that God had given an original "Natural Religion" to humanity, but that it had become perverted: "It can't be imputed to any defect in the light of nature that the pagan world ran into idolatry, but to their being entirely governed by priests, who pretended communication with their gods, and to have thence their revelations, which they imposed on the credulous as divine oracles."[199] Typically, Deists considered themselves Christians, in that they accepted Jesus' teaching as being an excellent moral standard, but they still denied his divinity and his authority in a religious sense. They were equally hostile to continuous revelations, in which the Divine might be said to interfere in human affairs, as they were to the discontinuous revelation of the Bible. Thus, without declaring themselves Atheists, they effectively removed religion from life.

The Rational and Scientific approach to truth raised in this process, and their proximity to atheism or to an absent and actionless God, was confined largely to the intellectual elite, and the main followers might include nobles and the higher class of the mercantile elite, sometimes also wealthier farmers, but by and large it was the religion of a small but highly influential elite. Given that it lies at the root of modern science and played a vital role in the political thought of the revolutionary period of the late eighteenth and early nineteenth centuries, it is not surprising that it receives more attention today, retroactively, than it had in its formative years.

Another solution to the problem of understanding and deciding on truth and revelation was an increasing turn to continuous revelation. Mysticism – a practice that allowed individuals to come into contact directly with the Other World through meditation or altered states of consciousness – emerged as an important part of the new religious order in the Post-Reformation world. Mysticism was old in the European church, and was widely accepted. A number of the founders of religious orders had been mystics, and their writing, sometimes composed in the midst of mystical experience, was accepted as valid revelation. Mystics like Theresa of Avila, eventually accepted as a saint and the founder of the Carmelite Order, continued to flourish after the Reformation. Cornelius Jansen, writing in early-seventeenth-century France and Flanders, was less successful in convincing the Church of the validity of his mystical experiences. Blaise Pascal, who was familiar with and friendly to Jansen's writing, was fully converted to mystical approaches by what he considered miracles in 1654–1657, most notably in which his niece was cured of an eye ailment by the touch of a holy relic. Although Pascal was fully in touch with the scientific and skeptical spirit of his day, he often spoke of miracles, of belief through faith,

---

[198] Matthew Tindal, *Christianity as Old as Creation...* (London, 1730 and many subsequent editions, online edition, 2003, online at http://celestiallands.org/library/christianity_as_old_as_the_creat.htm), cap. 1.

[199] Tindal, *Christianity*, cap. 14.

and of inner belief.[200] A somewhat later Spanish mystic, Miguel de Molinos, developed the mystical side of the theology more fully in the 1670s, arguing that people could contact God directly through spiritual exercises, a "soft and savory sleep of nothingness."[201] His approach was called "Quietism" because of the passive nature of its mystical exercises.

Mysticism emerged within Protestantism as a challenge to the institutionalism that crept back in as the religious tradition became more politicized. Protestant churches, having broken with Rome, needed to regularize their own doctrine, and in so doing Luther's follower Melanchthon developed a comprehensive system of faith that both reintroduced many of the concepts that had led to the break with Rome and imposed them on the rank and file of the church, and was institutionalized at universities like Wittenberg. In Switzerland, Calvin's primary residence, there was an attempt to consolidate his teachings into a systematic catechism, but by the seventeenth century, the community was too scattered to be easily forced to adopt any specific creed.[202]

By the end of the seventeenth century, a reform movement within the Lutheran Church, derisively called "Pietism" by its detractors, challenged the church's elite monopoly of interpretation.[203] Johann Arndt presented a first contestation with the publication of *Wahres Christentum* in several editions between 1605 and 1610, a book that relied on mystical ideas to connect believers to a knowledge of Christ through the development of the inner faith of the individual Christian – what he called a "heart religion" rather than a "head religion." Arndt's work was complemented by Philip Jacob Spener in his book *Pia Disideria* (1675), which called for the laity to be more involved in church and advocated a return to the idea that every person could interpret the Bible for themselves. To stress this he advocated that every household ought to have a Bible and that believers should meet together in small groups to discuss the Bible.

Pietists worked within Lutheran churches, where they stressed individual and group study, personal acts of charity, disciplined life, regularization of dress, and limitations of many activities considered pleasurable. Working, like Luther had, with the idea that salvation was through faith alone, and not through good works or performing sacraments, the Pietists developed a

---

[200] Blaise Pascal, *Pensées*, nos. 245, 248, 286; and in particular nos. 802–855 (on miracles). This work was published from his notes posthumously and the thoughts, actually on slips of paper, were arranged in various ways. This numbering fits the numbering system developed in the modern critical editions of his work.

[201] His work was presented primarily in *Guida spirituale che disinvolge l'anima...* (Rome, 1675, 1683 [GB], mod. ed. Giovanni Amendola, Naples, 1908 [GB]). An English translation of sections of it are in Joseph Henry Shorthouse, ed. and trans., *Golden Thoughts from the Spiritual Guide of Miguel Molinos, the Quietist* (New York, 1883 [GB]).

[202] W. R. Ward, *Early Evangelicalism: A Global Intellectual History* (Cambridge, 2006), pp. 70–73; see the various essays in W. Fred Graham, ed., *Later Calvinism: International Perspectives* (Kirkland, 1994).

[203] For a good general history of Pietism and its relationship to worldwide Evangelicalism, see Ward, *Early Evangelicalsim*.

concept of faith that approached mysticism. In 1695, Spener and his followers founded a new university at Halle to develop and teach their theology. Faith had to be personal, innate, and not confined simply to acceptance of the existence of Christ. While Spener remained within the Lutheran church, one of his students, the wealthy landowner Count Nicholas Ludwig von Zinzendorf, founded his own separate church, the United Brethren, in 1727, often called the Moravians because von Zinzendorf had his base in Moravia (today's Czech Republic). The Moravians, in turn, were fervent missionaries who reached as far afield as Tibet, the West Indies, Africa, and North America.

The emotional appeal of Pietism and its placing of salvation in faith, and faith in the emotions, gave Pietistic traditions a potential for mysticism and thus continuous revelation of a personal sort. It was characterized by the emotional discovery of God by each believer in a mystical manner, which was explained as the working of the Holy Spirit. The Moravians, like other Protestant groups, considered the conversion experience so important that they required church members to create a written record of their conversion by the Holy Spirit. Indeed, such an encounter became essential to full membership in the church.

The Pietists' ideas of a mystical inner conversion provided great help to Calvinist traditions, especially in England and America. For Calvinists, or Presbyterians as the Anglo-Scotch branch was known, the problem of knowing who was elect troubled many, and mystical experiences helped confirm in them knowledge that they were among the saved. Thus, like Moravians and their Anglican colleagues, English Calvinists focused on the idea of conversion and acceptance based on this sort of personal continuous revelation. Many of the English Calvinists were part of the Puritan movement, which sought to purify the English church of elements they conceived as Catholic.

Many English Puritans migrated to America, as persecution of them progressed in England, first in 1620 to Plymouth and then, when the Massachusetts Bay Company founded its colony at Boston in 1630, they created a colony where Puritan ideas could have full sway. The Puritans of North America were conscious of the role of the elect in both church and civil government, and also in knowing their status as elect. The mystical inner voice that reassured the Pietists of the validity of the Scriptures also provided a vehicle for Puritans in New England to know their election.

The Baptist movement, which began among English Anabaptists but gradually split with them to form its own community, adopted both the insistence on adult baptism, which was the hallmark of the Anabaptist movement, and the idea of adult revelation of divine grace, which was found widely among the Pietists. They were also antiauthoritarian, with informal meetings, focus on Scripture, and the closest acceptance of any of the major Protestant churches on the individual interpretation of Scripture. It was carried from England to America in 1639 by Roger Williams who founded the first Baptist congregation in Providence, Rhode Island.

Mystical thinking had a pronounced impact on the development of religion in English America. Moravian ideas that came to America with German settlers, both Moravians and others influenced by Pietist ideas, also interacted with Calvinist ideas through Presbyterian settlers from Scotland and ultimately Puritan ones in New England. At the same time in England, John and Charles Wesley formed a "Holy Club" to teach "inward religion, the religion of the heart" in 1725. The brothers visited America in 1734 and upon visiting the areas of New York, New Jersey, and Pennsylvania, where there was great interaction between German Pietists, English Calvinists, Anabaptists, and Moravians, encountered a freer exchange of these religious ideas that was usually possible in Europe. Upon his return to England, John Wesley found his "heart strangely warmed" and a complete assurance that Christ had forgiven his sins. Wesley took up a position in Georgia, where he encountered Moravians intimately. Taken by their approach, he subsequently visited their headquarters in Herrenhut (Silesia) in 1738, and the went back to England. Both preached in the open air, as the Anglican clergy, upset with their approach, banned his preaching in churches. It was this atmosphere that caused the Methodists to form study bands on the Pietist model, eventually breaking with the Anglican Church in 1791.

During their American visits, the Wesley brothers were joined by George Whitefield, a talented and emotional speaker with more Calvinist leanings, who developed an approach to preaching that would work the congregation into a collective emotional turmoil in which they would sense their salvation in a way that suggested possession by the Holy Spirit. Given the atmosphere in America at the time, Methodists like Whitefield found a welcome home among them, and his preaching tour of the English colonies in 1738 was immensely successful. This early opening to Methodist ideas in America was eventually followed up by Francis Asbury, who founded the American Methodist Church in 1771. Later historians would call this period of religious turmoil and reconsideration the "First Great Awakening."

The possession-like experiences of the Methodists and Great Awakening theologians (who could be found among Presbyterians, Anglicans, or Puritans, among others) were called "Enthusiasm" and were not wholly accepted by the religious leadership, so that these congregations often divided, as they did in New England, in the "Old Lights," who followed the more established path, and the "New Lights," who took after the new preachers. They were especially successful in the poorer and working-class areas and frontier regions in America where the established religious authorities had not provided much religious service. They would also take a Christian message to the African and indigenous communities within American towns, farms, and plantations, and beyond its frontiers into the Middle Ground of the American Midwest.

RENEWED CHRISTIANITY AND MISSIONS

English Protestant thinking underlay not only their own decisions to move to America, but also their attempts to convert their Algonquian hosts and neighbors. In many respects, their basic strategy resembled that of Catholic missionaries in dealing with free associations – that is, they were anxious to make them into what they conceived to be as civilized people, which required substantial changes. As with the Catholics in Mexico or Brazil as well, their first converts made in the late 1640s, the "Praying Indians," were drawn from groups that had allied themselves with the English formally.

In their understanding of indigenous religion, Puritans saw both potentially divine elements and diabolic ones. Puritan preachers, most notably John Eliot, believed that the indigenous people of New England had knowledge of the True God, sought to find examples of it, and toyed with the idea that they might be a lost tribe of Israel, finding parallels between Jewish ideas and customs and those of the Algonquians.[204] Roger Williams, whose linguistic treatise of 1643 is by far the most detailed inquiry into Algonquian religion, found evidence supporting an Algonquian idea of one god, but thinking that the English had another, or "they branch their God-Head into many Gods."[205] On the other hand, they were also convinced that the "powwows" – indigenous spiritual leaders with contacts to the Other World – were, according to Daniel Gookin, one of the early Puritan workers, "partly wizards and witches, holding familiarity with Satan" – a view widely shared by most Puritans.[206] Although Eliot believed they must be rooted out, his primary approach to them was simply to preach to them, in their own language, on selected verses of scripture using a Bible that he had translated.[207] He entertained their questions, a good number of which have been recorded, that show both a degree of curiosity and some skepticism, but also do not speak of powwows or other elements of their own religious system.[208] Williams appears to have taught in the same way, for he provided an example of such a question-and-answer dialogue in the Narragansett language.[209]

While these spiritual speculations may have been theoretically interesting, in practice, Puritan missionaries were little concerned with comparative theology, instead focusing on the mystical conversion alone. In 1659, a number of the older converts were admitted to church membership and made biographical statements of how they became Christians. The statements stress a dissolute younger life, most often tormented by lust, disinterest, and only occasional and passing reference to "powwowing," or to parents who "prayed to many gods,"

---

[204] See the appendix by "I. D." to Edward Winslow, *The Glorious Progress of the Gospel Amongst the Indians in New England* (London, 1649 [EEB]), pp. 22–24; and Daniel Gookin, "Historical Collections of the Indians in New England" (1677) in *Collections of the Massachusetts Historical Society* 1 (1792, online at http://www.digitalcommons.uri.edu/sc_pubs/13), cap 3.13, p. 154.

[205] Roger Williams, *A Key into the Language of America* (London, 1643), pp. 115–116.

[206] Daniel Gookin, "Historical Collections of the Indians in New England" (1677) in *Collections of the Massachusetts Historical Society* 1 (1792, online at http://www.digitalcommons.uri.edu/sc_pubs/13), cap 3.13, p. 154; Williams, *Key*, pp. 129–130.

[207] Gookin, "Collections," Cap 5.2–4, pp. 168–170.

[208] Large numbers of sample question were recorded in Winslow, *Glorious Progress*, pp. 12–14 and 20–21.

[209] Williams, *Key*, pp. 123–128.

or "When English men came first, we did pray to the Devil." Family pressures also played a role, as converted brothers or neighbors encouraged them to "pray to God."[210] Thomas Mayhew's report on his evangelical work in Long Island stressed the miraculous healings that had brought people to his side, and one occasionally meets hints of such experiences even in the testimonies of 1659.[211]

Presbyterian missionaries, like David Brainerd, who worked in New Jersey and Pennsylvania among Delawares for the most part after 1740, were not much concerned about the indigenous religion either, claiming that it lacked much in the way of specifics, and that multiple ideas prevailed, but noting that there were ideas of a creator god and a life after death.[212] In introducing the idea of the soul and afterlife, he found it only possible to explain by using Delaware concepts.[213] Unlike his Calvinist predecessors in New England, Brainerd did not find indigenous religion Diabolic, although he did think that the mystical revelations of "conjurers," one of whom he interviewed at length about his revelations, must have involved contact with the Devil in order to effect miraculous cures.[214] Instead, he focused far more on teaching a Christ centered message of salvation, leaving most theology behind.[215] A simple catechism which he used in his preaching and with his converts focused almost entirely on salvation in the Other World, and not Original sin or an angry God.

The Moravians, who came to America in 1740, played a major role in the evangelization of the people of what would become New York, Pennsylvania, and Ohio. Indeed, they were resented by European settlers, and driven out from their first settlements among indigenous people by local settlers. As they often operated on or near the frontier, they were required by circumstances to work within both the complicated indigenous politics of the area and still maintain some support from the colonial authorities and settlers – a difficult and sometimes deadly game to play.

As with the Presbyterians, the Moravians approached Native Americans by "the heart." By this, they meant that they intended to convert by teaching their would be converts to feel a sense of the God in their hearts, and that through this they would teach about Christ – indeed, their teaching was extremely Christ-centric.[216] From the beginning, when the theologian Count Ludwig von

---

[210] John Eliot, *A Further Account of the Progress of the Gospel Amongst the Indians of New England* (London, 1659). For a detailed commentary on these spiritual biographies, see Daniel Richter, *Facing East from Indian Country: A Native History of Early America* (Cambridge, MA, 2001), pp. 118–129.

[211] Mayhew's report of November 18, 1647 is in Winslow, *Glorious Progress*, pp. 3–5.

[212] Brainerd, "Appendix," ed. Edwards, *Life*, pp. 441–448.

[213] Brainerd, "Appendix," ed. Edwards, *Life*, pp. 451–455.

[214] Brainerd, "Appendix," ed. Edwards, *Life*, pp. 446–448.

[215] David Bernerd, "Rise an Progress of a Remarkable Work of Grace," June 19, 1745 in Jonathan Edwards, ed., *The Life of David Brainerd, Missionary to the Indians* (London, 1818 [GB]), pp. 417–419; the catechism is in "Appendix to the Journal," June 20, 1746, *ibid* pp. 435–438.

[216] See the excellent description of Moravian theology as it applied to mission work in the introduction to Hermann Wellenreuther and Carola Wessel, *The Moravian Mission Diaries of David Zeisberger, 1772–1781* (State College, 2005), pp. 51–59.

Zinzendorf arrived in Pennsylvania in 1742, the Moravians imagined that their task would be to convert individuals, not "nations," to Christianity using the same methods they would use with Christians of other denominations – that is, by long and serious discussions, perhaps over long periods, until the would-be converts felt the relevant stirrings in their hearts that would move them to accept the Moravian message.[217]

Moravian writing about indigenous religion, primarily concerning the Delaware, Shawnee, or Iroquois, stressed the concept of the existence of God, which Moravians firmly believed was manifested in all people, and also their general goodness. While von Zinzendorf, writing at the beginning of the mission in 1742, thought that the Native Americans might be a lost tribe of Israel, and Moravians considered reintroducing circumcision and other Jewish customs, Moravians spent little time sorting out Native American religious customs.[218]

Moravians were not advocates of a Diabolic theory of indigenous religion either. George Loskiel, who finished his treatise on the Native people of Pennsylvania and Ohio in 1784, gave a very matter-of-fact account of indigenous religion, noting both cosmology and ritual without comment, but also made it clear that he did not believe the Devil underlay any of it and criticized any who thought that the locals were worshipping the Devil.[219] John Heckewelder, writing a general description of the Delaware and their neighbors as he witnessed them after his arrival in America in 1754, had a similar approach, describing a devotion to an all-powerful creator god, and dismissed most of their religious devotions as the result of the manipulations of trickster "doctors" or "jugglers."[220]

The Moravian inner feeling of Christ in them, with its mystical transformation, was sufficiently like the vision quest that was characteristic of the indigenous people of North America that it was not difficult for them to have satisfactory co-revelations.[221] In the biography of Michael, one of the earliest Moravian converts in 1742, he only noted that he had been a mighty warrior in his youth, and that "he received a deep impression of the Savior's wounds

---

[217] "Zinzendorf's Account of his Mission among the Indians" (1743) in William Reichel, ed. and trans., *Memorials of Moravian History* (Philadelphia, 1870), pp. 116–117; 123–125.

[218] "Zinzendorf's Observations of the Indians of Canada" (1742), and "Zinzendorf's Narrative of a Journey form Bethlehem to Shemokin in August, 1742" both in Reichel, *Memorials*, pp. 18–20 (Israelite origin); 66 (Iroquois remote from Jesus); 98 (Israelite custom); MAB, Bethlehem Diary, June 24, 1742 (Moravian Digital Archive Project).

[219] George Henry Loskiel, *A History of the Moravian Mission to the Indians of North America* (London, 1794 [GB] [Original German edition, 1789]), cap 3, pp. 33–48. Although Loskiel did not travel to North America until 1801, he wrote his work out of a plethora of reports from missionaries.

[220] John Heckewelder, *History, Manners and Customs of the Indian Nations who once inhabited Pennsylvania and the neighboring States* (2nd rev. ed., Philadelphia, 1876 [original 1818]), Cap 6, pp. 100–102; Caps 31–32, pp. 231–244.

[221] The vision quest is described in Loskiel, *History*, p. 63, though not with reference to Moravian mysticism; see also his notes on dreams and their influence, pp. 45–46, one place where he thinks Satan might influence them.

on his heart," and that in giving witness of "what the Savior had done in his heart," only that formerly he had been a "mean person."[222]

The Moravians converts lived with them in villages that included both baptized and unbaptized people and adopted European ways in dressing and building to go with their new revelations, but the Moravians did not demand many changes in economy, dress, or the like. The mission diaries, of which there are many, describe a sort of desultory missionary work. David Zeisberger's diary in the 1770s is quite vivid on this. Moravians allowed indigenous groups to visit, and would feed them if they were hungry, even if they had no desire to be Christians, and gladly accommodated those with religious questions.[223] Groups of people came, sometimes large groups, sometimes small ones, but especially many in religious holidays, where they listened intently to Moravian teaching and asked relevant questions. Those who did not obey the rules were sent away, but many came back or stayed.[224] Their talk was frank and free; one visitor who said he was "not a non believer" thought they taught the truth, but could not join because two things stood in his way: hunting and drinking.[225]

Mystical Protestant ideas allowed a good deal of penetration of Christian ideas into Native American thought through continuous revelation, and it manifested itself in the emergence of indigenous prophetic movements. The prophets in question clearly had taken in some of the Moravian teaching, no doubt the result of long conversations that influenced them without converting them, according to the strict definitions Moravians required.[226]

The prophetic movements were founded in a series of new and dramatic revelations; an early one, recorded by David Brainerd's brother and successor John, on the Susquehanna in 1751, came to a "squaw in a trance" from the Great Power and it presented the idea of separate creations for the different races, and that each received its own religion, so that of the whites was not suited to them.[227] Neolin was perhaps the most famous of these prophets. According to a French account, he wished to visit Paradise, but lacking knowledge of how to get there, he had recourse to "juggling (*jongler*)" or the art of the

---

[222] MAB, Memoirs, Michael, 1758 online at the Moravian Digital Archive Project (http://bdhp. moravian.edu/personal_papers/memoirs/michael/michael.html).

[223] MAB, Bethlehem Diary, April 25, 1745.

[224] Zeisberger, *Moravian Mission Diaries*, ed. Wellenreuther and Wessel, see entries for September 23 (woman finally converts), September 28, 1774 (more strangers than ever), January 17, 1775 (an in-and-out relationship), January 27, 1775 ("strangers" camping there), February 24, 1775 (come for corn during famine); March 13, 1775 (a woman who had been in and out of Moravian community for many years).

[225] Zeisberger, *Moravian Mission Diaries*, February 9, 1775.

[226] Alfred Cave, "The Delaware Prophet Neolin: A Reappraisal," *Ethnohistory* 46 (1999): 265–290 considers the Christian element in the prophetic movements, which began as early as the 1730s.

[227] John Brainerd to Ebenezer Pemberton, August 30, 1751, in Thomas Brainerd, ed., *The Life of John Brainerd, Brother of David Brainerd and his successor as Missionary to the Indians of New Jersey* (Philadelphia, 1865), pp. 233–235. While the idea is clear enough, it is not clear that it came from the revelation mentioned earlier in the text.

spiritual leaders, and had a dream of such a journey. During his long journey to the Master of Life (*Maître de la vie*), he met a radiant woman and a man, both dressed in white, who helped him. At last the Lord told him that to be saved, Native people must abandon drinking, fighting, and conjuring, which evokes Manietout, who is the Devil. The Master also told him he created America for "you and not for others," and that the whites should not be allowed there, and further that they should abandon the material things they had obtained from this contact.[228] Moravians reported that he began his preaching around 1762, and had been given a map, a sort of cosmogram, by the Great Spirit.

Another prophet, Wangomend, a Munsi, had been taken so near to Heaven in 1766 that "he could distinctly hear the crowing of the cocks" there, and had been borne aloft "by unseen hands." Here he learned of three heavens: "one for Indians, one for the negroes and another one for the white people."[229] Perhaps the greatest innovation in this preaching was the idea that one might not enter heaven simply by living a good life, but that a special regimen of life needed to be followed – an idea that Moravians at least thought might have come from Christian teaching.[230] These traditions took on strong political roles, informing the unification and militant movements of Pontiac and Tecumseh in the late eighteenth and early nineteenth centuries.[231]

AFRICAN CONVERSION IN THE AMERICAS

Africans who were carried as slaves to Catholic countries, which were essentially all those who reached the Americas before 1617, had different experiences from those who would later come to Protestant countries. From 1516 onward, the official policy of the Portuguese crown was that all slaves should be baptized and given catechism in Africa before their departure for the Americas. It is unlikely that this stricture was taken very seriously by the captains of the ships, and an inquest into the process led by the Jesuits in the early seventeenth century revealed that it was only really carried out seriously in Angola where there was an African Christianity and a Portuguese colony. Elsewhere along the coast, there was little Christian presence and no colonial base, so that slaves were loaded directly on ships without any evangelization.[232]

The development of African Christianity in both Spanish and Portuguese America was shaped by the religious experiences of the slaves in Africa.

---

[228] "Journal ou Dictation d'un Conspiration," trans. Clyde Ford, in C. M. Burton, ed., *Journal of Pontiac's Conspiracy, 1763* (Detroit, 1912), pp. 22–33 (original French and English translation on facing pages). The "Master of Life" is once called *Le Bon Dieu* in this account.

[229] Heckewelder, *History*, Cap. 39, pp. 290–299.

[230] Loskiel, *History*, pp. 37–39.

[231] There is a substantial literature on this subject; see in particular, Gregory Evans Dowd, *A Spirited Resistance: The North American Indian Struggle for Unity, 1745–1815* (Baltimore, 1992) and *War Under Heaven: Pontiac, the Indian Nations, and the British Empire* (Baltimore, 2004), which seeks a larger context.

[232] For a fuller treatment of this, see Linda Heywood and John Thornton, *Central Africans, Atlantic Creoles, and the Making of the Americas* (Cambridge, 2007), pp. 224–225.

Initially, most slaves arriving in Spanish America came from the Upper Guinea region. A good number must have been Muslim, coming from Mali, Jolof, and the other states of the Senegal Valley; others – for example, from Sierra Leone and its vicinity or from Lower Guinea – were practitioners of traditional religions.[233] Those from farther south – from Kongo, for example – were already Christians in their homeland, because Kongo's conversion predated the voyages of Columbus.

How Muslim Africans fit into the Christianizing scheme is difficult to determine. The sources on the social and religious life of slaves in the Spanish and Portuguese worlds are very meager, and very few refer to Islam. Furthermore, we should remember that the Islam of Atlantic Africa was often very open and flexible, not necessarily committed to a rigid system, except for the marabouts (religious leaders), who were probably very rarely enslaved. The experience of Francisco Jolofo, enslaved in the early seventeenth century and living and working in Cartagena, is an example. When approached by Claver to become a Christian, Francisco Jolofo refused, claiming that he was a Muslim. Claver tolerated this for years, arguing with him but not applying force. When a Wolof named Francisco de Jesus testified in Claver's canonization inquest in 1659, he related that it was only when he saw the future saint's tireless efforts on behalf of the slaves over many years that he was moved to accept Christianity.[234]

The Christian element became extremely important after the founding of Angola in 1575. The "Angolan Wave" of slaves who came to Spanish America through the Portuguese-held asiento system, and the dominance of slaves from the same source in Brazil, could not help but lay down a pattern of Christianity that resembled that of Angola.[235] Mexico and Pernambuco were particularly notable for having vast Angolan-descended populations, as many as 85 percent, but some regions received less than about half as many Angolans as Mexico or Pernambuco (for example, Cartagena, New Granada in general, and Peru). Either way, it seems fairly clear that the Angolan model of conversion applied in all the regions – the only catechism in an African language printed in the Spanish Americas was in fact the Kimbundu catechism, published in Peru. To this core of Angolans must be added a handful of Christians from Portuguese posts in Senegal and Guinea, who knew the languages of the area and had developed some sort of compromise between the two religious traditions. The catechists who served Claver in early-seventeenth-century Cartagena were typically from such communities, either from Christian Africa or from the coastal zones.[236]

Perhaps it was because of this unusual situation that the Spanish and the Portuguese assumed that all the Africans arriving in their lands would soon

[233] Heywood and Thornton, *Central Africans*, pp. 38–48 on slave-trading patterns before 1650.

[234] BN Colombia, Claver Inquest, fol. 143v, Testimony of Francisco di Giesu, di natione Jolofo.

[235] On the "Angolan Wave," see Heywood and Thornton, *Central Africans*, p. ix.

[236] John Thornton, "On the Trail of Voodoo: African Christianity in Africa and the Americas," *The Americas* 44 (1988): 261–278.

be Christians, and unlike the indigenous people, they were placed under the jurisdiction of the Inquisition. In fact, the Church invested very little in training or evangelizing the slaves – the Jesuits did so in Vera Cruz and Cartagena, and in the latter port, Claver was eventually canonized as a result of his labors. Furthermore, his catechism, probably one adopted by Jesuits everywhere, was remarkably cut down. Divided into five parts, it only described the divinity of the Trinity and Jesus, his death and resurrection and the salvation of all, later followed by instruction on the laws of the church and the sacraments as well as minimal prayers. There was no apparent attempt to address other aspects of religion or what the slaves themselves may have believed, although Claver did disrupt ceremonies that he thought "heathen."[237]

In Brazil, Jesuits were also responsible for creating catechisms, but they do not appear to have given it much attention, at least to judge from their correspondence on the matter. In spite of this meager preparation, however, Spanish and Portuguese clergy seemed remarkably satisfied that Africans absorbed the principles of the faith without any apparent training. In the late sixteenth century, Jesuits in Spanish territories announced that Africans were anxious to be Christians, and on the whole they seemed satisfied with their progress.

For this early period, the Inquisition provides the best source for understanding what the actual religious life of Africans in America was. Given their proportion in the population, especially the urban population that was most prone to ecclesiastical attention, remarkably few Africans were tried for religious crimes. In Mexico, for example, many were tried because they renounced God while receiving punishment. Such a renunciation was considered a crime, so they were turned over to the Inquisition, and ultimately the frequent outcome was that they were removed from an abusive master.[238] While technically a religious crime, it smacks more of an attempt to manipulate the system of slavery than a question of belief or religious status.

When the Mexican Inquisition, whose late-sixteenth-century records are interesting on this topic, accused Africans of practicing witchcraft, because they invoked Other-Worldly beings in ways not approved by the Church, some – albeit not all – of the practices could be linked to African roots. Both the invocation and the response resemble that of the Kongo, often for the same sorts of crimes. Sometimes these records suggest what seems obvious, that they were essentially continuing their older religion in a new setting, but they also show clearly that even in the early periods, Christian or European magical practices were mixed in along with the ones of African origin.[239]

[237] BN Colombia, Claver Inquest, fols. 33v, 35v, 39–39v Testimony of Niccolo Gonzalez, September 7, 1658.
[238] Colin Palmer, *Slaves of the White God: Blacks in Mexico, 1570–1650* (Cambridge, MA, 1976), pp. 95–106.
[239] Palmer, *Slaves*, pp. 152–156; Gonzalo Aguirre Beltrán, *La Población Negra de México* (Mexico, 1946).

The Brazilian Inquisition similarly investigated claims of witchcraft among the newly arrived and sometimes long-settled African population. Given the very large number of Africans in Brazil, they account for a remarkably small number among the thousands of judicial investigations and processes the Inquisition examined. When religious crimes were investigated, as a recent study by James Sweet shows, they confirmed that religiously significant activities from African sources continued to be practiced in the Americas, even when the slaves had been baptized and converted to Christianity, or were already Christians from Angola or Kongo. The Inquisition's records of eighteenth-century Brazil reveal a bewildering combination of methods of religious practice, ranging from Christian to purely African, and with ample mixtures of both. Typically, religious practitioners were called on to find lost objects, heal the sick, or care for the afflicted. Many of their practices can be traced to African roots, some to roots in European magical practices, others perhaps to local innovation. A number mention spirit possession, a formidable type of continuous revelation, in which Other-Worldly beings are asked to testify directly about matters pertaining to this world.[240]

As imports of slaves became more varied after 1650 and non-Christian slaves from West Africa joined Central Africans, the religious situation became more complex. Both the acceptance of Christian concepts and a willingness to mix them with elements from older religious traditions probably derived from the fact that African religions relied so heavily on continuous revelation. This continuous revelation would undoubtedly have worked overtime in the Americas, where in effect the relevant spiritual powers would have to be located and approached. Without a fixed doctrine anchored in a text or a master prophetic message, African religions were open to innovation and change. They were more inclined to see religious syncretism – the mixture of ideas from different traditions – as acceptable, and tended to view the validity of the resulting system in terms of its efficacy in healing, prediction, or miracles. Any African with religious talent and the capacity to demonstrate connection to the Other World could have helped fuse a variety of African beliefs together in the new environment.

Such multicultural stews can be seen in the nationally oriented assemblies and dances recorded in various colonial records. Early missionaries were suspicious of national gatherings as places where unacceptable practices might be followed. Claver, for example, regularly broke up these social gatherings, seized musical instruments, and punished participants.[241] The Brazilian calandus, mentioned frequently in Inquisition records, for example, are often associated with the "Congo Nation" and include, among other things, the use of the cross or Christian prayers, but with mixtures of other elements that come from the Mina coast (Ewe and Fon as well). Similarly, Moreau de St-Méry, a resident in

[240] James Sweet, *Recreating Africa: Culture, Kinship and Religion in the African-Portuguese World, 1441–1770* (Chapel Hill, 2003).
[241] BN Colombia, Claver Inquest, fols. 40, 108v, 180v.

prerevolutionary Haiti, noted the various Vodu dances and assemblies, which included elements drawn from both Fon and Kongo backgrounds.[242] Although initially often associated with particular African nations, such religious organizations became quickly and thoroughly multicultural.

The Church organized lay fraternities over the national organization in order to teach Christian doctrine. These fraternities became, in time, the centers for national life, providing mutual aid, access to freedom, and patronage from older, better-off slaves and freemen, to poorer slaves and those slaves who had just arrived. To the degree that African religious practice found its way into the religious practice of Africans and their descendants in the Americas, they did so in their own respective nations with the Church's approval.[243]

The process of transmitting African Christianity from West Central Africa or creating multicultural, multireligious communities was more complex in the Protestant areas settled by the English and the Dutch. This is because the Protestant religious tradition had debated the proposition that Christians might not be held as slaves by other Christians. The Synod of Dort (Dordrecht) – a joint meeting of Calvinists to settle doctrinal matters, which involved theologians from both England and the Netherlands, held in 1618, just as the first Africans were being brought to Protestant American colonies – debated the question of the possibility of Christians holding other Christians as slaves and, although not reaching a definitive conclusion, certainly considered the possibility favorably.[244] Whatever formal gatherings might determine, the folk wisdom among a good number of Protestants was that Christian slaves had to be granted their freedom.

This widespread belief may explain why so many of the first generation of Africans carried to the Anglo-Dutch colonies obtained freedom, as the English and Dutch captured their African slaves before 1640 exclusively from Portuguese slavers, delivering overwhelmingly Central Africans to the Spanish Indies. Many of these slaves were Christians, and no doubt the decision to free them, such as that of Governor Krieft in New Amsterdam to grant freedom to eleven Africans and their families and children in 1643, might well have had this idea as a backdrop, given that Church records show they were accepted as Christians. Richard Ligon, visiting Barbados in 1647–1648, discussed Christianity with one of the slaves on the estate where he resided, when the man's master informed Ligon in no uncertain terms that he would not allow his slaves to become Christian as it would require him to free them. Thus, masters actively discouraged attempts of slaves to become Christian and, needless to say, did nothing to encourage missionary work. Legislation in Virginia also closed this door on the formal freedom of Africans who were Christian as

[242] Louis Médéric Elie Moreau de Saint-Méry, *Description topographique, physique, civile, politique, et historique de la partie française de l'isle de St. Domingue* (3 vols., Philadelphia, 1796) 1: 64–69.

[243] Thornton, *Africa and Africans*, pp. 200–202; 331–325.

[244] Heywood and Thornton, *Central Africans*, pp. 328–329.

changes in the slave trade brought in a more varied supply of Africans, most of whom came from non-Christian parts of Africa.[245]

However, even in the absence of missionary work by masters, African Christians might well have done their own missionary work. A tantalizing piece of evidence of this comes from a detailed description of how the Kongolese served as unofficial missionaries in the Danish Virgin Islands. The Moravian missionary Georg Christian Andreas Oldendorp related that during his time on the islands in the 1760s, it was a well-established practice for slaves from Kongo to baptize non-Christians arriving on the slave ships. The rite that they used was "that they have seen of the holy Catholic one or of blacks who once were accustomed to it or employed it themselves, or heard of it and described it." At least some of the Kongolese who performed this baptism, Oldendorp was told, had been "priests in their own country," probably the lay ministers (*mestres*) that are frequently mentioned in accounts of the day. Oldendorp's informant, an unnamed Kongolese who performed the rite frequently, was such a priest himself. His method was first to give the neophyte "five or six blows on his back ... for the sins he committed in Guinea" and then to place "a little water on the head of the person to be baptized, some salt ... in his mouth," and to say "a prayer in the Congolese language." But he was not alone, and there were other Kongolese doing slightly different ceremonies at other places in the island: "some pour water on the person to be baptized, others only dip their finger in the water, and sprinkle it three times on their face, then make the sign of the cross three times and sing in their language." Oldendorp believed that this was commonly done on all three of the Virgin Islands. Following their baptism, the Kongolese became something of godparents for the newly converted, as Oldendorp put it, "to provide the male and female Bussals [newly arrived Africans] who have no elders or kindred ... to look out for them as a mother," holding dances for them, giving them entertainment and advice, and when they died – which was all too frequently the case – making sure to give them a Christian burial. "This baptism," Oldendorp went on to relate, "is very common among the heathen Blacks of all three islands [of the Danish Virgin Islands]."[246]

This sort of informal missionary work was not confined to the Virgin Islands. Another interesting document from Brazil describes how a certain Pedro Congo spent much time in the 1750s holding makeshift teaching sessions for slaves from the Mina coast, presenting Christian doctrine. Pedro Congo, like the Kongolese in the Virgin Islands that Oldendrop describes, may have been a lay minister in Kongo, for in fact he dressed as a priest and conducted services in a way that suggested a good knowledge of the liturgy. Like others from his country, he also mixed in non-Christian elements, or at least elements that priests considered as having Diabolic origins, and fell afoul of the Inquisition.[247]

---

[245] Heywood and Thornton, *Central Africans*, pp. 330–331.
[246] Oldendorp, *Historie* 1: 843–814.
[247] ANTT, Inq Lx, Processos, no. 16001 (1754).

While we cannot see clearly the course of religious mixture that emerged in the Protestant areas, religious blending among them may well have resembled that documented by the Inquisition in Spanish and Portuguese America. The creole result of the blending, as in languages, was likely to be the colonial religion, in this case Christianity, albeit with numerous African elements within it, as these elements proved effective in healing or producing continuous revelation.

Slave life in many English colonies is poorly described in general, especially as it might touch on Christian practices. Nevertheless, English missionaries of the Society for the Propagation of the Gospel, sent in the early eighteenth century to attempt to convert slaves in South Carolina (and met with stubborn noncooperation among most slave masters), tried to bring some slaves in. Francis Le Jau, one of the most active missionaries, noted in 1710 that some of the slaves asked to be admitted to communion among the regular community, but he was reluctant, knowing them to have been Catholics. Le Jau seems to have felt that they were already observing Christianity as Catholics and had no desire to be Anglican, except to take communion from the priest. He proposed that he would admit them only if they renounced the "errors of the Popish Church."[248] Thirty years later, there were enough African Catholics from "Angola" in South Carolina that they would lead a rebellion, among the objectives of which was to flee to Spanish Florida to be with coreligionists.[249] What role might such people have played in introducing the Christian component to the mix of religious traditions that were merging among South Carolina's African population?

However important the African Christian background may have been, formal conversion, at least in North America, came through the Great Awakening. From a theological perspective, the Great Awakening came out of a controlled process of continuous revelation within the confines of the Protestant world. Some of the new religious movements, such as Methodists and Baptists, sought to enhance the possibility of having these mystical experiences of Jesus by conducting meetings that were very emotional and led to revelation. Such meetings, often with lengthy and emotional preaching, music, and even physical movement, led to what was called "Enthusiasm," which in turn caused the participants to find Jesus.

While these religious movements were sweeping the population of European origin in northern colonies, they were also reaching into the southern plantations and to Africans. The Methodists and Baptists did not hold that conversion led to freedom and were not troubled by the thought of preaching to slaves. Their focus on continuous revelation allowed the unconverted slaves to find the revelation necessary to finalize the place of Christianity in their mixture of

---

[248] Annette Laing, "'Heathens and Infidels?' African Christianization and Anglicanism in the South Carolina Low Country," *Religion and American Culture* 12 (2002): 197–228.

[249] John Thornton, "African Dimensions of the Stono Rebellion," *American Historical Review* 96 (1991): 1101–1113.

religious practice, and as a result most became Christian as a part of one or another of these sects. When George Whitfield brought the Great Awakening to South Carolina in 1740, his message reached both African- and European-descended groups, and even though his movement had relatively little formal impact after 1750, it sowed seeds that would eventually be taken up as the first black churches were organized after 1780 when Baptists began to be active.[250]

Although for much of the Atlantic world, Christianity arrived through the ministrations of European missionaries, the process of creating the local variants of the religion depended on a joint religious project. Co-revelation was crucial to this process, and although at times the more fundamentalist of the religious leaders (both among the Protestants and among the regular Catholic clergy) denounced it, in fact, African and Christian religious traditions merged. This merger resulted in mixed concepts and practices, particularly among indigenous people on the frontiers of empires (but sometimes even in core regions) and among the Africans.

---

[250] Sylvia Frey and Betty Wood, *Come Shouting to Zion: African American Protestantism in the American South and the British Caribbean to 1830* (Chapel Hill, 1998); Mechal Sobel, *Trabelin' On: The Slave Journey to an Afro-Baptist Faith* (Greenwood, 1979).

The Revolutionary Moment in the Atlantic

European possession of most of the Americas ended almost as abruptly as it had begun. While the Spanish had occupied vast tracts of American land in a little over a half-century between 1492 and 1550, even larger regions of the Americas won their independence in the half-century between 1775 and 1825. While there had been rebellions and disobedience in the earlier periods, there was nothing like the massive and successful resistance to rule from Europe that characterized the American revolutions.

These observations may make it appear that the American revolutions were fairly straightforward; in fact, the period was one of immense complexity. In many regions, the movement toward independence was as much an inter-American civil war as the ousting of an occupying power. Moreover, in many cases, the revolutions were social movements as well as political movements, and involved a complex dance between the revolutionaries who wanted a radical change in social order and the nationalists who wanted simply to rid American colonies of their overlords in Europe. Both sorts of movement were part of a pattern of a revolutionary age that began with the American Revolution in 1775 and extended to the end of the Spanish American Revolutions in 1825. In between there was the French Revolution and a powerful slave revolt and revolution in Haiti.

FISCAL PROBLEMS AND THE REVOLUTIONARY MOMENT IN THE ATLANTIC

The impetus to the revolutionary period came largely from fiscal difficulties experienced by Old World countries. In the eighteenth century, the European colonial countries all developed what John Brewer called the "military-fiscal state" involving substantial investments in armies and navies in order to pursue aggressive policies with regard to their neighbors.[1] The financial demands

[1] John Brewer, *The Sinews of Power* (London, 1989), the classic statement for England. The concept has been expanded and applied to most other European powers; for a full discussion of

of the military-fiscal state put tremendous strain on European mechanisms of revenue extraction and at times placed very uneven burdens on its population, creating systems that seemed more and more unjust as they evolved.

England was one of the leaders in this movement. England stepped outside of European politics following the Thirty Years' War (ended in 1648), mostly because of its own civil war, but became reengaged when the Dutch William of Orange was invited to become king in 1688. England's new military involvement often centered on the Low Countries and Rhine Valley, protecting them from expansionist policies of France, such as the Nine Years War (also called the War of the League of Augsburg) (1688–1697), the War of the Spanish Succession (1701–1714), and the Seven Years' War (1756–1763). As a result of this engagement in continental politics, the English army grew from some 40,000 soldiers in 1697 to more than 190,000 in 1784, and its military expenditure in the same period grew from about 5 million pounds sterling to more than 20 million pounds sterling. To meet this growth, the English state increased its total revenue from slightly less than 4 million pounds sterling to 12 million pounds sterling in the same period. These expenditures, however, still did not meet the costs of war, and public debt topped a staggering 240 million pounds sterling. In fact, the English crown spent somewhere between two-thirds and three-quarters of all its income on military affairs.[2]

Military expenses grew apace elsewhere in Europe as well. France, England's great rival in this period, showed a similar growth in military expenditure; indeed, some historians have described the series of wars between them (and involving other European powers as well) as the "Second Hundred Years' War."[3] Eighteenth-century French revenues increased from 207 million livres in 1727 to 344 million livres in 1768, and military expenses took up more than half their outlays.[4] Spain, even though it was the envy of other European powers because of the huge revenues it could extract from its colonies (and particularly New Spain, which transferred millions of pesos to its mother country), had managed to spend as much as it took in, and even borrowed more.[5]

the issues involved, see Jan Glete, *War and the State in Early Modern Europe: Spain, the Dutch Republic and Sweden as Fiscal-Military States, 1500–1660* (London and New York, 2002). For a broad overview, see the essays in R. Bonney, ed., *The Rise of the Fiscal State in Europe, c. 1200–1815* (Oxford, 1999).

[2] Brewer, *Sinews*, pp. 30, 40, 42.

[3] J. Meyer and J. Bromley, "The Second Hundred Years' War," in D. Johnson, F. Bédaria, and François Croizet, eds., *Britain and France: Ten Centuries* (Folkstone, 1980), pp. 168–171; François Croizet, "The Second Hundred Years' War: Some Reflections," *French History* 10 (1996): 432–450.

[4] James Riley, "French Finances, 1727–1768," *Journal of Modern History* 59 (1987): 223–228. Any attempt to calculate French revenues or expenditures has to overcome the difficulties of the loss of vital records; Riley's work includes a wide range of original source material. Martin Körner, "Expenditure," in Richard Bonney, ed., *The Origins of the Modern State in Europe* (Oxford, 1995), pp. 393–422; see charts on pp. 410–415, albeit generally for the less dramatic seventeenth century.

[5] Carlos Marichal, *Bankruptcy of the Empire: Mexican Silver and the Wars Between Spain, Britain, and France, 1760–1810* (New York and Cambridge, 2008).

The expense of raising armies and especially of maintaining them meant that larger European states continued to use mercenaries in time of war. In fact, the eighteenth century saw the rise of a peculiarity – polities that specialized in military service. Hesse-Cassel can serve as a prime example. It was a small state that controlled several noncontiguous districts in northern Germany, which developed a sizable and modern army, numbering almost 20,000 – a large number indeed relative to its fairly small population. It was able to pay for the army, and indeed reoriented its politics around being what Charles Ingrao dubbed a "mercenary state," by selling its services as a sort of portable army, typically in the service of England.[6] The famous Hessian mercenaries, recruited by Britain to fight in the American War of Independence, came largely from Hesse-Cassel.

The wars of the later eighteenth century did not involve larger armies than earlier ones; in fact, army size in some countries such as France may have been a bit smaller, but they were much more expensive. This is because armies became permanent and professionalized, and supplying them moved from foraging at the expense of the civilian population to carrying their own supplies. Troops were under strict discipline and were paid salaries and kept in barracks. While this reduced their rapaciousness, the problems of supplying armies to keep them from foraging and maintaining them in peacetime made them much more expensive.[7] Even so, the French army grew so rapidly in the seventeenth century that it completely outstripped the capacity of France's taxation system to support it, and so French battalions still pillaged the civilian population in the districts in which they were stationed. The crisis of military pillage, as the army's size reached as much as 400,000, ultimately created a crisis that forced new fiscal policies.[8]

The rise in the size and expense of fleets, especially Atlantic fleets, also increased the demands for revenue. Great Britain led the way in constructing ships, and by the 1760s had the best fleet in the world, and was particularly competent at land-sea operations, being able to outsail and outgun opponents as well as land large marine forces, which made them capable of conducting operations in the hotly contested Caribbean very effectively. Britain' fleet more than doubled between 1720 and 1760, from 174 ships to 375. This led to an inevitable race to keep up by France and Spain, Britain's principal rivals. In the same period, the French navy grew from 48 to 156 ships, and Spain's from 22 to 137. By 1775, the two smaller powers had nearly 200 ships each, so that when allied, as they often were, they had more ships that Britain's 350 or so vessels.[9]

---

[6] Charles Ingrao, *The Hessian Mercenary State: Ideas, Institutions and Reform under Frederick II, 1760–85* (Cambridge, 1987); for a view of the impact of this policy, see Peter Keir Taylor, *Indentured to Liberty: peasant Life and the Hessian Military State, 1688–1815* (Ithaca, 1994).

[7] Martin L. van Crevelt, *Supplying War: Logistics from Wallerstein to Patton* (Cambridge, 2004).

[8] John A. Lynn, *Giant of the Grand Siècle: The French Army, 1610–1715* (New York and Cambridge, 1997), pp. 184–217.

[9] Jan Glete has led the way in pointing out the importance to fleets to the development of the military-fiscal state; see *Navies and Nations: Warships, Navies and State Building in Europe and America, 1500–1860* (2 vols., Stockholm, 1993); these figures are drawn from his counts, 2: 256, 263, 271.

European countries all faced problems in raising the money to pay for the new military system. In many countries, especially in France and Spain, the government was incapable of taxing its citizenry freely, although Spain was remarkably free to tax its empire.[10] Nobles and the church were tax exempt, and thus the crown was impeded from raising revenue from its richest subjects. In addition to noble exemptions, many corporate bodies, towns, and even provinces had special privileges that had either reduced or eliminated their tax burdens. The combination of territorial, occupational, local, noble, and clerical exemptions from this or that tax produced a crazy quilt of tax liabilities.

Jacques Necker, the last French finance minister before the Revolution of 1789, wrote an extensive treatise on French taxation, in which he outlined the plethora of taxes and duties – the regular land tax yielded considerably less than a combination of salt taxes, sales taxes, and overseas revenues, for example. There were regional taxes paid in some counties and not in others, voluntary taxes of clergy, sales of offices and other matters, amounting, by Necker's assessment, to twenty-nine different articles (not all of which were strictly paid in money).[11] More than that, however, there were also a variety of indirect taxes leveled in a variety of ways. It was possible for two districts lying not far apart to have radically different tax rates per capita.[12] In addition to these difficulties in assessing taxes, it was expensive to collect them, requiring a substantial and costly bureaucracy to determine dues and to ensure that the state received all that it was due by law from reluctant taxpayers.[13] Because of this expense, state leaders had not updated records and were unwilling to pay the cost of a professional tax service. Hence they often "farmed" the taxes, meaning that they allowed private persons to collect taxes on their behalf in exchange for a share of the takings, which resulted in the state receiving substantially less that it was legally due.[14] Often these entrepreneurs failed to collect the amount they contracted for but managed to collect their share in any case. A great deal of what was called "reform" in fiscal matters in France, in Carlos III's Spain, or the Portugal of the Marquis of Pombal, all of whom are credited with mid- to late-eighteenth-century reform, was simply an attempt to create a single, efficient way to raise the taxes to which the crown was entitled, even without touching the special rights and privileges of the exempted orders (in fact, however, royal officials laid siege to these fortresses of exemption as well).

---

[10] Marichal, *Bankruptcy*, 48–80.

[11] Jacques Necker, *De l'administration des finances de la France* (3 vols., Paris, 1784; several English translations usually as *A Treatise on the Administration of the Finances of France*, 1786, 1787 [GB]), vol. 1, chapter 1.

[12] The inequities in France are discussed with frustration by Necker, *Administration*, vol. 1, chapter 2.

[13] Richard Bonney, "Taxation and the Problem of European Regions," European State Finances Database (http://www.le.ac.uk/hi/bon/ESFDB/frameset.html). For France, see Necker, *Administration*, vol. 1, chapter 3.

[14] Eugene N. White, "From Privatized to Government-Administered Tax Collection: Tax Farming in Eighteenth Century France," *Economic History Review* 57 (2004): 636–663 (and extensive literature cited therein).

Although noble and ecclesiastical wealth was the greatest untapped asset in most European countries, kings were reluctant to touch it. Thanks to the system of representation in existence since the Middle Ages, the crown could only get taxes from nobles or the church with their permission and through the acts of deliberative bodies like the parlements, estates, or cortes. Yet to summon these bodies also ran the risk of impeding the ability of the crown to centralize its decision-making and war powers, and this it was very reluctant to do. The French crown was sometimes able to get around these problems by summoning only the local or regional parlements when asking the nobility for money, but even then only in those provinces where the crown was sure they could manipulate and dominate the proceedings.

In general, the policy in France was to find money wherever it could be found, from whatever taxpayers could be located. Those that had fewer legal rights and privileges paid much more than those who could protect themselves. The burden of taxes increasingly fell on the Third Estate, legally commoners, whatever their incomes, who were often merchants and professionals as well as those of lower social status. The inherent unfairness and inefficiency of this system of taxation was widely criticized by spokespeople of those groups that bore its burden, and French economic thinkers, often drawn from that class, constantly reminded the kings that huge untapped revenues awaited them in the privileges of the nobles and the church.

In England, the process of royal centralization had run into trouble already in the seventeenth century, and England offered to Europe both a solution and a danger, at least from the royalist point of view. Thanks to the existence of a fairly coherent nobility and a parliament that stood for the whole country, attempts of the kings of the Stuart dynasty to raise funds through extra-parliamentary means failed, and following the revolution of 1649, Parliament actually executed the king (Charles I) and ran the country on its own in the atmosphere of civil war. The war and the dictatorship of Oliver Cromwell had proven problematic for Parliament to the point where they agreed to restore the king in the person of Charles II, but it was not until 1688, in what is called the "Glorious Revolution," that a final settlement was reached that firmly restricted the taxation power of the king, and placed such matters in the hands of Parliament. While this made English fiscal problems much lighter, it did not set an example other European monarchs wished to follow, for English kings were decidedly less capable of determining policy than those of the continent were. The English model was frequently invoked in Spain and France either as an undesirable outcome (for the crown and the protected classes) or as the solution to all problems by those who bore the taxes.

The costs of maintaining ready armies and fleets put an ever-increasing strain on the normal budgets of all the western European states, and the extraordinary expenses required when the soldiers went to war augmented that many times. European states were not able to raise the necessary cash from regular taxation, which could usually meet the "ordinary" expenses of peacetime but not the "extraordinary" ones of wars. Many schemes, especially ones of borrowing or releasing valuable assets by sale, produced sufficient money in the short run, but impinged on the long-run ability of the state to raise more income and sometimes even to meet ordinary expenses. This led to incredible debts: as noted, by the 1780s, English revenues ran about 12 million pounds sterling a year, but their national debt exceeded 240 million pounds sterling.

French finances in the eighteenth century showed similar trends. While revenues generally grew in tandem with expenses during peaceful years, in war years they skyrocketed, leaving the government far in arrears. The war of the Spanish Succession was particularly damaging, reaching a pinnacle in 1709, and the Seven Years' War almost as bad.[15] The mounting debts and the increasing inability to pay them led to partial bankruptcies or other government strategies designed to eliminate debt at the expense of the lenders. This made credit harder to obtain and ultimately worsened the situation.[16]

Not surprisingly, the European countries' colonies played a significant role in maintaining the finances of their mother countries. The colonial system had been created originally in such a way that there were far fewer exempt local bodies and people than in Europe, and the crown had far more power to tax and legislate in the colonies than in the home country. To tighten the colonial revenues, Spain and France both increased the monopoly control of metropolitan merchants, streamlined tax and customs collections, and increased the mercantilist regulations. In Spanish colonies, for example, the government of King Carlos III and his various finance ministers introduced the *intendant* system, in which paid, professional administrators sent directly from Spain were tasked with collecting information, assessing taxes, and carrying out other government functions. These reforms, often called the Bourbon Reforms, were particularly associated with the vigorous Visitor General of New Spain, José de Gálvez, in office from 1765 to 1771.[17] The results of their work were impressive. While revenues from Lima (Peru) rose relatively little (from 2 billion Spanish dollars in 1700 to slightly less than 4 billion Spanish dollars in 1800), Mexican revenues to the crown went from slightly more than 2 billion to nearly 30 billion in the same period, and were still climbing in the following years.[18]

In addition to the rise in taxation, England, France, Spain, and Portugal also increased and strengthened mercantile regulations. Although in the 1770s, Spain created a free trading zone within its colonial sphere, allowing colonial towns to trade with each other, which they had not been allowed earlier, it still

[15] Alain Guéry, "Les finances de la monarchie française sous l'Ancien Régime," *Annales: Economies, sociétés, civilizations* 33 (1978): 216–239; see especially graph 4, p. 228.
[16] James Riley, *The Seven Years' War and the Old Regime in France: The Economic and Financial Toll* (Princeton, 1986).
[17] Marichal, *Bankruptcy*, for a thorough study of colonial finance in the context of the military-fiscal system.
[18] Herbert Klein and J. J. TePaske, *The Royal Treasuries of the Spanish Empire in America* (4 vols., Durham, 1982–1990) 1: 284–421, and table in European State Finances Database, online at http://www.le.ac.uk/hi/bon/ESFDB/frameset.html; for further data and structure, see Marichal, *Bankruptcy*.

did not allow their colonies to trade with either France or England, although merchants from those countries were offering better prices and higher-quality products than Spanish merchants did. Similarly, the problems of monopoly trade and other imperfections bothered American producers everywhere. In addition to channeling trade, the mercantile system also hampered manufacturing, because in theory, the colonies could not manufacture any product that could be imported from the metropolitan country. In actual practice, however, colonial industry flourished in spite of the law, and most of the colonial regions had fairly vibrant metallurgical and textile industries in spite of fairly specific legislation to the contrary.[19]

The taxation and restrictions hurt the native-born merchants and large-scale producers such as plantation and mine owners. They were also hurt by the development of an upper administration under the intendant system that answered more directly to Spain. This administration was dominated by Spanish-born people (sometimes called *peninsulares*, but also *Europeos* and in Mexico the insulting *gauchopines*) and did not employ as many of the otherwise powerful local elites (*criollos*). Whereas rich and well-connected local elites and powerful corporations managed to work their way into the system, the lower-level elites felt the burden, particularly the non-Spanish elites of indigenous nobility. As intendants shouldered out *criollos* in lower levels of decision making, they created resistance and resentment. Even when *criollos* managed to obtain such positions, their freedom of movement was often hampered and there were strong prejudices against *criollos* among the Spanish-born elite. This lead to an increasing dissatisfaction with the colonial relationship and created the initial movement toward independence.[20]

Political and economic loss was exacerbated by European arrogance and chauvinism. In the eighteenth century, European scientists, led by Georges Louis, Comte de Buffon, argued that all manner of things became degenerate in the Americas, and his disciple de Pauw concluded that this included people as well. Thomas Jefferson, while in Paris, wrote a stirring riposte to the French challenge, but the theory remained for all the Americas.[21] *Criollos*, who had always regarded themselves as suitably white, guarded or promoted their past assiduously to accommodate the new "science" and in the wrestling for position and power applied it to the more unmistakably African or indigenous (or mixtures of all three) common people of their homes.

The spirit of constitutional revisionism that was the hallmark of the fiscal revolt was echoed all over the Atlantic world: in Africa, the Americas, and in Europe, various people and social groups were seeking to alter the way

---

[19] For a detailed discussion of colonial taxation and trade, see Peggy K. Liss, *Atlantic Empires: The Network of Trade and Revolution, 1713–1826* (Baltimore, 1983); and for Spain and Portugal in particular (but only the South American regions), see Jeremy Adelman, *Sovereignty and Revolution in the Iberian Atlantic* (Princeton, 2006).

[20] Marichal, *Bankrupcy*, pp. 48–80 for a summary of winners and losers in New Spain.

[21] Phillipe Roger, *The American Enemy: A Story of French Anti-Americanism* (Chicago, 2005), pp. 8–21.

government was handled. In North America, a movement to limit British fiscal and commercial policies also managed to produce a constitutional republic along the lines quite different from the English model. In Europe, there were strong constitutional challenges to the monarchies by various representational bodies, climaxing in the French Revolution in 1789 that established a new pattern of republic that vested authority in a popularly elected Assembly. The Haitian Revolution, after experimenting with monarchy, ended up becoming a republic as well, as did all the new states carved out by revolutionaries from Spain's American possessions. Finally, in all of the Americas, the unconquered free associations were trying to come to terms with the spread of settlers who threatened to dispossess or to encapsulate them in inegalitarian and authoritarian political systems, while balancing their relations with the European monarchies.

The champions and generally the beneficiaries of the new spirit of republicanism were the middle-class commercial elites, not yet wedded to the machine production of the Industrial Revolution (although it would follow shortly), and squeezed by royal taxation. The powerful monarchies of the early modern period had been built on lopsided taxation that avoided the nobility and the church and fell squarely on those commercial elites who could not buy nobility. This predicament was felt especially in the Americas, where virtually no one was exempt from taxation, and where the general thrust of monarchial money lust was combined with an additional burden of yielding to monopolies that favored the merchants of the metropoles. Thus, the spirit of the Enlightenment that swept Europe in the late eighteenth century often sought to develop "rational" taxation policy that would even out the tax burden while making the sovereign answerable to the taxpayers.

REVOLUTION AND REFORM IN THE AMERICAS

The fiscal crises in Europe led to increasing pressure on the colonies, and that in turn led to the desire to alter the arrangements that had grown up over two or three centuries of colonial rule. Colonial areas were at first inclined to avoid or simply to seek abatement of the new and more demanding relationship with their colonial masters, but as time went on, the demands were increasingly met with open and eventually armed resistance. Throughout Europe and the Americas, the initial resistance to the fiscal pressure was led by elite groups who were not protected by privileges from taxation and other onerous devices, but as the struggle descended into armed conflict, these groups and their colonial opponents searched for military allies to assist them. In this process, dispossessed lower classes were drawn into the struggle as foot soldiers, like the urban poor and peasants in the French Revolution or slaves and indigenous people (both "Indian" subjects in Iberian countries and independent indigenous groups everywhere) in the Americas. The inclusion of these groups and the crossing of racial, class, and status barriers created an unstable situation that all groups sought to exploit or to minimize.

It is not surprising, perhaps, that the first of the American revolutions began in the English-controlled areas. Not only was the English crown, like those of other powers, inclined to tax the colonial regions vigorously, but the fact that the home government had made a transition to fiscal rule by Parliament made Anglo-Americans angry, as Parliament refused to allow them either to sit in the English Parliament or decide their own fiscal fate with a local equivalent. The seventeenth-century English transformation was not lost on American colonists, and the idea that unjust governments might legitimately be overthrown had already been advanced in America by Jonathan Mayhew. In 1750, he used the occasion of the centennial of the execution of Charles I to assert the right of subjects to depose an unpopular government.[22]

In the mid-eighteenth century, aggressive monarchs of the Hanoverian dynasty had sought to take back royal power, only to be thwarted by Parliament. Parliamentary victories guaranteed that the English middle classes would be protected from excessive taxation, and could limit activities of the king in many ways. But these victories were strictly limited to the British Isles, and their fruits were not enjoyed at all in the Americas. This became particularly acute following the Seven Years' War (1756–1763) or the French and Indian War as it was called in North America. Directly on the heels of the war with France was a second set of operations against the Native American leader Pontiac, in which raids on the settlers who had moved into the Ohio Valley caused the temporary evacuation of large areas. The costs of English participation in the war and against Pontiac were high, and Parliament decided to tax Americans to pay at least some of the cost of both wars.[23]

The question of the relationship between the financing of war and representative government was broached even as the Seven Years' War was ongoing. Not only did the Parliament and its leaders seek taxation from the Americans, but they also used powers they had always had to overturn the acts of the American provincial assemblies. The touch points were many: to prevent friction with the Iroquois and Algonquians in the north and the Creeks, Cherokees, and others in the south of their colonies, and more immediately to confront the issues raised by Pontiac's war, the government forbade colonists from entering the territory (even though they could do little to enforce this). The American colonists saw this as an attempt to cut them off from lucrative markets and prevent settlement in fertile regions.

Taxation, both direct and indirect, was another issue. Following 1760, the British government began asserting stronger mercantile control, by issuing writs of assistance to customs officers, to ensure that colonial trade was channeled though approved merchants. Although apparently only an enforcement mechanism for older laws granting monopolies over colonial trade to Europe-

---

[22] Jonathan Mayhew, *Discourse Concerning Unlimited Submission* (London, 1750).
[23] For this and the paragraphs that follow, there is abundant literature. I have relied heavily on Middlekauf, *The Glorious Cause: The American Revolution, 1763–1789* (Oxford, 2005 [1st ed., 1985]).

based merchants, this new enforcement was viewed as a tax and was resisted in legal channels in Boston by James Otis.[24] The popularity of Otis's defense caused the government to limit the use of writs, but did not prevent the passage of other fiscal measures aimed at the colonies – the Sugar Act in 1764 and the Stamp Act in 1765. In another tax issue, King George personally vetoed a Virginia act intended to fix clerical salaries to their detriment, an act that came to be regarded as a reminder that American legislatures did not have the final say in revenue matters.

A variety of American writers and speechmakers hit on the Virginia case as an example of the enactment of fiscal measures against the colonies, and Jonathan Mayhew used the phrase "no taxation without representation" in a sermon, while John Otis provided a different variant, "taxation without representation is tyranny," to describe it. Significantly, Mayhew's 1750 essay on the justification of rebellion against tyranny was republished in 1767 in London, providing at least an initial justification for active and perhaps armed resistance against the measures.

Responding to the protests of the colonies, the British hesitated and repealed the stamp tax in 1766, and the next year Charles Townshend, the new British chancellor, introduced a new set of taxes that he declared would be expended in the colonies and not simply sent to England. But while these measures were intended to make the fiscal pressure of England more palatable, it made no difference – the various colonies began exploring ways to develop a joint response to British policies. The English government, concerned about the volatile situation in Boston, sent a garrison to occupy the city in 1768. Even though most of the Townshend taxes were repealed shortly after, the tea tax was retained, and in 1773, a group of Boston residents promptly threw a large shipment of taxed tea into the sea, leading England to close the harbor in 1774 and then to give the colonial governor broad powers against the Massachusetts assembly.

The Seven Years' War had also brought a good number of French territories under British control, including Canada and several islands in the Caribbean (notably Grenada, Trinidad, and other islands in the Lesser Antilles). In general, the British attitude to these colonies was harsh – local law was largely disregarded, British immigration was encouraged, and the settlers received important privileges that were denied the French-speaking residents. In the Caribbean, these anti-French measures, although deeply resented, were grudgingly accepted, but in Canada, the situation was different. Few English settlers went there, and the English government feared that the restive French residents would side against them in the looming conflicts farther south. To mollify these French interests, and to reestablish former French interests in the hinterland of Canada, Parliament passed the Quebec Act in 1774.[25] An important

---

[24] M. H. Smith, *The Writs of Assistance Case* (Berkeley, 1978), which corrects much of the patriotic image of Otis in the writing of his contemporary, John Adams, who saw Otis as a precursor to the revolution.

[25] Text, officially called 14 Geo. III c. 83, in English and French on facing pages in facsimile at http://www.canadiana.org/view/48786/0003

measure of the act granted the governor of Quebec formal control over the formerly French territories of the Upper Midwest as far south as the Ohio River. Colonists in the older British colonies regarded these areas as an extension of their own colonial claims, often established in their original charters as extending from their coasts due west until the other side of the continent, and thus to be their own reserves for settlement and trade.[26] The British government's formally hostile attitude toward continued settlement of the area from Atlantic coast colonies and Parliament's decision to honor French law and the Catholic religion in this area (a notable contrast to their relentless hostility to Catholicism in the French Caribbean colonies that fell to England at the same time as Canada) was also perceived as deleterious to the interests of the older colonies caused them to be dubbed the "Intolerable Acts."

Just as the British occupation of French territories had stirred resistance in the colonies, it had an immediate effect among the various indigenous people of the zone. While initially it appeared that Britain would abide by the treaties that France had made in the Upper Midwest, British soldiers soon occupied the French forts of the Ohio valley and the Great Lakes region. Britain concluded that the alliances formed in the war were no longer vital to her interests and sought to deal with the indigenous people as if they were subjects; among the most crucial decisions was to curtail sales of gunpowder. As soon as English intentions were clear, even before the formal end of the war, a large interethnic coalition formed in the Upper Midwest, partially led by Pontiac, an Ottowa, and seconded by Neolin, a religious leader preaching a strongly anti-European message. In 1764, the united forces attacked British and colonial positions all along the Ohio country, taking some forts and forcing settlers from the region.[27]

While a British counterattack did relieve some of the forts, and negotiations settled the disputes, at least temporarily, the incident helped reinforce the determination of the British government to restrict vulnerable settlers whose protection would be difficult as long as they held to their alliances. British policy makers were also relieved that although a large number of indigenous groups joined Pontiac, others, even in the Upper Midwest, did not; moreover, the Iroquois alliance – Britain's oldest – held firm and did not join against the British or the settlers.[28]

Just as postwar policies created a new sense of anti-British unity among formerly disparate Native Americans in the Midwest, so the settler colonies of the Atlantic coast began to pull together and coordinate their efforts. A network of interconnected elites in mercantile cities of the English colonies organized Committees of Correspondence to share news and discuss reactions.

[26] Paul Langston, "'Tyrant and Oppressor!' Colonial Press Reaction to the Quebec Act," *Historical Journal of Massachusetts* 34 (2006): 1–17.

[27] Colin Calloway, *The Scratch of a Pen: 1763 and the Transformation of North America* (Oxford, 2006) provides one of the best-integrated survey of the period between the Seven Years' (French and Indian) War and the Revolution (War of American Independence).

[28] Calloway, *Scratch of a Pen*, pp. 67–76.

These committees were often formed specifically to address a tax or sometimes a more local issue, but they coordinated their activities with similar committees in other colonies. Massachusetts formed such a committee in 1772, followed by similar bodies in Virginia, Rhode Island, Connecticut, New Hampshire, and South Carolina in 1773. As resistance to the Tea Act grew in 1774, New York also formed a committee.

In 1774, in response to the Intolerable Acts, representatives of the twelve colonies of British North America (Georgia did not send delegates) met at the First Continental Congress to develop a pan-colonial response to British activity. They compiled a list of grievances and decided to boycott English shipping to the colonies.[29] The English government, alarmed by the wave of dissention, sent troops from Europe to America to protect and ensure their interests, focusing their attention on Boston, which appeared an epicenter.

General Thomas Gage, the British commander at Boston, hoped to diffuse the growing conflict by seizing stores of powder that were used by militias in towns deemed less than loyal, and throughout 1774–1775, a series of confrontations between the British forces and colonial militias developed. Eventually, when Gage sent a force of 700 men to remove the powder from Concord, Massachusetts, on April 19, 1775, the militia confronted them at Lexington and an exchange of gunfire resulted. In response, the militia laid siege to the British forces in Boston and called on the other colonies to assist. The war for American Independence had begun.[30] In response to the actions in Boston, enthusiastic militia leaders managed to capture British Fort Ticonderoga in New York and used it as a staging point for an ill-fated invasion of Canada in 1775–1776, which did, at least, prevent British forces stationed there from launching an invasion immediately.

As fighting intensified, representatives from the various colonial assemblies met at the Second Continental Congress in 1775 in Philadelphia. They agreed to form a unified army to attack Boston and to appoint George Washington of Virginia to be its commander. Washington's army, composed mostly of Massachusetts militia (as Virginians and other colonial militias were reluctant to serve so far north), managed to drive the British from the city in March 1776, thanks especially to artillery captured from the British at Ticonderoga. The British forces withdrew to Halifax in Canada to regroup. By July of that year, British officials had abandoned all their posts in the thirteen colonies, and the Congress voted a Declaration of Independence on July 4, 1776. The British Parliament did not accept the declaration and began plans to mount a major expedition to reclaim the colonies. Military matters were now to come to the fore.

---

[29] The original documents of the various congresses as well as observers' reports are printed in Charles Tansill, ed., *Documents Illustrative of the Formation of the Union of the United States* (Washington, 1927), online at www.questia.com/PM.qst?a=o&d=61951136, pp. 1–22.

[30] An excellent military history of the Revolution is found in Jeremy Black, *War for America: The Fight for Independence* (New York, 1991).

The military situation that would decide the fate of the rebellion was complicated. The American colonies were defended in large measure by militias, most of whom regarded their service as local and short term. Such militias had primarily been raised to fight against the Native Americans on their borders and had adopted tactics and weapons appropriate to that style of war, which involved maneuver, ambushes, and short but sharp engagements. Native Americans were free associations, they had little fixed wealth and little incentive to protect any specific position, so they rarely stood and fought unless they had great advantage. In this situation, American militias were reluctant to serve in long campaigns, because the nature of frontier war never required it; they were anxious to attend to the agricultural cycle and were committed primarily to home defense.

On the frontier, both the indigenous people and settlers had a great deal of common ground, but the coastal regions were different, as they had cities that were the hubs of commerce and the residence of the colonial merchant and planter classes that were pressing for independence. To defend those points they had to engage in the European style of warfare, which involved massed formations of musketeers whose characteristics were that they could fire their weapons rapidly and remain calm while taking horrific causalities, culminating in bayonet charges.[31] If Americans expected to defend their cities or engage in European-style warfare, they needed to develop similar armies while making the most that they could of their own skills in the American style of war.

In the Seven Years' War – the last major engagement involving attacking cities and densely populated areas in North America – many operations had involved joint operations with Native Americans and European units (hence the name French and Indian Wars), but the situation was somewhat different in 1775. In the intercolonial war, the British subsidized the Five Nations of the Iroquois to fight on their side against the French, whereas the French used their own subsidies to the multiple nations of the Pay d'en Haut to promote their own military interests. After 1763, the British were paying subsidies and thus could claim alliance with all these groups, but their approach had alienated a great many and made their loyalty uncertain.

In 1775, British agents actively recruited Iroquois to fight in the war. From a strategic point of view, it might have been very effective for the British to encourage the Iroquois, or other more southern groups such as the Creeks or Cherokees, and other bordering groups to seek large-scale revenge on the encroaching colonizers, which would at the very least force the engagement of their militias in the west. But such a strategy was also hampered by the fact that the British hoped and indeed expected that many, and perhaps even most, of the colonial residents would favor peace over war and, whatever their grievances, join the British soldiers in rounding up the rebels. Turning indigenous fighters against the settlers in the western part of the rebellion might have some

---

[31] For the specifics of this style of warfare, and in particular its unique brutality for the soldiers, see John Keegan, *A History of Warfare* (New York, 1993).

advantages, but it would surely put them squarely in the camp of the rebels, and the government was not yet willing to take that step in hopes it could still win them over. As for the Iroquois, the group most significantly involved in the rebellion in the north, their experience with the British crown had been as ally, and at least to some degree as protector against their deadliest collective enemy – the colonial settlers whose steady encroachment all along their frontier, and whose violent anti-Native American attitudes made long-standing diplomacy with the Anglo-American settlers less fruitful. Recognizing that they were unlikely to win them to the cause of revolution, the colonies sent representatives to the Iroquois, encouraging them to declare neutrality.[32]

To preserve this option, it would be necessary to minimize the destructive power of their Native American allies, and to do the best they could with European-style fighting. British forces returned to North America in August 1776, where they landed 22,000 troops and captured New York, which then became the main base for British forces in North America. The colonial army, composed largely of militias, began disbanding, leaving Washington with only about 5,000 men to carry on the fight. After a series of small engagements, British forces took Philadelphia. In doing so, however, they neglected to carry out the two-pronged attack strategy originally intended to defeat the northern colonies.

The British plan had coupled the seaborne attack on New York with a land invasion from Canada, and at this point they were prepared to use their Iroquois allies. This army of some 10,000 British regulars, 4,000 Hessian mercenaries, and 650 Canadian militiamen and Iroquois, commanded by John Burgoyne, advanced down from Canada. The British hoped the Canadians and the Iroquois could serve as disciplined allies in their European-style military campaigns, but in this they were mistaken. Thomas Anburey, a lieutenant in Burgoyne's army, thought the Iroquois who aided them "were vast service in foraging and scouting parties ... [but] they will not stand a regular engagement." Indeed, neither the Iroquois nor the Canadian militia units, both used to the American style of war, proved effective for stand-up battles and showed themselves prone to desertion when pitched battle was imminent.[33]

The American force defeated Burgoyne's army in a series of battles around Saratoga, New York, in September–October 1777, and in the end some 5,000 troops surrendered. Horatio Gates, the American commander, had been able to win this victory over a powerful army by raising large militia forces to face it, making skillful use of the regular troops available, and skirmishing with the Anglo-German force constantly.[34] Anburey, the British officer in Burgoyne's army, noted that American riflemen, positioned in trees, picked off the officers

---

[32] Colin Calloway, *The American Revolution in Indian Country: Crisis and Diversity in Native American Communities* (Cambridge, 1995).

[33] Thomas Anburey, *Travels through the Interior Parts of America* (mod. ed. Boston, 1923 [LC Memory of America]), Letter 39, October 6, 1777, pp. 250–255 (quotation on p. 251).

[34] Richard Ketchum, *Saratoga: Turning Point of America's Revolutionary War* (New York, 1997).

regularly, and the Iroquois and Canadian troops deserted them.[35] This victory gave the colonial rebellion an important diplomatic coup, for Benjamin Franklin, who had been sent to France to seek an anti-British alliance, was able to persuade the French government to support the American cause. Dutch and Spanish armies also joined, and the subsequent war was fought in many theaters outside North America. In the meantime, the somewhat battered British army withdrew to New York and remained there, conducting no further campaigns following the Saratoga disaster.

The British, while retaining the city, could do little more than hope that the Iroquois could undo their losses, and became more willing to seek aid in that alliance. In 1778, an integrated English and Iroquois force defeated some 400–500 Pennsylvania and New York militia force at Wyoming, Pennsylvania. In this battle, the English commander noted the "Indians ... observed they should be upon an equal footing with them in the woods." Indeed, they delivered the decisive blow, killing many of the militia and torturing others, in what came to be called the "Wyoming Massacre."[36] Colonists' counterattacks in 1778–1779 met with some success, but the war had the effect of, on one hand, forcing the deployment of state militias in New York and Pennsylvania against the British, and on the other hand, preserving the commitment of otherwise neutral or even Loyalist colonists to the rebellion's side from fear of an Iroquois invasion.

In 1778, the British tried a second attack, this time on the southern colonies. In December 1778, a British force from New York took Savannah and, after repelling an attempt by a combined French and American force to retake it in October 1779, advanced northward, taking Charleston, South Carolina, on May 12, 1780. When General Benjamin Lincoln, the American commander, surrendered his command of some 5,000 troops, the British were free to control most of the coast. An attempt to retake the area by troops dispatched from New York under General Gates, the victor of Saratoga, was roundly defeated in August 1780. The British southern commander, Charles Cornwallis, then moved many of his forces northward into Virginia. However, his remaining forces in Charleston were unable to defeat the American militia and eventually were pinned in Charleston. French intervention ultimately sealed the fate of Cornwallis's army, which was trapped in Yorktown, Virginia. The French fleet under Admiral de Grasse defeated a British force at the Capes, and then nearly 11,000 French soldiers joined 8,500 Americans to press a siege. Thanks to the presence of European regular infantry and heavy artillery on the American side, Cornwallis was forced to surrender his force of 7,500 men unconditionally on October 19, 1781.

British commanders also hoped to call in the alliances that the British crown had negotiated with the indigenous people of the south to assist them militarily. The British hoped to coordinate their military efforts with the Cherokee

---

[35] Anbury, Letter 39, p. 254–255.

[36] BL Add MSS 21760, fols. 31–34, Jon Butler to Lt Col Bolton, July 8, 1778, online at http://revwar75.com/battles/primarydocs/wiom1778.htm

beginning in 1776. The British commissioner Stuart wished for them to work as auxiliaries for the British troops when they invaded, but instead, the Cherokee started their own war, reclaiming what they felt were their lands from the settlers. The militias of the Carolinas fought this war, with some success, and to the degree that they were distracted from British operations, the strategy worked to the British advantage. On the other hand, as with the British appeal to slaves, it also helped consolidate at least tacit support for the revolutionary cause by alienating many otherwise loyal settlers.

The southern campaigns raised different problems from a military standpoint than the northern ones had. In addition to the complexities of militia fighting, the divided loyalty of the colonial population (greater in the south than in the north), and the adherence of the Cherokees to the British cause and their willingness to engage the settlers on their contested frontier, the south was full of slaves. More than in the north, the aspirations of the slaves, and their potential to contribute to the military outcome, were crucial.

SLAVES AND REVOLUTION IN ENGLISH AMERICA

Most of the English colonies in the Americas faced similar fiscal demands from their European masters as did those of North America, but not all found armed revolt and revolution a viable solution. Any revolution that middle-class leaders might engineer had its dangerous side for them, namely that the lower classes may also catch the fever and make demands for more fundamental changes than just tax reform. In New England and even in the Middle Colonies, there was a fairly large population of people of modest means, who could fight in militias and be counted on to support the revolution. While some remained loyal to the crown, there was little pressure for radical social change from such people, and indeed on the whole their sense of exploitation was much less urgent than it was even for the laboring poor of Europe.

Slaves, on the other hand, did not fall into this category. For them, the potential in revolution was in the prospect of the overthrow of the existing order, gaining freedom either individually through their service on one or the other side in the fighting, or independently through revolt. The fear of a slave revolt could prove a serious damper on those societies of British America where they made up a sizable proportion of the population as they did in all colonies south of Virginia, and particularly in South Carolina where slaves were very close to a majority of the population.

The problem of the potential for slave revolt is best illustrated not as much in South Carolina as in the West Indies, where slaves generally made up a vast majority of the population. This issue was clearly revealed in the writing of the Jamaican planter and historian Edward Long, whose *History of Jamaica* appeared in 1774, on the eve of the revolution in North America. Long's chapter on the government of Jamaica stressed its constitutional similarity to the government of England: "the form of government here resembles that of England almost as nearly as the conditions of a dependent colony can be brought to resemble that of its mother country."[37] But Long's description of this constitutional system did not prevent him from seeing the same sort of inequities that Bostonians saw in their relationship with England. In his introduction, for example, Long alluded to the tyranny of royal officials operating far from England and taking on arrogant attitudes.[38]

In describing its government in detail, he complained that the governors could not function exactly as the king did, as the former must await the "king's pleasure" at such a distance; moreover, the lower house of the assembly – which he equated with the House of Commons – did not have the judicial or fiscal authority of its English counterpart, for the crown and its officials routinely pressed Jamaica for revenue outside of the sort of fiscal control that the English Commons exercised.[39] But whatever his complaints about government, Long did not think that a revolution, such as he saw brewing to the north, would work in Jamaica because of the danger of a slave revolt. Even in his introduction he remembered bitterly that Jamaicans had been advised in England that they were slave masters, and ought to "give freedom (say they to others) before you claim it for yourselves."[40]

Long had good reason to fear slave revolts. He remembered well, and gave a detailed account of, the great slave revolt of 1760–1765, known as Tackey's War. In this revolt, the slaves had risen simultaneously in five parishes, and the colonial militia, even when reinforced with Maroons, failed to make headway against the rebels. Indeed, it was only when regular English soldiers joined the fighting that the revolt was finally suppressed. Jamaicans, he believed, could not afford to cut this cord with England when thousands of exploited Africans labored in the sugar estates and dreamed of revolt.[41] Long was not wrong in this – in addition to the obvious desire that such vigorously exploited people might have to be free or even to have revenge, Afro-Jamaicans had considerable capacity. Of those who were born in Africa, a good many had military experience from African wars, as was revealed in the weapons and tactics of Tackey's War.[42]

The demography of Jamaica, particularly its brutal labor regime and unbalanced sex ratios, made it far from a self-sustaining population. Every year, thousands of newly arrived Africans came to fill in the gaps in Jamaica's population, and with them they brought military skills from Africa, honed in the

---

[37] Edward Long, *A History of Jamaica...* (3 vols., London 1774), Book 1, chapter 1, 1: 9.

[38] Long, *History*, introduction 1: 2–4 (complaints about tyranny of a very indirect nature); see also p. 7 where he complains that governors who might have written an impartial history have not done so.

[39] Long, *History*, Book 1, chapter 1, 1: 9–26.

[40] Long, *History*, introduction 1: 5.

[41] Long, *History*, Book 3, chapter 3, pp. 447–455.

[42] John Thornton, "The Coromantees: An African Cultural Group in Colonial North America and the Caribbean," *Journal of Caribbean History* 32, nos. 1–2 (1998): 161–178; and *idem*, "War, the State, and Religious Norms in Coromantee Thought," in Robert Blair St. George, ed., *Possible Pasts: Becoming Colonial in America* (Ithaca, 2000), pp. 181–200.

very wars that had enslaved them. Moreover, they had no families and had suffered traumatic experiences, so they had little to lose in making war. Such people needed to be treated with great care. The slave population of North America was different, however. In colonies like Virginia, for example, the slave population was stable and self-reproducing. The slave trade brought very few newcomers to the colony after 1770, and even in South Carolina, where there were more slaves and more of them newly arrived, the balance still favored the native born. Slaves born in the colonies did not have military experience; moreover, they had local families and dependents, which considerably reduced their willingness to risk everything in armed combat.

Although they may not have been aware of all the dynamics of a slave revolt and its potential, both military and political, the English sought to make use of the aspirations that American slaves had for their freedom to undermine the rebels' cause.[43] The potential of exploiting social tension was quickly seized upon. The colonial office in London, considering the situation in North America difficult, declared that "things are now come to a crisis, that we must avail ourselves of every resource, even to raise the Negroes in our cause."[44]

As the rebellious Massachusetts militia was laying siege to Boston and the call to other colonies to send soldiers went out, John Murray, 4th Earl of Dunmore, governor of Virginia, found himself in a difficult place.[45] With only 300 regular soldiers at his command, he could easily have been captured or killed, and indeed took refuge on a warship in the harbor at Norfolk. Dunmore, like other British officials at the outset of the revolution, believed there were more potential loyalists in the general population and issued his own call-up for a militia. Compelled, he claimed to take this "most disagreeable but now absolutely necessary step" of calling on "every person capable of bearing arms to his Majesty's Standard." But he augmented this call-up for royal service with a telling addition to "declare all indentured Servants, Negroes, or others free that are able and willing to bear arms, they joining his Majesty's troops as soon as may be."[46]

Some 800 slaves joined Dunmore, many of them women, and he was able to form Lord Dunmore's Ethiopian Regiment of 300 men from them, with uniforms that bore the motto "Liberty to Slaves." The rebellious Virginia authorities responded quickly: the *Virginia Gazette* asking slaves to not be "tempted by the proclamation to ruin your selves," and later the Virginia Convention agreed to pardon any runaways who returned to their masters. In the end, Dunmore,

---

[43] Sylvia Frey, *Water from the Rock: Black Resistance in a Revolutionary Age* (Princeton, 1991).

[44] Unreferenced in Black Loyalist page at National Archives Web site.

[45] Dunmore had been considering the enlistment of slaves since at least 1772 and occasionally threatened rebellious Virginia elites with it; Gerald Mullin, *Flight and Rebellion: Slave Resistance in Eighteenth Century Virginia* (New York, 1972), p. 131.

[46] Lord Dunmore to Major General William Howe, November 30, 1775, in William Bell Clark, ed., *Naval Documents of the American Revolution* (Washington, DC, 1966) 2: 1209–1211; a broadside of the proclamation is online at www.nationalarchives.gov.uk/pathways/blackhistory/work-_community/loyalists.htm

like the other British officials, left Virginia, taking some 300 of the runaways with him, in August 1776. Nor was Dunmore alone, for when General William Howe from the army of New York invaded the Chesapeake in 1777. before the debacle of Saratoga forced him to hole up in the city, he issued a similar proclamation granting protection to slaves who ran away to him.[47]

These attempts to recruit slaves were just precursors to the British actions in their major invasion of the southern colonies under Henry Clinton in 1778. Clinton, like Dumore before him, issued orders that all slaves who ran away to English forces to serve in the army would be granted freedom.[48] Many answered the call: according to British records, some 20,000 slaves ran away to the British as a result of their proclamations, although many – perhaps half – died during the smallpox epidemics that raged in British camps, and some 8,000 were eventually evacuated by the British when they left.[49] This was despite the fact that the British had no real intention of ending slavery, and indeed were reluctant to employ the slaves as anything other than laborers, even giving them to soldiers and selling them as need be.[50]

The order inviting slaves to run away sent a chill across the South and brought many slave owners over to the side of the revolution. Indeed, in South Carolina, where many of the planters were very loyal to the crown, the war developed as a civil war between loyalists and revolutionaries. The slave defections, runaways to the British, and those who simply melted away or went to maroon camps like the Great Dismal Swamp, represented the third wing of the revolutionary war. Planters responded to the British challenge in various ways. Jamaica received more than 60,000 new slaves between 1775 and 1785, and very few of them were from Africa; presumably British American colonists in North America were sending their slaves to the stable slave environment of Jamaica where their property could be safe. Another response was to grant, reluctantly, counteroffers for slaves to serve in the revolutionary armies in exchange for freedom.

The British offers of freedom or the counteroffers from planters may have accounted for a certain amount of liberation – and much more consternation and fear on the part of slaveholders – but in fact, the disruptions of the war, particularly in South Carolina but even in northern areas like New York, led to many slaves simply running away, moving and changing their status or taking advantage of the situation in other ways.[51]

---

[47] Cited in Cassandra Pybus, "Jefferson's Faulty Math: The Question of Slave Defections in the American Revolution," *William and Mary Quarterly* 62 (2005): 243–264, at p. 260 n. 16.

[48] Pybus, "Jefferon's Math," p. 265 n. 20 citing document in British National Archives.

[49] For a detailed discussion of the numbers involved, see Cassandra Pybus, "Jefferson's Faulty Math," pp. 243–264.

[50] Frey, *Water*, p. 80–87.

[51] For the New York example, see Paul Gilje, "Between Slavery and Freedom: New York African Americans in the Early Republic," *Reviews in American History* 20 (1992): 163–167, especially 164.

The slaves who fled to the British were generally recruited under military aegis, although as it happened, from Dunmore's appeal onward, a good many women and children were accepted. However, only a few were organized as combat units – Dunmore's Ethiopian Regiment and a few other units, such as the Black Carolina Corps – while the vast majority served in the Pioneer Corps. Pioneers were not combat units and served as support troops, most in sanitary and construction work. They were valuable to the British effort, not only for their services, but more for the damage they inflicted on the American economy. They were commanded by white officers and to the degree that they possessed obvious military training and efficacy it came from their European-style training rather than anything they brought from Africa, even though the "Negro Book" that noted by name one group taken from South Carolina did record a fair number of African-born among them.

When the British withdrew from North America, they took a good number of the runaways with them. The majority of them went to the Bahamas and Jamaica. Although many of them were slaves and were dragooned into leaving with their loyalist masters, others had fought on the side of the British in return for their freedom. Members of the Black Carolina Corps organized in South Carolina in 1779 later saw service on Grenada, Martinique, and other islands. They and others became the nucleus of the West India regiment used for the defense of the West Indies. These black loyalists were scattered throughout the West Indies, Europe, and Nova Scotia, while others, abandoned by the British, fled Spanish West Florida to escape being reenslaved by the victorious southerners.

GRIEVANCE AND PROTEST IN IBERIAN AMERICA

The Spanish and Portuguese colonies also had their grievances; the centralization of the Spanish Empire under the Bourbon Dynasty had led to general discontent among the *criollos*, as the locally born Spanish inhabitants were called. As elsewhere, this middle class wanted fiscal reform and freedom from domination by monopolists and crown officials, but not at the expense of their special social position.

Criollos were at times driven to revolt. With the spirit of the American Revolution in the air, the Comuñero revolt in New Granada (modern-day Colombia) broke out in 1781. The initial leaders were the same sort of men who had led the movement against the English in North America, primarily merchants and tradespeople who suffered with taxation policies and trading restrictions.[52] A particularly ruthless tax collector, named Juan Francisco Gutiérrez de Piñeres, sent to Bogotá in 1779, so irritated the local elites with his tax increases and brutal collection procedures that they revolted. A large band of insurgents attacked the government officials in Socorro and drove them out, replacing them with officials that they elected themselves. The supporters of the

---

[52] A standard interpretation and history is John Phelan, *The People and the King* (Madison, 1978).

initial leader, Juan Francisco Berbeo, were mostly farmers, traders, and local municipal officials, but as the revolt spread to other towns, they were joined by a number of indigenous people. They marched in Bogotá, the colonial capital, and demanded the recession of taxes and other onerous duties. Once this was granted, however, Berbeo dispersed his men, allowing the Spanish authorities to reassert control.

As in North America, there was the danger of revolt unleashing discontent from the lower classes that might unhinge the social order that the *criollos* hoped to maintain. For many regions of Spanish America, the threat was not so great from the slaves as it was from the restive Native American population. In Peru, for example, there had been many revolts among the population classed as "Indian" and still living under the descendants of their ancient rulers, known in Peru as *curacas*. The idea that there might still be a *pachacuti*, or "reversal," and the Spanish would be thrown out had never been stilled since the days of the Taki Onoqi in the sixteenth century. In the eighteenth century, these beliefs were represented by the idea that the last Incas had somehow built a secret state in the densely wooded interior, and that they would return to drive out the Spanish. The Bourbon reforms and subsequent centralization had caused disproportionate problems for the *curaca* class, which lost some of its prerequisites, and businesses of others suffered through the commercial reorganization. The possibility of a restoration of the Incas was in the air, and in the 1740s, Juan Santos Atalhalpa led a rebellion that claimed to restore the descendants of Atahualapa, the Inca ruler executed by Pizarro. Peru suffered five rebellions in the 1740s, eleven in the 1750s, twenty in the 1760s, and another twenty in the 1770s. Most were small and easily suppressed, but their frequency indicated that the reforms had shaken society.

Then, just before the Comuñero revolt would divide Colombia, Peru was shaken to its core by the greatest of the colonial revolts, the Tupac Amaru. The revolt began as a simple protest of Jose Gabriel Condorcanqui, a *curaca* of Tinta in the region near the old Inca capital of Cuzco, who was well educated and thoroughly Hispanicized, married to a mestiza, and counted Spaniards and mestizos among his closest friends. He had sought to demonstrate his blood relationship to earlier Incas, especially the last independent Inca, Túpac Amaru I, whose semi-independent kingdom had been extinguished by the Spanish in 1572. Like many other disaffected *curacas* of his day, he read with great interest the work of Garcilasco de la Vega, a mestizo of the late sixteenth century, whose mother was of royal Inca blood, and who had presented an idealized view of pre-conquest Inca society.[53]

---

[53] There is substantial literature on the rebellion; see most recently, Ward Stavig, *The World of Tupac Amaru: Conflict, Community and Identity in Colonial Peru* (Lincoln, 1999) for context; for the events themselves, see Nicholas Robbins, *Genocide and Millenialism in Upper Peru: The Great Rebellion of 1780–82* (Greenwood, 2002), esp. pp. 23–58 for historiography. The Peruvian National Archives published a large, seven-volume collection of documents relevant to the rebellion (but only in Peru) in *Colección documental del bicentenario de la revolución emancipadora de Túpac Amaru* (Lima, 1980–1981).

On November 4, 1780, Condorcanqui ordered the *corregidor* Antonio Arriaga, a notoriously cruel and ruthless official, arrested and executed under the ancient Inca law, which he claimed had been falsely suppressed by the Spanish occupation. He issued orders in his own name, but also in the name of the Spanish king, eliminating many Spanish institutions. In a letter to his relative, the *curaca* Diego Chuquiguanaca, he noted he had received from "a superior order" a commission to extinguish *corregidors* – that no more would come – as well as the totality of the "mitas of Potosí," fiscal measures, customs restrictions, "and many other pernicious novelties."[54] Shortly afterward, he issued a proclamation, noting that he hoped to unite the indigenous population and the locally born "creoles, mestizos, zambos [offspring of African and Native American parents] and Indians" against the "oppression and tyranny of the Europeans," assuring those *criollos* who join him that they would remain under his protection. He signed the letter and the proclamation as "D. Jose Gabriel Túpac-Amaru, Inca."[55] Indeed, the lower-class elements of Túpac Amaru's followers were pressing to eliminate Christianity, and in the end even Túpac Amaru himself told his forces besieging Cuzco that they must not invoke the name of Jesus or confess.

Although Túpac Amaru carried out this rebellion with limited aims and a limited agenda, he decided to take up arms against the government, and initially defeated the colonial force sent against him at Sangarará. He then took his forces to Cuzco and laid siege to the city, while at the same time sending them messages and pleas to join his movement and take common cause against Spain.[56] Although he appealed to the powerful *curacas* descended from the governing families of Inca Peru, they refused to budge in their loyalty to the crown, much to his dismay. Peru had been held, more or less jointly, by Spain and Inca nobles, but these nobles were best represented by the ancient alliance between the "Lords of Cuzco" and the governors rather than by the *curacas* of the countryside. It was Túpac Amaru's mistake to assume that the division of the country would be Indian against Spaniard, and not along the lines of the same civil war that had brought the Spanish into Peru in the first place.[57]

The Spanish government responded to this threat by mobilizing a large force, which included a substantial number of Native American and mestizo troops, which broke the siege and captured Túpac Amaru. He was ordered to be executed on May 18, 1781, and to witness the prior execution of his wife, family, and a number of followers. Moreover, Governor José Antonio de Areche also decided to suppress the wearing of Incan clothing, including the long-held customs of dress among the elite, so as not to recall either the Incas or the rebellion.[58]

---

[54] Túpac Amaru to Cacique D. Diego, November 15, 1780, in *Documentos para Tupac Amaru* (Buenos Aires, 1836), pp. 15–16.

[55] Don José Gariel Túpac Amaru, Inca, December 15, 1780, in *Documentos*, pp. 13–14.

[56] Texts of the several letters in *Documentos*, pp. 15–30.

[57] David T. Garrett, *The Shadows of Empire: The Inca Nobles of Cuzco, 1750–1825* (Cambridge, 2005), pp. 183–210.

[58] Sentencia pronunciada en el Cuzco por ... contra José Gabriel Tupac-Amaru ..., n.d. [1781], in *Documentos*, p. 48 (whole text is pp. 44–51).

Although Túpac Amaru's rebellion was initially led by reform-minded *cura-cas*, it was accompanied by an independent and much more radical movement led by Tomás Catari in the province of Chayanta in Upper Peru. Whereas Túpac Amaru was content with governmental reform and the ending of Spain's rule (while ironically somehow still remaining under the Spanish king), Catari and his brothers, who continued the rebellion following Túpac Amaru's execution in 1781, wished to drive out all Europeans, *criollos*, mestizos, and Afro-Peruvians and to return to a purely indigenous way of life. After the suppression of the Cuzco rebellion and Túpac Amaru's capture and execution in 1781, the stronger attitudes of the Cataris' movement prevailed and spread southward into what would be modern-day Bolivia and even northern Argentina. Julián Túpac Catari and his followers laid siege to La Paz on March 13, 1781 with some 40,000 followers until colonial troops raised the siege on July 1, forcing the Amaristas to retreat to the hills, only to resume it when royal troops evacuated the city. However, a larger royal army arrived and captured Julián Túpac Catari.

Even as La Paz was under siege, yet another would-be Inca, Tomás Catari, started attacks around Potosí, which soon spread to Tucumán in upper Argentina. Even farther away, there were demonstrations in favor of the movement without reaching the point of armed insurrection. The Indians began to advocate anti-Spanish attitudes, including attempts to purge their language off all Spanish words, to end using Spanish tools and clothing, and to return to an idealized – but actually radical – past in which the ayallu governed all affairs. Despite its anti-Spanish rhetoric, however, the movement still had Christian elements in its ideology. Spanish authorities under the Viceroy Agustin de Jáuregui declared a general amnesty on 1September 17, 1781 in hopes of breaking the rebellion, and included a number of palliative measures, abandoning tax measures and forced labor. On the whole, however, these were not followed by the Spanish, who pressed the war on, capturing most of the remaining leadership by August 1783. Ironically, although much of the Indian nobility of Peru had stood by the colonial government during the rebellion, the crown's long-term reaction was to make a long-lasting but effective attack on the whole cacique class. Indeed, the punishment of the highlands of Peru was simply more, and heavier, taxes with fewer privileges for all.[59]

The initial phases of the Túpac Amaru revolt coincided with the Comuñero movement in New Granada, and when that revolt spread from its initial home in Socorro to the Llanos, the flat plain in the interior of the colony, the leaders of the revolt – who, like those farther north, were largely locally born criollos and some mestizos – abolished the tribute that indigenous people paid to win their loyalty; moreover, their leader swore loyalty to Tupac Amaru and declared himself governor of the province.[60] In this case, the rebellion spread

---

[59] Garrett, *Shadows of Empire*, pp. 211–224.
[60] This phase of the rebellion is covered in Jane M. Loy, "The Forgotten Comuneros: The 1781 Revolt in the Llanos of Casanare," *Hispanic American Historical Review* 61 (1981): 235–257.

to new ethnic groups, ones that had not in fact been part of the historic Inca Empire, and combined with an existing revolt by the local elites, even though they actually had fought separately and cooperated only warily. The possibility of collaboration between such diverse groups was raised by the revolt, although Spanish authorities were eventually able to restore order.

These various tensions and dangers, revealed as they were in the American Revolution, made the idea of a violent break from France, Spain, and Portugal unappealing on the whole. However, all three of these countries would be caught up in the events that stemmed from the French Revolution, first in France and its colonies and then in Spain and Portugal as the latter were drawn into war with France. Monarchies were overthrown or challenged in Europe, and the colonies were drawn into the affairs of Europe. Whereas the English colonies had reacted after a century to the establishment of parliamentary rule in 1688, the other European colonial powers were literally hurled into independence and self-government, almost in spite of themselves, by the rapid changes in Europe.

FRANCE AND SAINT DOMINGUE

The first American revolution in the British colonies of North America might be said to have had its starting point in the Glorious Revolution of 1688 and certainly in the establishment of the parliamentary system in England which took firm hold in the eighteenth century. Although participants on both continents took advantage of the aspirations of the lower classes or exploited and marginal people at times, the American Revolution was not in general a social revolution. This was not the case with the French Revolution in Europe or its American cousin, the Haitian Revolution, and the independence movements in Spanish America also had more radical social objective than the American Revolution. Both engaged the lower and exploited classes fully, if not always successfully from their point of view, and both found the social element of the revolution coming to the fore at times.

The French Revolution started from a fiscal crisis in 1788–1789, which ultimately came about from the expenses the state incurred in supporting the American Revolution as well as other late-eighteenth-century wars. By 1788, it was clear that the usual means of redressing the crisis were not adequate, and King Louis XVI summoned the Estates General to propose general taxation to the noble and ecclesiastical orders. The Estates had not met since 1614, and there was no clear-cut agenda or method of procedure, because France in 1789 was far from being the same country as it had been a century and a half earlier. From the beginning they ran into problems, because the nobles and the church, which made up the first two Estates, were primarily anxious to protect their fiscal privileges, while the non-nobles of the Third Estate (most of whom were also wealthy and propertied) wished to see the burden shared more equitably. When the noble Estates made it clear that they were not going to entertain grievances of the Third Estate, it met separately and declared itself the National Assembly.

As this standoff reached crisis proportions, the king brought troops into Paris, with the intention of dissolving the Assembly and the whole project. At that moment, the ordinary people of Paris, who had been suffering for several years from famine and high prices, rioted in favor of the Assembly. Fearful of their threat, the king backed down and met the Assembly, and the noble Estates renounced their privileges. The first Revolution was complete.

But the continued wrangling over the shape of the constitution and the role of the king did not resolve the crisis or lead to a return to normal politics. Foreign powers – Prussia, Austria, Russia, and Brunswick, to name just a few – expressed fear and saw opportunities in France's troubles and sent troops to invade France. But the French were able to secure the loyalty of most of their royal army and augmented it with thousands of volunteers, who soon formed a large army of their own. This new army in turn became a force in Paris, and in a new run of conflict in 1791 turned the revolution in a distinctly more radical direction. The king was tried and executed, and the country was declared a Republic. Rural peasants began to attack the royal chateaux, military force could not hold them back, and eventually the lands of the church were nationalized to help defray both the debt and the war costs. Even though very few of the members of the various French governing bodies that came in this period were truly sympathetic to the seizure of land by peasants or the demands of the urban mobs, they did not hesitate to recruit them into their own less dramatic struggles with rival parties in the emerging legislature.[61]

Across the Atlantic, European, African, and American roots of revolution came together in the French colonies of America. The French Revolution was far more radical, even as a purely elite political movement, than eighteenth-century English political institutions that gave rise to the American Revolution, and moreover, gave more opportunities for social forces to be released. Throughout the French Caribbean, there were tensions between France and its colonial elites, and there were also inter-elite conflicts, especially as the French Caribbean had a large number of African-descended and mixed-race landholders relative to the English colonies in either the Caribbean or North America. These mixed-race elites had been politically and socially excluded from participation in colonial decision making and thus nursed grievances that they were quick to press when the opportunity presented itself.

In addition to the elite politics, the French Caribbean, like all the Caribbean colonies, held a vast number of slaves, who outnumbered the European-descended and mixed-race people considerably, and who might be recruited into the politics of revolution as deemed necessary. Indeed, the colony of Saint Domingue would be the theater of such recruitment, but there, slaves also acted on their own accord.

Saint Domingue in the late eighteenth century was France's most prosperous colony, and as with the other American colonies, the elite of the merchants

---

[61] For a survey of the French revolution, see William Doyle, *The Oxford History of the French Revolution* (2nd ed., Oxford, 2002).

and planters there had strong grievances about commercial restrictions and government on the island. It had a highly varied social structure: some half a million slaves, half of whom were African-born, labored on its plantations. The majority worked in sugar estates in the northern half of the island, but other crops such as coffee, cotton, and indigo also used slave labor. These crops were often grown on small plantations, especially in the south of the colony. Saint Domingue was unusual in that it possessed a large, free, and wealthy population of African origins – the *gens de coleur*. Many were the descendants of the earlier planters who had left lands and slaves to the offspring of their slave wives and mistresses, and had waxed prosperous, especially in the lesser crops like coffee, which required relatively low capital inputs. Some had served in the French forces that had fought on the colonial side in the American Revolution, where they formed their own ideas about colonial freedom.

When the French Revolution broke out, a number of colonial factions sought to capitalize on it to gain new rights. As the Third Estate called for representatives from across France to form the National Assembly, Saint Domingue's wealthy planters sent a delegation, and after a discussion, six of them were seated. In the debates of 1790, they lobbied for the elimination of the colonial restrictions (such as the metropolitan control of exports) that were most onerous to them.[62] At the same time, poorer European residents of Saint Domingue formed revolutionary clubs, and local assemblies were formed in the major towns, most of them hostile to recent French policy and seeking at the very least greater political autonomy of the island. Two assemblies were eventually established: one at Saint Marc in the south, dominated by the coffee and indigo planters who hoped to see the end of many of the commercial policies that hurt their profits; the other in the north at Cap François, the capital, dominated by the large planters of the Plaine du Nord and the merchants who sided more firmly with the royal policy.

While the French Assembly discussed the demands of the major colonial planters, they received with interest petitions sent by middle-class planters drawn from the *gens de coleur* in Saint Domingue, who were residing in France.[63] The leaders of this group were slave owners themselves, but were irked by the explicitly racist legislation of colonial Saint Domingue. Among them were Julien Raimond and Vincent Ogé, mixed-race planters, who were supported by French intellectuals opposed to racism and slavery, most notably the radical priest Henri Grégoire and an antislavery organization, *Les amis des noirs*, founded in 1787. Raimond, who was wealthy enough to own more than 100 slaves in Saint Domingue, had moved to France in the mid-1780s, and had written pamphlets demanding that the French colonial officials refuse to accept laws that not only excluded wealthy *gens de coleur* from political

---

[62] A good narrative history of the revolution is Laurent Dubois, *Avengers of the New World: The Story of the Haitian Revolution* (Cambridge, MA, and London, 2004). He relies heavily on the work of Gabriel Debien, *Les colons de Saint-Domingue et la Revolution: Essai sur le Club Massiac (août 1789–août 1792)* (Paris, 1951) for the French side.

[63] Dubois, *Avengers*, pp. 71–85.

privileges, such holding many offices (including military ones, in spite of their forced service in the militia), but even forbade them from wearing certain types of clothing or participating in cultural events.[64]

Once the revolution had created the Assembly, and particularly after it passed its famous Declaration of the Rights of Man in 1789, the colored leaders hoped they could use these principles to obtain further rights in Saint Domingue. Within the colony, *gens de coleur* had been systematically rebuffed in their attempts to join the local Assemblies. Raimond and Ogé lobbied the French Assembly to abolish racial distinctions and allow the wealthier class of colored men to be represented in local government, but they also wanted the whole colonial government revised to allow qualified (that is, wealthy) property owners to be considered as legislators regardless of color or origin. On the other hand, they were more equivocal on the question of slavery; as slave owners, they were reluctant, in spite of the radical claims of some of their French allies, to rail against slavery (although Ogé did argue that there might be gradual abolition, and others argued that mixed-race slaves might be free).[65] The result was sufficiently alarming to the wealthy white colonial delegates that they formed an organization, the Club de Massiac, to counter its propaganda.

While some in the Assembly considered Raimond and Ogé's vision carefully, the final result was that granting them rights would compromise the loyalty of the planters and push the colony toward independence. Thus, in spite of their initial support for extending full citizenship rights to the non-European-descended elite, the Assembly ultimately capitulated to the wealthier representatives and accepted the idea that all citizens could vote, but refused to acknowledge that the mixed-race inhabitants could be citizens.[66] Bitterly disappointed by this capitulation, Ogé returned to Saint Domingue in July 1790 with weapons to arm mixed-race citizens against the local assemblies that had steadfastly refused to grant them the franchise. His revolt won immediate support, and he occupied several towns. From there he wrote to demand the vote, while noting that his petition said nothing about the slaves who were to "remain in their slavery." The revolt was crushed, however, and Ogé was brutally killed. Although the National Assembly in France did grant some franchise to free colored people that year, it was a dead letter when it arrived in the colonies, and many planters were prepared to invite the English or another slave-owning power to take over and drive out the French rather than change the social order.[67]

[64] Julien Raimond, *Observations sur l'origine et les progrès du préjugé des colons blancs contre les hommes de couleur* (Paris, 1791) is the final product of earlier, more ephemeral efforts. See also his petition to the Assembly, *idem, Observations adressées à l'Assemblée Nationale par un deputé des colons américains* (Paris, 1789).

[65] Dubois, *Avengers*, p. 81.

[66] David Geggus, "Racial Equality, Slavery, and Colonial Secession during the Constituent Assembly," *American Historical Review* 94 (1989): 1290–1308.

[67] Dubois, *Avengers*, pp. 82–90.

Just as the French Revolution had started with the middle class and worked its way down to the urban mob and peasants, so the Saint Domingue civil war worked its way to revolution. In part, this may have been because the wealthy planters began arming their slaves to meet the challenge of the colored militia, but in part it was quite an independent movement among the slaves.

The slave revolt of 1791 undoubtedly took its cue from the dissentions and fighting going on in the previous year. Its leaders were not oblivious to the course of the French Revolution, but on the whole it grew out of the slave condition and was not summoned forth by the colonial leadership to buttress its own efforts, as slave recruitment had been in the American Revolution and would be again in Spanish America.

The slave revolt broke out in September 1791 on the Plaine du Nord, the great sugar-growing region of Saint Domingue's north coast. The initial leadership was, like that of the revolution in general, the "middle class" among the slaves. These were the skilled slaves, and especially the *commandeurs d'atelier*, or slave drivers. As the Swiss visitor to the island, Justin Girod de Chantrans, commented in the mid-1780s, the typical estate was a highly centralized and structured society, which he likened to the Ottoman Empire, the European paradigm of autocratic centralization and stratification, and in this empire, the *commandeur d'atelier* enjoyed great power and authority.[68] Most of them were born on the island and spoke creole French rather than an African language. While they organized production, disciplined the workforce, and made the fundamental decisions, as slaves they enjoyed only a mildly better lifestyle than the slaves they supervised. They watched as the *economes*, or European employees of the absentee owners, many of whom were not competent to run the daily life of the estate, enjoyed a much higher lifestyle and faced none of the restrictions that slaves and even free people of African descent endured.[69] Some 200 plotters, the majority of them *commandeurs*, met in a secret conspiracy at Bois Caïman and planned to order the ordinary slaves to revolt in support of their demands, which were largely to be free and able to enjoy the fruits of being skilled and being supervisors.[70]

The slave revolt began so soon after the death of Ogé, and in the politically charged atmosphere of dissention and discussion among the slave owners, the *petit blancs*, or landless people of European descent, and colonial maneuvering in Paris and on the island, it was inevitable that some would hear one of the interested parties involved in it. The idea that one or another group of outsiders, either local whites or Europeans, had incited the revolt for their own ends was bandied about at the time, and has found some support among modern

---

[68] Justin Girod de Chantrans, *Voyage d'un Suisse dans les colonies d'Amérique* (1785, mod. ed. Pierre Pluchon, Paris, 1980), p. 124.

[69] On the role of *commandeurs d'atelier*, see Dubois, *Avengers*, pp. 36–39.

[70] John Thornton, "'I Am the Subject of the King of Congo': African Political Ideology in the Haitian Revolution," *Journal of World History* 4 (1993): 181–214, at p. 199.

historians.[71] By and large, however, most historians see the slave revolt of 1791 as yet another large-scale slave rebellion, like the massive flight of slaves in the Dutch wars in Brazil that led to the creation of Palmares, or perhaps the several revolts that had wracked the Caribbean, such as the Saint John revolt of 1733 or Tackey's War in Jamaica in 1760. The circumstances of the French Revolution and other political situations made it far more successful than those earlier attempts.

While the Bois Caïman plot and subsequent uprising coordinated by *commandeurs d'atelier* certainly point to a straightforward operation of the hierarchy of slave society, this leadership group was not capable of raising or leading the sort of military forces that would lead to victory. To achieve this, they had to rely on the military skills of the African-born slaves who had served in African wars. It was the presence of these African slaves that allowed the rebels to create a remarkably disciplined and effective military force, apparently out of nothing.[72] The role of African veterans and the goals of the *commandeurs* were made clear in a letter that Jean François, one of the early leaders, wrote to some commissioners sent from France a few months after the revolution began. After first proposing that he and a small group of his coconspirators be granted freedom and amnesty in exchange for turning in his followers, Jean François complained that his soldiers were all "negroes [*nègres*] of the coast [that is, newly arrived Africans] who for the most part can scarcely make out two words of French, but who above all were accustomed to warfare [*à guerroyer*] in their country." The military necessity of using them had made him uncomfortably subject to their "general will," which he could not control.[73]

The revolution rapidly freed a large segment of the land in the Plaine du Nord and developed its own organization, usually built around fortified estates. Military units, often called "*bandes*" in the contemporary documentation, operated around these estates. The bands were frequently set up on the basis of African nations and brought together people from similar cultural and military backgrounds.[74] Initially, the *commandeurs* sought to coordinate the activities of the many bands that made up their following, but as Jean François noted very early on, bodies that formed in this way were unstable, and the higher-level leaders were often challenged by the leaders of the bands. By 1792, however, Toussaint Louverture, a *commandeur* who would rise to become the general leader of the revolt, was organizing his own military forces, generally from slaves loyal to him, but trained to fight in European manner by Spanish and French renegades or by *gens de coleur* with militia experience who, after at first fighting hard against the rebellion, gradually came to join it. These military

---

[71] A number of examples of contemporary claims are cited in Dubois, *Avengers*, pp. 102–105; for modern interpretations, see Ralph Korngold, *Citizen Toussaint* (London, 1945); and more recently in the novel by Madison Smart Bell, *All Soul's Rising* (New York, 1997).

[72] For the specifically military aspects of this, see John Thornton, "African Soldiers in the Haitian Revolution," *Journal of Caribbean History* 25 (1991): 58–72.

[73] ANF D-XXV, I, 4, doc. 6, Jean François and Bissau to Commissioners, October 12, 1791.

[74] Thornton, "King of Kongo," p. 203.

units would become the demi-brigades that fought with him against opponents of the revolution.[75]

Thus within a year or two, the slave revolt had developed two distinct military organizations. The first were military units organized largely by the slave elite, former *commandeurs* for the most part, like Toussaint L'Ouverture, Jean-Jacques Dessalines, or Henri Christophe. These demi-brigades that fought in European style would come to form a formidable regular army that could hold its own against French or English units. For their officers, the end of the revolution was independence, the formal end of slavery, and the recognition of the former *commandeur* as the owner or manager of estates, which continued to function effectively – if not formally – exactly as slave plantations had.

The second organization were the bands that had been organized on African regional or ethnic lines, often headed by a "king" and fighting using African techniques and tactics. Their leadership was drawn from among the slaves and particularly the African born, and almost surely drew on seasoned veteran soldiers of African wars, perhaps with their leadership drawn from enslaved elements of former officers in African armies.[76] Neither group could win the war of liberation on their own, and when British forces invaded the island in 1793, and especially when Napoleon sent a strong army there in 1802, they had to cooperate, uneasily as it happened, to carry the day.

Whereas the *commandeurs* clearly wanted to gain their freedom and obtain the income of estates operating as they had under slavery, the ideology of the bands was different. We can glimpse some idea of the ideologies of rebel slaves from both Africa and earlier revolts. In the formation of Palmares, for example, Angolans with military experience built a kingdom with a system of military ranks – undoubtedly the product of the necessity to fight to defend themselves – that included capturing and holding others as slaves.[77] In the 1739 conspiracy alleged to have been formed on Antigua, slaves from the "Coromantee" nation elected a king among themselves and presented this king as a potential local broker through enacting an Akan ennobling ceremony.[78] Where authorities recognized such brokers for slaves, as happened in Pernambuco, Brazil, for example, the system might be institutionalized, although it was suppressed on Antigua. Jamaican Maroons at about the same time (1739–1740) also used an ennobling ceremony to demand recognition of an independent polity headed by a "captain," much as it happened when a new town was built in the Gold Coast.[79] Tackey's War also featured a king and was probably an attempt to build a larger Akan nation in Jamaica, controlling part of the island. In short, slaves on the verge of rebellion typically sought to create an independent society

[75] Thornton, "King of Kongo," pp. 204–206.

[76] Thornton, "King of Kongo," and Thornton, "African Soldiers."

[77] John Thornton, "Les États de l'Angola et la formation de Palmares (Brésil)," *Annales: Histoire, Sciences sociales* 63/4 (2008): 769–797.

[78] John Thornton, "War, the State, and Religious Norms in Coromantee Thought," in Robert Blair St. George, ed., *Possible Pasts: Becoming Colonial in America* (Ithaca, 2000), pp. 181–200.

[79] Thornton, "War, the State and Religious Norms."

under their direction within or outside the colonial setting, and were prepared to establish an elected monarchy of a sort that was far more achievement-based and democratic than was found in the polities of Africa.

National or ethnic loyalties were as prominent among the Saint Domingue rebel slaves as they were elsewhere among rebellious slaves in the Atlantic world. We know of bands formed from Igbo, Yoruba, and Ewe-Fon origins from among the documents and records, but the Congo nation was perhaps the most numerous. Roughly half of all slave imports into Saint Domingue had been from Kongo, and the Congo nation was augmented by a wave of new arrivals, from the civil war in Kongo that gained intensity after the death of Afonso V in 1785. Macaya, one of the revolution's lesser leaders, told the French commissioners who came to enlist him in the Republican army in 1793 that he served three kings: "The King of France who is my Father, the King of Spain who is my mother, and the King of Congo, who is lord of all the blacks."[80] Thus the monarchical model found in other slave revolts was repeated here, using Kongo models of royalism and limited government reflected in, for example, Kongo's coronation oaths, and cloaked in Christian religious symbolism that Africanized Jesus.[81]

While the slave revolt had created both a free zone and a group of armies in the north, the other parts of the colony went their own way. The *gens de coleur*, no friends of slave revolt, formed their own party, and in the changed circumstances declared their own assembly in 1791; when the governor ordered it disbanded they took up arms, led by André Rigaud. After forming an alliance with some of the bands of former slaves (affectionately called "The Swiss" after the Papal Guards), they proved capable of defending themselves, and won some white planters to their side, but not enough to stop a civil war from breaking out in which both sides armed their slaves or brought rebels into their ranks. In the confusion, slaves ran away, formed bands, and soon had created their own "republic" in the Platons region.[82]

At the end of 1791, the French National Assembly sent commissioners to rule Saint Domingue as a colony, but one in which slavery continued and free colored people were excluded from citizenship. The commissioners were unable to get the planter-dominated local government to accept even amnesty for the elite slaves who offered to use their authority to end the rebellion. In 1792, the National Assembly, now more radical, declared that all who met property qualifications could vote and serve in the Assembly, and their commissioners made immediate alliances with the *gens de coleur* while maneuvering to bring the leaders of the slave insurrection under government control. They met bitter political resistance in both France and Saint Domingue by the planter classes, various colonial white groups, and merchants.[83]

---

[80] François-Joseph Pamphile Lacroix, *Mémoires pour server à l'histoire de la revolution de Saint-Domingue* (2 vols., Paris, 1819) 1: 125 (quoting a lost original document).
[81] Thornton, "King of Kongo."
[82] Dubois, *Avengers*, pp. 117–122; 134–139.
[83] Dubois, *Avengers*, pp. 139–147.

In 1793, events in Saint Domingue took a new turn, when England and Spain declared war on France and then used the opportunity to seek to occupy the French colony for their profit. Spanish officials soon contacted some of the slave insurgent leaders to enlist them as auxiliaries in the Spanish armies, although in fact they were independent units under their own command. The English, on the other hand, worked with planters who hoped that the arrival of seasoned European troops would end the rebellion and put the slaves back to work.[84] The Republican commissioners, Sonothax and Polverel, sought to make concessions to find the forces to counter this threat. The commissioners tried hard to enlist forces to put down their political opponents. In a desperate move to secure the loyalty of more insurgents, they abolished slavery on October 31, 1793 and gave all former slaves the rights of citizens.[85]

The abolition of slavery appears to have won over Toussaint Louverture, one of the most powerful band leaders, who joined the Republic against the Spanish (whom he had formerly served) early in 1794. He was soon at war with other prominent leaders from the slave elite, such as Jean François and Biassou, who eventually accepted commissions in the Spanish armies and enjoyed further careers in that state.[86] As Louverture became recognized by the French revolutionary government as the effective military ruler of the island in 1794, they worked with him to try to restore order. With his assistance and those of other band leaders, the Republicans were able to push back the Spanish and tie the British down to a relatively small area in the west and south.

One of the ironies of the revolution was that while great parcels of the country passed under control of the rebels, many plantations never revolted and continued producing sugar as if there was no revolution. Neither Rigaud nor Louverture wanted the plantation economy to end, although Louverture, like other *commandeurs*, supported abolishing slavery. As the situation in Saint Domingue calmed following the expulsion of the English, Louverture, who enjoyed the de facto status of ruler, brought as many bands under his authority as he could. To reinstate the plantation system, which had been destroyed in much of the island by the revolution, he invited French landowners to return and restored properties to French owners who had not fled as long as they accepted his rule and redistributed the remaining estates to his officers.[87]

However, Louverture could not easily persuade the former slaves to return to the harsh labor regime that made sugar production so profitable, and he was compelled to institute forced labor to keep plantations running. Thus, even as

---

[84] For the English role, see David Geggus, *Slavery, War, and Revolution: The British Occupation of Saint Domingue, 1793–1798* (Oxford, 1982).

[85] Dubois, *Avengers*, pp. 152–167.

[86] Dubois, *Avengers*, pp. 171–180, 183. For the further adventures of Jean François and Biassou, see Jane Landers, "Rebellion and Loyalism in Spanish Florida," in David Barry Gaspar and David Geggus, eds., *A Turbulent Time: The French Revolution and the Greater Caribbean* (Bloomington, 1997), pp. 156–171.

[87] Dubois, *Avengers*, pp. 184–193, a position very sympathetic to Toussaint; for a more critical position, see Pierre Pluchon, *Toussaint Louverture: De l'esclavage à pouvoir* (Paris, 1979).

Louverture managed to drive off French and British attempts to reestablish the old system in Saint Domingue, he all but reinstated slavery in it himself.[88] The regime of forced labor was difficult to institute, because many former slaves still bore arms and were integrated into bands with their own command structure. A moment of clear tension came when Macaya, a Kongo band leader with a considerable following, revolted against Louverture in 1796 and went to raise his army. Civil war loomed and at times broke out during this period.[89]

These tensions probably explain why Louverture was prepared to cooperate with French forces sent by Napoleon to the island in 1802, ostensibly to restore order and to regularize relations with France. In fact, Napoleon planned to reinstate slavery, disband all other military forces, and, if possible, arrest or neutralize all former slave leaders. The commander of the expedition, Charles Leclerc, cooperated with Louverture against the rebel band leaders, but Leclerc overplayed his hand when he arrested Louverture. The game revealed, Louverture's lieutenants revolted, rejoined the bands, and fought to drive the French out. As in the 1790s, the combination was successful: Leclerc's forces were defeated, and Napoleon was forced to abandon the island. In 1804, Saint Domingue became independent as Haiti, though not yet recognized by any other country.[90] Its further history, as the tension between the bandes and the elite played out into the 1820s, is beyond the scope of this book.

The French Revolution had its own impact elsewhere in the Caribbean, and here France sought to use its revolutionary ideology and radical social agenda to wage social warfare. France had done this even prior to the Revolution. When French forces that had seized Dominica from the English during the American Revolution in 1778 were told to evacuate following the transfer of that colony back to England in accordance with the Peace of Paris in 1783, Governor Duchailleau refused to accept the result and sent weapons to the runaway slaves of the hinterland, who, joined by some slaves held by French settlers and other Frenchmen, conducted a vigorous resistance that lasted until 1786. It was only by forming "legions" of free Africans, local creole Europeans, and some slaves that the English were able to defeat the rebels and take their strong points, but even then the war continued on a lesser scale.[91]

Following the declaration of war in 1793, Britain, working with royalist elements, had occupied many of the other French colonies in the Caribbean. A former planter of Saint Domingue, Victor Hugues, was dispatched to Guadeloupe in 1794 where, by using France's abolition of slavery as a tool, he mobilized slaves into military units and expelled the English and the royalist garrison. He mobilized these ex-slaves into an army; indeed, the majority of the military forces Hugues mobilized to make attacks on St. Lucia, Grenada, and other places were former slaves. At the same time, like Toussaint in Saint

---

[88] Pluchon, *Toussaint.*
[89] Thornton, "Soldiers" and "King of Kongo."
[90] Dubois, *Avengers,* pp. 194–231.
[91] Thomas Atwood, *The History of Island of Dominica* (London, 1791), pp. 227–250.

Domingue, he sought to require the former slaves to work to keep the plantation economy going, using the sequestered estates of former royalists for state income, but promising wages.[92] He sought to exploit reserves of French sympathy and hostility to England among former French colonies with a social program to reverse the colonial past in the Caribbean. He turned to three areas of discontent: Grenada, where a fair number of free colored planters were chafing under an anti-French, anti-Catholic regime; St. Lucia, where publicizing the abolition of slavery led to anti-British revolt; and St. Vincent, to support Carib claims against an encroaching English government.

Grenada had been a French colony until 1763 when it passed into English hands (and was briefly back under French control from 1771 until 1783). English discrimination against all French and Catholic elites resulted in the flight of the white planters elsewhere, especially Trinidad.[93] Colored planters then became more prominent, and a group of them began acquiring more property and slaves. However, the English government continued social, religious, and particularly racial discrimination against them. Some colored planters, led by Julien Fédon, began to plot against the English as the war with France heated up.[94] By 1793, Fédon and his associates had gathered munitions at his estate, but felt they lacked resources to revolt on their own, and began to look for support among slaves and maroons.

Fédon's opportunity came in 1795, when Hugues began to organize anti-English forces in the Caribbean. Hugues needed to augment his army beyond what he could do with the ex-slaves (and his own privateer navy), so he sought allies. He retook Saint Lucia and Dominica for France, and tried unsuccessfully to attack Grenada and Saint Vincent.

When Huges promised Fédon support, the planter revolted, captured English towns, and successfully resisted several attempts against his fortified estate.[95] However, he was unable to win over the militia, even though its members were largely colored, and so civil war ensued.[96] Both sides would turn to the slaves to break the stalemate, beginning with Fédon. As John Hay, a doctor who was captured early on by the insurgents, reported, the slaves – mostly from French estates – came up to Fédon's camp from the earliest days of the rebellion, and

---

[92] Laurent Dubois, "The Price of Liberty: Victor Hugues and the Administration of Freedom in Guadeloupe, 1794–1798," *William and Mary Quarterly* 56 (1999): 363–392.

[93] Beverley Steele, *Grenada: A History of Its People* (Oxford, 2003), pp. 66–148, for a history of Grenada based on careful research, and the best general account of Fédon's rebellion.

[94] Curtis Jacobs, "The Fédons of Grenada, 1763–1814," University of West Indies (Cave Hill) Grenada Conference (2002), online at http://cavehill.uwi.edu/bnccde/grenada/conference/papers/Jacobsc.html. A study of Fédon's family and its connections, using especially Grenadian land records.

[95] Gordon Turnbull, an English officer of the reoccupation force, noted that the prisoners were guarded by their own slaves; [Gordon Turnbull], *A Narrative of the Revolt and Insurrection of the French Inhabitants of the Island of Grenada* (Edinborough, 1795), p. 75.

[96] John Hay, *A Narrative of the Insurrection in Grenada…* (London, 1823), pp. 22–23. Hay was a resident of the island and captured by the insurgents.

were organized by him into companies of 60 to 100 for foraging, armed mostly with pikes and commanded by "a Captain of their colour."[97]

Fédon promised his slave supporters freedom. Hay saw Fédon address a group of slaves belonging to an English master named McBurnie and asked them if they would "take a part with them," and "after some hesitation" they opted to join with the rebels. Thereupon, Fédon took them outside and said that "they were as free as he was."[98] Perhaps Gordon Turnbull, another eyewitness, was right in saying that Fédon's followers were mostly from the slave elite, and claimed that the field hands remained rather indifferent, but Hay noted his abusive guards were formerly field hands.[99] Samuel Carey, an American then working in Grenada, believed the insurgents were largely colored but with a few French whites, that the French slaves had all gone to the insurgency, and some of the English as well, but most of the rest of the "English Negroes" had gone into the woods, seeking perhaps a third route to emancipation as maroons.[100]

The English were slower to seek to arm slaves, given that an early assessment of the situation led the English leaders to believe that the "hostile disposition of almost all the gangs of negroes" precluded using them as soldiers.[101] But circumstances forced a reassessment, and the English reconsidered. According to Hay, those who found the country desolate and without food sided with the English, whereas those who "still adhered to the delusive but flattering promises of liberty and equality" followed Fédon.[102] The English initially armed a corps of 300 slaves and subsequently augmented their numbers to attack Fédon, but made no promise of freedom.[103]

Thus between Fédon's and the British actions, the island was more or less divided up between the two, and in the confusion and slave flight, all the plantations were burned down.[104] By the time English reinforcements eventually ended the rebellion and restored all the slaves they could recover to their masters, considerable numbers of slaves or former slaves were found in both camps. In any case, slaves suffered horribly, for the assessment following the revolt considered that one-fourth of the slaves were "killed, dead or otherwise lost to their masters."[105]

---

[97] Hay, *Narrative*, p. 42.

[98] Hay, *Narrative*, p. 29.

[99] Turnbull, *Narrative*, pp. 11–12, and K. F. McKenzie to Colonel Horsford, n.d. [c. 1795], quoted in Turnbull, *Narrative* p. 56; Hay, *Narrative*, pp. 49, 80.

[100] Samuel Carey, Jr. to Samuel Carey, Sr., August 12, 1795, in Joel Montague, Mariam Montague, and Shanaz Montague, eds., "The Island of Grenada in 1795," *The Americas* 40 (1984): 535.

[101] Hay, *Narrative*, p. 57.

[102] Hay, *Narrative*, pp. 140–141.

[103] Turnbull, *Narrative*, pp. 114–115; Hay mentions a corps raised at Guyave; *Narrative*, p. 131. They were not promised liberty for their fighting, however, and the masters were paid; pp. 143–144.

[104] Turnbull, *Narrative*, pp. 68–69; Hay, *Narrative*, pp. 32, 34 (both thought that the slaves were engaged primarily in "plunder" of the English estates).

[105] Turnbull, *Narrative*, p. 163.

In St. Lucia, Huges managed to set off what was called the Brigands' War by publicizing the freedom decree, which in turn led many slaves to desert their plantations and take to the woods. As in Dominica earlier, the English who captured the island were forced to mobilize local forces, including slaves, to fight the war that dragged on for some time.[106]

St. Vincent promised to provide Huges a different sort of support. The island had been declared neutral in Franco-English Treaty of Aix-la-Chapelle in 1748, even though French colonists had established themselves on the island as early as 1700. This treaty, however, was abrogated by the Seven Years' War, and in the settlement of that war, St. Vincent was awarded to Great Britain, which moved rapidly to establish a government there, settling with the Caribs in 1763. The Caribs further accepted a treaty with England in 1768, which allowed English settlers to acquire lands, and in turn impinged on Carib understanding of their sovereignty. For the most part, Carib leaders had increasingly rejected English demands, leading to a war and a new treaty in 1773, which did not lower the tensions much.[107]

Shortly after Fédon's revolt, Huges sent a delegation to the Carib leader in Saint Vincent, Chatoyer (whom he addressed as "chief of a free nation"), promising "friendship and assistance in the name of the French nation to you and your comrades," and asked their assistance in driving the English out, promising to return usurped lands.[108] M. A. Moreau de Jonnès, the French delegate, met Carib leaders in a large joint session during which the Black (African-descended) and Red (indigenous) Carib leaders agreed to join to drive out the English.[109] The Caribs had initial success, but powerful English reinforcements that later retook Grenada defeated them in 1796–1797. Some 5,080 Caribs were captured, whom the English divided into "Black" and "Yellow" based on their degree of admixture with African runaways. While the Yellow Caribs were ultimately allowed to return to St. Vincent, the Black Caribs, numbering some 2,400, were deported to Roatán Island off the coast of Honduras in 1797. The Caribs did not remain on Roatán for long; many displaced themselves immediately to the nearby Spanish town of Trujillo, where there were welcomed as settlers. Many subsequently found their way into the independent Miskito Kingdom and to Belize, where the English admitted them in 1802. Those who remained in Trujillo entered Spanish service and ended up successfully defending the town against a French invasion in 1820.[110]

---

[106] D. Barry Gaspar, "La Guerre des Bois: Revolution, War, and Slavery in Saint Lucia, 1793–1838," in D. Barry Gaspar and David Geggus, eds., *A Turbulent Time: The French Revolution in the Greater Caribbean* (Bloomington, 1997), pp. 102–130.

[107] William Young, *An Account of the Black Charaibs in the Island of Saint Vincent's* (London, 1975), pp. 20–97.

[108] Curtis Jacobs, "Brigands' War in Saint Vincent: The View from French Records," Conference proceedings, 2003, online at http://www.cavehill.uwi.edu/BNCCde/svg/conference/papers/jacobs.html

[109] M. A. Moreau de Jonnès, *Aventures de guerre au temps de la République et du Consulat* (2 vols., Paris, 1858) 1: 246–248.

[110] Nancie Gonzalez, *Sojourners of the Caribbean: Ethnogenesis and Ethnohistory of the Garifuna* (Urbana and Chicago, 1988), pp. 19–24; 39–49; 52–57, provides a well-researched and thorough overview of the Carib/Garífuna adventure.

INDEPENDENCE IN SPANISH AMERICA

The violence and social possibilities of the Haitian Revolution had a distinctive dampening effect on other would-be rebellious leaders in the Americas. In 1795, slaves in Coro, Venezuela, inspired by the Haitian Revolution, revolted and demanded an end to slavery and excessive taxes. Coro's slave rebellion was matched by the middle-class demands of mostly free blacks in Brazil in what was known as the "Revolt of the Tailors" in Bahia in 1798. For the tailors, who were mostly free blacks, abolition of slavery joined with demands to extinguish differences in law by color and to allow maritime free trade.

The distaste of *criollo* elites of Spanish and Portuguese America for disturbing a social order founded in large part on slavery or the exploitation of indigenous people outweighed their desire for independence, even in light of the emergence of an independent United States in 1783. Between the fears engendered by Tupac Amaru in Peru and slave insurrections in Venezuela, the elite of Spanish America took few steps to agitate for independence or even for more autonomy.

The revolution in Spanish America came as much from developments in Europe as from action in America. After losing a war against Revolutionary France, Spain was forced to cede territory in America and to conclude a formal alliance with France in 1796. The British then began an effective blockade of the Spanish coast, cutting off relations between Spain and its colonial empire. Left on their own, without new directives or governors from Spain, the colonies were put in a position of de facto independence.

When Britain tried to take Buenos Aires in 1806 as a part of this blockade, the local elite, acting on their own, managed to defeat them. While they showed their continued loyalty to Spain, the criollo elite of the town also noted that they were capable of raising military forces and defending themselves on their own.

Following a string of victories in Europe, crowned by the Treaty of Tilsit in 1807, Napoleon sought to counter the British blockade by declaring the Continental System that would restrict all trade with the English. To ensure its success, French diplomats demanded that Portugal declare war on Britain, and although the Portuguese court was divided on the matter, the French invaded from Spain, forcing the Portuguese court to flee to Brazil. On November 19, 1807, King João V left Lisbon bound for Rio de Janeiro in a large armada with 6,000 courtiers and 9,000 sailors and marines of the Portuguese fleet, escorted by the British fleet.

French troops sent to occupy Portugal also turned to Spain, forcing King Carlos to abdicate in favor of Napoleon's brother Joseph Bonaparte, but when Joseph was installed in Madrid in 1808, riots broke out, which were suppressed by French troops and followed by violent reprisals, including the execution of thousands of people (immortalized by Goya's paintings), which hardened Spanish resistance. Most of the Spanish army deserted Joseph and rallied to the cause of Carlos's son Fernando, who the Spanish nobility declared King

Fernando VII in Seville, a new capital. The nobles loyal to Fernando organized local committees – juntas – to maintain government in Fernando's name both in Spain and in America. French attacks on Seville forced the junta to withdraw to Cádiz, but with British support it maintained itself as the legitimate ruling body of insurgent Spain and the Americas.

FIRST TRIES FOR INDEPENDENCE IN SPANISH AMERICA, 1808–1814

Starting in 1808, juntas were formed in most of Spain's American colonies as they had in Spain itself. These juntas were created from the self-governing institutions of the urban cabildos and provincial audiences that had long been a subordinate part of Spanish administration. The new juntas, dominated by *criollo* elites, declared allegiance to Fernando VII, largely symbolic as he had little power to support or defend them, but also no capacity to collect taxes or give orders.

In retrospect, we can recognize that these juntas and their criollo leaders would be the root of independence for most of the Spanish Empire. But it is fairly clear that at the time, the sentiment for independence was limited, and only a few people imagined that they would achieve self-government. At most, colonial elites hoped to reverse or alleviate the Bourbon Reforms, return power to the criollos to the extent that they possessed local power in the mid-eighteenth century, and modify economic policies to support local rather than metropolitan interests. As it turned out, Spain – whether the Junta of Cadiz or the king – was unwilling to reverse or indeed even relent on the fiscal system that so greatly favored it, especially as the colonial revenue stream was vital to the Spanish state as a whole. Thus royal resistance ultimately forced those criollo leaders who might have been perfectly happy in a reformed colonial situation to see independence as the only viable option to preserve their interests.[111]

In a similar retrospect, it is easy to see the contending parties in Spanish America as the monarchy (or, more generally, Spain) on one side and the criollos on the other. Postindependence writing about the period often sees it as those who were pro-independence against those who opposed independence, and to use terms like "patriot" and "royalist" to characterize them – a tendency that also dominated historical literature until well into the twentieth century. In fact, the situation was much more complicated. Many vital regions remained quite firmly against any move toward independence, and in other cases, war broke out between those who would eventually lead independence movements and those who would oppose them over issues that did not involve independence. Because Spain had very little formal presence in the colonies during much of the period, these wars were internal civil wars between parties who had different interests, although it usually did involve those who had been

[111] José Maria Portilla Valdés, *Crisis atlantica: Autonomía y independencia en la crisis de la monarchía hispana* (Madrid, 2006).

royal officials, recent Spanish arrivals, and elements of the colonial govern-ments (often the military elements) against upstarts who dominated the instru-ments of local authority such as audiencias and town councils.

At the same time, the presence of this civil war encouraged socially subor-dinate groups – indigenous communities and sometimes the indigenous elite, slaves, and nonelite people of whole or partial European origin – to seek their own new paths. Sometimes this converged with the interests of the criollos and at other times with that of the royal government and its agents. Given the gen-erally weak professional military forces available to all sides, a force of 5,000 was very large in the revolutionary era, and the potentially quite strong – at times – military potential available to indigenous auxiliaries or slaves resulted in them being courted by both sides with promises of social advancement – a desperate exigency in a crisis situation, which threatened to upset the social balance for criollo or royalist alike.

The movements that came to support independence developed in areas that were in some ways peripheral to the main centers of wealth and power in Spanish America. Three centers – New Spain, Buenos Aires, and Caracas – led the way, and their success drew in other regions like Peru, which were often not involved in the movement at all, or even actively opposed it.[112] In many cases, independence was won by those who got support from the zones that we have defined as "Contact" areas rather than the ones of "Conquest," in no small part because military skills and resources were concentrated there.

The first center was New Spain, to become independent at first as Anáhuac and then as Mexico. The movement began in the mining areas north of the main center of Spanish settlement, and relied heavily on indigenous peo-ple, before moving to the south and into another area of lighter Spanish settlement and heavily indigenous population. The second center was in Venezuela, at first in the Caracas area and involving New Granada right away, which could not succeed until it was able to mobilize the apparently marginal and heavily indigenous Orinoco Valley. The third center was in Buenos Aires, a newly rich city that benefited from the trade generated by its being a part of the new Viceroyalty of Rio de la Plata. Here, too, success was won primarily by mobilizing indigeneous or mixed populations in Upper Peru (both Potosí and the frontier zones like Chayantas and Moxos) and in the Banda Oriental, the region that had once been dominated by the Jesuit reductions.

MEXICO

Mexico was the first Spanish colony to make independence a goal.[113] From the very start, the Mexican War of Independence took on aspects of a civil

[112] See the observations in Lockhart and Schwartz, *Early Latin America*, pp. 424–426.
[113] Much of the general story of Mexican independence that follows is based on *Brian* Hamnett, *Roots of Insurgency: Mexican Regions, 1750–1824* (Cambridge, 1986).

war, in which most Spaniards and a significant faction of criollos lined up against the majority of criollos. The very first divisive issue was the question of New Spain's relationship to Spain, especially as Spain's own government was divided and unable to assert itself. José de Iturrigaray, president of the first junta formed by the cabildo of Mexico City and the Audiencia, moved to establish an essentially independent country, but Spanish residents deposed him, setting up a situation of tension and conflict between these Spanish residents and the criollos. Criollos, in turn, began a series of plots in various parts of the Viceroyalty with the aim of overthrowing the junta and advancing various agendas, but frequently adhering to the goal of an independent state, with many looking to the United States as a model.

Winning independence in Mexico, as indeed everywhere else in the Americas, was going to require military action, for both royalists and independence factions were unprepared to surrender without a fight. As there were no soldiers from Europe in Mexico (although many of the officers were), the question immediately arose as to how the professional military forces would line up, and in the end, a very substantial portion of the armed forces in Mexico stood with the crown and the Spanish officials. Criollos, while having success with some units – and there were constant negotiations with those standing for Spain – needed to find alternate military forces.

Some among the criollos saw hope for a military solution through the mobilization of Mexico's vast indigenous population. Both indigenous communities and their leaders had often suffered from the intrusions of Spanish-born entrepreneurs who had all but invaded the richest areas of Mexico following the Bourbon Reforms, taking land and shifting power to them.[114] At times, these Spaniards were met with spontaneous fury, often ending in murder, at the hands of the indigenous peasants – fury that criollos hoped to mobilize and control.[115]

Father Miguel Hidalgo y Cosillos, a parish priest in the mining town of Querétaro, just north of Mexico City, led the most visible and successful of these alliances of criollo and *naturales* (the most common term of the time for indigenous people).[116] Querétaro lay in the Bajío, a district that lay north of the northern frontier of the ancient Aztec Empire and had been incorporated into New Spain piecemeal though the settlement of miners and colonies drawn from the former Aztec and Trascan empires. The indigenous people had raided

[114] For a good overview and detailed research, see John Tutino, *From Insurrection to Revolution in Mexico: Social Bases of Agrarian Violence, 1750–1940* (Princeton, 1986).

[115] This aspect has been explored most fully in the work of Eric Van Young. See "Millenium on the Northern Marches: The Mad Messiah of Durango and Popular Rebellion in Mexico, 1800–1815," *Comparative Studies in Society and History* 28 (1986): 385–413; "The Messiah and the Masked Man: Popular Ideology in Mexico, 1810–1821," in Steven Kaplan, ed., *Indigenous Responses to Western Christianity* (New York and London, 1995), pp. 144–174.

[116] A classic overview is Hugh Hamill, *The Hidalgo Revolt: Prelude to Mexican Independence* (Gainsville, 1966).

and fought these colonists and had been incorporated through the efforts of missionaries in reduction. In the eighteenth century, the region had seen increasing settlement both because of mines and because the region was close enough to the central zones of Mexico City that it became a center for agriculture and ranching.[117] Bourbon Reforms had brought a good many Spaniards (disdainfully known there as gauchopines), who had benefited disproportionately in the economic growth of the period.

For their part, the indigenous communities had lost lands, and many of their people were impoverished by the process, and continued social and legal discrimination assisted in making them potentially a group interested in violent revolution. In this way Hidalgo's movement might be said to resemble that of the earlier Túpac Amaru movement in Peru, except that its indigenous people had not been historically part of the Aztec Empire, and were thus approached as *naturales*. Unlike the Peruvian movement, its ideology was cast in social terms of land reform and communal privilege, rather than an idea of the restoration of the Aztec Empire.

Knowing the sentiments of the region well through his role as a parish priest, Hidalgo appealed to indigenous people, and as an indication of this he placed his movement under the patronage of the Virgin of Guadeloupe, as his enemies said, "to better seduce the people, especially the Indians as he knew the devotion they had of this image."[118] He was probably telling the truth, however, when he denied the charge that he wanted to create a wholly Indian movement and return the country to them.[119] His first supporters were, in fact, the "Indians and rancheros" who appeared at Mass when the conspirators, their plans discovered, had to start the revolt early, on September 16, 1810; others, he testified at his trial, joined his movement spontaneously.[120] In fact, they were a variety of people, local *criollo* ranchers whose hands assisted, some military units, with bureaucrats, tradesmen, and artisans often serving as officers.[121]

Hidalgos' followers rallied to him from all sides and were of wildly different opinions, for in addition to regular troops, various leaders formed their

---

[117] D. A. Brading, *Haciendas and Ranchos in the Mexican Bajío: Leon, 1700–1860* (Cambridge, 1979).

[118] Declaración del cura Hidalgo, May 8, 1811, in Hernández y Dávalos, ed., *Colección* 1: doc. 2, 12th question, pp. 15–16. These declarations, made in the course of his trial after his capture, are probably as close as we can come to his actual thoughts and motivations, and here he denied that it was a special appeal and that his followers used the image as much as he did (although as a man on trial, perhaps his declarations were motivated by hopes of avoiding execution).

[119] Declaración de Hidalgo, May 8, 1811, in Hernández y Dávalos, *Colección*, 1: doc. 2, 28th question, 30th question, pp. 22, 24–25.

[120] Declaración de Hidalgo, May 7, 1811, in Hernández y Dávalos *Colección*, 1: doc. 2, 3rd question, p. 6, and 4th question, p. 7. His confederate Juan Aldema gave their number as 500 "on foot and on horseback," Declaración de Juan Aldemas, May 20, 1811, doc. 27, p. 5.

[121] "Informe sobre lo que resulta en las causas de los jefes insurrectos," June 29, 1811, in Hernández y Dávalos, *Coleción*, 1: doc. 38.

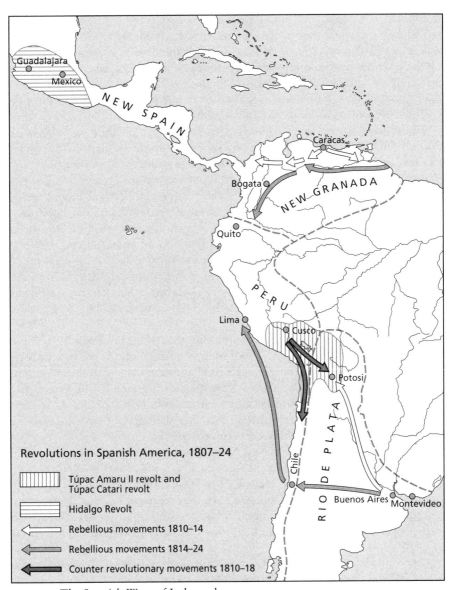

MAP 11. The Spanish Wars of Independence.

own companies. For example, the indigenous inhabitants of Xichu formed a company, including their priest, and another priest, José de Vargas, was named "General of the Indians."[122] Likewise, an independently organized band of 300

---

[122] "Informe, expresando muy por extenso la opinión general de las falsedades que contiene, nulidad y desprecio con que ha sido visto por los sacerdotes y el público el edicto de la Inquisición," February 22, 1811, in Hernández y Dávalos, *Colección* 1: doc. 47, p. 21.

drawn from the Nola, Tula, and Palma, led by Bernardo Gomez de Lara (nick-named Huacal), operated in the northeast part of Mexico (Santander) until Huacal was killed in 1811.[123] At least some of them were interested in revers-ing the fortunes of the conquest and restoring, if not the Aztec empire, at least indigenous control. Garcia Conde, a Spanish officer captured by Hidalgo's allies, thought that the sentiment was that the movement was about restoring the Indios to power, to make an "Indiada."[124]

While Hidalgo may have appealed to Indians, it did not mean that all answered his call, especially once one moved beyond the Bajío. New Spain was not simply divided into "indios" and Spaniards; the conquest had been made with the cooperation of many different indigenous groups and leaders. Many of the "indios amigos" groups of the conquest period had become more or less military units in the colony and were prepared, as milita units often were, to support the king. In 1808, the indigenous governors of Querétaro offered the king the services of 10,000 Otomis should he need them.[125] When one of Hidalgo's lieutenants moved northward into Sinaloa, he was joined in his march by numerous indios from the Bajío, who were drawn from the peasant classes and without much military skill, but in Sinaloa, royal officials called on the services of Opatás, an ethnic milita unit, to fight against the insurgents.[126]

In this light, it would hardly be surprising that Tlaxcala, Spain's principal ally in the conquest and beneficiary of numerous exemptions because of their service, stood firmly in the royalist camp. The junta along with the city coun-cil of Tlaxcala issued a statement roundly denouncing Hidalgo on October 6, 1810, and promising to defend the king "with their last drop of blood." In their statement they reminded their readers that Tlaxcala had been "assistants in the conquest of this kingdom" three centuries earlier.[127]

Similarly, the government of New Spain had been built in large part and in many sections on the services of the local caciques. The Bourbon Reforms had hurt them, as had the Spanish incursions in landholding and economic power, but like the criollos who had also been hurt, they were not necessarily prepared to join in the insurgency, especially if it had a social program that threatened their property and enterprises. In fact, Eric Van Young estimates that if 50–60

---

[123] Letter of Deputy Elosua, quoted in Carlos Maria Bustamante, *Cuadros Historicos de la Revolución de Mejico* (Mexico, 1823), Carta 18, pp. 7–9.

[124] Garcia Conde to Virey, December 8, 1810, in Hernández y Dávalos, *Colección* 2, doc. 156, pp. 268–270.

[125] Representación de los naturales de Querétaro, July 27, 1808, in Juan Evaristo Hernández y Dávalos, ed. *Colección de Documentos para la Historia de la Guerra de Independencia de Mexico 1808 a 1821* (6 vols., Mexico, 1877–1882 [GB]), cited by document number for refer-ence in the digital edition, http://www.pim.unam.mx/catalogos/juanhdzt.html, 1: doc 215.

[126] [Francisco de Parra], Expedición al Rosario ... 1810–1811, in Hernández y Dávalos, *Colección*, 1: doc 153, pp. 378–383 (Opatás on p. 382).

[127] Ayuntamiento de Tlaxcala, October 6, 1810 in Hernández y Dávalos, *Colección*, 2: doc. 73, pp. 143–144, and October 20, doc. 93, pp. 173–174.

percent of the rebel movement was composed of indigenous people, the traditional leadership was underrepresented among them. Many were cautious, others quite staunch loyalists.[128]

To pay politically for the support of the poorer indios, Hidalgo had to extend concessions, and these in turn pushed him to a social agenda. He not only ended onerous legislation that effected indigenous communities, but also ended slavery and spoke of land reform. To meet this challenge, the royal government also stopped Indian tribute, issuing their decree in both Spanish and Nahua.[129] These were not topics that criollos on the whole would want to support, and Hidalgo's evocation of them was a necessary mobilizing strategy, but one that set off forces he could not control and that often engaged as much in looting and murder as in disciplined warfare. During the course of the insurrection, several cities fell to his followers, and many were sacked, looted, and people were indiscriminately killed. Hidalgo blamed these actions on his indigenous followers, operating under the command of little-known leaders and perhaps only partially under his control. He had tried to avoid public scenes of execution as "only the Indians and the riff-raff [*canalla*] wanted these." Indeed, he contended, all such public executions were carried out by the Indians.[130]

Hidalgo's army, which his contemporary, Garcia Conde, estimated at 80,000, was not well organized and included the families and children of his followers, who came in groups under local leaders – anyone who brought a thousand fighters with them was named a colonel.[131] He was helped by the fact that militia units often deserted to the revolution, and even some indigenous units, created by royal officials to combat the rebellion, deserted.[132] The regular soldiers who came from the militia thus provided him with a core of trained fighters, which was awkwardly supported by the thousands of naturales. After winning a number of engagements, he advanced on Mexico City, but in the end was unable to take the city; his army was defeated and broke up into smaller units, and he himself was captured while trying to flee northward to the United States. He was tried and executed as a heretic by the Inquisition in 1811 before he could organize anything of a countergovernment; as he noted, "I adopted no plan for the whole or in part, having as a goal only the extension of the insurrection, leaving everything as it was and only changing the

---

[128] Eric Van Young, *The Other Rebellion: Popular Violence, Ideology, and the Mexican Struggle for Independence, 1810–20* (Stanford, 2001), pp. 142–147.

[129] Bando del Virey, May 26, 1810, in Hernández y Dávalos *Colección*, 2: docs. 70 and 71, pp. 137–141.

[130] Declaracíon de Hidalgo, May 8, 1811, in Hernández y Dávalos, *Colección*, 1: doc. 2, 16th question, pp. 17–18. He went on to describe a number of such public executions that were all carried out by Indians.

[131] Garcia Conde, in Hernández y Dávalos, *Colección*, 2: doc. 156, p. 271.

[132] Michael Ducey, "Village, Nation, and Constitution: Insurgent Politics in Papantla, Veracruz, 1810–21," *Hispanic American Historical Review* 79 (1999): 470–472.

officials."[133] Even though the criollos of New Spain were badly frightened by the thought of a general uprising of indios, which Hidalgo seemed to lead, they supported his anti-Spanish sentiments; the decision to execute him was widely disparaged by all classes of American-born people as being the corrupt work of Europeans.[134]

Hidalgo's movement was the most famous, and is widely regarded as decisive in today's Mexico; still, he was only one of the many conspiratorial groups working for a variety of interests, and his execution hardly brought political or military activity to an end. His former army broke up but continued fighting as dispersed bodies, mostly mounted, and supported by a few artillery pieces, in the Bajío and northward into Guadalajara and Zacatecas. Reports of military officers such as Rosindo Porlier described these units as they engaged them throughout 1811: an action against "11–14,000 enemies mostly on horses" or another battle against "Indians and horsemen"; another battle against 8,000–10,000 insurgents, in which the royalists captured arrows, canon, and horses; yet another action against the united gavillas (the term of choice for military bodies) of insurgents; and yet another action against some 10,000 insurgents in which priests, often prominent in the insurrection, played a special role.[135] By the end of 1811, however, the royalist commander Felix Maria Calleja felt confident that he had the situation enough in hand that he proposed that his regular forces be dispersed in towns, and he organized militias to watch the roads and hunt down rebel bands, while disarming the whole population not enlisted in the militias.[136] While he may have felt confident that the main threat of insurgent action had passed or could be contained, he was also aware that many bands, smaller and sometimes resembling bandits, continued to operate.

Leadership of Hidalgo's supporters who continued in the field passed into the hands of a loosely structured group that tried to coordinate the various armed groups fighting against continued Spanish control. Hidalgo's secretary Inacio López Rayón, along with several other prominent followers of Hidalgo, took over the remnants of Hidalgo's army and on August 19, 1811 established a governmental body, the Junta Suprema Nacional Americana (Supreme American National Junta), to coordinate the actions of the other local leaders.

[133] Declaracíon de Hidalgo, May 8, 1811, in Hernández y Dávalos, *Colección*, 1: doc. 2, 27th question, p. 23.

[134] "Informe," February 22, 1811, in Hernández y Dávalos, *Colección*, 1: doc. 47.

[135] See the reports of royalist officers in Hernández y Dávalos, *Colección*, 3: docs. 11, pp. 281–282 (11,000–14,000 enemy fighters, mostly on horses); 19, pp. 256–257 (action against a gavilla of Padre Calvillo); 25, pp. 263–266 (battle against "Indians and horsemen"); 31, pp. 271–272 (battle against 8,000–10,000 insurgents; arrows, canon, and horses captured); 32, pp. 274–276 (battle against united gavillas of insurgents, action against some 10,000 insurgents, with clergy playing a special role); 34, pp. 277–278 (small-scale operations to "restore order"); 38, pp. 282–283 (another engagement with insurgents); 39, pp. 283–284 (action against 3,000 horsemen with 4 canons), primarily concerning operations of Rosendo Porlier in 1811.

[136] Don Félix Calleja propone al virrey un proyecto para armar y pacificar el reino, June 8, 1811, in Hernández y Dávalos, *Colección*, 3: doc. 44, pp. 289–290.

The Junta Suprema met at Zitácuaro in Michoacán, east of New Spain's capital city. Calleja's forces drove the Junta from that city in 1812, and for a time its constituent leaders separated, finally being brought together again as the Congresso de Chilpancingo (a town in the western mountain range) in 1813, this time under the leadership of José Maria Morelos y Pavón, the Junta Suprema's most successful military leader. Although the Junta Suprema had issued newspapers, coined money, and sought international recognition (while still maintaining its loyalty to Fernando VII), its real power was limited and was primarily held by local military leaders who supported its overall cause. The Congresso was hardly more powerful as a government than the Junta Suprema, but it declared Anáhuac (their new name for New Spain) independent of Spain on November 6, 1813.[137]

Jose Maria Morelos, a priest by training and profession and a person of mixed European, African, and indigenous ancestry, emerged as the most effective commander after Hidalgo's demise. Hidalgo had sent him to the west coast in 1810 to take Acapulco, and he became the revolutionary leader all along the coast in subsequent years. Whereas Hidalgo's movement was specifically anti-European, and his followers inclined to massacre them, Morelos was against wealth of any sort, regardless of ethnic identification. Even before the official declaration of independence, Morelos declared in 1812 that only people born in America could represent the country (thus effectively declaring independence), and

as a consequence, from here on no distinction shall be made in categories of qualities, being that generally all of us call ourselves Americans, and looking each to the other as brothers, we ought to live in the Holy Peace that our Redeemer, Jesus Christ has left us … that there be no motive for those groupings that are called castes, which only want to destroy each one the other, the whites against the blacks, and these against the indigenous people [*naturales*].[138]

He wrote to his commanders that they ought to "consider as enemies of the nation, and adherents of the party of tyranny all the rich people, nobles and first order owners, both criollos and gachupines (European), as they authorized the vices and passion of the European legislation system."

Although this decree also protected the property of rich people, a year later Morelos was ordering the expropriation of all the property of wealthy people and its redistribution, "half going to the poor, half going to the army." He was also anxious that the redistribution not enrich anyone, while also striking against export crops and ordering export-oriented plantations such as those producing sugar to be destroyed.[139] This plan called for widespread redistribution of land and wealth, to take place as soon as his soldiers occupied a village

[137] "Acta Solemna de la Declaración de la Independencia de America Septentrional," November 6, 1813.
[138] Jose Maria Morelos, "Bando … sobre embargos de bienes de europeos y otras materias de buen gobierno," October 13, 1812, in Hernández y Dávalos, *Colección*, 3: doc. 95, pp. 401–402.
[139] Wilbert H. Timmons, *Morelos: Priest, Soldier, Statesman of Mexico*.

or town. They were to immediately inform the rich to turn over all their money and wealth, half to go to the poor, the other half to the army. They were also to break up estates in the favor of the poor and to seek an equitable distribution of land.[140]

Many of these ideas were combined in Morelos's 1813 text, "Feelings of a Nation," anticipating both the declaration of political independence from Spain and a constitution, ratified in 1814, that abolished slavery, Indian tributes, caste systems, and other forms of discrimination.[141] Coupled with the policy of land redistribution, the movement was more radical than Hidalgo envisioned, and indeed than most of his criollo colleagues would have liked, although military necessity made this option attractive. His field of operation was also different; whereas Hidalgo operated north of Mexico City in the agricultural, mining, and industrial center, Morelos's operations were fixed on the southwest Pacific Coast region. Although Morelos captured fewer large cities, his movement endured longer than the more dramatic actions of Hidalgo. As regular forces coalesced, the insurgents' capacity to maintain real field armies declined. In a report of 1813, for example, the commander Callejon noted the insurgents had broken into "numerous bands (*gavillas*)" who were "naked [and] poorly armed," which forced him to deploy his troops in "small divisions," separated from each other and unable to communicate effectively or aid each other, while provoking general misery.[142] Nevertheless, the ultimate success of the movement was probably ultimately caused by the low-level but constant activities of small, local guerilla bands who had only tenuous ties to the larger movement.[143]

Strengthened by vast support from his lower-class followers, Morelos was able to achieve much more military success than Hidalgo had. The appeal to indigenous people revealed the ancient and deep-seated social divisions within Mexican society, especially as the movement achieved sufficient military success to begin governing. The ordinary peasants of indigenous origin were generally enthusiastic backers of Morelos, but the indigenous leadership, drawn from the traditional cacique class, was more divided. They had been undermined by Bourbon reforms and looked for changes to restore their income and authority; others feared the radical elements in the movement that threatened their position. Leaders like Hidalgo and Morelos won support from some of the indigenous caciques, but many remained neutral, having benefited personally from the regime enough to keep them cautiously loyal. A handful became supporters of the movement, but a good many more actively participated in its

---

[140] Decreto del señor Morelos sobre repartimiento de intereses, in Hernández y Dávalos, *Collección*, 1: doc. 287.

[141] "Sentimentos de la Nacion," September 14, 1813; "Decreto Constitutional para la Liberdad de la America Mexicana" (Apatzingán, October 22, 1814).

[142] AGI Estado, 31 (México), n. 20 [PARES], "Virrey sobre el estado de la revolución de aquel pais," enclosing letter of Felix Maria Callejon, March 15, 1813.

[143] Van Young, *The Other Rebellion*, is an invaluable book, based on painstaking research in local sources.

suppression, hoping to obtain further rewards and exemptions from taxation for their loyalty.[144]

Morelos's own background and social program led him to exploit other social divisions than those on which Hidalgo had targeted. When he decided to carry the war into Veracruz on the Atlantic coast, for example, his earliest armed advances focused on the sugar estates of the region and deliberately sought to provoke revolts among enslaved Afro-Mexicans, many of whom fled the estates and soon formed independent or semi-independent camps in the hills. Francisco Severiano Gomez, acting with a license from Morelos, entered the province in 1812 and "stirred up the Negros" of the sugar estates of the area, where they gathered under the leadership of two mulatos at camps at Chiquihuite and Palma Sola.[145]

But Morelos's social programs were too much for many of his followers, and after an attempt to besiege Mexico City failed in 1813, many of the elite criollos deserted him. Morelos was captured and executed by royalist forces in 1815. The radical movement he had started continued, however, much as it had before, in the hands of small units of guerillas, most notably or most successfully in the south of Mexico under Vicente Guerrero – like Morelos, a person of mixed European, African, and indigenous descent. Subsequent irregular fighting, raids, and a good number of atrocities convinced the wealthier of the criollos to stay with Spain, and in turn the Viceroys pardoned them. As the low-level war continued in the countryside, it increasingly took on the overtones of a social war of class and color. In much of the country, the royalists managed to hold on to the towns, but the rural areas were given over to unsubdued but also uncoordinated bands of guerillas.[146]

The situation as it existed by 1815 might well have continued colonial rule indefinitely, as the guerilla bands were as much like bandits as coordinated followers, and as royalist fighters hunted down the most effective of them, one by one. The veteran Augustín de Iturbide had great success against the bands of Vicente Guerrero in Oaxaca although he had been unable to win the final victory. However, when the Spanish government restored the 1812 constitution, which revoked many criollo rights, Itrubide began a complicated series of negotiations with both local Spanish elites, the Church, and Guerrero, eventually reaching a compromise that declared Mexico independent on September 28, 1821. Various Spanish expeditions attacked Mexico between 1822 and 1829, but all of them failed, and Spain finally recognized Mexico's independence formally in 1836.

[144] On indigenous elites, see Van Young, *Other Rebellion*, pp. 142–147.

[145] Anonymous, "Comentários desde el año de 1811 hasta el 1820; de los sucessos de Córdova..." (manuscript of c. 1820, 2nd ed., Adriana Naveda Chávez-Hita, as *La guerra de independencia en Córdoba, Veracruz. Narración de un testigo* [Xalapa, 2007]), pp. 49–50.

[146] Ducey, "Village Nation and Constitution," pp. 472–474.

REVOLUTION IN RIO DE LA PLATA, CHILE, AND PERU

As in Mexico, the Spanish viceroyalties of South America met the challenge of the Napoleonic occupation of Spain by forming juntas to run local affairs in the towns and cities. Some of these juntas embarked on a path that would lead them to independence, but in the struggle to achieve that goal would also open social wounds, empower the previously powerless, and create sometimes radical programs of reform. In South America, the primary center of royalist strength was in Peru, and it would fall on it and its governor, José Fernando de Abscal y Sousa, to hold down its own restive population as well as intervene in that of the neighboring viceroyalties. Abscal y Sousa did not have many soldiers to use outside his province. His report to Spain in 1810 revealed that he had twelve companies of troops – ten urban and two provincial – but also noted that they were "without the least bit of discipline and instruction," under officers "of the same class." Only three companies were considered notable and their service was in the Túpac Amaru rebellion, thirty years earlier.[147] However, he did have another important resource, which was the loyal indigenous militia, estimated in 1811 at 40,000 strong, under Mateo Pumacahua.[148]

If Peru remained loyal, other regions were not. In 1809, criollo rebels in Upper Peru (modern-day Bolivia), the westernmost section of the Viceroyalty of Rio de la Plata, took over government in Chuquisaca (today's Sucre) and La Paz, declaring that "now is the time for a new system of government," which would be free from the "bastard politics of Madrid."[149] The region, which had witnessed a revolt by the cacique Tomás Catari during Tupac Amaru's rebellion, had been restless since then, with revolts in 1798, 1801, and 1805.[150] Given the danger of this movement to the silver revenues from Potosí, Abscal y Sousa dispatched a powerful force and soon brought the rebels to heel.

But rebellion was not yet quashed, for the criollo-dominated junta of Buenos Aires seized power on May 25, 1810. Although they declared their allegiance to Fernándo VII, the junta declared that "the people" would rule as stakeholders for the king until he was free. Viceroy Baltasar Hidalgo de Cisneros and the Spanish officials denied this, claiming that as royal officials they enjoyed the king's grace and authority. The conflict was settled by the recourse to military force. Popular riots broke out in Buenos Aires, and the local criollos persuaded

---

[147] AGI Estado 74 (Lima), no. 36, image 21 [PARES], José Manuel Goyeneche to Marqués de las Hormazas, September 8, 1810.

[148] John Fisher, "Royalism, Regionalism, and Rebellion in Colonial Peru, 1808–1815," *Hispanic American Historical Review* 59 (1979): 242, quoting AGI Cusco 8 Pedro Antonio de Cernadas to the Council of Regency, April 26, 1811.

[149] Quoted in Manuel José Cortés, *Ensayo sobre la historia de Bolivia* (La Paz, 1861), p. 29. Cortés, well known as a poet as well as a historian, does not cite sources specifically, but did make use of many manuscript and unpublished sources.

[150] José Luis Roca, *Ni con Lima, ni con Buenos Aires: La formación de un estado nacional en Charcas* (Lima, 2007), pp. 167–190.

the militia commanders to join them, forcing Viceroy Cisneros to flee on a British ship.

The Junta Grande, formed from this seizure of power in Buenos Aires, petitioned other cabildos in Rio de la Plata to join a unified government. The western province of Córdoba refused, and its governor, the former viceroy Santiago de Liniers, and his colleague Francisco Javier de Elío in Montevideo, a port across the Rio de la Plata from Buenos Aires, also remained loyal. In response to the initiative from these royal officials, Abscal y Sousa declared that most of western Rio de la Plata would be placed under the authority of Peru.

Given these conflicting developments, Rio de la Plata was thrown into civil war. The junta in Buenos Aires raised an army of about 1,000 men, called the Army of the North, formed from militia companies, including those of African descent and pardos who had served in the 1807 defense against the British. This force marched to Córdoba, and by the middle of 1810 had captured and executed Liniers, but they were unable to prevent the remnants of his forces from joining Peruvian forces in Upper Peru, where the real showdown between the Peruvian-backed royalists and those who threw their lot with Buenos Aires took place.

As in Mexico, the battle for Upper Peru quickly involved indigenous people. Antonio Gonzáles Balcarce, the commander of the Army of the North, entered Upper Peru and was immediately aided by a sympathetic revolt in Cochabamba, which supplied his army with troops. At the same time he made a crucial advance by promising to end tribute payments to the indigenous inhabitants of La Paz.[151] Moreover, he sought to extend his actions into Peru by sending calls to revolt to Peruvian towns. In June 1811, criollos in Tacna, led by Francisco Antonio de Zela, responded to the call and declared their allegiance to the junta of Buenos Aires, with substantial support from local indigenous people.[152] However, the royalist forces defeated the Army of the North, and without external support, the junta was suppressed. Meanwhile, the indigenous inhabitants of Huánaco revolted in April 1812 and raised an army of some 2,000 fighters, but were quickly suppressed by royalist forces.[153]

Although the royalists had defeated the Army of the North and the Huánaco revolt, other indigenous allies fought on. The caciques of the Omasuyo, Pacaje, and Larecaja of the region around La Paz, along with priests of the region and local authorities, revolted to form the "Army for the Restoration of the Indians of Peru" (*Ejercito Restorador de los Indios de Peru*) and laid siege to La Paz.[154] The royalists counterattacked, bringing in troops, including some 3,500 Inca

[151] Cortés, *Ensayo*, p. 34.
[152] R. Cúneo Vidal, *Historia de la insurreciones de Tacna por la independencia de Perú* (Lima, 1921).
[153] Fisher, "Royalism," pp. 250–252.
[154] *Gaceta Oficial de Buenos Aires*, quoted in Juan Ramón Muñoz Cabrera, *La guerra de quince annos en el Alto-Perú* (1867 [GB]), pp. 216–220. The title of the army is given in a manifesto by Juan Manuel Cáceres, October 7, 1811, in *Gaceta Oficial*, quoted in Muñoz Cabrera, *Guerra*, p. 221.

(Quechua-speaking) fighters from Cuzco under Mateo Pumacahua. For much of 1811, Upper Peru was the scene of sustained fighting involving substantial antiroyalist indigenous forces (though usually with regular soldiers as well), which were only defeated with great difficulty.[155]

In the aftermath of the uprising, and even after the defeat of the Army of the North, local commanders, often leading forces of mixed milita troops and allied indigenous fighters, continued in operation, taking over government in some districts and resisting the attempts of the royalist forces to contain them.[156] Thus, much as in Mexico after Hidalgo's defeat, more local, loosely organized guerilla fighters kept advancing the cause. These local centers, often called "republiquetas" or "little republics," kept up a low-key guerilla war: they would surge forward to assist the Army of the North when it made new expeditions into Upper Peru as it did in 1813 and again in 1815, each time meeting defeat in the battlefield. But in spite of these defeats and the fact that the royalists held the important towns, the combined forces of the insurgency could not be defeated either.[157]

The forces of the republiquetas included indigenous people, guachos (often called "cholos" in the contemporary sources, a scornful term for a person of mixed race) who rode horses and carried lances, and some regular soldiers with artillery.[158] When the republiqueta leader Manuel Asencio Padilla fell on royalist forces during the third expedition of the Army of the North in 1816, he commanded a force of a few regular troops and "a great number of indios"; later that year he appeared with a force of 150 fulisiers, a few horsemen, and 1,000 indios.[159] Royal troops massacred a group of some 2,000 indios, apparently also a military unit of the republiqueta led by Ildefonso Carillo and his associates.[160] José Vicente Camargo also mobilized many indigenous people in the same war; more than 800 were lost in one action, seeking to wrest bayonets from the royal troops.[161] Ignacio Warnes, another local leader, recruited slaves into his small army, promising them freedom and forming the Battalion of Free Pardos, as well as incorporating indigenous people to form the Hunter Battalion in 1815. In addition to the fighters allied with the independence movement, there were the indigenous people of the frontier – Chiriguanos, Moxos, and Chiquitos – who were connected to the colony more through missionaries and their fear of Brazilian raids than real administration.[162]

---

[155] Roca, *Ni con Lima*, pp. 233–241.
[156] Marie-Danielle Delémas, "De la 'petite guerre' à la guerre populaire: Génese de la guérilla comme valeur en Amérique du Sud," *Cahiers d'Amérique Latine* 36 (2001): 17–35.
[157] Roca, *Ni con Lima*, pp. 301–368.
[158] Marie-Danielle Delémas, *Nacimiento de la guerra de guerilla: El Diario de Jose Santos Vargas (1814–25)* (Lima, 2007).
[159] Cortes, *Ensayo*, pp. 67, 70.
[160] Cortes, *Ensayo*, p. 67. The text makes it ambiguous whether the massacre was of civilian or military indios, but it does note that only the drum major survived, implying a military unit.
[161] Cortes, *Ensayo*, p. 68.
[162] Roca, *Ni con Lima*, pp. 257–300 (for the Moxo rebellion of 1810–1811).

The continued rebellion in Upper Peru also had its impact in Peru itself, especially as Buenos Aires continued to communicate with Peruvian elites and kept its army, even if inactive, nearby. At the end of 1813, a number of criollo officers, led by José Angulo and his brothers Mariano, Vicente, and Juan Angulo Torres, were arrested by the Royal Audience in Cuzco, but escaped and raised a revolt in the city in August 1814. Lacking support to take on the royal forces, they involved Mateo Pumacahua, the influential high Inca noble who had led forces in the suppression of the Upper Peru revolt of 1811–1812. Pumacahua was disappointed by the continued policy of Spanish domination in this, the most loyal of Spain's colonies, and threw his military support to the rebels. Flush with this support, the rebel leaders sent large forces into Upper Peru and to several locations within Peru itself, including more than 25,000 indigenous fighters. In presenting the Spanish government as an occupation of the former Inca Empire, and adopting Inca iconography, the movement made themselves an indigenous movement, which caused the numbers of criollo supporters to dwindle as the movement's indigenous element grew.[163] But royal forces rallied, especially after the return of troops from Upper Peru, found their own (less numerous) indigenous allies, and managed to put the rebellion down by 1815, although many of the defeated soldiers continued fighting with republiquetas in Upper Peru.

Even as the junta of Buenos Aires was fighting in Upper Peru, they were dealing with another front to the north, created by the continued occupation of Montevideo by royalist forces. The junta sent the same requests to Paraguay and the other districts along the major rivers (Paraguay, Paraná, and Uruguay) in 1810, as they did to the western regions, asking them to join with the junta. This area was traditionally connected to Asunción, the original core of Spanish settlement and the "mother of cities" for the whole basin, including even Buenos Aires. The shift in power to Buenos Aires, created by the formation of the viceroyalty, had left Asunción less powerful and important, and thus jealous of the newly rich port city.

The royalist governor of Paraguay, Bernardo de Velasco, convoked a general assembly in the district, which initially declared its loyalty of Fernando VII and solidarity with Buenos Aires. However, as it became clear that Buenos Aires planned to subordinate Asunción and Paraguay to its interests, the relations soured. Eventually Buenos Aires sent a military force under Manuel Belgrano, ostensibly to prevent a Brazilian takeover, but in fact to bring Paraguay under its control. Although Belgrano believed that the sentiments of the Paraguayan elite would favor the expedition, he soon discovered that the anti-Buenos Aires sentiments were stronger than expected. Even though he recruited additional forces from the Guaraní of the former Jesuit missions to assist, the Paraguayans forced him to withdraw.[164] Subsequently, the criollos of Asunción deposed

---

[163] Fisher, "Royalism," pp. 252–257.
[164] The classic initial statement of the history is Blas Garay, *La revolución de la independencia del Paraguay* (Madrid, 1897 [GB]).

Governor Velasco for plotting with Portugal to turn the province over to Brazil, and then declared an independent junta in June 1811, which expressed solidarity with Buenos Aires but explicitly stated the autonomy of Paraguay.

As Paraguay moved to independence, the Banda Oriental, which lay downstream from Asunción and included Guaraní regions formerly under Jesuit control, presented other problems. This area had, in addition to a large indigenous population, a number of farms and ranches of settlers who had devoted their time and energy to raising horses and mules to be used for supplying Peru. Its most prominent member was perhaps Francisco Candioti, the "prince of the Gauchos," who had made a fortune in the mule trade and owned ranches up and down the Paraná which were managed on his behalf by junior kinsmen and the descendents of his mistresses.[165] The Banda Oriental also bordered on the unconquered equestrian free associations of the Gran Chaco and had a tradition of near-constant fighting with them. The mixed-race Gauchos were the military backbone of the region, and the government had organized formal military units from them, called the *Blandengues*, who were well known as lancers and formidable horsemen.

Hoping to mobilize some of these forces against Montevideo, the junta won the support of the formerly royalist Jose Gervasio Artigas, the commander of the Blandengues. In addition to forces that had been officially enrolled in units, he had the support of many other Gauchos. His troops also included some 250 African lancers, whose descendants still live near Asunción.[166] Artigas rapidly defeated royalist forces and in 1812 (thanks to additional desertions from the royalists in mid-battle), he briefly laid siege to Montevideo.[167] Artigas's successes, however, alarmed the Portuguese in Brazil, who feared the republican tendencies of the Junta in Buenos Aires and were anxious to obtain a strategic foothold in the Rio de la Plata invaded the Banda Oriental; in the upshot, in 1812, the authorities in Buenos Aires agreed to return the Banda Oriental to royalist control in exchange for the withdrawal of Portuguese forces.

Artigas was not satisfied with Buenos Aires's role in the Banda Oriental and withdrew with some 16,000 followers across the Uruguay River, where he formed a countergovernment, hostile to both the Spanish authority in Montevideo and the junta in Buenos Aires. Artigas's followers included many indigenous people as well as the mixed-race nonelites of his home region. The Scotch trader William Parish Robertson, traveling through Artigas's country in 1814, commented on the raids and military power of the Artigueños and the fear they provoked in Buenos Ayres, even though he thought of Artigas as a raider and outlaw as much as a political leader.[168]

---

[165] John Robertson visited and described the economic activities of this man in 1812; see John and William Parish Robertson, *Letters on Paraguay: An Account of Four Years' Residence in That Republic* (2 vols., London, 1838 [GB]) 1: 208–212.

[166] John Lipski, "Un remanente afrohispánico: El habla afroparaguaya de Camba Cua," *Lingua Americana* 10 (2006): 13–14.

[167] John Street, *Artigas and the Emancipation of Uruguay* (Cambridge, 1959), pp. 118–155.

[168] Robertson and Robertson, *Letters* 2: 178–192.

Thus when a coup in Buenos Aires led to the creation of a government that wanted a centralized authority in Rio de la Plata in 1813, Artigas organized a counter-congress dedicated to a federal solution that granted the former provinces more autonomy. Indeed, the struggle between unitarians who wanted a centralized authority led by the elite of Buenos Aires and the federalists who wanted more autonomy in the provinces would shape the politics of the region until well after independence was attained. In 1813, Artigas created his own national assembly, which reflected the aspirations of his largely non-elite followers when it enacted important reforms including ending the use of forced indigenous labor, the system of encomiendas, titles of nobility, and the Inquisition. In 1814, Artigas reorganized his holdings and created the League of Free People (*Liga de Pueblos Libres*), governed by the Instructions of the Year XIII, which created a federal structure not only for his own followers, but for most of Rio de la Plata. Provincial juntas joined the league, which was loosely structured under the Congresso Oriental, which declared itself independent of "all foreign powers" on June 29, 1815. In 1815, Artigas adopted even more radical reform measures, breaking up estates, abolishing caste and race distinctions, and redistributing lands to all.[169]

If Artigas declared independence from Spain on behalf the League of Free Peoples, the United Provinces of Rio de la Plata declared its own independence, as the United Provinces of South America, on July 9, 1816. The Congress of Tucumán was its governing body. For a time, the two governments shared portions of the same territory and presented conflicting claims on the loyalty of provincial juntas.

The war diverted military interests, and as a result, the various free associations of the Gran Chaco recommenced raiding the river towns with great success, carrying off much in spoils. Robertson, negotiating trade between Buenos Aires and Asunción, commented on the ravages of these indigenous raiders. In 1814, the federal government in Buenos Aires, which had nominal control of the lower towns on the Paraná, negotiated a treaty with them, certified by fifteen caciques.[170] Although this peace was likely to be shaky, at least as Robertson understood its prospects, it could potentially serve the interest of Buenos Aires or Artigas, depending on who might win the loyalty of the Gran Chaco people.

While Buenos Aires and the provinces of its interior sought to create a governmental system and union with Artigas, while fending off royalist counterattacks in Upper Peru or Brazil, the Captaincy of Chile was moving toward independence. As juntas formed in Chile, a complex power struggle between local criollos and loyalists ended with the emergence of José Maria Carrera

---

[169] Lucia Sala de Touron, *Nelson dela Torre, Julío Rodriguez, Artigas y su revolución agraria, 1811–1820* (Montevideo, 1967), pp. 114–153, 208–212; Eduardo Azcuy Ameghino, *Historia de Artigas y la independencia argentina* (Montevideo, 1993), pp. 214–228.

[170] Robertson and Robertson, *Letters* 2: 194–196 (these letters are by William and relate to the period after 1814).

in 1812. On October 27, 1812, the junta under Carrera's leadership created the Provisional Constitutional Rule (*Reglamento Constitucional Provisorio*), which effectively declared Chile independent by claiming that "no decree or order issued by any authority outside of Chile shall have any effect," while still claiming to be loyal to Fernando VII. To defend their new freedom and to forestall problems, the assembly declared all slaves to be free as soon as they enlisted in the army, and when the numbers were inadequate declared they would be forced to serve, but still to be freed upon enrollment.

The activities of the Chilean junta alarmed Viceroy Abscal y Sousa in Peru as much as those of Buenos Aires or the rebels in Upper Peru. As a result, he sent a number of military expeditions into Chile, but with his forces spread thin by the war in Upper Peru, he had little initial success. Fortunately for the royalist cause, Chile continued to be rifted by factions, and Carrera managed to alienate enough followers by high-handed management that when a second expedition attacked Chile in 1814 (following the victory in Upper Peru), the junta's leaders were so divided that the royalist army dealt them a crushing defeat. Chile returned to royal control and Abscal y Sousa's subordinate governor, Vicente San Bruno, launched a full-fledged repression of *criollos* known to have favored independence. In 1815, a good number of these *criollos* fled from Chile across the Andes to Mendoza, a small town then in the hands of the United Provinces of Rio de la Plata and protected by their general, de José de San Martín.

San Martín was busy organizing an army modeled on Napoleonic lines, and to strengthen its numbers he created two regiments of black and mulatto soldiers through promises of freedom after the wars. When soldiers lacked, he freed more slaves or requisitioned them from their masters to serve in the army. In this way, one-third (1,500) of his 4,500-man army were composed of former slaves. Just as Chilean exiles arrived in San Martín's jurisdiction, Buenos Aires decided to open a front there, as compensation for its lack of success in neighboring Upper Peru.

In 1817, San Martín led this army into Chile, defeated the royalists' army on at Chacabuco on February 12, then occupied Santiago. He defeated a royalist counterattack from Peru at Maipú on April 5, 1818, which gave San Martín the opportunity to invade Peru itself. He commanded a mostly Chilean force of slightly more than 4,000 men, of which almost half were freed slaves, aided by the Scottish naval captain Lord Thomas Cochran, whose navy provided valuable support. The army set sail on August 20, 1820 for Peru, landed at Pisco, and on July 12, 1821 entered Lima after Viceroy Jose de la Serna e Hinojosa abandoned it. On July 28, San Martín, with a newly designed Peruvian flag in his hand, declared Peru independent.

The independence could not count for much, however, as long as substantial royalist elements were still active in the countryside. Upper Peru was still in royalist hands, and the royalist army and the viceroy established themselves in Cuzco. In Chile, O'Higgins, the soldier San Martín left in charge, found that the defeat of the royalist army was not the end of the war. Mapuche leaders along with surviving royalists led by Vicente Benavides continued a long struggle in the mountains and the south – a war so ruthless that it was dubbed The War to the Death (*Guerra a Muerte*) by commentators.[171]

Lacking forces to continue the war against these enemies, San Martín declared the north coast of Peru a protectorate and withdrew, temporarily, to Chile. In 1822, he met with Simón Bolívar who, advancing from Venezuela and New Granada, had driven royalist forces from northern South America at Guayquil.

THE REVOLUTION IN VENEZUELA AND NEW GRANADA

The rise of Bolívar originated in the juntas formed in 1810 at Caracas, Barcelona, Cumaná, Merida, and Trujillo in Venezuela. Most of these juntas were composed of the wealthiest of the *criollo* group, and the one at Caracas ousted the Spanish Captain General Vicente Emparán on April 9, 1811. They sent to England to recall Francisco de Miranda, a widely traveled Venezuelan who had lived in the United States and had close ties with England. Miranda wrote about a unified Spanish America, which he often called Colombia in honor of Christopher Columbus, and in 1805, with British help, he had sought to land a small army in Venezuela to begin the process of freedom. Miranda expected a spontaneous support from all quarters upon his landing; instead, the expedition failed rapidly.

Now that the junta of Caracas had led a more successful seizure of power, they sent to England to bring Miranda back to be the first president. On July 5, 1811, soon after Miranda's arrival, Venezuela declared its independence as what would come to be called the First Republic. However, not all juntas in Venezuela were behind either Caracas's lead or the move to independence, convinced that the junta of Caracas was simply a group of "mantuanos," a pejorative local name for wealthy criollos who had grown rich from cacao production. Juntas in Maracaibo, Guyana, and the district of Coro never recognized the junta of Caracas's authority, and raised military forces to resist it in support of continued loyalty to Spain. To bolster the royalists, General Domingo de Monteverde, with a small force of 230 soldiers from Cuba, landed in Coro.

His first support came from indigenous people who had served Spain in the area, led by Juan de los Reyes Vargas, the cacique of Siquisique (often just called "el Indio"). Reyes Vargas augmented Monteverde's force with 300 musketeers and 100 archers, both indigenous and mestizos, which soon grew to 1,500. Thanks to this timely assistance, Reyes Vargas subsequently became a notable regional commander, fiercely loyal to the crown, and was even granted a title.[172] Monteverde scored another important coup when he accepted Tomás

[171] Manuel Ramírez Espíndola and Eduardo Téllez Lugaro, "Vicente Benavides: Reacción y devoción en el seno de la post-independencia americana," *Revista de Historia*, 15 (2005): 31–42.

[172] A celebrationary biography of this cacique is in Rafael María Rosales, *Reyes Morales: Paladin del procerato mestizo* (Tachira, 1950).

Boves, a Spaniard who had great influence in the Orinoco River provinces (called the Llanos), as part of the royalist coalition. Boves's forces were largely mestizos who were renowned for their equestrian skills, honed in raising and raiding cattle. By July 1812, Monteverde had forced Miranda to come to terms and took him prisoner. Some of the Republican leaders managed to escape, notably Simón Bolívar, who fled to Cartagena, and Santiago Mariño, who fled to Trinidad (and then to nearby Cumaná, his home region).

As Venezuela was declaring its independence, a number of cities in New Granada also formed their own juntas; the junta of the viceregal capital of Bogotá claimed supremacy, deposed the viceroy, and declared the province a constitutional monarchy under Fernando VII in 1811 as Cundinamarca. However, Bogotá's claim was not widely accepted – other major towns and even lesser towns each claimed to be their own sovereign entities. The juntas of Cartagena, Tunja, Antioquia, Casanare, Pamplona, and Popayán joined to form their own constitutional entity called United Provinces of New Granada. These two entities soon came to conflict over the question of whether the new political entity would have a centralized government or a weaker federation, just as Bolívar arrived.

In Cartagena, Bolívar wrote his famous pamphlet, the "Cartagena Manifesto" which warned the leaders of New Granada to avoid the mistakes that had lost Venezuela, namely failing to adopt a strongly centralized government in the struggle against "our born, implacable enemies, the European Spaniards." The federal system, he argued, while the best in the long run, could not defend itself adequately, and allowing too much free voice, or even elections, hampered that effort to form a united front. He urged strong measures, including the death penalty, for those who conspired against united, centralized action.[173] He was given command of the army of the United Provinces to carry on the civil war, attacking first the royalist towns of the Magdalena Valley and then attacking Bogotá, thus forcing Cundinamarca to join the United Provinces.

Having secured a base in New Granada, he launched a campaign to retake Venezuela, and in the "Admirable Campaign" (January–July 1813), his relatively small army was able to advance rapidly eastward to join forces with Mariño's forces coming west to drive the royalists from Caracas. There Bolívar declared the Second Republic in July 1813 and accepted the title of dictator. But Bolivar and Mariño still faced royalist resistance from Tomás Boves and his supporters in the llanos of the Orinoco. Excellent horsemen and lancers, Boves's followers defeated republican armies; then, in a devastating campaign in 1814, Boves attacked the central highlands and captured Caracas, forcing Bolívar and many of his supporters to flee the country.[174]

---

[173] First published as a pamphlet in Cartagena on December 15, 1812, subsequently reprinted in many compilations (an online version is at http://www.analitica.com/bitblioteca/bolivar/cartagena.asp). An English translation is found in Frederick Fornoff, trans., and David Bushnell, ed., *El Liberator: Writings of Simon Bolívar* (Oxford, 2003), pp. 3–12.

[174] Jesús Ignacio Fernández Domingo, *Boves: Primer caudilo de América* (Oviedo, 2008).

Boves's victory over Bolívar coincided with the restoration of Fernando VII to the throne of Spain, who was determined to bring his American colonies back under control. In 1814, Fernando sent some 11,000 Spanish soldiers under Pablo Morillo to Venezuela to use as a base for the full reoccupation of Venezuela and New Granada. Morillo's troops landed in Margarita and then advanced rapidly, crushing resistance as they met it. Even before the forces arrived, a number of republican leaders went into voluntary exile. Bolívar himself, trying to organize resistance, left for Jamaica when he was unable to get forces from Cartagena for the defense. He tried to organize several counterattacks while in Jamaica, but none were successful.

The most successful republican resistance was led by Manuel Piar, who took a small force down the east coast of Venezuela, a long distance from Morillo's forces or interests, and entered the province of Guayana at the mouth of the Orinoco River. Piar was probably of mixed African and European origin, the only *pardo* among Bolívar's closest circle. Piar's diary of his journey shows his attention to indigenous people and mestizos as allies – on November 2, 1816, he met and incorporated a force with 200 "archers and criollos," and later the same day a band of Caribs joined; on February 21, 1817, 28 indigenous fighters joined his battalions; on March 3, 100 more joined; 31 joined at Santa Marta; another 20 at Altagracia; and so on.[175] As he moved along, he wrote that "neither the Indios nor the Fathers hid from us, they presented themselves openly" – a development he thought would help hold the areas.[176] He ordered his followers to protect indigenous rights as well.[177] Even so, the bulk of those who opposed his advance were also indigenous people.[178]

Piar's success was sufficient that Bolívar joined him in Guyana in 1817 and founded the Third Republic with its headquarters at Angostura. Using the wealth of the region in cattle, precious stones, and other resources, Bolívar was able to procure additional arms, including the British Legion, a volunteer mercenary group composed of more than 1,000 British, Irish, and German veterans of the Napoleonic Wars, the sort of regular trained infantry that could counter Spanish soldiers.

Bolívar's future depended, in fact, on the sort of alliance with marginal people of color – slaves, former slaves, mestizos, and other groups generally labeled "pardo" in the vocabulary of Venezuela. During a stay in Haiti during his exile, Bolívar had taken the advice of Alexandre Pétion, his host, and made freeing the slaves a part of his agenda. Even as Bolívar was gathering his forces, he worried both publically and privately about the dangers of creating "pardocracía" through giving too much power to such social groups.[179] Full of

---

[175] Diario de Operaciones del General Piar, in *Memorias del General O'Leary* 15: 105, 204, 207, 208.
[176] Piar to Miguel Armas, February 4, 1817, in *Memorias*, 15: 152.
[177] Instructions to General Chipía, February 4, 1817, *Memorias*, 15: 152.
[178] Piar to Pedro Chipía, February 7, 1817, *Memorias*, 15: 165.
[179] For a good survey of Bolívar's life and his social attitudes, see John Lynch, *Simon Bolivar: A Life* (New Haven, 2006).

suspicion, he put Piar on trial, then executed him for conspiring to "dissolve this precious army" by separating pardos and other lower-class soldiers from it. Hostile witnesses accused Piar of saying he wanted to "gather together all the pardos and kill all the whites."[180]

Given that the llanos of the Orinoco had been the seat of Boves and the source of his undoing, Bolívar seemed unlikely at first to be able to achieve much with such a strategy, but he managed to hold the army together in spite of his jealousy and fears. Fortunately for Bolívar, Boves was killed in 1814, and Morillo's Spanish forces were just as inclined as Bolívar to distrust pardos. In a report of his position in 1818, Morillo described the inhabitants of the llanos as restless and violent people, who even in peacetime robbed and attacked their neighbors, and in wartime needed only a strong leader to direct their activities. Bovés, Morillo argued, provided that leadership and had delivered Venezuela from the "rebels." To reestablish good government, Morillo argued he had to send those people "who are not able to live except on their horses" back to their homeland. There, "among their cattle and ranches," they had "reunited in small parties and declared their independence," which reinforced their desire to rob.[181] This policy of effectively renouncing the alliance between royalist goals and pardo power would be Morillo's undoing. This had caused the inhabitants of the Llanos to reunite under a new leader, José Antonio Paez, who was now "following the pathway left open by Boves." In fact, backwoodsmen's cavalry had defeated and driven out Morillo's forces out, and he attended to trying to raise an equivalent force that he hoped could, when combined with European infantry, turn the situation around.[182]

Bolívar conceived a bold – and, some thought, reckless – plan to recover the coastal areas by attacking from the Orinoco Valley. Targeting New Granada as the most vulnerable of the areas, Bolívar moved a small force up the Orinoco in the rainy season, when no one would expect such a movement, then across the mountains to surprise the Spanish soldiers. The Battle of Boyacá on August 7, 1819 sealed the fate of Morillo's position and brought New Granada into the Third Republic, which Bolívar renamed the Republic of Gran Colombia upon his return to Angostura. More fighting eventually culminated in the battle of Carabobo, where the last of Morillo's forces, now commanded by Miguel de la Torre, were crushed on June 24, 1821.

After Bolívar's forces defeated the Spanish in Gran Colombia, he turned to complete the conquest of Peru, begun by San Martín's taking of Lima but subsequently stymied by Spanish resistance in Cuzco and Upper Peru. As a result of a meeting of the two at Guyaquil in 1822, San Martín decided to leave Peru and allow Bolívar to conquer it. Bolívar, who had occupied parts of

---

[180] Processo of Piar, *Memorias*, 15: 355, 366.
[181] Pablo Murillo to Ministro de la Guerra, February 26, 1818, in Antonio Rodriguez Villa, ed., *El Tenente General Don Pablo Murillo, Primer Conde de Cartagena (1778–1837)* (4 vols., Madrid, 1908 [GB]) 3: 511–512.
[182] Murillo to Ministro de la Guerra, February 26, 1818, in *Pablo Murillo*, 3: 512.

the province of Quito, sent some 6,000 troops to Lima, but in 1823, a strong royalist force under general José Canterac attacked the city and forced its evacuation, the republican forces withdrawing to El Callao. In the interim, bickering broke out among the various leaders of Peruvian cities, and as a result, Bolívar himself moved to Peru and took charge of affairs, even putting down a rebellion by the Rio de la Platan elements in the army. Meanwhile, the royalists, now led by the General de Serna, were themselves split into those who supported the constitutional monarchy in Spain and those who still supported absolute rule. Sucre, Bolívar's general in Peru, met the royalists in a final battle at Ayacucho on December 9, 1824, and was victorious, thus sealing the fate of the royalist cause and guaranteeing the independence of Peru as a part of the now-massive new state of Gran Colombia.

IMPERIAL INDEPENDENCE: BRAZIL

Unlike Spanish Americans, whose communications with the court had been curtailed by the British blockade of Spanish ports, and who thus were left to fend for themselves, the Brazilians were more directly under the Portuguese crown than ever following the arrival of the court in Rio de Janeiro in 1808. Following the withdrawal of French forces in 1814, João VI reorganized the empire in 1815 as a United Kingdom of Portugal, Brazil, and the Algarve, each of which was held to be an equal partner, while he remained in Rio de Janeiro.

The Portuguese presence in Brazil had mixed impacts in the country. Portuguese soldiers came to command many Brazilian army units, and Portuguese army units occupied much of the country. Many high posts and positions that Brazilian-born people had occupied were passed to the Portuguese. The Portuguese crown was generally solicitous of the region around Rio de Janeiro, and many Brazilians of that region benefited financially from the crown's support. Elsewhere, however, the movement of the court was less well received. On the other hand, the Portuguese also thought to intervene in the neighboring eastern provinces (Banda Oriental) of Rio de la Plata in 1816, and the low-intensity war waged by Artigas against them proved to be more and more costly.[183]

In Pernambuco, a conspiracy led by Domingo José Martins to overthrow the Portuguese governor and create a republic developed, and the conspirators took over Recife on March 6, 1817 as well as the other northern states of Para, Paraíba, and Rio Grande do Norte along the coast. These provinces had enjoyed none of the benefits of the presence of the court, but had been saddled with the increased taxation that the court imposed to support the war in eastern Rio de la Plata. They also had to accept a much stronger group of the Portuguese in both administrative and commercial life. But the crown responded quickly to the revolt, and ground and naval forces quickly surrounded Recife and

---

[183] Street, *Artigas*, pp. 295–298, 313–329.

smashed the resistance. By June 1817, the revolt was over, its leaders dead or imprisoned, and as punishment, the province was dismembered.[184]

In 1820, however, a liberal revolution broke out in Portugal and declared a constitutional monarchy. The leaders of the revolt demanded that the royal family return to Portugal, now free for some years from French control. João VI returned to Lisbon, leaving his son Pedro as the Regent in Brazil. They also demanded, however, that the old colonial order be restored, with Brazil demoted to the status of a province, and the many Bourbon-era restrictions be reinstated. To forestall any resistance, Portuguese troops were dispatched to Brazil, and Brazilian army units placed under Portuguese command. These demands were met with determined resistance, and a number of Brazilian towns declared juntas with the aim of obtaining independence. At the same time, the regent Pedro refused to obey the orders from Portugal, and then ordered the troops to be sent back to Portugal. In response, Portuguese officers sought to take over Brazilian army units, at which point violence broke out in Bahia and Pernambuco. Whereas in Pernambuco, the Portuguese units were forced to withdraw in November 1821, in Bahia, the Brazilian forces, which revolted in February 1822, were expelled by their Portuguese counterparts and withdrew into the country to begin a low-key guerilla war.

After consolidating support in São Paulo and Minas Gerais, Pedro declared Brazil to be independent, with himself as a constitutional emperor, on September 7, 1822, and was duly accepted and installed on December 1. Although Pedro controlled the south of the country, Portuguese forces were strong in the north, from Maranhão at the Amazon to Bahia; reinforced with Napoleonic War veterans from Portugal, they waged a bitter struggle to hold onto the Portugal's colony. In addition, Portuguese forces also held onto Montevideo in the south.

To defeat these powerful forces with only militias would be very difficult, but Pedro was able to gain assistance from Great Britain and from various European mercenaries, including his naval commander Thomas Cochran, who had lately served in Peru with San Martín. In addition, other Spanish, French, and English troops arrived to assist, and in a series of battles and sieges, the Portuguese troops were forced to withdraw, finalizing Brazilian independence.

In virtually all of the Americas, independence was won through a complex struggle of interlocking elites in which no one side was clearly able to win the day. Just as the conquest of the Americas had been in part a local civil war, so almost all American independence movements had the overtones of civil war in them. In these struggles, the lower class and the marginalized often played a large role, taking charge in Haiti and winning some power and freedom everywhere. Working out how to handle the demands that these groups tried to make as a result of their participation would be the task for the independent American governments to decide.

---

[184] Carlos Guilherme Mota, *Nordeste 1817* (São Paulo, 1972) and Glacyra Leite, *A Insurreção Pernambucana de 1817* (São Paulo, 1984).

Index